The Study
of the Middle East

The Research and Training Committee of the Middle East Studies Association 1972-1973

Roger M. A. Allen
Morroe Berger
Leonard Binder, Chairman
Robert A. Fernea
Oleg Grabar
Ira Lapidus
Ernest McCarus
John Simmons
I. William Zartman, ex-officio

The Study of the Middle East

RESEARCH AND SCHOLARSHIP
IN THE HUMANITIES AND THE SOCIAL SCIENCES

A Project of the
Research and Training Committee
of the
MIDDLE EAST STUDIES ASSOCIATION

Edited by
LEONARD BINDER

A WILEY-INTERSCIENCE PUBLICATION

JOHN WILEY & SONS
New York • London • Sydney • Toronto

Library of Congress Cataloging in Publication Data:

Main entry under title:

The Study of the Middle East.

"A Wiley-Interscience publication."
Includes bibliographies and index.
1. Near East studies. 2. Near East-Bibliography.
I. Binder, Leonard. II. Middle East
Studies Association of North America. Research and
Training Committee.

DS61.8.S78 956'.007'2 76-7408
ISBN 0-471-07304-0

Printed in the United States of America

10 9 8 7 6 5 4 3 2 1

Notes

TRANSLITERATION OF NAMES

The system of transliteration for Middle Eastern languages is that employed by the *International Journal of Middle East Studies*. It will be noted that anomalies occur when an Arabic loan word is transliterated into Persian or Turkish, according to context—and vice versa. In the bibliographies, in citations, and when titles of works are included in the text we have retained the original transliteration. Classical authors' names and those of modern authors who have not been translated or whose preferred transliteration of their own names is unknown to us have been transliterated systematically. We have tried to maintain a similar distinction between the authors and titles of works in Ottoman as opposed to modern Turkish. Middle Eastern loan words commonly found in English have been employed as English words without italicization or transliteration except in the case of a few technical terms or where certain authors insisted. Every effort has been made, at considerable expenditure of time and money, to do a consistent and reasonable job.

INDEXING

Muslim names are indexed alphabetically, using the most widely known nominal element, usually the last. The IJMES system of transliteration is used for Arabic, Persian, Turkish and Ottoman names except where the name occurs in the text in some other form. The individual's preferred way of transliterating his or her own name is generally the way in which the name is listed here. At times, the name of a classical author will be transliterated in more than one language. Names are not alphabetized by the definite article "al-," but "ibn" and "abû" are employed as any other nominal element might be.

Contents

CHAPTER ONE

Area Studies: A Critical Reassessment

LEONARD BINDER

The basic motive in the development of area studies in the United States has been political. As many observers have pointed out, responsible leaders realized during World War II that this country lacked an adequate number of specialists trained in the languages and cultures of other parts of the world. This deficiency applied not only to European specialists, but to the specialists in the developing areas or in countries that were in 1939 subject to European imperialism. Our fundamental political motivation was to gain influence and to combat hostile forces in these areas; hence we tended to discredit a good bit of European scholarship, which was consciously or unconsciously motivated by imperalist considerations. Nevertheless, it is difficult to discern a consistent political line in the organization of area studies in the United States, or in the patterns of funding that have emerged and changed over the last quarter of a century. In nearly every area confraternity there are as many or more who oppose U.S. foreign policy as there are those who support it. Those who enter upon area studies are as often motivated by their attachments to, or fascination with, the objects of their study as by the urge to represent, or define, or defend American interests in that area.

Political sophisticates will say that in a liberal bourgeois state one does not expect scholarship to follow a party line or even to have a party line laid down in such subjects as literary criticism and philosophical theology. Pluralist and competitive ideals should prevail, so that it is not the State Department that determines the nature of area studies, but area studies which will constitute one more among the many nongovernmental pressures that determine our foreign policy. From this point of view, the political forces that determine the orientation of area studies are to be sought among the groups, organizations, and individuals who are in positions or have the resources to influence scholarship and academic programs in this country. Nor are the academics themselves altogether passive in this situation, for it is considered seemly that scholars take the initiative in acquiring both private and governmental support for their scholarly enterprise. In some universities, not only is such initiative condoned, but it is positively encouraged. As a result no single perspective is dominant in the various branches of area studies. The reason for this academic pluralism is to be found in the large number of university centers, the technical orientation of relevant government agencies, the multiplicity of funding sources, and the autonomous if relatively weak organization of the academics involved in area studies.

I would not argue that area studies are therefore nonpolitical. I think that the opposite is the case. Although thus far no single view has become dominant, conditions might change.

We are in fact faced with an anomaly. Area studies were fostered for political reasons. These studies were characteristically viewed as instrumentalities and not as ends. Area studies were and are considered to be accumulations of knowledge rather than areas of inquiry and interpretation. But area studies are also new and still lack widely accepted standards of excellence. We have still not decided which are the things worth knowing, which problems require additional research, how the various subjects are to be defined, and all of the rest of the limitations that determine the ways in which more traditional studies are organized and standards of scholarship are set. To borrow a much abused term from Thomas Kuhn, the paradigms of area studies, and of Middle East studies in particular, have not yet been fixed. They are in the process of being determined—by means of pluralistic interaction involving government, foundations, scholarly groups, university boards of trustees, community groups, foreign governments, large corporations, religious organizations, and others. This book attempts to sum up where this process has taken us and, frankly, to enhance the influence and the autonomy of the scholars themselves by means of setting the criteria by which scholarship is to be judged. Many will argue that scholarship is too important to be left to the scholars themselves, but in our system if it is not left to the scholars, then it must be left to those who pay the scholars.

So long as there were many different groups "paying" the scholars this problem was not so severe. But we have entered upon a period of sharply declining funding for area studies, and even Middle East studies have been affected. It is difficult to say whether we are facing a real crisis of funding. There is no doubt that the international political and economic significance of the Middle East has increased tremendously in recent years and especially after the war of October 1973. It is safe to say that interested parties will come to believe that they will be benefited if their points of view become better known and more sympathetically presented. I am sure that there will be increased funding for Middle East studies, but I am not sure where it will come from and what affect it will have on scholarship. Heretofore the sources of funding have been the U.S. Office of Education in the Department of Health, Education and Welfare, the Ford Foundation, and the universities themselves (or their supporters, both public and private). Scholarly research, as opposed to the support of teaching programs, has been funded by a wide variety of agencies including the National Science Foundation, the Rockefeller Foundation, the Guggenheim Foundation, and the Fulbright faculty research program. Of course, the major sources of faculty research support have come from the Social Science Research Council and the American Council of Learned Societies, but these have been sustained, for the most part, by the Ford Foundation.

The major supporters of Middle East studies are now reducing their contributions by substantial amounts. The Ford Foundation is in 1975, thinly spreading only a little more than $500,000 a year across the board of Middle East studies. The Federal government is squeezing hard on the National Defense Education Act scholarship allocation, though its language and area center grants have remained more or less steady in recent years. All universities are in financial difficulty, and although some are looking to Middle East related sources to solve some of these difficulties, few administrations are inclined to invest more in the area without guaranteed superprofits.

We might have expected some financial support from the large number of business enterprises that are sending salesmen and promoters scurrying around in Middle Eastern and especially Persian Gulf capitals in search of business. Perhaps these firms have not been properly approached, perhaps they feel that they do not wish to make large contributions during a period of economic recession, or perhaps they see no value to themselves in supporting Middle East studies. In fact, except for a few long-standing arrangements with oil companies, very few universities receive much support from private industry or commerce for their Middle East programs.

It is natural that many should look to the Middle East itself for financial support of area studies, both because of the great interest and because of recent accumulations of great wealth in some of the countries. It is unfortunately true that the wealthiest countries with the exception of Iran, perhaps, are those that least value the Western ideal of scholarship. All Middle Eastern countries are inclined to view higher education as a political matter, and given their political experiences, this is not surprising. At present, it is highly unlikely that any single Middle Eastern country or group of countries will follow the example of Japan and simply present 10 endowed chairs to 10 American universities with no strings attached. This will be particularly unlikely if relations between the United States and the more conservative (and wealthier) regimes become strained. Nevertheless, I suppose that some financial support will be forthcoming from the Middle East itself, even though I do not now believe that such financing will ever constitute more than a relatively small fraction of the cost of Middle East programs. Individual universities may hit the petroleum jackpot, but most of us will have to rely on the traditional sources of university finance.

If it is true that no windfall support is in the offing, then we must face the prospects either of a sharp decline in the manifold activities included in Middle East studies or of considerably greater effort to sell what we do to prospective donors. The temptations will be great, for this is the way we make our living, build our empires, and serve our ego needs. It will become increasingly difficult to keep one another honest under such conditions, and we will require all the help we can get.

THE LAMBERT REPORT: THE STANDARD OF AREA TRAINING

To my mind, keeping one another honest means maintaining, or at least pursuing, high standards of scholarship and of objectivity in the classroom, in research, and in the organization of our programs. To achieve these ends we need to fulfill two preconditions: we must have a corps of well-qualified scholars and we must have established disciplinary standards.

One of the most disappointing products of the massive Lambert report on area studies is the discovery that after all these years only 16.7% of the so-called Middle East specialists are "language and residence-qualified" according to the simple criteria he employed.[1] Lambert himself writes concerning all area specialists, "These figures are disturbing. I suspect that many of the self-ratings are a bit optimistic and that the true figures, if objective standardized tests could be given, would be considerably lower."[2] About our present concerns he writes, "A little surprising is the tolerance of the lack of language skills among Middle East specialists."[3] Only about one third of those tabulated by Lambert were fully skilled in at least one Middle Eastern language,[4] and only half that number had high skills in two of the major Middle Eastern languages (i.e., Arabic, Persian, Turkish, and Hebrew).[5]

The same sort of statistics describe the residence of so-called area specialists in the countries of their scholarly interest. Less than one half of all Middle East area specialists have spent more than two years in the area.[6] Less than half of those reporting have resided in any one Middle Eastern country for at least six months, and less than 20% have resided in more than one country for at least six months. Most of this residence was in Egypt, Israel, Turkey, and Lebanon.[7] It is to be further noted that such residence does not indicate that the respondent engaged in field research or any form of scholarly activity. There were 158 (22.2%) nonacademic specialists in Professor Lambert's sample, which made it even more difficult to ascertain just how much academic competence there is in Middle East area studies. It is of some additional interest that the proportion of non-academic Middle East specialists in government was the lowest among all areas and that the proportion in church-related activities was the highest.[8]

It seems to me that these data lead us to the unavoidable conclusion that most of those who claim to be Middle East area specialists are certainly not qualified on the basis of their language competence or their length of residence in the area. Is it possible that they have attained an area expertise by mastering a social scientific or humanistic discipline?

Over 80% of Lambert's sample identified themselves with a discipline and about 3.5% stated that they were engaged in professional or applied fields. Nevertheless, the "general" area studies group engaged in Middle East studies was the largest for any area: 10.3%.[9] We suspect that the nearly 23.2% in history include a great many "generalists" who cannot claim high language skills, but some are among the 6.8% in religion and even the 6.8% in linguistics. Admitting that our area expertise is wanting, we merely ask just how good our disciplinary skills are.

Unfortunately, Lambert's data tell us almost nothing about the quality of the disciplinary skills of Middle East area specialists, nor does he seriously explore the criteria for determining the quality of such skills. Assessments of scholarly quality appear to be based on reputation and the relevance of area expertise to certain disciplines. Lambert writes[10]:

> The message seems to be clear. The field, in judging the quality of a program, is not so concerned with program style . . . as it is with the academic quality of the faculty (presumably reflected in the academic quality of the university as a whole).

Lambert does not further probe this issue, but instead presents some correlations of program productivity. His concern with program quality reflects the interest of the government and the foundations that have typically made grants to study centers, i.e., to collections of scholars, academic entrepreneurs, and administrators rather than to individual professors. The only relevant criterion used by Lambert is that of the *number* of faculty publications. Not only does mere quantity tell us little about quality but this statistic (which is not broken down by area) correlates with *no* other criterion of program productivity. It is unlikely, therefore, that program support has been closely correlated with academic quality, except as reflected in the general reputation of the university to which the Middle East area specialist has been attached.

If my guess is correct, it is not unlikely that some good area specialists will be found in universities that do not have strong reputations. On the other hand, very few of these universities also have strong Middle East centers, because of the way of determining quality.

Even in distinguished universities, the quality of departments varies greatly, so that one might wish to rely instead on the reputation of individual departments in assessing the disciplinary skills of Middle East area specialists. Similarly, we might generally rate these skills by the reputation of an individual scholar among his disciplinary fellows. Unfortunately not only do we lack data of this sort, but some disciplines do not regard area specialization as at all relevant. In some cases, area specialization is a positive detriment to advancement. It is my guess that the individual reputations of Middle East area specialists among their disciplinary colleagues would vary directly with the percentage of disciplinary specialists who also claim to be area specialists. Lambert gives us relevant data for all areas:

Subject	Percentage of all Specialists Who Are Area Specialists
Linguistics	33.5
Anthropology	84.5
Economics	9.5
Political science	36.0
Psychology	.4
Sociology	7.1

To pursue our quasi-structural interpretation of Lambert's data, it might be suggested that we have not so much the accreditation of area expertise in certain disciplines, but the emergence of area enclaves within some departments under conditions of more or less intellectual segregation. Thus, on the average, political scientists and historians are more prevalent, have more influence, and have better reputations among their colleagues than do economists or sociologists who specialize in the Middle East.

Our attempt to assess the disciplinary standing of Middle East area specialists has been indecisive. It appears that the standing of most specialists in the eyes of their disciplinary colleagues is not very high. It also appears to be the case that many of those who are most accepted by their disciplinary colleagues are least qualified (in terms of language and area residence) in the eyes of their area colleagues. Moreover, Middle East studies seem to have more than their share of nonspecialized scholars and of non scholarly specialists. Part of the reason for this sorry state of affairs is the failure to apply firm academic standards during the recent period of rapidly induced growth of area specialists. Many accomplishments have occurred over the past 30 years of which we can be proud, as shown in this book. But there are great extremes of achievement in this field, and it was awfully easy to become an area specialist and to get a job up until very recently. If the first phase of the development of Middle East studies was the expansion of the number of specialists, I think that task has been more than adequately achieved. The second phase, the new area studies, requires the adoption of far more stringent standards in terms of area skills and, especially, of disciplinary competence.

THE GOALS OF THIS PROJECT

The project of writing this book originated in the meetings of the Research and Training Committee (RAT) of the Middle East Studies Association. Our intention was to provide a review of recent research and a guide for younger scholars. We hoped to provide some intellectual justification for the selection of research topics and for the allocation of research and program support funds. We were not primarily concerned with the pluralistic values and distributive mechanisms that governed Lambert's essentially political approach. We were concerned with the improvement and the diffusion of scholarship and the encouragement of cumulative research. We were therefore concerned more with what Middle East specialists were doing than with how many of what kind there were.

The Research and Training Committee proposed a rather elaborate program to the executive of the Middle East Studies Association. MESA accepted our proposal and Bill Zartman, its Executive Secretary, drew up a request which was then presented to the Ford Foundation. The Foundation trustees approved the recommendation of the Middle East program officers and we were on our way. RAT proceeded to select the authors for each chapter. According to the letters of invitation we sent out, each author was called upon to canvass his colleagues, to make surveys, and generally to make sure that all points of view were taken into account. At the same time, we urged the authors to make their contributions intellectual arguments rather than simple accounts of recent research. The authors were then invited to participate in a workshop held at the Center for Advanced Study in the Behavioral Sciences during August 1973. At the workshop each author presented a preliminary draft of his paper, which was then subjected to criticism by his colleagues and invited specialists. The authors were encouraged to remain at the workshop and to make immediate revisions. Each of the revised papers was reviewed by additional readers during 1974, and several were revised yet again for this publication.

So often, in projects of this kind, the first steps are the most crucial, and once the thing has been begun one cannot conceive of its being done differently. Most of those who participated in the original planning received training in Middle East studies after World War II, that is, after both area studies and the integration of Middle East studies into the existing academic disciplines appeared on the scene. The Ford Foundation's Foreign Area Fellowship program is largely responsible for developing area specialists, and National Defense Education Act grants frequently helped them to get jobs, but the SSRC–ACLS Joint Committee on Middle East Studies became increasingly concerned with the application of more universal disciplinary standards in Middle Eastern research. The Joint Committee has always been a bit frustrated because of its limited funds, its limited impact on the training of area specialists, and its marginal influence on the policies of university area centers—in contradistinction to HEW. In a sense the Joint Committee felt that it was left trying to pick up the pieces scattered about by the injudicious policies of the two giants. Despite this tension, there is little doubt the Joint Committee has had an enormous influence on a relatively limited but quite active group of Middle East specialists.

It was therefore not surprising that our initial conception of the project was in terms of disciplines and that the disciplines were conceived of as basic subdivisions of the general field of Middle East studies. Our problem was much more one of determining which were the disciplines, than of deciding just how to describe that art, the state of which we were seeking to determine. Our problem was less theoretical than it was practical. We had to limit the number of disciplines in order to make our task feasible.

This practical need raised a number of important issues that bear on the definition of the art itself. We had to make value judgments and we sought to attain a measure of intellectual integrity in our solutions. Hence we had to decide which were the more important disciplines or topics, which could be subordinated to others, and which might be reasonably combined. The result is a compromise, which, though not ideal, nevertheless is a comprehensive view of what Middle East studies are or should be. At the very least we may say, and not without some misgivings, that the view of Middle East studies presented here is more or less at odds with the ideas of both Orientalism and area studies. We have sought to put each segment of Middle East scholarship in the context of a discipline for purposes of criticism, while at the same time demonstrating that there is a community of understanding and purpose among those engaged in Middle East studies.

That these were our goals, or that we had to any degree achieved these goals, was not clear to any of us in advance of the discussions we held at the workshop at the Center for the Advanced Study in the Behavioral Sciences. Most people who were at the workshop for any length of time felt that we could establish this community precisely because people engaged in the different disciplines were not only able to communicate about Middle Eastern matters, but also to grasp the nature of the other fellow's problem from the point of view of his relationship to his discipline. We gained something of a sense of the task of relating Middle Eastern realities to the scholarly paradigms which have recently emerged in the various social science and humanistic schools. I suppose that the most awkward, and, in the long run, the most revealing question was, "What has work in your field contributed to the discipline [rather than to Middle East area studies]?" The point of the question was to discover of what scholarly use it was to have more "information" about the Middle East—a matter of great interest to those of us who are employed in university departments and engaged in general education.

ORIENTALISM VERSUS AREA STUDIES

The method of scholarship which those who specialize in the Middle East call "Orientalism," a term drawn largely from the German usage, is aimed at the study of nonextant civilizations, and even then emphasizes the intellectual history or ideal self-image of such civilizations. Orientalism is based on the methods developed for the critical restudy of the classic literatures in Greek, Latin, and Hebrew. Although influenced to a substantial degree by the historiographic theories of the nineteenth century, Orientalism remained essentially a philological discipline in which knowledge of the language and its history was the primary basis for the hermeneutical explication of texts. As practiced on the literatures of the Islamic world, Orientalism had little influence on the European-centered disciplines from which it had sprung. The imagination of some Europeans may have been captured by the exoticism and the reputed hedonism of Middle Eastern cultures, but in the main the Islamic cultural heritage was treated as an incomplete or distorted version of the Judaeo–Hellenic–Roman–Christian tradition, with the exception that the rationalist and functionalist (Comtian and Darwinian) elements of the hermeneutic were less restrained when applied to an alien and "deviant" tradition. Furthermore, in the many works tinged with imperialist interest, there was even less evidence of empathy, regardless of the claims of present-day schools of hermeneuticists.

Despite all this, the orientalists have achieved immense works of scholarship, and their attainments stand like the monuments of the ancients which induce awe in us even though our technology far exceeds theirs. Orientalists have given us the basic outline of Islamic history, religion, and society. They have introduced us above all to the idealized self-image of Islamic civilization in the major, orthodox tradition. For all their intellectual and political biases, as products of an important, even a formative, historical period in the relations between Christian Europe and the Islamic Middle East, the orientalists must be credited with providing us with the basic hermeneutical frame of reference, the intellectual and historical context which is the sine qua non of understanding the worldly meaning of anything called Islamic. Regardless of our contemporary disciplinary orientation, it must be recognized that we do not and cannot start with a tabula rasa, but rather with a highly elaborated Orientalist tradition of scholarship which, moreover, has its own national variations.

We are nearly all agreed now that we wish to study Islamic civilization as related to the living societies of the Middle East today. This goal leads us beyond the possibilities of Orientalism and must naturally subvert the orientalist's notion of good scholarship. Orientalists were all too often content to sum up the meaning of a civilization on the basis of a few manuscripts, but at least they could say their conclusions were based on all of the then-known evidence. The contradictory evidence of contemporary practice was not taken as evidence of possible historical social patterns, but simply as the corruption of modern Middle Easterners, a conclusion, incidentally, which all too many Muslims were willing to accept.

The problem of studying another culture or an alien civilization is by no means a simple one. The formal disciplines are pretty much committed to the view that it is possible for people in one culture to understand, or to know what people in another culture "mean." Most of us, nevertheless, entertain serious doubts about the limits of such understanding and about the consequences of defining knowledge in terms of a specific disciplinary paradigm. That is, we wonder whether knowing what someone else means depends upon how we define meaning or how they define meaning. If, in Husserl's terms, meaning depends essentially on subjective intentionality, then the study of another culture is always achieved in terms of our own subjectivity. If our goal is to understand the subjective intentionalities of the other culture, is that understanding possible only in the terms of that other culture, or is there a kind of universal, objective intentionality of scholarly knowledge that transcends particular cultures and that can guide scholars toward synthesizing observational experiences into a statement of a cultural reality acceptable to alien and native alike? These questions are asked from the perspective that views our scholarly endeavors as a collective process of establishing truths, rather than as the more mechanical task of verifying assertions by measuring them up against the facts. I suppose that we can all agree that cultural facts are problems and not solutions, and therefore are not simply given.

To put the matter more simply we can ask, is it possible to understand Islamic civilization without being a Muslim? A more difficult way of posing the question is to repeat it for every period in Islamic history and for every part of the Islamic world. The claim that the outsider never quite knows what it is like to be an insider is, of course, unexceptionable as far as it goes. It may, however, be questioned whether the goal of scholarship is to ascertain how it feels rather than how it is. At any rate, even though we can never prove that pain, pleasure, enlightenment, or consciousness are the same for any two individuals, it is a gross exaggeration to claim on that account that we can have no knowledge of other minds, not to speak of other societies and other cultures. Such negative estimates of the possibilities of knowledge cannot cope with the evident facts that Middle Easterners travel to the West, study there, become acculturated, and sometimes write and teach about their own countries of origin. Similarly, Westerners travel, learn languages, adopt Islam, and otherwise become in some degree acculturated. It is consequently clear that it is possible to have some understanding of other cultures, even though it may not be possible to empathize perfectly.

The problem is really concerned with the level of adequacy of the knowledge we seek. Do we seek knowledge adequate for the making of foreign policy? Do we seek knowledge adequate for carrying out business dealings? Do we seek knowledge adequate to allow us to persuade others of the value of our projects? Do we seek knowledge adequate to explain certain historical and social phenomena?

It is certainly not enough that we have faith that it is possible, in some ways, to know about an alien culture. We must be more specific about the type of knowledge we think we can have and its level of adequacy. To specify such criteria is, obviously, to define area studies. After all, the whole point of area studies is the argument that what we know about ourselves is an inadequate basis for understanding others. In a sense, area study casts doubt on the idea of a universal history, the whole of which has some single meaning, or which, taken in its entirety, lends itself to a single definition of man. At the very least area study argues that there are very significant differences among peoples and cultures, as well as among historical periods, and that for some people at some times the differences are far more important than the similarities.

Some area specialists hold that it is fundamentally wrong to use the criteria of meaning of one culture to understand cultural phenomena in another. Each culture must be understood in its own terms, and no simple standard of value is applicable to all. To do otherwise is not merely to misunderstand, but also to subordinate and to exploit the other. Such distorted knowledge would be inadequate for any purpose save that of reassuring ourselves of our superior virtue. This view does not hold that you cannot know one without being one. It merely asserts that knowing a culture is possible only within the meaning context of that culture. Hence even translation is suspect, but more importantly the common dualistic distinction between the "real" and the "apparent" is rejected, and an acceptance of all phenomena as appearances beyond which we cannot go is affirmed. In its extreme form this view rejects anthropology's favored functionalism and argues that a culture is simply what it says it is, and therefore even if we do not use its language we must use its terms in translation. Naturally, there is more substance to this position when we are dealing with a highly elaborated and self-conscious culture which has its own science and philosophy than when we are dealing with localized, undifferentiated, and nonliterate cultures.

Despite the fact that Islam meets these criteria of providing an alternative ontological perspective, most area specialists do not go so far. They are content to argue that there are certain things about the Middle East (or any other area) that we must know in order to understand everything else. They do not argue that Islamic culture is inaccessible except in its own terms, but rather that access from the outside and even in a comparative perspective is possible only if certain prerequisites have been fulfilled. According to this orientation, there are kinds of evidence acquired by some forms of observation which are bound to be misleading unless the observer has the correct interpretive key. In many ways this view is derivative of the earlier Orientalist attitude toward hermeneutical analysis. Here, too, the area specialist insists that knowledge is possible in a transcultural sense, but that interpretation is necessary. For some the key to valid interpretation lies in intuition, empathy, long familiarity, and intersubjective apperception, whereas for others that key is to be found in the ubiquitous influence of certain cultural "constants," such as Islam or the "genius" of the Arabic language, or in certain structural constants, such as cousin marriage.

In its most extreme form, this position invites mystification or obscurantism, since it rejects or is suspicious of straightforward reporting of observations, or descriptions, or the tabulation of responses to questionnaires. Since the facts never speak for themselves we must speak for them; in addition, people do not always say what they mean or mean what they say. In its less extreme form the possibility of discerning patterns and trends of change is often precluded by a preoccupation with the continuing significance of what once was. We are all acquainted with standard works in the field which generalize about Muslims without qualification as to time and place.

In my own opinion area study rests upon a single key idea, which is that the object of study, the thing we want to know, is the determining and organizing principle of the intellectual enterprise and not the method or discipline. Research methodology and disciplinary paradigms are not to determine what is selected for study, and they are not to limit observation. Area study, from this perspective, holds that true knowledge is possible only of things that exist, whereas methods and theories are abstractions that order observations and offer explanations according to nonempirical criteria. In taking this perspective (usually implicitly) many area specialists join with important segments of scholars in nearly all the disciplines who argue against nominalist, positivist, and scientistic tendencies in their own fields of study. The question that separates these area specialists and the antipositivists is whether Middle Eastern events constitute a valid unity so that the consequence of their study could reasonably be called knowledge.

In other words, even though we may reject the "logical atom" for the "meaningful event," we still must establish the criteria or the "ground" for determining which is the meaningful event. More especially we must ask whether it is in any epistemologically essential way a *Middle Eastern* event, rather than a social event, a political event, or a linguistic event.

The fourth orientation to area studies is a simpler one, in that it argues the need for interdisciplinary study rather than for the existence of a special discipline called Middle East studies. There are a number of sources of this interdisciplinary interest, but none so influential as the post-World War II concern with development. It was, of course, this concern with the role of the underdeveloped countries of the "Third World" in the "Cold War," as well as the momentum of the 1939–1945 struggle itself, that gave rise to area studies. The career of Western theories of development is a fascinating story of intellectual inventiveness and ideological self-delusion; yet as the search for a formula became even more frustrating, so did the conclusion that an interdisciplinary approach was necessary become more general. It was argued that development or its absence is not the result of a single sequence of causal events, but that it is the consequence of many possible combinations of a great many factors. If we are to get at the problem of development, admitting that the problem is an interdisciplinary one, then we must resolve the issue of whether each discipline constitutes an isolated universe of discourse, whether several disciplines together form such a universe of discourse, or whether all the human sciences together do. If we take the view that each discipline is logically separate from the others, then it follows that the problem of development cannot be resolved, or can be resolved only to the satisfaction of the nontransferable meaning requisites of that discipline.

We can see how the demand for interdisciplinary approaches may lead to attacks on disciplinary consistency or to efforts to articulate the unity of the human sciences.

AREA STUDIES VERSUS THE DISCIPLINES

For those who see the disciplines as formalistic, abstract, and positivistic, it is clear that the study of development must stress the situational above the theoretical or even the ideal typical. For those who are oriented to the situational, interdisciplinary studies often mean nondisciplinary, but even for those who would not go so far, the application of disciplinary methods or "laws" must be adapted to another kind of knowledge. That knowledge is of certain conditioning factors without which the abstractions of the disciplines are meaningless.

There are substantial groups of social scientists seeking to articulate the unity of the human sciences. The most important among them are the behavioral scientists, the functional sociologists, and some of the phenomenologists.

In their application to the Middle East, or to any historically and situationally bound set of phenomonena, these approaches have serious consequences in terms of limiting what may be observed. All these approaches are willing to recognize that there may be significant situational differences among particular regional and historical phenomena, but the functionalist seeks to reinterpret culturally defined appearances, the behaviorist seeks to measure the degree of conformity to a general law under special conditions, and some phenomenologists seek the universal meaning of each situation in its relation to the nature of the world or the human condition which is itself revealed bit by bit by the study of just such situations.

Ideologically, such orientations tend to reject the notion that cultures are unique. These orientations are compatible with the view that to know one society is to know what is essential to all: the rest is merely translation. An alternative way of putting it, and one more congenial to many, is that the task is to understand man or human nature, and that is essentially the same everywhere. From this perspective area study is concerned with accidents and not essences, with exotic curiosa, the usefulness of which is limited to establishing the universal validity of scientific findings even when appearances are to the contrary. The greatest value consequently is placed on the universal, and much less on the unique; or else the unique is explained away in terms of functionalism, retarded development, or the phenomenologists' dialectic of meaning and unintelligibility.

The urge to organize all of knowledge into a single architectonic structure is not the inspiration that has led some area specialists to opt for interdisciplinary studies. Nor can we easily accept the view that to be interdisciplinary in orientation is to be eclectic, moderate, and reasonable. To be interdisciplinary is to take a position with regard to the disciplines and their aims, with some arguing that the disciplines go too far and others arguing that they don't go far enough.

In his *Cartesian Meditations*, Husserl contrasts the terms adequacy of evidence with apodicticity of evidence. His emphasis upon the importance of evidence appears to be a welcome reference to the decisive character of empirical observation in supporting scholarly assertions. But the way in which these two terms are used greatly vitiates any purported empirical bent in Husserl. By adequacy he appears to mean all evidence, or every case of the occurrence of the phenomenon in question. Since complete adequacy entails all future cases, the requirement of adequate evidence precludes the possibility of science, especially of social science. Apodicticity of evidence requires only that it be sufficient to prove the assertion without any doubt. Such evidence, for Husserl, is produced by the subjective process of the eidetic reduction. Neither of these concepts offers us a solution to the problem of validating area studies knowledge, the former being unattainable and the latter being neither public nor replicable. What we require, of course, is a functional equivalent of apodicticity, in the sense of a measure of a level of adequacy which satisfies the restricted purposes of a given inquiry rather than seeking to answer all questions or seeking to answer any question at all with a zero probability of error. What we require is a way of linking area studies, which determine to a large extent the purposes of our inquiry, and the disciplines that are supposed to tell us what we can know and how well we can know it. In striving to determine this nexus, however, we must continuously bear in mind the distinction between these two.

That distinction has many philosophical referents, but none so clear as the Aristotelian distinction between the practical and the speculative sciences. The Kantian distinction between synthetic and analytic discourse points to the same issue. The area specialist would side with those followers of each discipline in the human sciences who hold that *the human sciences are practical, that the logic of their discourse is synthetic, that their evidence is always incomplete, that analysis is comparison, and that the first principles are normative.*

Area study poses as its preliminary problem the description, or explanation, or understanding of a part of the existent world. What must be disallowed, however, is the belief that we can achieve scientific adequacy in the description of a part of the world without reference to the rest. In other words, this orientation toward the human sciences is not essentially ideological as some would have it, but it holds that their subject matter is properly constituted in history and that complete answers must always elude us so long as we cannot take account of all cases including those of the past, the future, and the present, and all of these without geographical limit.

From the point of view of our concern with area studies, then, the basic problem of the disciplines is whether they are to be considered as tools that help us to find out what we want to know or whether they determine what can be known. In more practical terms the payoff in the first case is a higher degree of confidence in the validity of statements made about the Middle East, and in the second case is in terms of more highly validated general laws or propositions. The position of most area specialists who practice a discipline, and that group includes myself, tends to be closer to the former rather than the latter—but that position must be clearly differentiated from the view of the area studies specialist who denies the value of the disciplines.

The basic problem that concerns the would-be area–discipline amphibian if that of objectivity as opposed to the questionable claims made for the significance of subjective understanding. The psychological phenomenologists have set up the optimistically named goal of "intersubjectivity" as the ground of all the human sciences, but the more pessimistic and dualistic social phenomenologists such as Schutz deny that a truly individualistic intersubjectivity is possible. Instead, only the intersubjectivity that is entailed in the understanding of a Weberian ideal type is possible. The difficulty with this moderate position is that such intersubjectivity is not between two ideal types but between one scholar's empathetic understanding and his reconstruction of an ideal typical understanding prevailing in the society he is studying. The asserted self-image of the society being studied is frequently arrived at by subjective processes or by methods that cannot be replicated short of living the researcher's life all over again. Nor is this objection merely theoretical or exaggerated in its importance.

The fact is that Middle Eastern studies are beset by subjective projections, displacements of affect, ideological distortion, romantic mystification, and religious bias, as well as by a great deal of incompetent scholarship. To my mind the greatest problem is that of incompetent scholarship, but incompetence can often be disguised or even defended as the application of a subjective, nonquantitative, phenomenological, or anti-positivist approach. None of these approaches is without merit, but every application of such a method must be justified and explained if it is to persuade the reader. The area specialist, basing his arguments on his own long residence in the area or on his knowledge of the languages of the area asserts an arbitrary authority. This assertion can be countered by the equally arbitrary authority of another specialist who has as much experience. Ultimately, we cannot rely on the reputation or attributed authority of the scholar; we must rely on the evidence and the sound reasoning by which he supports his statements. We cannot escape the fact that we study the Middle East because we are *interested* in it, in all the senses of that word.

From the point of view of the area specialist, the discipline ought to be subordinate to the thing we want to know about. We may indeed question the original constitution of the "thing we want to know about," but to be too precious about the sociology of knowledge at this level not only leads to an infinite regress but also loses for us the immediate context of meaning which lends at least situational (not essential) significance to the determination of objects of study. It is in this sense that determination of the objects of study may be said to be ideological in the broad sense in which *everything* is ideological. The "things we want to know about," therefore, arise in the context of life, in the *Lebenswelt;* they are formulated or constituted within a culture in a matter of fact manner. Each of us, as a member of a society, confronts these things from his own perspective, but it is nevertheless of the utmost importance that we do not lose our grasp of the original stimulus to questioning and research. For the area specialist, at any rate, that stimulus does not arise within the framework of a disciplinary paradigm. It is, however, absolutely essential that we distinguish between the situational context which gives meaning to the phenomena we wish to study and the intellectual and institutional context within which we try to resolve or explain those problems. The situational context is not an explanation—the more so if we insist that that context is sui generis. The situational context is itself problematical because it is in a general sense ideological.

From this perspective, area study poses the problem of the human sciences in a far more realistic manner than is the case when the absence of transcultural difficulties lulls one into the belief that there is no tension between situationally determined problems and institutionally developed intellectual disciplines. When this somnolence is joined with the ethnocentrism by which one takes our own society to be an authentic and complete microcosm, its victims are often led to the conclusion that the careful study of their own situation can be an adequate guide to knowledge, not only of this world, but of all possible worlds. Other societies can then be known by extrapolation and deduction.

The difficulty with this orientation is its assumption that everything of world cultural and social significance has already happened, and has happened within the confines of a single historical culture. If we deny these assumptions—and we must as area specialists—then it follows that we must question the formulation of problems for research as determined by a given situational context, we must compare the experiences of many different societies, and we must realize that all the evidence is not in yet, that history is not yet complete.

The principle of becoming must replace the arrogant and parochial complacency that is expressed by so many scholars who see in the historical events of their own country expressions of the essential being of man. But the view of the world as process which is entailed in the principle of becoming, despite its potentially liberal, pluralistic, and tolerant implications, can as well sustain an arbitrariness based on a rigorous relativism. Consequently, if the disciplines cannot be grounded on absolute, a priori knowledge, they are themselves necessarily synthetic to a considerable degree. The disciplines do not supply us with infallible methods and practical means of validation and verification. Since they are synthetic, and since they depend upon our knowledge of human events, the disciplines of the human sciences must also be comparative. The disciplines must include cases drawn from different situational contexts, or from contexts that are situationally irrelevant, but that are extremely relevant in terms of that part of each discipline which is speculative, philosophical, or normative. All the human disciplines are speculative, philosophical, and/or normative insofar as they assume that there is a common human nature, that there are characteristic human activities such as communicating and governing, and that these activities may be performed in better or worse ways.

In spite of these aspects of the human disciplines we also know that the disciplines themselves have historical and situational beginnings, and they have been developed within specific academic institutions under the patronage of particular regimes. They have been borrowed and transferred or even imposed at various times and under various circumstances, but their universality is a claim that is difficult to sustain, or rather one that is still being realized. Nevertheless, as in the case of the situational origin of the problems that we wish to explore, so also in the case of the situational origins and development of the human sciences are these defects also virtues if properly understood.

Now it seems to me that the crucial merit of any given discipline resides in the extent to which it reflects the historical and situational development of prevailing perspectives of certain subject matters and at the same time provides for a self-conscious criticism of those perspectives from a base of reasoned understanding of whose interests they may serve, of how they got started, and of why they have been maintained. Thus a discipline must be self-critical, even suspicious, of its own paradigms, and it must constantly question why we think we know what we say we know: that is, why we consider some things to be political knowledge or literary knowledge or legal knowledge. But this self-criticism must be relevant to the kinds of distortion of reality to which each subject matter is especially prone and not simply skeptical of any assertion of the possibility of knowledge in the most general sense. The only justification that the separate disciplines can have is their divergent subject matters, and these differences are conceptual and not empirical. It follows that a discipline is defective if it does not constantly inquire into the consequences of its selection of concepts and if it does not inquire into the situations that have determined that a given set of phenomena shall be taken to constitute a separate subject matter.

THE DISCIPLINARY ORIENTATION OF THIS BOOK

The perspectives that I have outlined are certainly not shared by all my coauthors, but I take them to be quite decisive in support of using a disciplinary framework in order to assess the state of the art in Middle East studies. Not every author has given extensive attention to these epistemological questions, although they were broached in our original correspondence and they were discussed at length in our workshop. There was certainly a good deal of concern with the fact that the disciplines as practiced in contemporary universities are not indigenous to the Middle East, and hence their utility might be limited by their own lack of universality. For this reason we were very much concerned with the question of what our studies could contribute to the disciplines, and although in most cases we cannot be very proud of contributions of this kind, in some disciplines work on the Middle East has been of great theoretical significance.

Another reason for emphasizing the disciplines in this survey is that most work is now being done within the framework of the disciplines, and most of us need the criticisms of our disciplinary colleagues as much as we need the criticisms of other area specialists. We hope that this arrangement will encourage those less concerned with Middle East studies to read this book.

When examined in the light of the disciplines, it seems to me that our recent achievements are not unimpressive. One can discern a cumulative quality, as well as an intellectual dialectic which lends an intelligible unity to much that we have been doing. We have wasted no time congratulating ourselves on these achievements. Instead the generally agreed method is to point to gaps and defects in the hope that someone will try to remedy the situation. Nevertheless, I think we can celebrate two rather tentative accomplishments of the last quarter century. The first is the academic institutionalization of the discipline. Middle East specialists may still be fascinating curiosities in academic departments, but by now we are familiar ones. The second is that we have joined the disciplines with a good deal of skepticism and some epistemological sophistication. If we have not yet had a heavy impact on the disciplines, the essays in this volume clearly illustrate that we are aware of their limitations. We have, therefore, committed ourselves to turn away from the merely rhetorical justification of our prejudices without at the same time accepting some alien model as an arbitrary authority. As these essays show, we have only begun to move along this path, but it is a decisive change from the situation prevailing when some of us, now in mid-career, started out. I think it can fairly well be said that Middle East studies have come of age, and this book marks the rites of passage.

At this stage it is to be expected that in many cases, the historically and situationally defined phenomena of the Middle East fit ill with the categories of the established disciplines. In general there seems to be less of this tension in the social sciences than in the humanities, even though the scholarly achievements may be greater in the humanities. But the main point is that the present integration of area and discipline represents an early stage in a process. This is why these essays have been written more or less as arguments, usually reflecting the views of the author most strongly, but not neglecting alternative perspectives. We were fortunate, indeed, in being able to enlist the cooperation of authors who are recognized authorities in Middle East studies and who are also well socialized into their respective disciplines. We have thus benefited from the integrated processes which each of these authors has made his life's work as well as from the unique opportunity to discuss one another's papers during the four weeks of the workshop. I think I am echoing the general consensus of those who attended the workshop in stating that it made a substantial difference in the way in which the authors have completed their extremely difficult tasks. Since we feel that those sessions were productive it is worth drawing the moral that the participants represented various disciplines and various generations, but they did not in fact lose touch with one another during the course of the discussions. The more we learned about the other fellow's discipline the more we gained respect for the problems he faced and for the achievements of his colleagues in that discipline. Furthermore, it became increasingly clear that it was not only a concern with the Middle East that we have in common, but also a concern for objectivity, for systematic analysis, for sound theory, and for intellectual integrity. It also became clear that we cannot hope to be adequate as area specialists knowing but a single discipline. In the future, it is unlikely that we shall speak of an "amphibian" who combines Orientalist knowledge and disciplined knowledge. Experience of the phenomena of an area is not yet knowledge because it is not systematized, tested, compared, and evaluated. The amphibians of the future are those who will master more than a single discipline, and especially those who will be able to work in the humanities as well as in the social sciences. The new definition of area specialization will be multidisciplinary, and there is no doubt that we shall require higher standards of linguistic competence, more sophisticated knowledge of philosophic orientations, and a sounder and more critical mastery of the history of the area.

Nor does it appear to be at all clear what alternative organizing principle might have been used. The categories of geographical region and historical period obviously reflect particular disciplinary views. What then are the natural categories of area studies? Any answer that might be proposed will, in effect, be but a hypothesis regarding which are the independent variables and which the dependent. Do we start with religion or with social structure? Do we start with political institutions or with per capita incomes? Moreover, the values implicit in an area approach are far too specific in their implications for objective study than are those implicit in disciplinary study.

There is a profound difference between the attempt to define a good government and the attempt to judge the quality of the existing regime in a given country. The value orientations of Middle East studies are manifestly more subtle in most cases than the perspectives of government information agencies, but the problem cannot therefore be avoided. Thus all studies of Lebanese politics are concerned with whether Lebanon ought to remain an independent political entity, even though the tests of democracy or "integration" may be used. Linguistic studies of Arabic are relevant to controversies over Arab unity, and they are a fundamental component of nationalist theory. Historical interpretations are essential elements in contemporary nationalist ideologies. Literary analyses are presumed to express the views and sentiments of the inarticulate masses. Economic studies are often trenchant criticisms of government policies or condemnations of foreign economic intervention, but their primary value orientation is support of or opposition to a particular country and its regime. Economic performance is an implicit ground of legitimacy. Certain controversial issues in Middle East anthropology are but thinly veiled polemics on the Arab–Israeli dispute. Some of the issues in art history and in philosophy are residuals or revivals of the *Shu'ubiyya* question.

This is not to argue that these questions ought to be avoided. It is rather to argue that the value orientations of area studies are not innocuous and that references to the "sociology of Middle East studies" is not merely an Hegelian knee jerk. The greatest danger to objectivity, however, is, not the obvious advocate but the subtler pragmatist who argues against any intellectual or normative constraints that might prevent judgments from according with short-term policy considerations. The normative orientations of the disciplines are more consistent, even if diverse schools of thought ask different questions. One cannot, for example, ask about the stability of Middle East governments without reflecting on the stability of the American government after the Watergate and Agnew scandals. In essence, the disciplines state the normative issues in more general terms, and in that sense they not only militate against ad hoc judgments, but they also present us with methods for exploring those moral issues which arise in the context of the area. Comparison is one of the ways in which we can judge the conduct of one agent as though it were a general role for the conduct of all.

SOME SPECIAL PROBLEMS

These issues are not specific to Middle East studies; they are common to all area studies, but there are a number of other problems more specific to Middle East studies that emerged during the course of our discussions. There was a general consensus that many of these problems affected all or nearly all branches of Middle East studies and hence might better be mentioned in this introductory chapter.

Most of our authors made substantial efforts to contact their colleagues at other universities in the West and in the Middle East. They sought to consult Soviet literature when accessible, and we were fortunate in having several European and Middle Eastern scholars with us. Nevertheless, there was a great deal of uneasiness expressed over the sense that the state of the art we were surveying was much more the state of the art in North America than anything else. We felt that a great many of the important non-American works were known and mentioned in the papers, but we lacked confidence that our information was adequate, and on more than one occasion it was obvious that we know little of recent scholarly developments in the Middle East and in certain European countries. Though each author agreed to do as much as possible to fill in the gaps in our knowledge, we could not but conclude that there is a very great need to improve international scholarly communication and, in particular, to devise efficient methods for scholarly exchanges with Middle Eastern academic and research institutions.

In a few cases it was felt that important new contributions in fields like art history and the history of the early caliphate had not been incorporated into recent synthetic works. Some argued that existing paradigms were too fixed, and others that current standards were too lax, in explaining these failings. There was, however, surprising agreement that such innovations are frequently disregarded. There was some discussion of ways of remedying this defect, but no concrete proposals were hit upon despite the seriousness of the question. Manifestly, few scholars will long feel the incentive to question existing perspectives if no one is listening. Perhaps the best way of dealing with this problem is by means of periodical reviews of just this kind, in which the emphasis is less on inclusive reporting than on an analysis of the problems being worked on and an identification of the gaps.

Perhaps the most universally acknowledged source of difficulty in advancing the art of Middle East studies is the lack of adequate scholarly communities in the universities. It is true that some institutions have fairly large groups of scholars specializing in the Middle East, but most do not. Even where there are larger Middle East centers we rarely find more than a single scholar in a given discipline. It was this condition that many of our colleagues felt was a grave barrier to advancement of the field. Some believed that particular schools ought to specialize in one or two disciplines (or language areas) whereas the larger centers ought to be encouraged to appoint at least two persons in each discipline. Others argued that the appropriate scholarly community was, in the first place, the academic department in which the individual scholar held his appointment. It was widely agreed that Middle East specialists are often isolated within their departments and at the same time intellectually estranged from other Middle East specialists of different disciplinary persuasions. Because of existing financial limitations, few expected that solutions to the problem of adequate scholarly communities will be resolved by the ubiquitous enlarging of Middle East faculties. Instead, I think it is apparent that interuniversity organizations such as MESA, with its annual meetings and publications, will have to do the job.

There is little doubt, however, that we must increase the number of scholarly meetings and exchanges, while reaffirming the importance of the disciplinary alternative community as a means of upgrading Middle Eastern studies.

An important suggestion, bearing both on the question of the size of the scholarly community and on the problem of interdisciplinary cooperation, is that interdisciplinary task forces be encouraged to formulate and undertake specific projects of research. Conceivably a single university could be encouraged to assemble the requisite skills and interests, or it may be preferable to arrange for the short-term cooperation of scholars from different institutions. Presumably, the problem to be researched would be defined in historical or journalistic terms so that it might then be translated into relevant categories of each discipline. As in the case of urging large centers to appoint more than a single scholar in each discipline, so this solution is expensive, and it also does not take account of the different requirements of teaching and research. This book is devoted to research problems rather than teaching, although the Research and Training Committee of MESA has undertaken to investigate the problems of teaching in the near future. It is clear, however, that a good educational program does not require a "critical mass" in any one discipline; nor would the skills required for a specialized research effort be of more than ad hoc relevance. Educational requirements will continue to emphasize the role of the generalist in introductory and undergraduate courses for a long while.

The distinction between research and teaching seems less relevant when we turn our attention to the need for scholarly tools. During our workshop discussion attention was frequently turned to the need for specialized dictionaries and for carefully edited texts, as well as for more information regarding the whereabouts or availability of manuscripts, archival material and statistical data. In some cases, the provision of these tools is an essential aspect of the "art" of Middle East studies. In others, such tools appear more necessary to the "craft" of teaching, to use the rather arbitrary and invidious terms that have come into the lexicon of the Research and Training Committee. It doesn't seem useful to try to draw too fine a line between these two activities especially with regard to their need for these important references. Every discipline suffers from their lack of availability or from the inadequacy of the reference works we have. In fact, so central are these needs that it seems wise to urge that substantial efforts be made at an interuniversity level, and certainly at an international level, to provide for continuous production and updating of such references. It is from the perspective of the general need for these tools that we can recognize Middle Eastern area studies as a relevant field of study; it is from the same point of view that we can transcend the intellectual limits of each national tradition of scholarship. Hence for those who sense some danger in the overemphasis on disciplinary orientations, it is obvious that they must work to expand the common effort to produce works of general reference, text editions, specialized dictionaries, data banks, and annotated archive catalogs.

Throughout this introduction we have referred directly and indirectly to the tension between descriptive and prescriptive studies; that tension affects every discipline. In all cases it is not at all easy to distinguish the boundary between description and prescription, because the definitions and terms of classification may incorporate value judgments and prejudices. Yet in several of the humanistic disciplines there is a more obvious distinction than, say, in political science and history. It was especially in the areas of literature, or art history, and to a lesser extent philosophy that we felt that the traditional or Orientalist self-definition of the discipline was descriptive rather than prescriptive. The distinction is valid for all disciplines, regardless of their relationship to the Orientalist tradition, and this distinction is of the most crucial importance in dealing with our most difficult and important question. That question is one of priorities.

In a world without scarcity (both financial and intellectual) there would be no need to consider the matter of priorities except from the point of view of what questions are logically prior to others. The lack of academic resources compels us to try to use those we have most efficiently, but we do not wish to have these decisions made on the basis of extrinsic criteria. Certainly we should be uneasy if such decisions were to be made in terms of short-run political considerations or even with regard to the competitive interests of Middle East centers. We would gladly prefer to let each scholar follow his own interests, but since we cannot disregard existing scarcities, we must decide on what basis we shall proceed to determine research priorities. I don't think it is possible to choose among the various disciplines since they define their own values. If we are to step outside the disciplinary framework for such judgments we shall have to press the point with the advocates of an area approach. From the perspective of area studies, the expected subjects of history, language, and religion generally loom largest; but even such an evaluation does not determine what is prior at any given time. If area studies could provide us with a comprehensive rationale for determining priorities, it would have the structure of a developed discipline. I find no evidence that area specialists think in these terms, because they do value description above prescription. Hence what is a prior need for an area specialist depends upon those phenomena that have not yet been adequately described. So long as the criteria of adequate description have not been determined, there will be a tendency for area studies to press us in the direction of the more remote or esoteric and the more contemporary. In general, the more accessible and the historically earlier will already have been described. It is the disciplines that help us to critically evaluate the adequacy of descriptions, and it is such criticism that leads to revisions and to the recognition of inconsistencies.

Each author has attempted to deal with the question of priorities in his own paper. To a considerable extent, these sections on priorities represent the views of the authors themselves. In all cases, the authors have been urged to take account of alternative views and the priority consequences of opposing disciplinary approaches. The authors have also been urged to make explicit the ground for their own decisions regarding priorities. Nevertheless each author has approached the issue in his own way: some more explicitly and some less so. All have expressed some diffidence about trying to tell other people what to do. Therefore we have not attempted to preempt the policy making functions so widely diffused throughout the academic community. Instead we have made proposals, and occasionally these proposals have been forcefully put. We have also set a framework within which any alternative proposals will have to be justified. The framework referred to is not one of explicit suggestions, but rather a framework of the logic of decision. It may be taken for granted that when substantive values are read into this logical frame, priorities will vary not only from discipline to discipline but from country to country. Recognition of this likelihood ought not deter us from looking upon our scholarly endeavors as those of a potential, if not actual, worldwide academic community.

ACKNOWLEDGMENTS

In this project, and especially in our workshop meetings during August 1973, we tried to make this global perspective more of a reality, and though we did not fully succeed, whatever we did accomplish is largely due to the cooperation of our colleagues here in North America, in Europe, and in the Middle East. We are most grateful to all those who took the time to answer the various questionnaires that the authors sent out. We are also grateful to those who took even more time to write at length about some aspect of their special fields in order that such material might be incorporated into the more general work of the authors. Such contributions have not been acknowledged in every case, although in most cases they have been cited or quoted extensively. Regardless of whether these contributors wished to be known, we are thankful for their help.

Those who accepted invitations to attend the Palo Alto workshop deserve a special vote of thanks because of the great contribution which they made in direct and friendly dialogue with the authors. The discussions were informal and forthright, and the more remarkable when one considers the variety of national backgrounds and scholarly interests represented. We tried to get critics and commentators from all disciplines and from many countries. Unfortunately, several of those invited could not take the time from other responsibilities, and one or two of the scholars invited were denied passports by their governments. In spite of all these problems we were pleased to have the following scholars with us for one or more days:

Ahmad Abu Zaid, Professor of Anthropology, Alexandria University (Egypt).
Charles Adams, Professor of Religious Studies, McGill University.
Roger Allen, Professor of Arabic, University of Pennsylvania.
Walter Andrews, Professor of Turkish, University of Washington.
Richard Antoun, Professor of Anthropology, State University of New York, Binghamton.
Gabriel Baer, Professor of Near Eastern History, Hebrew University.
Morroe Berger, Professor of Sociology, Princeton University.
Willem Bijlefeld, Professor of Islamics, The Hartford Seminary Foundation.
Leonard Binder, Professor of Political Science, University of Chicago.
Edmund Burke III, Professor of History, University of California, Santa Cruz.
Hamid Enayat, Professor of Political Science, University of Tehran.
Paul Ward English, Professor of Geography, University of Texas at Austin.
Richard Ettinghausen, Department of Islamic Art, Metropolitan Museum of Art.
Robert Fernea, Professor of Anthropology, University of Texas at Austin.
Lisa Golombek, West Asian Department, Royal Ontario Museum, University of Toronto.
Oleg Grabar, Professor of Fine Arts, Harvard University.
William Hanaway, Professor of Persian, University of Pennsylvania.
Iliya Harik, Professor of Political Science, Indiana University.
Elbaki Hermassi, Professor of Sociology, University of California, Berkeley.
Albert Hourani, Professor of History, St. Antony's College, Oxford.
George Hourani, Professor of Philosophy, State University of New York, Amherst.
Charles Issawi, Professor of Economics, Princeton University.
John Kennedy, Professor of Sociology, University of California, Los Angeles.
Mounah Khouri, Professor of Arabic, University of California, Berkeley.
Ira Lapidus, Professor of History, University of California, Berkeley.
Ragaei El Mallakh, Professor of Economics, University of Colorado.
Ernest McCarus, Professor of Linguistics, University of Michigan.

Michel Nabti, Assistant Curator of the Middle East Collection, Hoover Institution Library.

Laura Nader, Professor of Anthropology, University of California, Berkeley.

Nader Afshar Naderi, Professor of Sociology, University of Tehran.

Seyyed Hossein Nasr, Professor of Philosophy, University of Tehran.

Ayyad al-Qazzaz, Professor of Sociology, California State University.

William Quandt, Professor of Political Science, University of Pennsylvania.

George Rentz, Curator, Middle East Collection, Hoover Institution Library.

Hans Robert Roemer, Professor, Orientalisches Seminar, Der Universität Freiburg im Breisgau, Der Erste Vorsitzende, der Morgenländischen Gesellschaft.

George Sabagh, Professor of Sociology, University of California, Los Angeles.

Hikmet Sebuktekin, Professor of Linguistics, Boĝaziçi Universitesi, Istanbul.

John Simmons, Economist at the World Bank, Visiting Fellow in Public and International Affairs, Princeton University.

Charles D. Smith, Jr., Professor of History, San Diego State College.

David Smock, Deputy Head, Middle East and Africa, International Division, The Ford Foundation.

Elias H. Tuma, Professor of Economics, University of California, Davis.

Gernot Windfuhr, Professor of Iranian Studies, University of Michigan.

I. William Zartman, Professor of Political Science, New York University.

Farhat J. Ziadeh, Professor of Arabic, University of Washington.

Those of us who attended the workshop are very much aware of the great contribution which the setting, the administration, and the staff of the Center for Advanced Study in the Behavioral Sciences made to the success of our meetings.

This project has made an especially heavy demand on the time of our authors and of the members of the Research and Training Committee of MESA. We are all in their debt, but as the one charged with developing and administering this project I am deeply grateful for their willingness to cooperate and for their patience with me. We worked as a team. Our plan was to complete this project within a year of its approval by the Ford Foundation, and I am happy to say that this goal has been achieved. Last, but by no means least, all of us in the Middle East Studies Association owe a vote of thanks for the confidence reposed in us by the Ford Foundation and its Middle East division. Bob Edwards and Tom Scott have watched over us with sympathetic enthusiasm, and no small part of the credit for what we have accomplished must go to them.

NOTES

1. Richard D. Lambert, *Language and Area Studies Review*. Monograph 17 of the American Academy of Political and Social Science. Philadelphia, 1973, p. 59.
2. Ibid. p. 59.
3. Ibid. p. 59.
4. Ibid. p. 78.
5. Ibid. pp. 69, 70.
6. Ibid. p. 53.
7. Ibid. p. 93.
8. Ibid. p. 38.
9. Ibid. pp. 109, 110.
10. Ibid. p. 282.
11. Ibid. p. 117.

CHAPTER TWO

Islamic Religious Tradition

CHARLES J. ADAMS

DEFINITIONS

Among the greatest difficulties that this chapter faces is to justify the limits set to its subject matter. The difficulties arise from two key elements, Islam and religion. How is each to be understood, and what decision is to be made concerning their use in this context?

Islam

For Muslims themselves Islam has always been a civilization and an orientation to the world. It is not merely a religion in the usual, limited, modern sense (whatever religion may mean). In the Muslim view, ideally, there are few or no aspects of individual and social life that may not be considered as immediate expressions of Islam or the working out of its implications. Since the Muslim vision of the world—at least for most people and until fairly recent times—has always been integral and whole, with the religious commitment seen as the central point from which all else flows, it is all but impossible to draw the line between those facets of Islamic experience that are religious and those that are not. Indeed, many Muslim thinkers would insist that it is illegitimate even to try to do so. The closer such people stand to the traditional culture of the Islamic world, the more likely they are to be firm in this insistence. A great deal of covert secularism and also some overt espousal of a secularist view have been evident in the Muslim mentality in recent times, to be sure, but the majority of Muslims are uneasy with them. Muslim thinkers adopt a number of devices to escape secularism's more radical implications. There is a deeply ingrained impulse among Muslims to think and to try to live in terms of an Islamic world view. Such an impulse persists along with conscious efforts to change aspects of social life, even when these amount to a veritable transformation of traditional Islamic society. Means are sought, though not always as a conscious process, to bring the changes desired under the perspective of a traditional Islamic outlook. Historically, when one generation of Muslims has departed from modes of behavior or ways of thinking already established in the community (and therefore, because of the Islamic view of history, correct and righteous ways), succeeding generations have usually found the means to extend the cloak of legitimacy over the acceptable parts of these innovations. Among Sunni Muslims what was innovative, and perhaps therefore questionable, for one generation has become authoritative for those who follow by being considered part of the ongoing tradition of the righteously guided community. For Shi'i Muslims the agent of this accommodation to change has been the authority of the living Imam as exercised by the *mujtahidîn* of the community. Whatever the mechanism at work, Muslims have been enabled through the ages to sustain a lively faith in the integrity of their world view and the rightness of their social forms by the continued expansion of a religiously based understanding of life to include the emergent aspects of Islamic experience.

In more recent times when the Islamic world has faced the painful dilemma posed by its relations with the dominant force of modernity and its own failure of dynamic, means have been pursued to enable the borrowing that is essential to survival, means that would at the same time not compromise the Muslim sense of identity, of special destiny, and of living under the law of God. Characteristically the device chosen, in von Grunebaum's words, is to consider the heterogenetic to be orthogenetic (von Grunebaum, 1962). The possibly disruptive effects of the profound impulse to change have in large part been blunted by giving an Islamic coloring to the processes at work. Thus one witnesses the phenomenon among our Muslim contemporaries of radical changes in social life being pursued on the ground that such changes truly represent traditional Islamic values.

The relevance of such thinking to our present purpose may be seen, to take but one example, in the case of Pakistan where the agonizing—and from the standpoint of many persons nonreligious—matters of forming a constitution, agreeing upon the structure of a government, and designing a policy to foster the well-being of the population are seen as the working out of Islamic principles, that is, as in some basic way a religious enterprise true to the original guidance in the revelation, the life of the Prophet, and the early community. That the quest for a state where they might live out the implications of Islam has led Pakistanis to adopt, as being Islamic, ideas and institutions that prior generations of the pious ancestors did not know and would have rejected unceremoniously, constitutes in Pakistani eyes no valid argument against this process. What is at stake is the compelling necessity to feel that one is faithful to the highest truth he knows. It is to be emphasized that the appeal to an

Islamic frame of reference is not merely a manner of speaking, a deliberately dishonest perversion of historical fact, or a cheap trick of political leaders to enlist the loyalty of ignorant lower classes, but rather represents the way in which Pakistanis, including the elite, largely think of their state (or, if that is somewhat less true after the disaster of the country's breakup, how they largely *thought* in the days of Pakistan's infancy). In consequence, these matters pertain as much to the history of religions as to the concerns of a political scientist or an historian.

The problems that arise in reaching a useful understanding of the concept of Islam stem both from the breadth of the concept, the fact that it implies a multitude of matters beyond the narrowly religious in the more customary sense, as in the above example, and from the rich variety comprehended by the historical Islamic community. The question, "What is Islam?" proves to be extraordinarily difficult to answer both for Muslims and for scholarly students of religion, though it is perhaps no more so than the similar queries, "What is Christianity?" or "What is Buddhism?" The points of view from which the question might be approached are as numerous as those who dare attempt an answer, and the answers given will be as diverse and contradictory as the points of view from which they are constructed. In my opinion there is no hope for the realization of an essentialist definition of Islam that will find close to universal agreement. If the matter is to be dealt with at all, Islam must be seen from the perspective of history as an always changing, evolving, and developing response by successive generations of Muslims to their deepest vision of reality and the meaning of human life. It is not, however, only the expressions of this vision that change but the very vision itself as the ideals of the Islamic community readjust themselves to the differing demands of differing ages. The link among this diversity of responses is their common origin in the prophetic experience and their common agent, the Islamic community. Thus Islam cannot be one thing but rather is many things, not a system of beliefs and practices, etc., but many systems (or non-systems) in a never ceasing flux of development and changing relations to evolving historical situations. Often the historical content of Islam shows several different systems coexistent, in competition, sometimes even in conflict, with one another, but in every case marked by strong mutual differences. No attempt to reduce this diversity to uniformity by emphasizing common elements is tolerable for an historian. Nevertheless, there is a widespread and recurrent tendency to look upon Islam as monolithic and to treat its emergent aspects, especially in the modern period, as somehow being betrayals of the clearly established normative tradition or departures from it. Whatever may be meant by Islam, so far as that is accessible to study, is always a part of history (even the believers' reference to the reality of God who transcends history is accessible to us only in the variety of ways in which this belief has been expressed in the concreteness of historical situations) and reflects the universal character of historical existence, which is one of change. Thus the best that one can do in response to the question, "What is Islam?" is to point to an ongoing process of experience and its expression, which stands in historical continuity with the message and influence of the Prophet.

Religion

There is no less difficulty inherent in the effort to define what is meant by religion. There exists as vast a literature on this matter as on any to which men have given attention, and the subject is proverbially controversial. In scholarly writing religion has been variously seen as man's response to the great and uncontrollable forces of nature, as a disease of language, as the outgrowth of fear and the drive for security and assurance, as an instinctive mechanism for the enshrinement of the chief values of a society, as a principal means for social integration, as response to an inherent sense of the infinite in man's consciousness, as commitment to the deepest values that men recognize, and so on. Discussions on this matter continue with great liveliness as may be witnessed in Spiro's revival, on new grounds, of the old view that religion is belief in gods (Spiro, 1966).

Many of the theories that scholarship has generated, beside complicating the problem of understanding religion, have great potential as interpretive devices for Islamic materials. Such theories, however, have seldom been applied to illuminate Islamic experience. The reasons are several: (1) the fact that students of religion are more interested, on grounds not altogether clear, in the archaic religions than in the higher religions; (2) the relative neglect of Islam in Western scholarship having to do with higher religion; (3) the fact that the desire genuinely to understand the experience of others is often less when the object of study is Islam than in the case of Indian or Far Eastern religions; and (4) the domination of the field by persons with largely philological or historical interests. Among the foremost desiderata, if the field of study is to advance, is the greater application to Islamic materials of the methods and theories used elsewhere for the study of religions generally.

Even if one were able to devise an understanding of religion in general terms that would satisfy him, there would still remain the question of what materials constitute the object of his inquiries. At what things must one look in order to find out about religion, Islamic or otherwise? Again the answer is not easy, for man's religiousness shows itself as affirmations of doctrinal or creedal statements, as the formulation of philosophical systems, as acts of worship, as modes of behavior governed by moral sanctions, or as association with and participation in the life of religiously oriented groups. But are these observable things in themselves adequate keys to the understanding of religion? Is there not also behind them, as their ground and stimulus, a variety of nonobservable experience peculiar to each individual—though fashioned, to be sure, by the historical tradition in which he stands—experience that lies closer to the heart of whatever is meant by religion than its external manifestations? In short, there is an inwardness to religions, a personal and incommunicable area of awareness, feeling, and response, that is at best only partially accessible to others and often not at all. Religion is a matter both of man's inward experience and of his outward behavior, and the student of religions must attempt to the best of his ability to explore both the hidden and the manifest if he is to be adequate to his task. In some of his recent writings W. C. Smith has illuminated this problem by his suggested distinction between tradition and faith, the former standing for the external, observable social and historical aspects of religiousness in the case of any given community, and the other for the internal, ineffable, transcendentally oriented, and private dimension of religious life (see especially Smith, 1963). These two stand in a necessary and indissoluble relationship with one another, each pointing to the other and each incapable of existing independently.

Although the ultimate goal of the student of religion may be to fathom the secrets of the inner life, his attention must necessarily be focused on the historical tradition with which he is concerned, for that alone is public and accessible to the methods of historical inquiry.[1]

There is no corresponding sophistication of methods for approaching directly the mysteries of the inner life of individuals and communities, and the scholar must be content with using the tradition as a stepping stone from which his own ability at putting himself into the place of others may permit him to rise to some degree of genuine insight. Neither the tradition nor the concern for what nourishes it can be neglected in the study of Islam; indeed, they are far from being understood with even a minimum of adequacy. As challenging as that task may be, the study of Islam as a religion implies going beyond the tradition (on which the study has largely been concentrated to this point in our history) in order to come to terms in some fashion with the structure of the inner life of the Muslim peoples. Not only is there involved here a need for the outreach of scholarship, but also for a flight of the soul. Only he who can feel himself able in some degree, if only in imagination, to advance on the path of Islam can enjoy hope of seeing something of the significance of Islam for Muslims themselves. Furthermore, the man who embarks on this path also takes upon himself an onerous moral responsibility to be just and open toward those whose deepest values he claims to understand and to represent in his scholarly work.

It is not the purpose here to attempt to develop another theoretical approach to religion that might be convincing to any large group of scholars but only to set out the terms of reference that have governed the approach of this position paper. When we speak here of Islam as a religion, we have in mind all that was associated with the revelatory experience of the Prophet and all that has followed in more or less direct fashion from it. The direct, as opposed to the more indirect, outcome of the basic Islamic urge may be seen in the traditional body of religious sciences.[2] The Islamic experience is one of a Sovereign Deity who is self-disclosing through His books and His prophets and in the life of the community of those who have committed themselves faithfully to obey Him.[3] As a religion, then, Islam is the experience of the reality of the Sovereign Lord and His demand upon mankind, the response to this experience, and the expression and renewed cultivation of the experience through intellectual modes, structures of worship, and the formation of distinctive types of social groupings.

APPROACHES

A number of perspectives that have governed and still govern the approach to Islam may be distinguished. It is our purpose here to discuss the more important of these.

Approaches to Islam may be located along a continuum, ranging from the normative to the descriptive, or in somewhat different terms, may be classified according to those that have a basis in the religious commitment of the investigator and those that do not. The distinction would seem to be most clear in the case of those who study Islam (or any other religion) with the goal of proselytizing on the one hand, and those who appear to respond to motives of intellectual curiosity on the other hand. It would be a mistake, however, to place too high stakes on such a division because the attempt to maintain such a distinction is in constant danger of breaking down. In spite of strenuous efforts to build an independent and truly scientific study of religion (*Religionswissenschaft*) in the Western universities, it has proven formidably difficult to conduct studies that are neutral in their relation to normative matters and to the philosophy of religion. Evidence of the difficulty may be seen in many of the theories of the nature of religion developed in the last century which, when fully understood, often amount to judgments, and usually negative ones, of the truth and reality of religion. Other evidence of a different kind is afforded in the thought of the founding fathers of the European science of religion or *Religionswissenschaft* whose avowedly scientific motivations often coalesced with theological predispositions. This problem arises because of the nature of religion. Although it is a human and historical phenomenon in one of its aspects, religion claims to have a transcendental reference. In all cases it involves deep commitment and strong emotion on the part of religious men who can at best be restless with efforts to play down the normative demands of religious experience. The business of sorting out normative considerations from what some might consider more properly scholarly concerns becomes acute when the scholar is discussing a religious faith not his own, as in the instance of Western students of Islam. Good scholarship, even though its orientation be scientific, must make every effort to preserve and communicate the sense of transcendental value that accompanies all genuine religious experience. At this point not only is a large measure of empathy called for in the scholar, but the line between normative and more descriptive approaches to the study of religion, between those approaches religiously motivated and those which are not, necessarily becomes blurred, for the scholar is dealing with matters whose significance consists precisely in their pointing to a transcendental dimension that makes the most compelling claims on human life.

Normative or Religious Approaches

Among the approaches to Islam that fall near the normative or religiously motivated end of the continuum are the following: (1) the traditional missionary approach, (2) the Muslim apologetic approach, and (3) the irenic approach of some recent Western writers.

TRADITIONAL MISSIONARY APPROACH. In the nineteenth century there occurred a vigorous outburst of missionary activity on the part of a variety of Christian churches, sects, and denominations that corresponded with the growth of European political, economic, and military influence in parts of Asia and Africa. This new interest in missionary activity was doubtless largely due to the deepened awareness of non-Western civilizations and peoples that followed the advent of colonialism, but it also had deep roots in Christian thought. As a consequence of the missionary movement large numbers of dedicated individuals journeyed to Asia and Africa in the wake of colonial officials in order to convert the populations of those distant places to Christianity and to confer on them the supposed benefits of Western civilization. As a group missionaries necessarily had, and continue to have, strong motivations for establishing close ties with the people among whom they labor. Like colonial officials, they are under the necessity to learn the languages and to participate to some significant extent in the cultural life of those with whom they work if they are to be effective. Consequently among missionaries there have been a number of individuals who have excelled in their use of Muslim languages and whose continued exposure to Islamic culture has given them a deep, if not always sympathetic, knowledge of it. These two classes of persons, missionaries and colonial officials, were among the earliest serious contributors to the growth of a science of Islamics, and until recent times were a basic constituent of the scholarly community. Their contribution should not be underestimated because of disagreement with their goals; all who now work in the Islamics field owe them a great debt.

In the early days of the missionary movement conversion was the uppermost aim of most who left their homes to live abroad in the midst of an alien population. There was much interest in knowing Islam better because deepened knowledge might help in fashioning approaches to Muslims or be useful in the sometimes bitter religious polemics that occurred. Much attention was given to comparisons between Islamic faith and Christian faith, always to the detriment of Islam. From the beginning, however, the motives animating the missionary movement were doubtless mixed. With the passage of time the concern for conversion among the old-line missionary groups has receded more and more into the background, and the desire simply to be of service to people in other parts of the world, still inspired, to be sure, by Christian motives, has come to the fore. Developments in Christian thinking in more recent times, especially among liberal Protestants, have undercut the theological justifications for attempts at proselytization, and the long-established missionary groups have turned to a largely service function, ministering to native Christians and providing teachers, medical personnel, social workers, and the like to the less fortunate areas of the globe. This trend is reinforced by the growing hostility of governments and individuals in the Islamic world toward activities aimed at conversion. It seems fair to say that the missionary movement, insofar as it involved a large number of Western Christians from the principal religious bodies, is past its prime.

One serious qualification, however, must be made in this judgment of the trends in the missionary movement. Though the older groups have in significant ways relinquished the goal of evangelism, since World War II there has emerged an important new element in the form of the so-called "faith" missions. These missions, which are normally ultrafundamentalist Protestant in their convictions, have flooded many parts of the Islamic world with eager souls desirous of helping Muslims to see the error of their ways. At the same time the drive for conversion and the complex of attitudes that accompanies it have been taken up by many Asian and African Christians who perpetuate some of the condemnatory, polemical, and judgmental stances toward Islam that were characteristic of the early years of missionary involvement. Through the agency of such persons the traditional missionary approach to Islam is still very much alive.

APOLOGETIC APPROACH. Among the chief characteristics of Muslim thought in the twentieth century has been a preoccupation with apologetics. Stimulants to adopt an apologetic attitude have been so strong, and the tendency has become so well entrenched, that in some parts of the Islamic world, such as the Indian subcontinent,[4] it is difficult to find Muslim writers who do not, to a greater or lesser degree, reflect apologetic concerns. This burgeoning apologetics can be understood as a response of the Muslim mentality to the situation of the Islamic peoples in modern times. During the past century Muslims have developed a new self-consciousness and dynamic, arising from a sense of internal decay in the community and from the desire to counter the intrusive forces of Western civilisation. Brought to the brink of crisis, the community has felt a need, at times desperate, for reassurance about the basic values of the tradition. It has also sought the means to modernize, which it has considered the key to regaining a lost power and glory, while at the same time struggling determinedly to retain its identity and the principal stamp of its traditional heritage. Apologetics has been one of the principal devices by which the community has met its need for reassurance and asserted the capability of Islam to carry the Muslims into a bright new age.

The themes upheld by modern apologists are familiar to all students of Islamics and need not be catalogued in detail, such as the insistence on Islam's essential rationality, its accord with science, its progressive spirit, its liberal ethical oulook, and its history of conferring benefits upon mankind. Any who are interested can read the classical expression of these themes in Sayyid Amir 'Alī's famous *The Spirit of Islam* ('Alī, 1922) or find them analyzed with perception and some acerbity in W. C. Smith's *Modern Islam in India* (Smith, 1946) and *Islam in Modern History* (Smith, 1957).

To the apologists' credit it must be recorded that they have served the Islamic community positively in several ways. Most important, perhaps, is their evocation of a new sense of identity with Islam among several generations of young Muslims and the creation of a strong pride in this heritage. Their efforts have also resulted in the rediscovery of many aspects of Islamic history and achievement that had been forgotten by the community. The result has been much activity of research and writing that has strengthened Muslims' knowledge of their own religious, intellectual, and cultural heritage. Any study of the Islamic renaissance of the past 100 years must take these contributions of the apologetic movement into account.

Like the missionary interest in Islam, however, the apologetic movement has a number of characteristics which show it in an equivocal light when it is considered from the standpoint of scholarship. Because apologetics is concerned above all else with presenting Islam in a favorable manner, it has frequently fallen into errors that vitiate its scholarly value. In a fashion similar to Christian polemic attacks on Islam, to which it is in part a response, apologetic literature is guilty of distortion, selectivity, and exaggeration in the use of evidence, of romanticizing the history and achievements of the Muslims, of making false comparisons to score debating points, and of other serious faults that betray its tendentious character. The fundamental failing of modern Muslim apologetics, as of its counterparts elsewhere, is to be seen in its motives, which are defensive and polemical, not scholarly. Although much of the apologetic literature exhibits great learning and is presented with all the paraphernalia of scholarship, it is devoted to the exposition of a preconceived position. Its service to scholarship is, in consequence, greatly compromised.

IRENIC. In the years since World War II there has grown up a distinctive movement in the West, represented in both religious circles and the universities, whose purpose is the greater appreciation of Islamic religiousness and the fostering of a new attitude toward it. One is justified in considering this movement in connection with the missionary approach to Islam because those who have participated and been its leaders have been religiously involved individuals, animated in large part by religious and moral purposes in addition to intellectual ones. In a number of instances they have also been missionaries. The thrust of this movement has been toward a deepened grasp of the values which Islam represents to Muslims themselves and toward a truly positive evaluation of Islamic piety. Much of its effort has been given to overcoming the generally prejudiced, antagonistic, and condescending attitudes of Westerners, particularly Western Christians, toward the Islamic tradition. At the same time it has sought "dialogue" with Muslims in the hope of building bridges of mutual sympathy between religious traditions and nations. Insofar as individuals who share this approach have remained true to the tradition of critical scholarship, they have faced extraordinary difficulties in cultivating relations with Muslims because of the suspiciousness with which Muslims, in the light of past experience, tend to regard Western Orientalist study.

In one of its branches the irenic approach to Islam is best exemplified in the work of Bishop Kenneth Cragg. Cragg is a capable Arabist and a trained theologian; in addition, he has for years cultivated relationships with learned and pious Muslims in an effort to bring about a greater degree of accord between Muslim and Christian insights (see Cragg 1956 and 1959). Through a series of studies written in elegant style and with the sensitivity of a poet, Cragg has endeavoured to show to a Western and Christian audience some of the elements of beauty and religious value that animate the Islamic tradition and the duty of Christians to be open to these. This he does by demonstrating that Muslims are concerned with many of the same problems and issues that are fundamental for Christians, but use different terms and are guided by awareness of a different set of priorities in their exposition of the great religious insights. In the same works and at the same time, however, he has in view a Muslim audience to whom he also directs a message. The substance of the message is that the most profound meaning of Islamic faith is realized in Christian experience. His method proceeds by demonstrating that the seminal insights and realizations of Islamic faith when pursued to their ultimate level of significance, prove to be congruent with the Christian understanding of God and the world, and man's relation to them. Further, these insights find a more adequate and profound expression in Christian than in Muslim terms. In effect, he declares that Muslims are in reality Christians who have never pursued their religious experience far enough to recognize that fact, and his effort is to achieve such recognition on both sides of the Muslim–Christian religious boundary. Thus in the final analysis Cragg's purpose remains evangelical, for in spite of his insight into the Muslim soul and his genuine appreciation for the urges that move there, Cragg ultimately believes that Muslims should be Christians and that only in becoming so will they be Muslim in the fullest sense.

Cragg has penned some of the most evocative and appealing work on Islam as a religion that has ever been done in English. His contribution is especially valuable as a means of combatting the negative view of Islamic faith so prevalent among the generality of Westerners. Nonetheless there is, from the scholarly standpoint, a fundamental flaw in his efforts. Cragg's argument is developed by deliberately seeking and finding Christian meanings in Islamic experiences and doctrines Both his interpretation of the nature and structure of Islam and the foundations of the "dialogue" with Muslims that he seeks are achieved by Christianizing the Islamic, by insisting that the Islamic religious tradition means not what Muslims have always thought it to mean, but something else that Christians are in a better position to understand. Such a manner of reasoning does extreme violence to the historical reality of the Islamic tradition by forcing it into categories of interpretation and meaning drawn from a different historical stream of piety and experience. That which Cragg describes is in the final analysis not Islam but the product of his own wishful, though doubtless sincere, religious striving. No matter how thorough or how clever the effort to find congruities between Muslim doctrines and views and those of Christians may be, the stubborn fact remains that Muslims are not Christians. As a way of looking at the world and at the nature and significance of human existence, Islam has a peculiar character of its own. The uniqueness of the Islamic world view is somewhat obscured by the fact that Muslims use terms and concepts in common with Christians and Jews, but the place which these notions find in the total structure of Islamic piety is often radically different from that which they occupy in the competing religious perspectives Of paramount importance to students of religion is the meaning of Islam for Muslims, and that meaning will be seen, it may be suggested, only by considering the Islamic tradition in its own terms as an integral whole.

A second branch of the movement that has broken the link with evangelical motives completely is exemplified in the work of W. C. Smith. Perhaps the most relevant of his works in this connection is the booklet *The Faith of Other Men* (Smith, 1962), and his essay "Comparative religion, whither and why?" (Smith, 1959). In Smith's eyes it is arrogance supreme to call upon the Muslim (or anyone else) to redirect his faith and thus to fail to appreciate that the divine communicates itself to Muslims through the symbols and forms of Islamic piety, just as it communicates itself to others through their respective symbols and forms. His concern is to understand the faith of other men, not to transform it, but this concern is itself a religious matter and a moral duty. Thus there is a strong element of theological interest, though not evangelical motivation, running through Smith's writing.

Taking note of the fact that religious diversity is characteristic of the human race as a whole and religious exclusiveness is characteristic of that segment of mankind who have been affected by the so-called prophetic religions, Smith holds that three different types of questions are to be asked about this diversity. The first is a scientific question, to ask in what the diversity consists, and how and why it has come to be. The second is a theological question, to ask how each religious group accounts to itself in its own normative framework for the fact that others do not share its faith. Finally, there is a moral question, to ask how one should behave toward those of different faith. It is the last that most occupies Smith's attention, for underlying all his work in comparative religion is the drive toward world community and preoccupation with the means of achieving it. Smith holds that the precondition for world community is a proper sympathetic (participative?) understanding of the basic values that form the foundations of the world's cultures, and further, that these values are approached nowhere more immediately than in the study of the religious faiths of mankind. Thus the study of comparative religion, of which the study of Islam is but a part, is in his view the most compelling urgency of our time. Such thinking ranges in its implications far beyond the relatively narrow field of Islamics, and its basic thrust is perhaps ultimately religious and theological.

In his more recent writings Smith has shown increasing interest in the broad issues that arise from the comparative study of religion, especially in their theological and religious implications for the scholar himself, and his interest in the more technical aspects of Islamics has accordingly declined (Smith, 1963). Nonetheless, Smith has made one of the foremost contributions to the understanding of Islam in this generation, and his influence has touched many others in both oriental and theological studies. His works that treat of trends in the contemporary Islamic world rank as standard reference volumes, impressive both for their breadth of learning and the acuteness of their analysis.

By choosing Cragg and Smith as examples of variations on the irenic approach to Islam, we do not intend to ignore the numerous others who should be classified in the same category with them. Mention might be made of Montgomery Watt, whose books (Watt, 1963, 1969) are animated by the irenic spirit, as is Geoffrey Parrinder's study of *Jesus in the Qur'an* (Parrinder, 1965). The point here is only to underline the existence of this approach, which has brought about a revived interest in Islamic religiousness, and to demonstrate some of the forms it has taken.

Philological and Historical Approach

There can be no doubt that the most productive perspective on the study of Islam has been that of philological and historical scholarship. Over the past 100 years scholars equipped with the principal Muslim languages and trained in the methods of philology have devoted themselves to the textual materials that are the most accessible part of the Islamic religious heritage. The work of philologists has not always followed directly from interest in Islam as such, at least in the beginning, but has often come about as a side result or additional benefit of other concerns, such as comparative semitics or Biblical studies. Because of Arabic's status as the most highly developed of the Semitic family of languages, the most widely known, the oldest in continuous living use, and that with the vastly greatest literary heritage, it has been indispensable for students of Semitics, even when their primary interests lay elsewhere. Arabic has often been the key to understanding non-Arab elements in the Semitic linguistic tradition. Once having become acquainted with Arabic, for whatever reasons, some scholars have gone on to explore the literature of the language and to contribute to our knowledge of Islam. In North America it appears that the first formal study of Arabic in a university in the nineteenth century was undertaken in connection with Biblical studies, as a means for better understanding the Hebrew Bible through comparison with a living Semitic tongue. However it may have come to be, the result of philological study is an impressive literature touching upon almost every aspect of Muslim life and piety. Not only has this literature been the principal storehouse of Western knowledge of Islam and its history, but it has played a vital role in the Muslim world itself where the outcome of philological and historical inquiry has been eagerly taken up and exploited by reformers, intellectuals, politicians, and others. Scholarship has brought about a rediscovery of the forgotten glories of Islamic culture among Muslims that is one of the important factors in the present-day Islamic revitalization.

There also can be no doubt of the vital role that philological work must continue to play in the study of Islam. The richest mine of material for students of Islamics lies in the numerous documents from the past bearing on history, theology, law, mysticism, etc., a literature that is one of the most extensive the world has known and that, except for the tiniest fraction, has not been translated into European languages or studied outside the Islamic lands. Unfortunately, even in the Middle East, the greatest part of this rich store is still unexploited.

Language, therefore, stands in the first rank among the tools that a scholar must command in order to achieve significant penetration into the Islamic heritage. Although this matter is appreciated in principle by most who are concerned with the organization of Middle Eastern studies, the formation given to students does not always reflect a place of priority for linguistic and philological competence. This shortcoming is especially evident in area-study and social-science oriented programs that tend to turn students toward a disciplinary tradition rather than toward Islamic culture as a whole. North American students today, as in the past, continue to lag behind their counterparts in Great Britain and on the Continent in essential linguistic skill. The reasons for the difference seem to lie in the greater emphasis that British and European training places upon literature as the key field for all Oriental studies, the opportunities given to students at the undergraduate level to lay a proper foundation for their future research involvements, and perhaps, though it is debatable, to superior methods of teaching language. Of at least equal importance is the fact that more is demanded and expected in the way of language competence from European students relative to their American colleagues. Fewer may survive their course of studies than in North America, but the inevitable by-product of such training is a highly developed competence in language. Although strictly linguistic matters should more properly be considered elsewhere, it must nonetheless be said here that one of the basic needs for the development of studies of Islam as a religion is greatly increased attention to more effective teaching of languages such as Arabic, Persian, Turkish, Urdu, Malay, and Indonesian and the literatures of which these are the vehicles. Serious study of Islam without acquaintance with Arabic is an absurdity, and ideally the scholar should have more than superficial knowledge of at least one other major Islamic tongue and its literary heritage.

Philological–historical methods thus continue to have the most vital relevance to the study of Islam; indeed, in the peculiar circumstances obtaining in North America there is reason to give first priority to the admittedly old-fashioned but essential field of philological training. It is perhaps time that more adventuresome approaches to the field of Islamics should be sought, but these can only be additions to traditional philological work, never replacements of it. It is philology that provides the bulk of material for understanding and analysis and without it sound progress in the understanding of Islam would be impossible.

To set the picture right it must be granted that philological work is often dull and overly engrossed in minutiae of language, or in tracing literary allusions and the antecedents of terms and ideas. Further, there is no guarantee that even the most extensive and detailed acquaintance with a textual tradition will result in meaningful interpretations of the culture that has produced it. Very many philologists have been content to remain historicists, seeing the value of their work in the very details with which they are concerned. Others who have worked on Islamic matters have been hostile or unappreciative toward the materials they have unearthed and studied. In short, trivial philological scholarship exists alongside more important work. None of this, however, undercuts the vital relation between philology and the study of Islam. There may be no guarantee that philological expertise will issue in genuine cultural understanding, but it is certain beyond question that no depth of understanding can arise where there is ignorance of the literature, which is the principal expression of cultural values still accessible to us from ages past. Before anything else, the study of Islam must know to as great a degree as possible what the tradition has been and is; philology is still today, as in the past, the basic tool for acquiring this information.

As a further disclaimer, it should be explained that there is no intention here to set aside or derogate the methods of social scientists employed for the investigation of contemporary Islamic life in favor of purely philological effort. Contemporary behavioral studies have a contribution of significance to make to our knowledge of Islam as a living religion, and the cultivation of such knowledge belongs among the priority aims of Islamists in the near future. The point is rather that philology is the key to the past or to the so-called Great Tradition where the greatest part of Islamic experience lies, and it is my conviction that investigations of the present reality of practice and institutional life proceed on doubtful grounds if they lack reference to the accumulated heritage of the Islamic past. The methods of the behavioral sciences should be used where they are applicable but not at the expense of neglecting traditional philological inquiry.

One of the brighter hopes for the future, though a somewhat idealistic one, is that a type of scholar may emerge who is equipped with the tools of philological and historical inquiry and also conversant with the methods and approaches of the behavioral sciences. Up till now the behavioral scientists interested in Islamics and the traditional students of philology and history have been two different groups of people having little intercommunication and some degree of mutual suspicion and distrust. One of the important contributions that persons interested in interdisciplinary approaches to Islamic and Middle East studies might make is to conceive and carry through a series of steps to lessen the distance that separates older and newer approaches in the field. Although the drive toward interdisciplinary communication has been strong and prominent in the universities in recent years, it has been tied to the social sciences and for the most part its goal has been to break down the tight compartments into which the social scientific disciplines tend to separate themselves or to be forced by the organization of university faculties. The time has perhaps arrived to enlarge the scope of these efforts and to endeavor to attain perspectives that will, to whatever extent possible, combine the more humanistic concerns of traditional historical and philological study with the analytic interests of social scientists

Social Scientific Approach

The emergence of the social sciences and their flowering is unquestionably among the most important developments in intellectual life and in the organization of the sciences in the universities in the present century. For many different reasons social scientists interested in the Middle East have found it important to concern themselves with Islam. In North America, if one thinks in terms of the sheer quantity of work devoted to aspects of the Islamic religious tradition, particularly in the modern and immediately pre-modern periods, the vastly greater part has been pursued by social scientists, not by persons with humanistic orientations and not by individuals trained in the study of religions. Much of this work has great value. It has enormously increased the information available to students of the Middle Eastern area, and its methods have in many instances provided means of analysis that have enlarged our understanding.

It is very difficult to characterize what may be meant by "a social scientific approach" to the study of religion, since there are wide variations of opinion among social scientists themselves about the nature and validity of the studies in which they engage. Intense preoccupation with their methods and with defining the precise scope of their activity is one of the most evident characteristics of social scientists. As a result the approaches and stances they adopt are in a perpetual state of flux and advance. The uninstructed outsider, such as I, who attempts to characterize what is happening in simple terms, places his head in the proverbial lion's mouth, where it is more than likely to be bitten off. For example, may one consider the traditional discipline of history to be a social science? There are those who would wish to do so and those who would not. In my opinion the study of history is not a social science in the same way that sociology may be considered to be so. The basic difference consists in the fact that the sociologist marks off a certain sphere or segment of human activity as his interest and seeks to develop methods peculiarly suited to the study of that segment, whereas the historian entertains broader purposes and uses different methods. There are thus some factors that one can point to as constituting the elements of a "social scientific approach." The relative decline of the humanities in our day and the ebullient faith in the social sciences as keys to the real understanding of human behavior make it important to consider the social scientist as a student of religion, even at the risk of losing one's head.

One of the factors in the outlook of at least a great number of social scientists is a conviction of the possibility and the need to objectify the forces that mold human behavior. If these forces can be conceived and treated as distinct objective entities, then they become observable by empirical methods and in many instances can be quantified. As a further step in the thinking process it then also becomes possible to see broad principles that shape the operation of these objective forces. Such broad principles are similar to universally valid laws that govern human conduct. Typically, social scientific activity is not thought to reach its full fruition until it issues in theoretical constructions that "explain" whatever particular body of factual information may have been gathered or that show the relation of specific situations, developments, etc., to a more comprehensive framework of human behavior. It is the outreach beyond the particular and unique to a (hopefully) universal stance that affords social science its claim to be scientific; otherwise one is studying only history. Many social scientists would claim much more modest goals for themselves than to formulate and understand universal laws of behavior in the area of human activity that interests them most, and probably none would be so bold as to hold that our present grasp of the broad principles of human conduct is exhaustive or definitive. Nevertheless there is an underlying confidence running through the social sciences that man is capable of understanding himself and the way he behaves and possibly even of improving his lot by pursuing social scientific inquiry and acting on the insights it provides. This confidence rests on the assumption that the formative forces in human life are observable as objective realities and involves the impulse toward universal formulae as well.

Among many social scientists the attempt is also made to conceive religion in objective terms so that it, too, may be "explained" and its role in human societies understood. The desire of inquirers is to discover the hard or empirical aspects of religiousness in the belief that uncovering these will allow one to come to terms with what religion in reality is. Unfortunately this way of thinking contains a danger, for it may lead to reductionist views of human religiousness. The history of thought about the nature of religion is replete with theories that "explain" religion as an extension of social values, as a mechanism of social integration, as a device for dealing with the unknown and uncontrollable, etc. The hard or empirical aspect of religion, its true reality, thus shows itself in these theories not as what the religious man thinks or claims it to be, but as the influence of social norms, the instinctive drive for social stability, the human incapacity to live with unresolved fear, etc. In this way religious reactions are deprived of any possible transcendental reference and are brought down into the world of materiality. They are subsumed under a theoretical structure that "explains" religiousness on the same plane as responses to a market situation of supply and demand are explained. Not infrequently in the past social scientific approaches to religion that assume its objectifiable character have become veiled attacks upon the meaning and validity of religious commitments. Although the situation has changed to some degree in recent years, prior generations of social scientific students of religion were in the majority personally and intellectually hostile to their subject. If they escaped the pitfall of reductionism, they still ran the risk of missing the most essential thing in the study of religion. The matter that causes so much trouble in coming to terms with religion in human history is precisely the fact that religious men feel themselves, and sincerely and deeply so, to be reflecting in their pious responses the ultimate character of reality itself. How does one legitimately objectify the transcendental or the ultimate to make it observable, or to subsume it under some still larger conception that accounts for it and shows its "real" nature? Much, though to be sure not all, social scientific thinking holds religious men to be deluding themselves when they think themselves responding to a transcendental vision. In reality they are motivated by other forces, social, psychological, economic, or whatever.

Our purpose here is not to deny the numerous ways in which social scientific inquiries have advanced the state of knowledge. Although one may criticize the theories of the nature or origin of religion that social scientists have produced and continue to produce, each one of them has opened new vistas for all who are interested in the study of religion. Each has been a contribution, and each is more than welcomed by every student of the subject. The point is rather to suggest, as we have already done in the opening sections of this chapter, that one confronts an especially subtle and difficult methodological issue in the study of religion. An aspect of human experience that claims to be rooted in a trans-historical and transcendental realm is to be made the focus of study. Every means must be sought not to blunt the force and significance of the claim for transcendental grounding, for to do so diverts the study from its most central concern. If ways of thinking are adopted that serve to undercut the transcendental dimension of religion, or to deny it altogether by reducing it to more mundane aspects of reality, then the study will be prevented from getting at the heart of religion. If one's purpose is to understand the quality of religiousness, to know what is happening to a man when he sincerely responds to life in a typically religious way, he must be on his guard against conceptions that will mislead.

Another characteristic of social science that may not reflect the ideal of social scientists but that has much practical significance is the tendency to approach the study of man by dividing human activity into discrete segments. There is no quarrel to be raised against the division of a large subject matter into its component parts so that it may be studied more readily. We are familiar with a social science devoted to political behavior, another devoted to social organization and interaction, another devoted to economic behavior, and the like. Each of these has evolved its own methods and tends to a large degree to be self-contained. The best evidence of the trend is to be seen in the existence of separate departments in the universities for these sciences. This fact, however, gives rise to a problem because there is often difficulty in achieving communication among these. Indeed, communication appears to become more difficult with the passing of time as each science refines its approaches to an always greater degree. Evidence exists in plenty to show that social scientists are uneasy with the fragmentation of approaches and the possibly fragmented conception of human nature that it might seem at times to imply. Nevertheless, the much prized attempts to create truly interdisciplinary approaches to the study of human culture have not been conspicuous for their success. It has been enormously difficult for social scientists to understand one another's concerns and to speak one another's language. Instead of communciation, there exist a number of solitudes in the social sciences that encourages each disciplinary group to feel its own concerns to be more fundamental and its methods more trustworthy than those of the others. All this has an effect on the results achieved when social scientists turn their attention to the study of religion.

Most social scientists who have contributed to work on Islam in the recent period have done so from a base within one of the recognized social scientific disciplines. They write as political scientists, as sociologists, as anthropologists, etc., who happen to be interested for some reason or another in the Middle East as a region or in one of the Islamic peoples. To the extent that they see their studies as expressions of a disciplinary interest, they are normally concerned with Islam only as it affects the subject to which the discipline is devoted. Thus questions are raised about the effect of Islam on politics in one country or another, or about the relation of religious orientations to economic development or social change. This approach skirts dangerously near a fragmented view of human nature, for it may slip into looking upon religion, politics, economics, social behavior, etc., as separate, comparable, and reified entities capable of influencing one another and interacting with one another. Whether this danger always exists at a theoretical level and with each individual scholar or not, writings from a disciplinary perspective tend to assess religion and its meaning in terms of something else, namely, its relevance to politics or to economic behavior, or whatever. From such a perspective religion attains its meaning as a function of another realm of activity. A great deal of valuable insight may be won in this way, and social scientists have done an incalculable service in illuminating political, economic, and social facts in the Middle East against the background of the

Islamic heritage. One may question, however, whether studies of this kind do justice to the phenomenon of religion since they are not principally directed at the investigation of the Islamic experience for its own sake. Because their scope is determined by a certain focus of interest, they are likely to take into account only those aspects of Islam that seem relevant for their purposes. On the aspects of Islam that are important for them the social sciences have a great deal to say, and it is valuable. However, it is not all that must be said for Islam to be understood as a religion. Simply put, political scientists and sociologists are not historians of religion, and their writings about religion are as little likely to be complete and satisfactory as would be the writings of a student of comparative religion about politics or social forces. There is no reason why social scientists should be interested in the character of religion for its own sake; they have their own peculiar concerns. By the same token social scientists who write from a disciplinary perspective have a limited, though important, function in contributing to the understanding of Islam.

Perhaps the most significant exception to the pattern of social scientific study of religion described above is to be seen in the case of anthropology. In many respects the anthropologist and the historian of religions approach one another very closely. Because they are interested in the whole life of society, though normally a folk society, anthropologists tend more than political scientists, sociologists, or economists to be also interested in the whole of the religious life of the societies they study. The breadth of their focus allows them to take into account and to render more or less adequate account of even those societies, such as the Islamic, where religious experiences and insights are apprehended as the basis of all else. In short, anthropologists have an interest in the phenomenon of religion for its own sake, and in every aspect of its expression. In certain of the contemporary varieties of anthropological thought religion takes on a special kind of importance. We refer to those anthropologists who would characterize themselves as structuralists, as phenomenologists, or as having adopted a symbol system approach to the people whom they study. Particularly the latter school, among whom the name of Clifford Geertz is the most prominent, have been interested to enter into and represent the value outlook and world view of the folk societies on which they concentrate. Since the religious expression of a people brings together and focuses its value orientations as does no other expression of cultural life, religion becomes almost the equivalent of culture from this perspective. The approach has proven very fruitful in producing illuminating studies of the regional expression of Islamic piety in different places among peoples of differing life styles. Its great strength has been its insistence upon presenting the self-understanding of the subject group in addition to an analysis in the categories and terms of the inquirer.

There are other social scientists who defend the type of study devoted to segments of human activity, arguing that such study, though its angle of vision may be relatively narrow, still constitutes an important, even neglected, avenue of approach to the study of religion. C. A. O. van Nieuwenhuijze gave vigorous expression to this point of view in a paper which he called "The Next Phase of Islamic Studies: Sociology?" published with the proceedings of *Colloque sur la sociologie de l'Islam* held in Brussels in 1961. The opinions expressed in the paper are the more important because of van Nieuwenhuijze's interest in the history of religions and his highly sophisticated awareness of its methodological problems. Although the nature of religion may never be made explicit by the unaided efforts of the sociologist, yet the role of religion as it affects the segment of life that is the concern of sociology may be clarified. There is thus need for a sociological study of religion that gives its attention to Islamic data. Van Nieuwenhuijze is persuaded that the methods of sociology and other social sciences hold the possibility of important new advances in understanding the Islamic religious tradition.

Phenomenological Approach

Among others who have devoted time and energy to the study of Islam are some whose primary interest has been religion or *Religionswissenschaft*. These are persons who received their formation in the European tradition of the study of religion which was born in the last quarter of the nineteenth century, and which has striven for a scientific approach to religion as one of the universal and most important phenomena of history. Their effort has been given to marking out a separate discipline for the study of religion with objectives and methods of its own, independent of theological and philosophical concerns. In the North American context work of this kind is generally known under the rubrics comparative religion or history of religions. For this chapter we ignore the changing conceptions of *Religionswissenschaft* as they have emerged in methodological discussions and use the term phenomenology to characterize this approach to the study of religion. We do so because of the dominance of a school of phenomenologists in the discipline in recent times. Phenomenology of religion is difficult to define since almost every contemporary student of *Religionswissenschaft*, no matter what his differences from his fellows, would identify himself with the phenomenology of religion. Nevertheless, we can distinguish two important concerns that seem to characterize the phenomenological approach. The first of these may be expressed by saying that phenomenology is a method for understanding the religion of another which involves an attempt on the part of the scholar temporarily to set aside or neutralize ("put into parentheses" is the phrase used by van der Leeuw, high priest of the movement) his own preferences and commitments as a preparation for deliberately trying to reconstruct in his mind the experience of another. Such an act of self-renunciation is called *epoche*; the attempt that follows, to relive in one's imagination the experience of another, to stand in his shoes, as it were, is what is meant by understanding. It implies a common ground in human personality for religious experience and a fundamental sameness of religious reaction among all men, no matter how separated in time and space and how different in cultural expression.

This aspect of the phenomenological approach is of fundamental importance for the study of Islam. It holds the key to making restitution for the sins of unsympathetic, hostile, or interested approaches that have plagued the tradition of Western Orientalism, and it opens the door to a penetration of Islamic religious experience on both a broader and a more profound scale. The great achievement of the phenomenologists is to have seen, and uncompromisingly to have insisted, that the norm in all study of religion is the experience of the believer himself. What the study must attempt to do is to elucidate the meaning of his religiousness to the religious man. The categories for understanding and organizing religious experience are those that the religious man has established for himself through the working of his own historical tradition upon him and his own personal experience. Phenomenology abjures any reductionist explanation of religion in other terms or any application of categories drawn from sources outside the experiences one is attempting to comprehend. The matter of basic importance, indeed the only legitimate concern for a student of religion, is what the religious man himself has experienced, felt, said, and done, but above all, what these experiences mean to him, how they are presented to the consciousness. The thrust of phenomenological studies is toward the elucidation of meanings, to make clear what rites and ceremonies, doctrines, or social reactions connote to the actors in the religious drama. As part of its equipment phenomenology makes the fullest use of a variety of auxiliary disciplines which supply its raw material, such enterprises as history, philology, archaeology, literary studies, psychology, sociology, anthropology, and others. The collection of materials and the description of religious phenomena, however, are only the preliminary part of the phenomenologist's task, for there follows the need to interpret the data turned up by investigation, in the sense of discerning the structure and interrelationship that the data exhibit in the consciousness of the community or individual which is the object of interest. Ideally the criterion that should inform the phenomenologist of religion who studies Islam is the question: can Muslims themselves recognize as true and accept what is put forward by the scholar as a description of their faith? If this question cannot be answered in the affirmative, if there are serious shortcomings in conveying the quality of Islamic life as Muslims live and see it, then one must conclude that the thing described is not Islamic faith. It is clear that the task phenomenologists have set for themselves is most demanding, one that requires far more than hard work, rigor, and the refinement of tools and techniques. As is suggested at another point in this chapter, what is required is a flight of the soul, an outreach toward the world view and feelings of others that reshapes the personal commitments of the scholar.

The meaning of the phenomenological method or spirit for the study of Islamics and the revolution in approach for which it calls will be appreciated by all who are acquainted with the tradition of Western scholarship having to do with the Islamic religious tradition. Until the emergence of irenic attitudes in very recent times, it would be fair to say of the vast majority of Western Orientalist writings on Islam that they are at best indifferent and often openly hostile or contemptuous toward the religious perceptions and values of Islamic faith. This fact is so widely known and so often commented upon that it requires no further documentation here. In any event there can be no doubt that Muslims perceive the scholarly tradition in this way. Not only is this situation an evidence of moral insensitivity to the deepest commitments of other men on the part of Western students of Islam, but more to the point for our purposes, it is also an evidence of faulty scholarship. Before all else what the phenomenological approach would demand is that Islamic experience be taken seriously as an object of study, valuable for its own sake. Only if it is so considered is an adequate account of its significance for the community likely ever to be achieved. With very few notable exceptions, there is now no scholarly work on Islam from Western pens that seeks to penetrate the Muslim horizons to offer an authentic representation of Islam's impact on the lives of the millions who call themselves Muslims. The phenomenologists of religion through their discussion of methods in their field have called attention to the paramount task of observing, comprehending, entering into, and *re*-presenting the experience of religious men. The stimulus they offer is perhaps the brightest hope for the advance in our understanding of Islam as a religion.

The second aspect of a phenomenological approach is the construction of taxonomic schemes for classifying phenomena across the boundaries of religious communities, cultures, and even epochs. Gathering material as widely as possible, phenomenologists seek for the categories that will group together phenomena showing similarity of basic nature. Underlying this activity is the search for structure in religious experience, for the broad principles that seem to operate in forming the manifestations of human religiousness as a whole. Though the process of gathering material concerning religious phenomena involves the phenomenologist in historical and philological inquiry into the particularities of various religious traditions, the effort to systematize these and to demonstrate the character of religion and the dynamics inherent in its makeup through isolating structures goes beyond the strictly historical to become almost a philosophy. The urge to construct taxonomic schemes stems from the conviction that each type of religious phenomenon (e.g., sacred man, sacred time, sacred place) follows an inherent logic, obeying a principle extrinsic to the historical event itself, in the course of its historical expression and development. Thus, it is argued, one cannot grasp the meaning of a religious phenomenon if he confines himself to the historical particularity of the event, but must search beyond in a larger realm for the structural, universal, or archetypical force which the particular phenomenon exemplifies.

Such thinking comes very near to holding that each religious phenomenon has an independent and universal meaning in itself, and it tempts many phenomenologists to neglect the historical structures of particular religious communities and the religious perceptions of particular men in favor of the search for the broad meaning of religion. In my opinion the ground upon which this aspect of phenomenological inquiry rests is not as firm as the foundations of the first aspect of the approach discussed above. For many inquirers the search for the universal meanings of religious phenomena is transmuted into an hermeneutical device useful for forming a religious interpretation of the religious history of mankind or for building a theology of the history of religions. For others who focus their interpretations around such key concepts as myth or symbolism, the culmination of phenomenological activity is the resacralization of a world that has progressively lost its sense of the holy. Phenomenology thus seems in danger of leading *Religionswissenschaft* back into the maze of theology and philosophy from which it has struggled so valiantly and so long to escape.

In one respect, however, the systematizing efforts of phenomenologists undoubtedly have a validity and a great importance, for it is precisely this aspect of the approach that lifts the study of religion to a scientific level. Not contenting itself with the particular and unique, phenomenology is interested in the general rules or characteristics of all religious life, or in what might be loosely called the laws governing the emergence and expression of human religiousness. Application of its methods to the study of Islam, to take an example, would afford the scholar an opportunity to assess the place of the Islamic tradition as a whole, or any part of it, in the universal religious history of the race. In this respect the goals of the phenomenologist respecting religion are very close to the aims and aspirations of social scientists in their respective fields.

Although the phenomenology of religion has enjoyed a great vogue in North America in recent years because of the influence of Mircea Eliade and his disciples, there has been almost no attempt to apply the methods and insights of this approach to Islamic materials. Nor is the case much better in Europe, the home of the phenomenological approach as of so many other things in the study of religion. To judge from the use made of it, the phenomenological method appears much better adapted to the investigation of religious communities that express themselves primarily in nonverbal and prerational modes, and for this reason phenomenologists have devoted the greater portion of their attention to so-called primitive and archaic religions.

There are some beginnings, to be sure, but Islam, which is always the poor relation of the family of religions in North America, receiving far less attention than the other major religious communities of the world, has come in for relatively little consideration. Islam, however, offers an extraordinarily rich field for cultivation by those who are skilled in the use of phenomenological and other methods developed specifically for the study of religions. In view of the importance of religion throughout the whole of the historical adventure of the Islamic peoples, professional students of the Islamic world could only benefit from enlisting the insights and skills of scholars in religion as these bear upon the field of interest.

It is a sad but undeniable fact that the study of Islam as a religion is grossly underdeveloped in the centers of higher learning in North America. The two types of locale where studies of this kind might best be pursued are the major centers of Near and Middle Eastern studies and university departments of religion, but in neither type is the requirement for Islamic studies adequately met. In the major centers of Near and Middle Eastern studies it is a rarity to find staff members trained in religion, and there is little evidence of recognition of a major place for studies of Islam as a religion in the requirements set for students or the courses offered them. Although the majority of these centers are interdisciplinary in character, their organizers have not seen fit to include *Religionswissenschaft* among the disciplines represented. In most departments of religion, which are a recently emergent but increasingly important element in university life, Islamics comes very near to or at the bottom of their priorities for a variety of reasons, which it would be interesting to explore. Very few such departments offer opportunities for more than an introductory semester on the Islamic tradition, and none can sustain more advanced work in Islamics. Progress in the understanding of the Islamic tradition would seem, therefore, dependent upon two quite fundamental things: (1) recognition of Islam as one of the truly major segments of human religious involvement deserving of the studious attention that other such segments receive; and (2) recognition that there is a sophisticated and vigorous discipline of the study of religion, with insights and methods of its own, whose resources should be utilized for the better understanding of Islamic religious experience. The latter of these amounts to a plea that

Religionswissenschaft should find its representatives and expressions in the major programs of Middle and Near Eastern studies.

THE ISLAMICS FIELD

The subject matter relevant to the study of Islam as a religion may be broken into the following subdivisions: (1) pre-Islamic Arabia; (2) studies of the Prophet; (3) Qur'anic studies; (4) prophetic tradition (*hadîth*); (5) *kalâm*; (6) Islamic law; (7) *falsafah*; (8) *taṣawwuf*; (9) the Islamic sects, especially the Shī'a; (10) worship and devotional life; and (11) popular religion. An entire chapter is devoted to Islamic philosophy, and for that reason no mention is made of the matter here. Nor does it seem necessary to survey in detail the existing literature in each of the other subdivisions. I have devoted two lengthy essays to this subject, (Adams, 1965 and 1970, 71), and there are other resources available in addition. We content ourselves here with attempting to assess where we now stand and with some brief remarks on some of the more outstanding developments and possibilities in these various aspects of the subject.

Pre-Islamic Arabia

There is an element of arbitrariness that must be acknowledged from the beginning in the decision to limit discussion of the background of Islam only to pre-Islamic Arabia. Any who have reflected on the matter, especially students of the religions of the ancient Near East, will recognize that no adequate account of the religious heritage upon which Islam drew and the religious backdrop against which it emerged can even be attempted without tracing the religious evolution of the Semitic peoples as a whole and seeing that heritage in relation to the simultaneously evolving religious insights of the other peoples who inhabited the ancient Middle East. The store of religious insight, experience, and tradition available to Muhammad and his contemporaries, which they partially utilized and partially reacted against, was not drawn strictly from the confines of Arabia. Islam is the culmination and working out of trends in the religious life of the Near East that preceded the birth of the Prophet by centuries, and it exhibits an unmistakable continuity with that heritage, a fact that the Islamic tradition itself affirms on theological as well as historical grounds. The background of the rise of Islam is, therefore, the history of ancient Near Eastern religion as a whole. To pursue so broad a field, however, is clearly beyond the scope of this chapter, especially since ancient Near Eastern studies is a vigorously pursued area of inquiry with an already rich but still growing literature. We restrict ourselves, therefore, to some considerations on Arabia prior to the rise of Islam.

Although we do not go into the matter, it is important here to underline the continuity of Islamic experience with the great Near Eastern religious tradition that preceded it for the reason that the close connections between the two are often forgotten or ignored. A somewhat anomalous situation exists in studies of Near Eastern religious history which is not to be seen elsewhere. In a brilliant article, "Islam and Image," the late Marshall G. S. Hodgson called attention to the fact that religious life in the ancient Near East is not normally looked upon as a developing continuity but is studied and conceived as a series of discrete and somehow exclusive religious communities, one supervening upon the other (Hodgson, 1964). This trend is no doubt due to the essentially theological convictions of uniqueness that cling to the two Biblical traditions. For many Jewish and Christian scholars a view of their own religious communities which holds them to be outgrowths or further developments of previous religious insights represents a compromise of their claims to special and unique truth. They have, therefore, insisted that their own traditions are sui generis, not to be viewed in developmental historical terms as concrete expressions of an ongoing Near Eastern tradition. Such an approach is in sharp contrast to the way in which scholars approach the Indian, Chinese, and Japanese traditions, where a picture is drawn of a developing religious consciousness, which though continuous with a past heritage, passes through continually new and emergent phases in the course of history. Hodgson also suggests that the manner of organizing studies in Near Eastern religions resulting from such a point of view is among the powerful reasons why Islam does not hold the same interest and attraction for students and scholars that the Far Eastern and Indian religions exhibit.

Knowledge of religion and of other conditions of social life in pre-Islamic Arabia was for a number of years at a kind of plateau from which it could not rise because of the unwillingness of governments in Arabia to permit archaeological work or free travel by foreigners. The essential interpretative studies on pre-Islamic Arabia were done by scholars such as Goldziher, Wellhausen, Margoulioth, Nöldeke, Lammens, Lyall, and Nicholson, all great names from past generations, whose work is of continuing importance down to the present. Most of these pioneers in Islamics drew the material for their work on pre-Islamic Arabia from literary sources: from the *Jâhilî* poetry, from the *sîra* literature, from the accounts of Arab historians, or from such compilations as the *Kitâb al-Aghânî* and even from the Qur'an. They have given us a picture of the outlook and attitudes of the pre-Islamic Arabs among whom Muhammad appeared, which is clarified but not greatly changed by more recent work. Among the more significant contributions to the enlargement of understanding are the efforts of Toshihiko Izutsu to mark out precisely the elements in the moral outlook of the Arabs to which the teachings of the Qur'an have immediate relevance (Izutsu, 1959); the studies of Montgomery Watt on the economic and social backgrounds of the rise of Islam and the functioning of tribal relationships in his books on Muhammad (Watt, 1953 and 1959), and the anthropological studies of R. B. Serjeant (1962) relating to certain of the religious institutions of the Arabs before Islam. The important critical question about the authenticity of the *Jâhilî* poetry on which studies of this kind depend so much has not been pursued beyond the point where it was left after the explosion that greeted the publication of Ṭâhâ Ḥusayn's *al-shi*^{c}*r al-Jâhilî*. Both Izutsu in *The Structure of the Ethical Terms in the Koran* (Izutsu, 1959) and A. J. Arberry in *The Seven Odes* (Arberry, 1957) return to the matter but only to say that the question is no longer a lively one, a kind of general consensus on the authenticity and genuinely pre-Islamic nature of the poetry having somehow been reached. Neither discusses convincingly or in detail the arguments and considerations that have led to their convictions in the matter. There is important new information, however, especially on the written transmission of pre-Islamic poetry in the first Islamic century, made available in Fuat Sezgin's *Geschichte des Arabischen Schriftums* (Sezgin, 1967). Sezgin's supplement to Brockelmann, when its impact is fully felt, will do much to change the picture of the early Islamic period and the developments that occurred there.

One of the ways in which studies on the religious heritage of the Arabian peninsula have been advanced in recent years is through archaeological work on the ancient history of the region. Although it is by no means easy, even today, to gain permission to dig in the interior of Arabia, a good bit of work has been undertaken in the recent past, and the outlook for more such activity is good. Several foreign expeditions have been permitted (Belgian, Danish, American), and there is greatly increased interest by governments in the region to foster specialized training in archaeology for a number of their own nationals. The growth of a highly capable, thoroughly trained, and adequately supported group of local people concerned with exploring and preserving the archaeological heritages of their countries is among the very promising factors in the present situation. In the Western world the University of Louvain has emerged as the most important center of new work on ancient Arabia, and G. Ryckman has established himself as the leading authority on the religious life of the era. At this point in the development of studies the most important gain to be registered is the accumulation of a vast new store of materials for analysis and interpretation. Much of this, however, is still fragmentary to the point of preventing a connected and reliable account of the ancient religious outlook of the area. It is still impossible to give a satisfactory answer to questions about the meaning to the ancient Arabs of the deities discovered or the rites and ceremonies evidenced by the archaeological remains. Some of the results of this scholarly activity can be seen in the writings of Ryckman (1951) and J. Pirenne (1955), both of Louvain, and in the series of six massive volumes edited by Franz Altheim and Ruth Stiehl entitled *Die Araber in der alten Welt* (Altheim and Stiehl, 1964–1968). The purpose of these volumes is to describe the role of the Arabs in the ancient world as a whole. Its authors uphold a thesis about the deep involvement of the Arabs with the classical and Hellenistic civilizations of the Mediterranean basin before the rise of Islam. Volume 3 of the series is devoted to the study of religion in ancient Arabia and argues that much that is characteristic of later Islam was already to be found there, including a belief in monotheism and the use of Neoplatonic modes of thought. The contributions of archaelogy in southern Arabia to a firmer construction of the history of the area may be perused in a sumptuously published volume by Brian Doe which contains an excellent bibliography and a number of illustrations; it is entitled *Southern Arabia* (Doe, 1971). Hermann von Wissman of Tübingen also has a number of works dealing with pre-Islamic Arabia. For one example see his *zur Geschichte und Landeskunde von alt Süd-Arabien* (von Wissman, 1964).

The greatest advance in systematic description of aspects of religious life in pre-Islamic Arabia has been registered by French scholarship, where three names have special importance: Bishr Farès, Joseph Chelhod, and Toufic Fahd. Farès' contribution is his *L'honneur chez les arabes avant l'Islam* (Farès, 1932), a study of the values that were central to the self-conceptions of Arabs in pre-Islamic as well as later times. The starting point is Goldziher's emphasis upon the concept of *Muruwwah* as the basic virtue of Arab life. As a result of criticism, Farès is able to show that the pursuit of manliness serves a further purpose beyond itself, namely, to establish the *ᶜirḍ* or reputation of a man in the eyes of his fellows. *Muruwwah* and the other virtues, such as generosity, bravery, and faithfulness to one's word, which make it up, find their meaning in the honor they confer upon their possessor. Chelhod's interest lies in matters that are more evidently religious in nature. He has written on *Le Sacrifice chez les arabes* (Chelhod, 1955) and on *Les Structures de sacré chez les arabes* (Chelhod, 1964). The method employed in these studies reflects the systematic impulses of the phenomenologists of religion, for Chelhod classifies the types both of sacrifice and of the sacred as they are found among the Arabs in order to present a fully rounded picture. The work of Toufic Fahd (1966) began with his *La divination arabe.* Part of the material which he originally gathered for this study proved to be of such interest and so abundant that it was published as a separate volume entitled *Le Panthéon de l'Arabie centrale à la veille de l'Hegire* (Fahd, 1968). A major element in the value of all these studies is the fact that they range over material drawn from both the pre-Islamic and the Islamic eras. They serve in this way to show the continuity of religious life in the area and to illuminate the relationships between Islamic ideas and practices and those which antedated them in the peninsula. In his studies of sacrifice, for example, Chelhod discusses the sacrificial cultus that predated Islam but goes on to give a major element of his attention to the sacrifice that occurs in connection with the ceremonies of the *ḥajj* and to the other sacrifices that mark aspects of both civil and religious life among Muslims. Similarly, his analysis of the sacred comprehends both the jinns and spirits of the Jahiliyya and the high Islamic conception of the unique Sovereign Lord. In his work on divination, Fahd elaborates the relation between divination and prophecy and offers a full discussion of the attitudes of eminent Muslim authors of the medieval period toward this important subject. The appearance of studies of this kind marks the transition from archaeological work on the pre-Islamic remains in Arabia to a fuller and more systematic understanding of the character of religious life and outlook there and its continuing influence in the piety of the Islamic community.

Muhammad

The study of Muhammad's life has been favored in the years since World War II by the appearance of several important works. Watt's full-scale biography underlined the social and economic dimensions and background of the Prophet's activity and illuminated the brilliance of his relations with the tribes (Watt, 1953 and 1956). It also explores the knotty question of the reliability of the source materials for Muhammad's life and career and argues for a much greater dependence on traditional materials than a previous generation of scholars was willing to grant. Among the important features of Watt's work is his sensitivity to the moral issues that any non-Muslim inquirer who studies Muhammad must face. Watt seeks to avoid overt statements and even language that would by implication judge the religious meaning that Muslims see in Muhammad. Since it covers the whole of the Prophet's career and touches most of the problems raised there, Watt's must be judged to be the most important study of Muhammad since the biography of Frants Buhl (*Das Leben Muhammeds*) which was the previous standard in Western scholarship (Buhl, 1961).

A different kind of study that represents another major contribution to work on the Prophet is A. Guillaume's translation of Ibn Hishâm's *Sîrat al-Nabî* (*The Life of Muhammad*) (Guillaume, 1955). This Arabic biography of Muhammad, prepared on the basis of an earlier work by Ibn Ishâq, is the earliest and most fundamental source for information on Muhammad, his activities, his companions, and his times that has been preserved for us. It is a very large book and a most difficult one to use, even for the trained Arabist, in its original version. Works of this kind are seldom rendered into European languages. Its translation cost Guillaume an immense labor over a long period of time, but he has provided his colleagues with a most important resource. It must be added that Guillaume's translation has been sharply criticized in some of the review literature for a number of its features (see R. B. Serjeant, 1958), but in a work of such length and fraught with such difficulties, errors and disagreements are unavoidable. In spite of caveats about points of detail the basic source of material for Muhammad's life is now readily accessible to the English reading public.

Mention of work on source materials must also take notice of Marsden Jones' new edition of al-Wâqidî, whose account of the Prophet's *maghāzī* is perhaps an even more vital source of information on the latter part of Muhammad's life than much of the *sîra* literature (Jones, 1966).

As remarked in connection with Watt's work, considerable attention has also been given in recent times to the critical problems that affect the authenticity and reliability of the information available on Muhammad. These matters are considered with brevity, clarity, and acuteness in the small volume of Régis Blachère entitled *Le Problème de Mahomet* (Blachère, 1952). Blachère is somewhat pessimistic in his conclusions, proving that the Prophet is far from being the well-known historical figure that he is claimed to be, and demonstrating the existence of a host of trenchant problems that can be resolved only by the discovery of new evidence if they can be solved at all. His volume describes the state and situation of biographical work on Muhammad with precision and lays down the criteria by which any future reworking of the literary materials bearing on Muhammad will have to be judged.

The new departures in this field that appear to hold promise are R. B. Serjeant's anthropological work among the Arabs of South Arabia (Serjeant, 1958) and Harris Birkeland's studies of the Qur'an, (Birkeland, 1956). Serjeant believes it possible to find elements in the life of contemporary tribal Arabia that will help to understand the Arabia of Muhammad's time. He is sharply critical of the work of some others, especially Watt, regarding Muhammad, arguing that insufficient account is taken of the nature of tribal life among the Arabs. He has sought to remedy the shortcomings of scholarship by extensive anthropological and ethnological work among Arab tribes in the extreme south of the peninsula. The fundamental assumption of his method which has earned him strictures from critics, is that tribal society is massively conservative and virtually static, tending to change very little even over the course of centuries. It is today, in its essential characteristics, very much as in Muhammad's time. If this is true, it should be possible to extrapolate from contemporary tribal experience and outlooks to reconstruct the environment in which Muhammad functioned and many of the practices that characterized it. Serjeant (1958) has carried out a number of studies of religious institutions in South Arabia and has offered comparisons between the "holy men" of the area and the Prophet, arguing that Muhammad often acted in the same way as these "holy men" now act and rested his activity upon a similar kind of institutional base. Thus much that is otherwise puzzling in the behavior of Muhammad becomes for the first time understandable. Some of the results he has achieved are indeed striking and illuminating, and he is reportedly preparing a full-scale study on his research among the South Arabian tribesmen.

Harris Birkeland (1956) has been principally interested in the content of the Qur'an; his work is for that reason relevant to matters that are discussed below. Of importance for the present is his belief that a careful analysis of the Qur'an's text will reveal aspects of Muhammad's personal religious development that have not been previously appreciated. He thinks it possible, from a combination of careful perusal of the text and reference to the early *tafsîrs*, to describe some of the earliest stages in Muhammad's thinking. He believes it possible even to show from the early *sûras* that there was a time, after the beginning of the prophetic experience, when Muhammad was not yet a firm monotheist. This amounts to the radical claim that the Qur'an in some of its parts does not uphold monotheism. The evidence for this point of view, however, is admittedly slim and the interpretations subtle. Further, Birkeland's work rests firmly upon the historicist Western view that interprets the Qur'an as the product of Muhammad's mind and experience, and his interest is in questions of development rather than of religious meaning.

One area of importance in the study of Muhammad, however, has been little advanced in recent time though it is most vital for those concerned with the exploration of the religious life of Muslims. We refer to the role that Muhammad plays in Islamic piety, his religious function for the community, and the place that prophecy occupies in the Islamic understanding. The best work on the subject is still Tör Andrae's book, *Die Person Muhammads* (Tör Andrae, 1918); it is, in fact, the only full-scale work on the matter known to me. For the purposes of one interested in religion, the place of Muhammad in the thinking and devotions of Muslims is of greater importance than the facts of his biography and personal development. Of central concern is Muhammad the Prophet rather than Muhammad the man, the Muhammad perceived by Muslims, whether or not he be the same as the Muhammad of history. There is no intention to deny the worthiness and interest of scholarly work on the prophetic biography and all the problems that surround it. These matters are of great concern to historians and to Islamists alike and ought to be pursued with all the vigor the scholarly community can summon.

The point is rather that strictly historical and critical studies do not necessarily cast light upon the religious perceptions of Muhammad as a Prophet. It matters more to one who wishes to explore the spiritual realm of Islam to know what Muslims think of Muhammad, even if what they think is wrong from the historical and critical perspective, than to set the historical picture straight. More or less exclusive concern with the person and biography of Muhammad in recent Western scholarship has led to neglect of the fact that the view and meaning of Muhammad, as of most everything else, have evolved in the course of the Islamic community's development and continue to do so. In spite of Qur'anic denials, the earliest generations attributed miraculous powers to the Prophet, and later theologians made the possession of such abilities the very touchstone of prophecy. Philosophers and mystics also embroidered the image of the Prophet according to their own peculiar visions, and the process continues with the modernists and revivalists of our time. These matters are the very stuff of the study of religion, and they deserve the fullest measure of attention. We would emphasize once again the relevance of the phenomenological stance which asks, "What is the meaning for the believer?" The appearance of writings in answer to this question by an established scholar such as W. Bijlefeld together with the interest of some younger people is very much to be welcomed. In view of the availability of new materials in fields such as Sufism, there now exists an opportunity for further work to demonstrate the highly varied and extremely rich role that Muhammad has played in the history of Islamic thinking and devotion. Of great relevance to this concern also is a recent proposal for the translation and publication of Haykal's *Life of Muhammad*, probably the most widely read and respected biographical effort from a Muslim pen in the twentieth century, and a work that expresses the thrust of contemporary Islamic thought about the Prophet.

The Qur'an

Closely resembling the situation in studies of Muhammad, Western scholarship on the Qur'an has principally concerned itself with what may be called the critical problems that surround the Islamic Scripture. Such matters as the formation of the Qur'an text, the chronology of the materials assembled in the text, the history of the text, variant readings, the relations of the Qur'an to prior literature, and a host of other issues of this kind have been investigated thoroughly. Much of the basic work on these problems was done by nineteenth-century scholars, the most important of whom was unquestionably Theodor Nöldeke (1909) whose *Geschichte des Korans*, as supplemented by the later efforts of Bergsträsser and Pretzl, remains the fundamental work in the field. Advances have been made on these early studies in more recent times, as for example Richard Bell's attempt to refine Nöldeke's scheme for establishing the chronology of Qur'anic materials,* but the basic framework of critical Qur'anic studies remains that laid down in the preceding century. Probably the most significant effort to carry a critical approach to the Qur'an to new levels of exactitude in the twentieth century was the ill-fated project by a group of German scholars in cooperation with others to produce a critical text of the Qur'an. The project was brought to an end by the Allied bombing of Munich in World War II, which destroyed the manuscripts and other materials that had been assembled. The late Arthur Jeffery, who was one of the group of interested scholars, has published some of the relevant materials in his *Materials for the History of the Text of the Qur'an* (Jeffrey, 1937). The degree of loss was so great that it may never again be possible to mount a similar effort. The problem is further compounded by the deaths of most of the persons involved. To my knowledge no extensive critical work on the text of the Qur'an is now being undertaken in either the Muslim or the Western worlds.

The surprising fact about the state of Qur'anic scholarship in the West is the degree to which critical concerns have dominated the field. In spite of its overwhelming importance for Muslim religious life, the Qur'an has received astonishingly little study aimed at discovering, explaining, and expounding more clearly what that famous book says. There is a large literature analyzing Qur'anic teachings scattered through the pages of periodicals and embedded in larger discussions of Islam, but there exist only a few major works that have study of the contents of the Qur'an as their aim. Better understanding of the Qur'an is of such importance for the whole range of Islamic life that the present situation should not be allowed to continue. Encouragement of studies in this field deserves the highest priority.

Fortunately the picture is not altogether bleak. Daud Rahbar has written a major work which upholds the thesis that the Qur'an's message centers in the notion of the justice of God, from which the work gets its title. (Rahbar, 1960). Rahbar has been especially concerned with disentangling the Qur'an's point of view from the Greek ideas and concepts that later generations of Muslims, and especially the theologians, have used to interpret it. His work supports the idea, held by a number of others, that the Qur'an possesses a distinctive world view of its own that should be appreciated for its own sake. This he sees as a prerequisite for understanding the Qur'an itself and for a proper reading of the development of Muslim thought. Probably the most impressive effort of recent days toward a detailed exposition of selected Qur'anic concepts and ideas is the work of Toshihiko Izutsu (1959, 1966, and 1964) *The Structure of the Ethical Terms in the Koran* and its revised version

* See his *Introduction to the Qur'an* (1953).

Ethico-Religious Concepts in the Qur'ān plus his *God and Man in the Koran.* Izutsu employs a highly sophisticated method of semantic analysis which develops the meaning of key words and concepts in the Qur'anic text in great depth, and in addition demonstrates the structural relationships among these concepts in the Qur'an as a whole. These works constitute the most thoroughgoing studies of aspects of the Qur'anic message now available in English, and the method expounded and used there offers a promising tool to researchers who are prepared to employ it with diligence for further explorations. To these developments must be added mention of Birkeland's studies cited above (1956), and those of Willem Bijlefeld (1969) who has given particular attention to the Qur'anic teachings about prophecy. His work, together with a doctoral study submitted to McGill University in 1973 (Fiegenbaum, 1973) show that the Qur'anic import of even this fundamental Islamic religious idea has been misunderstood by many of the scholars who have studied it. A great deal remains to be done in the way of painstaking analysis and exposition of Qur'anic ideas before we shall have a firm grasp on the Qur'an's message in its own terms.

A kind of variation on the method of semantic analysis has been developed by a group of scholars at the Université St. Joseph in Beirut for the study of the Qur'an (see Allard, 1963). The technique employs a subject index to the Qur'an and a group of punched cards; by utilizing them in conjunction with one another it is possible to investigate the interrelationships among some of the basic ideas of the Qur'an. Development of this method is a move toward the use of computing devices in Qur'anic studies, and there will doubtless be a great deal more attention given to the possibilities in this area in view of the growing importance of computers in almost every field of scholarship, humanistic as well as scientific. In its present stage of development, however, the system is disappointing. Not only is it somewhat difficult to use, but in addition the question may be raised whether the categories employed in the index are adequate for opening up and truly representing the message and the text of the Qur'an.

The most impressive effort by an European scholar in the field of Qur'an interpretation on a broad scale is beyond doubt the work of Rudi Paret in *Der Koran, Kommentar und Konkordanz* (Paret, 1971) which is a companion volume to his earlier German translation of the Holy Book (1966). Paret's commentary covers the whole text of the Qur'an, much in the fashion of a traditional Muslim *tafsîr*, offering explanations and comments on terms, usages, and references that are difficult and unclear or that have been the objects of earlier scholarly attention and controversy. Although his comments are necessarily brief, the commentary is rich and constitutes the best of the works presently available in European languages to help the reader in gaining an understanding of what the Qur'an may have meant to Muhammad and to those of his contemporaries who witnessed the proclamation of the revelations. Paret emphasizes that his purpose is to understand the Qur'an historically in the peculiar circumstances and milieu in which it came, not to trace the later history and development of its key terms and concepts. One of the great values of the work is its citation of previous scholarly literature in connection with each of the individual words or passages that require interpretation. Thus it offers a comprehensive bibliography on interpretation organized in a way that makes it easy to pursue whatever issue may interest one. The appearance of this wide ranging volume, representing a summation of Western learning in Qur'an interpretation, is a highly important development in scholarship.

One of the major reasons why greater attention has not been given to expounding the Qur'an is to be found in the domination of historical concerns among former generations of scholars. Where the text has been studied, the inquirer's aim has often been to discover the origins of Qur'anic ideas or to demonstrate the dependence of the Qur'an on Jewish and Christian teachings. The result has been a failure to appreciate the uniqueness and integrity of the Qur'an's peculiar vision of the world and a persistent downgrading of the Qur'an's significance as being but a copy, and often a distorted one, of already existing ideas. A second and related reason for inattention to the text as such has been the primary place of biographical interest in the Prophet among the motives animating scholarship. One of the Qur'an's great attractions to a critical scholar is its unquestioned authenticity as a document originating in the experiences of Muhammad. In an area of study where so much else is uncertain and doubtful, the Qur'an stands forth as the single unimpeachable source for information on Muhammad's life and experience. The Qur'an is studied for the light that it can shed upon the prophetic personality and especially upon the process of its progressive development, hence the great concern with the chronology of the separate revelatory declarations that make up the text. In short, attention is directed not to the ideas set forth for their own sakes nor to the world view they constitute, but rather to the figure of the man who stands behind the words and whose expressions the words are considered to be. The distortion effected by this perspective may be subtle, but it is important, for it has forestalled serious grappling with what the Qur'an has to say. Liberation from these viewpoints is underway through the efforts of the scholars mentioned above. The study of the Qur'an for its own sake as the basic document of the Islamic community must now be fostered and encouraged, and study of this kind stands in the first rank of importance for the deepened understanding of Islam as a religion.

Qur'anic study is also badly neglected in another of its aspects, that which deals with the traditional interpretation of the Scripture in the Islamic community itself. Again one may urge that the most basic of all considerations in the study of Islam is the meaning to the believer of his own faith in all of its various aspects. There is a specific religious science, the discipline of *tafsîr*, or of Qur'an explanation and exposition, which enshrines the efforts of devoted Muslim scholars over the centuries to lay bare the meaning of the Scripture for themselves and their contemporaries. There is probably no richer or more important key to the basic but always evolving significance of the Qur'an in the Muslim religious consciousness than this tradition of *tafsîr* writings. The extent of the *tafsîr* literature is enormous, every generation of Muslims through the ages, in every place where Islam has flourished, having turned its hand to interpreting and reinterpreting the revelations given to the prophet. A single *tafsîr* may run to many volumes in length, and such works exist in great numbers in every one of the principal languages that the Muslim peoples have employed. Further, they continue to be written and published in our own day. It is, perhaps, the very extent of this imposing literature that discourages scholars from making it the object of critical historical study. Whatever the explanation, there is a paucity of works dealing with *tafsîr* in Western languages despite the crucial importance of Qur'an interpretation for both the traditional Islamic sciences and the modern scientific study of Islam alike.

The standard analytical work on the subject is Goldziher's *Die Richtungen der islamischen Koranauslegung* (1952) which provides an historical framework for the development of the most important and widely used *tafâsîr* in Arabic. The only significant advance over Goldziher's basic work has taken place in relation to the study of *tafsîr* in the modern period, which *Die Richtungen* did not treat in adequate fashion. J. M. S. Baljon (1961) and J. Jomier (1954) have written full studies specifically on modern *tafsîr* developments. Others have touched on the subject in their analyses of Islamic modernism and revivalism. These older studies of modern developments were supplemented by J. J. G. Jansen's *The Interpretation of the Qur'ān in Modern Egypt* (1974). This slim book surveys a number of *tafsîrs* composed in this century, lists the more important of them, and describes in considerable detail the tendencies which they exhibit. It offers the most thorough-going treatment of modern *tafsîr* available, but unfortunately it is limited to works done in one country and one language. It does, however, point the way to scholarly possibilities that others, better equipped to study other regions, will hopefully exploit. Some account must also be taken of Nabia Abbott's and Birkeland's contributions to the knowledge of the very early development of *tafsîr* and of studies by Rahbar on the Indian tradition of *tafsîr*. More recently doctoral work at Harvard and McGill has been devoted to this subject. Two theses (unpublished) at McGill deal with *Ithna 'Asharî* Shî'î Qur'anic interpretation in the form of a *tafsîr* by al-Ṭabarsî (Abdul, 1974) and with Ṣûfî *tafsîr* through consideration of the well-known work of Sahl al-Tustarî (Böwering, 1974). Both of these subdivisions of *tafsîr* literature are virtually unrepresented in the analytical writings of Islamists, and both are worthy of far more attention than they have received. The Harvard doctoral dissertation by Jane K. Smith (1970) takes up a particularly promising approach to *tafsîr* that hopefully will be adopted by others. Professor Smith endeavors to trace the development of an important theological concept by following its exposition through a series of commentaries on the Qur'an. Other such studies concentrating upon fundamental terms and ideas of the Islamic religious tradition could do much to reveal the range, depth, and complexity of the Islamic religious vocabulary and to establish signposts for distinguishing the stages in the historical development of religious terminology.

Ḥadîṯh

The state of studies respecting traditions of the prophet may be measured in terms of the work of four persons: Ignaz Goldziher (1910), Joseph Schacht (1945), Nabia Abbott (1967), and Fuat Sezgin (1967). Of somewhat lesser importance but still a significant contributor to recent discussions is Fazlur Rahman in his *Islamic Methodology in History* (Rahman, 1965). Fazlur Rahman takes particular issue with some of the assertions that are basic for Schacht's reconstruction of the development of Islamic law and the connection of *ḥadîṯh* literature with this process.

Miss Abbott presented her work to the public in 1967 in Volume 2 of her *Studies in Arabic Literary Papyrii*. Her purpose is not to dispute directly the question of the authenticity of the prophetic *ḥadîṯh* as it was raised by Goldziher; indeed, though her material at many points bears on this issue, she is extremely cautious in setting out its possible implications. Neither is her interest concentrated especially upon the legal *ḥadîṯh*, as was the case with Schacht. Nonetheless, she has set the stage for the next steps in the discussion by demonstrating, among other things, the existence of interest in both the *ḥadîṯh* and the *sunna* of the Prophet in the first century, the existence of written collections of *ḥadîṯh* from the earliest times and their continuous transmission up to the third century, and the fact that the science of tradition was not, as commonly thought, simply an offshoot of the developing legal interests of the community. Future debate on the authenticity of the tradition and studies of the *tadwîn al-ḥadîṯh*, or recording of *ḥadîṯh*, will have to take account of the material that Miss Abbott has so painstakingly gathered and analyzed. In the same year in which Miss Abbott published her volume of papyri studies that deals with Qur'anic commentary and tradition, there also appeared Volume 1 of Fuat Sezgin's *Geschichte des Arabischen Schrifttums*.

In discussing the *ḥadîth* it both supports and goes beyond the conclusions reached by Miss Abbott. This large reference work, which is an expansion, correction, and updating of Brockelmann's basic study of the history of Arabic literature, includes in Volume 1 a lengthy section devoted to the *ḥadîth* literature. In the introduction to that section Sezgin subjects Goldziher's reconstrcution of the *tadwîn al-hadîth*, as set out in Volume 2 of *Muhammadanische Studien*, to a thoroughgoing criticism. Although Goldziher and his predecessors such as Sprenger had in their possession all the evidence that would have permitted a proper understanding of the process of *ḥadîth* transmission, Sezgin charges them with having failed to understand its significance or with having overlooked parts of it. For Goldziher the result was the puzzling position taken in *Muhammadanische Studien*, where the great Hungarian scholar acknowledges the existence of written collections of *ḥadîth* materials (in the form of *ṣuḥuf*) in the hands of the Companions of the Prophet, but nonetheless believes the process of recording *ḥadîth* to have begun in earnest only in the second century. Sezgin insists that the process began much earlier and was, in fact, continuous and uninterrupted from the time of Muhammad to the emergence of the great *ḥadîth* collections of the third century. He bases this assertion upon both the extant manuscript material and arguments from formulas employed by transmitters to indicate the ways in which given *ḥadîth* came to them. It is the latter in particular that have not been understood, since according to Sezgin many of these formulas imply the existence and use of written documents in the process of *ḥadîth* transmission, although they do not explicitly say so. Goldziher's views on the development, history, and significance of the *ḥadîth* literature have carried almost the authority of gospel for Western scholars from his time until now. Sezgin's essay is one of the few attempts to make a fundamental examination of Goldziher's position that is not tainted by theological presuppositions, and it is therefore of the first importance. If his argument can be sustained, we shall have passed beyond Goldziher's reconstruction of the history to a new stage of understanding of the *ḥadîth* literature. The fundamental difficulty yet remains, however, that there are no known *ḥadîth* collections from the first century.

Generally speaking, the matter of the authenticity of prophetic *ḥadîth* and, beyond that, the broad problem of the reliability of oral materials in circulation among Muslims is perhaps the knottiest problem that contemporary scholarship in Islamics faces. The greater part of our historical information about early Islam and its development is derived from such materials. The issue poses extraordinary difficulties for the critical scholar because of the paucity of primary materials in written form from the first Islamic century and the necessity to resort to methods that are at best obtuse in order to reconstruct what may have occurred. For Muslims the matter is highly emotionally charged because of the authoritative role of the *ḥadîth* in the traditional structure of Islamic law and religiosity. The time would appear ripe, however, for a proper study of the matter in the light of the work of Goldziher, Schacht, Abbott, and Sezgin, if for no other reason than to clarify the issues needing further investigation. The four scholars did not envision the same purposes in their writings and were, in fact, interested in quite different problems. Because of the divergent thrusts of their interests the state of scholarship is somewhat confused, awaiting the intelligence of someone who can properly assess past accomplishments and point the directions of the new steps that must be taken.

Among the newer developments in the study of *ḥadîth* are some that serve in part to answer the question about the meaning of prophetic tradition for the community. One of these is an emerging interest in contemporary debates among Muslims over the authority of the *aḥâdîth*. Such debates have occurred from time to time in Islamic history, but they are particularly intense in our own time. In several different Muslim countries works have appeared that question or attack the traditional place of *ḥadîth* in Muslim religious thinking or that otherwise have attempted to assign it a new and more limited role. Of particular interest are the book by Mahmûd Abû Rayyah (1967), an Egyptian writer, called *Aḍwā ᶜalâ al-Sunna al-Muḥammadīyya*, and the numerous publications of Ghulâm Gîlânî Barq, Ghulâm Aḥmad Parvêz, and Abû al-Aᶜlâ al-Mawdûdî, all three Pakistanis. Writings on this subject have evoked a vigorous controversy between more conservative and more liberal Muslims, a controversy that is very much alive and that is of the greatest importance for the community's attempt to reconstruct its doctrine of religious authority in a manner more directly relevant to the modern world. Interestingly, these modern controversies often turn on the very historical issues that are central for the problem of the authenticity of *ḥadîth*. This aspect of modern Muslim religious life and thought has gained some attention from Western scholarship though not as much as it merits. G. H. A. Juynboll in his published doctoral research, *The Authenticity of the Tradition Literature: Discussions in Modern Egypt*, has studied the matter in Egypt, and (unpublished) theses dealing with Barq and Parvêz have been submitted to McGill University. There is also work in progress dealing with Mawdûdî and Shiblî Nuᶜmânî, both of whom are important contributors to the discussions in the Indian subcontinent.

As another facet of developments that help in appreciating the meaning of the *ḥadîth* mention may be made of the penetrating study by William Paul McLean of the role and nature of Jesus as set out in the authoritative *ḥadîth* collections. He convincingly demonstrates that the Jesus portrayed in the *aḥâdîth* is not only different, but radically so, from the Jesus portrayed in the Qur'an. In the *ḥadîth* Jesus belongs essentially to an eschatological context and therefore takes on a new focus for this significance and a vast new range of meanings not to be discovered in the pages of the Scripture. There do exist some studies which expound the content of *ḥadîth* on particular problems or doctrines but few that are as successful as this and few that afford as much understanding of the religious significance of the subject matter. Again, one sees here a type of scholarly work that hopefully will be taken up by others. McLean's work is available in his (unfortunately unpublished) thesis entitled "Jesus in the Qur'ān and Ḥadîth Literature," submitted to McGill University for the M.A. degree in 1970.

Kalâm

The area of *kalâm*, or of Muslim scholastic theology, is one in which the state of studies is particularly difficult to assess because of the complexity and breadth of the subject matter and the considerable activity there. Theology or the systematic intellectual expression of religious faith, however, is necessarily of primary interest to students of religion, and must receive its due. There is perhaps a tendency on the part of Western scholars, particularly those familiar with the Jewish and Christian traditions, where theological speculation stands in the first rank, to assign a somewhat exaggerated role to theology in their efforts to come to terms with the Islamic tradition. Once the formative period of Islamic thought was passed, roughly around the middle of the tenth Christian century, the *kalâm* tended to recede into the background for Muslims themselves and other types of religious expression came to the fore, namely, the law and mysticism. The peculiar structure of the Islamic view of the world must always be kept in mind when approaching this and other aspects of Islamic religious life. Here, as elsewhere, the normative consideration for the scholar is the attitude of the believer and the place which the community, in the appropriation of its religious experience, gives to theological speculation. Another factor which conditions the study of *kalâm* is the close interrelationship of this particular kind of activity with other facets of Islamic thought, especially in the early period. One who is interested in the emergent theology of the first three Islamic centuries often finds himself considering matters that might be seen more properly as aspects of the study of philosophy and at other times seems to be trespassing upon the realms of the jurist or the student of tradition. Through much of Islamic theology there runs as well a lively awareness of the political background against which the various positions were developed, so much so that many scholars see the significance of theology as being the working out of stands toward the great political issues of that early time. In any event there can be no doubt that early Muslim theological thought was near the heart of the pulsing life of the community, a matter of immediate and perceptible relevance for daily existence, even though in its form may it appear excessively formal and dry.

The task of establishing the main outlines or framework of the history of Islamic theological thought was accomplished by the pioneering scholars of the nineteenth century and the period up to World War I. Such writings as Goldziher's justly famous *Vorlesungen* (1910), Duncan Black MacDonald's *The Development of Muslim Theology, Jurisprudence and Constitutional Theory* (1903), and the books of Max Horten still have fundamental importance in providing an orientation to the field of study (Horten, 1912). At a somewhat later date (1932) A. J. Wensinck's *The Muslim Creed* brought more clarity to the matter by exploring some of the basic themes of early theological thought in detail and with great erudition (Wensinck, 1932). At the present time the fundamental study of the formative history is the volume by M. M. Anawati and Louis Gardet (1948) called *Introduction à la théologie musulmane* in which the authors adopt a systematic stance towards the scholastic theology of the Islamic tradition that is informed by the scholasticism of their own Catholic Christian backgrounds. Almost all this work on the history of Islamic theology, from the beginning to our own day, is based upon the heresiographical works of the early Islamic centuries. Of principal importance are al-Shahrastânî's *Kitâb al-Milal wa al-Niḥal*, al-Baghdâdî's *al-Farq bayn al-firaq*, and in a somewhat different category, al-Ashᶜarî's *Maqâlât al-Islâmiyyin*. These works purport to describe the variety of doctrinal stands and of sectarian groupings that emerged in the early centuries and to classify them. They are the fundamental sources for our knowledge of many individuals and groups who left no writings or other evidences of their views behind them.

In addition to work on the broad outlines of theological history, scholarship has also dealt with a number of the important figures of the Islamic theological tradition in some detail. Probably the most widely studied is al-Ghazâlî, about whom there now exists a very considerable literature that includes text editions, translations, monographic studies, and biographies. It is al-Ghazâlî the mystic or philosopher, however, rather than al-Ghazâlî the Ash'ari theologian, who tends to occupy the center stage. Detailed attention has also been given to other figures such as Aḥmad ibn Ḥanbal, Ibn Taymiyya, Ibn Hazm, al-Ashᶜarî and Ibn ᶜAqîl. Work of this kind is especially valuable in providing solid material that may be used to fill the gaps in our altogether too sketchy grasp of the general history.

The important new developments of interest in the realm of *kalâm* studies have to do with the history of early Islamic theological speculation and with the later development of the major school of Sunni orthodoxy, the so-called *Ashâᶜira*. The revived interest in the early period has several aspects. One of these is the appearance of efforts to reconstruct and deepen the understanding of the development of thought in the period as a whole. W. Montgomery Watt's *Free Will and Predestination in Early Islam* was perhaps the first of these, and it has been followed by his *Islamic Philosophy and Theology* in the Islamic Survey Series and his quite recent *The Formative Period of Islamic Thought* (Watt, 1948, 1962, 1973). The latter is a major effort to bring together the numerous strands that affected the growth of the classical Islamic synthesis of thought which began to emerge in the tenth century. One of the real advances Watt has achieved is to have subjected the heresiographers to criticism in the attempt to get behind their biased and overly systematic descriptions of schools and groupings to lay bare the highly complex and fluid milieu in which classical Islamic thought was born. Another work devoted to the general history of thought including the early period is Majîd Fakhry's *A History of Islamic Philosophy* (1970).

A second aspect of renewed interest in the early period of theological speculation may be seen in the appearance of a considerable number of highly technical studies of particular figures and texts, some of them relatively obscure but important, nonetheless, for assessing the character of the development. The foremost name in this aspect of the study is that of Josef van Ess of the University of Tübingen who has published a series of text editions of early fragments, translations, and monographic studies. Van Ess's interests range very widely, and his scholarship is of the highest order. He has given attention to such diverse subjects as the problem of *qadar wa qaḍâ*, on which he has several articles, and early *Mu^ctazilî* heresiography, to which he has devoted an entire volume (van Ess, 1971). These writings take up a variety of the important individuals of the time such as al-Ḥasan al-Baṣrî, Dirâr ibn ᶜAmr (see *Der Islam*, 44), al-Dâraquṭnî, Ba<u>sh</u>r al-Marîsî, and ᶜAmr ibn ᶜUbayd. The value of this painstaking work is to make the background of the great *Muᶜtazila* more understandable and to elucidate the situation out of which the synthesis we call Sunni Islam has emerged. Worthy of mention also is the long and careful study that Richard Frank has directed to Abû al-Hudhayl al-ᶜAllâf, reputed by some to have been the founder of the *Muᶜtazili* system. (See his *The Metaphysics of Created Being According to Abû l-Hudhayl al-ᶜAllâf: a Philosophical Study of the Earliest Kalam.* Istanbul: Nederlands Historisch-Archaeologisch Institut, 1966.)

The third aspect of studies on early Islam is the revival of interest in the *Muᶜtazila*. This branch of study received a special stimulus through the discovery in the Yemen in 1951 of a major work by an important *Muᶜtazili* thinker, Qâḍî ᶜAbd al-Jabbâr. The book known as *al-Mu<u>gh</u>nî* is the most extensive treatise on *Muᶜtazili* theology to have survived. One of the formidable difficulties in assessing the role of the *Muᶜtazila* in early Islamic history has been the lack of first-hand source materials and the need to learn of their doctrines and activities through the reports of those who disagreed with them. The *Kitâb al-Intiṣâr* of al-Khayyât, first published in the 1920s, provided some authentic Muᶜtazili material, but *al-Mughnî* offers it in great abundance though it is scarcely material that is either transparent or easy to use. The way now lies open, however, for important new work on the *Muᶜtazila* who, it is commonly agreed, are the founders and strongest stimulus of the *kalâm* in its precise sense. Most, if not all, of *al-Mughnî* has now been published by a commission in Cairo, and George Hourani, (1971) has translated small portions of it into English. Full exploitation of this new source material on an important early group has a strong claim to priority for those interested in the history of Islamic thought.

To my knowledge no full-scale work on the school of the *Muᶜtazila* has been attempted in a Western language since Steiner's nineteenth-century effort (*Die Muᶜtaziliten oder die Freidenker im Islām* [Steiner, 1965]). A start toward a more precise assessment of the school and its contribution to the history of Islam was made in Albert N. Nader's *Le Système philosophique des Muᶜtazila* (Nadir, 1956), but more is now possible and desirable. It is probably true to say that H. S. Nyberg's article in the *Shorter Encyclopedia of Islam,* where he characterizes the *Muᶜtazila* as religious propagandists for the ᶜAbbâsîs, commands the greatest respect as an interpretation of the movement, though W. M. Watt has subjected it to criticism in *The Formative Period,* mentioned above. There has been a great deal of work done and material accumulated on the *Muᶜtazila,* and the ground for a new critical assessment perhaps has now been adequately prepared. If such an assessment does see the light of day, it will be facilitated and enriched by a numerous literature on lesser figures of the school, such as al-Jâḥiẓ (studied by Charles Pellat and others), who do not deal directly with the great theological issues but reflect *Muᶜtazilî* attitudes and doctrines.

The other area, in addition to studies of early Islamic thought, where progress has been made in understanding Islamic theology has to do with the history of the school of thought that bears the name of al-Ashᶜarî. In the majority of writings on the Islamic religious tradition this school is identified with Muslim orthodoxy, and the assumption is made that the ideas of its founder were simply perpetuated by his disciples. The validity of this assumption, however, is now called into question. The first to raise the matter was Joseph Schacht (1945) in an often cited article, "New Sources for the History of Muhammadan Theology" where he calls attention to the inconsistency of approach and viewpoint in the writings attributed to al-Ashᶜarî himself. Thus he poses the possibility that supposedly authentic Ashᶜarî writings are not the works of the master but of a disciple who differed from him in important respects. George Makdisi has taken up this matter in a pair of articles [*Studia Islamica,* 17 (1962), 18 (1963)] entitled "Ashᶜarî and the Ash^c^arites in Islamic Religious History," in which he reexamines the role and nature of Ash^c^arism in the later history of Islamic religiosity, investigating the relationship between the thought of the alleged founder of the school and that of his later disciples. His conclusions support the thesis that Ash^c^arism is not identical with the views of al-Ash^c^arî, that the school has a history which exhibits change and development in doctrine, a history requiring to be ascertained in detail. In other of his writings dealing with the *Ḥanâbila*, Makdisi discusses the role of Ash^c^arism in the Madrasahs of the ^c^Abbâsî era and successfully disputes the thesis that these institutions existed primarily to foster the Ash^c^arî position.

The single most weighty work in later Islamic theology, though its scope is by no means limited to the postclassical period, is Josef van Ess's translation and commentary on the first book of the *Kitâb al-Mawâqif* of al-Ījî, a fourteenth-century thinker and theologian. The work is entitled *Die Erkenntnislehre des 'Adudaddīn al-Īcī* (van Ess 1966). Not only does van Ess set the particular subject of his book into its historical context, but he exploits the opportunity to trace the historical antecedents of references made in the text and doctrines discussed there. The book is a major piece of scholarship by one of the best Islamic scholars in the Western world.

There are, of course, many frameworks other than the historical in which the study of Islamic theology might be approached. One of these is the systematic consideration of principal doctrines, and there has been some excellent scholarship of this type in recent years. Particular attention may be called to works by Michel Allard, Louis Gardet, and Toshihiko Izutsu. Allard (1965) has studied the problem of the divine attributes that lay at the heart of the controversy between the *Mu^c^tazila* and their opponents over the divine unity in his *Le Problème des attributs divins dans la doctrine d'al-Ash^c^arī et de ses premiers grands disciples*. Following their *Introduction* Gardet and Anawati have undertaken a more detailed study of the *kalâm* in a two-volume work with the general designation *Les Grands problèmes de la théologie musulmane*. The first of these by Gardet, called *Dieu et la destinée de l'homme* (Paris: J. Vrin), appeared in 1967 and in five parts deals with God's acts and man's freedom, prophecy, resurrection and future life, faith and works, and the problem of leadership in the community with its implication of promoting the good and forbidding evil. So far as I have been able to discover the promised companion volume by Anawati, which will treat of *Dieu, son existence et ses attributs*, has not yet been published. Gardet and Anawati are concerned here, as in their previous study of *kalâm*, with a comparison of Muslim and Christian insights on the great theological issues. Izutsu's contribution to this type of study is his *The Concept of Belief in Islamic Theology: a semantic analysis of īmān and islām* (Izutsu, 1965). The book "purports to present a detailed description of the historical process through which the concept of belief was born, grew up, and was theoretically elaborated among the Muslims." In addition, "it aims at making a careful semantic analysis of 'belief' and other related key-concepts together with the conceptual networks which the latter formed among themselves" (Preface, p. i). There is a great need for more analytical studies of doctrine of this kind and in particular for analyses that trace the historical evolution of doctrinal positions in addition to sketching their essential structures, as do the works cited above.

Although a great deal has been accomplished in the study of *kalâm* it may be said that two important things still are lacking. The first is an attempt to push the boundaries of knowledge in some considerable degree beyond studies of the more well-known figures of the tradition. There are schools of thought and individuals among the Muslims outside the *Ashaᶜira*, the *Hanâbila*, and the *Muᶜtazila* who deserve to be investigated, indeed, who must be investigated before an adequate historical treatment of the *kalâm* is possible. Source materials for the purpose exist in overwhelming abundance. In spite of the work of previous generations and the more recent synthesizing efforts of Gardet, Anawati, and others, there exists no fully framed history of Muslim theological thought that does justice to the richness of the tradition by providing a place for minor and divergent figures and schools. A history of Islamic theology is needed that would parallel von Harnack's famous *Dogmengeschichte* in comprehensiveness. That no such exists and that it is perhaps impossible to conceive of undertaking one in the light of the state of scholarship is a commentary on the underdevelopment of the field.

The second thing of which there is a paucity is interpretive studies of Islamic theology that attempt to get behind the forms of expression to make clear the underlying concerns of the thinkers of the tradition. Much medieval writing on theology from Muslim pens, like similar medieval Christian writings, is exceptionally dense material. It is couched in terms of formal arguments on the scholastic mode, and although the sophistication and subtlety of the positions advanced may be considerable, very little is revealed of the authors who stand behind the words. All too often treatises on *kalâm* leave the impression of being a lifeless exercise, a kind of obscurantist game conducted among cognoscendi, with no vital relationship to real life. What, one is left to ask, is it all about? Are there real human beings with deep commitments and warm feelings who are attempting by these dry and stilted modes of discussion to express experiences and orientations of real meaning to them? If the theologians be such people, then what are they attempting to convey, and what is its vital importance for them personally and for their fellows in the community? Is there a problematic for Islamic theology that is capable of being understood in broad and general human terms? Again, the essence of the matter is the meaning for the believer. Treatises on theology must be read, not only to discover what is said there and the relation of this content to the views of previous and contemporary thinkers, but also to discern what is implied between the lines but never explicitly set out. Work of this kind has not yet even begun, but it is the type of enterprise that will invest the study of *kalâm* with vitality and that will reveal the genuine religious meaning of this very important discipline among the Islamic religious sciences.

Sufism

Of all the subdivisions of Islamic studies Sufism is that which has probably drawn the most widespread interest in recent times, though to be sure, the interest has not always been scholarly in nature. The growing attention is a good thing for the profession, however, in that it holds the possibility of attracting students and of opening doors to a more profound encounter with Islamic civilization than many would otherwise make.

The study of Islam as a religious tradition cannot avoid taking account of the profound mystical strain that has been present among the community from an early time, perhaps even from the era of the Prophet himself. Our knowledge of Muslim mysticism, however, suffers from underdevelopment relative to the place that mystical elements have occupied in Islamic religious life. From at least the fifth Islamic century, when the great mystical brotherhoods began to be organized and to gain influence, until modern times, mystical types of piety and expression have been a principal manifestation of Islam for a great portion of the community, both the lowly and the mighty, the unlettered and the sophisticated. Despite its importance Islamic mysticism or Sufism—which, it must be noted, is not necessarily the same thing—does not yet have a systematic or firm basis in scholarly studies. The problem is illustrated by works, or rather the lack of them, on the history of Sufism. Although there are many books that discuss the lives, activities, and thought of principal figures and delineate stages in the broad unfolding of the Sufi experience, the scholarly grasp of what has happened in this engaging area of Islamic spiritual life remains shaky and uncertain. Fundamentally the problem seems to be one of an insufficient amount of preparatory work that would enable a history to be written. In his *An Introduction to the History of Sufism* (Sir Abdullah Suhrawardy Lectures), A. J. Arberry (1943) wrote that it was not then possible to compose a history of Sufism and called attention to the need for a greatly increased range of preliminary studies in the form of text editions, translations, monograph studies of individual Sufis, analyses of significant texts, and the like. In spite of his reservations, Arberry (1950) published a small volume entitled simply *Sufism* which is ostensibly a history of the major stages through which the mystical movement among

Muslims has evolved. The volume is far from satisfactory; it is too small in size to treat any aspect of its broad subject in depth, and it serves only to tantalize the reader.

Very recently a new treatment of the history and development of Sufism by Annemarie Schimmel (1975) has become available; it is entitled *Mystical Dimensions of Islam.* Professor Schimmel has great sensitivity to the aesthetic appeal of Islam, and her study especially concentrates upon the expression of mysticism in poetry. This concern takes her beyond the relatively well known writers of the Arabic and Persian traditions into the exploration of poets who wrote in some of the less well known Islamic languages such as Sindhi and Pashto. The work, however, is not merely an effort at literary study but offers, as well, a wide ranging analysis of Sufism in all its aspects.

The scholarly works that offer the best historical reconstructions of the development of Sufism do so in passing, as it were, for it is not their primary purpose to sketch the course of history. The earliest and perhaps still the most important of these is Louis Massignon's famous *Essai sur les origines du lexique technique de la mystique musulmane* in its later revised and enlarged edition (Massignon, 1922). In Chapters IV and V Massignon traces the antecedents of al-Ḥallâj among the early community in minute detail, showing how the great martyr mystic was but the culmination and working out of tendencies that had germinated from the time of the Prophet and the revelation of the Qur'an. His treatment of the subject amounts to an historical account of the classical or early period of Islamic mysticism. In Massignon's view the high point of the development was reached in the person and teachings of al-Ḥallâj, who alone dared, at the cost of his life, to make explicit and to live according to a doctrine that had been only implicit in the outlook of his predecessors. Thereafter, there was only decline and falling away, reaching its nadir in the theosophic pantheism of Ibn ᶜArabî and his disciples such as the school of Suhrawardî. For this reason Massignon is not interested in the later development of the Sufi experience. It is in response to somewhat similar motivations that Helmut Ritter in his *Das Meer der Seele* (Leiden: 1955) has studied the classical period and the formation of a mystical outlook among Muslims. The purpose of his study is to elicit the teachings about God, man, and the world, the great themes of all theological thought, as they are set out in the writings of the Persian mystic, Farîd al-Dîn al-ᶜAṭṭâr. To do so he first found it necessary to trace the roots of ᶜAṭṭâr's thought among Sufis of prior generations. This study is one of the finest attainments of scholarship in regard to Sufism, and its elaboration of the history and development during the early period is of equal importance with the earlier work of Massignon. Among historical works mention may also be made of *La Mystique musulmane* by M. M. Anawati and Louis Gardet, 1961). The portion of the book that is of interest to historians is that written by Anawati. The purpose there is straightforwardly historical; the remainder of this important book is devoted to an analysis of the structure and major themes of Sufi experience.

Before passing on we must also call attention to the importance of another aspect of Massignon's *Essai*. This work has had a decisive effect in forming the method by which European scholarship has approached the study of Sufism. Almost every European scholar of stature from the time of the *Essai's* first appearance in the early 1920s to the present has been persuaded by Massignon's emphasis upon the role of technical vocabulary and the need to elucidate its meaning by painstaking and patient research and analysis. The Sufi lexicon has been built up through the interiorization of basic concepts and the experience of their meaning in cultic practice. The task of the scholar is to follow this process and thereby to come to comprehension of the great Sufi themes. Massignon described the process as one of confronting the works of an author with the stages of his personal history so that the development and deepening of his insights may be understood. Subsequent scholarship, through the study of a variety of individual Sufis and their works, has carried this process forward, seeking both to understand the ways in which particular mystics have appropriated and developed fundamental concepts and to elucidate the evolution of the grand themes through the phases of Sufism's growth as a whole. There appears to be common agreement in the scholarly community that the task first described by Massignon is still the desideratum that will advance the cause of understanding. Among recent noteworthy work that fills the need is the book by Jean Michon, *L'miᶜrâj de Muṣṭafâ al-Bakrî al-Khalwatî* (Paris: J. Vrin, 1973), which consists of a translation with commentary and explanation of a dictionary of technical Sufi terms written by a mystic of the seventeenth century.

In Sufi studies devoted to topics other than history it is possible also to distinguish several developments of importance in more recent scholarship. One of the most imposing of these for both its bulk and its accomplishment is the emergence of a very considerable literature on Iranian mysticism, especially the *ishrâqî* or illuminationist school, and its relationship to Twelver Shiᶜism. In this case we have used the word "mysticism" rather than Sufism since many of the Iranian mystics, including some of the greatest among them, have emphatically rejected the Sufi identification. The most important name in connection with this development is that of Henry Corbin, a prolific author and editor whose many works elucidate almost every aspect of Islamic thought and experience from worship to philosophy (see Corbin, 1970, 1971–1972, 1964). Corbin established and has served as chief editor of the series known as *Bibliothèque Iranienne*, published by the Institut Franco-Iranien in Tehran, whose volumes (22 at present) are one of the most important resource collections for the study of Islamic mysticism and philosophy ever to have been assembled. Books in the series consist of those from Corbin's own pen, some done in collaboration with others, and some done under Corbin's direction. It may be said with justice that a school of thinkers under Corbin's influence has come to exist. Of his own numerous works the two that deserve special mention here are his *Histoire de la philosophie islamique*, prepared in collaboration with Sayyid Husayn Nasr, and his *En Islâm iranien*, a four-volume work that represents the culmination and summing up of Corbin's long and fruitful career. The first of these is notable for its insistence upon the existence of a philosophical tradition among Muslims in the eastern Islamic areas after the decline of the peripatetic variety of philosophy, largely dependent upon Aristotle, in the West. This Eastern type of philosophy Corbin holds to be mystical in nature. Its origin lies in the work of Shaykh al-Ishrâq, al-Suhrawardî, who was killed by the Ayyubid sultan in Aleppo, and finds its climax in Ṣadr al-Dîn Shîrâzî, known as Mullâ Ṣadrâ, who by common agreement is the most profound and subtle member of the illuminationist school to have lived in Iran. The larger work, *En Islâm iranien*, is concerned with many different facets of Iranian religious life and is therefore one of the important resources for the study of Shiᶜism and its relation to what preceded it in the history of the people among whom it has taken strongest root. The second of the four volumes is devoted to the *ishrâqî* school, which is the focus of Corbin's interest. An English version of this work is in preparation at McGill University; it has already been translated into Persian and Arabic. There runs through the whole of Corbin's work an overriding interest in the esoteric, which he holds to be the key to the most profound interpretation of the phenomena he has studied. Although there are many scholars who feel that the emphasis on the esoteric tradition of the Muslims is one-sided and likely to result in underestimating other aspects of Islamic experience, there can be no doubt that Corbin's studies are among the most impressive monuments of Islamics scholarship in this century.

A second recent development in Sufi studies is the appearance of a number of works on the much neglected subject of the mystical brotherhoods. These brotherhoods, which made their appearance in the twelfth Christian century, are the most visible aspect of the mystical life of the community in its later history, and they have the closest and most vital of relationships to a number of other important Islamic institutions such as the craft guilds, the ᶜulamā' corps, and the *futuwwa* organizations. There was some noteworthy work of previous generations on this subject, for example, the book of O. Depont and X. Coppolani (1897), *Les Confréries religeuses musulmanes* (1895), the basic study by John Kingsley Birge (1937), *The Bektashi Order of Dervishes*, and others; older periodical literature is also rich in articles on particular orders and their specific teachings. The greatest depth is to be found in studies of the orders in North Africa, most of it done by French scholars and published in French journals. As the realization of the orders' importance has grown, the scholarly literature available has also become more extensive. E. E. Evans-Pritchard (1949) devoted a work to *The Sanusi of Cyrenaica* which grew out of his war experiences in the area. The element of greatest interest about the Sanûsiyyah for Evans-Pritchard appears to have been the history of their conflict with the Italian colonial authorities and not the nature of the order or its mystical experience as such. Nicola A. Ziadeh (1958) also has a useful book on this important North African order called *Sanūsiyya.* The study by Abun Nasr on *The Tijanniya* shares with Evans-Prichard's work a primary concern for something other than the order and its mystical life (Nasr, 1965). In this case the author has studied the Tîjâniyya principally in the light of their role in the several *jihâd* movements that occurred in West Africa in the eighteenth and nineteenth centuries. Another substantial contributor to analysis of the orders and their role in various Islamic societies is H. J. Kissling, who has composed a number of essays and other short pieces in English and German.

The most extensive study of the Sufi orders and the unique effort to present their history and development as a whole is the volume by J. Spencer Trimingham, *The Sufi Orders in Islam* (1971). Trimingham is interested in the study of mysticism in all its many aspects, and he has undertaken the truly monumental burden of attempting to organize the information available to scholarship according to historical and systematic criteria. His study is a vast collection of information; and though, as Arberry warned, it suffers from the unavailability of preparatory studies that would make the character of the development in some crucial areas more clear, for the first time it gives proper recognition to a subject matter of first importance for the Islamic religious tradition. Its significance arises from the attempt to treat all the orders known to the author and to bring about an understanding of the course and nature of the historical development from the beginnings to the present. Attention may be called especially to the bibliography of *The Sufi Orders in Islam,* which is as comprehensive a guide to both the older and newer writings on Sufism as may be readily found. Trimingham has also devoted considerable attention to the Sufi orders found on the African continent; he has published writings on them beginning in 1949.

Another work of a general kind on the orders is in progress at the hands of Richard Gramlich, professor in the theological faculty at the University of Freiburg, who is attempting a broadly based study of the Sufi *tarîqah* in Iran. Only one volume, however, has appeared in which the *salâsil* or tables of the genaeology of the Iranian orders are presented together with a bibliography. It is called *Die schiitischen Derwischorden Persiens,* (Gramlich 1965).

In my opinion the most promising work on the orders in recent days may be seen in the detailed consideration of the thought and life of certain ones of them. I have in mind the studies of M. Molé (1961, 1963) and Fritz Meier (1957) relative to the *Kubrawiyya*, and the work of P. Nwyia on the *Shâdhiliyyah*. Meier's magnum opus is his *Fawâ'ih al-Jamâl wa-Fawâtih al-Jalâl ... Die Fawā'ih al'gamāl wa-fawātih al-galāl des Nagm ad-Dīn al-Kubrā: Eine Darstellung mystischer Erfahrungen im Islām aus der Zeit um 1200.* In publications in periodicals he has studied other writings of the founder of the *Kubrawiyya* and those of certain of his disciples such as ᶜAlî-i-Hamadânî. Partially under Meier's influence, his student Hermann Landolt has carried the study forward in the publication of *Correspondence spirituelle echangée entre Nuroddin Esfarayeni et son disciple 'Allaoddawleh Semnani* (Landolt, 1972) and in his article "Der Briefwechsel zwischen Kâšânî und Simnânî über Waḥdat al-Wugûd," (1973) concerning the rejection of pantheistic thought by the *Kubrawî* mystic al-Simnânî. Molé's contributions to the understanding of this important order, the outlines of whose history and significance have now become clear, are offered in two articles. One is his "Les Kubrawiya entre sunnisme et shiisme aux huitième et neuvieme siècles de l'hégire" (1961), and the other is "Traités mineurs de Nağm al-dīn Kubrā" (1963).

What Meier has done for the *Kubrawiyya*, P. Nwyia has accomplished for the widespread order of North African origin, the *Shâdhiliyya*. Nwyia has three major studies of the *Shâdhiliyyah* in addition to a significant contribution to the study of the technical Sufi vocabulary. He has published an Arabic text (*al-Rasâ'il al-Sughrâ*) whose title is translated as *Les Lettres de direction spirituelle d'Ibn ᶜAbbād de Ronda* (1958), the latter an important Shâdhilî mystic. The text edition was preceded in time by a monographic study of this man, his thought and life called *Ibn ᶜAbbād de Ronda* (1332–90) (1956). His other work on the *Shâdhiliyya* is *Ibn ᶜAta' Allāh ... et la naissance de la confrérie Sadilite* (1971) which consists of an edition and translation of the wise sayings or *ḥikām* of the mystic named in the title. The part of this volume of the greatest significance, however, is its introduction, which sketches the history and development of the order. Nwyia's contribution to the *lexique technique* is his *Exégèse coranique et langage mystique* (Beirut: Dar al-Mashriq, 1970), which is an analysis and study of the mystical *tafsîr* of Jaᶜfar al-Ṣâdiq, a key figure in the formative period of Islamic thought, who played a prominent role in the development of both Sufism and the Shiᶜa. The work is not strictly a study of a single *tafsîr* but is rather a contribution to understanding the growth of a technical Sufi vocabulary. Here Nwyia follows the lead of Massignon and confirms his work.

Studies of the kind mentioned here show the possibilities for the enlargement of our knowledge inherent in work on the Sufi orders. Their recent emergence, the recognition of the importance of the orders which they imply, and the fact that both traditional Islamics scholars and social scientists have found the subject of interest all point to the desirability of giving priority to this type of study.

Other aspects of work in the area of Sufi studies, of which there are many, are not so easy to classify or organize, but they are nonetheless important. The past decade has witnessed the appearance of significant work on individual mystics such as the writings of Henry Corbin and Toshihiko Izutsu on Ibn al-ᶜArabî. The English translation of Corbin's book is entitled *Creative Imagination in the Ṣūsfim of Ibn ᶜArabi* (1970). Izutsu's comparative study of Ibn al-ᶜArabî, Lao-tzu and Chuang-tzu, was published under the title *A Comparative Study of the Key Philosophical Concepts in Sufism and Taoism* (1966–1967); the first of the two volumes is the part most relevant to the student of Sufism. The side-by-side reading of these two works, both by highly skilled scholars with unimpeachable qualifications, is instructive; they present quite different pictures of the famous Andalusian mystic, illustrating in this way the need and the possibility for further study as a prerequisite to better understanding of one of the central personages of the Sufi development. Muḥammad ᶜAbdur Rabb has written *The Life, Thought and Historical Importance of Abu Yazid al-Bistami* (Dacca; 1971) giving particular attention to his *shaṭaḥât.* S. de Beaureceuil has studied the life and work of *'Abdullah-al-Harawî Anṣârî* (Cairo: 1962), Maṭbaᶜat al Maᶜhad al-ᶜIlm î al-Faransi lʿal-Āthar al-Sharqiyya the well-known Hanbali mystic who established a *khânqa* in Herât in western Afghanistan that still today houses his disciples. As the study of a particular mystic, the book on al-Junayd by A. H. Abdel Kader (1962) is also worthy of mention, though reservations might be expressed about the felicity of some of the translation. It is entitled *The Life, Personality and Writings of al-Junayd.* Works on individual mystics also include the attractive book by Martin Lings (1961), which has as its subject a contemporary Sufi leader. We refer to *A Moslem Saint of the Twentieth Century: Shaikh Aḥmad al-ᶜAlawî.* All these works belong to the type of detailed monographic studies which Arberry signaled as the foremost need if understanding of the Sufi tradition as a whole is to be advanced.

To conclude this sketch we may mention several other writings that have marked substantial steps forward in scholarship. First is the book by the Italian scholar, A. Bausani (1959), called *Persia Religiosa,* in which the principal figures of the Sufi tradition in Iran, including the great mystical poets, are considered. The book is valuable in particular for its exploration of the difficult subject of connections and relationships among the Sufis, the Twelver Shiᶜa, and the various groups of the Ismaᶜiliyya. Of considerable interest also is the doctoral dissertation by Benedikt Reinert which analyzes one of the most fundamental of Sufi technical terms. He calls his work *Die Lehre vom Tawakkul in der klassischen Sufik* (Berlin; 1968). Finally, there is a pair of writings which treat the vexing question of the relationship between the mysticism of the Islamic tradition and that of the religions of the Indian subcontinent. One is R. C. Zaehner's *Hindu and Muslim Mysticism* (1960) and the other is M. M. Moreno's "Mistica musulmana e mistica indiana" (1948).

At the present point in their development Sufi studies are among the divisions of Islamics that stand to profit most from the dedicated pursuit of philological objectives. What these studies most require is the editing and publication of more of the numerous texts of Sufi writers that are as yet unexploited, the translation of some of the more important of these into European languages, and the composition of analytical monographs along the lines laid out by Massignon. Only thus will it eventually become possible to gain a broader view of the nature of the Sufi phenomenon, to understand its development, and to assess its place in the religious history of Islam. In many respects the study of Sufism is comparable to studies of Islamic theology and philosophy. In no one of these fields is there yet the range of primary material and the depth of preliminary study that will permit the scholar any degree of confidence about his grasp of even the essentials.

At the same time it must be noted that Sufism is one of the aspects of Islamic experience that lends itself most readily to investigation by the methods that phenomenologists and historians of religion have evolved and employed elsewhere. Not only are the Sufis and their literature rich in a kind of legendary lore which embodies and perhaps explains the more important motifs of the movement, but they are equally well endowed with a variety of ritual practices and of social forms. This diversity and the intense emotional involvement that accompanies it invite comparison with mystical phenomena in other traditions and lend themselves more readily to the hermeneutical purposes of the phenomenologist than does the somewhat iconoclastic tradition of classical Islam, with its preference for more rational modes of religious expression. Because it promises more, Sufism might well serve as the *Anknupfungspunkt* for phenomenologists of religion who wish to extend their studies to comprehend Islamic material.

Shiᶜism

With very few exceptions the Western scholarly tradition tends to look upon Islam as a monolithic structure, having well-defined norms for belief and practice. These are usually identified with the reigning attitudes among Sunni Muslims, for which reason the latter are often called "orthodox." When in the course of Islamic history groups have differed from the alleged norms, or chosen other norms, the tendency has been to consider such people deviant, to assign them a role somewhere outside the main stream of Islamic life, or perhaps to ignore them altogether. The assumption of a monolithic Islam explains the difficulty that many students of religion experience in understanding the place of Sufism in the Islamic tradition or in dealing with groups such as the Aḥmadiyya, to take but one example.

Such a set of mind also goes far to elucidate the problem that many encounter in coming to terms with the developmental nature of Islam; i.e., the fact that Islamic religious experience is a human and historical phenomenon constantly changing and evolving in response to the differing situations of various segments of the community. If one insists from the beginning, even unconsciously, that the truly Islamic must conform to a dogmatic or other fixed scheme, the complexity and depth of the Islamic experience is likely to escape him. Although it is true that one segment of the community, that which we call Sunnism, became notoriously conservative after the formative period of Islamic thought was past, even in this instance there has been development and change as well as wide tolerance of divergent opinion. Above all, it must be remembered that the great synthesis of ideas, practices, and institutions that resulted in Sunni Islam is itself the end product of a long and highly variegated historical development.

The most important scholarly casualty of the "monolithic" set of mind are the *Ithnâ ᶜAsharî* Shiᶜa, the great majority Shiᶜi community of Iran, Iraq, and the Indian subcontinent. Because the Shiᶜa have not belonged to the heart of Islam as scholars have conceived that heart, they have received only a fraction of the attention devoted to the Sunni community. In consequence, when scholars write of Islamic theology, their attention is given exclusively to Sunni thinkers; when they discuss the development of Islamic law, the subject for consideration is jurisprudential development in Sunni Islam. Acknowledgment is normally given to the fact that the Shiᶜa differ from Sunni opinions, but the differences are minimized, and it is seldom thought necessary to consider Shiᶜi views at length in order to understand their peculiar spirit and religious *Weltanschauung*. The fact is that developments among the Shiᶜa have often followed a course radically different from that of the Sunni community, and these developments deserve to be studied and understood. Up till now they have not been sufficiently noted and analyzed. To take one example, the usual book on Islamic jurisprudence takes no notice at all of the fact that the *uṣûl al-fiqh*, whose emergence as principles was all-important to Sunni law, do not play a similar role among the Shiᶜa, that the rationalization and structuring of law among the Shiᶜa occurred much later than in the Sunni case and proceeded on quite different principles. A similar fundamental difference may be perceived between the Shiᶜi and the Sunni approaches to theology. Not only are the names of the important thinkers different, al-Ḥillî instead of al-Ashᶜarî, etc., but the systems of thought are permeated by a totally different spirit. Whereas Sunni *kalâm* tends to argue from authority, Shi^ci *kalâm* affords rationality a much greater place. In this respect it resembles the discredited thought patterns of the *Mu^ctazila*, much of whose speculative approach it has preserved. These differences are undoubtedly related to the contrast in the understanding of religious authority between the two groups. The important facts are that differences do exist between Sunni and Shi^ci Muslims, that these differences are great and important, that they are little noted in contemporary scholarship, and that they deserve the fullest and closest treatment. One may go so far as to say that the fundamental ethos of Shi^cism differs from that of the Sunnis. Whereas the Sunni Muslim is preoccupied above all else with the awesome majesty of a Sovereign Lord who has commanded men to live in a prescribed way, his Shi^ci brother builds his religious devotions around the themes of suffering and martyrdom, normally exhibiting a far greater element of emotional outpouring in the expression of his piety. Further, the Shi^ca feels himself to have a closer and more personal relationship to the divine reality through the living imam and his representatives among the *mujtahids* of the community. The citation of basic differences could be multiplied in other fields such as the science of *ḥadîth* or the role accorded to philosophy. European, particularly French, scholarship has paid more attention to the unique character of Shi^ci Islam than has North American study. We cited above the numerous writings of Henry Corbin, who is perhaps the principal figure. There is, however, a clear need for greater attention to this field of endeavor. The desideratum is a series of works detailing the unique history of Shi^ci thought, practice, and institutions for their own sakes and without the stigma of their being considered "heterodox" and "deviant." There is an incalculable wealth of both primary materials and secondary studies in Arabic and Persian awaiting the attention of assiduous scholars.

In one area of the study of non-Sunni Islamic groups there is no need for lament. Perhaps because of their more radical nature the Isma^cilis have received a great deal of scholarly attention, both from individuals within their various communities and from outsiders. A great number of documents of interest for the history of the group has been edited and published, and there are many excellent studies available ranging from strict history to subjects of more interest to an historian of religions. Relatively speaking Isma^cili studies are one of the healthier subdivisions of Islamics.

Popular Religion

Worship, devotional life, and popular religion are elements in the study of Islam that must again be considered as neglected but priority areas. More emphasis on the nature of Islamic piety and the quality of the believer's experience is sorely needed to offset the prevailing view that Islam is a religion of formalistic legal requirements, a highly sophisticated set of detailed rules for the conduct of life without corresponding fervor, warmth, or satisfaction in the devotee's heart. The book of several years back by Constance Padwick (1961) entitled *Muslim Devotions* has done more to reveal the quality of Islamic experience to the interested observer than many of its more weighty fellows. A great deal more work of this kind must be undertaken before the religious texture of Islamic involvement will be properly revealed. Miss Padwick's book is based on a collection of materials from Sufi prayer manuals, harking back to a time when forms of Sufi piety were pervasive in Islamic society and one of the principal factors in its social cement. Investigations of this kind must be carried beyond the bounds of Sufism into other facets of Islamic religiousness. Study of devotional life is one of the areas where the methods and concerns of the historian of religions again become relevant for the understanding of Islam.

There exists a very rich literature from the past on what may be called the popular religion of the Muslim peoples. Much of this is contained in travelers' accounts and in writings by such persons as colonial officials as well as in more scholarly treatises. This material, though it often has no clear relation to the great themes of classical Islam and may even appear subversive of those themes in some ways, is of the first importance for understanding Islam as a living faith. At the risk of repeating the thought too often, we say once more that the vital thing in the study of religion is to discover the meaning of religious phenomena for the believer. The demarcation of a theoretical religious ideal for a community has its place in religious studies, but more germane to the heart of the inquiry is the way the pious faithful feel, think, and behave, even when these depart drastically from the ideal. Among the scholarly works of earlier generations that deal with popular religion and that still have great value is Duncan Black Macdonald's *The Religious Life and Attitude in Islam* (MacDonald, 1909) and Max Horten's *Die religiöse Gedankenwelt des Volkes im heutigen Islam* (1917–1918).

More recent scholarship has returned to this matter and exhibits several significant achievements. A major work in two large volumes called *Volksglaube im Bereich des Islams* (Wiesbaden: 1960 and 1962) represents the efforts of Rudolf Kriss and Hubert Kriss-Heinrich, two folklore specialists whose early studies had been devoted to European folklore. The volumes treat the countries around the Mediterranean basin but find their principal focus in the Arab lands. Volume 1 discusses pilgrimage and saint worship in these areas and Volume 2 deals with amulets, magical formulas, and oaths. Attention may also be called to works such as that by E. Dermenghem, *Le Culte des saints dans l'Islam maghrébin* (1954) and H. Granqvist's inquiries into the beliefs and rites connected with death. Her volume, which is the outcome of two different field studies, is called *Muslim Death and Burial: Arab customs and traditions Studied in a Village in Jordan* (Granqvist, 1965).

The last work mentioned is but one of a number of studies by anthropologists who in the last decade have become increasingly interested in looking at Islam as it is actually lived and experienced in a variety of Muslim countries. The approach has many virtues apart from its intrinsic interest: it serves strongly to counter the assumption of a monolithic Islam; it demonstrates the real and important differences in the nature and meaning of Islam in its various regional manifestations; it evidences the manner in which the classical or great tradition of Islam has adapted itself to a variety of cultural contexts; and it shows much of the actual meaning of Islam for simple believers who share the faith. Perhaps the outstanding name in this development is that of Clifford Geertz whose work in Java and in North Africa has proven valuable, attractive, and influential. His *The Religion of Java* is a careful observation of religious life in a small Javanese town with its mixture of the classical Islamic and the non-Islamic (Geertz, 1960). Of perhaps even more significance, though it is not so carefully crafted a study, is the volume of published lectures called *Islam Observed*; Geertz attempts to compare the ethos or spirit of Islamic faith in Indonesia with that in Morocco (Geertz, 1968). He effectively demonstrates the fact that two peoples, both considering themselves Muslim and striving sincerely to be so, nevertheless appropriate the Islamic heritage in such different ways that an uninstructed observer might well overlook any relation between them at all. Studies of the type that Geertz has undertaken are among the ways that social scientists have aided in comprehending Islam and where they may yet make a most substantial contribution; every encouragement should be afforded to such endeavors.

One may easily cite a number of other works of a similar type. Ernest Gellner, for example, in *Saints of the Atlas* has carried out an essentially ethnographic study of the saintly families of the High Atlas range, showing their social role among the Berber tribesmen (Gellner, 1969). Our purpose here, however, is not to be comprehensive, but to note where scholarship now stands and to delineate the trends it may exhibit. Gellner's study is indicative of one of the prevalent trends, namely, the concentration upon North Africa and especially upon Morocco by social scientists interested in the Islamic world. There is perhaps an element of follow-the-leader in this suddenly awakened interest, for fashions sometimes reign in scholarship as they do elsewhere. More basic to the trend, however, is the fact that Morocco and other parts of North Africa continue to be receptive to field work by foreign scholars as some of the other regions of the Islamic world are not. As valuable and welcome as growth in the understanding of North Africa assuredly is, means must continue to be sought for the conduct of similar researches in other regions of the Islamic lands where it is now more difficult to gain access.

Future Studies

In the foregoing discussion a number of considerations and emphases have emerged that offer the possibility of suggestions for the future development of studies devoted to Islam as a religion. We shall set down several of these here as firm recommendations. The recommendations made arise either from the promise that a given aspect of studies shows in the light of recent developments or from the importance of the subject matter for its own sake. In my opinion students of Islam should strive on a priority basis to promote the following:

1. Qur'anic studies, especially those dealing with the teachings, ideas, and world view of the Qur'an.

2. The history of early Islamic theology with special attention to the *Mu^{c}tazila*. The editing, publication, and translation of texts in Islamic theology is a continuing need of the field.

3. Sufi studies, with special emphasis going to the preparation of detailed works on individuals, movements, texts, and the great mystic orders. These studies should give a place of priority to text editing, publication, and translation as part of the preparatory buildup for an eventual history of Sufism.

4. Shi^{c}i studies focusing attention upon the uniqueness and richness of the Shi^{c}i contributions to the religious sciences.

5. Studies of popular religion among Muslims and of Islamic devotional life.

6. The cultivation in the Islamics field of the methods and insights gained through the emergence in Europe and America of a discipline concerned with the scientific study of religion. This type of study is most often called the history of religions or *Religionswissenschaft*.

NOTES

1. It is important to clarify what is meant here and, especially, to emphasize that focusing attention on the historical tradition does not exclude either the desire or the possibility for some grasp of the faith or inward experience of religious men, including the faith of individuals. Major attention falls on creeds, acts of worship, moral codes and actions, and social groups because these are the elements in which the inner experience finds expression. Although the method is one of indirect approach to religious experience, this roundabout path is unavoidable because we do not possess means of fathoming directly the inner life of others or, perhaps even of probing our own inner lives to the fullest. Study of religious experience must be made, therefore, in the light of two things: (1) what religious men say about their encounters with ultimate reality, i.e., the hearsay evidence; and (2) the indications of the quality of the underlying experience that shine through the various modes of response to it and expression of it, i.e., evidence by implication. Thus it follows that all religion is an historical phenomenon in that it involves the experience and response of individual men who are part of the historical stream. It also follows that all study of religion, in its inward as well as its outward aspects, is study of history since the science of religion has no other object of study but what has happened to individual actors in history.

This long explanation has been added because of the tendency of some students of religion, who in their zeal to know the inner experience of *Homo religiosus*, derogate the significance of studying the manifest elements of religiousness with all that this implies. Reasoning that the inward encounter with ultimate reality is the true essence or core of man's religious adventure, they discount the varied forms of religious expression as accidental and secondary. Although one may sympathize with the intention of such thinking, it is erroneous, for there is no way to approach the inwardness of human religious involvement except along the manifest historical pathway of its expression.

2. See the categories into which the subject matter of the Islamics field is divided below.

3. There are scholars who have argued with considerable cogency that what is disclosed according to the general Muslim understanding of revelation is not the divine nature, the divine personality or self, but rather the divine will for mankind or as such part of it as God thinks it important for men to know. Thus they would speak not of a self-disclosure, but of the disclosure of truths, prescriptions, and proscriptions that constitute a pathway for men with the ultimate mystery of the divine nature remaining hidden from human perception. The debate between these two interpretations of Islamic understanding is an interesting substantive problem in the history of Islamic piety, but it is not possible here to enter into it.

There are two other controversial elements in this brief characterization of the Islamic experience. One is to be found in the assertion that, according to Muslim thought, revelation has occurred for Muslims and continues to occur, outside the books sent to mankind, in the personalities and lives of the prophets and in the cumulative experience of the community. If relevation is conceived as the sum of normative guidance which the community has at its disposal, these latter sources of direction for men, though different in quality, clearly deserve to be counted as revelation because they serve the same ends and exercise much the same kind of authority as the divine words set down in the Qur'an. Nor does the matter stop even here, for one may venture to add that evidence exists to show that Muslims are also conscious of a continuing revelation in nature, and to some extent in human reason. As it actually operates in the life of the community religious authority is not limited to the Qur'an, the revelation in the strict sense, but derives very largely from those extra-Qur'anic elements that, in effect, become secondary sources of revelation or perhaps sources of indirect revelation.

A second controversial element has to do with the applicability of this brief characterization to the Shiᶜa, in both their more and their less radical branches, and to the mystics of the community generally. Both the Shiᶜa and the *mutaṣawwifîn* hold at the center of their religious consciousness the concept of a continuing guidance available to the community through specially endowed individuals who represent the ongoing presence of the Divine in the midst of the material world of humanity. The notion of a living and ever-present mediator of divine truth is the fundamental and most vital element in their understanding of religious authority; whatever the revelation of the Qur'an and the experience of past generations may mean is to be understood as these living persons interpret them and declare their relevance. In a broad sense the teachings of the Imam of the Age or of the *awliyâᶜ Allâh* are a kind of revelation. Of equal importance is their very existence as a metaphysical principle that serves to sustain the universe. In the case of each there is available immediate access to divine truth, not through the agency of experiences that belong to the past, but in the living present. The content of revelation is thus not finally fixed and uniform, nor is its form literalistic as for Sunni Muslims; rather these elements of the Islamic community live with a sense of an infinitely expanding and directly accessible truth. It is of great importance to call attention to this difference in modes of thinking and feeling, for it is not merely a matter of formal doctrine that must be noted to keep the historical record straight. Corresponding to the differing intellectual formulations is a qualitative difference in the piety, i.e., in the substantive religious experience, of these groups of Muslims. If one were to characterize the ethos of Sunni Islam in comparison with that of Shiᶜi Islam, he would find it necessary to emphasize in the latter case the elements of emotionalism, purgation, grief, suffering, injustice, and martyrdom that figure so prominently in the everyday religious reactions of the Shiᶜa, none of which is present in the same degree or occupies the same position in the structure of Sunni religious life. The differences in the content and meaning of the religious experience are reflected even in the major festivals celebrated by Sunni and Shi'i Muslims and the relative emphasis given to them.

Ideally speaking, any brief descriptive statement characterizing Islam as a religion should be broad enough to cover the varieties of Muslim experience, reaction, and expression. The fact that a need was felt to include this long footnote shows the difficulty of achieving such a formulation, even when it is couched in abstract terms such as those chosen here. The variety and richness of piety comprehended in the stream of historical Islam and the subtlety of much that is found there defy facile compression into a formula.

4. After a period in the late nineteenth century and the first half of the twentieth century when apologetics was a basic factor in the religious writings of Arabs, the trend seems now to be waning. Its absence is perhaps most noticeable in the Maghreb, and it was not a vital element in the Iranian reaction to the modern scene until recently. Within the last decade, however, the emergence of apologetic attitudes coupled with hostility toward Western Orientalism has become evident in that country. In the Indian subcontinent, where apologetics has drawn the energies of several entire generations of Muslims, the trend continues to be very much alive.

5. Chapter 8 in *A Reader's Guide to the Great Religions* (New York: 1965, with a second revised and enlarged edition in preparation) and No. VIII of the State of the Art Series in the *MESA Bulletin* in two parts [**4**, 3 (October 1970); **5**, 1 (February 1971); correction in **5**, 3 (1971)].

Appendix

LAW*

The kinds of activities and concerns that are normally designated by the term Islamic law in English lie closer to the heart of the Muslim outlook on the world than perhaps any other of the traditional religious sciences. Effort to spell out the specific rules of conduct that should govern society as a whole is the fundamental and most typical Muslim religious activity.

*The section of this chapter on law was intended only as a supplement to a more extensive treatment of the subject elsewhere in this volume and for that reason has purposely been kept brief.

The bench mark of all modern studies on the history and development of Islamic law is found in the writings of the late Joseph Schacht. Not only has Schacht sketched the broad outlines of development in a manner that other scholars increasingly tend to confirm, but he has also set the guidelines of work in this field for some time to come by his masterly orientation toward the problem areas that require consideration. His basic work is the famous but difficult *The Origins of Muhammadan Jurisprudence* (Schacht, 1950) where the investigations leading to his conclusions about the history of Islamic law are set out in detail. Far easier to understand and follow is his *An Introduction to Islamic Law* (1964) where the development of the law is discussed in systematic terms and in historical sequence. These two books are of such basic import for understanding the law that they form the beginning and the reference point for virtually every other modern scholarly writing in the field. There is a large literature devoted to criticism of Schacht, either to disputing his basic position (which Muslim authors in particular find difficult to accept because of its rejection of the validity of legal *ḥadîṯẖ* ascribed to the Prophet, its refusal to accept the classical theory of the law as a sober description of historical fact, and its insistence upon development of the law) or to refining some of the details of his assertions. In spite of this often hostile consideration, Schacht's basic view has stood firm, with only the modification of some details. For example, the writing of Noel J. Coulson, who after Schacht's death is now perhaps the leading scholar in the field, accepts the framework that Schacht described and supplies some additional evidence in its support, but at the same time Coulson is not as skeptical as Schacht about the validity of all the legal *ḥadîṯẖ* attributed to the Prophet and holds some different, though hardly fundamental, views about the early schools of law. Coulson's *A History of Islamic Law* (1964) in the Islamic Surveys series is another of the significant achievements of legal scholarship devoted to Islam.

This important work on the history and early development of the law is more than matched by an interest in the legal evolution of contemporary Muslim states. Although in most instances the positive law of these modern states has little or nothing to do with the *s̱ẖarîᶜa*, there is a lively and continuing sense of the relevance of the community's past heritage and a felt need to come to terms somehow with the problems posed by the adoption of principles that have no foundation in that heritage. Among the institutional changes that the Muslim world must undertake in its quest for modernization, and the restoration of its lost power and prestige, legal reform and evolution stand foremost. In view of the fact that Muslims are the inheritors of an immensely rich religiously based legal tradition which spells out a host of normative demands for life, the discussions about the nature and content of law in the Muslim world pose some of the liveliest and most vital religious issues of our time for the community. A number both of legal scholars and social scientists have interested themselves in legal changes in the Islamic countries. The outstanding contributor to the field is J. N. D. Anderson, who has written several books and a number of articles, too numerous to be cited in their entirety; we may take note only of his *Islamic Law in the Modern World* (1959) and *Islamic Law in Africa* (1954). Coulson, mentioned above, and the incomparable Joseph Schacht have also interested themselves in the study and description of the modern situation. Generally speaking, there is available a competent literature that treats the recent evolution of the law among our Muslim contemporaries. One of the finest examples is Coulson's *Succession in the Muslim Family* (1971) which surveys both the classical stand on problems of inheritance and the state of legislation on this matter in the principal Muslim countries of our day. The law of inheritance is the most complex of the sub-divisions of Islamic law, but Coulson has given it a treatment that is lucid in addition to being comprehensive. Surveys of a specific area of the law that contrast the old with the new as Coulson has done are of the highest scholarly value.

Scholarship on the law thus may count several achievements to its credit. It has made accessible soundly based histories of the law's origins and development and of its modern expression. In addition, there is a large store of scholarly work from previous generations that explores the content of the medieval Islamic legal heritage. This literature is comprised of text editions and translations, studies of the various schools of law, comparisons of the teachings of legal schools, *fatâwâ* or decisions of jurisconsults, handbooks for quick reference, studies of judicial institutions, descriptions of the principal elements of the public law of the community, analyses of sectarian law, work on the status and use of Islamic law under various colonial regimes, and so forth, in all a formidable accumulation of available knowledge.

From the standpoint of the primary interest in religion that animates us here, there are two aspects of legal study of particular significance for the future. One is the continued assessment of the role of *sharîa* in the modern world and of the legal changes being brought about as the result of the revolution that is transforming Muslim life everywhere. The second is related to the first, namely, the need for close theoretical analysis of the jurisprudential principles that have informed both the positive law and the ideal law of the Islamic world in the past and that figure prominently as the basis of the accelerating legal evolution of our own time. There is very little study of Islamic law from the kind of perspective that determines Western speculative analyses of jurisprudence. This is so in spite of the fact that rich material is at hand to make such studies possible, for Muslim legal thinkers invoke abstract principles to justify their rulings on particular points of law and to provide rationality for the system as a whole. One thinks, for example, of the Spanish jurist al-Shâṭibî, whose principle of *al-maṣlaḥa al-mursala* has been a principal tool in the equipment of the Islamic modernists. In addition the Islamic literature on the *uṣûl* is characterized by the presence of a great deal of discussion of a straightforwardly philosophical nature. The study of these matters is of interest to scholars but of vital importance to the Muslim world in the light of the ongoing reassessment of the legal heritage and the need for insight into the implications of what is happening.

BIBLIOGRAPHY

Abbott, Nabia, *Studies in Arabic Literary Papyrii.* Vol. 2. Chicago: Univ. Press, 1967.

Abdul, Musa A. O. The Qur'an: Tabarsî's Commentary, unpublished Ph.d. dissertation, McGill University, 1974.

Abun-Nasr, Jamil M. *The Tijanniya.* London: Royal Institute of International Affairs Oxford Univ. Press, 1965.

Adams, Charles J. "Islam," in *A Readers Guide to The Great Religions.* New York: The Free Press. London: Collier-Macmillan, Ltd. 1965, pp. 287–337.

———. No. VIII of The State of the Art Series in the *MESA Bulletin.* 4, 3 (October, 1970), and 5, 1 (February 1971) and 5, 3 (October 1971).

ᶜAlī, Sayyid Amir. *The Spirit of Islam.* London: Christopher's Ltd., 1922.

Allard, Michel. *Le Problème des attributs divins dans la doctrine d'al-Ashᶜari et de ses premiers grands disciples.* Beirut: Institut les lettres orientales, 1965.

———. et al. *Analyse conceptuelle du Coran sur cartes perforées.* Paris and the Hague: Mouton, 1963, (2 vols, and cards).

Altheim, Franz, and Ruth Stiehl, eds. *Die Araber in der alten Welt,* 5 vols. Berlin: de Gruyter, 1964–1968.

Anawati, M. M., and Louis Gardet. *Introduction à la théologie musulmane.* Paris: Vrin, 1948.

———. *La Mystique musulmane.* Paris: Vrin, 1961.

———. *Les Grands problèmes de la théologie musulmane.* Vol. 1. *Dieu et la destinée de l'homme.* by Louis Gardet. Paris: Vrin, 1967. Vol. 2. *Dieu, son existence et ses attributs,* by M. M. Anawati. Not yet published.

Anderson, J. N. D. *Islamic Law in Africa.* London: Her Majesty's Stationery Office, 1954.

———. *Islamic Law in the Modern World.* New York: New York Univ. Press, 1959.

Andrae, Tör. *Die Person Muhammads in Lehre und Glauben seiner Gemeinde.* Stockholm: Lundell, 1918.

Arberry, A. J. *An Introduction to the History of Sufism.* Sir Abdullah Suhrawardy Lectures, 1942. London and New York: Longmans, Green and Co., 1943.

———. *The Seven Odes.* London: Allen & Unwin, 1957.

———. *Sufism.* London: Allen & Unwin, 1950.

Baljon, J. M. S., *Modern Muslim Koran Interpretation,* 1880–1960. Leiden: Brill, 1961.

Bausani, A. *Persia Religiosa da Zaratustra a Bahâ'u'llâh.* Milan: Il Saggiatore, 1959.

de Beaureceuil, S. *'Abdullah al-Harawī Anṣārī.* Cairo: Matbaᶜat al-Maᶜhad al-ᶜIlmî al-Faransî lil Âthâr al-Sharqîyah, 1962.

Birge, John Kingsley. *The Bektashi Order of Dervishes.* London: Luzac, 1937.

Birkeland, Harris. *The Lord Guideth.* Oslo: H. Aschehaug, 1956.

Blachère, Régis. *Le Problème de Mahomet.* Paris: Presses Universitaires de France, 1952.

Böwering, Gerhard. A Textual and Analytic Study of the Tafsīr of Sahl al-Tustarī. Unpublished Ph.D. dissertation. Montreal: McGill Univ., 1974.

Buhl, Frants. *Das Leben Muhammeds*, Hans Heinrich Schaeder, trans. Heidelberg: Quelle & Meyer, 1961.

Chelhod, Joseph. *Le Sacrifice chez les arabes*. Paris: presses universitaires de France, 1955.

———. *Les Structures du sacré chez les arabes*. Paris: Maisonneuve and Larose, 1964.

Corbin, Henry. *Creative Imagination in the Ṣūfism of Ibn ᶜArabi*. London: Routledge and Kegan Paul, 1970.

———. *En Islam iranien*, 4 vols. Paris: Gallimard, 1971–1972.

———. with S. H. Nasr. *Histoire de la philosophie islamique*. Paris: Gallimard, 1964–.

Coulson, Noel J. *A History of Islamic Law*. Edinburgh: Univ. Press, 1964.

———. *Succession in the Muslim Family*. Cambridge: Univ. Press, 1971.

Cragg, Bishop Kenneth. *The Call of the Minaret*. New York: Oxford Univ., 1956.

———. *Sandals at the Mosque: Christian Presence Amid Islam*. London: SCM Press, 1959.

Depont, O., and X. Coppolani. *Les Confrèries religeiuses musulmanes*. Algiers: Jourdan, 1897.

Dermenghem, E. *Le Culte des saints dans l'Islam maghrébin*. Paris: Gallimard, 1954.

Doe, Brian. *Southern Arabia*. London: Thames and Hudson, 1971.

Evans-Pritchard, E. E. *The Sanusi of Cyrenaica*. Oxford: Clarendon Press, 1949.

Fahd, Toufic. *La Divination arabe*. Leiden: Brill, 1966.

———. *Le Panthéon de l'Arabie centrale à la veille de l'Hégire*. Beirut: Institut Français d'Archéologie. Paris: Geuthner, 1968.

Fakhry, Majid. *A History of Islamic Philosophy*. New York: Columbia Univ., 1970.

Farès, Bishr. *L'honneur chez les arabes*. Paris: Adrien-Maisonneuve, 1932.

Frank, Richard. *The Metaphysics of Created Being According to Abu l-Hudhayl al-ᶜAllaf: a Philosophical Study of the Earliest Kalam*. Istanbul: Nederlands Historisch-Archaeologisch Institut, 1966.

Fiegenbaum, J. W. Prophethood from the Perspective of the Qur'an. Unpublished Ph.D. dissertation, McGill University, 1973.

Geertz, Clifford. *The Religion of Java*. Glencoe: Free Press, 1960.

———. *Islam Observed*. New Haven: Yale Univ., 1968.

Gellner, Ernest. *Saints of the Atlas*. London: Weidenfeld and Nicholson, 1969.

Goldziher, Ignaz. *Vorlesungen über den Islam*, 2nd rev. ed. Heidelberg: Winter, 1910.

———. *Die Richtungen der islamischen Koranauslegung*, 2nd ed. Leiden: E. J. Brill, 1952.

Gramlich, Richard. *Die Schiitischen Derwischorden Persiens*. Wiesbaden: Deutsche morgenländische Gesellschaft, 1965.

Grandqvist, H. *Muslim Death and Burial: Arab Customs and Traditions Studied in a Village in Jordan*. Helsinki: Societas Scientiarum Ferinica, 1965.

Guillaume, A. trans. *The Life of Muhammad*. (*Sîrat al-Nâbi*. Ibn Hishâm). London: Oxford Univ., 1955.

von Harnack, Adolf. *Grundriss Der Dogmengeschichte*. Freiburg im Breisgau: J. C. B. Mohr (P. Siebeck), 1889.

Haykal, Muḥammad Ḥasanayn. *Ḥayât Muḥammad* (Life of Muhammad). Cairo: Maktabat al-Naḥda, 1963.

Hodgson, Marshall G. S. "Islam and Image," *History of Religions*, **3**, 2 Winter, 1964.

Horten, Max. *Die philosopischen Systeme der specülativen Theologen im Islam*. Bonn: 1912.

———. *Die religiöse Gedankenwelt des Volkes im heutigen Islam*. Halle: Niemeyer, 1917–1918.

Hourani, George. *Islamic Rationalism: the Ethics of ᶜAbd al-Jabbār*. Oxford: Clarendon Press, 1971.

Izutsu, Toshihiko. *The Structure of the Ethical Terms in the Koran*. Tokyo: Keio Institute of Philological Studies, 1959.

———. *God and Man in the Koran*. Tokyo: Keio Institute of Philological Studies, 1964.

———. *The Concept of Belief in Islamic Theology: a Semantic Analysis of Īmān and Islâm*. Tokyo: Keio Inst. of Cultural & Linguistic Studies, 1965.

———. *Ethico-Religious Concepts in the Qur'an.* Montreal: McGill Univ., 1966.

———. *The Key Philosophical Concepts in Sufism and Taoism,* 2 vols. Tokyo: Keio Inst. of Cultural and Linguistic Studies, 1966–1967.

Jansen, J. J. G., *The Interpretation of the Qur'an in Modern Egypt.* Leiden: Brill, 1974.

Jeffery, Arthur. *Materials for the History of the Text of the Qur'an.* Leiden: Brill, 1937.

Introduction to the Qur'an. Edinburgh: Edinburgh Univ. Press, 1953.

Jomier, J. *Le Commentaire coranique du Manār.* Paris: Maisonneuve, 1954.

Juynboll, G. H. A. *The Authenticity of the Tradition Literature: Discussions in Modern Egypt.* Leiden: Brill, 1969.

Kader, A. H. Abdel. *The Life, Personality and Writings of al-Junayd.* London: Luzac, 1962.

Kriss, Rudolf, and Hubert Kriss-Heinrich. *Volksglaube im Bereich des Islams,* 2 vols. Wiesbaden: Harrassowitz, 1960 and 1962.

Landolt, Hermann. *Correspondence spirituelle echangée entre Nuroddin Esfarayeni et son disciple 'Alaoddawleh Semnani.* Bibliothèque Iranienne, Vol. 21. Tehran: l'Institut Franco-Iranien, 1972.

———. "Der Briefwechsel zwischen Kāsānī und Simnānī über Waḥdat al-Wugūd," *Der Islam,* 50 (April 1973).

Lings, Martin. *A Moslem Saint of the Twentieth Century: Shaikh Aḥmad al-ᶜAlawī.* London: Allen & Unwin, 1961.

MacDonald, Duncan Black. *Development of Muslim Theology, Jurisprudence and Constitutional Theory.* New York: Scribner's Sons, 1903.

———. *The Religious Life and Attitude in Islam.* Chicago: Univ. Press, 1909.

Makdisi, George. "Ash'arī and the Asharites in Islamic Religious History," *Studia Islamica,* **17** (1962), **18** (1963).

Massignon, Louis. *Essai sur les origines du lexique technique de la mystique musulmane,* rev. and enlarged. Paris: Geuthner, 1922.

Meier. Fritz. *Die Fawāᶜiḥ al-gamāl wa-fawātih al-galāl des Nagm ad-Dīn al-Kubrā: Eine Darstellung mystischer Erfahrungen im Islām aus der Zeit um 1200.* Wiesbaden: Steiner, 1957.

Michon, Jean. *L'mi'rāj de Muṣṭafâ al-Bakrī al-Khalwatī.* Paris: Vrin, 1973.

Molé, M. "Les Kubirwiya entre sunnisme et shiisme aux huitième et neuvième siècles de l'hégire." *Revue des études islamiques,* **29** (1961).

———. "Traités mineurs de Nagm al-dīn Kubrā," *Annales Islamologiques,* **4** (1963).

Moreno, M. M. "Mistica musalmana e mistica indiana," *Annali Lateranensi,* **12** (1948).

Nader, Albert N. *Le Système philosophique des Muᶜtazila.* Beirut: Editions les lettres orientales, 1956.

Nasr, Abun. *The Tijanniya.* London: Royal Institute of International Affairs, Oxford University Press, 1965.

Nöldeke, Theodor. *Geschichte des Korans,* 2 vols. Second revised ed. prepared by F. Schwally. Leipzig: Dieterich, 1909.

Nwyia, P. *Les Lettres de direction spirituelle d'Ibn ᶜAbbād de Ronda.* Beirut: Imprimerie Catholique, 1958.

———. *Ibn ᶜAbbād de Ronda* 1332–90. Beirut: Imprimerie Catholique, 1956.

———. *Exégèse coranique et langage mystique.* Beirut: Dâr al-Mashriq, 1970.

———. *Ibn ᶜAtā' Allāh ... et la naissance de la confrèrie Sadilite.* Beirut: Dâr al-Mashriq, 1971.

Padwick, Constance. *Muslim Devotions.* London: SPCK, 1961.

Paret, Rudi, *Der Koran, Kommentar und Konkordanz.* Stuttgart: Kohlhammer Verlag, 1971.

Parrinder, Geoffrey. *Jesus in the Qur'an.* London: Faber, 1965.

Pirenne, J. *La Grèce et Saba.* Paris: Imprimerie Nationale, 1955.

Rabb, Muḥammad 'Abdur. *The Life, Thought and Historical Importance of Abu Yazid al-Bistami.* Dacca: 1971.

Rahbar, Daud. *God of Justice* Leiden: E. J. Brill, 1960.

Rahman, Fazlur. *Islamic Methodology in History*. Karachi: Central Institute of Islamic Research, 1965.

Rayyah, Maḥmûd Abû. *Aḍwâ ᶜalâ al-sunna al-Muḥammadiyya*. Cairo: Dâr al-Maᶜârif, 1967.

Reinert, Benedikt. *Die Lehre vom Tawakkul in der klassischen Sufik*. Berlin: de Gruyter, 1968.

Ritter, Helmut. *Das Meer der Seele*. Leiden: Brill, 1955.

Ryckmans, Jacques. *Les religions arabes préislamique*. Louvain: Bibliothèque du Museon, 1951.

Schacht, Joseph. "New Sources for the History of Muhammadan Theology," *Studia Islamica*, **1** (1945).

——— *The Origins of Muhammadan Jurisprudence*. Oxford: Clarendon Press, 1950.

———. *An Introduction to Islamic Law*. Oxford: Clarendon Press, 1964.

Schimmel, Annemarie. *Mystical Dimensions of Islam*. Chapel Hill: U. of North Carolina Press, 1975.

Serjeant, R. B. "Professor A. Guillaume's translation of the Sīrah," *Bulletin of the School of Oriental and African Studies*, **21** (1958), 1–14.

———. "Haram and Hawtah, the Sacred Enclave in Arabia." In *Ilā Ṭāhā Ḥusayn*. ᶜAbd al-Rahmān Badawī, ed. Cairo: Dâr al-Maᶜârif 1962.

Sezgin, Fuat. *Geschichte des Arabischen Schriftums*, 5 vols. Leiden: Brill, 1967–

Smith, Jane K. *An Historical and Semantic Study of the Term 'Islam' as seen in a Sequence of Qur'an commentaries*. Boston: Harvard University, 1970.

Smith, W. C. *Modern Islam in India*. London: Gollancz, 1946.

———. *Islam in Modern History*. Princeton: Univ. Press, 1957.

———. "Comparative Religion, Whither and Why?" In *The History of Religions*. Mircea Eliade and Joseph Kitagawa, eds. Chicago: Univ. Press, 1959.

———. *The Faith of Other Men*. Toronto: Canadian Broadcasting Corporation, 1962.

———. *The Meaning and End of Religion*. New York: Macmillan, 1963.

Spiro, Melford E. "Religion: Problems of Definition and Explanation," *Anthropological Approaches to the Study of Religion*. ASA monographs, no. 3. London: Tavistock, 1966.

Steiner, Heinrich. *Die Mu'taziliten oder die Freidenker im Islam*. Leipzig: Hirzel, 1865.

Trimingham, J. Spencer. *The Sufi Orders in Islam*. Oxford: Clarendon Press, 1971.

Van Ess, Joseph. *Die Erkenntnislehre des 'Adudaddīn al-Īcī*. Wiesbaden: Steiner, 1966.

———. *Frühe Muᶜtazilitische Häresiographie*. Wiesbaden: Steiner, 1971.

al-Wâqidî. *The Kitāb al-Maqhāzi of al-Wâqidî*, 3 vols., Marsden Jones, ed. Oxford: Univ. Press, 1966.

Watt, Montgomery. *Free Will and Predestination in Early Islam*. London: Luzac, 1948.

———. *Muhammad at Mecca*. Oxford: Clarendon Press, 1953.

———. *Muhammad at Medina*. Oxford: Clarendon Press, 1956.

———. *Islamic Philosophy and Theology*. Edinburgh: Edinburgh University Press, 1962.

———. *Truth in the Religions*. Edinburgh: Univ. Press, 1963.

———. *Islamic Revelation in the Modern World*. Edinburgh: Univ. Press, 1969.

———. *The Formative Period of Islamic Thought*. Edinburgh: Edinburgh University Press, 1973.

von Grunebaum, *Modern Islam; the Search for Cultural Identity*. Berkeley: U. of California Press, 1962.

von Wissmann, Hermann. *Zur Geschichte und Landeskunde von alt süd-Arabien*. Wien: Hermann Bühlaus, 1964.

Zaehner, R. C. *Hindu and Muslim Mysticism*. London: Athlóne Press, U. of London, 1960.

Ziadeh, Nicola A. *Sanūsīyah*. Leiden: Brill, 1958.

CHAPTER THREE

History

ALBERT HOURANI

The civilization of which Islam was the dominant religion, and which expressed itself mainly in Arabic, Persian, and Turkish, was always aware of its own past, and produced a succession of historians, whose aim was not only to commemorate the deeds of the rulers who were their patrons, but also to record all that was known about the times and places in which, according to the belief of Muslims, the word of God had been revealed to the Prophet Muhammad, and about the chain of witnesses by whom the deeds and sayings of the Prophet had been passed on to later generations, and the scholars who had articulated and transmitted the systems of law and thought derived from prophecy and tradition. This historical tradition has not quite died out. In the early years of the nineteenth century, a full-scale chronicle on the same level of importance as the great medieval ones, the *ᶜAja'ib al-Athâr* of al-Jabarti,[1] was produced in Egypt; later in the century there appeared works lying halfway between medieval and modern styles of historiography, like Mubarak's *Khiṭaṭ*,[2] Cevdet's *Tarih*,[3] al-Naṣirî's *Kitâb al-Istiqṣâ*,[4] and also the last great biographical dictionaries recording the lives of scholars and saints, al-Bitâr's *Ḥilyât al-Bashar*[5] in Syria, al-Kattani's *Ṣalwât al-Anfâs*[6] in Morocco. By the end of the nineteenth century, however, traditional historiography could no longer provide a frame within which Muslims of modern education could see their own past, or Western scholars could understand the development of Islamic society and civilization.

In Europe and North America, the professional study of Islamic history by historians scarcely goes back two generations. For a long time Islamic history

This chapter was completed before the publication of M. G. S. Hodgson's *The Venture of Islam*, 3 vols. (Chicago: University of Chicago, 1974). Some of the author's judgments would have been different, or would have been expressed in a different way, if he had been able to read this important work before revising his chapter.

was part of "Islamic studies," and Islamic studies were themselves a by-product of studies more central to the great concerns of the nineteenth-century mind: comparative philology, Biblical criticism, and the "science of religion."[7] It was only with the generation of I. Goldziher (1850–1921) and C. Snouck Hurgronje (1857–1936) that the study of Islam became an independent discipline demanding a scholar's whole attention, and a generation later, with C. H. Becker (1876–1933) and W. Barthold (1869–1930), that some of those who studied Islam began to think of themselves as primarily historians, concerned with bringing the highest standards of historical scholarship and interpretation to bear on Islamic history; it is only in the present generation that, in some universities, some of those who think of themselves as historians have been able to devote all or most of their time to teaching Islamic history.

Thus the study of Islamic history lies at least 100 years behind that of European history, and there has been no time yet to lay all the necessary foundations or create cumulative traditions of craftsmanship. Even in the present age, the study of Islamic history has not attracted enough scholars for all the urgent tasks. It has not moved the imagination of European and American scholars as China and Japan are doing. At a rough estimate, the serious teaching of Islamic history, above the level of an elementary survey course, takes place at perhaps 20 universities in North America, 20 in western Europe, and 20 in the Middle East and North Africa. In North America, there are perhaps between 30 and 50 university teachers who can give their main attention to Islamic history; in each of Great Britain, France, and Germany perhaps 15 to 20; similar numbers in Egypt, Turkey, and Israel; and fewer in other Middle Eastern countries. Altogether, therefore, there may be 200–300 scholars who can be regarded primarily as Islamic historians. In western Europe and North America some hundreds of university students are exposed each year to elementary courses on Islamic history, and in the Middle East and North Africa some thousands; but only a small proportion of them are studying for a first degree of which Islamic history forms a major part, and only a few dozen go on to higher study. In some parts of the field, those who emerge as fully trained historians are scarcely numerous enough to fill vacant teaching posts.

The simple fact that there are so few teachers and research workers has certain results. Few of them can specialize; most of them have to teach over too wide a range. However hard they work as scholars and writers, they cannot fill all the gaps. To take some obvious examples, few collections of documents have been properly cataloged; not all the basic chronicles have been published; there are few general surveys of periods or regions incorporating recent research; there are few monographs, even on periods or personalities of major importance; and there are almost no satisfactory biographies, even in the modern period. (We shall return to some of these points in other contexts.)

Even those workers who exist live for the most part in isolation: physical isolation first of all, scattered as they are by ones and twos in many universities, but also intellectual isolation. Each studies his own subject—there is a kind of tacit agreement that scholars do not impinge on each other's field, and there is a lack of those scholarly controversies which provide a stimulus to further research and thought. Students of English history, for example, are familiar with such great and fruitful arguments as those about the gentry in the seventeenth century or the structure of politics in the eighteenth. In the Islamic field there are few equivalents to them: recent discussions among French and North African historians about the invasions of Beni Ḥilâl,[8] and the arguments about Jamâl al-Dîn al-Afghânî to which Kedourie and Keddie have contributed,[9] but not many others, although Islamic history is full of problems in regard to which the discussion of different explanations may offer the best way of advance.

The obstacles posed by the shortage of European and American historians in this field are all the greater because of the relatively backward state of indigenous scholarship. Any Western scholar working on Chinese or Japanese history knows how much he owes, in the way of solid foundations, stimulus, and fruitful collaboration, to Chinese and Japanese scholars. In the Middle East, however, although narrative histories and biographical dictionaries of an old-fashioned kind continued to be written in this century (those of al-Râfiᶜî in Egypt,[10] al Ghazzî,[11] al Ṭabbâkh,[12] and Kurd ᶜAlî in Syria,[13] and ᶜAzzâwî[14] in Iraq), the emergence of modern historiography in the full sense was slow, and hindered by obstacles such as the slow development of higher education, the absence of an environment conducive to research, and the existence of political limitations upon free inquiry and publication.

In some countries this situation has changed. In Egypt there is now a genuine historical tradition which shows itself in the publication of Arabic texts and documents and the production of some good work on local history. In Israel the methods and standards of European scholarship were brought in by immigrant scholars and have taken root. The development of Turkish historiography is perhaps the most interesting because it took place in the same kind of circumstances as those of Europe in the nineteenth century: the growth of national consciousness and the emergence of the nation-state. In Turkey as in Europe this stimulated the desire to understand one's own past and provided a guiding concept, that of the nation, which, however much it has been criticized by thinkers, provides a satisfactory focus for some kinds of historical work. The Kemalist revolution tried to explain and justify itself in explicitly historical terms, to remake the historical self-consciousness of a nation. This impulse, working on ideas derived from the French sociologists of the nineteenth century, produced the seminal work of Fuat Köprülü as scholar and teacher, and his students, doing research in the Ottoman archives, have formed a considerable historical school.

In other countries, however, progress has been slower and there are fewer historians; in Lebanon, for example, the long tradition of local history is virtually carried on by one scholar. This is harmful in more ways than one. Self-interpretation is an important element in historiography, and there is something lacking in the history of a society written mainly from outside. Moreover, there are some things which indigenous scholars can do better than others, such as the collection of local documents and the editing of texts. In North Africa, a number of striking interpretative essays have appeared in recent years (for example, Laroui's *Histoire du Maghreb*[15]), but they still await the painstaking research that will make it possible to test or modify the ideas in them.

* * *

In such circumstances, progress in historical inquiry is bound to be slow, but nevertheless it has been made, and there is now a separate academic discipline of Islamic history. Like all historical disciplines it consists of two closely related activities: the discovery, collection, and editing of sources, and the interpretation of them. For purposes of exposition we must separate them, and it is perhaps truer to the nature of historical thought, which is oriented toward the particular, to begin with the sources.

The Islamic historians of the classical tradition built upon each other's work: each chronicle contained, in some form, the substance of earlier chronicles. In a sense the earlier European historians of Islam followed the same procedure. Their basic sources were the chronicles, and to find and edit them was an important task of scholarship. A large number of the essential chronicles are now available in printed form, but some are lost in whole or in part, some are still unpublished, and some have been published only in old and uncritical editions, for example the Arabic works published in Cairo in the nineteenth century, and the Ottoman histories published in Istanbul. Only a few new and more satisfactory editions have appeared, for example, the new Cairo edition of al-Ṭabarî.[16]

The use of the literary sources will always remain an important part of the Islamic historian's work. For some periods, in particular the early centuries of Islam, few other kinds of source exist. Even when they do, significant results can still be obtained by a traditional method: the careful study of written sources, whether they are chronicles, biographies, or works of quite a different kind (for example, legal texts), by scholars who combine a full philological training with the historian's craft of asking questions that will uncover their latent meaning and implications. The literature of Islamic studies provides some classic examples: Goldziher's use of the *ḥadîth* literature to illuminate the political and theological controversies of the early centuries,[17] and Lammens' use of the *Kitâb al-Aghânî* to throw light on pre-Islamic and early Islamic society.[18] More recent works show how effective such a method can be, for example, Udovich's study of legal texts to explain the organization of medieval commerce,[19] and Sha'ban's careful examination of the precise meaning of the relevant chronicles in order to explain the nature of the Abbasid revolution.[20]

Nevertheless attention has moved in the last years, here as in other fields of historical study, from the use of literary sources to the collection and use of documents, that is, texts written for an immediate practical purpose such as trade or administration, but which can be used by the historian for other purposes. It is sometimes said that Islamic history, at least before the Ottoman period, can never be as firmly based as is that of medieval Europe because of the lack of solid documentary evidence. It is true that no complete and organized archives of medieval governments appear to have survived, similar to the papal archives or those of the kings of England and France. But there are usually more sources than one thinks, and the discovery of them waits for the scholars with the curiosity to ask new questions and the enterprise and luck to find new materials to provide the answers. A more systematic and successful attempt is now being made to collect and study chancery and diplomatic documents. They have been found in many places: in monasteries and synagogues, in European archives, in libraries of Istanbul to which documents from many countries occupied by the Ottoman armies found their way, or incorporated in manuals and chronicles. Works such as the two volumes edited by S. M. Stern (*Fatimid Decrees* and *Documents from Islamic Chanceries*)[21] show how much can be learned from them. Medieval *waqfiyas* also exist, and some of those for the great Mamluk foundations in Cairo are now being used. For one country, Egypt, the mass of documents is particularly great because of the dry climate and the continuity of administrative life in spite of political changes. They include papyri, containing administrative and financial material, which are important because they are so detailed and can be used together with similar material from pre-Islamic times; they have in fact been little used, and since Grohmann there have been few Arabic papyrologists. There are also the commercial and legal documents preserved, together with religious and literary works, in the genizah of the Fusṭâṭ synagogue; many of them have now been published and studied, and they form the basis of a major work now being written, Goitein's *A Mediterranean Society*.[22] It seems unlikely that any other hoard of this size will come to light, but Richards has published a smaller collection of documents from the Karaite synagogue in Cairo,[23] and D. and J. Sourdel have found (significantly, in Istanbul) a collection of documents from Damascus in the tenth century.[24]

For the early modern period, that of the great empires, there are above all the inexhaustible riches of the Ottoman archives, which throw light not only on the central institutions of the empire but on all the provinces it ruled, including the North African regions where its hold was light, and on all the countries with which the Ottoman sultan had dealings, eastern and central Europe, Russia, the Caucasus, and Iran. They contain information not only about the period of Ottoman rule, but about earlier periods as well.

The archives of Ottoman provincial governments have been to a great extent destroyed or scattered, but they still exist in some cities which had considerable autonomy or a developed bureaucracy, for example, Sofia, Cairo, and Tunis. Recently an Egyptian historian, ᶜAbd al-Raḥîm, has found and used documentary sources for Egyptian local history in the eighteenth century.[25] For the history of the provinces, however, there is another rich source, the archives of the religious courts which contain not only records of judicial cases but a variety of other documents both public and private (for example wills) which were registered in them; Raymond has recently used those of the Cairo court to investigate the structure of property and wealth in eighteenth-century Egypt.[26] In Syria and other countries they are now being collected and made available for study.

Of the other states of the same period, archives exist in Morocco but have scarcely yet been studied. There are no surviving organized archives for Safavid Iran, but some attempts have recently been made to collect documents, and a work by Busse shows how much can be gathered even from a small number of documents.[27] For the eastern part of the Muslim world there is a source of vast potential importance, the Chinese archives of the Ming and Ch'ing dynasties.

For the Middle East in the nineteenth and twentieth centuries, much of what has been written is based on British and French diplomatic and consular papers. They will continue to be used for many different purposes, but so far as the internal history of the Ottoman, Qajar, and Alawi states is concerned they are too well-known to make it likely that the study of them will generate exciting new ideas. The introduction of the "thirty years' rule" in the British Public Record Office has made it possible, however, to study the period of British ascendancy in depth, and to illuminate the colonial relationship from one side at least. The archives of other European states, in particular the Austro-Hungarian Empire and Russia, have not been used so fully, and each will add something of its own: in the last phase of Ottoman history each consulate and embassy had its own group of clients and derived from them its own picture of Ottoman politics and society. But there is more to be learned from indigenous archives, which exist in abundance and have scarcely been used. Apart from Ottoman sources, the Egyptian state archives are particularly rich; organized for the use of scholars in the reign of King Fuad, they were used at that time by some historians for the history both of Egypt and of Syria under Muḥammad ᶜAlî (A. Rustum published a large calendar of those dealing with Syria under Muḥammad ᶜAlî,[28] and Deny a catalog of the Turkish documents[29]). More recently, A. Schölch has made them the basis of a new study of the ᶜUrabî period,[30] which now for the first time can be seen through Egyptian rather than British eyes. Of other archives, perhaps the most unexpected discovery was that by Holt of the records of the Mahdist government in the Sudan,[31] a proof that all governments, however, remote they seem from the ideal of bureaucratic order, rest upon paper, and paper is more often forgotten than destroyed. The Israeli state archives are also very complete and well-organized. In almost all Middle Eastern and North African countries a determined effort is now being made by local historians, with help from their governments, to discover and collect the documents for their national history.

Also for the modern period, the papers of banks and companies have scarcely been looked at, except in such pioneer works as Landes's *Bankers and Pashas*.[32] There are also more family and personal papers than might be expected. The private papers of British diplomats, officials, and businessmen are being collected at Durham (for the Sudan) and Oxford (for other countries); there is no similar plan for collecting the papers of French officials in North Africa and Syria. Middle Eastern politicians keep more papers than they admit: in Egypt those of Nubâr Pâ<u>sh</u>â have been used by at least one historian, and those of Za<u>gh</u>lûl Pâ<u>sh</u>â also exist; for general Arab politics there is a large collection of <u>Sh</u>akîb Arslân's papers; for the development of the Jewish National Home, the Central Zionist Archives and the Weizmann Archives are of basic importance.

Rural records are the most difficult to find and use in any country where a traditional social order exists, but even they are coming to light. There are a large number of agricultural contracts among the papers of the <u>Kh</u>âzin family in the Lebanese Museum, and similar materials are now being used for work in progress in Morocco and Jordan. The writings of some French officials in North Africa contain a mass of precise and detailed observations of rural processes which have almost the value of documentary evidence: special mention can be made of Berque's *Structures sociales du Haut Atlas*.[33]

Archives and documents once discovered must be well looked after, and here all scholars are conscious of difficulties. The great archives of western European states are open, well arranged, and easy to use; the Russian Foreign Ministry papers are closed to most foreigners, although other Russian archives are open; those of the Middle East tend to lie somewhere between these two points—sometimes open, sometimes not, access given to some scholars and not to others. Political strains, the desire of officials to use their authority, and of scholars to preserve their cultural capital all play a part. Even when open the archives are not always easy to use: they may be badly arranged, badly indexed, and cataloged badly if at all; there may be few trained archivists to look after them, and few or no facilities for photocopying. In Turkey, a commission has been studying the reorganization of the archives and there is a plan to train archivists, but here and elsewhere there is a long way to go.

There are two types of document which, in Bernard Lewis's words, have survived "because they are written on metal and on stone": coins and inscriptions. The study of coins can of course help to elucidate not only the history of dynasties but economic and financial history and, within limits, the transmission of artistic forms. Much work has been done to collect and study them, largely under the inspiration of G. C. Miles, and collections exist for many of the Muslim dynasties. Inscriptions are more valuable still. As Sauvaget has said (following van Berchem),[35] most Islamic inscriptions illustrate one or the other of two great themes, divine power and political authority, and there are fewer administrative inscriptions than in classical antiquity; but those that record endowments can be used to date buildings and identify patrons, and so to trace the lines of trade or conquest and the accumulation of wealth. Medieval Arabic inscriptions have been collected on a large scale in the *Corpus Inscriptionum Arabicarum*[36] and the *Répertoire chronologique d'épigraphie arabe*,[37] but little has been done to collect Persian inscriptions, or Arabic ones in Iran.

Buildings and the sites or ruins of them could also be more fully used as sources of historical information. There have been surprisingly few serious excavations of Islamic sites since Hamilton excavated at Khirbat al-Mafjar[38] and Schlumberger at Qaṣr al-Ḥayr al-Gharbî and Lashkari Bazar. Only a handful of recent or current excavations exist: those of Scanlon at Fusṭâṭ, Whitehouse at Sirâf, Grabar at Qaṣr al-Ḥayr al-Sharqî, a few done by the Iraqi Department of Antiquities, and a few in Iran. The reasons are obvious, shortage of trained personnel and money: it is natural that whatever funds are available should go mainly to excavations of ancient sites of periods for which no written sources exist. But lack of funds can only partly explain the long delay before definitive reports are published; those on Schlumberger's work will perhaps never be written or published in full.

Rather more has been done to study buildings which still stand. Sauvaget's classical studies of Muslim cities in Syria,[39] Creswell's of Cairo,[40] and those of G. and W. Marçais in North Africa[41] have provided solid foundations on which a few scholars are building: Kessler in Cairo,[42] Sourdel-Thomine in Syria and Iran,[43] Pugachenkova in Central Asia,[44] and Ayverdi[45] and Kuran[46] in Turkey. Very recently, however, it has been possible for a reviewer to describe Golombek's study of the shrine at Gazur Gah as "the only major study of any Timurid monument in a western language."[47] There are still major cities and buildings for which no adequate study exists, and the need is the more urgent because many of the monuments are in a bad state of repair; at least work is now starting on a French survey of medieval buildings in Cairo and a British one in Jerusalem.

When cities have still to be studied it is too much to expect that much work should have been done on the archaeology of the countryside. Adams' *Land Behind Baghdad*[48] is a good example of the way in which archaeological and other techniques can be combined in order to study the changing pattern of land use in a single district. In regions like the inner plain of Syria and the Sahel of Tunisia, where land use has shifted throughout history, the excavation of abandoned villages might help us to understand the interaction of settled and pastoral life.

A historical method now used profitably in other parts of the world, but scarcely at all in the Middle East, is that of recording "oral history." This expression covers two very different kinds of activity. The first is the recording of the memoirs of people who have played a part in public life; the only systematic attempts being made are those at the Hebrew University of Jerusalem and the American University of Beirut, but Seale's *The Struggle for Syria*[49] shows how a book can be built upon hundreds of interviews with politicians, whose replies to skillful questions have been subtly analyzed. By oral history we can also mean, however, the recording of the collective memory of a community, particularly of a small-scale, self-enclosed, illiterate community. This method has been much used in sub-Saharan Africa to supplement the limited written sources, and its use is one of the reasons for the rapid advance made in African history in the present generation. For the Middle East there are only a few works (done more by anthropologists than historians) in which personal observation and interviews are used together with documentary sources: good examples are Evans-Pritchard's *The Sanusi of Cyrenaica*[50] and Berque's *Histoire sociale d'un village égyptien au XXème siècle*.[51]

* * *

If the sources are to be properly used there is a need for various "tools," not all of which exist. In some ways indeed the worker in Islamic history is well favored. As bibliographical aids he has Sauvaget's *Introduction to the History of the Muslim East*,[52] revised by Cahen and translated into English with further revisions; the older biobibliographical work for Arabic literature by Brockelmann,[53] a more recent one by Kahhala,[54] and the latest by Sezgin[55]; a similar work by Graf for Christian Arabic literature;[56] and for Persian that by Storey (of which the revised version only exists in Russian).[57] But catalogs or even simple lists of manuscripts, archives, and collections of documents are defective, for example, those for the Ottoman archives. Published selections of documents with annotations, which can serve as manuals of diplomatics, are not entirely absent; apart from those by Stern and Busse already mentioned, different kinds of Ottoman document have been published in English by B. Lewis[58] and Heyd,[59] in French by Sauvaget and Mantran, and in Turkish by Barkan[61] and others.

For articles in European languages, the *Index Islamicus*[62] is an excellent working tool; an *Index Hebraicus* is just beginning, and similar works for Turkish and Persian would be useful. So would cumulative lists of books newly published in Middle Eastern countries where the practice of reviewing books is not widespread, and abstracts of books and articles in languages not widely known among scholars (in particular, Russian, but in future, Japanese as well), to supplement those which appear in *Abstracta Islamica* and *Orientalistische Literaturzeitung*.

Of handbooks which offer a wide range of basic information, the *Encyclopaedia of Islam*,[63] in both the first and second editions, is a magnificent product of sustained international cooperation; it should be supplemented by the Turkish *Islam-Ansiklopedisi*.[64] The *Handbuch der Orientalistik*[65] and the "index documentaire" in D. and J. Sourdel's *La Civilisation de l'Islam classique*[66] are also useful for quick and reliable reference. For genealogies there are are Zambaur's *Manuel*[67] and now Bosworth's *The Islamic Dynasties*,[68] and for chronology, Freeman-Grenville's *The Muslim and Christian Calendars*.[69]

Other kinds of tools are more defective, however. A need felt by historians of all periods is for better maps and plans. Roolvink's *Historical Atlas of the Muslim Peoples*[70] is excellent for introductory teaching purposes, but not detailed enough for research. Of modern maps showing towns and routes as well as physical features, those produced by the French administrations in Syria and Lebanon and in North Africa are admirable, but for some other regions there seems to be nothing more reliable and full than the maps produced by European General Staffs before World War I. Of city plans, those for Cairo compiled by Bonaparte's savants and published in the *Description de l'Egypte*[71] are unique; for most other cities there can be nothing so full, but Sauvaget's plans of the growth and development of Aleppo and Damascus[72] provide a model to follow.

Another need historians share with others working in Islamic studies is for more adequate dictionaries. For Ottoman Turkish, a reprint of Redhouse's *Lexicon*[73] appeared recently, but for Arabic and Persian there is a need for dictionaries on historical principles. The task of compiling them, however, is probably too great—the prototype of them, the Oxford English Dictionary, took half a century to complete in more spacious days. Failing this, what is perhaps most urgently needed is an Arabic dictionary which gives special attention to the middle period of Arabic, when the specialized vocabulary for every sphere of knowledge had been more or less fixed in the form it retained until the nineteenth century. Dozy's *Supplement*[74] is still the best guide to it, but it needs to be expanded and brought up to date.

It would be helpful, too, to have more dictionaries for Arabic dialects, and detailed studies of the development and meaning of technical terms, which are living beings undergoing continuous change. Massignon's study of the growth of the technical language of Sufism provides a model,[75] and some suggestive essays by B. Lewis have traced the evolution of political terms.[76] The language of poetry is of particular importance for all researchers, as almost every work contains a wealth of allusions to Arabic and Persian poetry which lie at the heart of secular culture; the Hebrew University of Jerusalem has built up on index cards a valuable concordance of early Arabic poetry, and something like it is needed for Persian.

Adequate facilities for publication are also needed. The editing of texts goes on all the time, but important works too numerous to mention still lie in manuscript, and many of those printed long ago need to be republished in critical editions, and some of them with subject indexes. Of editions of Arabic histories, among those for which many scholars feel the need are the *Kâmil* of Ibn al-Athîr, the *Masâlik al-absâr* of al-^{c}Umari, the *Muqaddima* of Ibn Khaldun, and al-Jabarti's *^{c}Ajâ'ib al-Athâr*. The vast bulk of the Ottoman chronicles also needs reediting.

It has become increasingly difficult to publish academic theses and monographs in the traditional form, even with a subsidy. Most American theses can be obtained on microfilm, but this is not satisfactory for general use. A combination of offset printing with direct distribution through exchange between universities and advertisement in periodicals would seem to be the most promising approach. This has already been tried in Germany with the series *Islamkundliche Untersuchungen*.

The general opinion seems to be that there are enough learned periodicals. Apart from general historical periodicals of a kind which are open to articles dealing with non-Western history, like *Annales* or *Comparative Studies in Society and History*, there are now almost too many general "Orientalist" and "Islamic" periodicals. It would be useful if some of them could become more specialized in their interests; *The International Journal of Middle East Studies*, *Middle Eastern Studies*, and *The Journal of the Economic and Social History of the Orient* show how valuable it is to have periodicals focused, through the personal concern of an editor, on a certain type of problem. Apart from learned journals in the strict sense, there is a need for regular "newsletters," which give news of recent publications, conferences, and work in progress and publish bibliographical or other "notes and queries," and also for yearbooks or special issues of periodicals which could include works of, say, 100 pages, too long for an article in a journal, but too short for a book.

In a discipline practiced by so few, and where most of the few are scattered and isolated, it is essential to have some kind of framework within which ideas can be exchanged. There is a place, although it tends to be a marginal one, for Islamic historians in general congresses of historians or Orientalists, but perhaps the most fruitful exchanges now take place among small groups of scholars discussing a limited and carefully defined problem: to give two examples, a series held in London (*Historians of the Middle East*,[77] *Political and Social Change in Modern Egypt*,[78] *Studies in the Economic History of the Middle East*[79]) and a series held in Oxford (*The Islamic City*,[80] *Islam and the Trade of Asia*[81], *Islamic Civilization 950–1150*).[82]

With so few specialists, it is probably too much to expect that there should be permanent organizations of Islamic historians in most countries, but mention should be made of the historical associations in Turkey which both express and have helped to direct that effort to rethink the Turkish past, which was one of the essential parts of the Kemalist revolution: the Turkish Historical Society, the Institute for the Study of Turkish Culture, and the Institute for Seljuk History and Civilization.

* * *

It might be useful at this point to take stock of the progress made by our few dozen specialists, working for two generations or so with such sources and tools as we have described. It would be long and tedious to make a detailed survey of the field, period by period and country by country, but it may be possible to make some broad general statements.

First of all, there is a marked difference between the work done on different kinds of history. Most work has been done on explicitly political history, the narrative of wars and conquests, rulers, and governments. After that comes "intellectual history": movements of thought, legal schools, and the scholars and writers who have carried on the inner process of Islamic history. Less has been written on social history, even if that term is used in the loosest possible way, and even less on economic history, even for the modern period where statistical material exists. (But there has been a change, as we shall see, in the last few years.) Some kinds of history are just beginning to be written, for example, those of technology and demography.

Secondly, there is a marked difference also between the extent to which different regions of the Muslim world have been studied. Most attention has been given to the lands lying around the eastern end of the Mediterranean, Asia Minor, Syria in the broader sense, and Egypt. The reasons for this are obvious: the close connection between these countries and the rest of the Mediterranean world, the richness of the historical sources, and the relative strength of the indigenous tradition of historiography, both medieval and modern. For similar reasons, much attention has been paid to the history of Muslim Spain and its interaction with Europe. But less work has been done on the North African coast, the Sudan and the Arabian Peninsula, and Iraq after the first few centuries, and least of all on Iran and the lands beyond the Oxus.

Thirdly, some periods have been more thoroughly studied than others, although none of them is near being exhausted. In spite of the paucity of literary sources, the study of Umayyad history has been renewed by archaeological methods, and has probably reached a point where a new synthesis could be made to supplement that of Wellhausen. But the same cannot be said of the Abbasids; the revolution by which they took power has recently been studied by Shaᶜbân,[83] and there is some work on some of the institutions of their rule, notably Sourdel on the Vizirate,[84] but later Abbasid history has been little studied except in patches (for example, Makdîsî's work on eleventh-century Baghdad[85]). Various chapters in the fifth volume of the *Cambridge History of Iran*[86] provide at least a chronological and institutional framework for the history of the Seljuks; in an early work, *La Syrie du nord à l'époque des croisades*,[87] Cahen studied Syria during the Seljuk period, and in a later one, *Pre-Ottoman Turkey*,[88] the extensions of the Turks and Islam into Asia Minor. There is very little about the Fatimids or about early Maghrebi history, although there is more for the later Middle Ages—Brunschvig's *La Berbérie orientale sous les Hafsids*[89] deserves special mention. About Spain, there is above all the work of Lévi-Provençal.[90] For the Ayyubids, Gibb has written some penetrating essays[91]; for the Mamluks of Egypt even the basic institution, the military society, has not yet been thoroughly studied, although Ayalon has laid very solid foundations[92] and Darrag has studied one reign in depth.[93]

For Iran in the same period, the work of Spuler is important.[94] For the Safavid period, there are a number of monographs, mainly by German scholars, and there has been a certain concentration on the origins of the dynasty[95]; Minorsky's annotated translation of *Tadhkirat al-Mulūk*[96] elucidates the administrative system, and Aubin's studies[97] throw light on the way in which the regime inserted itself into Iranian society.

In general, however, much less work has been done on Safavids than on the Ottomans, and it is easy to see why: the immense range of Ottoman rule or influence, and the existence of the archives. Already 20 years ago, before the archives had been explored, Gibb and Bowen[98] tried to provide a framework within which later Ottoman history at least could be understood. This has stood for a generation, but has probably now served its purpose of stimulating thought. Detailed research in the archives and other manuscript sources has made it possible to form a clearer, fuller, and in some ways different view of the nature and working of the central government and the system of taxation. Much of this work has been done by Turkish scholars, notably by Uzunçarşili[99] and Inalcik, whose recent book, *The Ottoman Empire: the Classical Age 1300–1600*,[100] offers a clear summary of the present state of research.

The strength of such work lies in its grasp of the working of the central government. Less has been done on other aspects of Ottoman society. For the legal system, some articles by Heyd and his posthumous book on Ottoman criminal law[101] go beyond the textbooks to the ways in which law was actually interpreted and administered. The organization of industry and trade has also attracted some attention, in particular the international trade, for which European sources can be used in conjunction with Ottoman, as they have been by Inalcik in his study of the silk trade.[102]

It is inevitable that more attention should have been paid to the central government and the capital than the provinces, and right that it should be so; any attempt to write the history of the provinces, even of remote ones which appear to have been virtually independent, must take full account of Ottoman policies and methods if the picture is not to be distorted. A considerable amount of work on administration, taxation, and land has been done in the Balkans, where a number of Ottomanists in the successor-states have worked effectively on local records, in Hungary, Bulgaria, Albania, Rumania, and above all Yugoslavia. Apart from them, a great advance has been made in the study of the province of Egypt. Until a few years ago most of what was written was still based on three sources, Jabartî's chronicle, the *Description de l'Egypte*, and Volney's *Voyage*. But in the last few years three historians asking different questions have changed our understanding. Shaw, basing himself on fiscal records, has explained in great detail the administrative structure[103]; Holt, using a wide range of chronicles, has analyzed the nature and history of the Mamluk beys[104]; and Raymond has studied, among much else, the delicate balance between government control and political activity in Cairo.[105] For other provinces less work has been done. In Anatolia there are some local histories of varying quality; in Syria, two or three works on the cities and—something very rare—Salibi's investigations of the rural nobility of Mount Lebanon.[106] For Ottoman North Africa (and for Morocco in the same period) there is least work of all; but articles by Hess[107] and by Mantran[108] remind us that here also the Ottoman presence was a reality.

For modern history much the same can be said; considerable work has been done or is in progress, but it is not evenly spread over the field. The greater part of it deals with two kinds of subject. The older books dealt mainly with the relationships of the European powers with each other and with the Ottoman Empire, Iran, Egypt, or Morocco; these states appeared only as the passive body over which the powers argued and negotiated, or as the scene of disturbances which led to a readjustment of their relations with each other. Langer's *The Diplomacy of Imperialism*[109] is a classic example of the meticulous research produced within such a framework, and Anderson's *The Eastern Question*[110] a useful summary of the results of such work. The opening of the British archives to the end of World War II has made possible a large amount of new work, in particular on the relations between the powers and the nationalist movements of the Middle East during the World War I.[111] But only a few articles, for example, those of Naff[112] and Cunningham,[113] try to see the local governments as active parties.

More recent work has somewhat shifted the point of view, and deals mainly with the attempts of central governments to "reform" or "modernize" their countries in the light of ideas derived from Europe. In this perspective the local governments are seen as active, but only with an activity derived from Western models, whereas the societies they ruled appear as passive masses. Much work of this kind has been done by Turkish as well as Western scholars, and two important works of synthesis, Lewis's *The Emergence of Modern Turkey*[114] and Davison's *Reform in the Ottoman Empire 1856–1876*,[115] represent this tradition at its best. On the similar movement in Egypt there is old work by French, Italian, and Egyptian scholars, but little up-to-date critical work. There is a rapidly increasing amount of work on "reforming" policies carried out by European imperial governments; the older books tend to accept uncritically the imperial rulers' own explanation of their motives and assessment of their success but more recent work, based on archives and private papers, try to relate reforming policies more realistically to imperial interests, and to set them in the context of a relationship between peoples rather than dealing with them in a vacuum. Here again most work has been done on Egypt (books by Tignor[116] and Lutfi al-Sayyid[117] come to mind), and less on French than on British dependencies, apart from a few works like Ageron's important analysis of French policy in Algeria.[118]

By a logical extension, the ideas or ideologies in terms of which "reform" or modernization could be justified or criticized have attracted much attention. On movements of Islamic reform, there are important works by Adams[119] and Jomier,[120] and a deep critique by Gibb[121]; on Pan-Islam as a political movement, Keddie's life of Jamâl al-Dîn al-Afghânî summarizes recent research and answers some but not all questions; S. Mardin's *The Genesis of Young Ottoman Thought*[123] investigates the origins of one kind of nationalism; for Arab nationalism, works by Zeine,[124] Dawn,[125] Haim,[126] and Kedourie[121] query an older interpretation derived from Antonius' *The Arab Awakening*.[128]

On the changes of social structure that underlie political change or are molded by it, not much was written until a few historians began to look at the Middle East from a new angle.

* * *

If we were concerned with quantity alone, the picture which has just been sketched would be one of a field in which not much work was done in the past, but more is now being done (at least in parts of it), and still more will be done in future. But no one working in the field or looking at it closely would feel quite so confident about the progress being made. In the discussions out of which this chapter arose, considerable disquiet was expressed about the quality of the work being produced. It was generally felt that the standard of work being done on Islamic history was of course far lower than that on European or American history, which have had a 100 years' start, but also lower than that on Chinese and Japanese history. When we talk of lower standards, we may mean something which can be perceived but is difficult to define: standards of "craftsmanship" shown in the use of sources, the arrangement of materials, and the mastery of argument, for example. But we mean here something more specific: the extent to which attention is paid to the kind of problems that absorb historians today, and to ideas derived from the general historical culture of the age.

When we speak of a historian's "ideas," we do not mean that he need work in the same way as a social scientist, by framing a hypothesis and looking for materials by which it can be tested. In the mind of every historian the particular has a certain primacy; there is something, which perhaps he cannot put into words, that moves his imagination toward some country, some age, some person, or some aspect of the human scene. Of course he must have a principle of selection and emphasis when he works on it, but he can derive it from more than one source. He may have an explicit theory, a hypothesis about causal or logical connections, or an "organizing concept," an "ideal type" which particulars imperfectly embody; or ideas may come to him hidden and implicit in a moral norm, in some other work of history which has excited his mind, or diffused throughout his general culture. From these principles and ideas there flows in turn a certain definition of the subject matter: what is meant by "Islamic" or "Middle Eastern" history, and how it should be divided into periods or into regions of the "Islamic world."

To many of those who took part in the discussions from which this chapter sprang, it seemed that the structure of ideas around which historical writing on Islamic history has been built is inadequate, in the sense that it does not enable the historians to explain many of the features of Islamic history, or to answer the questions or satisfy the demands of historians working in other fields. In other words, too little work in Islamic history has been written by those whom other historians would recognize as genuine historians sharing in their historical culture. In spite of changes in the past generation, most work has been done by "general orientalists." At one time it was inevitable that this should be so, as the only scholars genuinely interested in the Muslim world, and the only ones who possessed the essential key to unlock its secrets, the knowledge of its languages, the Orientalists of an older generation, were called upon to do many things without being fully prepared to do all of them: to teach languages, appreciate literature, study history, explain religious and legal systems, even to advise governments and enlighten public opinion on political matters. The greatest of them wrote and taught well over an amazingly wide field, and showed a breadth of knowledge and understanding to which few modern scholars can aspire, but they did so at a price. In some parts of their vast field they had to be content with a lower standard of craftsmanship than perhaps they would themselves have liked; most of them were at home in philology and religious studies, less so in pure literature, less still in history, and least of all in the social sciences. When writing history, they tended either to transpose into the field of historical study concepts drawn from fields in which they were more at home, for example that of religious studies, or else to take over the commonplaces of the general culture and information of their age—the political ideas of the day, or the historical or sociological ideas of yesterday—and to work within a framework already being discarded or refined by historians contemporary with them.

* * *

Very roughly, we can distinguish two main types of writing about Islamic history which sprang from these sources: the "cultural–religious" and the "political–institutional." Of course these are ideal types and not mutually exclusive, and most writers on Islamic history belong to some extent to both, but as preliminary descriptions of leading ideas they may be useful.

In what we call the cultural–religious approach, the organizing concept is that of a "culture," a system with various aspects but unified by a single mode of perceiving the world and one which persists in time. This culture could be defined in either of two main ways: first, in terms of a particular religious experience which, so far as the Islamic culture was concerned, was that of a prophet preaching a message which was later embodied in a tradition, that is to say, in systems of practices, beliefs, and laws. From this leading idea sprang a historiography of which the characteristic problems were those of the way in which the prophetic message gave rise to the tradition, and the way in which the tradition molded the lives of those who accepted the message, so that even the most "secular" aspects of life could be seen as specifically "Islamic," and it was possible, for example, to speak of an Islamic city, an Islamic countryside, and Islamic governments or armies. Secondly, the unifying factor in the culture could be seen in terms of a human "world view," transmitted from one culture to another and modified by the transmission. The Islamic world view was created by the transmission of that of classical antiquity and its modification (to a greater or lesser extent) by Islam; thus the characteristic problems are those of the ways in which the Muslim world adopted classical culture, and the ways in which it preserved, developed, or distorted it before handing it on to western Europe. With all the necessary reservations, we might regard Goldziher,[129] Arnold,[130] and Gibb[131] as falling within the first group, and Becker,[132] von Grunebaum,[133] and Sauvaget[134] within the second.

The political–institutional approach also starts from a general concept, that of an organized system of government. Insofar as books in this category went beyond narrative—of the ways in which power was seized, used, and lost—to interpretation, they too tended to fall into two groups: those concerned with the analysis of institutions, for example, fiscal institutions; and those concerned with politics as the expression of a certain "spirit," defined in Islamic or in "national" terms. The typical problems of this kind of history were problems about how power was obtained, organized, justified, used, and lost; there was an underlying assumption that society was molded by political power. This kind of writing can be traced back to von Hammer[135] and Wellhausen,[136] and forward through Barthold[137] and Gibb again. For those like Gibb, who combined the political with the cultural approach, there was a special concern with the kind of culture which rulers patronized and from which they derived their moral or political concepts.

Both these schools of historians had a concept of Islamic history as something distinct and to be understood in its own terms. Of course even the firmest believer in Islamic history would have agreed that the Islamic world was contiguous with other worlds in time and space, but awareness of this was more fully present in intellectual than in political or social history. Schacht, following Goldziher, could show that elements from Roman, Byzantine, Talmudic, and Sassanian law had infiltrated into the nascent religious law of Islam,[138] but historians tended to look at the Islamic state as something produced by internal processes. Thus most books on Islamic history begin with a chapter on pre-Islamic Arabia but say almost nothing about Byzantium and the Sassanians. In the same way, the "social system of Islam" was explained from within. What happened in the regions where Islam was the dominant religion was explained in terms of the nature of Islamic tradition, and a knowledge of Islam was regarded as the main key to an understanding of this tradition.

As a result, what Muslim countries and peoples had in common tended to be seen as more important than the differences between them; this meant in practice that, given the disproportionate amounts of work done in different parts of the field, a stereotype taken from the "Turco–Arab" parts of the Near East was applied to other parts of the Muslim world. In the same way, there was a tendency to periodize Islamic history in terms of "rise" and "decline": Muhammad plants a seed, which grows to its full height under the early Abbasids, in terms both of political power and cultural "renaissance"; after that, political fragmentation and cultural stagnation lead to a long decline from which the Muslim world does not begin to awaken until the nineteenth century, with the impact of Western civilization and the stirrings of "national spirit."

* * *

It is only in this generation that historical work on the Middle East has begun to be fertilized by a new concept; that of "social history," of which the principle is that of a "social system," a whole system of human relationships in which a change in any part reacts on every other part. This idea can of course be developed and used in more than one way. There is an empirical English and American tradition, which springs less from an elaborate theory than from a shift of sentiment and interest away from rulers and governments to "how ordinary people lived." But three types of systematic thought about society and its past have also had an influence on historians of the Middle East: that of Max Weber, that of Marx, and that of the *Annales* school of French historians, with their care for quantitative precision and their willingness to learn from other disciplines and to subject Islamic, like other, history to questions drawn from the general scientific activity of the age. In particular, the work of Braudel has had a profound influence, because of its underlying concepts and its methods, and also because of its obvious relevance to the history of the Middle East and North Africa.

For those who would call themselves social historians in one sense or another, "Islamic history" means something different and must be subdivided in different ways. Few historians would wish to abandon the concept of Islamic history completely. Most would find it valid and useful within limits, and are aware of the danger of looking at the world in which Islam was the dominant religion as having no reality of its own, and having to be explained in terms of something other than itself: in its medieval phase as being simply a stage in the transmission of classical culture to Europe, a "Middle East" in time as well as space, and in the modern phase a passive body on which Europe imposed itself.

But it is necessary to try to make sharper definitions and distinctions than earlier historians would have done. First of all we should separate two different groups of characteristics which seem to be common to most countries where Islam is the dominant religion. There are those which can be explained in terms of a common acceptance of Islam as a system of beliefs and worship: systems of law, certain kinds of social institutions molded by law, common intellectual concerns, a certain relationship with the non-Muslim world, and a certain tradition of political discourse. On the other hand, there are similarities connected with the fact that, at least west of the Indian subcontinent, Islam has spread and taken root mainly in regions with a certain geographical and therefore socioeconomic structure: regions where land and water resources are most effectively used by a combination of sedentary cultivation and transhumant pasturage, a combination unstable and shifting by its nature; where long-distance trade routes have made possible the growth of large urban conglomerations in fertile areas; and where the combination of these two factors has produced a certain kind of symbiosis between cities and their rural hinterlands. It is important not to misinterpret the relationship between these two types of similarity. It is tempting and dangerous to suggest that Islam spread in areas of a certain kind because it was specially suited to them, and it is safer to look at the relationship as a sociologist would, as one between two separate elements interacting within a single system, Islam "embodying" itself in different forms in different ecological areas but also modifying the ways in which people live in them.

Secondly, it is important to distinguish different periods, in each of which terms like Islamic history must be understood in different senses, and also where necessary to use varying periodizations for different types of history. So far as political history is concerned, a rough periodization would be this: an early period in which a Muslim élite ruled a society still largely non-Muslim in culture and norms, and did so within a single political structure; a second or medieval period marked by the dissolution of the unified structure and the establishment of a new kind of relationship between a ruling élite, mainly Turkish, and a society which had become predominantly Muslim by conversion and the extension of Islamic law; a third period, that of the five great integrative states, Alawi, Ottoman, Safavid, Uzbek, and Mogul; and the modern period of the dissolution of all except one of these states, the domination of Europe, and the emergence of "nation-states." In this last period the concept of Islamic history loses some but not all its value as a principle of explanation, and that of Middle Eastern history, itself a creation of British imperial policy, does not adequately replace it. (This explains why the term "Islamic history" rather than "Middle Eastern history" has been used throughout this paper.) But it should not be assumed without further thought that economic or intellectual history would fall into the same periods.

Thirdly, we must make certain geographical distinctions. All Iranian historians are aware, as we have said, that the categories in terms of which we tend to see Islamic history are mainly derived from a study of the western or "Turco–Arab" part of the Muslim world. The eastern or "Turco–Iranian" part needs to be interpreted in other terms: because of the different forms that Islamic belief and culture took there, different ecologies, and geographical links with India and Inner Asia. So too does the Maghreb, which can be regarded as a separate unit culturally and ecologically; in a striking article, Burke has shown that the framework into which Gibb and Bowen fitted Ottoman history in the eighteenth century cannot be used for that of Morocco.[139] These broad divisions of course can in their turn be subdivided.

It is clear, then, that words like Islamic history do not mean the same things in different contexts, and that in no context are they enough by themselves to explain all that exists. In other words, "Islam" and the terms derived from it are "ideal types," to be used subtly, with infinite reservations and adjustments of meaning, and in conjunction with other ideal types, if they are to serve as principles of historical explanation. The extent to which they can be used varies according to the type of history we are writing. They are least relevant to economic history; as Rodinson has shown in *Islam et capitalisme*,[140] the economic life of societies where Islam is dominant cannot be explained primarily in terms of religious beliefs or laws. In spite of the influence of Islamic law on commercial forms, other kinds of explanation are more relevant; as Cahen[141] and others have suggested, concepts such as "Near Eastern," "Mediterranean," "medieval," "preindustrial" society are more useful than that of Islamic. For sociopolitical history, Islam can furnish some elements of explanation but by no means all that are needed. The institutions and policies of even the most fervently "Islamic" states cannot be explained without taking into account geographical position, economic needs, and the interests of dynasties and rulers. Even the history of those institutions that seem to be based upon Islamic law cannot be wholly explained in these terms: a concept like "Islamic slavery" dissolves if one looks at it closely; as Milliot's examination of the *ᶜamal* literature of Morocco suggests,[142] there were always ways in which local customs were incorporated into Islamic law as it was actually practiced. Only some kinds of intellectual history, at least before the modern period, can be explained in mainly Islamic terms, as a process by which ideas from outside were blended with those generated from within Islam itself to form a self-maintaining and self-developing system; even the *falâsifa* must now be seen, not as Greek philosophers in Arab clothes, but as Muslims using the concepts and methods of Greek philosophy to give their own explanation of the Islamic faith.[143]

* * *

New concepts of "social history" lead also to a different emphasis in the choice of subjects, in particular, to a new preference for economic subjects, for the study of those gradual and long-term changes in production and trade which can modify the basic social and even ecological structure of a society. A little work is now being done in medieval economic history; to older works on Iraq by Duri[144] and el-ᶜAlî[145] can now be added newer ones on Egypt by Rabie[146] and Goitein[147] and a joint article by Lopez, Miskimin, and Udovich,[148] which places Islamic trade in a wider context of the Mediterranean world. For the early modern period sources become more reliable, in the form of the Ottoman archives and the papers of European trading companies; works by Inalcik[149] based on the former and by Davis,[150] Valensi,[151] and Svoronos[152] on the latter show how effectively the methods of economic history can now be applied to these sources. For the nineteenth and twentieth centuries quantitative materials become fuller and more reliable, but surprisingly little use has been made of them, apart from the works of O'Brien,[153] Owen,[154] and Chevallier,[155] dealing with basic problems of development, and some suggestive essays by Issawi.[156] A newer kind of history, that of population and all the factors which affect it, has scarcely begun to be written for the Muslim world, but once more there are exceptions: writings on Ottoman population by Barkan,[157] Issawi,[158] Todorov,[159] and Cook;[160] some remarks about disease and epidemics in North Africa by Valensi;[161] and a completed but unpublished work by Musallam on Muslim attitudes to birth control,[162] as shown in the legal, medical, pharmacological, and erotic literature.

But something else is beginning as well, an attempt to rethink old subjects by placing them in a new framework, that of society considered as a whole. Thus a new kind of political history can be written, in which governments are seen not as bodies acting freely upon a passive mass of subjects, but as one element in a system all parts of which are active in some sense. In political history conceived in this way, all kinds of questions arise in addition to the traditional one of the way in which control over the machine of government is seized and used. What are the ways in which those who control the government, whether rulers, soldiers, or officials, are themselves rooted in the society they rule and molded by it? By what mixture of obedience, resistance, or acquiescence do different social groups react to the attempts of governments to control them? What are the different ways in which governments try to achieve their aims, by pressure and manipulation as well as bureaucratic control? What are the ways in which those who stand outside the machine of government in fact secure a share of political power or influence? And how do those inside the government machine try to secure a certain freedom of action through access to the ruler or control of part of the bureaucracy, or through wealth and social power within the society they rule?

In the same way, while there will always be a type of intellectual history which considers the development of systems of ideas and their relationships with each other in abstraction, there are other ways of studying it as well, as a constituent part of a social process. To reduce ideas simply to "expressions" of some social reality is probably not useful, but they can be studied validly from the point of view of the influence they have on life as it is lived in different social contexts, and the process of "selection" by which some ideas take root and spread and others do not; what is still more important, thinkers can be seen not just as thinkers but as products of a social milieu and as performing certain social roles. Thus the *ᶜulamâ* are not just the preservers and transmitters of a certain intellectual tradition, but hold certain offices, enjoy certain privileges, have links with various social groups, and the fact that they are *ᶜulamâ* is not enough by itself to explain their roles; a recent book edited by N. Keddie shows this clearly.[163] In the same way, there can be a social history of the arts, architecture, and science; but so far little has been done to open up such subjects.

So many different historical themes can be seen in these new perspectives, that it is possible only to make a personal choice among them. Here, then, are four different kinds of theme which have excited at least one mind. First, urban history: since so much of the source material deals primarily with cities and their inhabitants, it is natural that social historians should find a particularly rich field here. There is a relatively long tradition of Islamic urban studies, but the older works were concerned mainly with the city as an artifact, that is, the ways in which streets and buildings were made and arranged, and were modified and changed in course of time. In this tradition can be placed the important studies of Hautecoeur and Wiet,[164] Sauvaget,[165] Marçais,[166] and by extension, more modern works concerned with the growth of cities in space, their division into quarters, and other problems of this kind, for example, Abu Lughod on Cairo[167] and Ayverdi on Istanbul.[168] In later work, however, the main interest has shifted to the city as a social organism, the way in which the different parts interact so as to maintain a certain equilibrium, the lines along which their strength is mobilized, the bargains they can strike with the government, and the relations of economic change and political dependence between its constituent groups—*ᶜulamâ*, merchants, and skilled artisans; Christians and Jews; proletarians and temporary dwellers in the towns. This is a subject mainly exploited by French historians: Cahen on "Mouvements populaires et autonomisme urbain,"[169] Le Tourneau on Fez,[170] Mantran on Istanbul,[171] and Raymond in a number of articles and a comprehensive book on Cairo[172]; to these we should add Lapidus' *Muslim Cities in the Later Middle Ages*,[173] which, beyond its explicit subject, defines an ideal type of wider relevance.

Closely connected with this, but extending far beyond the city, is the study of the systems of patronage around which society was organized for political purposes: those pyramids of relations of protection and dependence which ran all through society, linking the most remote and "closed" community with a broader society and ultimately with the great cities and their governments, providing a certain protection for the powerless, and a machinery for political mobilization for the "notables" at the top, and a means of "manipulation" for governments to extend their influence even beyond the range of bureaucratic control. By their nature they were unstable, because they were always tending to move in both directions, those above trying to strengthen their control over those under them, and those below trying to extend their power of independent action: governments trying to turn "notables" into bureaucrats, and bureaucrats trying to become "notables." Only a study of such systems can enable us to understand the dynamics of sociopolitical action in a "traditional" society (but also, to some extent, in a "modernizing" society as well). Lapidus' book again provides an "ideal type" of such systems in an urban environment; for the countryside and steppe, Lambton's *Landlord and Peasant in Persia*[174] analyzes in depth the three-cornered relationship of government, landowner, and cultivator as it shifts according to the relative strength of the first two; an article by G. Baer[175] describes the ambivalent position of those who occupy intermediate positions in the pyramid, the village *ᶜumdas*, at the same time agents of the government and leaders of the local community.

Thirdly, the study of what appear to be recurrent "tribal" or nomadic movements in Islamic history needs to be carried further. With many variations, the normal type of Middle Eastern rural community is a mixed society of sedentary cultivation and transhumant pasturage. That being so, it is no longer possible to fall back on an old interpretation of Islamic history in terms of an inherent antagonism between "the desert and the sown." Pastors and cultivators may be the same people, or belong to the same community, or live in some kind of symbiosis with each other. The real problems are of two kinds. First, how can we explain the long-term shifts of the balance between cultivation and pasturage? It would be unsafe to assume that they are what they may seem to be, movements of population, with one group pressing against another; they may be so, but they may also be changes within an existing community, from one type of land use to another, and this may be caused by changes of climate, technology, or commercial demand. Secondly, how can we explain those great political movements which lead to changes of ruler and appear to have a nomadic basis? There seems to be a contradiction here between what historians tell us about the rise of great tribes and federations that overrun countries, capture cities, and found empires, and what seems to be the inability of pastoral people to generate from within themselves groupings larger than those necessary for economic life—the units of herding or migration. The beginnings of an answer can be found by carefully distinguishing names from things. Old tribal names may continue to be used although the reality within them has changed, like those of Qays and Yemen in eighteenth-century Lebanon or nineteenth-century Palestine; the use of those names may mean that the language of kinship is being used to denote not a real kinship group but a "political" construction, a grouping of different elements, not all of them kin and not all of them nomadic, around a leading man or family. This grouping may be brought about by a leader who himself comes from within a nomadic community, but is more likely to be brought about from outside, by one who controls fixed resources and means of political action in the city.[176]

Fourthly, a special importance attaches to small-scale studies of limited regions and communities within a broader framework as it is only through them that we can understand what really happened in history. States act differently in different parts of their domains; beliefs mean something different to different communities; the symbiosis between citizens, villagers, and tent dwellers varies for geographical, economic, and political reasons. This is true of all periods of history, but let us take the earliest period as an example. The "Islamic conquest" can be understood further only by regional studies of the process of conquest, the process of Islamization, and the way in which the new rulers adopted and changed the legal and administrative systems they found. So there is a need—where sources permit—for the study of individual cities or quarters of them, of districts and villages, and of particular social groups and religious communities. Here again, some work is now being done: Goitein's investigations of the Jewish community of medieval Cairo,[177] Salibi's minute inquiries, already mentioned, into the origin of Lebanese families[178], Chevallier's study of the way in which the small-scale economy of the Lebanese villages was affected by the industrial revolution in Europe, and the political results of this[179], and K. Brown's still unpublished work on a small seaport in Morocco.[180]

* * *

The social historian must of course look beyond history to the social sciences for some of the concepts and methods he uses. This is most obvious in economic history: a comparison of Davis' book with older work by Masson and Wood on the Levant trade[181] will show how much more a trained economic historian can extract from the sources. In the same way, Owen's book on *Cotton and the Egyptian Economy*[182] is clearly a product of recent discussions about economic development, and sets Egypt in the nineteenth century in a perspective derived from studies of India and Japan in the same period.

From sociology historians seem to have derived little. Some, for example Lapidus, have been influenced by the ideas of Max Weber, but sociology does not seem to have generated a method which can be validly applied to the past, and to preindustrial societies. Human geography, in the sense in which French scholars understand it, has had a greater influence. More than American scholars, French historians seem almost all to have a vivid sense of ecology, of the relationship between the land and the people.

Few historians would claim to have learned much from political science, and this perhaps is an example of the time lag which exists between changes in the ideas and methods of a subject and the spread of an awareness of them to those practicing other disciplines. An old kind of political science, which was concerned with the analysis of formal political institutions, was clearly not relevant to ages and societies which had no such institutions. The theories of political development or modernization, which were current a few years ago, seemed to most historians too general to help much in studying particular societies, particularly those of previous ages. In the last few years, however, there has developed a new kind of analysis of noninstitutional modes of politics, of the different ways in which social groups become political forces oriented toward the acquisition of power. So far, only one or two attempts have been made to apply these concepts to the past: notably by Harik in *Politics and Change in a Traditional Society*,[183] an attempt to see eighteenth- and early nineteenth-century Lebanon in the framework of a certain theory of politics.

The social science from which many historians claim to have profited most is social anthropology, and it is easy to see why. It deals with societies as a whole; it has developed through the study of small, closed, preindustrial communities. As such it has concentrated on creating tools for the understanding of societies which work by habit and convention rather than formal rules and institutions; its methods are therefore particularly well adapted to the understanding of such aspects of Islamic society as the nature of patron–client relations, the distribution of power in a segmentary society, the role of kinship as a language to express and give depth to social relations, the integrative function of religious leaders and orders, and the relations of urban entrepreneurs and rural communities. Moreover, it has provided some important studies of Muslim societies, for example, those of Robertson Smith[184] and Evans-Pritchard.[185] For all these reasons social historians are turning more and more to anthropology. This is profitable, but it may be a little dangerous: in the absence of historical sources about small rural communities, we may assume that they have never changed, and that what anthropologists have observed in the present or immediate past has always been true. Historians can use the findings of social scientists with safety only if they do not forget that they are historians.

* * *

Social history seems likely to be the dominant mode of history writing for the present generation, but as it gathers force its own limitations become clearer. Unless it is practiced in the most sensitive way, the individual may disappear, and consciousness may disappear. Thus an even more complex type of history may be needed; just as for the social historian politics must be seen within an entire social system, so it may be necessary to see the social system within a larger whole: in other words, to see it not only in itself but as it and its changes are mirrored in minds molded by a particular culture, and not only mirrored but themselves changed by the way in which those minds see them. There would be two main ways of writing such a history. It could be done in terms of a kind of collective mind: that of a whole age, a social group, or a nation. For medieval history, events and changes as reflected in the minds of the urban literate class, the *ᶜulamâ*, could well be studied; it would be difficult to do this for any other group. For the modern age, Berque's *L'Egypte, impérialisme et revolution*[186] provides a remarkable example of social and political changes seen simultaneously in two perspectives, as events which lead both to a loss of collective national consciousness through the loss of symbols and to its recovery. It might however be difficult to carry out the same kind of study in countries where a unified national consciousness, molded by geography and history, and preserved and developed by forces radiating from a single great city, does not exist. As an alternative, it might be possible to study an age as reflected in the mind of a single man. P. Brown's life of St. Augustine[187] shows how this might be done, but so far it has not been done for the Muslim world, apart from brief sketches, such as a study by Berque of a Moroccan writer of the seventeenth century.[188]

* * *

The ideas which guide us in writing Islamic history will also guide us in forming the historians of a new generation. Clearly Islamic history, as it is now coming to be conceived, cannot be taught in a vacuum, as the only element in a higher education, but what is the larger framework into which it should be fitted? Should those who are primarily interested in Islamic history, and who are the teachers and research workers of the future, be taught within departments of history, or within departments of "Oriental studies"?

In the Middle East itself, the study of the history of the area forms the core of the curriculum of history departments. But in most universities in Europe and some in North America, Islamic history is mainly taught within departments of Oriental studies. Most Islamic historians appear to be uneasy about the present situation. They feel that departments of Oriental studies are for the most part dominated by the interests of those who teach languages and literature and are without a full understanding of the nature and needs of historical study, and that history departments are hostile or indifferent to Middle Eastern history, because they do not want to spread limited resources too thinly, or because of a limitation of interests or imagination—or perhaps because Islamic historians have failed to make their subject a part of the general historical culture.

Perhaps the formal problem is not so fundamental as it may appear to be. The real problem is that in most universities there are too few Islamic historians for their views about the special needs of their subject to carry much weight, no matter which department they belong to. Islamic history will flourish as an academic discipline only if there are in some places enough teachers interested in it to be able to put into practice their ideas about how the historians of the future should be trained.

But how *should* they be trained? This is a question to which there could be many different answers, and it is possible only to put forward some personal ideas, which seem, however, to command much support. First, there is no doubt that those who wish to practice Islamic history seriously should sooner or later make a thorough study of Islamic civilization in a broad sense, and of the languages in which it expressed itself. But it may be best for this study in depth to come after, not before, they have acquired a good general historical culture. In western Europe in particular, where specialized study may begin at the age of sixteen or so, the first degree can give a student's mind a basic formation it will never lose, and it is best that this formation should be in the fullest sense a historical one. (There would of course not be universal agreement on this, and that is not harmful; there are irreducible differences of temperament and approach, and disputes about how to teach history can themselves stimulate historical inquiry.)

Secondly, what we call "historical culture" should include from the beginning elements drawn from elsewhere than Islamic history alone, which cannot generate entirely from inside itself the stimulus to its own advance. What those elements should be will depend on the interests of teacher and student: certainly some European history, and perhaps some training in one or other of the social sciences.

Thirdly, within the teaching of Islamic history itself, it is not easy to attain a proper balance between "medieval" and "modern." Probably most teachers would feel that a thorough knowledge of classical Islamic history and civilization is important even for those who wish ultimately to study the modern world. It can provide a rich education by making the student familiar with great historical events and original ideas; it demands techniques so difficult, and a grasp of a way of thought so different from ours, that it can be acquired only by transmission from teachers. Besides, its legacy survives in the modern world. On the other side, however, there are dangers in approaching the modern world with a mind formed in the study of medieval history. He who wishes to understand modern history must have a deep knowledge of the great worldwide changes in thought, sentiment, and society that have occurred in recent times. A classical Islamist who looks at the modern Middle East may fall into a kind of "reductionism," and minimize the extent to which even "traditional" ideas and institutions have changed.

* * *

Just as some tools of research are defective or lacking, so are some teaching instruments. There are few introductory books that can be put into the hands of a beginner, at least in English-reading countries. Most students still begin, as they have done for 20 years, with Gibb's *Mohammedanism*[189] and Lewis's *The Arabs in History*,[190] but it is not easy to find books to read after them.

There are perhaps four kinds of books needed for teaching. First come works of *vulgarisation* or tentative synthesis (it can be no more than that in the present state of research). It is too early to hope for such a synthesis of the whole of Islamic history; the new *The Cambridge History of Islam*,[191] in spite of some excellent chapters, lacks a conceptual framework, a shared understanding of Islamic history. But the time has come when it should be possible to synthesize recent research on the first few centuries of Islamic history; French readers are better served here than English, by D. and J. Sourdel's *La civilisation de l'Islam classique*[192] and Cahen's *L'Islam des origines au début de l'empire ottoman.*[193] Something similar might be done for Ayyubid and Mamluk Egypt. For the first centuries of the Ottoman empire we now have Inalcik's book,[194] and for North Africa Julien's history in a revised edition,[195] and Abun-Naṣr's more recent book,[196] but for Iran there is virtually nothing of an introductory kind except for a suggestive sketch by Bausani.[197] More generally, there is no comprehensive work on the development of Shi'i Muslim society. In spite of all the interest shown in modern history, there are no good surveys that go much beyond a narrative of political events on the eastern Mediterranean seacoast.

Secondly, teachers need books of a different kind, oriented toward problems rather than periods, surveying the present state of a problem and suggesting directions for future research. A good example of what is needed is provided by L. Valensi's *Le Maghreb avant la prise d'Alger*[198] in the series *Questions d'histoire*, a summing up, on the basis of current research, of the problem of whether or not the coming of French colonialism was a reaction to the socioeconomic stagnation of the Maghreb.

Thirdly, some teachers feel the need for source books, translated and annotated extracts from Islamic writings and other primary sources, which can be used to supplement the introductory surveys. Some good ones do exist, Sauvaget's *Historiens arabes*,[199] Williams's *Themes of Islamic Civilization*,[200] Gabrieli's *Arab Historians of the Crusades*,[201] and Issawi's volumes on economic history in the nineteenth century,[202] but more are needed. (Some teachers, however, prefer to make their own selection of sources, appropriate to the content and direction of their own teaching.)

Fourthly, there is a general demand for translations into English or French of some at least of the chronicles and other sources, so that students may have some kind of contact with the original sources and the men who wrote them, even before they are able to read them in the original languages. Here once more the French student is better served than the English, thanks to the institution (now abolished) of the *thèse complementaire*, for which an edition or translation of a text was acceptable.

* * *

All through this chapter, it has been clear that work of every kind is needed. But this makes some kind of understanding about priorities more, rather than less, urgent, since research workers and resources are so scarce.

The scholar's imagination moves as it will, and it would be quite impossible to make decisions about priorities as between different countries or periods of history. But it might be possible to form a general opinion about the kind of work which should be encouraged and funded. There would probably be wide agreement about the urgency of such tasks as the following:

1. So far as *sources are concerned*, there seems an equal need for (*a*) the critical edition or reedition of important chronicles in Arabic, Turkish, and Persian; and (*b*) the collection of documents of governments, law courts, religious communities, business concerns, and families, their proper classification, cataloging, and maintenance, and, as a necessary complement to this, the training of archivists.

2. So far as *tools* of research and teaching are concerned, a particular urgency seems to attach to (*a*) the publication of large-scale dictionaries of Arabic and Persian, dealing in particular with the language of the fully developed Islamic society and culture; and (*b*) the publication of large-scale historical maps and atlases.

3. So far as the *organization* of teaching and research is concerned, there seems a need for (*a*) the creation of groups of Islamic historians in at least a few universities, and (*b*) the maintenance of close relations between historians through the organization of specialized meetings and visits.

4. So far as the *content* of research is concerned, as we have said, in the last analysis every scholar must go his own way, but bodies that organize or finance research might pay special attention to projects concerned with

(*a*) economic history, and more generally any work that tries to go beyond impressions and lay down firm quantitative bases; (*b*) detailed work on a small scale, such as the precise study of regions, cities, villages, families, religious communities, or administrative institutions; and (*c*) work that tries to insert political and religious history into the total history of a society, in other words, by tracing the interaction between political institutions and movements, movements of thought and ideology, and the societies in which they exist, to form a more accurate and comprehensive, sensitive and living picture of "Islamic history."

NOTES

1. ^{c}A. al-Jabartî, *^{c}Aja'ib al-âthâr*, 4 vols. (Cairo: al-Maṭba^{c}a al-Kubrâ al-Amîriyya, 1880).

2. ^{c}A. Mubârak, *al-Khiṭaṭ al-tawfîqiyya*, 20 vols. (Cairo: al Maṭba^{c}a al-Kubrâ al-Amîriyya, 1888).

3. A. Cevdet, *Tarih-i Cevdet*, 12 vols., 2nd ed. (Istanbul: Dar Sa^{c}âdet, 1891).

4. A. al-Nâṣirî, *Kitâb al-istiqsâ*, 4 vols. (Cairo: al-Maṭba^{c}a al-Miṣriyya, 1895).

5. A. Bitar, *Hilyat al-bashar*, 3 vols. (Damascus: Maṭbû^{c}ât Majma al-Lugha al-^{c}Arabiyya, 1961–1963).

6. M. al-Kattânî, *Kitâb salwat al-anfas*, 3 vols. (Fez: hand copied, 1898–1899).

7. For Islamic history and other studies, cf. B. Lewis and P. M. Holt, *Historians of the Middle East* (London: Oxford Univ. Press, 1962); J. J. Waardenburg, *L'Islam dans le miroir de l'occident* (Paris: Mouton, 1963); A. Hourani, "Islam and the philosophers of history," *Middle Eastern Studies*, **3** (1967), 206 ff.

8. C. Cahen, "Quelques notes sur les Hilaliens et le nomadisme", *Journal of the Economic and Social History of the Orient*, **11** (1968), 130 ff; J. Poncet, "Le mythe de la 'catastrophe' hilalienne", *Annales*, **22** (1967), 1099 ff.; H. R. Idris, "De la réalité de la catastrophe hilalienne", *Annales*, **23** (1968), 660 ff.; J. Berque, "Du nouveau sur les Beni Hilal", *Studia Islamica*, **36** (1972), 99 ff.

9. E. Kedourie, *Afghani and 'Abduh.* (London: Cass, 1966); N. R. Keddie. *Sayyid Jamâl al-Dîn "al-Afghânî": a Political Biography* (Berkeley: University of California Press, 1972).

10. ^{c}A. al-Râfi^{c}î, *Tarîkh al-ḥaraka al-qawmiyya*, 3 vols. (Cairo: Maṭba^{c}at al-Nah ḍa, 1929–1930), and subsequent works.

11. K. al Ghazzî, *Nahr al-dhahab fî tarikh Ḥalab*, 3 vols. (Aleppo: al-Maṭba^{c}a al-Marûnîyya, 1923–1926).

12. R. al-Ṭabbâkh, *A^{c}lâm al-nubalâ' bi-târîkh Ḥalab al-shahbâ*, 7 vols. (Aleppo: al-Maṭba^{c}a al-^{c}Ilmiyya, 1923–1926).

13. M. Kurd^{c}Alî, *Khiṭaṭ al-shâm*, 6 vols. (Damascus,: al-Maṭba^{c}a al-Hadîtha, 1925–1928).

14. ^{c}A. M. al- Azzâwî, *Târîkh al-^{c}Irâq bain iḥtilâlain* (cover title: *Historie de l'Irâq entre deux occupations*), 8 vols. (Baghdad: Maṭba^{c}at Baghdad, 1935–1956).

15. A. Laroui, *L'Histoire du Maghreb* (Paris: F. Maspero, 1970).

16. M. al-Ṭabarî, *Târîkh al-rusûl wa al-mulûk*, 10 parts (Cairo: Dar al-Ma^{c}ârif, 1960–1969).

17. I. Goldziher. *Muhammedanische Studien*, vol. 2 (Halle: M. Niemeyer, 1889–1890). See note 129.

18. H. Lammens, *Études sur le siècle des Omayyades* (Beirut: Imprimerie Catholique, 1930) and other works.

19. A. L. Udovich, ed. *Partnership and Profit in Medieval Islam* (Princeton: Princeton Univ. Press, 1970).

20. M. A. Shaban, *The Abbasid Revolution* (Cambridge: Cambridge University Press, 1970).

21. S. M. Stern, *Fâṭimid Decrees* (London: Faber and Faber, 1964); S. M. Stern, ed., *Documents from Islamic Chanceries* (Cambridge: Harvard Univ. Press, 1965).

22. S. D. Goitein, *A Mediterranean Society*, 2 vols. (Berkeley: Univ. of California Press, 1967, 1971).

23. D. S. Richards, "Arabic documents from the Karaite community in Cairo," *Journal of the Economic and Social History of the Orient*, **15** (1972), 105 ff.

24. J. Sourdel-Thomine and D. Sourdel, "Nouveaux documents sur l'histoire religieuse et sociale de Damas au Moyen Age," *Revue des Etudes Islamiques* **32** (1964), 1 ff.

25. ᶜA. ᶜA. ᶜAbd al-Rahîm, *al-Rîf al-miṣrî fî al-qarn al-thâmin ᶜashar*. Unpublished Ph.D. dissertation (ᶜAin S̲h̲ams University, 1973).

26. A. Raymond, "Les bains publics au Caire à la fin du XVIIIe siècle," *Annales Islamologiques*, **8** (1969), 129 ff.

27. H. Busse, *Untersuchungen zum islamischen Kanzleiwesen* (Cairo: Kommissions-verlag Sirović Bookshop).

28. A. Rustum, *al-Maḥfuẓât al-malakiyya al-miṣriyya*, 4 vols. (Beirut: al-Matbaᶜa al-Amrîkiyya, 1940–1943).

29. J. Deny, *Sommaire des archives turques du Caire* (Cairo: Institut français d'archéologie orientale du Caire pour la Société royale de géographie d'Egypte, 1930).

30. A. Schölch, *Ägypten den Ägyptern* (Zurich: Atlantis, 1972).

31. P. M. Holt, *The Mahdist State in the Sudan 1881–1898* (Oxford: Clarendon Press, 1958 and 1970).

32. D. S. Landes, *Bankers and Pashas* (London: Heinemann, 1958).

33. J. Berque, *Structures sociales du Haut Atlas* (Paris: Presses universitaires de France, 1955).

34. B. Lewis, "Sources for the economic history of the Middle East." In *Studies in the Economic History of the Middle East*, M. A. Cook, ed., (London: Oxford Univ. Press, 1970), reprinted in Lewis, *Islam in History*, (New York: Library Press, 1973).

35. J. Sauvaget, *Introduction à l'histoire de l'Orient musulman*, 2nd ed., C. Cahen, ed. (Paris: Maisonneuve, 1961), p. 57; *Introduction to the History of the Muslim East*, English translation (Berkeley: Univ. of California Press, 1965).

36. M. van Berchem and others, *Matériaux pour un Corpus Inscriptionum Arabicarum* (Cairo: Imprimerie de l'Institut français d'archeologie orientale, 1894–1956).

37. E. Combe, J. Sauvaget, and G. Wiet, *Répertoire chronologique d'épigraphie arabe* (Cairo: Imprimerie de l'Institut française d'archeologie orientale, 1931–).

38. R. W. Hamilton, *Khirbat al-Mafjar* (Oxford: Clarendon Press, 1959).

39. J. Sauvaget, *Alep* (Paris: Geuthner, 1941), and "Esquisse d'une histoire de la ville de Damas." *Revue des Etudes Islamiques*, **8** (1934), 421 ff.

40. K. A. C. Creswell, *The Muslim Architecture of Egypt*, 2 vols. (Oxford: Clarendon Press, 1952–1959) and *Early Muslim Architecture*, 2 vols. (Oxford: Clarendon Press, 1932–1940).

41. G. Marçais, *L'architecture musulmane d'Occident* (Paris: Arts et Métiers Graphiques, 1955).

42. C. Kessler, "Mecca-oriented architecture and urban growth of Cairo," *Atti del Terzo Congresso di Studi Arabi e Islamici* (Naples, 1967), 425 ff.

43. J. Sourdel-Thomine, "La mosquée et la madrasa, types monumentaux charactéristiques de l'art islamique médiéval," *Cahiers de civilisation médiévale,* **13** (1970), 97 ff.

44. G. A. Pugachenkova, "The architecture of Central Asia in the Time of the Timurids," *Afghanistan,* **22** (1969–1970), 15 ff.; "Les monuments peu connus de l'architecture médiévale de l'Afghanistan," *Afghanistan,* **21**, i (1968), 17 ff.

45. E. H. Ayverdi, *Osmanli mimârîsının ilk devri,* 3 vols. (Istanbul: Baha Matbaasi, 1966–1973).

46. A. Kuran, *The Mosque in Early Ottoman Architecture* (Chicago: Univ. of Chicago Press, 1968).

47. J. M. Rogers, review of L. Golombek, *The Timurid Shrine at Gazur Gah,* in *Kunst des Orients,* Vol. 7 (1972), p. 175.

48. R. M. Adams, *Land Behind Baghdad* (Chicago: Univ. of Chicago Press, 1965).

49. P. Seale, *The Struggle for Syria* (London and N.Y.: Oxford Univ. Press, 1965).

50. E. E. Evans-Pritchard, *The Sanusi of Cyrenaica* (Oxford: Clarendon Press, 1949).

51. J. Berque, *Histoire sociale d'un village égyptien aux Xème siècle* (Paris: Mouton, 1957).

52. See note 35.

53. C. Brockelmann, *Geschichte der arabischen Litteratur,* 5 vols. (Leiden: Brill, 1967–1971).

54. ^{c}U. R. Kaḥḥâla, *Mu^{c}jam al-mu'allifîn,* 15 parts (Damascus: al-Maktaba al-^{c}Arabiyya, 1957–1961).

55. F. Sezgin, *Geschichte des arabischen Schrifttums,* **1**, **3**, **4** (Leiden: Brill, 1967–1971).

56. G. Graf, *Geschichte der chrislichen arabischen Literatur,* 5 vols. (Rome: Biblioteca Apostolica Vaticana, 1944–1953).

57. C. A. Storey, *Persian Literature: a bio-bibliographical survey,* 4 parts (London: Luzac & Co., 1927–1971); Russian trans. *Persidskaya Literatura,* **1** (Moscow: Hayka, 1972).

58. B. Lewis, "Studies in the Ottoman archives," *Bulletin of the School of Oriental and African Studies,* **16** (1954), 469 ff.; and *Notes and Documents from the Turkish Archives* (Jeruslaem: Israel Oriental Society, 1952).

59. U. Heyd, *Ottoman Documents on Palestine 1552–1615* (Oxford: Clarendon Press, 1960).

60. R. Mantran and J. Sauvaget, *Règlements fiscaux ottomans* (Beirut: Institut français de Damas, 1951).

61. Ö. L. Barkan, *XV ve XVI asırlarda osmanlı imperatorluğunda ziraî ekonominin hukukî ve malî esasları* (Istanbul: Bürhaneddin Matbaasi, 1943).

62. J. D. Pearson, *Index Islamicus* and supplements First three vols. (Cambridge: Heffer, thereafter London: Mansell, 1958–); *Tûrkiye makaleler bibliografyasi* (Ankara, 1952–); I. Afshar, *Index Iranicus,* 2 vols. (Tehran: l'Université de Tehran, 1961–1970).

63. *Encyclopaedia of Islam,* 1st ed., 4 vols. and supplement (Leiden: Brill, 1913–1942); 2nd ed., 3 vols. to date (Leiden: Brill and London: Luzac & Co., 1960–).

64. *Islâm ansiklopedisi,* 10 vols. published so far (Istanbul: Maarif Matbaasi, 1940–).

65. B. Spuler, ed., *Handbuch der Orientalistik: I Abteilung, Der Nahe und der Mittlere Osten* (Leiden: Brill, 1952).

66. D. and J. Sourdel, *La Civilisation de l'Islam classique* (Paris: Arthaud, 1968).

67. E. de Zambaur, *Manuel de généalogie et de chronologie pour l'histoire de l'Islam* (Hanover: H. Lafaire, 1927).

68. C. E. Bosworth, *The Islamic Dynasties* (Edinburgh: Univ. Press, 1967).

69. G. S. P. Freeman-Grenville, *The Muslim and Christian Calendars* (London and New York: Oxford Univ. Press, 1963).

70. R. Roolvink, *Historical Atlas of the Muslim Peoples* (Djakarta and Amsterdam: Djambatan, 1957).

71. *Description de l'Egypte: Etat moderne*, 4 vols. (Paris: Imprimerie Impériale, 1809–1812).

72. See footnote 39.

73. J. W. Redhouse, *A Turkish and English Lexicon*, 2 vols. (Constantinople: Amer. Mission, 1890; reprint, Beirut: Libraire de Liban, 1974).

74. R. Dozy, *Supplément aux dictionnaires arabes*, 2 vols. (Leiden: Brill, 1881).

75. L. Massignon, *Essai sur les origines de lexique technique de la mystique musulmane* (Paris: P. Geuthner, 1922).

76. B. Lewis, "Islamic concepts of revolution," and "On modern Arabic political terms." In *Islam in History* (New York: Library Press, 1973).

77. B. Lewis and P. M. Holt, eds., *Historians of the Middle East* (London: Oxford Univ. Press, 1962).

78. P. M. Holt, ed., *Political and Social Change in Modern Egypt* (London: Oxford Univ. Press, 1968).

79. M. A. Cook, ed., *Studies in the Economic History of the Middle East.* (London and New York: Oxford Univ. Press, 1970).

80. A. Hourani and S. M. Stern, eds., *The Islamic City* (Oxford: B. Cassirer, and Philadelphia: Univ. of Penn. Press, 1970).

81. D. S. Richards, ed., *Islam and the Trade of Asia* (Oxford: B. Cassirer, and Philadelphia: Univ. of Penn. Press, 1970).

82. D. S. Richards, ed., *Islamic Civilization 950–1150* (Oxford, 1973).

83. See footnote 20.

84. D. Sourdel, *Le Vizirat ᶜabbāside de 749 à 936*, 2 vols. (Damascus: Institut français de Damas, 1959–1960).

85. G. Makdisi, "Autograph diary of an eleventh-century historian of Baghdād," 5 parts, *BSOAS*, **18** (1956), 9 ff. and 239 ff.; **19** (1957), **13** ff., 281 ff., and 426 ff.

86. J. A. Boyle, ed., *Cambridge History of Iran*, Vol. 5. (Cambridge: Univ. Press, 1968)

87. C. Cahen, *La Syrie du nord à l'époque des croisades et la principauté franque d'Antioche* (Paris: P. Geuthner, 1940).

88. C. Cahen, *Pre-Ottoman Turkey* (London: Sidgwick and Jackson, 1968).

89. R. Brunschvig, *La Berbérie orientale sous les Hafsids*, 2 vols. (Paris: Adrien-Maisonneuve, 1940, 1947).

90. E. Lévi-Provençal, *Histoire de l'Espagne musulmane*, 3 vols. (Paris: Maisonneuve, 1950–1957).

91. H. A. R. Gibb, "The achievement of Saladin." In *Studies on the Civilization of Islam* (Boston: Beacon Press, 1962), and *The Life of Saladin* (Oxford: University Press, 1973).

92. D. Ayalon, *Gunpowder and Firearms in the Mamluk Kingdom* (London: Valentine, Mitchell, 1956); and "Studies on the structure of the Mamluk Army," *BSOAS*, **15** (1953), 203 and, 448 ff., and **16** (1954), 57 ff.

93. A. Darrag, *L'Egypte sous le règne de Barsbay* (Damascus: Institut français de Damas, 1961).

94. B. Spuler, *Die Mongolen in Iran* (Berlin: Akademie-Verlag, 1955 and 1968).

95. Most recently, E. Glassen, *Die frühen Safawiden nach Qāzī Ahmad Qumī* (Freiburg im Bresgau, 1968) and M. Mazzaoui, *The Origins of the Safawids* (Wiesbaden: F. Steiner, 1972).

96. V. Minorsky, *Tadhkirat al-mulūk* (London: Luzac & Co., 1943).

97. J. Aubin, "Etudes safavides I: Shah Isma'il et les notables de l'Iraq persan," *Journal of the Economic and Social History of the Orient*, **2** (1959), 37 ff.

98. H. A. R. Gibb and H. Bowen, *Islamic Society and the West*, Vol. 1, 2 parts. (London: Oxford Univ. Press, 1950–1957).

99. I. H. Uzunçarşılı, *Kapıkulu Ocakları*, 72 vols. (Ankara, 1943–1944); *Osmanlı devletinin merkez ve bahriye teşkilâtı* (Ankara: Türk Tarih Basimevi, 1948); and *Osmanlı devletinin saray teşkilâtı* (Ankara: Türk tarih Basimevi, 1945).

100. H. Inalcik, *The Ottoman Empire: the Classical Age 1300–1600* (London: Weidenfeld and Nicolson, 1973).

101. U. Heyd, "Some aspects of the Ottoman fetva," *BSOAS*, **32** (1969), 35 ff., and *Studies of Old Ottoman Criminal Law* (Oxford: Univ. Press, 1973).

102. H. Inalcik, "Harir." In *Encyclopaedia of Islam*, Vol. 3, 2nd ed., 211 ff., and "Bursa and the Commerce of the Levant," *Journal of the Economic and Social History of the Orient*, **3** (1960), 131 ff.

103. S. J. Shaw, *The Financial and Administrative Organization of Ottoman Egypt 1517–1798* (Princeton: Univ. Press, 1962).

104. P. M. Holt, "Studies in Egyptian History." In *Studies in the History of the Near East*, 151 ff. (London: Cass, 1973).

105. A. Raymond, "Essai de géographie des quartiers de résidence aristocratique au Caire au XVIIIème siècle," *Journal of the Economic and Social History of the Orient*, **6** (1963), 58 ff.; "Quartiers et mouvements populaires au Caire au XVIIIème siècle." In *Political and Social Change in Modern Egypt*, P. M. Holt, ed. (London: Oxford Univ. Press, 1968); "Problèmes urbains et urbanisme au Caire aux XVIIème et XVIIIème siècles." In *Colloque internationale sur l'histoire du Caire*. (Cairo, n. d.), 319 ff.

106. K. S. Salibi, "The Maronites of Lebanon under Frankish and Mamluk rule," *Arabica*, **4** (1957), 288 ff.; "The Buhturids of the Garb," *Arabica*, **8** (1961), 74 ff.; "Northern Lebanon under the dominance of Gazir," *Arabica*, **14** (1967), 144 ff., "The Muqaddams of Bsarrī," *Arabica*, **15** (1968), 63 ff.; "The Sayfās and the Eyalat of Tripoli," *Arabica*, **20** (1973), 25 ff.

107. A. C. Hess, "The Forgotten Frontier." In *The Islamic World in the Eighteenth Century*, E. R. J. Owen and T. Naff, eds. (in press).

108. R. Mantran, "L'évolution des relations entre la Tunisie et l'Empire Ottoman du XVIe au XIXe siècle," *Cahiers de Tunisie*, **7** (1959), 319 ff.

109. W. L. Langer, *The Diplomacy of Imperialism 1890–1902*, 2nd ed. (New York: Knopf, 1951).

110. M. S. Anderson, *The Eastern Question 1774–1923* (London: Macmillan, 1966).

111. For a survey of recent work see C. E. Dawn, "Hashimite Aims and Policy in the Light of Recent Scholarship on Anglo-Arab Relations During World War I." In *From Ottomanism to Arabism* (Urbana: U. of Illinois Press, 1973).

112. T. Naff, "Reform and the Conduct of Ottoman Diplomacy in the Reign of Selim III 1789–1807," *Journal of the American Oriental Society*, **83** (1963), 295 ff.

113. A. Cunningham, "Stratford Canning and the Tanzimat." In *Beginnings of Modernization in the Middle East*, W. R. Polk and R. L. Chambers, eds. (Chicago: U. of Chicago Press, 1968).

114. B. Lewis, *The Emergence of Modern Turkey* (London: Oxford Univ. Press, 1961).

115. R. H. Davison, *Reform in the Ottoman Empire 1856–1876* (Princeton: Univ. Press, 1963).

116. R. L. Tignor, *Modernization and British Colonial Rule in Egypt 1882–1914* (Princeton: Univ. Press, 1966).

117. A. Lutfi Al-Sayyid, *Egypt and Cromer* (London: Murray, 1968).

118. C. R. Ageron, *Les Algériens musulmans et la France*, 2 vols. (Paris: Presses Universitaires de France, 1968).

119. C. C. Adams, *Islam and Modernism in Egypt* (London: Oxford Univ. Press, 1933).

120. J. Jomier, *Le Commentaire coranique du Manar* (Paris: Maisonneuve, 1954).

121. H. A. R. Gibb, *Modern Trends in Islam* (Chicago: U. of Chicago Press, 1947).

122. See note 8.

123. S. Mardin, *The Genesis of Young Ottoman Thought* (Princeton: Univ. Press, 1962).

124. Z. N. Zeine, *The Emergence of Arab Nationalism* (Beirut: Khayats, 1966).

125. See note 111.

126. S. Haim, *Arab Nationalism* (Berkeley: Univ. of California Press, 1962).

127. E. Kedourie, *England and the Middle East* (London: Bowes and Bowes, 1956).

128. G. Antonius, *The Arab Awakening* (Philadelphia and New York: J. B. Lippincott, 1939).

129. I. Goldziher, *Muhammedanischen Studien*, 2 vols. (Halle, 1889–1890), English trans. by C. R. Barber and S. M. Stern. 2 vols. (London: Allen & Unwin, 1967, 1971).

130. T. W. Arnold, *The Caliphate* (Oxford: Clarendon Press, 1924); *The Preaching of Islam*, 2nd ed. (London: Constable, 1913).

131. H. A. R. Gibb, *Studies on the Civilization of Islam* (Boston: Beacon Press, 1962).

132. C. H. Becker, *Vom Werden und Wesen der islamischen Welt: Islamstudien*, 2 vols. (Leipzig: Quelle & Meyer, 1924–1932).

133. G. E. von Grunebaum, *Medieval Islam* (Chicago: U. of Chicago Press, 1946).

134. See note 39; and "Comment étudier l'histoire du monde arabe." In *Mémorial Jean Sauvaget* (Damascus: Institut français de Damas, 1954), 167 ff.

135. J. Von Hammer-Purgstall, *Geschichte des Osmanischen Reiches*, 10 vols. (Pest: C. A. Hartleben's Verlage, 1827–1835).

136. J. Wellhausen, *Das Arabische Reich und sein Sturz* (Berlin: G. Reimer, 1902). English trans. by Margaret Graham Weir, *The Arab Kingdom and its Fall* (Calcutta: U. of Calcutta, 1927).

137. W. Barthold, *Turkestan down to the Mongol Invasion*, Eng. trans., 2nd ed. (London: Luzac, 1958).

138. J. Schacht, *The Origins of Muhammedan Jurisprudence* (Oxford: Clarendon Press, 1950).

139. E. Burke, "Morocco and the Near East: Reflections on Some Basic Differences," *Archives europées de sociologie*, **10** (1969), 70 ff.

140. M. Rodinson, *Islam et capitalisme* (Paris: Editions du Seuil, 1966).

141. C. Cahen, "L'histoire économique et sociale de l'Orient musulman médiéval," *Studia Islamica*, **3** (1955), 93 ff.

142. J. Berque, "ᶜAmal." In *Encyclopedia of Islam*, 2nd ed., Vol. 1, p. 427 ff.

143. See R. Walzer, *Greek into Arabic* (Cambridge: Harvard Univ. Press, 1962).

144. A. Duri, *Târîkh al-ᶜIrâq al-iqtiṣâdî fî al-qarn al-râbiᶜ al-hijrî* (Baghdad: Maṭbaᶜat al-Maᶜârif, 1948).

145. S. el-Alî, *al-Tanẓîmât al-ijtimâ^{c}iyya wa al-iqtiṣâdiyya fî al-Baṣra fî al-qarn ai-awwal al-hijrî* (Baghdad: Maṭba^{c}at al-Ma^{c}ârif, 1953).

146. H. Rabie, *The Financial System of Egypt A. H. 564–741/1169–1341 A. D.* (London: Oxford Univ. Press, 1972).

147. See note 22.

148. R. Lopez, H. Miskimin, and A. Udovich, "England to Egypt 1350–1500: Long-term Trends and Long-Distance Trade." In *Studies in the Economic History of the Middle East*, M. A. Cook, ed. (London and New York: Oxford Univ. Press, 1970).

149. See note 102.

150. R. Davis, *Aleppo and Devonshire Square* (London: Macmillan, 1967).

151. L. Valensi, *Le Maghreb avant la prise d'Alger* (Paris, 1969).

152. N. G. Svoronos, *Le Commerce de Salonique au XVIIIe siècle* (Paris: Presses universitaires de France, 1956).

153. P. O'Brien, *The Revolution in Egypt's Economic System* (London: Oxford Univ. Press, 1966).

154. E. R. J. Owen, *Cotton and the Egyptian Economy 1820–1914* (Oxford: Clarendon Press, 1969).

155. D. Chevallier, *La Société du Mont Liban à l'époque de la révolution industrielle en Europe* (Paris: Librairie Orientaliste P. Geuthner, 1971).

156. C. Issawi, "The Decline of Middle Eastern Trade 1100–1500." In *Islam and the Trade of Asia*, D. S. Richards, ed. (Oxford: B. Cassirer, 1970); "Egypt Since 1800: a Study in Lop-sided Development." *Journal of Economic History*, **21** (1961).

157. O. L. Barkan, "Essai sur les données statistiques des registres de récensement dans l'Empire Ottoman au XVe et XVIe siècles," *Journal of the Economic and Social History of the Orient*, **1** (1957), 9 ff.

158. C. Issawi, "Comment on Professor Barkan's Estimate of the Population of the Ottoman Empire in 1520–30," *Journal of the Economic and Social History of the Orient*, **1** (1957), 329 ff.

159. N. T. Todorov, *La Ville balkanique aux XVe-XIXe ss* (In Bulgarian with French summary, Sofia, 1972).

160. M. A. Cook, *Population Pressure in Rural Anatolia 1450–1600* (London and New York: Oxford Univ. Press, 1972).

161. See note 151.

162. B. Musallam, *Sex and Society in Islam: the Situation and Medieval Techniques of Birth Control*. Unpublished Ph. D. dissertation (Harvard, 1973).

163. N. R. Keddie, ed., *Scholars, Saints and Sufis* (Berkeley: U. of California Press, 1972).

164. L. Hautecoeur and G. Wiet, *Les mosquées du Caire* (Paris: E. Leroux, 1932).

165. See note 39.

166. See note 41.

167. J. Abu Lughod, *Cairo, 1001 Years of the City Victorious* (Princeton: Univ. Press, 1971).

168. See note 45.

169. C. Cahen, "Mouvements populaires et autonomisme urbain," *Arabica*, **5** (1958), 225 ff.; **6** (1959), 25 ff, and 233 ff.

170. R. Le Tourneau, *Fez avant le protectorat français* (Casablanca: Société Marocaine de librairie et d'édition, 1949).

171. R. Mantran, *Istanbul dans la seconde moitié du XVIIe siècle* (Paris: Maisonneuve, 1962).

172. See notes 26 and 105.

173. I. M. Lapidus, *Muslim Cities in the Later Middle Ages* (Cambridge: Harvard Univ. Press, 1967).

174. A. K. S. Lambton, *Landlord and Peasant in Persia* (London: Oxford Univ. Press, 1953).

175. G. Baer, *Studies in the Social History of Modern Egypt* (Chicago: U. of Chicago Press, 1969), in particular "The Village Shaykh, 1800–1950," p. 30 ff.

176. See T. Asad, *The Kababish* (New York: Praeger, 1970); C. Cahen, "Nomades et sedentaires dans le monde musulman du milieu du moyen age." In *Islamic Civilization 950–1150*, D. S. Richards, ed. (Oxford, 1973).

177. See note 22.

178. See note 106.

179. See note 155.

180. K. Brown, *The Social History of a Moroccan Town: 1830–1930.*) Ph.D. dissertation, UCLA, 1969); and "An Urban View of Moroccan History: Salé 1000 to 1800," *Hesperis-Tamuda*, **12** (1971), 5 ff.

181. See note 150; A. C. Wood, *History of the Levant Company* (London: Oxford Univ. Press, 1935); P. Masson, *Histoire du commerce française dans le Levant au XVIIe siècle* (Paris: Hachette & Co., 1896), and *Histoire . . . au XVIIIe siècle* (Paris: Hachette & Co., 1911).

182. See note 154.

183. I. Harik, *Politics and Change in a Traditional Society: Lebanon, 1711–1845* (Princeton: Univ. Press, 1968).

184. W. Robertson Smith, *Lectures on the Religion of the Semites* (New York: D. Appleton & Co., 1889), and *Kinship and Marriage in Early Arabia* (London: A. and C. Black, 1903).

185. See note 50.

186. J. Berque, *L'Egypte, impérialisme et révolution* (Paris: Gallimard, 1967). Eng. trans. by Jean Stewart, *Egypt, Imperialism and Revolution* (London: Faber, 1972).

187. P. Brown, *Augustine of Hippo* (Berkeley: U. of California Press, 1967).

188. J. Berque, *Al-Yousi* (Paris: Mouton, 1958).

189. H. A. R. Gibb, *Mohammedanism* (London: Oxford Univ. Press, 1949).

190. B. Lewis, *The Arabs in History* (London: Hutchinson's Univ. Library, 1950).

191. P. M. Holt, A. K. S. Lambton, and B. Lewis, eds. *The Cambridge History of Islam*, 2 vols. (Cambridge: Univ. Press, 1970).

192. See note 66.

193. C. Cahen, *L'Islam des origines au début de l'Empire Ottoman* (Paris: Bordas, 1970).

194. See note 100.

195. C. A. Julien, *Histoire de l'Afrique du Nord de la conquête arabe à 1830* (Paris: Payot, 1951—1952).

196. J. M. Abun-Nasr, *A History of the Maghrib* (Cambridge: Univ. Press, 1971).

197. A. Bausani, *I Persiani* (Florence: Sansoni, 1962); Eng. trans. by J. B. Donne, *The Persians* (London: Elek, 1971).

198. See note 151.

199. J. Sauvaget, *Historiens arabes* (Paris: Maisonneuve, 1946).

200. J. A. Williams, ed., *Themes of Islamic Civilization* (Berkeley: Univ. of California Press, 1971).

201. F. Gabrieli, *Storici arabi delle Crociate* (Turin: G. Einaudi, 1957); Eng. trans. by E. J. Costello, *Arab Historians of the Crusades* (Berkeley: U. of California Press, 1969).

202. C. Issawi, ed., *The Economic History of the Middle East 1800–1914* (Chicago: U. of Chicago Press, 1966), *The Economic History of Iran 1800–1914* (Chicago: U. of Chicago Press, 1971).

CHAPTER FOUR

Anthropology

RICHARD T. ANTOUN
with
Appendices by David M. Hart and Charles L. Redman

BACKGROUND

As a discipline modern social anthropology, in particular Middle Eastern anthropology, cannot be understood apart from its traditional locus of study, the small community, and apart from its traditional type of people studied, to use the term anthropologists used themselves, the "primitives."[1] The humanistic and social scientific implications of such study for the development of social anthropology have been spelled out in a classic statement by Evans-Pritchard (1954), which one can not do better than to quote in the following paragraphs.[2] What did anthropologists mean by the term "primitives"? This designation indicated societies that were "small in scale with regard to numbers, territory, and range of social contacts, and which have by comparison with more advanced societies a simple technology and economy and little specialization of social function." Why did anthropologists first devote themselves to the study of primitive societies and communities? They were interested in them because they believed that:

> They displayed institutions in their simplest forms, and that it was sound method to proceed from examination of the more simple to examination of the more complex . . .; this last reason . . . gained in weight as the so-called functional anthropology . . . developed, for the more it is regarded as the task of social anthropology to study social institutions as interdependent parts of social systems, the more it is seen to be an advantage to be able to study those societies which are structurally so simple, and culturally so homogeneous that they can be directly observed as wholes, before attempting to study complex civilized societies where this is not possible. Moreover, it is a matter of experience that it is easier to

> make observations among peoples with cultures unlike our own, the otherness in their way of life at once engaging attention, and that it is more likely that interpretations will be objective.
>
> Another . . . reason for studying primitives [even at the present time] is that they are rapidly being transformed and must be studied soon or never. These vanishing social systems are unique structural variations, a study of which aids us very considerably in understanding the nature of human society, because in a comparative study of institutions [and social anthropologists are committed to comparison at one level or another] the number of societies studied is less significant than their range of variation.

Finally, social anthropologists began by studying primitives and continue to study them, though now they also study, perhaps dominantly, peasants, pastoral nomads, and urbanities, because "they are interesting in themselves in that they provide descriptions of the way of life, the values, and the beliefs of people living without what we have come to regard as the minimum requirements of comfort and civilization."

The consequences of the early preoccupation with small-scale societies and communities for the development of modern social anthropology are profound and in part explain the methodological, theoretical, and stylistic differences between it and its fellow social sciences. Since the societies the social anthropologist studied were small-scale, they could be studied as wholes; that is, the social anthropologist studied the ecologies, economies, and legal and political institutions of the societies as well as their family and kinship organizations, their religions, and their technologies—and he studied them as part of what he conceived to be general social systems.

> But once it was accepted that a custom is more or less meaningless when taken out of its social context it became apparent both that detailed and comprehensive studies of primitive peoples in every aspect of their social life would have to be undertaken, and that they could only be undertaken by professional social anthropologists . . . The functionalist insistence on the relatedness of things has thus been partly responsible for, as it has been partly the result of, modern field studies.

In order to carry out a thorough detailed investigation of a whole social system, whether that system was conceptualized as a single community or a small-scale society, the anthropologist had to "spend sufficient time on the study," at least a year and often two years; he had throughout to remain "in close contact with the people among whom he was working"; he had to communicate with them in their own language; and he had to "study their entire culture and social life." "Though he may decide to write a book on a people's law . . . or religion . . . or . . . their economics, describing one aspect of their life and neglecting the rest, he does so always against the background of their entire social activities . . . ."

The implications of learning the native language are particularly important: "The language must be mastered as thoroughly as the capacity of the student and its complexities permit, not only because the anthropologist can communicate freely with the native," but because "in learning the language one learns the culture and the social system which are conceptualized in the language." Indeed, "the most difficult task in anthropological field work is to determine the meaning of a few key words, upon an understanding of which the whole investigation depends." The anthropologist's commitment to the study of language is not, however, merely a reflection of the tradition of intensive observation undertaken in small-scale societies, as Evans-Pritchard has suggested; it is also the most striking illustration of the anthropologist's intellectual commitment to the concept of culture. The study of language, the development of descriptive linguistics, and its inclusion as a normal part of training in American and, increasingly, European departments of anthropology have given the anthropologist his best model for the study of culture patterns. It is the search for these patterns and the cultural focus they represent that orients his research, at least in his first field trip. Thus if the anthropologist conducts research among a people who are obsessed by witchcraft, he focuses on witchcraft rather than markets, even though his theoretical interests may lie in the latter direction. Likewise, if he conducts research among a community rent by factionalism he studies politics rather than religion or myth. Moreover, his interest in comparison is only in part a reflection of a social scientific interest in nomological inquiry. It is in part a reflection of a commitment to humanistic and philosophic goals: the anthropologist is interested in human nature. Unlike the philosopher, however, who is content to speculate about the unity or variety of human types, the anthropologist ventures into the field to discover what in fact that range is. One must hasten to add that the social anthropologist is not uninterested in the development of statements of general validity regarding such subjects as social control, social stratification, political power, or social change. He is also interested in comparison for social scientific purposes. But it is only after gaining the corrected vision that comes with understanding the cultural patterns of particular communities and societies that he feels he can approach such problems with any probability of their successful formulation, investigation, and validation.

This capsule summary of the development of anthropology indicates that the development of Middle Eastern anthropology is not simply a product of distinctive Middle Eastern facts, e.g., political instability, attitudes toward Islam, the Orientalist tradition, and the changing availability of counterpart funds, but also a reflection of a problem built into the discipline itself: its simultaneous commitment to humanistic and social scientific goals. The former is reflected in the continued production of ethnography and in the emphasis on values, the latter in the increasing attention being given to the formulation of research problems and to the methodologies appropriate to them.

I have written thus far almost as if anthropology has remained stationary since the days when Bronislaw Malinowski was interned on a Pacific island among the Trobrianders during most of World War I, and, making sweet the uses of adversity, later wrote four volumes on that people and established at the London School of Economics a "school" of anthropology which made extended fieldwork the badge of courage. But social anthropology has changed radically, first in respect to the kind of people it studies; it has moved from the study of isolated, politically autonomous, economically self-sufficient primitive and tribal populations to the study of peasants. This shift has radical implications for both theory and methodology because peasant societies and communities are complex, for they are "part-societies." That is, whether the anthropologist addresses himself to the economic, political, or religious aspect of such societies, he finds his investigation necessarily taking him outside the local community to an investigation of the connections between it and urban and tribal populations and, not least important, the state and other formal legal and educational institutions. Because individuals in the community in which he is located are interpreting sophisticated religious traditions to their parishioners, he becomes interested in "the social organization of tradition;" because villagers have important economic ties outside the community he becomes interested in markets and rural–urban migration; and because village leaders and councils are carrying out (or not carrying out) ordinances from the central government he becomes interested in the role of "political brokers." Moreover, because interconnections (e.g., between town and village, village and village, state and countryside) are as important as the communities that are connected and because ready-made frameworks for analyzing tribal populations (e.g., clans, lineages, moieties, age-grades) are often lacking, he must develop or borrow new concepts (e.g., social networks, reference groups, bridge actions). Finally, because participant observation is often no longer sufficient by itself or appropriate in the new situation, he must develop new methods and techniques not only for gathering data but also for alerting himself to the new possibilities of data collection.

In part for the above reasons and in part for others that cannot be discussed here, anthropology has changed in other respects; nomological inquiry from an evolutionary perspective has once again become a focus of investigation, particularly by prehistoric archaeologists, after a century of disrepute. Although much research continues to be guided by the homeostatic view associated with functionalism, the notion that social systems are self-regulating systems has been called into serious doubt, and studies of change and process, e.g., politics, feud, assimilation, urban domination, and mediation, have become increasingly important. Increasing self-consciousness about methodology and potential cross-cultural comparisons is reflected in the growth of ethnoscience, which has developed techniques for eliciting in a more systematic fashion aspects of cognitive structure from specific informants. In fieldwork, regional approaches have been developed in prehistoric archaeology and social anthropology as well as geography. Finally, there has been a development of models for the description and analysis of social structure politics, and ethnicity.

With all these new developments in theory, methodology, and style of research, social anthropology has remained constant in certain critical respects—in its demand for detailed case studies, its insistence on field research, its commitment to language study, its holistic approach, the priority given to cultural focus, and its humanistic concerns. Thus, I have selected a number of works as significant not only on the basis that they contributed something new to the field of social anthropology by the above-mentioned criteria, but also that they continued to operate in terms of the traditional canons of social anthropological excellence.

Because, as suggested above, social and cultural anthropology in North America and much of Europe and the Middle East is perhaps distinctive among the social sciences in requiring its students with few exceptions to carry out an extended piece of field research, the analysis of Middle Eastern anthropology must necessarily consider the geographical range of fieldwork undertaken, the background of the personnel undertaking it, the methods employed, and the goals of research. In this chapter five aspects of the state of the art of Middle Eastern anthropology are discussed: stages of development, significant works, results of the survey questionnaire, problems of development, and directions for future research.

STAGES OF DEVELOPMENT

Four stages in the development of Middle Eastern anthropology can be discerned: dominance by Orientalists; dominance by travelers, political officers, and amateur anthropologists; dominance by professionally trained anthropologists guided, consciously or unconsciously, by a homeostatic model of communities; and influence (not yet dominance) of professional anthropologists consciously guided by a diachronic model of social systems and a comparative point of view. The relationship of the above-mentioned stages is cumulative, with each building on the work of the preceding one without displacing it.

Orientalists have written valuable studies of particular Middle Eastern milieus based on their long-time immersion in the study of Islamic institutions and/or their long-time residence in the area. Notable among these studies are Lane's *Manners and Customs of the Modern Egyptians* (1836); Hurgronje's remarkable study of *Mekka in the Latter Part of the Nineteenth Century* (1889); Lammens' *Le Mecque a la veille de l'Hegire* (1924); and Smith's classic, *Kinship and Marriage in Early Arabia* (1903). More recent work of primary social anthropological significance includes the work of the French Orientalists on North Africa, e.g., LeTourneau's *Fes avant le protectorat, les villes musulmanes d'Afrique du Nord* (1957) and *Fez in the Age of the Merinides* (1961), and on the Fertile Crescent and Egypt, e.g., Berque's *Histoire sociale d'un village egyptien au XXeme Siecle* (1957), and Cahen's "Movements populaires et autonomisme urbain dans l'Asie musulmane du Moyen Age" (1959). It also includes the work of British and French Orientalists who have occasionally cut loose from the particularities of time and place and generalized about matters of social organization and culture within the Middle Eastern Muslim world, e.g., Gibb's brilliant essay on kinship and social organization (1958), Lewis' stimulating monograph, *Race and Color in Islam* (1970), and Montagne's classic, *La civilisation du desert* (1947). Lapidus' *Muslim Cities in the Later Middle Ages* (1967) and "Muslim Cities and Islamic Societies" (1969) and Makidisi's "Muslim Institutions of Learning in Eleventh Century Baghdad" (1961) represent three of the best examples of American scholarship. Notable Middle Eastern contributions include Baer's *Studies in the Social History of Modern Egypt* (1969) and El-Ali's *The Social and Economic Strata of Basra in the First Islamic Century* [*al-ṭabaqât al-ijtimaᶜiyya wa al-iqtiṣadîyya fi al-Basra fi al-qarn al-awwal al-hijri*] (1953). A glance at these titles—an arbitrary selection from hundreds—indicates three things about the character of the Orientalist contribution to Middle Eastern social anthropology: (1) it provides considerable data and analysis of Middle Eastern urban institutions, which have been sadly neglected in social anthropological research until just recently; (2) it attempts the study of rural and nomadic societies and cultures; and (3) it ranges from monographic studies on particular communities to studies of particular regions to generalizing studies about particular social structural or cultural attributes of Islamic civilization. Moreover, for anthropologists literate in Middle Eastern languages, the works of native scholars, ranging from the boring but still useful biographical (*ṭabaqât*) records of the likes of Ibn al-Jawzî to the scintillating essays of al-Jâḥiz to the herioic Shahnameh of Firdawsi, remain invaluable for the study of various Middle Eastern cultures and societies. It would be a shame for future generations of cultural and social anthropologists to neglect this vast significant literature as the past generation has done.

For many centuries, travelers' accounts have poured out of the Middle

East, but although all have some degree of social anthropological significance, depending on the biases of the observer and the regularity of the recording of observations, a few are outstanding in that regard. Doughty's *Travels in Arabia Deserta* (1888) marks one of the first of a distinctive tradition of English traveler's accounts; others in the grand tradition include Philby's *The Empty Quarter* (1933); Thomas' *Arabia Felix* (1932); and most recently and not least, Thesiger's *Arabian Sands* (1959) and *The Marsh Arabs* (1954). Supplementing these accounts are those of the British political officers posted in various parts of the Middle East including Bell, Lawrence, Glubb, and Dickson. Excluding Smith's evolutionary study of kinship, all the above-mentioned works, though varying in their literary worth and in their systematic observations and insights into the culture, lack a theoretical perspective; they are not social science and do not claim to be so. Dickson's *The Arab of the Desert* (1949), which most clearly purports to be an ethnographic study, is organized in such an aimless and transparent manner (with chapter headings ranging from sandstorms to camel disputes, and from smoking to morality) that the description of anthropology as a thing of shreds and patches is in this case an understatement. The best ethnographic work by far in the immediate pre-World War II period was done by Hilma Granqvist, a Finnish student of the Bible and disciple of the folklorist Edward Westermark. From 1931 to 1965, she published a series of monographs dealing with childbearing, kinship, marriage, and religion, all on the village of Artas in Palestine. An entirely different genre in the prewar period, also of high quality, was the work of the French school of human geography, whose work in North Africa and the Levant included the works of LeCoz, Lesne, Weulersse, de Planhol, Despois, Mercier, and Goddard. They laid the foundation for later regional and urban studies.

Following World War II, for the first time a number of professional anthropologists undertook fieldwork in the Middle East. With a few notable exceptions, e.g., the work of Peters among the Bedouin of Cyrenaica, these anthropologists broke sharply with the tradition established by travelers and political officers—they studied peasants rather than nomads; more important they carried out extended participant observation (usually a year) in particular communities.[3] Many of these anthropologists were much concerned with social change, but others explicitly or implicitly considered the communities to be things worthy of study in and of themselves. The aim of such studies, although the authors often failed to state so explicitly, was to study the "nature" of the community, that is, its social structure, its functions, its ideology and values, and the forces that maintain its cohesiveness. Thus the model of study followed was homeostatic.

The final stage of development of Middle Eastern social anthropology is characterized by the incipient development of comparative studies, diachronic studies, ecologically oriented studies, studies of urban life, and regional studies. Communities are studied less as things in themselves and more as "samples," that is, as convenient milieus for investigating particular theoretical problems. There is also an incipient development regarding personnel; a core of Western-trained Middle Easterners has begun to undertake research in their own countries and to publish their results.

SIGNIFICANT WORKS[4]

Two works by an Orientalist and student of the "higher criticism," both written before the turn of the century (1885 and 1889), are important in the development of modern social anthropology: the works are *Kinship and Marriage in Early Arabia* and *Lectures on the Religion of the Semites*, and the author is William Robertson Smith. Because the author accepted an evolutionary perspective that was repudiated by the students of Malinowski and Radcliffe-Brown in England and Boas in the United States, his works have been neglected by three generations of social anthropologists and, when considered, branded for their evolutionism rather than appreciated for their sensitive analysis of social groups and religious symbolism. As a social anthropologist, Smith was a pioneer in that he recognized the fundamental importance of the local descent group (Edmund Leach (1951) rediscovered its importance in 1951), its nature as a corporate group (in blood feud and in the distribution of inheritance and booty), and that all other ties above the level of this corporate group (the *hayy*) were necessarily labile in order to allow men (here, the Bedouin) to unite for offense and defense and to disperse to exploit surrounding economic resources (Murphy and Kasden rediscovered this lability and its functions in 1959). Smith also clearly delineated the patrilineal paradox, later spelled out in a more comprehensive way by Fortes for the Tallensi and readjusted for a matrilineal society by Malinowski; namely, in a patrilineal polygnous society, the most powerful idiom of unity is necessarily traced through women and the critical index of power is the ability of the father to violate descent-phrased rules of succession and inheritance for the benefit of most-favored others. That Smith was a "social" anthropologist is most clearly indicated by the fact that even when he studied religion, he focused on religious social relations, i.e., rituals (rather than creeds); he was quick to note not only that human social structural dyads are descriptive models for God–man relationships, but also that changes in social structure are reflected in changes in religious ideology. Indeed, logically speaking, his functionalism was better grounded than the more famous proponents of functionalist anthropology, Malinowski and Radcliffe-Brown, since functional interdependence can be established only by investigating relationships at several points in time, that is, by diachronic studies rather than synchronic studies lacking both a comparative and a historical framework. Smith, however, was not simply a social anthropologist who reduced all data to their significance for intra- or intergroup relations; on the contrary, he saw that every act in every ritual had mental correlates that had to be inferred and related to one another. Moreover, if his delineation of evolutionary stages was in terms of our own hindsight, simplistic and static and not actually focused on how change occurs, it also recognized the need for abstraction, for statements of regularity, and by implication for cross-cultural typology. Thus although Smith was careful to limit his studies to "the Semites," and although he immersed himself in the historical and philological data pertinent to them, he was not concerned about just their social structure and religion, but by implication about his own, and by extension humankind's. It is only very recently that cultural and social anthropologists have looked beyond their own field studies or explored their implications for wider areas of relevance, an indictment for which the early evolutionists could not be held accountable.

The publication of the first two volumes of Hilma Granqvist's five-volume monograph on the village of Artas near Bethlehem, *Marriage Conditions in a Palestinian Village* (1931–1935), marked a significant departure from the works of the Orientalist, traveler, political officer, and romanticist. Granqvist was the student of the noted folklorist, Edward Westermark, and she originally intended to undertake a study of Biblical custom by studying it in situ. What she discovered after arriving in Palestine, apart from the questionable theoretical basis of her study (had the culture of the local population remained unchanged for 1900 years for her convenience?), was that the living culture of the community as she observed it was worthy of study in and of itself. In this discovery she reflected the fundamental humanistic point of view of modern cultural and social anthropology, a point of view that often separates it philosophically from the fields of sociology, psychology, and political science, which are avowedly social scientific in their aspirations and methodologies. If people in and of themselves are worth studying, then it follows that an extended period of field research is necessary to delineate the patterns of their culture; Granqvist spent about 16 months in the field. Her field research was significant not only for its length and its reliance on participant observation, but also for its intensity, which is attested to by the substantial documentation found in appendices: genealogies, detailed census of household composition, and marriage charts and lists. Although she did not cast her net as widely as Malinowskian functionalism dictated (she ignored such matters as land tenure, social stratification, and politics) and gathered much more data on what people said happened or said should happen than on what actually happened, by comparison with previous work of anthropological interest in the Middle East her work was a substantial achievement. That achievement was not merely in techniques of fieldwork and size of documentation but also in analysis, for her discussion of the ambivalent status of the "stranger bride" and "the flight of anger" remain classics in the study of kinship. Finally, her study of Artas—a Sunni Muslim Arab peasant community—broke sharply with the tradition of studying romantic (e.g., Bedouin) and/or esoteric (e.g., Druze) populations, and began the more modern tendency of studying the dominant social, cultural, and economic strains in the Middle Eastern mosaic (e.g., villages, Sunni Muslims, and peasants).

One of the most important postwar contributions to social anthropology appeared in 1960 with the publication of Emrys Peters' prize essay, "The Proliferation of Segments in the Lineage of the Bedouin in Cyrenaica." Peters, a professional social anthropologist, spent almost twice as long in the field as Granqvist (27 months) and combined historical and ethnohistorical with traditional social anthropological data to produce a superb social structural analysis. In several respects the essay represented a new departure in Middle Eastern anthropology. First, rather than treat the physical environment, the social structure, and the ideology of the group under separate rubrics, as had been common, he related them in an intimate manner showing that the form, recruitment, and composition of groups and their accompanying ideologies were closely related to environmental conditions and their fluctuations. Yet the relationship was not a completely determinative one, since certain aspects of ideology (e.g., genealogy) remained impervious to environmental and social structural changes, and other aspects of social structure (e.g., the affiliation of *laff* groups) reflected these changes very closely. In this respect the essay is as valuable for Middle Eastern historians as it is for anthropologists, not only because Peters combined historical and social anthropological data but also because he demonstrated beyond doubt that tribal genealogies heretofore taken as historical documents by many historians are primarily indicators of the social structural realities at one level and the ideology of the tribe on another. Second, the focus of the article was not on the social structures per se (i.e., the various kinship groups) but on the process of adjustment, the adjustment not only of groups to the environment but also of ideology to groups and of groups to one another; the focus was on structural dynamics rather than structural form or typology. This essay on the process of proliferation foreshadowed his classic analysis of another vital social process, the feud (1967). Finally, the essay was the first to call attention to the critical structural importance of ties through women in what are ostensibly male-dominated patrilineal, patrilocal, and patripotestal societies. Perhaps the most salutary consequence of Peters' detailed case studies is that after reading them with any degree of attention, one cannot continue to parrot the clichés about the feud-ridden, irrational, male-dominated Bedouin and, by extrapolation, Middle Easterner.

Six years after the publication of Peters' essay, Paul English, a geographer, published a monograph entitled *City and Village in Iran.* This too was a case study but, rather than concentrate on a particular community or tribe or ethnic group, English selected a region, the Kirman basin. The selection of a region for study was in itself significant, for the traditional anthropological approach to the study of the Middle East had trichotomized the area into peasants, urbanites, and nomads, each with its characteristic structure and culture; anthropological research in the area was usually confined to one type of community or the other, and introductory texts accepted the above rubrics as natural divisions for pedagogical purposes (see, for instance, chapter headings in Coon, 1951, and Patai, 1962); moreover, field research in the area was usually confined to one type of community or the other. English demonstrated that there was constant communication between the urban elite of the region and the peasantry; that a series of contracts tied urban landlord to peasant, urban wool merchant to herdsman, and urban carpet manager to rural weaver; and that it was no longer possible to uphold the view that villages were either isolated or homogeneous communities. They varied in size (from 50 to more than 4000), complexity (from mountain hamlet to village to regional subcenter), and the structure of occupations (with dominance alternatively in agriculture, herding, weaving, or fuel collecting). Moreover, he held that the organized exploitation of regional resources from a city base and involving continuous cooperation and communication between all economic factors was not some new phenomenon brought about by the introduction of wheeled vehicular traffic (as students of modernization sometimes argue); rather, it was a traditional pattern of interdependence that was merely intensified with the building of roads and the introduction of buses and automobiles. He argued further that communal patterns of exploitation, e.g., of land and water, were not related to tribalism or kinship but rather to the overarching feudal ties existing between the urban elite and rural population. In sum, by focusing on the socioeconomic ties between what had until then been regarded as discrete and isolated social types, English was able to challenge both the pedagogical assumptions of introductory texts and the implications of research designs that confined themselves to an examination of a single community within a given social type.

In the same year as the publication of English's monograph, an extremely important study appeared by a prehistorian, Robert M. Adams, entitled *The Evolution of Urban Society: Early Mesopotamia and Prehispanic Mexico.* The study was important in several respects. First, like English's work, it stressed the importance of a regional point of view for understanding complex society, although it arrived at this conclusion entirely independently by sifting through archaeological data. Adams suggested, for instance, that the Mesopotamian temples acted as collecting points for the products of adjacent ecological niches as well as redistribution points for such products, that important conflicts could be understood only in terms of the competition of upstream and downstream cultivators, and that marginal cultivators of the hinterland probably played critical political roles in Mexico, and seminomads played similar roles in Mesopotamia.

Second, Adams' study, based largely on Middle Eastern materials, was responsible for encouraging the rethinking of archaeological and historical data from an evolutionary perspective. He suggested that certain kinds of social structures, e.g., "conical clans," were "preadapted" for the formation of the complex, flexible hierarchies that characterized the growth of the state itself. Of special interest for social anthropologists in this regard was his view that "class" and "clan" were by no means polar opposites.

Third, Adams' study was both comparative and processual. He demonstrated that although the development of the Mexican and Mesopotamian elites had certain broad similarities, there were critical processual differences. The latter represented the growth of stratification as an organic process related to local differentiae in irrigation and agricultural management by owner-administrators; the former represented the growth of stratification as a result of royal largesse distributed to a predatory military nobility. Again, Adams' analysis is of particular interest to social anthropologists since, unlike Childe and Steward, he saw social organization as the key to transformation rather than technology or extracultural factors such as the physical environment or population pressure.

Adams' study, at once regional, evolutionary, and comparative, focused on process and, drawing heavily on Middle Eastern materials, certainly represents a significant and auspicious contribution to Middle Eastern anthropology.

In 1968, Clifford Geertz's interpretive lectures on the religious development of Indonesia and Morocco were published under the title *Islam Observed.* Geertz sought to delineate at the same time the distinctive ethos of each country in its classical period, the challenge to each rendered by Islamic "scripturalism" (the turn toward the Qur'an, the *ḥadîth*, and the *sharîᶜa*, together with standard commentaries upon them as the only acceptable bases of religious authority), and the consequences of colonialism not only for religious and political institutions but also for the minds of men. Geertz's essay is important not only because it represents the first attempt to apply his own distinctive view of religion to an overall Islamic context but also because it focuses on what must be a critical process for modern man, the decline in "the aura of factuality" that has made religion "another world to live in" for the vast majority of mankind until recent times. Geertz studies the options available to man, here Muslim man, when religious traditions falter and the quandaries posed to both politicians and savants when a disassociation occurs between the symbols of legitimacy (e.g., in Morocco, the Sharifian court), the locus of power (e.g., until 1956 the French), and the instruments of authority (e.g., tribal leaders). The value of *Islam Observed* is not so much in particular delineations of Javanese versus Moroccan ethos (for instance, in the insightful contrasts of the conversion experience in the two cultures) or the encapsulation of history in the lives of key personalities (e.g., al-Yusi and Muhammad V in Morocco and Kalidjaga and Sukarno in Indonesia). Rather, it is in Geertz's capacity to pull down the old stereotypes and in their place to make us aware of the immense variety that is comprehended by such terms as mysticism, animatism, and Sufism, not only between different parts of the Muslim world but within a single cultural tradition. Thus Moroccan Sufism comprehends not only the cult of saints around tombs, and the variety of relgious brotherhoods, but also the Sharifian court which in itself combines both the "intrinsic" and the "contractual" theories of legitimacy. Thus *baraka* means not merely blessing, divine favor, or magical power, but also material prosperity, physical well-being, and completion. Geertz's view that concepts should be viewed as fans of meaning, coupled with the view that vital processes are often uncovered in the most unlikely institutional settings, if accepted must lead both to the development of more systematic study of symbolizing and symbol systems and to more intensive fieldwork over longer periods of time.

One of the most recent significant works is Reinhold Loffler's "The Representative Mediator and the New Peasant" (1971).[5] On the basis of data collected among tribal villagers in western Iran, Loffler breaks new ground in the study of political brokers, skillfully demonstrating in a case study that a new breed of mediator occupying no established position of authority and drawn from the peasantry itself has emerged in rural areas. Indeed, Loffler holds that it is just because he is drawn from the peasantry rather than the local gentry—as the anthropological literature has suggested in the past—that the "representative" mediator is able to discern traditional preadaptive patterns (for instance, Ni'matullāhi Sufism) and also to manipulate them symbolically to promote change. Although the delineation of this hitherto largely unrecognized type of mediator is an insightful contribution to the study of leadership, the main value of Loffler's essay is not in the field of political anthropology. Rather it is in the new perspective the author provides for the study of peasantry and for the study of "modernization," "nation building," and "developing nations." Loffler argues that the stereotype of the peasant nourished by some anthropologists—the immobile, passive (in action), defensive (in strategies), desperate (in revolt), unimaginative (in planning and execution) fellow addicted to subsistence and, in his own view, to fate and luck—represents a view appropriate to the nineteenth and early twentieth century, but not to the present. It is a stereotypical view not in accord with current reality since it fails to take into account either the communications revolution or the change in the relative power position of peasants in the polities into which they are becoming increasingly integrated. Loffler's greatest contribution is the broad delineation of this process of integration: the combination of traditional "vertical" mediation (in which one jumps outside the hierarchy to get something done within it) with a modern ethos (demanding on the basis of withheld rights rather than entreaty on the basis of favoritism); the development of village-based organization to replace kinship organization; and last but not least, the development of "representative" rather than "patron" mediators. The appearance of Loffler's essay is not only significant in itself for its contribution to political anthropology, peasant studies, and modernization but also auspicious for the state of the art of Middle Eastern anthropology, for it demonstrates that after 20 years of field research in peasant societies, Middle Eastern anthropologists are contributing insights that are important not only for Middle Eastern anthropology, but also significant for important theoretical problems in the discipline at large.

THE STATE OF THE ART

As a graduate student in anthropology I attended my first annual meeting of the American Anthropological Association in Washington, D.C. in 1958. At the time I was appalled and somewhat intimidated to find so many persons who classified themselves as professional anthropologists, particularly because I had just entered the discipline and was far from possessing the credentials. Equally surprising and no less a cause of chagrin was that not only was the Middle East unrepresented by specific panels or symposia—whether problem oriented or area oriented—but also only three papers in social anthropology related directly to the Middle East! At the time the Middle East Studies Association did not exist.

By contrast, at the annual meeting of the Middle East Studies Association held in Binghamton, New York in 1972, anthropologists delivered 19 papers and wholly comprised one panel while being represented on seven others, including those on law in Muslim society, nineteenth-century Ottoman society and economic history, form and content in Persian literature and society, the problems in the historiography of Iran, class, tribalism in modern Iran, facets of political and social life in Tunisia, and history and social anthropology in the study of Islam. At the meeting of the American Anthropological Association in Toronto four weeks later, one panel numbering nine papers was devoted exclusively to the Middle East, and another symposium on patterns of visiting in the eastern Mediterranean focused on Lebanon, Turkey, and Iran as well as Greece; Middle Eastern anthropologists participated in a variety of other problem-oriented panels during the sessions. The titles of the papers in the Middle Eastern panel give some sense of the topical areas of interest and the points of view taken as well as the geographic spread of fieldwork: "Linguistic Strategy and Social Order: The Case of Iran"; "The Relationship Between Sedentarization and Social Stratification Among the Iranian Nomads: A Critique of Barth"; "The New Bedouin: Adaptive Changes in Bedouin Nomadism in Modernizing Oil-Rich Arabia"; "Cultural and Social Structural Dimensions of Trust in Turkey"; "Dowry and Alliance in the Sephardic Jews of Istanbul"; "Women's Honor, Men's Shame: Mediterranean Values Reconsidered"; "Brokers of Religious Truth and Supernatural Power" (in Afghanistan); and "Education and Value Conflicts in a Turkish Community." The symposium on visiting and the panel on the Middle East reflect the state of the art of Middle Eastern anthropology in a number of ways. First, the symposium focused on a social process, visiting, rather than on formal social structure; second, the cues for analysis were emic, e.g., *shirkets* in Beirut, *qubûl* in southern Anatolia, *dørøstluk* (trustworthiness) in a Turkish factory; third, the analyses demonstrated the wide variety of functions served by the same institution in different cultures and societies. Visiting can serve economic goals (saving) in a highly competitive economy, ensure trade in a nomadic society where it is vital for survival, provide social insurance and welfare in an urban milieu where the state does not provide welfare and the petty bourgeois is in chronic debt, set social styles of life in small towns, or reflect the necessities of the ecological cycle in small subsistence farming communities.

On the other hand, the most important point of nearly every paper on the Middle Eastern panel of the American Anthropological Association related to a myth prevalent among social scientists and historians. One paper clearly demonstrated that religiosity and fatalism are not necessarily or even usually concomitant; another challenged the view that pastoral nomadism is a traditional, anachronistic and passing way of life and the assumption that there is a linear progression in modern times from nomadism to sedentarization; a third critically examined the widely held view that the male code of honor provides little leeway for women and that its sanctions are absolute; and a fourth rejected the view that the establishment of factories fosters the breakdown of old class (feudal) ties and the establishment of new (proletarian) ties. Now one of the results of anthropological research must certainly be the exploding of myths and the stereotypes associated with them—exploding them not only for the public but for anthropologists who have too often nourished them. In this respect, the panel alluded to was very successful and intrinsically interesting. However, the explosion of myths should be a by-product of anthropological research, not its central tendency. The papers referred to were successful either in demonstrating the variety of functions served in different cultural milieus or in exploding prevalent myths but did not aiming at accomplishing more than that, e.g., the suggestion of hypotheses or the delineation of models; this reflects exactly the state of the art of Middle Eastern anthropology in the year 1972.

The results of a questionnaire that I sent to more than 300 scholars, who (1) identified themselves as social anthropologists and (2) had a serious research interest in the Middle East, as well as to a number of Middle Eastern geographers reflect the state of the art in another fashion.[6] These scholars were asked how many field trips they had made to date. Fifty seven of the 72 respondents to this question stated they had done fieldwork, with the largest number stating that they had made two (19) or three (14) field trips. Five other respondents stated that they were permanent residents of the area in which they were doing research.[7] In all, more than 227 field trips were made by these respondents. When asked the length of time spent in the field on each trip, the largest number (32) said their field trips took between 1 year and 18 months; the second largest number (31) took between 6 months and 1 year; and the third largest number (23) took between 18 months and 2 years Most field workers (25) went alone, although 17 stated they had assistants. The above record of field research is truly remarkable, not so much for the number of persons who have undertaken fieldwork, but for the number of trips made—repeated rather than single trips are the norm—and for the long periods spent in the field. Thus field research in the Middle East, insofar as it takes place, seems to be based on a solid ethnographic foundation.

Indicative of the state of the art of Middle Eastern anthropology were the replies to the following three questions on the above-mentioned questionaire. What is the title or subject of your present research as opposed to your past research? What is the probable direction of your future research? Finally, in what directions, areas, or problems would you like to see future research done in the Middle East? The largest number of answers for past research, own future research, and opinion as to directions of future research can be classified as relating to the study of a particular geographic area or people within it.[8] For instance, one respondent replied that in the past he had studied the oasis of al-Hasa; another said that in the future he wished to study peasants in Turkey, a third, the Sa'ar tribes of southern Arabia; a fourth said that in the future he would like to see research done on the Mongols; a fifth would like to see work done on Shi^{c}ite groups in Iraq (see Table 3 in Appendix I). There is still a very pronounced tendency to identify research interests in terms of geographic areas or the peoples within them. Despite this tendency, however, not a single person identified his past, present or future research interests in terms of the study of a region, as a special perspective. This is the case despite the work of Geertz's students in Morocco, Fernea's and Kennedy's in Nubia, and the pioneering work on regionalism of English in Iran (see above).

The tendency to focus on a particular geographic area and a particular people in it, i.e., to collect "ethnographic" facts, is accompanied by and almost certainly encourages the publication of "ethnography"; when asked to cite their outstanding publications, respondents cited 29 items that referred directly either to ethnography or to studies of tribal social structure; the trend is not only for the collection of ethnographic facts and for the publication of ethnography, but also for teaching and, by inference, thinking in terms of ethnography. Thus when respondents to the questionnaire were asked what courses they were currently teaching involving the Middle East over half the courses cited (24 of 47) referred to ethnography, only one referred to culture and personality, only two to politics, and only two to ethnicity; however, four courses did cite change in their titles. Likewise, out of the 46 Middle Eastern courses cited as being taught in the past, by far the largest number (24) referred to ethnography; by contrast, two referred to social stratification, one to social change, one to women in the Middle East, and one to the sociology of Islam. By far the largest number of course titles cited in response to both the above questions simply stipulated "Ethnography of the Middle East" or much less frequently, "Ethnography of the Kurds," "Ethnography of Ethiopia," of "Rural Moroccan Ethnography," for example (see Appendix I, Table 4, for exact tabulations).

Statements of future research interests and opinions about the direction of future research revealed a sharp increase in the number of respondents indicating that ethnicity was their focus. Such replies varied from those that merely indicated an interest in interethnic relations to those that specified an interest in a particular ethnic group (such as the gypsies) or groups (e.g., relations between Israelis and Arabs) to those that framed their interest in more theoretical terms (e.g., the role of *dhimmi* and outcaste populations in maintaining economic and social equilibrium). The focus on ethnicity indicates both a continuance of the old interest in peoples and geographic areas and, to some people, a new determination to place their study in a more explicitly theoretical framework (See Appendix I, Table 3).

Opinions about directions of future research revealed a very sharp break with past and present research with respect to the necessity of combining two or more disciplines in anthropological research. Whereas no respondent stated the subject of his present research in terms of combining disciplines, 10 respondents urged the necessity of such research. Among the combinations urged were sociology and linguistics, sociology and psychology, history and anthropology, and demography, ecology, economics, and social structure. It may very well be that the establishment of numerous Middle East centers and Middle East area programs in the United States and Canada—programs encouraging interdisciplinary approaches—is in part responsible for this new development.

Certain more theoretical or problem-oriented subjects were consistently neglected in the answers of the respondents. Not a single person identified the subject of his past research as comparative studies, only one identified it as the subject of his present research, and only two urged it as a direction of future research. On the positive side, in answer to the question, what are your research problems and research design, six respondents identified comparative research; this research, however, is both topically and geographically restricted since it deals in the main with the adjustment of various immigrant groups in Israel. A single respondent identified culture and personality as the subject of his past research and a single respondent identified it as the subject of his future research. Specific subjects of research that have received attention in society at large, in the social sciences, and in anthropology have been consistently neglected by Middle Eastern anthropologists: only one respondent stated that the subject of his research at present involved sex roles (including the rights of women), and only one identified it as a subject of future research. Not a single respondent identified colonialism as the subject of past or present research, although four urged it as a subject of future research. Finally, in an area where tribal codes of honor are replete and religious ethics often reinforces them, not a single respondent identified honor as the subject of present of future research, and not a single respondent urged it as a suitable direction for future research.

The analysis of the responses to the question; what are the titles of your outstanding publications, sheds further light on the state of the art of Middle Eastern anthropology in 1973.[9] The largest number of published items (26) related to religion. This result may seem to contradict what is said in the next section about the exiguous research and publication relating to the social anthropology of Islam; a closer examination of the responses reveals otherwise. Only eight of the 26 items related to Islam; five of those eight were by two authors. Seven of the 26 items related to Judaism and only one related to Christianity. The remaining 10 items were not directly related to the three great religious traditions in the area but rather to subjects such as witchcraft, spirit possession, circumcision, and shamanism. Thus the social organization of tradition has been neglected for all the major religions of the area and not merely for Islam.[10]

The third largest number of published items coded (20) related to ethnicity, a fact that confirms the increasing importance of this subject.[11] The growth in importance of ethnicity as a subject of research is clearly related to the influx of Jews of varying ethnic origins into Israel in the last 25 years.

Ten of the 20 published items related to Israeli Jews; another four items related to Jews in other Middle Eastern countries, leaving only six that dealt specifically on an ethnic basis with the numerous other peoples that make up the vast yet intricate Middle Eastern mosaic. Seven of the 20 items related to specific ethnic groups, for instance, the Jerusalem Sephardim, the Sulabba, and the Ma'dan; two ethnic groups related to morbidity and mortality; and two others dealt with ethnic stereotypes. Only two items indicated a specific focus on interethnic relations, and only four items indicated an interest in ethnicity as distinct from ethnic groups; that is, less than a third of all items approached the subject as a problem and a process, e.g., the problem of ethnic boundaries (Barth) or the problem of the politics of ethnicity (Cohen, see below).

The fourth largest number of published items (19) referred to nomads; this response may indicate the continued importance of the aura of romance that has influenced research in the past, but to a greater degree it may indicate the increased importance of an ecological approach since the physical environment and the economics of pastoralism must necessarily be taken account of in such studies. If the items on nomadism are combined with those explicitly referring to ecology (10), a total of 29 items can be said to be ecologically oriented. Thus ecology seems to be one of the fields in which Middle Eastern anthropologists have done important work; in fact, Barth's work (1956) among the nomadic Basseri and among the hill peoples of Swat was at the time pioneering. It cannot be said, however, that Middle Eastern anthropologists are pioneering in the field of cultural ecology at present; the implications of Rappaport's ecological model worked out with data from New Guinea (and stated in his monograph, *Pigs for the Ancestors*, 1968) have yet to be applied in the Middle East; nor has Dyson-Hudson's call (1972) for more refined demographic and economic data on animals been met. To my knowledge, the one exception is the work of Naderi on the economics of herd-keeping in the Zagros chain of Iran. Naderi was able to demonstrate on the basis of more refined data that several of Barth's assumptions and conclusions about ecological processes including sedentarization were erroneous; unfortunately, Naderi's work has yet to be translated from the original Persian.

The fifth largest set of published items (17) referred to village studies, as might be expected, but surprisingly, also to applied anthropology. However, almost half the items on applied anthropology (8) related to research conducted in Israel. The enormous Israeli contribution in this field is more properly judged when it is considered that an additional 14 published items related to immigration; 13 of these 14 items related to problems of assimilation, adjustment, and resettlement of immigrants in Israel, i.e., to applied anthropology. Thus the publication in the field of applied anthropology is substantial but considerably restricted both geographically and topically; important problems of applied anthropology such as overpopulation and refugees have been almost completely neglected. It is also interesting to note that although a large number of published items related to applied anthropology, only one respondent urged future research to be directed toward that subject.

The sixth largest number of published items (16) referred to cities. Although a number of anthropologists have done research in particular towns and cities, among the respondents only one, Gulick, has made urban anthropology a subject of special interest as evidenced by the fact that only he among the respondents has published extensively on the subject. Several anthropologists have approached the study of the city from the perspective of the countryside, i.e., in terms of rural–urban ties, but very few have examined the dynamics of urbanization; a recent exception is Eickelman's (1973) attempt to describe the making of a quarter in a Moroccan town. The French work on urban social structure in North Africa is exceptional in this regard and is treated separately in Appendix III. Again there seems to be a tendency among Middle Eastern anthropologists to shy away from problem-oriented approaches to the subject. Thus despite English's provocative hypothesis of urban domination over particular regions (as stated in the study of Kirman referred to above) and the interesting critique of his thesis by two anthropologists, Salzman and Spooner (1969), not a single published item on urban life or a single item of proposed research recorded by respondents was related to this hypothesis.

There is one set of published items that augurs well for the state of the art of Middle Eastern anthropology; that is the set of items relating to change. When those subjects that related directly to change, i.e., modernization immigration, applied anthropology, and process, were combined with those that cited change in their titles, a grand total of 61 items was recorded, far more than any other subject (see Appendix I, Table 5). Of particular interest were those items relating to process; both past and present research and opinions as to the direction of future research placed a high priority on studies of process (see Table 5 in Appendix I); the processes of assimilation adjustment, population dynamics, local politics, and socialization were mentioned as the subjects of present research; urbanization, nonverbal communication, and the manipulation of social relations through changes in speech style as suitable directions of future research; and faction and conversion, sedentarization, gossip in encounters, and the dynamics of cognitive descent as a sampling of published items.

Attention has been called at a number of points to the tendency of Middle Eastern anthropologists to identify their research interests very strongly with particular countries, peoples, or geographic areas within the Middle East;

this tendency was brought out most dramatically in questions where respondents were *not* asked specifically to identify geographical or political loci of interest. Thus when informants were asked to identify the "directions, areas, or problems" in which they would like to see future research done, the largest number of replies designated geographic areas (Appendix I, Table 6). Again, when respondents were asked, "What is the probable direction of your future research in the Middle East?" the stipulation of a geographic area or a country was the second most frequent reply (Appendix I, Table 3). Specific geographic clusterings were brought out when respondents were asked to stipulate the geographic areas of interest of present, past, and future research. The largest number of respondents ranked Israel first for all time periods (See Appendix I, Table 7A). Morocco, which was stated to be an area of past research interest for 15 respondents, had only two respondents state a research interest in the future. Turkey, which had 13 respondents state a research interest in the past, had only three state such an interest in the future. Not a single respondent stated a present or future research interest in Syria, Iraq, or Jordan. On the other hand, Iran and Afghanistan elicited a number of positive responses for all periods. Although the uneven replies to this question must be taken into account, an inference that can be drawn is that field research in the Middle East is peculiarly susceptible to the vagaries of political stability in particular countries, to the growth of anti-Westernism, particularly anti-Americanism, to the changing availability of counterpart funds, and to the level of international tensions current in the area.[12] The replies to a question asking respondents to list the locales of their past field trips do not differ significantly from the above pattern. The six most popular locales, with the number of individuals having done research in each, are as follows: Israel (18), Iran (18), Afghanistan (16), Turkey (12), Morocco (11), and Egypt (10) (see Appendix I, Table 7B). Since publication lags many years behind fieldwork, we are just now beginning to enjoy the published results of work in Turkey and Morocco; we shall soon begin to enjoy the results of research in Iran and Afghanistan. On the other hand, we are just beginning to enter a period of dearth, after substantial publication, for the Arab world. The restrictions on field research in Turkey, Libya, and most recently, Morocco, probably will be reflected in a drop in publication about seven years hence. The drop in publication for Syria, Iraq, and Jordan has been felt for some time. Fieldwork in Israel flourishes and continued relatively high-quality publication can be expected.

What, then, is the state of the art of Middle Eastern anthropology? The answer to this question reflects not only the tabulated results of the questionnaire but also the review of the periodical literature I undertook prior to writing this chapter and, for better or worse, my own evaluations of strengths and weaknesses of the field. First, there is no doubt that certain theoretical, methodological, and applied orientations important in the discipline of anthropology have been neglected, namely, law, the social organization of tradition, myth, urbanization, comparative studies, ethnoscience, and applied anthropology; other problem areas of interest to the discipline such as ethnicity and social change have been investigated, but not with the degree of sophistication present in the discipline at large. Other subjects that have received attention in society at large and/or in the other social sciences such as colonialism, sex roles, and game theory have been neglected by anthropology and, as part of that neglect, by Middle Eastern anthropologists. On the other hand, Middle Eastern anthropologists have done some of the early pioneering work in cultural ecology and have contributed recently both to the renewed interest in evolution as a theoretical perspective and to the development of a regional rather than a community approach, both in social anthropology and prehistoric archaeology. Moreover, individual anthropologists and geographers have made important contributions to the study of such processes as feud, mediation of political brokers at the local level, and urban domination. Indeed, one of the most auspicious developments in the growth of the social and cultural anthropology of the Middle East is the increasing commitment of anthropologists to the study of process—whether in the study of kinship, political organization, interpersonal relations, language, peasantry, or tribal life—rather than strictly formal studies of social and culture structure.

The significance of ethnography is important in this regard. In the discussion of the tabulation it was pointed out, perhaps with a degree of implied criticism, that Middle Eastern anthropologists continue to conceive of their research and carry it out in terms of ethnography and an interest in particular peoples and geographic areas. Although this tendency may be decried, particularly from a social scientific view, it can also be defended in terms of the anthropologist's theoretical commitment to the study of culture patterns. In addition, and, for the social scientist, more pertinent, ethnographic works often provide valuable insights into important processes that have more than local significance. To cite only one example, Fernea's *Shaykh and Effendi* (1970) has eight chapters, only two of which deal directly with social change, but the culmination of the ethnography is in the last two chapters, in which the author demonstrates the remarkable capacity of a segmentary tribal social structure to adapt to the demands of modern irrigation systems. These chapters have rather startling implications both for theories of development of hydraulic societies and for modernization; in that respect they are not atypical of recent ethnographic work in social anthropology in particular.

Finally, in any evaluation of the state of the art of Middle Eastern anthropology, as the introductory remarks of this section indicate, numbers cannot be overlooked with respect to either strengths or weaknesses. Middle Eastern anthropology has developed to the degree that it can and does, on an increasing scale, organize its own symposia at professional meetings in addition to providing numerous volunteered papers. Ninety one full- and part-time Middle Eastern anthropologists were listed in the American Anthropological Association's annual guide for 1972–1973, and over 250 social anthropologists with an interest in the Middle East were listed in the International Directory of Anthropologists of *Current Anthropology* for 1970. Thirty two Middle Eastern programs offering cultural and social anthropology were listed in the *Middle East Studies Association Bulletin* for 1972 (Vol. 6). In addition, anthropologists hold important positions as directors of research at the American University at Cairo, the University of Colorado, Harvard University, the University of Michigan, Tehran University, and the University of Texas.

PROBLEMS

The Social Anthropologist and the Study of Islam

Because anthropologists have greatly emphasized the unique, the esoteric, and the exotic in Middle Eastern culture, it is surprising and ironic to note that little attention has been given to the cultural tradition that has stamped its impress on all countries considered Middle Eastern and on all types of communities within them, be they nomadic, rural, or urban—the tradition of Islam. In the survey undertaken, when respondents were asked to list the title or subject of their present research, only seven of 58 responses mentioned Islam or religion in their titles, and none out of 48 mentioned Islam or religion as being a subject of past research. This is all the more interesting when one considers that since World War II, a considerable number of professionally trained anthropologists have conducted studies in Sunni Muslim communities (see above). For those who have been influenced by the so-called structural–functional, antihistorical, largely British, social anthropological school of thought associated with Malinowski and Radcliffe-Brown, such neglect may be understandable. I have heard British colleagues dissuade graduate students in anthropology from reading the Qur'an and the Traditions of the Prophet in the original Arabic on the grounds that it would require too much of an investment of time to master the intricacies of the grammar, and therefore the likelihood of really being able to understand such texts in an ungarbled fashion was small. I have been chastised by another anthropologist in a professional journal for daring to use the Qur'an and Qur'anic commentaries in an attempt to write about the social organization of tradition in a village in Jordan (Abu-Zahra, 1970); the implication of the criticism was that social anthropologists ought to stick to their own business—

the study of small communities—and not tamper with great cultural traditions which are best left to Orientalists and native theologians and jurisprudents. Of course, anthropologists will never achieve the proficiency in the written language achieved by the Islamic historian or Islamic philosopher or by scholars of Middle Eastern religions or literatures, and the understanding these scholars bring to the texts studied cannot be matched by the anthropologist. However, social anthropologists can make a unique contribution to the study of Islam by demonstrating how in fact the Islamic tradition is disseminated to thousands of local communities —villages, urban quarters, nomadic camps, suburbs, bidonvilles—and more important, by studying the process by which that tradition is accommodated to the thousands of diverse local customs that may range from extreme compatibility to extreme incompatibility with Muslim law and ethics. Now to analyze any great religious tradition in relation to its local environment assumes a reading knowledge of the language of its scriptures and related writings. It is interesting to note in this regard that of the 91 respondents who recorded their language proficiencies in Arabic, Persian, Pashto, and Turkish, only about half (43) stated that they could read the language. Next to Pashto the lowest percentage of literacy was in Arabic; whereas 9 of 13 were literate in Persian, and 8 of 10 in Turkish, only 25 of 63 were literate in Arabic.

If North American and European anthropologists persist in their reluctance to become literate in the languages and literatures of the Middle East, the social anthropology of Islam must and perhaps should become the special forte of insiders, that is, native Middle Easterners well versed in their own cultural and linguistic traditions. Fortunately, a large and ever growing number of native Middle Easterners are receiving training in anthropology and returning to the area to do research, as evidenced by the names of the authors of recent articles in professional journals and papers at professional meetings: Abu-Zahra, Abu-Zeid, Gavrielides, Fakhouri, Fazel, Farsoun, Hamalian, El-Shamy, El-Zein, Ansari, Naderi, Nakhleh, Khuri, Mohsen, "Amal" Vinogradoff, Lutfiyya, Eglar, and Yalman.

However, the reluctance of social anthropologists to deal with Islam in the Middle East in the way that social anthropologists have dealt with Hinduism in India or Christianity in Latin America is not just a reflection of a lack of advanced linguistic skills or the dogma of a particular school of anthropology. It is a reflection of the great demands made on time and effort to gain some degree of familiarity with the literatures that have communicated the Islamic tradition to the peoples of the Middle East. It is also a reflection of the intimidating character of a sacred tradition which has as a concomitant a substantial tradition of Western scholarship, namely, the Orientalist tradition. The anthropologist, however proficient in the language and however knowledgeable about the cultural background of the area, is always subject to self-doubt and to the whispers of his area colleagues: "But he really doesn't know Arabic, does he?"

Not completely irrelevant here is the historical image of Islam developed in the Christian West over the course of 1000 years: the view that Muhammad was a licentious hypocrite, that polygamy and concubinage indicated the affirmation of self-indulgence, and that Islam was a religion with a special propensity toward violence and power; the insistence upon misunderstanding the content and meanings of Islamic rituals, for example, ablutions amounted to false baptism (since one had to be clean on the inside), Friday congregational prayers were analogous to the Jewish Sabbath and the Christian Lord's Day, and the Muslim fast was a travesty of Lent. Of course, Norman Daniel, who has carefully documented the creation of this historical image in his *Islam and the West*, has also pointed out its subsequent alteration as Europe grew more powerful in *Islam, Europe and Empire*. However, the negative intellectual inheritance so long in the making has not disappeared. Indeed, as late as 1947 Sir Hamilton Gibb in reviewing Northrop's *The Meeting of East and West* said:

> The most striking example of this deficiency is offered by his treatment of Islam and the Mohammedan world. Indeed, the omission of any study of Islam as a whole and its relegation to a few superficial and inaccurate paragraphs in the context of India, brings the student of Islamic culture up with a jolt. How has it come about that a philosopher who is so obviously in earnest in his study of world cultures has found nothing significant to say about the spiritual and philosophical foundations of Islam? To some extent Islamic orientalists have themselves to blame, by their failure to furnish nonorientalists with adequate materials for a study of this kind. Yet it is difficult to believe that if Professor Northrop had searched the available sources, he would not have found enough to correct his excessively political interpretation of Islam with its fantastic picture of 80 million Mohammedan Indians "instilled over the centuries with the dictatorial, frenzied, aggressive militant theism of a Mohammed." This refusal to extend to Islam the benefit of that charity and largeness of mind which is accorded to every other system of thought and belief is not only regrettable in itself, however. Within Islam there were made some of the earliest attempts to solve the very problem which he has set before himself, the integration of the positivist religious intuition with a theoretical analysis of the structure of things.

Of course, neither Orientalists nor social anthropologists hold the images referred to above, but the fact that Western scholarship on Islam seems to be off in a corner, so to speak, in relation to scholarship on religious traditions at large does not encourage the commitment to the study of Islam by those for whom Islam is not the sole or dominating frame of reference.

Recognizing the historical background and the practical difficulties of the endeavor, but also the unique contribution that anthropologists can make because of the locus of their studies in particular communities, I believe that the social anthropology of Islam should proceed in four directions. First, we should direct ourselves to the collection of data on the local level regarding Islamic beliefs and rituals. Since 1959 when I recorded a number of sermons (khutbahs) on the occasion of the Friday congregational prayer in a Jordanian village, I have been searching for comparative data from other parts of the Middle East.[13] Today, 14 years later, I have yet to find a single sermon recorded by a social anthropologist working in the rural areas of the Middle East. Ironically, the single collection that has come to my attention is that (recorded in urban milieus) made by a political scientist, Ralph Crow, working at the American University in Beirut; interestingly enough, the collection was analyzed by another political scientist, Borthwick, at the University of Michigan (1969). It is surely strange that political scientists should find sermons significant for the study of politics, but that social anthropologists should not find them significant for the study of beliefs, social structure, and ethics. Though it must be the case that the insiders referred to above are in a better position to understand the classical Arabic in which such sermons are delivered, it must also be the case that it is exactly the insider who finds it most difficult to record and analyze them, unless, of course, he has heeded Clyde Kluckhohn's advice and undergone psychoanalysis before undertaking fieldwork. Thus the outsider does not simply bring the advantages of another perspective to the study of another culture; he brings a capacity and an inclination to record and analyze without the inhibitions placed upon him by the norms of the culture studied. And yet, "outsider" anthropologists have not utilized this natural advantage to good account. In a brilliant ethnographic and ethnological monograph, *The Religion of Java*, Geertz writes at length about the Muslim educational, political, and legal system, but spends only 10 pages on *Islamic* ritual—and 96 pages on various aspects of *non-Islamic* peasant rituals. In his *Islam Observed*, referred to above, Geertz deals with the learned men of Islam, the students of the Qur'an, traditions, and religious law—the producers of Friday sermons—in a chapter called, significantly, "The Scripturalist Interlude." The propagators of Orthodox Islamic doctrine are variously referred to as "pilgrim zealots" (in Indonesia) and "withdrawn pedants" (in Morocco), and the logical conclusion of the Scripturalist movement was "radical and uncompromising purism." As a result of the successful proselytization by Muslims (in Indonesia), "the spiritual balance of power which ... had kept the Indic, the Islamic, and tree-god minded, if not integrated, at least out of one another's way, was definitively and, so far as I can see, irretrievably lost." I think Geertz, in common with many other anthropologists who have worked in the Middle East, has viewed the indigenous cultural traditions as being somehow better—for they lament their passing—and the

Islamic tradition as being imposed and somehow less worthy—for they regret its victory. Thus in Morocco, the symbol for the "classical style" is a marabout, al-Yûsî, and not an Islamic scholar, and the symbol of the "classical style" in Indonesia is a mystic, Sunan Kalidjaga, and not an Islamic scholar. The indigenous tradition has been the tribal tradition, nomadic in the first instance, sedentary in the second, and although there has been an increasing tendency to study peasants wherever they are and an incipient tendency to take account of urban life, anthropologists continue to head for the hills in large numbers (Iran is the most recent example of this phenomenon). In light of this ethical predilection and geographic concentration, the paucity of data on Islamic belief and ritual can better be understood, though deplored.

Once data on Islamic ritual and belief are collected, how can they form the basis of a social anthropology of Islam? Three possibilities stand out: first, we can study "the social organization of tradition." Since Redfield first advanced the idea, it has, in the Middle East at least, remained a programmatic statement rather than a guide to ongoing research. The basic assumption that Redfield made was that both the great (here, Islam) and the little (here, tribal or peasant) tradition had to be taken account of, and the accommodation of each to the other, as an ongoing process, had to be investigated without reducing either one to the other. I wish to suggest here that "the social organization of tradition" does not mean merely the concentration on belief, to be precise, the accommodation of beliefs (including the possibilities of their complete acceptance, complete rejection, juxtaposition, reinterpretation, etc.) as Redfield suggested, but the relationship of the accommodation of belief to the accommodation of action—to the process of "social organization" as Firth conceived of it. Thus the success or failure to achieve political accommodations between particular groups in particular situations (say, in a case of honor) is intimately related to the working out of an accommodation between beliefs (say, regarding the modesty of women), and between ideal and practical norms, or even the necessity of having to work out such an accommodation (for examples, see Antoun, 1968). Accommodation may come in the field of action by ordering norms among different elements in the population, by rituals of reversal, by women's management of custom, or by the development of functional analogues; intellectual accommodation can also occur in many ways, most of them still to be discovered by research.

In this endeavor Middle Eastern anthropologists can follow the lead of the social anthropologists of the Indian subcontinent. Singer, for instance, in analyzing the congregational devotional worship of an incipient Hindu cult in Madras (Singer, 1966), developed a particular mode of data collection and analysis. In order to determine the meaning of the ritual, in this case devoted to Krishna, he first observed the ritual and the social relations entailed by it; then he questioned learned men and examined scriptures for theological interpretations; finally he solicited explanations from the ordinary participants in the ritual. In this particular case he discovered that the story of Krishna and the *gopis* (milkmaids) found in the Bhagavata Purana was taken as a parable of the individual's spiritual odyssey and was reflected in the critical ritual acts of the congregational worship service. Marriott, in the same volume (see Singer, 1966), focused on the social relational significance of the greatest religious celebration of the year, that dedicated to Krishna, and found that it was the single occasion when all significant social relations of deference were reversed, whether they were of caste, kinship, sex, or marriage. In these two cases, in order to extract the meaning of rituals or to analyze their significance for the social structure, it was necessary to resort to the exegesis of the learned men of the community and to the scriptures of the religion as well as to the observations of the ritual situation by the anthropologist. In both cases it became apparent, as I think it must when the analysis is detailed and thorough, that the social organization of traditions is a complex process involving, for instance in Marriott's case, universalization, parochialization, reinterpretation and revival, and mingling local, regional, national, and quite remote religious movements.

To speak of *a* great tradition and *a* little tradition as global concepts in confrontation seldom, if ever, reflects the particular situation. In the Middle East Islam, Judaism, and Christianity are separate and yet historically related traditions. Often they are all represented in a particular community. Moreover, they are competing or accommodating with other great traditions, such as those espoused by secular nationalist bureaucrats or raconteurs of tribal lore. It is this accommodation of one great tradition to another, as it is worked out in thousands of local contexts, be they guesthouses, *hammams*, suburbs, grocery shops, bidonvilles, coffeehouses, or bazaars, as much as the processes of universalization and parochialization of the single great tradition in its own peculiar contexts, be they mosques, *zawiyyas*, *ḥussayniyyas*, *imamzades*, or *zurkhanes*, that is the subject of the social organization of tradition.

The third direction that the social anthropology of Islam can take is the analysis of the texts that heretofore have been the exclusive domain of historians, philologists, and students of belles lettres, as well as the reanalysis of the secondary works based on these texts from a social anthropological perspective. It would not be an exaggeration to say that anything done in this direction will constitute genuine pioneering, since hardly anything has been done. Wolf's analysis of the origins of Mecca (1951), though a noble effort, is marred by its rather rigid adherence to an evolutionary perspective and its failure to consult primary sources. Eickelman's analysis of Musaylima (1967) in terms of competing prophecy and "revitalization" is noteworthy but hampered by the lack of data. Ironically, the best efforts in this direction have come from the Orientalists themselves, including Ayalon (1967),

Chelhod (1964), Hurgronje (1888), Lewis (1970), and Watt (1962). In Watt's book *Muhammad at Medina*, there is a brilliant chapter on "the reform of the social structure"; moreover, in the excursus of the book, interesting information is compiled regarding such subjects as slaves and freedmen, marriage and the family, *zakât* and *sadâqa*, and Muhammad's marriages. Unfortunately, Watt's analysis suffers, as expected, from his lack of professional training in social anthropology; he confuses filiation with descent, makes questionable inferences about social structure on the basis of philological evidence, and attributes to matrilineal descent what might be better understood as the concomitants of complex patrilineal descent groups. However, his social anthropological analysis remains far superior to anything undertaken by anthropologists working with historical materials. More and more these materials are becoming available in translation, e.g., Guillaume's translation of Ibn Isḥâq's *The Life of Muhammad.* Surely the transition from the pre-Islamic social structure and belief system to the Islamic social structure and belief system is worthy of some attention by social anthropologists not only for its historical importance but also for the paradigm it displaced—or reinterpreted or accommodated or universalized—and the paradigm it laid down for future generations of Middle Easterners.

The fourth direction for the development of the social anthropology of Islam ties in directly with two burgeoning areas of research in anthropology itself, the study of local politics and interethnic relations. It is the study of Islamic movements as informal interest groups, usually attached to particular occupations and serving essentially political purposes. In Africa, this study is often related to the process of retribalization by which an occupational group reorganizes its traditional customs or develops new customs under traditional symbols. Pioneering work in this field has been done by Abner Cohen, who has demonstrated how the conversion of the Hausa of Ibadan to the Tijâniyya order with the accompanying localization and intensification of ritual and social activity enabled the Hausa to defend their interests in a dominant Yoruba milieu (Cohen, 1969). Here the parochialization of a great Islamic tradition served to strengthen one Muslim group against another, to confirm its identity, and to nullify the advantage of numbers possessed by the dominant group. This example demonstrates the three directions for research outlined above are not unrelated in the analysis of particular situations. It is just when the social organization of tradition is handled in a historical perspective and in relation to some process such as politics or ethnicity that the analysis becomes most significant. Unfortunately for students of the Middle Eastern heartland Cohen's earlier analysis of Arabs in Israel (1965) does not follow this mode of analysis; the fact that the populations studied were "Arabs" and "Muslims" is somehow lost in the shuffle of preoccupation with the analysis of *ḥamûlas* and the tracing of a supposed line of development from a "Joint Estate Period" to "The Mandatory Period" to the "Ḥamûla Period." This third politically and ethnically oriented approach will yield new insights into such diverse movements as the rise of the Safavid order in Iran and the Black Muslims in the United States—if only social anthropologists will turn to them with the same degree of fervor that they display in the study of cousin marriage.

Exotica: The Museum Approach to the Middle East

Related to the above-mentioned problem is that of the social anthropologist's focus on the unique and apparently esoteric aspects of Middle Eastern culture. A pertinent example is the attention given in professional anthropological journals to the "institution of father's brother's daughter's marriage" and to the practice of "lineage endogamy"; Barth (1954), Patai (1955), Ayoub (1959), Murphy and Kasden (1959), Markarius (1960), Patai (1962), Patai (1965), Gilbert and Hammel (1966), Murphy and Kasden (1967), Goldberg (1967), and Khuri (1970). In most of these papers, there has been no full recognition that an analysis of marriage on the basis of ethical norms (rules of "cousin right" or "cousin preference") has implications quite different from an analysis on the basis of marriage incidence, both for the kinds of marriage pattern resulting and the explanations offered for them. If there had been such recognition, it seems strange that not a single author systematically compared statements regarding norms of marriage (whom persons ought to marry) and statements of whom they say they do marry (suppositional data) with the actual incidence of marriages in particular communities. Murphy and Kasden, (1957) for instance, base their analysis on norms although they admit the necessity of rigorously collected census data "... for a more complete resolution of problems raised in this paper"; Patai, although reviewing the literature with regard to norms and incidence, and thereby pointing out the substantial discrepancy between them (statistical incidence varies from 43% in tribal Kurdistan to 2% in Lebanon), explains the discrepancy in terms of diffusion and Westernization rather than social structure and "social organization" (in Firth's terms); Khuri, the only author who presents detailed data on the incidence of cousin marriage (and not just father's brother's daughter's marriage) in a particular community, does not present similar data on the normative and suppositional aspects of marriage. What is surprising, then, even at the descriptive level, is a failure to provide data detailed enough for refined analysis.[14] Aside from Murphy and Kasden, who stipulate a societal point of view, it is also surprising that most authors fail to specify the point of view of the analysis: Barth's analysis clearly reflects the point of view of the fathers of bride and groom; Patai (1962), when he discusses the preservation of property within the lineage, reflects the point of view of the girl's father; when he discusses the preexisting tie of sympathy, he reflects the bride's point of view. Only Khuri systematically reviews the sociopsychological consequences of marriage from the points of view of a number of dyads, although even here the weight of the analysis is primarily with respect to the bridegroom and secondarily the bride, in relation to their parents-in-law.

A further source of confusion, still at the descriptive level, is the failure of authors to distinguish between rules of descent (defining membership in particular groups), descent-phrased rules (such as succession or inheritance), the functions (political, economic, religious, recreational) attached to groups defined by the rule of descent, and the ideology of descent together with its underlying values. No one of the above four attributes implies any one of the other three, although all four often coincide. Thus when Patai (1965) suggests that endogamous unilineal descent groups do not disappear or become reduced in importance with political centralization or occupational differentiation, as Fortes (1953) suggests, what he is really saying is that the ideology of descent is not sloughed off with such developments, but on the contrary, may become accentuated as the appropriate ideologies of urban economic associations on the one hand and overarching political structures on the other.

Explanations of the persistence of father's brother's daughter's (FBD) marriage and its endogamous extensions seem to be of four kinds: in terms of an overall societal marriage model (Murphy and Kasden), role conflict (Barth and Khuri), demographic-spatial limitations (Ayoub, Gilbert and Hammel, and Goldberg), and diffusion (mainly Patai, but including all others cited above with the exception of Khuri). Patai, in particular, explains the increasing incidence of rules of "cousin preference" over rules of "cousin right" in terms of the geographic location of the ethnic group or its position of "cultural marginality." The assumption behind such explanations is that patrilateral parallel cousin marriage diffused like an item of material culture—sherd or a black tent—with the spread of Islam; thus groups on the margin of the Islamic heartland as well as religious minorities within it display much lower incidence of such cultural rules. This rough and ready age-area hypothesis has been accepted by Murphy and Kasden (1967) and has become a commonplace assumption of the major comparative works on kinship and marriage, e.g., Murdock (1949). Only Khuri correctly states that FBD marriage is prescribed by neither the Qur'an nor the Traditions of the Prophet. Indeed, Patai, the chief proponent of the diffusionist thesis, presents much evidence against his own thesis. He notes that al-Ghazzali, the famous Muslim jurist and theologian, opposed close cousin marriage; more important, in the two cases cited (Patai, 1962, pp. 151 and 165) in which Islamic jurists played a part, they opposed cousin marriage rather than supported it. However, since myth has a life of its own, and absorbs or emasculates the facts to serve its own ends, the mythical connection between Islam and FBD marriage will surely receive future affirmation.

In a report on the state of the art of Middle Eastern anthropology, why is a fuss made about father's brother's daughter's marriage in particular and endogamous unilineal descent groups in general? The first reason is precisely to point out that a fuss *has* been made, despite the low statistical incidence of such marriages in most communities (10–15%) and despite its being only one of a number of marriage preferences. Why a variable statistical incidence of marriage and a single marriage norm among many other norms which in different locales perform a variety of functions, latent and manifest, should be treated as a single institution relevant to a particular problem is puzzling, unless one recognizes that, just as much of the early interest in the Middle East by travelers and political officers focused on the exotic (e.g., the Bedouin nomad), the later anthropological interest has focused on what appear to be the unique and esoteric. The second purpose is to note the lack of genuine case studies, the virtual disinterest in process, and the absence of that flesh and blood component which we all know to be involved in the contraction, maintenance, and dissolution of all marriages. Instead of treating this preference in relation to all the other preferences—for the MBD, for the FSD, for the MSD, for more distant cousins, for fellow villagers, for strangers—and analyzing the social structural, sociopsychological, economic, and political factors governing such choices, in particular communities (in order to form the basis for enlightened comparison), anthropologists have isolated an "institution" (FBD marriage) and its accompanying "problem" (lineage endogamy).[15] The isolation of some data from other pertinent sets of data violates the holistic approach traditional in social anthropology; the focus on a particular item of culture content almost to the point of its reification leads away from the most significant development in modern social anthropology, i.e., the study of process rather than culture content on the one hand, or formal structure on the other. In fact, descent groups in the Middle East are exogamous as well as endogamous, and therefore the very formulation of the problem in terms of "endogamy" banishes important data (relating to preferences as well as incidence) to the background. The collection of data, then, should be on all marriage forms rather than a few, and the analysis of such forms should be not in isolation from but in relation to one another and in terms of a decision model which outlines the possibilities of choice, the limitations upon it, and the factors and processes that transform marriage from one kind of institution into another.[16] It would be a shame if anthropologists who have been trained to cast the net of inquiry in a wide and sweeping manner in the field milieu should now restrict the scope of their studies of marriage in either the collection of data or its analysis. To quote a colleague, "The Middle East is not a museum into which one can pass to study one apparently exotic artifact in isolation from its overall relational context."[17]

Ambivalence Within the Discipline

In the preceding two sections, it has been suggested that the state of the art of Middle Eastern anthropology is related mainly to things Middle Eastern rather than to things anthropological. That is, it is the Middle Eastern anthropologist's preoccupation with the unique, the esoteric, and the romantic aspects of the culture and the negative popular image of a hostile Islam that accounts for the state of the art. It could also be argued that the cultural antiquity of the region requires a relatively greater commitment to the study of history and language and, consequently, a lesser commitment to the study of social anthropological theory and method. A correlate would be that those who have entered Middle Eastern anthropology are primarily interested in the area and only secondarily interested in the discipline. One could argue on a more practical level that the relative unconcern of the Middle Eastern anthropologist with intellectual issues of current concern, both generally and within the discipline (see tables in Appendix I), is related to the emphasis established by the U.S. Government and private American foundations on producing area specialists and the energetic action of American universities in furthering such goals. One could also argue that as a result of all this, the atmosphere has been created in which Middle Eastern anthropologists often find their intellectual peers among other Middle Eastern specialists rather than other anthropologists. With each of the above-mentioned factors probably related in an interdependent and self-reinforcing manner, one could then explain the preponderant interest in Middle Eastern ethnography (rather than ethnology and social anthropology) and in particular ethnic groups and countries to the exclusion of others (see above for a discussion of this trend and see also the appropriate tables in Appendix I).

The tabulated results of the questionnaire do not support some of the assumptions made above (see Table 9, Appendix I). Anthropologists were asked how they became interested in Middle Eastern anthropology and whether they were interested in the Middle East before they were interested in anthropology, or vice versa. Fifty-one out of 83 respondents stated they were in the discipline *before* they were interested in the area. The anthropologists who filled in the questionnaire were also asked to list their outstanding publications; a large proportion of such publications were published in journals. These journals were classified as to whether they were (1) Middle Eastern journals, (2) anthropological journals, or (3) other journals. It was discovered that the number of titles published in anthropological journals

(35) was slightly more than the number of titles in Middle Eastern journals (32); but by far the largest number of titles (74) appeared in journals that were neither Middle Eastern nor anthropological in their orientation; these journals included, to list a few, the *California Folklore Quarterly*, *Germanic Review*, *The Scotsman*, *Music Council*, *Health Education Journal*, *Journal of the American Institute of Planners*, *Proceedings of the American Philosophy Society*, *Urban Affairs Quarterly*, *Jewish Journal of Sociology*, *Mankind Quarterly*, *Journal of Economic and Social History of the Orient*, *International Journal of the Family*, *Speculum*, *International Journal of Psychitry*, *The Geographical Journal*, and *Bulletin De La Societe D'Histoire Du Maroc*. Thus this group of Middle Eastern anthropologists is not provincial with respect to either areal or disciplinary interests, at least as far as publication goes.

The problem then is not entirely, perhaps not even mainly, Middle Eastern; the problem is also one built into the discipline of anthropology. Evidence for this view is the fact that in those issues of intellectual concern and in those theoretical problem areas where Middle Eastern anthropologists have lagged behind, for example, in comparative studies of values—particularly honor, colonialism, and sex roles (see preceeding section for a discussion of the tabulation of the questionnaire)—anthropologists in general have also lagged behind their colleagues in the other social sciences and humanities. For instance, anthropologists in general, not just Middle Eastern anthropologists, have been absorbed in the study of kinship roles and occupational roles without paying much attention to the roles "man" and "woman."

As was mentioned in the introduction, the built-in problem of anthropology is that many anthropologists define themselves at least in part as "social" anthropologists and as such are interested in the development of statements of general validity regarding such subjects as social control, social stratification, political power, or social change; such a commitment implies at the very least a comparative view in both description and analysis, and at the fullest, explicit cross-cultural studies within a regional or worldwide context. At the same time, most "social" anthropologists also define themselves as "cultural" anthropologists. That is, they recognize a commitment to the study of culture and of cultural patterns. Indeed, many anthropologists become interested in particular theoretical problems as a result of their experience in a particular field locale and not as a result of a prior commitment self-consciously cultivated in the halls of the university. The "cultural" anthropologist recognizes that his first obligation is to describe and analyze the "cultural focus" of the people he studies (that is, the ideas, beliefs, values, customs, myths, and attitudes that *they* regard important and that *they* have elaborated, rather than to validate particular hypotheses related to particular theoretical problem areas. This inclination is in line with the humanistic and philosophic goals of the cultural anthropologist (he is interested in human nature)—goals that always influence his social scientific aims. It is only at a late stage in his research, often only after a second field trip—over a period of 10 or 15 years—that he addresses himself to the particular theoretical problem areas his fellow social scientists regard as important, e.g., the circulation of elites, urbanization, deviance, exchange systems, or modernization. Thus significant publication about these problems is long delayed. Since Middle Eastern anthropology developed much later than in other geographic areas, e.g., than in Africa or Polynesia, the relative amount of its research has been small, the incidence of publication restricted, and the theoretical importance of its conclusions minor. This state of affairs may be felicitous since the development of theoretical problem areas and the delineation of particular hypotheses related to them can come only after gaining the corrected vision that comes with understanding the cultural patterns characteristic of particular communities and societies. Thus the slow, steady, and somewhat unexciting growth of Middle Eastern anthropology has its peculiar advantages.

The built-in problem of sociocultural anthropology is not related to its history and intellectual commitments alone. It relates also to the structure of departments of anthropology, particularly in the United States. These departments are conceived as being composed of four subdisciplines: prehistoric archaeology, linguistics, physical anthropology, and social and cultural anthropology. Within each of these subdisciplines the expectation is that the widest possible range of theoretical interests is represented; thus it is not often the case that a social anthropologist has a colleague working in the same department with the same set of theoretical interests. Moreover, in the recruitment of area specialists, a wide representation of various areas is sought rather than a concentration on one or two. This arrangement has a particularly detrimental effect on Middle Eastern anthropologists, who because of their small absolute numbers are siphoned into different departments across the country and hardly ever have another colleague in the same department with the same area interest. They meet with them only once or twice a year at professional meetings. Some have argued that high-quality scholarship is a product not of numbers but rather of sophistication in training; I would argue that it is a product of both. Personal communication and feedback among anthropologists are particularly important owing to the added requirement of fieldwork, which results in a long hiatus between research and publication, not unusually amounting to 10 years or more. Thus personal contact is the only means by which the anthropologist can become aware of the latest developments in the field. It is not a matter of chance that the significant theoretical "schools" of American anthropology have developed at the very largest academic institutions where the size of the department has permitted some degree of replication of both theoretical and areal interests. An ameliorating factor is the presence of a Center for Middle Eastern Studies on the university campus; if there is such a center the anthropologist at least has the oppotunity of maintaining an active link with others who have the same area interest and, more important, the opportunity to improve his linguistic proficiency and his historical understanding of the area. In Europe, particularly England, the problem of institutional organization and numbers is less critical since departments of social anthropology or ethnology tend to reinforce both theoretical and area interests, creating in many cases an active community of scholarship with its implications for excellence in teaching and research.

Problems of the Native Middle Eastern Anthropologist

Thus far the problems of the development of Middle Eastern anthropology have been discussed from a Western point of view, more specifically from the viewpoint of Western anthropologists interested in the Middle East. The development of Middle Eastern anthropology must also be discussed from the point of view of the native Middle Eastern anthropologist. In order to discuss problems and priorities from this point of view it is necessary to review briefly the distinctive birth and growth of the discipline in the Middle East and current teaching, research, and publication in the area. For lack of space and personal knowledge the following comments are confined to the growth of the discipline in Egypt and Iran.[18]

Anthropology is a relatively recent import into Egypt, other parts of the Arab world, and Iran. In Egypt, although a number of eminent British anthropologists taught in "The Egyptian University" (now Cairo University) in the 1930s, e.g., Hocart, Evans-Pritchard, and Peristiany, they were regarded as "professors of sociology," and in fact they taught in the departments of geography, philosophy, and sociology. This was not unusual in that the French school of sociology identified with the name of Durkheim was and still is dominant in Egypt, and its orientation was toward philosophy on the one hand and social problems on the other. It was not until 1947 when Radcliffe-Brown came to Alexandria University that the word "anthropology" was used by social scientists in Egypt, although Radcliffe-Brown occupied the chair of sociology there. Apart from introducing anthropology at the graduate level, Radcliffe-Brown established the "Institute of Social Sciences" at Alexandria University to provide graduate courses in anthropology and sociology. But the first chair in anthropology was not established in Egypt until 1970. By 1973 four chairs of anthropology had been established there, one in Kuwait, but none in other Arab countries, although native

Middle Easterners teach anthropology in a number of universities in other countries, including the American University of Beirut, the American University at Cairo, and universities in Baghdad, Basra, Benghazi, and Kuwait.

Anthropology in Egypt was marked from the very beginning by intensive field research. Since the hypotheses were largely derived from the writings of French sociologists there was considerable continuity between the earlier sociological tradition and the new fieldwork-oriented tradition. Thus anthropological studies have never been simple ethnographic or descriptive accounts of the institutions or communities studied. As an example, the first M.A. thesis in anthropology accepted at Alexandria (by Abou-Zeid) dealt with "Funeral Rites among the Moslems of Egypt" and drew its theoretical argument from the writings of Hertz, Van Gennep, and Radcliffe-Brown. Most recently, Egyptian anthropologists have been directing their attention, and will probably do so to an increasing degree, to social and economic problems related to Egypt's most pressing problem, overpopulation; thus interest grows in family structure and family planning, urbanization, industrialization, and the resettlement of peasants in newly reclaimed lands. It is not accidental then that the past and ongoing research carried out in the Department of Sociology and Anthropology at Alexandria University and the Social Science Research Center of the American University at Cairo is oriented to such problems, as witnessed by the subjects of Ph.D. theses, e.g., "New Nubia," "The New Valley," childhood and socialization, and law and order in rural communities. Unfortunately, most of the theses produced by the national Egyptian universities on these subjects remain unpublished.

In Iran, as in Egypt, the French sociological tradition has dominated the development not only of academic work in the social sciences but also for a time political life as evidenced by the fact that a number of the French-educated sociologist-philosophers became ministers in Mossadegh's government. For over 20 years sociology was taught as a course at the School of Literature at Tehran University for those who were working toward a B.A. degree in philosophy and education. It was only in the fall of 1958 that the Institute for Social Studies and Research offering an M.A. degree in social sciences was created. Courses taught at the Institute included general sociology, demography, economics, social psychology, ethnology, statistics, and research methods in "the social sciences." The Institute carried out a wide variety of research projects organized around its eight research sections—urban studies, rural studies, demographic studies, tribal studies, social psychology, sociology of Iran, and political science. Representative titles of publications of the Institute, nearly all of which are in Persian, include the following: *The Social Psychology of Industry in Iran; Birth, Death, and Sex in Society and Popular Culture in Iran;* "*The Carpet Industry* (five volumes)*; A Cost Effectiveness Report on the Work-Oriented Adult Literacy Pilot Project; The Case* *of Isfahan; "Socioeconomic Studies of Khorosan, Azarbaijan, and Bandar Abbas Rural Areas* (30 volumes)*; The Socio-economic Impact of Land Reform in Seven Provinces; The Rural Cooperatives in Seven Regions; Study on the Fertility and Some Demographic Characteristics of Married Women in Four Rural Zones of Iran; Employment and Underemployment in Iran; Shah-Sovan: an Example of Sedentarization with Cultural Transplantation, Informal Education of Children in Traditional Societies of Iran;* and *Study on the Parliamentary Deputies.* The Institute also has seven monographs on six tribes of Kohguiluye, seven ethnographic documentary 16-mm color films, and 500 taped interviews of women's attitudes toward number of children, sex of children, and family planning. At this time, in addition to a number of other projects, the Institute is carrying out a study of squatters in 16 cities in Iran.

Aside from the growth of anthropology out of a dominant orientation toward French sociology, the growth of anthropology in Egypt and Iran is similar in two other important respects. First, anthropology departments are usually joint departments with sociology, as in Egypt, or with sociology, demography, and cooperative studies in the same faculty, as in Iran; this trend toward close multidisciplinary research is becoming even more pronounced as the applied aspects of these disciplines become more important to Middle Eastern academicians and government planners. Second, research priorities in all social sciences will be established more and more by the national governments, which alone have the capacity for funding research.

This consideration leads directly to a discussion of the problems involved in the development of Middle Eastern anthropology in the Middle East. The Middle Eastern countries are all undergoing directed social change; the developing private sector is supported and financed to a great extent by the government. Thus all research priorities have to take account of government priorities and also the problems of the people in urban, rural, and tribal areas. Research proposals that do not take account of the orientation toward current problems or practical solutions for them are unlikely to be funded. The situation is even more structured: because all research institutes are funded by the government, all research proposals emanate from it. A practical problem often arises when government research goals are partly oriented toward the realization of ideological commitments rather than well-conceived research goals or practical solutions, and for this very reason, the recommendations of researchers based on substantiated research are often ignored.

There are some very practical problems involving time and money that face native Middle Eastern anthropologists dedicated to research that do not face their Western colleagues, at least not to the same degree. In order to make ends meet Middle Eastern social scientists are forced either to enter the government service or to teach; research as such is not highly rewarded and is often assumed to be an obligation without provision for added time or supplementary grants; thus, for instance, one finds that the graduates of the Department of Social Anthropology and Sociology of Alexandria University are scattered in teaching positions over the whole of the Arab world; although this may be advantageous to the countries concerned, it certainly reduces the effectiveness of the social scientific effort in Egypt. In Iran, the overwhelming majority of those with B.A. or M.A. degrees in social science are immediately recruited by the ministries of the government, most of which have added "survey and planning" sections.[19] Again, although this development is advantageous for the government and the nation it retards the growth of academic disciplines. With regard to publication, social scientists produce and translate numerous introductory texts rather than monographs based on their own research.

There is also a distinctive social psychological problem often affecting native Middle Eastern anthropologists. Since they were Western-trained, they taught their students and encouraged the type of research that was currently of importance in the universities at the time they earned their degrees, such as bridewealth, kinship systems, honor and shame, myth, and such general theoretical orientations as social structure and social control. In the present academic and national climate of opinion such subjects and orientations are regarded as intellectual luxuries; thus anthropologists find themselves torn between the desire to fulfill their purely theoretical academic interests and the equal desire to meet the needs of their society.

From the point of view of the native Middle Eastern anthropologist, what are the solutions to some of the problems mentioned above? First, it seems wise to recognize the constraints established both by national governments and by the climate of opinion among intellectuals, which hold that certain kinds of research are more urgent than others. Second, related to the above, it might be worthwhile to carry out a study of the research priorities of government, public, and social scientists to discover areas of convergence in which profitable and motivated research could be supported by all segments. Third, whatever the research focus or methodology, research should help the local social scientist deal with problems that are of national significance, whether that help is primarily of a theoretical, methodological, fact gathering or practical nature. This may not be as problematic as the Western anthropologist might imagine, since most anthropologists would not find it difficult to relate their research to some aspect of urbanization, industrialization, rural development, nomadism, or family structure, or to such institutions as education, administration, or Islam. The fact that Middle Eastern governments favor practical problem-oriented research does not necessarily prevent the researcher from undertaking his own basic research.

From a Middle Eastern point of view perhaps the most pressing problem is the lack of time. Although the Middle Eastern anthropologist and sociologist often is able to gather data, whether as part of the work of a research institute or independently, he rarely has time to analyze those data. Thus both in Iran and Egypt a great deal of data has been gathered—many volumes filled with social and economic data from various locales—but remains unanalyzed. The analysis of these data, particularly from a comparative point of view, would be very significant both from a social scientific and a practical policy point of view. Private Western foundations should be encouraged to subsidize individual Middle Eastern scholars to undertake such a task. Alternatively, they could support exchange of professors between Middle Eastern and Western universities, with the researcher analyzing his own materials during the first part of the year, and delivering lectures to the host institution at the end of the year. Western private foundations and governments should also be encouraged to subsidize translation and publication of the growing body of anthropological and sociological literature in Middle Eastern languages. Finally, joint research between Middle Eastern anthropologists and their Western colleagues would, perhaps, help resolve the practical difficulties of a Western anthropologist doing research in a new and often less receptive climate of opinion and also the practical economic difficulties (time and money) of the Middle Eastern anthropologist with a commitment to research.

FUTURE DIRECTIONS OF RESEARCH

Ethnicity, Class, and the Mosaic

There is a growing interest in ethnic groups and interethnic relations among Middle Eastern anthropologists; this trend is marked whether one examines the tables on past, present, and future research, on opinions as to directions of future research, or on subjects of outstanding publications; interestingly enough, this trend runs parallel to that in the discipline of anthropology at large. It might be expected, then, that in this theoretical problem area Middle Eastern anthropology would be abreast of the discipline, particularly since one of the first major works that made ethnicity a central interest was Carleton Coon's *Caravan*. Coon's book, still the best popular introduction to the Middle East as a culture area, was published in 1951 and antedated the recent interest in ethnic groups and boundaries by more than 15 years. In this book, Coon discussed the Middle East as a "mosaic" of peoples and noted that although ethnic heterogeneity was by no means unique to the Middle East, the correlation of ethnic groups with the division of labor and the enshrinement of that ethnic division of labor in cultural difference, that is, styles of life (e.g., distinctive clothing, physical appearance, gait, speech, education, leisure activities, diet, and days of worship and rest), were unique in their degree of accentuation and defined the Middle East as a culture area. Coon thus established a framework, albeit metaphorical, for the study of ethnic groups and various other minority groups and social types (since the ethnic division of labor was only one part of a fivefold division of labor) that at the same time allowed for the diversity of Middle Eastern cultures and communities but also stressed their integration both historically and synchronically, the "cement" of the mosaic being Islam on the sociocultural level and the marketplace on the socioeconomic level.

The remarkable fact about the research on ethnic groups alluded to in the preceding section is that it has almost completely ignored Coon's framework for study and concentrated on the descriptive characteristics of particular ethnic groups, the stereotypes held by particular ethnic groups of other ethnic groups, or the assimilation of ethnic groups into the national polity.[20] This gap in the literature may be partly attributable to Coon, himself, since he stated that he was *not* describing Middle Eastern society as it existed today but rather as it had existed in the nineteenth century. His theoretical pretext for doing so was made explicit:

> A culture in transition is hard to describe and harder to understand; we must find some period of history when the culture was, relatively speaking, at rest. Then when we know the background, we can bring in the automobiles and the movies and the parliaments and the radio broadcasts; and the presence of these bits of plastic and broken glass in our mosaic will no longer obscure the plan of the picture. [Coon, 1951, p. 8]

Many anthropologists and a majority of other social scientists seem to have focused on "the bits of plastic and broken glass" rather than on "the mosaic," viewing the latter as passé.

There may be another reason, however, why anthropologists now ignore Coon's framework for description and analysis. The units he depicted as being integrated in "the mosaic" were often discrete types or stereotypes, e.g., "nomads," "villages," "towns." As research has proceeded, and largely on the basis of this trilogy,[21] it has become increasingly apparent that (1) many social structural units historically and currently span these three social types and they include a wide variety of institutions such as tribal segments, religious parishes, and national administrative units; and, perhaps more importantly, that (2) to approach the description and analysis of Middle Eastern society in terms of this trilogy directs attention away from important processes, e.g., modernization, integration, migration, parochialization, and universalization.

This tendency to ignore Coon's mosaic model,[22] the above caveats expected, is one of the most unfortunate tendencies in Middle Eastern studies for three reasons. First, Coon's model provides a framework for studying both the diversity of Middle Eastern cultures and social structures and their integration without reducing such diversity to the "thing of shreds and patches" that an approach by diffusion must entail.[23] Second, Coon's mosaic framework must eventually lead away from the ethnocentric interests of scholars in particular social types (e.g., cities, villages, or nomadic camps) and in particular ethnic groups (e.g., Arabs, Berbers, Jews, Persians, or Turks) and to a consideration of their interaction in an overall societal framework. One of the most alarming discoveries of the empirical review of research cited above is the tiny number of anthropologists who have done work in geographical areas representing more than one linguistic tradition or more than one social type; the tendency is to work on Arabs, Jews, or Turks, or on peasants, nomads, or townsmen. The mosaic model carried to its logical conclusion is interested in the diversity of types only in relation to their socioeconomic and cultural integration. Third and most importantly, the mosaic model, if approached from a critical point of view and with a concern for its detailed working out in particular contexts, can lead to a better understanding of social change and in particular to an understanding of the critical transition from societies based on an ethnic division of labor to those based on differences of economic status, class, and modern ideology. A number of questions immediately arise given this point of view: was and is the ethnic division of labor in the Middle East confined mainly to the villages and traditional urban quarters of preindustrial economies of the nineteenth century, as Coon explicitly suggested, or does it have a wider incidence both historically and synchronically as Coon's intuition perceived (otherwise he would not have written the book)? If the ethnic division of labor persists and it is not centered around the passing of consummate skills from one generation to the next, in what contexts, other than traditional craft, does it survive? Has the large extended family associated with the ethnic division of labor disappeared or has it adapted to the circumstances of modern enterprise, as some recent research suggests?[24] More generally, has the ideology of kinship which has traditionally articulated the social ties of members of urban associations (e.g., religious brotherhoods, guilds, rifle companies, or gangs) as well as rural social structures lapsed in favor of other types of ideologies? Here the study of the mosaic naturally leads to an examination of the process of urbanization of rural peoples or, contrarily, "villagization" of cities.[25] To be more specific, if one assumes, as LeTourneau (1957) did for some cities in North Africa, that there are three types of urban population—long-term urbanites, fixed outsiders (who return from time to time to their place of origin), and a floating population (who come in crises such as drought and war and return when the crisis is over)—then it may be hypothesized that it is among the second group, fixed outsiders, that the ethnic division of labor remains strongest; it is this group that (1) regularly rejuvenates ties with ethnic groups in the hinterlands and (2) values the continuation of such ties for the social security it provides on the rural side and the job recruitment opportunities it affords on the urban side.

Finally, a study of the mosaic and in particular, its manifestations in the traditional pattern of ethnic urban quarters naturally leads to the important question: under what conditions do "ethnic" quarters become transformed into "class" quarters, and perhaps more realistically, what interesting in-between types occur, and what are the processes accompanying their development? Or to put the question in another form, at what point does the ethnic group label cease to signify ethnicity? After the group stops living together? Marrying together? Visiting together? Working at the same occupation? Wearing the same dress? When viewed in these terms Coon's metaphorical model becomes not merely a basis for the description of isolated social units but rather a means of analyzing important processes of a society in transition.[26]

Sex Roles

Unlike ethnicity, which has been a focus of strong and continuing interest, the study of sex roles, including related topics such as honor, has been consistently neglected (see Appendix I, Tables 3, 5, 6, and 8); thus when respondents were asked what problems were being researched and what research designs were being used (Table 8), not a single individual stipulated sex roles or honor as a reply. Women have not been entirely neglected in the social anthropological lieterature, as Eglar's splendid (1960) study of the critical economic role played by women in a Punjabi village indicates; students of culture and personality, Prothro (1961) and Williams (1968), have touched on sex roles from the perspective of socialization, and the subjects of honor, masculinity, and feminity have been directly addressed by Antoun (1968, 1970), Abu-Zahra (1970), and by a sociologist, Dodd (1973). The neglect of sex roles in the Middle East is not altogether out of line with the neglect of the subject in anthropological literature at large, but again the Middle East has lagged behind other cultural areas in the renewal of interest in the subject. Ironically, when Middle Eastern anthropologists have published on subjects such as honor and shame, they have often done so within the framework of Mediterranean studies (Peristiany, 1965); thus the impact on Middle Eastern anthropology as such has been much reduced. Moreover, the rationale for the grouping of such disparate societies and cultures as those found in Spain, Italy, Greece, Egypt, Algeria, and Lebanon under a single "Mediterranean" rubric, other than the fact that geographically they border on that body of water, is that the "Mediterranean" is ecologically a single region; most commonly, it is suggested that it is demarcated by the boundaries of olive growing; yet neither Egypt nor Libya is an olive-growing country! More significant (but not surprising) is the implicit assumption made in such "Mediterranean" studies that the historical and cultural implications of Islamic culture are of less importance for the study of such an eminently "cultural" problem as sex roles than the facts of the environment.

At this point, it may be legitimately asked, why should the study of sex roles, women, shame, and honor stand high in the order of priorities for research? Three answers may be given. First, within anthropology in general, all sorts of roles have been studied, including occupational, kinship, political, and religious roles, each sort embracing only one aspect of the individual's total identity. But anthropologists have shied away from describing and analyzing the global roles "man" and "woman" in particular cultures, and surely they are of no less importance than the roles "chief," "wage-laborer," "shaman," or "first cousin once-removed." Second, within the Middle East, the concepts of honor and shame are a cultural focus not only for nomads and peasants but also for urbanites. A look at the daily newspaper or a visit to the local cinema marquee in any Middle Eastern city will demonstrate that the crime of honor is regular fare—it occurs, it is understood, it is applauded, and it is celebrated—it is not satirized. Films such as "Seduced and Abandoned" or "Divorce Italian Style" are foreign not only to the Middle Eastern way of life but also to the Middle Eastern *Weltanschauung*. There is hardly a subject one can investigate—law, morality, family life, social control, social change, politics—without at some point impinging on the domain of honor and shame. Third, as John Gulick (1969) has pointed out in a recent review of anthropological literature, no question is more pertinent to the possibilities of controlling population growth and diversifying occupations, i.e., to "development," than the "definitions of the roles and 'natures' of men and women" and the possibilities and probabilities of their radical change in the near or distant future.

Fortunately, in spite of the rather pessimistic overview of research indicated here, it is my impression on the basis of unpublished manuscripts made available in the last few months that in the area of research on sex roles, the field of Middle Eastern anthropology is on the verge of breakthrough.[27] Sweet has argued forcefully that middle-aged peasant women, far from acting in the sheltered manner that purdah supposedly imposes, undertake critical household management functions that extend to the running of their husband's agricultural enterprises; Peters has pointed out that the sharp sexual division of labor itself gives women control over men. Nelson has pointed out the various tactics that women can employ to gain power[28] and the various resources at their disposal—food, honor, sex, sons, and the supernatural. Vinogradov, on the other hand, while pointing out that the freedom of women increases with every successive marriage, stresses that wives operate very self-consciously with regard to the constraints imposed by the husband's unilateral right to divorce. Rosen, on the other hand, discusses manipulation by men and women in terms of "reality bargaining," that is, with each attempting to impose his own definition of the situation in "encounter" situations.

What emerges from this research is that it is not only necessary to look at the constraints under which women operate both in Islamic law and local custom (Antoun, 1968), but also the power and influence they wield in terms of management functions (Sweet), sexual division of labor (Peters), manipulation of men inside the household (Nelson), and achievement of religious and magical roles outside it (Vinogradov); in addition, regard must be paid to the special rights given them under tribal custom (Mohsen, 1967) and Islamic law. Out of some such balanced treatment (considering power and rights as well as constraints and obligations), with due regard to the detailed analysis of "encounters"[29] between the sexes, will emerge a more satisfactory view of the "natures" of men and women in the Middle East and the possibilities and probabilities of change.

Process

It was stated above that Middle Eastern anthropology has moved from a mainly homeostatic view of human behavior to an increasingly diachronic point of view, a trend that reflects, belatedly, the trend in social anthropology at large. The discussion of the power and influence women may wield, have, or manipulate and the constraints under which they must operate also lead to a consideration of the ways in which this trend can be encouraged and accelerated, that is, the ways in which Middle Eastern anthropologists can formulate descriptions of social structure while maintaining an ongoing view of social relations that stresses processes as well as the formal attributes of groups. It leads to a consideration of how the anthropologist can maintain a role for the flesh-and-blood actor making choices under constraints, while elaborating the pattern of such choices both normatively conceived and statistically recorded. That the Middle Eastern anthropologist is interested in process is demonstrated not only by the number of responses (see Appendix I, Table 3, 5, 6, and 8) indicating an interest in "process" as such, but also in particular processes such as "politics" or "conflict." In the conviction that the focus on process is empirically necessary and heuristically worthwhile, three conceptual frameworks are briefly discussed below in the hope that they may help Middle Eastern anthropologists in both description and analysis of data.

Raymond Firth has been the pioneer in the study of the processual aspects of social structure, and his studies of "social organization" (Firth, 1951, 1954, 1955) are milestones in the development of a perspective that views human behavior as focusing on a human actor choosing from a limited number of alternatives in a patterned manner. What is remarkable is that both in anthropology at large and in Middle Eastern anthropology, very few attempts have been made to elaborate and refine a perspective that is both social scientific and humanistic and, for that reason, particularly valuable.[30] Since I have referred previously to the relationship of "social organization" at large to the process of the "social organization of tradition," in what follows I briefly allude to three approaches that focus on process, each in some way related to Firth's work, but at the same time quite distinctive.

For those interested in the development of a theoretical framework for the study of politics as process (as distinguished from the study of political organization), the work of F. G. Bailey assumes importance. In a series of monographs and articles (Bailey, 1957, 1960, 1963, 1968, 1969) he has systematically outlined an approach for the study of politics successively at the village, tribal, regional, and national levels. In his model he has broken up the processual continuum of political competition into "rounds" that are punctuated by events that result in the shift of resources. Three different political processes—"subversion," "confrontation," and "encounter"—characterize the competition which takes place under the constraints of both "normative" and "pragmatic" rules, the aim of the competition being to win or "subvert" "support" elements from the opponent's "core" to one's own "core." I must admit a personal bias in recommending Bailey's framework, for I found it useful in analyzing local politics in a Jordanian village. It is significant that Bailey's framework, developed by and large in the context of Indian local politics pervaded by an ideology of caste, was useful in analyzing data gathered in a Middle Eastern context with an entirely different ideological background (and without reference to Bailey's framework; at the time I gathered the data, I had not read his major works). Theoretically, Bailey's framework also has one major advantage over others with which I am acquainted; it deals successfully with the problem at the heart of politics, the problem of how ideological and economic resources are converted into political resources and vice versa, i.e., with the problem of "process."

The second framework, that of Keesing (1970), deals with the principles underlying "social organization," specifically with "principles for making decisions." Keesing, dealing with the institution of fosterage in a Melanesian society, outlines a model of cultural rules. Keesing, following Goodenough, defines culture as "standards for deciding what is ..., what can be, ... how one feels about it, and ... how to go about doing it." Keesing presents his decision-making model in the form of a flow chart in which the nodes represent contingent circumstances; he explains the contingent circumstance at each node and recounts the factors leading to alternative choices. Thus at one node, for instance, the widower must decide whether or not to remarry. He will abstain if he is getting old, if he becomes a priest, if he cannot afford to remarry, of if his daughter, sister, or other relative provides him with household services. Keesing makes clear that once a path through the sequence has been followed, it need not be final; that is, it is always possible to return to the choice situation at earlier nodes if the appropriate choice is made at the later node. Unlike Firth, Keesing is not analyzing a particular "social organizational" situation at each node, but rather presenting a summation of any and all possible factors entering into a decision at any particular node. Again, Keesing's framework allows the social anthropologist to present human behavior as a patterned outcome without eliminating the alternatives in the human situation.

Finally, game models represent another view of human behavior that focuses on actors making decisions. A game model is not a normative or behavioral model; it is a conditionally normative model. That is, quoting two game theorists (Luce and Raiffa, 1969):

> It states neither how people do behave, nor how they would behave in an absolute sense, but how they should behave if they wish to achieve certain ends. It prescribes for given assumptions courses of action for the attainment of outcomes having certain formal "optimum" properties.

As Selby (1970, p. 46) has pointed out.

> Many of the traditional anthropological problems are amenable to game theory formats; problems of marital choice, residence, political relations, brideprice, group formation, etc., processes in which either competition or cooperation is reasonable to assume, and in which the strategeies of the players, the value of the game or the equilibrium point (that set of strategies that maximizes the joint benefit of the players) is of interest.

Selby recognizes the restrictions of game theory: the model often imposes severe restrictions on the data and "tortuous maneuvers" are performed to fit the data into the necessities of the model. On the other hand, Selby holds that the advantage of game theory models is that they lead us "to think of our data in a less 'commonsensical' and more imaginative way; they force us to explicate our assumptions and they lead us to more abstract and general theories about the nature of cultural behavior" (Selby, 1970, p. 47). The best known application of game theory to Middle Eastern data is Barth's (1959) classic "Segmentary Opposition and the Theory of Games: a Study of Pathan Organization." Recently, anthropologists have become more aware, through the contribution of ethnographers, that several different strategies and indeed different "games" can be played by different members of the same population in relation to the same situation (Salisbury, 1969). I am not recommending that Middle Eastern anthropologists become mathematical anthropologists or game theorists unless that is their bent; I am recommending that models for the study of human behavior be examined that produce some general statement of patterning, at the same time allowing for human action and the possibility of change.

Comparison

In the last part of the preceding section, it was suggested that a critical attribute of social anthropology is the commitment to a comparative point of view; the most extreme form of this commitment is reflected in the belief of some anthropologists that the only certain route to scientific generalization (aside from statistical tests of validity and reliability) is through cross-cultural comparative studies, assuming, of course, the development of the typologies appropriate to such social structural and cultural variation. It was pointed out earlier that Middle Eastern anthropologists have been reluctant to engage in such studies. Of course, the propensity to engage in these studies will remain a matter of personal predilection, with a large number of anthropologists, I suspect a majority, preferring to conduct detailed case studies of particular milieus or ethnohistorical research. But the question remains, what can be done to encourage such research and in what particular directions should it be undertaken?

There is initially the question of the appropriate strategy for the collection of data. In a recent review article Gulick (1969) has suggested that Middle Eastern social anthropologists rest on the horns of a dilemma: either they can fill subregional gaps in descriptive knowledge—so that comparative generalizations can be made more confidently—or they can focus research on just a few subregions—so that they can generate more sophisticated hypotheses. In reality, the dilemma may be naturally resolved on the basis of political, economic, and practical factors. As indicated above, owing to chronic political instability, the current levels of international tension, and changing availability of counterpart funds in any particular period, research in the Middle East has been marked by oscillations from one country to another; e.g., flows to Libya, Jordan, Turkey, and Morocco have been reversed, whereas exiguous research in Iran and Afghanistan promises to become a flow. It is likely that similar oscillations will occur in the future so that in the long run, gaps in research and publication in particular subregions will be filled. On the other hand, for peculiar historical, political, and geographic reasons Israel and Lebanon will continue willy-nilly to be centers of field research in the future as they have been in the past, and as a result will produce the more sophisticated hypotheses. Thus insofar as funds can be allocated by universities, private foundations, or the U.S. Government, they should be supportive, when possible, of research outside the above two countries, in order to test the hypotheses developed there in a wider comparative context.

Second, there is the question of the range of comparative studies. Should Middle Eastern social anthropologists undertake interregional comparison (comparing cases or instances within the Middle East with those outside it) or intraregional, or even intrasubregional comparison (for instance, within the Levant, within the Arabian peninsula, or within the Maghreb)? Again the personal inclination of the anthropologist will probably be the deciding factor here. Owing to the paucity of the literature, any and all ranges of comparison will be welcome. Thus collections of essays based on fieldwork in different Middle Eastern locales but addressed to particular theoretical problem areas, e.g., politics, social change, social stratification, socialization, values, myth, the interchange between great and little traditions, markets, interethnic relations, sociolinguistics, and social control including the study of Islamic courts, civil courts, customary and tribal law, gossip, and extra-judicial proceedings all will be useful.[31] In addition, particular essays addressed to particular theoretical problem areas but incorporating data from different Middle Eastern locales would be useful. The problem with such comparative essays is that when they are based on previously published work whose data was not collected with an eye to examining the particular problem under investigation, the data are often not detailed enough to match the refinement of the hypothesis being tested. For instance, I undertook to examine politics and social control from the perspective of Bailey's theoretical framework and utilizing the data provided by ethnographers in seven Middle Eastern villages (Antoun, in Antoun and Harik, 1972). The interpretation of such studies tends to be strained, but if they are accepted as pioneering efforts whose purpose is heuristic rather than as conclusions bearing an aura of validity, they can be extremely valuable. Only by going out on the proverbial limb and risking the fall will major theoretical advances be made. This brief discussion of what Eggan (1954) has termed "middle-range comparison" (middling in the geographic range covered and the generality of the hypothesis) does bring out rather clearly that the either/or aspect of Gulick's dilemma is dangerous for the development of comparative studies. That is, the gathering of comparative data from particular subregions cannot be divorced from the development of sophisticated hypotheses pertaining to particular theoretical problem areas; to the extent that it is, comparison becomes difficult, if not impossible, since each investigator explicitly utilizes a separate conceptual framework in collecting data; the result is that the data become unfit for comparison both qualitatively and quantitatively. It seems that the most successful studies with comparative implications have been conducted in a subregional framework, as a result of work being done in particular institutions under the supervision of one or two anthropologists. Good examples are the works of Fernea and Kennedy and their students on social change in Nubia, conducted under the auspices of the Social Science Research Center of the American University at Cairo (see Fernea, 1966; Kennedy, 1967; Fahim, 1973: Geiser, 1973), the work of Geertz and his students from the University of Chicago in Morocco (see Geertz, 1968; Eickelman, 1973; and Rosen, in press), and the work of English and his students from the University of Texas on urban domination in Iran (see English, 1966; and Bonine, n.d.). Such studies are not explicitly cross-cultural; on the contrary, one of the controls applied, precisely to rule out such variation, is to consider particular regions or subregions. Yet the intensive study of such processes as social change, rural–urban migration, quarter formation, and urban domination by several investigators in a particular region at about the same time is bound to be productive for comparative studies both within other subregions of the Middle East and between regions in the future.

Finally, a criticism of non-Middle Eastern anthropologists interested in comparative studies is warranted. The Middle East has been ignored by theorists in the field of social structure, kinship, and culture and personality, despite the growing pool of ethnographic data from the area. Fortes, for instance, entirely ignored the Middle East in his important article on unilineal descent groups (1953); Levi-Strauss ignored the Middle East in his classic study on kinship and marriage (1949); and as Kennedy has pointed out (1970), Brown, Cohen, Whiting, and Young have either ignored the area in their samples devoted to the study of culture and personality or incorrectly coded the entries; pioneers in this field such as Freud and Bettleheim rarely mentioned the Middle East. As Kennedy (1970) has demonstrated for the study of circumcision and excision and as Patai (1965) has demonstrated for the study of unilineal descent groups, inclusion of the Middle Eastern data forces reconsideration of major assumptions about the operation of critical processes and significant social structures. This development is further evidence that Middle Eastern anthropology is ready to make an important contribution in the general field of ethnology and social anthropology.

Colonialism

The colonial experience has been of major importance in the development of the people and cultures of the Middle East. Nearly every Middle Eastern country has been subjected to some form of colonialism or another, whether for good or ill, and the establishment of the state of Israel, the incidence of four Arab–Israeli wars, and the operation of large Western industrial enterprises in the area indicate its continued importance. One revolution against colonialism in Algeria has only recently ended and another resistance movement (the Palestinian) continues to operate. Middle Eastern historians, political scientists, and economists have described and analyzed the phenomenon and the reaction to it at great length, as a cursory examination of any current general bibliography on the area indicates. As indicated above, however, Middle Eastern anthropologists have consistently neglected colonialism; only two published items on the subject were reported on the questionnaire and only two individuals designated it as the future subject of their own research.[32] Why this should be so constitutes as interesting problem in the sociology of knowledge with respect to Middle Eastern anthropology, a problem that will not be pursued at length here. However, it is exceedingly naïve for Middle Eastern anthropologists to think that their own research interests and methods have been unaffected by the heritage of colonialism, however altruistic they may believe their own motivations and actions to be. Practically all Middle Eastern anthropologists, including native Middle Easterners as well as Americans and Europeans, and whether or not they have past, present, or future ties or support from particular governments, have been trained in Western institutions of learning; the practical and ethical implications of Western-trained scholars studying non-Westerners has yet to be explored.

In an excellent paper entitled, "Pax Britannica and the Sudan," Faris (1973) has described the colonial encounter as it was represented in the theory and practice of one of the most distinguished anthropologists of our time, S. F. Nadel.[33] Faris points out that nearly all of Nadel's research among the Nuba of the Sudan was conceived as being of use to administrators: studies of land tenure, social organization, political structure, primitive mentality, intelligence testing, and social control including studies of witchcraft, suicide, and shamanism. He pointed out that it was British colonial policy to foster non-Islamic pagan cultures, and for the same reason, they fostered missionary activity; the aim of colonial policy in this case was keeping the people controlled by "keeping them Nuba" since "controlling people with sociology [in this case, anthropology] was easier than controlling them with troops" (Faris, 1973, p. 6). Faris pointed out that Nadel preferred to gather information from "raw savages"; indeed, he cautioned against using educated informants since sophistication, as Nadel put it, "blurs their view" (Faris, 1973, p. 10). Faris further holds that for the "colonial anthropologist," alienation is regarded as having its origins "in people's heads" rather than in the injustices of colonialism (Faris, 1973, p. 15). Now all this may seem somewhat removed from the present situation since, it may be pointed out, the sun has set on the British Empire, and few anthropologists today would take pride, as Nadel did, in their connections with the colonial offices of their own polities. The fact remains that the Middle East was, is, and will continue to be a focus for big-power rivalry and, perhaps more important little-power neocolonialism. Certain kinds of research, not necessarily overtly political research, facilitate the colonial power in the task of control. The individual anthropologist, if he recognizes this fact, must take some stand toward colonialism, pro or con; a position of neutrality or a claim of dispassionate intellectual objectivity usually amounts to a pro vote. Scholarship serves some purposes willy-nilly; let the Middle Eastern anthropologist be aware of what they are, let him choose from among them, and let him be responsible for his choice.

One of the most important aspects of colonialism is the false images it nourishes regarding Middle Eastern peoples. Reference has already been made to the image of the simple, gullible, illiterate, miserable, oppressed peasantry exploited by absentee landlords. Such images become pernicious when they are used by non-Middle Eastern governments and planners and by neocolonial propagandists to justify intervention or continued control of Middle Eastern peoples. Unfortunately such images gain stature when they are given credence by social scientists who, ironically enough, champion reform and modernization. For instance, one political scientist in a widely known and accepted book in the field of Middle Eastern studies (Halpern, 1963) heads a chapter on peasants as "A Majority in Misery." Misery, of course, is a psychological state, and without some psychological or social psychological instruments for measurement of such states, generalizations about them are not only impressionistic but dangerous since government plans and programs often assume some state in the population for whom they are planned. Of course, images of an opposite type are disseminated for the same purposes, as Faris has suggested. Thus in the Middle East, the uneducated nomad, be he Bedouin, Bakhtiari, or Baluchi, is romanticized, while the educated urbanite espousing nationalism is regarded as a hothead, a man with a blurred vision.

Again, anything anthropologists do by way of research and publication in this theoretical problem area, an area pregnant with practical political and ethical implications, will be valuable since so little has been done. For instance, the victims of the thrice-fought war, the Arab refugees, have been ignored by anthropologists although their newly established social networks in urban bidonvilles throughout the Arab world is of great interest entirely apart from the political and ideological implications. The most recent empirical studies have been by a political scientist (Buehrig, 1972) and two sociologists (Dodd and Barakat, 1969). No anthropologist has studied the Palestine Liberation Movement, and a psychiatrist (Fanon, 1965) has presented the most penetrating analysis of the changes that have occurred in the Algerian family as a result of the Algerian revolution. Finally, the myths created by the colonial and neocolonial powers and the countermyths created by Middle Eastern movements in reaction to such powers have scarcely been investigated from the vantage of myth. Thus the Zionist images of the Middle East widely circulated in the West have not been subjected to serious or systematic study, nor have the Arab nationalist images widely circulated in the Middle East. The myth of Iranian kingship and pre-Islamic Aryan brotherhood celebrated at an international fete amidst the ancient ruins of Persepolis in the autum of 1971 is surely worthy of study by at least one enterprising sociocultural anthropologist.

Practical Recommendations

Apart from the specific directions of research stipulated above, it is possible to suggest a few more general guidelines for funding agencies. First, theoretically oriented or problem-oriented or applied anthropology has the best chance of achieving significant results when it is coupled with and preceded by a period of extensive ethnography. Thus funding agencies should not discourage proposals that stipulate a considerable period (say, nine months) for the carrying out of ethnography as a preliminary to gathering the necessary data for the analysis of particular problems.

Second, centers for Middle Eastern studies are essential for the growth and development of Middle Eastern anthropology, and their weakening would cripple that development. At a number of points in this report allusion has been made to the importance of the study of Middle Eastern languages, Middle Eastern history, Middle Eastern literature, Middle Eastern religions, and Middle Eastern geography for successful anthropological research and teaching. Centers for Middle Eastern studies not only encourage training in such disciplines, but also help to coordinate such studies for faculty, graduate students, undergraduates, and the community at large.

Third, although the main thrust of this report has been that anthropology is and should be closely tied to field research, the constriction of funds to finance such research is a reality that must be faced. Significant research—significant from either a humanistic or a social scientific point of view—can be undertaken that does not require fieldwork. Reference has been made above to the desirability of comparative studies; such studies may now be undertaken on the basis of the secondary sources now available in university and other libraries. Mention has also been made of the desirability of examining historical texts and religious materials, increasingly available in Western libraries, from a social anthropological perspective. It must be recognized that much work in France and Germany, frequently characterized as "ethnology," is exactly of this character and deserves support.

Finally, although the geographical spread of research in the Middle East is at any given moment lopsided, reflecting current funding restrictions, international tensions, and the political stability of particular governments, there is a tendency for such lopsided distributions to be self-correcting. However, insofar as possible, funding agencies should encourage research in the subregions and among the broadly defined community types and ethnic groups which have thus far been neglected.

NOTES

1. I wish to thank the many colleagues and friends who have contributed to this report, in particular, the more than 100 anthropologists who were kind enough to respond to the questionnaire, the members of the State of the Art Seminar held in Palo Alto in August 1973, who contributed generously by way of comment and criticism, and the authors of special reports on North African ethnology, Middle Eastern prehistoric archaeology, and Middle Eastern folklore, David Hart, Charles Redman, and Yedida Stillman, respectively. I also wish to thank my colleagues in anthropology, Ahmed Abou-Zeid, John Gulick, John Kennedy, Laura Nader, and Nader Afshar Naderi for their many useful comments and criticisms. Special thanks are due to Robert Fernea, who from inception of the report to its final conclusion offered continuing advice, criticism, and counsel, and to Leonard Binder and I. William Zartman, who combined to facilitate our task at every stage and to make the State of the Arts Seminar a pleasurable personal as well as intellectual experience. I also wish to thank my research assistant, Mary Jane Berman, for her invaluable assistance in processing the results of the questionnaire discussed in the text and tabulated in Appendix I. Although many have contributed to the strengths of this report, I accept sole responsibility for its weaknesses and for the views expressed.

2. These quotations are taken from the first four chapters of Evans-Pritchard's *Social Anthropology*. It should be clear at the outset that this chapter focuses on social anthropology and does not include contributions either to Middle Eastern physical anthropology or linguistics; the latter is covered in Chapter 8. Certain aspects of prehistoric archaeology particularly significant for social anthropology are touched, but this chapter makes no pretension of covering or evaluating the substantial contributions to Middle Eastern archaeology; Chapter 5 is devoted to that subject.

3. Some of those who have published monographs or long articles on their fieldwork (with the dates of their fieldwork, when known, in parentheses) include the following. Again, with some exceptions, they worked mainly in the Levant: Hamed Ammar, Sunni Muslims, Upper Egypt (1954); John Gulick, Greek Orthodox, Lebanon (1952); William Schorger, Sunni Muslims, Morocco, (1948–1949); Jacques Berque, Sunni Muslims, Egyptian Delta (1957); Emrys Peters, Shiᶜite Muslims, Lebanon (1952, 1956); Alan Horton, Sunni Muslims, Syria (1954); Louise Sweet, Sunni Muslims, Syria (1954); Paul Sterling, Sunni Muslims, Turkey (1961–1962); Henry Rosenfeld, Sunni Muslims, Israel; Robert Fernea, Shiᶜite Muslims, Southern Iraq (1957); Abner Cohen, Sunni Muslims, Israel (1958–1959); Harold Barclay, Sunni Muslims, Sudan (1959), Toufic Touma, Maronites, Lebanon; Richard Antoun, Sunni Muslims, Jordan (1960–1966); Abdullah Lutfiyya, Sunni Muslims, Palestine (1960); Victor

Ayoub, Druze, Lebanon (1955); Shakir M. Salim, Shi^cite Muslims, southern Iraq (1953); Millicent Ayoub, Druze, Lebanon (1955); Zekiya Eglar, Sunni Muslims, Pakistan (1949–1955).

4. A number of significant works have been omitted owing to space limitations. Moreover, the omission of ethnographic works is glaring and is quite unjust in the sense that in delineating the social structure of culture or the community studied, such ethnographies provide valuable insights into important processes that have more than local significance. Included in this genre are the ethnographies of Ammar, Berque, Cohen, Eglar, Fernea, Gulick, and Lutfiyya and the articles of Rosenfeld.

5. Loffler's is not the only recent significant work. For instance, John Kennedy's "Mushahara: A Nubian Concept of Supernatural Danger and the Theory of Taboo" (1967), written on the basis of Middle Eastern data, represents a breakthrough in the study of taboo. William Irons' "Nomadism as a Political Adaptation: The Case of the Yomut Turkmen" (1974), represents a fresh perspective on Middle East nomadism; and Nader Afshar Naderi's *The Settlement of Nomads and its Social and Economic Implications* (1971) represents a breakthrough in the field of applied anthropology and nomadism. The works discussed in this section were selected on the purely arbitrary basis of my own familiarity with the literature, my own theoretical interests, and a limited amount of literature that has been made available as a result of the questionnaire. Thus in no way should this discussion be taken as a comprehensive or definitive evaluation.

6. The geographers were included at the behest of the Middle East Studies Association (MESA), and included only those who were members of MESA. The anthropologists from whom information was solicited were those who were members of MESA and those who listed themselves as social anthropologists with an area interest in the Middle East in the International Directory of Anthropologists of *Current Anthropology* for 1970.

Thus the questionnaire was sent to a selective group and does not claim to be either a comprehensive survey or a random sample. The roster of associates in *Current Anthropology* was used because it is the most comprehensive worldwide roster known to me. Of the approximately 300 scholars who were sent the questionnaire, 107 replied; of that 107 only 82 filled out all or most of the questionnaire. The responses of those that replied were very uneven. For instance, question 8 asked the respondents to list their outstanding publications; some did list such publications, others sent a complete list of all publications, and still others sent a complete list of publications, requesting that I make a judgment as to which were outstanding! Question 3 asked the respondents to state the geographic areas of interest of present, past, and future research; question 2 asked respondents to state the subjects of their present and past research. Some respondents answered all parts of the questions; others answered only the part concerning present research or only the part concerning past research, or some combination, without answering the full question.

7. See Appendix I, Table 2 for the tabulation of the results.

8. Coding the responses to these questions was primarily in terms of the titles or subjects mentioned and secondarily by inference from the titles. Thus a respondent stated that the subject of his past research was the Marri Baluchi; this response was classified as the study of tribal social structure and also as the study of nomads. Some titles and subjects were coded more than once since they clearly belonged to more than one category. For instance, the title of one respondent's reply was "The Ethnic Factor in a Local Election Campaign"; this reply was coded under "ethnic" and "politics." The same coding procedure was followed in processing replies to questions 2, 4, 8, 9, and 10.

9. See note 1 for the problems involved in coding this question; for its tabulation see Appendix I, Table 5.

10. Michael Fischer of the University of Chicago has finished a Ph.D. thesis on the social organization of tradition in Yazd. The thesis fills a major gap in the literature not only on Zoroastrianism, which is the major focus of the thesis, but also on Shiᶜite Islam in its local context. Work such as Fischer's is rare; published work is practically nonexistent.

11. The second largest number of published items coded (23) related to folklore. However, 11 of these items are by a single author; therefore the interest in folklore is less pronounced than might seem to be the case. In a brief survey of Middle Eastern folklore research. Dr. Yedida K. Stillman has concluded, "The study of North African and Middle Eastern folklore has been notably unrepresented in the mainstream of American and European folklore research." She goes on to say, quoting Aarne-Thompson, that "even today there are large areas almost completely unexplored, such as Arabia, Iraq, and Iran." She further notes that the only Middle Eastern country where the science of folklore is highly developed is Israel.

12. It should be noted that (see Table 7A) in all Middle Eastern countries there was a consistent decline from past to present to future in the number of scholars stipulating geographic research interests. In great part, this result is a reflection of the uneven responses on the part of the respondents. Whereas 133 responses stipulated a past research interest, only 52 stipulated a current research interest and only 40 a future research interest. Thus the drop in the number stipulating Israel as a research interest from 16 (past) to 10 (future) should not be interpreted as a decline. On the contrary, given the number of responses, it can be interpreted as an increase in interest; the same interpretation can be made for the figures on Iran. On the other hand, the far sharper drop in research interests in Turkey from 13 to 3 and in Morocco from 15 to 2 cannot be explained by the drop in the number of scholars indicating research interests.

13. Even such a valuable work as Ernest Gellner's *Saints of the Atlas*, specifically dealing with a religious lodge, lacks such data.

14. The exception is Millicent Ayoub's unpublished Ph.D. dissertation on marriage in a Druze community in Lebanon (Harvard, 1957).

15. Ayoub and Goldberg do this on a statistical basis only; Khuri again makes the best attempt to compare the sociopsychological implications of various cousin marriage preferences, but devotes very little space to the alternatives compared with the space given to FBD marriage.

16. See Antoun (1967) for an attempt to investigate the possibilities of choice in the contraction of marriage in one case study.

17. The interpretation given above of the focus on cousin marriage in the Middle East is mine. Two colleagues, Robert Fernea and Laura Nader, have pointed out that other explanations must be considered. Thus social anthropologists in general have concentrated on kinship and marriage as focuses for analysis since more descriptive data on these subjects have been made available in ethnographic monographs. Because the social anthropologist proceeds on a piecemeal basis it is natural that he should formulate concepts and problems regarding institutions that are comparatively well-known rather than those that are still obscure from a descriptive point of view. With this pronounced interest in both the descriptive and analytical aspects of kinship and marriage as part of his professional training it is not strange that the social anthropologist in the Middle East has given special attention to the subject. This attention is particularly appropriate in view of the fact that although the Middle East seems to share many of the characteristics that are identified with tribal organization south of the Sahara, it has an apparently unique feature, i.e., the norm and the practice of lineage endogamy. The discrepancy poses a problem for investigation.

18. For further information on the growth of the social sciences among native Middle Easterners, particularly in North Africa, readers should consult Sabagh's chapter on sociology (Chapter 10) and Zartman's on political science (Chapter 6).

19. It may be added in this regard that universities often have their own bureaucratic red tape which makes it difficult for young social scientists to gain positions in them.

20. There are a few exceptions to the above statement, e.g., Zenner's interesting ethnohistorical treatment of "The Strongman in the Traditional Ethnic Relations of Ottoman Galilee" (1972) and Cohen's *Arab Border-Villages in Israel* (1965), alluded to above in another context.

21. See English's excellent critical review of literature (1973) on this subject.

22. I use the term "model" here not in a strict sense (e.g., arithmetic model, mathematical models, and quantification of variables) but in a loose and metaphorical sense.

23. See my comments on Patai above.

24. See Khalaf (1966) on family firms in Lebanon and Farsoun and Farsoun on Palestinian middle-class family structures in Beirut.

25. See any of Janet Abu-Lughod's published works on Cairo for an excellent example of the latter process.

26. I do not wish to suggest that Coon's model, which is after all metaphorical, is the be-all and end-all of models for the study of ethnic groups and interethnic relations. Obviously, it should be combined with other models currently being developed in other cultural areas where the problems take a somewhat different twist but remain, nevertheless, pertinent for Middle Eastern anthropologists, e.g., Barth's work on ethnic boundaries (1969), Glazer and Moynihan's work on the unmelted melting pot that is New York City (1963), and Cohen's work on the politics of ethnicity in West Africa, previously discussed (1969). Furnivall's concept of "the plural society," developed much earlier, is also pertinent.

27. The manuscripts referred to are as follows: "Consequences of the Segregation of the Sexes among the Arabs" (Peters, 1966); "Sex and Symbol in the Treatment of Women: The Arab Wedding Rite in a Libyan Oasis Community" (Mason); "Between Social Worlds: Women and Power in Nomadic Societies of the Middle East; (Nelson, 1973); "The Rope of Satan; Social Relations and Reality Bargaining Among Moroccan Men and Women" (Rosen); "In Reality, Some Middle Eastern Women" (Sweet, 1974); "The Colonial Mirror: Reflections on the Politics of Sex in Morocco" (Vinogradov). E. Fernea's *Guests of the Sheik* (1965) represents an earlier published descriptive account of women's activities. Together with Dodd's work (1973) and Starr's work, soon to be published in Turkey, the publication of these manuscripts mark an auspicious beginning to the study of sex roles in the Middle East. It is interesting to note as possible harbingers of future development that two panels were devoted to sex roles at the 1973 annual meeting of the Middle East Studies Association and that John and Margaret Gulick have compiled an excellent annotated bibliography concerned with women's roles in the Middle East.

28. Playing men off against one another, seeking the help of women as a class, or minimizing contact with men, e.g., the wife's classic "flight of anger."

29. See Handelman, (1973) for an example of such detailed analysis in a Middle Eastern workshop setting.

30. I have attempted to apply Firth's concept of "social organization" to a Middle Eastern setting (Antoun, 1967); although others may have made similar applications, I am not aware of them.

31. For an example of such a collection on the subject of politics and social change, see Antoun and Harik. (1972).

32. See Eickelman's rare attempt to deal with the subject, "Islam and the Impact of the French Colonial System in Morocco" (1973).

33. Faris' paper was prepared for the conference, "Anthropology and the Colonial Encounter," University of Hull, Hull, England, September 1972.

BIBLIOGRAPHY

Abu-Lughod, Janet. "Rural Migration and Politics in Egypt." In *Rural Politics and Social Change in the Middle East*, R. T. Antoun and I. F. Harik, eds. Bloomington, Ill.: 1972.

———. "The Mass Media and Egyptian Village Life," *Social Forces*, **42** (1963).

———. "Migrant Adjustment to City Life: The Egyptian Case," *American Journal of Sociology*, **67** (1961).

Abu-Zahra, Nadia M. "On the Modesty of Women in Arab Muslim Villages: A Reply." *American Anthropologist*, **72** 5 (October 1970).

Adams, Robert M. *The Evolution of Urban Society: Mesopotamia and Prehispanic Mexico.* Chicago: Aldine, 1966.

Ammar, Hamed, *Growing Up in an Egyptian Village.* New York: Grove Press, 1954.

Antoun, Richard T. "Social Organization and the Life Cycle in An Arab Village," *Ethnology*, **6** 3 (July 1967).

———. "On the Modesty of Women in Arab Muslim Villages: A Study in the Accommodation of Traditions," *American Anthropologist*, **70** (1968).

———. "Antoun's Reply to Abu-Zahra." *American Anthropologist*, **72** 5 (October 1970).

Antoun, Richard T. and Iliya F. Harik, eds. *Rural Politics and Social Change in the Middle East* Bloomington Ill.: 1972.

Ayalon, D. *Gunpowder and Firearms in the Mamluk Kingdom.* London: 1956.

Ayoub, Millicent. "Parallel Cousin Marriage and Endogamy: A Study in Sociometry," *Southwestern Journal of Anthropology*, **15**, 266–275.

Baer, Gabriel. *Studies in the Social History of Modern Egypt.* Chicago University of Chicago Press, 1969.

Bailey, F. G. *Caste and the Economic Frontier.* Manchester: 1957.

———. *Tribe, Caste and Nation*, Manchester: 1960.

———. *Politics and Social Change*, Berkeley: 1963.

———. "Parapolitical Systems." In *Local Level Politics.* Marc Swartz, ed. Chicago: 1968.

———. *Strategems and Spoils.* New York: 1969.

Barth, Fredrik. "Father's Brother's Daughter Marriage in Kurdistan," *Southwestern Journal of Anthropology*, **10** (1954), 164–171.

———. "Ecologic Relationships of Ethnic Groups in Swat North Pakistan," *American Anthropologist*, **58** (1956), 1079–1089.

———. "Segmentary Opposition and the Theory of Games: A Study of Pathan Organization." *Journal of the Royal Anthropological Institute of Great Britain and Ireland*, **89** (1959).

———. *Nomads of South Persia: The Basseri Tribe of the Khamseh Confederacy.* Oslo: Universitetsforlaget, 1964.

———. *Ethnic Boundaries*, 1969.

Berque, Jacque. *Histoire sociale d'un village Egyptien au XXeme siecle.* Paris: Mouton, 1957.

Borthwick, Bruce. "The Islamic Sermon as a Channel of Political Communication in Syria, Jordan and Egypt." Ph.D. Thesis, University of Michigan, Ann Arbor, 1969.

Buehrig, Edward H. *The UN and the Palestinian Refugees.* Bloomington: Ill.: Indiana University Press, 1972.

Cahen, Claude. "Mouvements populaires et autonomisme urban dans l'Asie Musulmane du Moyen age," *Arabica*, **6** (1959).

Chelhod, Joseph, *Le Droit dans la societé Bedouine.* Paris: 1971.

Cohen, Abner, *Arab Border-Villages in Israel.* Manchester: 1965.

Cohen, Abner. *Custom and Politics in Urban Africa.* Berkeley: University of California Press, 1969.

Coon, Carleton. *Caravan: The Story of the Middle East.* New York: Holt, Rinehart and Winston, 1951.

Daniel, Norman. *Islam and the West: The Making of an Image.* Edinburgh: Edinburgh University Press, 1962.

———. *Islam, Europe and Empire.* Chicago: Aldine-Atherton Press, 1966.

Dickson, Harold R. *The Arab of the Desert: A Glimpse into Badawin Life in Kuwait & Saudi Arabia.* London: Allen & Unwin, 1949.

Dodd, Peter and Halim Barakat. *River Without Bridges: A Study of the 1967 Palestinian Refugees.* Beirut: 1969.

Dodd, Peter. "Family Honor and the Forces of Change in Arab Society," *International Journal of Middle East Studies*, **4**, 1 (1973).

Doughty, Charles M. *Travels in Arabia Deserta.* New York: Random House, 1937.

Dyson-Hudson, Neville. "The Study of Nomads," *Journal of Asian and African Studies*, **7**, 1972.

Eggan, Fred. "Social Anthropology and the Method of Controlled Comparison," *American Anthropologist*, **56** (1954).

Eglar, Zekiye. *A Punjabi Village in Pakistan.* New York: Columbia University Press, 1960.

Eickelman, Dale. "Musaylima: An Approach to the Social Anthropology of Seventh Century Arabia." *Journal of the Economic and Social History of the Orient*, **10** (1967).

———. "Islam and the Impact of the French Colonial System in Morocco: A Study in Historical Anthropology," *Humaniora Islamica* (1973).

———. "Is There an Islamic City? The Making of a Quarter in a Moroccan Town," *International Journal of Middle East Studies*, **5**, 4 (June 1974).

El-Ali. *The Social & Economic Strata of Basra in the First Islamic Century* (in Arabic) 1953.

English, Paul W. *City & Village in Iran.* Madison, Wis.: University of Wisconsin Press, 1966.

———. "Geographical Perspectives on the Middle East: The Passing of the Ecological Trilogy." University of Chicago, Department of Geography, Resource Paper, 1973.

Evans-Pritchard, Edward E. *Social Anthropology.* Glencoe; Ill.: Free Press, 1954.

Fahim, Hussein M. "Change in Religion in a Resettled Nubian Community, Upper Egypt," *International Journal of Middle East Studies*, **4**, 2 (April 1973), 163–177.

Fanon, Frantz, *A Dying Colonialism.* New York, 1965.

Faris, James. "Pax Britannica and the Sudan: S. F. Nadel in Theory and Practice," *Anthropology and the Colonial Encounter.* T. Asad, ed. London: 1973.

Farsoun, Karen and Farsoun. Samih. "Class and Patterns of Association Among Kinsmen in Contemporary Lebanon," *Anthropological Quarterly*, **47**, 1 (January 1974).

Fernea, Robert, ed. *Egyptian Contemporary Nubia*. New Haven: Human Relations Area File Press, 1966.

———. *Shaykh and Effendi*. Cambridge: Harvard University Press, 1970.

Firth, Raymond. *Elements of Social Organization*. London: Watts, 1951.

———. "Social Organization and Social Change," *Journal of the Royal Anthropological Institute of Great Britain and Ireland*, **84** (1954).

———. "Some Principles of Social Organization," *The Journal of the Royal Anthropological Institute of Great Britain and Ireland*, **85** (1955).

Fortes, Meyer. "The Structure of Unilineal Descent Groups," *American Anthropologist*, **55** (1953), 17–41.

Furnivall, J. S. *Colonial Policy and Practice: A Comparative Study of Burma and Netherlands India*. New York: 1965.

Geertz, Clifford. *The Religion of Java*. Glencoe, Ill.: Free Press, 1960.

———. *Islam Observed: Religious Development in Morocco & Indonesia*. New Haven: Yale University Press, 1968.

Geiser, Peter. "The Myth of the Dam," *American Anthropologist*, **75**, 1 (February 1973), 184–194.

Gellner, Ernest, *Saints of the Atlas*. Chicago: 1969.

Gibb, Hamilton A. "Review of the Meeting of East and West: An Inquiry Concerning World Understanding" by F. S. Northrop. *The Middle East Journal*, **1**, 3 (July 1947), 336–337.

Gilbert, John and Eugene Hammel. "Computer Simulation and Analysis of Problems in Kinship and Social Structure," *American Anthropologist*, **68** (February 1966), 71–93.

Glazer, Nathan and Daniel Moynihan. *Beyond the Melting Pot*. Cambridge, Mass.: MIT Press, 1963.

Godlberg, Harvey, "FBD Marriage & Demography Among Tripolitanian Jews in Israel," *Southwestern Journal of Anthropology*, **23** (1967), 177–191.

Granqvist, Hilma. *Marriage Conditions in a Palestinian Village*, Vols. 3 and 4. Helsinki. Societas Humanarum Litterarum, 1931, 1935.

Guillaume, Alfred. *The Life of Muhammad: A Translation of Ishaq's Sirat rasul Allah*. Karachi, Pakistan Branch: Oxford University Press.

Gulick, John. *Social Structure and Culture Change in a Lebanese Village*. New York: Wenner-Gren Foundation for Anthropological Research, 1955.

———. "The Anthropology of the Middle East," *Middle East Studies Association Bulletin*, **3**, 1 (February 1969.)

Halpern, M. *The Politics of Social Change in the Middle East and North Africa*. Princeton: 1963.

Handelman, Don, "Gossip in Encounters: The Transmission of Information in a Bounded Social Setting," *Man*, **8** (1973).

Horton, Allen. *A Syrian Village in Its Changing Environment*. Ph.D. Thesis. Harvard University: 1961.

Hurgronje, C. Snouck. *Mekka in the Latter Part of the Nineteenth Century: Daily Life, Customs and Learning of the Muslims of the East-Indian Archipelago*, Leiden: Brill, 1970.

Irons, William. "Nomadism as a Political Adaptation: The Case of the Yomut Turkmen," *American Ethnologist*, **1**, 4 (November 1974).

Keesing, Roger M. "Kwaio Fosterage," *American Anthropologist*, **72**, 5 (October 1970).

Kennedy, J. G. "Mushahara: A Nubian Concept of Supernatural Danger and the Theory of Taboo," *American Anthropologist*, **69**, 6 (December 1967).

———. "Circumcision and Excision in Egyptian Nuba," *Man*. **5**, 2 (June 1970).

Khalaf, Samir. "Family Firms and Industrial Development: The Lebanese Case," *Economic Development and Cultural Change*, **15**, 1 (1966).

———. "Industrialization and Industrial Conflict in Lebanon," *International Journal of Comparative Sociology*, **8**, 1 (1967).

———. "Primordial Ties and Politics in Lebanon," *Middle Eastern Studies*, **4**, 3 (1968).

Khuri, Fuad. "Parallel Cousin Marriage Reconsidered: A Middle Eastern Practice that Nullified the Effects of Marriage on the Intensity of Family Relationships," *Man*, **3** (December 1970), 597–618.

Lammens, H. "La Mecque a la Vielle de l'Hégire." In *Melances de l'Université S. Joseph, IX*. Beirut: 1924.

Lane, Edward W. *Manners and Customs of the Modern Egytians*. London: Dent Press, 1954.

Lapidus, Ira. *Muslim Cities in the Later Middle Ages*. Cambridge, Mass.: Harvard University Press, 1967.

———. "Muslim Cities and Islamic Societies," *Middle Eastern Cities: A Symposium on Ancient, Islamic and Contemporary Middle Eastern Urbanism*. Berkeley: University of California Press, 1969.

LeCoz, Jean. *Le Rharb: Fellahs et Colons*. 1964.

Lesne, Marcel. *Evolution d'un groupement Berbere: les Zemmour*, Rabat: 1959.

LeTourneau, Roger. *Fès avant le protectorat, les villes Musulmanes d'Afrique du Nord*. Rabat: Institut des Hautes Etudes Marocaines, 1957.

———. *Fez in the Age of the Marinides*. Norman, Oklahoma: University of Oklahoma Press, 1961.

Levi-Strauss, Claude. *Les Structures élémentaires de la parenté*. Paris: 1949.

Lewis, Bernard. *Race and Color in Islam*. New York: Harper Torchbooks, 1970.

Loffler, Reinhold. "The Representative Mediator and the New Peasant," *American Anthropologist*, **73**, 5 (1971).

Luce, D. and H. Raiffa. *Games and Decisions*. New York: 1969.

Markarius, Raoul. "Le Mariage des cousins paralleles chez les Arabes." In *Des Actes du VIe Congrès International des Sciences Anthropologiques et Ethnologiques*. Paris: 1960.

Makidise, George. "Muslim Institutions of Learning in Eleventh Century Baghdad," *Bulletin of the School of Oriental and African Studies*, **24**, (1961).

Mohsen, Safia. "The Legal Status of Women Among the Aulad 'Ali," *Anthropological Quarterly*, **40**, 3 (1967).

Montagne, Robert. *La Civilisation du désert: nomades d'Orient et d'Afrique*. Paris: Hachette, 1947.

Murdock, George. *Social Structure*. New York: Free Press, 1949.

Murphy, Robert and Leonard Kasden. "The Structure of Parallel Cousin Marriage," *American Anthropologist*, **61** (1957), 17–29.

———. "Agnation & Endogamy: Some Further Considerations," *Southwestern Journal of Anthropology*, (1967) 1–13.

Mason, J. T. "Sex and Symbol in the Treatment of Women: The Arab Wedding Rite in a Libyan Oasis Community," Unpublished manuscript.

Naderi, Nader Afshar. *The Tribe of Bahma'i* (in Persian). Tehran; 1947.

———. "The Settlement of Nomads and Its Social and Economic Implications." Tehran: Institute for Social Studies and Research, Tehran University, 1971.

Nelson, Cynthia. "Self, Spirit Possession and World View: An Illustration from Egypt," *International Journal of Social Psychiatry*. **17**, 3 (Summer 1971).

———. "Between Social Worlds: Women and Power in Nomadic Societies of the Middle East." In *The Desert and the Sown*. Cynthia Nelson, ed. Berkeley: 1973.

Patai, Raphael. "The Dynamics of Westernization in the Middle East," *Middle East Journal*, **9** (1955).

———. "Cousin Right in Middle East Marriage," *Southwestern Journal of Anthropology*, **11** (1957).

———. *Golden River to Golden Road*. Philadelphia: University of Pennsylvania Press, 1962.

———. "The Structure of Endogamous Unilineal Descent Groups," *Southwestern Journal of Anthropology*, **21** (1965), 325–350.

Peristiany, J. G., ed. *Honour and Shame: The Values of Mediterranean Society*. London: 1965.

Peters, Emrys. "The Proliferation of Segments in the Lineage of the Bedouin in Cyrenaica," *Journal of the Royal Anthropological Institute of Great Britain and Ireland*, **90** (1960).

———. "A Muslim Passion Play," *The Atlantic Monthly* (October 1956).

———. "Consequences of the Segregation of the Sexes Among the Arabs." Paper delivered at the Mediterranean Social Science Council Conference. Athens: 1966.

Peters, Emrys. "Some Structural Aspects of the Feud Among the Camel-Herding Bedouin of Cyrenaica," *Africa* **37** (1967), 261–282.

Philby, Harry S. *The Empty Quarter*. New York: Holt, Rinehart & Winston: 1933.

Prothro, Edwin T. *Child Rearing in the Lebanon*. Cambridge, Mass.: Harvard University Press, 1961.

Rappaport, Roy. *Pigs for the Ancestors*. New Haven: 1968.

Redfield, R. *Peasant Society and Culture*. Chicago: University of Chicago Press, 1956.

Rosen, Lawrence. "The Rope of Satan: Social Relations and Reality Bargaining Among Moroccan Men and Women," To appear in *Male-Female Relations in the Mediterranean World*. L. A. and M. Fallers, eds.

Rosenfeld, Henry. "Change Barriers to Change and Contradictions in the Arab Village Family," *American Anthropologist*, **70** (1968), 730–752.

Salisbury, Richard F. "Formal Analysis in Anthropological Economics: The Rossel Island Case." In *Game Theory in the Behavioral Sciences*, Ira Buchler and Hugo Nutini, eds. Pittsburgh: 1969.

Salzman, Phillip and Brian Spooner. "Kirman and the Middle East: Paul Ward English's City and Village in Iran," "Settlement and Economy in the Kerman Basin," *Iran*, **7** (1969), 107–113.

Schorger, William. *The Stonecutters of Mediouna*, Ph.D. thesis. Harvard University.

Selby, Henry A. "Continuities and Prospects in Anthropological Studies," *Current Directions in Anthropology*, Ann Fischer, ed. *Bulletin of the American Anthropological Association*. **3**, 3, Part 2 (September 1970).

Singer, Milton. *Krishna: Myths, Rites and Attitudes*. Honolulu: East West Center Press, 1966.

Smith, William Robertson. *Lectures on the Religion of the Semites*. London: A & C Block, 1889.

———. *Kinship and Marriage in Early Arabia.* Cambridge: Cambridge University Press. London: A & C Block, 1903.

Stirling, Paul. *Turkish Village.* London, 1965.

Sweet, Louise E. *Tell Toqaan: A Syrian Village.* Ann Arbor; Michigan. 1960.

———. "In Reality: Some Middle Eastern Women." In *Many Sisters: Women in Cross-Cultural Perspective.* C. Matthiasson, ed. 1974.

Thesiger, Wilfred. *Arabian Sands.* London: Longmans, Green, 1959.

———. *The Marsh Arabs.* New York: Dutton Press, 1964.

Thomas, Bertram. *Arabia Felix.* London: J. Cape, 1932.

Vinogradov, Amal. "The Colonial Mirror: Reflection on the Politics of Sex in Morocco." Unpublished manuscript.

Watt, Montgomery. *Muhammed et Medina.* Oxford: Clarendon Press, 1966.

Williams. Judith. R. *The Youth of Haouch El Harimi: A Lebanese Village.* Cambridge: Harvard University Press, 1968.

Wolf, Eric. "The Social Organization of Mecca and the Origins of Islam," *Southwestern Journal of Anthropology,* **4** (1951), 329—353.

Zenner, Walter D. "Aqiili Agha: The Strongman in the Ethnic Relations of the Ottoman Galilee," *Comparative Studies in Society and History,* **14**, 2 (March 1972).

ADDENDUM

Fernea, Elizabeth. *Guests of the Sheik.* New York: Doubleday, 1965.

Leach, Edmund. "The Structural Implications of Matrilateral Cross-Cousin Marriage," *The Journal of the Royal Anthropological Institute of Great Britain and Ireland,* 81 (1952).

Appendix I

TABLE I
Language Facility

Reading, Writing, and Speaking	Speaking Only	Reading Only	Reading and Speaking Only
Arabic			
21, of which: 2 Moroccan dialect 1 classical 1 stated that his writing was poor 1 stated "a dialect"—unspecified 3 Egyptian dialect 1 It is understood that for reading, it is in classical Arabic only 12 unspecified	20, of which: 3 Moroccan dialect 1 Cairene and Khartoum dialects 1 Palestinian dialect 1 Egyptian dialect 1 Iraqi dialect 1 North African dialect—unspecified 1 Tripolitan dialect 7 did not specify which dialect, but felt they spoke it poorly 1 Saudi Arabian dialect 1 Tunisian dialect 1 Libyan dialect 1 did not specify quality	3 (classical)	4 poor
Hebrew			
15, of which: 1 said his skill was poor	3	1	2
French			
31	7	18	8
German			
25	5	6	4

Continued

TABLE 1—*continued*

Reading, Writing and Speaking	Speaking Only	Reading Only	Reading and Speaking Only
English (for non-native speaker only)			
22	8	0	0
Spanish			
13	3	5	1
Turkish			
6	4	1	2
Persian			
6	10, of which: 8 said that they spoke it poorly 1 Afghan Persian	0	3
Italian	0	0	1
Berber			
0	3, of which: 1 Riifian 1 Tashelit	0	0
Baluchi			
1	1	0	0
Pashto			
1	0	0	0
Amharic			
1	0	0	2
Tigrinya			
1	0	0	0
Yiddish			
1 (fair)	0	0	0
Dutch			
0	0	5	0
None			
5	0	0	0

TABLE 2A*

Fieldwork: Number of Field Trips Made

Number of Field Trips	Number of Persons
0	6
1	4
2	20
3	14
4	7
5	2
6	2
7	0
8	1
9	1
10	1
>10	6
Residents of area in which he is doing research	5
No answer	3
Doesn't remember	1

* 72 replies coded.

TABLE 2B

Length of Time Spent in the Field

Length of Time Spent	Number of Field Trips
1 week–3 months	10
3 months–6 months	13
6 months–1 year	31
1 year–18 months	32
18 months–2 years	24
2 years–30 months	3
30 months–3 years	7
4 years	1
5 years	2
6 years	2
7 years	5
8 years	1
9 years	0
10 years	0
11 years	1
12 years	1

TABLE 2C

Total Time Spent in Area but not Spent Continuously in the Field

Total Time Spent	Persons
3 years	1
5 years	1
9 years	1
No answer	11
Doesn't remember	1

TABLE 2D

Type of Research Team

Individual	26
With assistants	17
With wife	5
With husband (obviously not everyone answered this)	1
Total	48

TABLE 3

Past, Present, and Future Research

Topics	Past Research	Present Research	Future Research
Geographic area	7	0	9
Process	7	8	3
Ethnicity	4	5	10
Ecology	4	3	4
Tribal structure	4	2	0
Village	4	3	1
Applied anthropology	3	1	4
Ethnography	3	3	0
Two disciplines	3	0	1
Sex roles	3	1	1
Change	3	7	3
Conflict	2	5	6
History	2	3	3
Politics	2	5	3
Peasants	2	0	4
Small community studies	2	4	1
Class, stratification	2	1	2
Urban studies	2	3	6
Immigration	2	3	2
Folklore	1	2	5
Honor	1	0	0
Linguistics	1	2	2
Marriage and family	1	2	5
Personality	1	4	1
Social science	1	3	3
Modernization	1	0	1
Medicine	0	1	0
Physical anthropology	0	0	0
Archaeology	0	0	0
Comparative research	0	1	1
Diffusion	0	0	0
Demography	0	3	1
Economics	0	0	1
Literature	0	1	2
Material culture	0	3	3
Regional studies	0	0	0
Religion	0	8	5
Social types	0	0	0
Training	0	1	0
Colonialism	0	0	2
Nomads	0	2	6
Biography	0	0	2

TABLE 4*
Teaching

Present Middle East courses

1. Ethnography of the Middle East (Peoples and Cultures of the Middle East): graduate course, 2; undergraduate course, 3; do not specify, 19
2. Culture and Personality in Context of Kuwaiti Society
3. Prehistory of Central and South Asia
4. Jewish Oral Literature
5. Prophetic View of History
6. Seminar in Literary Forms of Old Testament (graduate course)
7. Seminar in Israelite Institutions
8. History and Problems of Nubia–Social Anthropology of Nubians
9. Africa and the Middle East, survey course
10. Anthropology of North Africa
11. Islam and Social Change
12. Status and Power in Peasant Societies (concentration on Middle East)
13. Mediterranean Culture Area: 2
14. Village Studies (concentration on Middle East): 2
15. Politics of Middle East and North Africa
16. Regional Studies of the Middle East
17. Ethnicity, Religion, and Change in the Middle East: 2
18. Hindustani Music
19. Aspects of Israeli Society
20. Ethnology of Europe and the Mediterranean (see no. 13)
21. Settlement of Bedouins in Jordan
22. Ethnic Groups in Israel
23. Preindustrial City in the Arab World (seminar)
24. Changing society of Persia
25. Topics of research in Southwest Asia
26. Many Things Dealing with the Middle East (title person gave) (graduate seminar)
27. Seminar on Islamic Religious Movement
28. Identity and Change in the Middle East
29. Methods of Research with Focus on Urban Cairo (seminar; projects with students)
30. Geography of the Middle East
31. Cities of the Middle East

Past Middle East courses

1. Ethnography of the Middle East (Peoples and Cultures of the Middle East): 18
2. Nomads of the Middle East: 2
3. Ethnography of North Africa
4. Ethnography of Iraq

continued

TABLE 4—*continued*

Past Middle East courses—continued

5. Archaelogy of Bible Lands
6. Archaelogy of South Asia
7. Romani Languages and Folktales
8. Afghan, Pakistan, and Bangladesh: Tribalism, Nationalism, and Regionalism
9. Sociology of Islam
10. Ethnography of the Kurds
11. Ethnography of Ethiopia
12. Ethnography of Russia and Central Asia
13. Face-to-Face Interaction in Urban Settings
14. History of North Africa
15. Culture and Society in Arab Africa
16. Rural Moroccan Ethnography
17. Social Stratification in the Middle East
18. Modern Middle East
19. Middle Class in Egypt (seminar)
20. Traditional Middle East
21. Social Change in the Middle East
22. Women in the Middle East
23. Ancient Near East
24. Introduction to Islamic Society: The Arabs, first semester; Non-Arabs, second semester
25. Problems in the Anthropology of the Middle East
26. Precolonial Africa (includes North East Africa, Egypt, and the Sudan)
27. Middle Eastern Societies in Detroit, Michigan

Courses Currently Taught

Number of Courses	Number of Persons
1	24
2	8
3	3
4	1
5	1
0	27
Retired	2
Museum work	3
No answer	9
Total	77

* Forty-one respondents were currently teaching or doing museum work.

TABLE 5*

Subjects of Outstanding Publications

Subjects	Number of Published Items
Religion	26
Folklore	23
Ethnicity	20
Urban studies	19
Nomads	19
Applied anthropology	18
Tribal structure	15
Ethnography	14
Material culture	14
Immigration	14
Politics	13
Change	13
History	12
Marriage and family	12
Regional studies	12
Ecology	11
Class, stratification	11
Physical anthropology	10
Process	10
Linguistics	8
Archaeology	7
Village	7
Modernization	7
Conflict (including law)	7
Economics	5
Personality	5
Sex roles	5
Demography	4
Medicine	3
Comparative research	3
Small community studies	3
Training	3
Diffusion	2
Colonialism	2
Peasants	1
Social science	1
Geographic area	0
Honor	0
Literature	0
Social types (broad)	0
Two disciplines	0

* Total number of published items coded: 101.

TABLE 6

Opinions as to Directions of Future Research

Subject	Number of Opinions
Geographic area	15
Two disciplines	10
Ethnicity	8
Change	7
Process	7
Stratification	6
Religion	6
History or ethnohistory	5
Training	5
Ethnography	4
Ecology	4
Urban	4
Politics	4
Colonialism	4
Conflict	3
Folklore	3
Social science	3
Nomads	3
Marriage and family	3
Local level	3
Comparative research	2
Diffusion	2
Regional studies	2
Women	2
Socialization	2
Archaeology	2
Modernization	2
Applied anthropology	1
Linguistics	1
Physical anthropology	1
Village studies	1
Peasantry	1
Medicine	1
Immigration	1

TABLE 7A*

Geographic Areas of Research Interest

Geographic Area	Past	Present	Future
Israel	16	11	10
Morocco	15	4	2
Iran	14	8	7
Turkey	13	4	3
Egypt	10	3	4
Tunisia	8	0	1
Saudi Arabia	7	2	6
Afghanistan	6	6	6
Ethiopia	5	0	0
Lebanon	5	1	0
Algeria	5	0	2
Pakistan	4	3	1
Syria	4	0	0
Immigrants in the United States and Canada	3	0	0
Sudan	3	0	1
Libya	3	2	0
Arabian peninsula	3	2	0
Iraq	2	0	0
Jordan	2	0	0
Caucasus	0	1	0
Yemen	1	1	1
Persian Gulf	0	0	1
Kuwait	1	1	1
Iran and West India	0	1	0
Canary Islands	0	1	0
European societies	0	1	0
Any Middle Eastern country	0	0	3

* 133 replies were coded for past research, 52 for present research, and 40 for for future research. The numbers do not refer to individuals since particular persons often specified more than one locale in their answers.

TABLE 7B

Locales of Field work

Locales of Field Trips	Number of Persons at Locales
Israel	18
Iran	18
Afghanistan	16
Turkey	12
Morocco	11
Egypt	10
Saudi Arabia	6
United States and Canada (studying Middle Eastern immigrants)	5
Lebanon	5
Jordan	5
Pakistan	4
Iraq	4
Ethiopia	3
Sudan	3
Syria	3
Tunisia	3
Kuwait	2
Libya	2
Yemen	1
Turks in Russia	1
Turkestan	1
Total	137

TABLE 8

Research Problems and Research Design

Research Problem	Number of Respondents
History	12
Change	8
Religion	8
Ethnicity	7
Conflict	6
Comparative research	6
Marriage and family	6
Politics	6
Complex society	6
Social science	5
Urban studies	4
Ecology	3
Material culture	3
Class, stratification	3
Two disciplines	3
Archaeology	2
Demography	2
Economics	2
Folklore	2
Process	2
Small community studies	2
Nomads	2
Immigration	2
Medicine	1
Physical anthropology	1
Applied anthropology	1
Ethnography	1
Linguistics	1
Regional studies	1
Training	1
Tribal structures	1
Village	1
Modernization	1
Biography	1
Socialization	1
Encounters	1
Diffusion	0
Geographic area (includes people)	0
Honor	0
Literature	0
Peasants	0
Personality	0
Social types	0
Sex roles	0
Colonialism	0

TABLE 9

Number of scholars interested in anthropology first	51
Number of scholars interested in some aspect of Middle Eastern studies first	32
Total number of scholars	83
Number of articles appearing in a journal of anthropology	35
Number of articles appearing in a journal dealing with Middle Eastern studies	32
Number of articles appearing in a journal other than anthropology and Middle Eastern studies	74
Total number of articles	141

QUESTIONNAIRE

Dear Colleague:

The Research and Training Committee of the Middle East Studies Association is organizing a comprehensive review and evaluation of the state of the art of Middle Eastern studies organized by discipline. I have been asked to coordinate the chapter on anthropology, and I am interested in the broadest participation in its formulation. Indeed, without such participation the report would not only be incomplete, but also misleading. I will be very grateful if you would take the time to answer briefly or at length the following questions:

1. How did you become interested in Middle Eastern anthropology? Were you interested in anthropology before you became interested in the Middle East, or vice versa?
2. What is the title(s) or subject(s) of your present research? Past research?
3. What are the geographic areas of interest of your present research? Past research? Future research? In what countries have you conducted research?
4. What are the problems being researched and what is the research design? Do these problems differ from those researched in the past?
5. Fieldwork experience: how many field trips have you made? What are the locales of each trip and what was the length of time spent there? Did you conduct individual or team research?
6. What are your language proficiencies (speaking, reading, writing)?
7. How many courses involving the Middle East are you currently teaching? What are their titles? Past Middle Eastern courses taught?
8. What are the titles of your outstanding publications?

9. What is the probable direction of your future research in the Middle East?
10. In what directions, areas, or problems would you like to see future research in the Middle East?
11. Any comments are welcome.

Abstracts, offprints, copies of unpublished papers, etc. would also be welcome. Early replies would be appreciated, since I must have a first draft of the report ready by February 1, 1973. The report will be published by the Middle East Studies Association and will thus be made available to all scholars interested in Middle Eastern studies and anthropology. Thank you very much for your help.

Respectfully yours,

Richard T. Antoun

Associate Professor of Anthropology
State University of New York
Binghampton

Appendix II Anthropological Archaeology in the Near East

CHARLES L. REDMAN

During the past 20 years the pursuit of archaeology in the Near East has undergone a series of fundamental changes. What had been primarily a quest for objects of art and very generally directed programs of research for the most part has developed into problem-oriented expeditions for the elucidation of basic questions of human behavior and development (Adams, 1966b; Braidwood, 1973). No longer is it an adequate goal to field an archaeological project simply to discover what remains are in the area or to excavate what is located. Instead of a preoccupation with regional time–space systematics, anthropological archaeologists are framing specific questions on important problems to be pursued in the field. As a result several expeditions may share a common general goal, such as understanding the origins of agriculture. They collect information that is compatible, and hence are able to benefit by the work of others. This type of concerted effort on selected questions is leading to more detailed knowledge and understanding of developments which have only been speculated about until recently (G. Wright, 1971).

Two significant methodological developments reflected in the organization of archaeological fieldwork were caused by a shift in the interpretive perspectives used by anthropological archaeologists in the Near East. The first phenomenon is the utilization of large multidisciplinary staffs for archaeological expeditions. The necessity for botanists, zoologists, geologists, pedologists, and other natural scientists for the solution of environmental and subsistence problems is widely accepted. The result is a better understanding of the subtleties of the archaeological record and its depositional history.

The second significant methodological development is the adoption of a regional approach to research. This shift is in large part a response to the recognition that many processes cannot be understood within the context of a single community. The necessity for systemic data is especially true of complex societies. Regional surveys combined with excavations have produced information of a different kind as well as in greater quantity. Whereas the archaeological survey had previously been little more than a reconnaissance to locate potential productive sites, it now is utilized as a major source of information on the demographic history of the area and as a means of measuring the nature and variability of all the communities in the area.

With the adoption of specific problem orientations two cultural stages have become the major focuses of research in the Near East. These two sets of substantive problems can be characterized as the origins of agriculture and the emergence of early cities. They are among the most fundamental accomplishments of the entire human career, and current data indicate that they were successfully achieved in the Near East as early as, if not earlier than, anywhere in the world. In addition, it is widely believed that these accomplishments in the Near East were in many ways ancestral to processes that led directly to Western civilization. Hence the temporal priority, the fundamental nature, and the special attraction of these problem focuses have led to widespread interest in their investigation by both professional archaeologists and the interested public.

Other time ranges and problems are currently being investigated in the Near East, but not on the same scale. Interest in the nature of the earliest human occupations has stimulated Paleolithic research at Shanidar Cave, Iraq (Solecki, 1963), Ubadiyah, Israel (Stekilis, M.), and Tabun, Israel (Jelinek, 1973). The investigation of prehistoric towns and the accompanying technological and social developments is pursued in many parts of the Near East [Hacilar (Mellaart, 1970); Catal Hüyük (Mellaart, 1967); Girikihaciyan (Watson, n.d.); Tepe Sabz (Hole, Flannery, and Neely, 1969); Beersheba (Perrot, 1968)]. Anthropological interest in the historic ranges of time has increased with the recognition of the great potential for formulating refined substantive models and a more detailed understanding of the society [Tell Abu Sarifa (Adams, 1970)] than is possible with the prehistoric time ranges.

ORIGINS OF AGRICULTURE AND SETTLED VILLAGE LIFE

The domestication of plants and animals was a major step in man's increasing control over the environment and a prerequisite for many subsequent accomplishments. This process has been generally viewed through an ecological perspective because of the close relationships among man, plants, animals, and the land. Subtle changes in the interaction of man with his surroundings led to successful agriculture and enabled permanent settlements. A detailed knowledge of the past climates and the potentially domesticable plants and animals available in each region is necessary for a thorough understanding of the relevant archaeological remains. The various forms and stages of domestication must be recognized in both the biological and cultural remains. These kinds of data have necessitated the inclusion of natural scientists on projects designed to elucidate the origins of agriculture. Robert J. Braidwood has been a pioneer in bringing together botanists, zoologists, geologists, and other specialists in large-scale archaeological projects in various parts of the Near East. His work in Iraq (Braidwood, Howe, et al, 1960), Iran (Braidwood, Howe, and Reed, 1961), and Turkey (Braidwood, Camberl, Redman, and Watson, 1971) has created a storehouse of data and encouraged other expeditions to follow his lead. Although American anthropologists have been active in the pursuit of this problem, they by no means monopolize this field. In addition to the recent projects by local Near Eastern countries, the French have done important work in the Levant (Perrot, 1966, 1968; de Conteson, 1971), the British in the Levant and Turkey (Kirkbride, 1966; Kenyon, 1957; Mellaart, 1970), and Canadians in Iran and Turkey (Bordaz, 1966).

Considerable research has been carried out and numerous preliminary reports have been prepared, but there is as yet a paucity of final reports concerned with domestication. One noteworthy exception is the report on the Deh Lurah Valley and particularly the site of Ali Kosh (Hole, Flannery, and Neely, 1969). The authors utilized the ecological approach to understand the introduction of agriculture within a regional framework. Sections on artifacts, botanical remains, zoological remains, and other aspects of the excavation and regional survey give a picture of the expedition's results.

One of the most exciting aspects of the increasing research into the origins of agriculture in the Near East is that it has provided the data base and stimulation for many theories on how and why this process took place. A series of variables are usually involved, with each scholar championing one or another variable as the most important. Climatic factors, population pressure, and margins of environmental zones are combined in a series of different models (Flannery, 1965, 1969; Binford, 1968; Smith and Young,

1972). It is apparent that considerable quantities of additional data are necessary before one or another theory can be accepted, but they have had the effect of increasing the interest in this important process and have outlined the specific kinds of data necessary for testing hypotheses.

EARLY CIVILIZATION AND THE FIRST CITIES

Interest in early civilizations is as old as archaeology itself. It is during the past 20 years that this problem has been increasingly pursued by anthropological archaeologists in the Near East as well as philogists, art historians, and Biblical scholars. The rich sources of early written records and ethnographic work in the region have made this a productive time range for anthropologists. The most significant contribution anthropological archaeologists have made to understanding the origin of cities is due to the regional approach they have utilized. The regional approach developed from the explicit recognition that a city is not an isolate. Cities and civilization can best be understood within their demographic and rural milieu. Cities functioned as central places and arose in response to the pressures and potentials within their surrounding countryside.

Anthropological archaeologists have concentrated on settlement pattern studies of specific areas over long periods of time. Knowledge of the changing patterns of community size and location during different periods enables questions to be asked that were not even previously considered. Demographic changes, spheres of interaction, and the importance of topographic or ecological setting can be more adequately evaluated with this type of data. A pioneer in this form of fieldwork is Robert McC. Adams, who has surveyed various areas within Iraq and Iran in an attempt to understand the origins of Mesopotamian civilization (Jacobsen and Adams, 1958; Adams, 1962, 1965; Adams and Nissen, 1972). The availability of this type of regional data has led to increased interest in problems of interaction and organization.

Recently a number of researchers have concentrated on the conduct and effects of long- and short-distance trade on the development of civilization. With the aid of trace element analysis it is often possible to determine the source of exotic materials. Concerning an earlier range of time, successful studies have been done on the origin of obsidian pieces found in early villages and the necessary routes of supply (Renfrew, Dixon, and Cann, 1966; G. Wright, 1969). Studies on trade routes, manufacturing industries, and sources of raw materials are more frequently being conducted in relation to early civilization (Renfrew, 1969; H. Wright, 1969, 1972; Lamberg-Karlovsky, 1970). These studies in various ways try to outline the importance of trade in the dissemination of ideas, the organization of specialists, and the accumulation of wealth. Further study on the effects of trade on the organization of communities is fundamental to an understanding of early civilizations. Currently several projects are being organized to investigate archaeologically the nature and the role of nomadism in early civilizations (Hole). Other important factors in the emergence of cities such as warfare, stratification, religious hierarchies, and differential access to resources are only beginning to be treated (Adams, 1966a).

The progress toward understanding early civilizations will depend on the success of both large-scale expeditions that investigate these societies in their full complexity (urban–rural, civic–domestic) and more specific projects that are aimed at individual elements in the systematic civilizational matrix. In perspective, anthropological archaeology in the Near East has grown rapidly in the past 20 years and is contributing to an understanding of some of the basic developments in the human career.

BIBLIOGRAPHY

Adams, Robert McC. "Agriculture and Urban Life in Early Southwestern Iran," *Science*, **136** (1962), 109–122.

———. *Land Behind Baghdad*. Chicago: University of Chicago Press, 1965.

———. *The Evolution of Urban Society*. Chicago: Aldine Press, 1966. (a).

———. "Trend and Tradition in Near Eastern Archaeology," *Proceedings of the American Philosophical Society*, **110** (1966), 105–110. (b).

———. "Tell Abu Sarifa," *ARS Orientalis*, **8** (1970), 87–119.

Adams, Robert McC. and Hans J. Nissen. *The Uruk Countryside*. Chicago: University of Chicago Press, 1972.

Binford, Lewis R. "Post-Pleistocene Adaptations." In *New Perspectives In Archaeology*. S. Binford and L. Binford, eds. Chicago: Aldine, 1968.

Bordaz, Jacques. "Superde," *Anatolian Studies*, **16** (1966), 32–33.

Braidwood, R. J. "Archaeology: A View From Southwestern Asia." In *Research and Theory in Current Archaeology*. C. Redman ed. New York: Wiley-Interscience, 1973.

Braidwood, R. J., Camberl, H. Camberl, C. L. Redman, and P. J. Watson, "Beginnings of Village Farming Communities in Southeastern Turkey." *Proceedings of the National Academy of Sciences*, **68** (1971), 1236–1240.

Braidwood, R. J., B. Howe, et al. "Prehistoric Investigation in Iraqi Kurdistan," *Studies in Ancient Oriental Civilizations*, Vol. 31. Chicago: University of Chicago Press, 1960.

Braidwood, R. J., B. Howe, and C. H. Reed. "The Iranian Prehistoric Project," *Science*, **133** (1961), 2008–2010.

Flannery, Kent V. "The Ecology of Early Food Production in Mesopotania," *Science*, **147** (1965), 1247–1256.

———. "Origins and Ecological Effects of Early Domestication in Iran and the Near East," In *The Domestication and Exploitation of Plants and Animals*. P. Ucko and G. Dimbelby, eds. Chicago: Aldine, 1960.

Hole, F., K. V. Flannery, and J. A. Neely. "Prehistory and Human Ecology of the Deh Lurah Plain." In *Memoirs of the Museum of Anthropology*. Ann Arbor: University of Michigan, 1969.

Jacobsen T. and R. McC. Adams. "Salt and Silt in Ancient Mesopotamian Agriculture," *Science*, **128** (1958), 1251–1258).

Jelinek, Arthur. "Preliminary Report on Excavation at Tabun," *Abstracts of the Society for American Archaeology*. 1973.

Kenyon, Kathleen. *Digging Up Jericho*. London: Ernest Benn, 1957.

Kirkbride, Dorothy. "Five Seasons At the Pre-Pottery Neolithic Village of Beidha in Jordan," *Palestine Exploration Quarterly*, **1** (1966), 8–72.

Lamberg-Karlovsky, C. C. "Excavations at Tepe Yahya, Southeastern Iran, 1967–1969." *Bulletin of the American Journal of Prehistoric Research*, **27** (1970).

Mellaart, James. *Catal. Hüyuk: A Neolithic Town in Anatolia:* London: Thames Hudson, 1967.

———. *Excavations at Hacilar*, 2 vols. Edinburgh: Edinburgh University Press, 1970.

Perrot, Jean. "Le Gisement Natoufien de Mallaha," *L'Anthropologie*, **70** (1966), 437–483.

———. "La Préhistoire Palestinienne," *Supplement Au Dictionnaire De La Bible*, **8** (1968), 286–446.

Renfrew, Colin. "Trade and Culture Process In European Prehistory," *Current Anthropology*, **10** (1969), 151–169.

Renfrew, C., J. E. Dixon, and J. R. Cann, "Obsidian and Early Cultural Contact in the Near East," *Proceedings of the Prehistoric Society For 1966*, **32** (1966), 30–72.

Smith, P. E. L. and T. C. Young. "The Evolution of Early Agriculture and Culture in Greater Mesopotamia: A Trial Model." In *Population, Resources and Technology*. B. Spooner, ed. Philadelphia: University of Pennsylvania Press, 1972.

Solecki, R. S. "Prehistory in Shanidar Valley, Northern Iraq," *Science*, **139** (1963), 179–193.

Watson, Patty Jo. "Girikihaciyan: An Halafain Site in Southeastern Turkey." Manuscript on file. Washington University.

Wright, Gary. "Obsidian Analyses and Prehistoric Near Eastern Trade: 7500 to 3500 B.C." *Anthropological Papers of the Museum of Anthropology*, **37**. Ann Arbor: University of Michigan, 1969.

———. "Origins of Food Production in Southwestern Asia: A Survey of Ideas," *Current Anthropology*, **12** (1971), 447–477.

Wright, Henry. "The Administration of Rural Production in An Early Mesopotamian Town," *Anthropological Papers of the Museum of Anthropology*, Vol. 38. Ann Arbor: University of Michigan, 1969.

———. "A Consideration of Interregional Exchange in Greater Mesopotamia: 4000–3000 B.C." In *Social Exchange and Interaction*. E. N. Wilmsen, ed. Ann Arbor: The University of Michigan, 1972.

Appendix III The French Contribution to the Social and Cultural Anthropology of North Africa: A Review and an Evaluation

DAVID M. HART

There is a very considerable, even voluminous, body of literature in French relative to the social and cultural anthropology of Northwest Africa. The term Northwest Africa, of course, is used in the wide sense to cover the Maghreb and the Sahara as well, for it is only natural that the great bulk of the total French anthropological literature on the Middle East at large, perhaps as much as 90% of it, is focused on its North African end. Hence it is to northwest Africa that this Appendix is confined; it in no way attempts to be an exhaustive bibliography, but tries rather to discern general trends and to pick out specific works which in my view stand out as anthropological landmarks. First, however, some essential historical background information should help to place the French anthropological contribution to the region in general in its proper perspective. Professional anthropologists and sociologists working there were long preceded by a tradition of ethnologically minded colonial-administrator army officers. This tradition started in Algeria as early as the 1850s, within two decades of the French conquest, much earlier than the development of any similar tradition in the British empire.

Yet it was the three-volume study by General Adolphe Hanoteau and the lawyer Ernest Letourneux, *La Kabylie et les coutumes Kabyles* (2nd ed., Paris: Augustin Challamel, 1893), which appeared originally in 1873, that was to have the largest impact on the administration of French Algeria because, far more than any other previous work, it created the "Kabyle myth" which, when later transported by the French to Morocco after 1912, became the "Berber myth." The work of Hanoteau and Letourneux contains an enormous amount of ethnographic detail on Kabyle sociopolitical organization and on their customary law, or *ᶜurf*, here understood as the core meaning of the word *coutume*. The study was very influential; it was considered by the administration to be a kind of tribal Bible until the virtual destruction of French Algeria in 1962—so much so, indeed, that it had the effect of stultifying further research on the Kabyles, who constitute the dominant Berber-speaking elements in the Algerian population and whose geographical center of gravity is the Jurjura mountain range.

Stripped to its essentials, the "Kabyle myth" conceives of Berbers as Noble Savages, living in a "basically democratic condition," one bordering on "anarchy" and missing it only because of the possession of the *Jma^c^a* type of representative council and the customary law alluded to above. This same customary law coexisted with the *Sharî^c^*a and even went counter to it in certain important respects. The council and customary law were held to combine in producing a vigorous resistance to outside forces, notably those represented by Arabs and Islam, for not only were the Berber languages and institutions considered worth preserving because of their own intrinsic value, but the Noble Berber also came to be viewed as a possible political counterweight to the Ignoble Arab and, what is more, one that might in time become susceptible to assimilation into French culture, and in effect Gallicized. (In Algeria the French *mission civilisatrice* was eagerly aided and abetted by the Catholic Church, and in point of fact a few Kabyles were actually converted to Catholic Christianity.) The myth was later to be imported, lock, stock, and barrel, to Morocco after the establishment there of the French Protectorate in 1912, where it became the "Berber myth." The French could hardly have imported it to Tunisia, which had and has very few Berbers in any case.

Yet the work of Hanoteau and Letourneux, albeit enormously colonialistic in tone, also influenced French sociologists in the metropolis, notably Emile Durkheim, who in his *The Division of Labor in Society*, originally published in 1893, developed an initial notion of "segmentary societies" from the Kabyle materials, which were also used by him as an example to buttress his theory of mechanical solidarity.[1] It would be interesting and instructive to know how much contact there was between administrators in Algeria and sociologists at home; certainly such contact had increased to the point where Edmon Doutté, one of the earliest and subtlest French investigators of Moroccan society, acknowledged his own debt to Durkheim in 1901.[2]

It was indeed in Morocco, rather than in Algeria, Tunisia, or the Sahara, that French colonialist sociology (now inspired by Marshal Lyautey and his team of officer advisors of the corps of the Affairs Indigenes) produced the bulk of its most interesing work; it is hence with Morocco that the greater part of this Appendix deals.[3]

Morocco presented, and presents, an overall social situation of extreme interest. Here was a well-defined sultanate and monarch, which, unlike Algeria or Tunisia, had undergone only local dynastic upheavals, never any occupation by alien Ottoman Turks. Morocco presented a magnificent sociopolitical dialogue between its own central government (the *makhzan*) and the urban seats of that government, and the tribal hinterland (for purposes of simplification, *siba*). This hinterland, often mountainous and often Berber-speaking, tended at times to opt away from the central authority's economic control, although identifying as part of the overall social system of the empire and recognizing the spiritual authority of the sultan. When strong sultans were at the helm, overt refusal by tribes to pay taxes was met with coercion on the part of the army. These facts, and other related ones, greatly impressed the earlier French observers. However, during the initial period (1900–1904), before the compound French sociological stereotypes of a dualistic kind, which Burke has aptly labeled the "Moroccan Vulgate"[4] (Arabs–Berbers, *Sharî^c^a–qasîda^c^urf* (customary law), town–tribe, urban orthodoxy–rural heterodoxy, the prevalence of saint worship and religious orders,[5] and *makhzan–siba*), began to harden. Doutté and Eugene Aubin wrote a remarkable sociopolitical account too sensitive to fall under the spell of the above stereotypes.[6] These authors were supported by the very voluminous output of Edouard Michaux-Bellaire.[7] But Michaux-Bellaire was far more an Arabist and historian in his orientation than an anthropologist, and not only does his work (which at its best is excellent) seem less sophisticated analytically than that of Aubin and the better work of Doutté, but in his attempts to unravel Berber from Arab origins, he paved the way for French colonial policy in Morocco.

Hence by the 1920s, when Robert Montagne appeared upon the Moroccan scene, the *makhzan* (governmental) versus *siba* (Berber and tribal) dichotomy was fully accepted, for the Lyautey administration had been in effect its prime advocate. The dichotomy itself came to represent, in brief, colonial thinking about Morocco, which was dominated by the series of dualistic absolutes already mentioned, the core of which was the myth of the Good Berber as opposed to the No-Good Arab. It culminated, of course, in the famous (or infamous) Berber Dahir of 1930.

Robert Montagne was one of the most important figures in French social science in the North African scene; he was also a thoroughgoing colonialist and extremely influential with regard to French administrative policy in Morocco. He was in addition, in my view, both brilliant and wrongheaded: brilliant insofar as when his ideas were right, they were very right, and wrongheaded insofar as when they were wrong, they were very wrong, with few half measures. His work therefore requires a certain amount of consideration and discussion. His most famous and important publication was *Les Berberes et le makhzen dans le Sud du Maroc: essai sur la transformation politique des Berberes sedentaires (groups Chleuh)* (Paris: Felix Alcan, 1930). Its conclusions are summarized in a much shorter work he published a year later and which has now become available in an English translation (by David Seddon) as *The Berbers: Their Social and Political Organization* (London: Frank Cass, 1973). Montagne's central thesis about Berber political life in the western Atlas mountains, as it was before the protectorate, is its oscillation between two very distinct political forms: egalitarian, democratic little tribal republics, in which political power was held only collectively by the assembled members of the tribal council, on the one hand, and the assumption of personal power and tyranny by ambitious individuals who from time to time were able to break out of the circle of their own tribal groups, so to speak, in order to impose their will on those of their neighbors, on the other hand. Even if one can quibble with Montagne's rather indiscriminate use of terms such as "anarchy," "democracy," and "republic," this part of his analysis is in the main very sound indeed, and the rise to personal power of three big caids of the western Atlas (the Mtuggi, the Guntafi, and the Glawi) is masterfully handled, with Montagne's caveat that the situation thus created in no way resembled European feudalism except perhaps superficially.

However, where Montagne went badly wrong in his analysis of Berber society was in two other directions entirely, both of them equally fundamental; he ignored or was unaware of Durkheim's earlier stress on the segmentary character of tribal structure in Kabylia, which was equally valid for Berber societies elsewhere. Hence he tried, mistakenly, to explain it wholly through the binary mechanism of intertribal alliances and hostilities as embodied in the "moiety" system known variously as *saff* or *liff*. His second error, too, was compounded, in my opinion, by his insistence on the "chessboard" character of *liff* systems, whereas in fact each tribe, with the occasional involvement of the neighboring clans of its neighbor tribes, represented the limit of its own *liff* system, which in its most typical form existed as a sociopolitical set of dual factions that conflicted with the segmentary system of the group concerned. Because the conflict might crystallize between two factions (often of unequal size and hence not properly moieties) of any given tribe and seldom spread actively beyond its tribal borders, I have chosen to view the whole mechanism less in terms of a chessboard[8] than in terms of a series of interlocking concentric circles, which is more expressive of the limits of tribal warfare. In any case, Montagne in his later years was preoccupied with *liffs* and their binary implications; in *La Civilisation du désert* (Paris: Hachette, 1947) he tried to postulate that they were the underlying feature of tribal social structure all over the Middle East. In addition, most Anglo-Saxon social anthropologists would be very skeptical about his constant tendencies to invoke theories of social evolution and not to control his comparisons adequately. Seddon (translation of *The Berbers*, op. cit., 1973) rightly criticizes his tendency to skate over tribal economics.

But Montagne made a very real contribution to Moroccan social anthropology all the same, and not only in the realm of Berber and tribal studies, for it was a collective inquiry under his direction that gave rise to the scientific study of the burgeoning urban proletariat in the bidonvilles (shantytowns) of Casablanca, Rabat, Algiers, Tunis, and elsewhere, in *La naissance du proletariat Marocain: enquête collective 1948–1950* (*Cahiers de l'Afrique et l'Asie*, Vol. 3, Paris: Peyronnet, 1951). This was the pilot study, giving rise to a number of others elsewhere in North Africa and culminating in the thorough, detailed, and generally excellent study by André Adam entitled *Casablance: essai de la transformation de société Marocaine au contact de l'Occident* (2 vols., Paris: Centre National de la Recherche Scientifique, 1968). This work is a major landmark in the urban sociology of not only North Africa but, one might say, the Third World in general, even though its author might have profited from an acquaintance with the concept of urban social networks currently being developed in African sociology by J. Clyde Mitchell and his associates at the University of Manchester (*Social Networks in Urban Situations: Analyses of Personal Relationships in Central African Towns*, Manchester University Press, 1969). This is not to imply that the late Roger LeTourneau (who by teaching at Princeton University and by writing some of his later work in English helped to bridge some of the gaps between French and Anglo-Saxon perceptions of North Africa), in his *Fès avant le protectorat: étude économique et sociale d'une ville de l'Occident Musulman* (Publications de l'Institut des Hautes Etudes Marocaines, XLV, Casablanca: Société Marocaine de Libraire et d'Edition, 1949) did not also make a very real contribution to the study of the intellectual and cultural capital of Morocco. But LeTourneau was essentially an historian, and there is a curiously static quality in his work which is entirely absent in Adam's highly dynamic sociological analysis of Casablanca. It is to be hoped that the present generation of young Moroccan social scientists will profit from Adam's example.

Before we leave Morocco to scan the rest of the Maghreb, however, we must return again to Berber society, as seen this time by a decolonizing sociologist, Jacques Berque, in his *Structures sociales du Haut Atlas* (Paris: Presses Universitaires de France, 1955). Despite the fact that this book often appears to be stylistically tortuous, it is a major work of enormous erudition by a *pied noir* who has (as André Adam notes, op. cit., 1972, pp. 32–33) never shared the prejudices of his peers and who has elevated the fieldwork techniques of the Algerian *Bureau Arabe* to the level of the College de France. Berque's grounding not only in the Arabic and Berber languages but in Muslim history, law, jurisprudence, and theology is colossal and his area knowledge is unrivaled. The work here under consideration is in many respects the best single piece of Moroccan ethnography yet published, and is particularly strong not only on the history and on the ecological–economic systems of the sedentary Berber agriculturists of the Seksawa, but on their whole complex of jural–religious institutions as well. The role of their female patroness saint Lalla Aziza in their lives is demonstrated with conviction and skill, and Berque too has grave doubts about Montagne's thesis on *liff* alliances. But it is by no means a complete ethnography: nowhere are we told anything about kinship and/or marriage, preferred or not, among the

Seksawa, and although we find numerous hints about the social structures which form the subject of the title, nowhere do we find a formal analysis of what (to any Anglo-Saxon social anthropologist) is meant by the term "social structure" in the narrow sense, i.e., the social groupings concerned, their composition and relationship to each other, and whether this relationship is or is not expressed politically in the idiom of segmentary lineage organization. Finally, and paradoxically, the book's greatest strength is also its greatest weakness: its author's unwillingness—which is most convincingly displayed—to find a single dominant social factor in the lives of the Seksawa; he gives us rather an idea of the wealth and complexity of existing social forms and behavior among them. We find a corresponding lack of preoccupation with the theory and method of social anthropology, which is perhaps typified by Berque's aversion to the construction of "models." In Jacques Berque's hands ethnographic riches become methodological poverty; but as two other very fine works by him, *Al-Yousi: problèmes de la culture Marocaine au XVIIIème siècle* (Paris: Mouton, 1958) and *Le Maghreb entre deux guerres* (Paris: Editions du Seuil, 1962), clearly show, Berque is more a social historian than he is a social anthropologist.

We may now return to Algeria, which we left intentionally in the limbo of Hanoteau's and Letourneux' colossal but intellectually stultifying nineteenth-century study of the Kabyles. It is truly astonishing that not until 1950 and the publication of G. H. Bousquet's *Justice Française et coutume Kabiles* (Algiers: Imprimerie Nord-Africaine, 1950) had anyone at all attempted to destroy the cult of Hanoteau and Letourneux by demonstrating, convincingly, that Kabyle customary law, even despite the extraordinarily tenacious community spirit of the Kabyles, was changing with the times. This fact was not recognized by the system of French justice to which the Kabyles were subjected (although they often secretly opted out of it; the blood feud was still practiced on the quiet in Kabylia long after the French had suppressed it in Morocco). In Algeria as in Morocco the areas of Berber speech were in general (there were exceptions) also areas in which Berber customary law was administered rather than the *sharî^ca*, and hence areas which, as Berque says, constituted the "Berber Park," a kind of jural deepfreeze.[9] One most undeniable result of the French magistrates' and colons' idolatry of Hanoteau and Letourneux is the fact that until the Algerian Revolution actually began in 1954, the French anthropological record there, in terms of significant works published, is close to zero. It was only on the very eve of independence that Jean Morizot, a civil administrator in Kabylia and former student of Montagne, published a most thought-provoking study entitled *L'Algerie Kabylisée* (*Cahiers de l'Afrique et l'Asie*, Vol. 6, Paris: Peyronnet, 1962), a work remarkable in terms of both its general lucidity and the amount of anthropological ground it covers. However, in the same breath we should also mention a general work on the sociology of Algeria by Pierre Bourdieu, which was translated into English as *The Algerians* (Boston: Beacon Press, 1961) and which contains capsule ethnographies of the Kabyles, the Shawiya Berbers of the Aures mountains, the Ibadhite Berbers of the Mzab Oases, the Arabic-speaking peoples, the common cultural heritage, disintegration and distress, and the revolution within the revolution, leading to radical social change and the espousal of state socialism once independence was achieved. The same author, with the collaboration of Abdelmalek Sayad, also published another noteworthy work in *Le Deracinement: la crise de l'agriculture traditionelle en Algerie,* (*Grands Documents*, Vol. 14, Paris: Editions de Minuit, 1964), in which the present uprooted character of the Algerian peasantry in general is graphically described. The French presence in Algeria lasted far longer, and had far greater impact, than in either of the other two countries of the Maghreb; far greater, too, was the cataclysm with which it ended. (Whether there are today any professional Algerian anthropologists or sociologists to take over where the French left off I do not know, but I have never met any.)

The French anthropological record in Tunisia is, in sum, even poorer than it is in Algeria, and to my knowledge it was (virtually) nil before independence in 1956. Even now there are no outstanding anthropological landmarks as exemplified by Montagne or by Berque in Morocco. To be sure, there is Jean Cusienier, *L'Ansarine: contribution à la sociologie du dévélop-pement* (*Memoires du Centre d'Etudes de Sciences Humaines*, Vol. 7, Université de Tunis, and Paris: Presses Universitaires de France, n.d., ca. 1961) and Pierre Bardin, *La vie d'un Douar: essai sur la vie rurale dans les Grands Plaines de la Haute Medjerda, Tunisie* (Paris: Mouton, 1965); both of these are good studies as far as they go. However, I found that the promise contained in one or two of Cusienier's earlier articles lacked complete fulfillment in his monograph, and Bardin's study, interesting and suggestive as it is (and it is one of the very few published nontribal-village studies on North Africa), is sketchy and impressionistic. Today, however, there are several young Tunisian sociologists and anthropologists who show great promise, and the *Revue Tunisienne des Sciences Sociales* seems to us to be unquestionably the best and the most professional social scientific journal published anywhere in the Arab world. (The Moroccans, on the other hand, have spread themselves too thin in this respect; they have upheld pure and applied sociology but have eschewed anthropology and ethnology in any form. At the date of writing the government has closed down the University Mohammed V in Rabat, so that no publications are emerging from Morocco at this time.) Hence in Tunisia, although the past has been undistinguished, there is much hope for the future.

For the Sahara, although it really forms another cultural world from the

Maghreb proper, we run into a further paradox. The best sociocultural anthropological study available is, in our view, not one by any Frenchman on, for example, any of the Tuareg groups (few of these studies are better than mediocre), but by a Spaniard on that part of the western Sahara still under Spanish domination today, the Ṣaghiyat al-Ḥamrâ and the Rio de Oro. The work in question is by Julio Caro Baroja, *Estudios Saharianos* (Madrid: Instituto de Estudios Africanos, 1955); and when one considers that its author spent only three to four months in the field, he truly covered an incredible amount of ground, in an area where nobody else, before or since, has been permitted to work. The book is nonetheless uneven, and contains sections of varying length on (1) the traditional social order in the Spanish Sahara, (2) the economics of the Sahil or West Saharan Atlantic coastline, (3) the structural analysis of a Saharan tribe, the Awlâd Tidrarîn (a group which, in our opinion, was badly chosen and with whom the author's analysis gets overinvolved), (4) a Saharan saint and his lineage (an excellent study of Sheikh Ma' al-ᶜAinain and his descendants), and (5) the wars of the western Sahara as recounted by the Bedouin nomads. Uneven though it is, however, this book remains one of the very best single pieces of North African ethnography to be published during the colonial period; it is primarily because of it that we have elected to include Spanish materials on North African anthropology. In Caro Baroja's writing, there is a strong sense of the work of Malinowski, Radcliffe-Brown, and Evans-Pritchard (Caro Baroja spent two years at Oxford), which is, when all is said and done, totally lacking in the whole of the French colonial output on North Africa.

The final paradox is that the kinds of problems concerning economic anthropology, systems of kinship and marriage, and systems of social and political structure which have been of basic concern to Anglo-Saxon sociocultural anthropologists did not *really* come to concern French scholars with any degree of acuteness until after the Maghreb achieved independence. French North Africa badly needed, for example, a Georges Balandier, but it never had one. Much good work was done by the French, during the colonial period, according to their own conceptions of what Islamic North African ethnography was all about. But in our view they placed a very great overemphasis on what they considered to be the formal particularities of Berber jurisprudence and customary law (plus misplaced comparisons with those of ancient Gaul or Germany), as opposed to on-the-spot field studies of individual Berber or Arab groups or subsocieties, stressing economic and sociopolitical organization; kinship, marriage, and family structure[10]; and localized and/or special manifestations of Islam, and its specific influence on the lives of its practitioners. In sum, there is more ethnology (as well as sociology—this at least is a good thing) than there is ethnography, and more ethnography than there is social anthropology. We who are the heirs of this French colonialist ethnography are also, regrettably, the losers, for the kinds of information they failed to gather, or at least to gather in depth, are now irretrievably lost.

There may well be, buried in the French and Spanish colonial archives in Paris, Aix-en-Provence, and Madrid, a number of anthropological nuggets of a sociocultural kind that may still emerge in the hands of discerning researchers[11]; but come what may, they will only reflect the social and cultural past of the Maghreb. Because the whole area today is in a state of kaleidoscopically rapid social change, it behooves younger anthropologists to get away from the "museum of traditionalism," to work in the North African countries, and to try to ascertain the patterns and directions of some of these newer social forms involved: for the transition from a tribal and/or an urban universe to a national one seems easy only to those who take it for granted.

NOTES

1. Durkheim also, in this connection, cites E. Masqueray, *La Formation des Cités chez les Sédentaires de l'Algérie*, 1886, a work considered important but which I unfortunately have never seen.

2. His best work is to be found in the journal *Renseignements Coloniaux et Documents Publiés par le Comité de l'Afrique Française et le Comité du Maroc*, supplement to the *Bulletin du Comité de l'Afrique Française*, for the period 1900–1904; in particular, his article on "L'Organisation sociale et domestique des Haha" in the same journal [**1** (January 1905), 1–16] is a miniature masterpiece as an ethnographic survey of a large Berber-speaking tribe on the Moroccan Atlantic coast between Essaouira and Agadir.

3. At the very outset, we are happy to announce the recent publication of an invaluable bibliography of Moroccan sociology, by Andre Adam: *Bibliographie critique de sociologie, d'ethnologie et de géographie-humaine du Maroc—Memoires du Centre de Recherches—Anthropologiques, Prehistoriques et Ethnographiques d'Alger*, Vol. 20 (Algiers and Paris: Centre National de la Recherche Scientifique, 1972). Although it lists only works published through 1965, this bibliography is a must for anyone interested in Maghreb studies, and its excellent introduction deals with the French (and other) bibliographical high points of Moroccan sociology in a way that cannot possibly be duplicated here. The main body of the work, the bibilography itself, is annotated, and most of the annotations are of value.

4. Edmund Burke, III, "The Image of the Moroccan State in French Ethnological Literature: A New Look at the Origin of Lyautey's Berber Policy," in *Arabs and Berbers: From Tribe to Nation*, Ernest Gellner and Charles Micaud, eds., (London: G. Duckworth, 1973), pp. 175–199.

5. On this last subject see two studies by Rene Brunel, *Essai sur la confrerie religeuse des Aissaoua au Maroc* (Paris: Paul Geuthner, 1972), and *Le monachisme errant dans l'Islam Sidi Heddi et les Heddaway, Publications de l'Institut des Hautes Etudes Marocaines*, Vol. 48 (Paris: Larose, 1955). Brunel's Heddawa study is nicely supplemented by one in Spanish which appeared at the same time, by Ramon Toüceda Fontenla, *Los Heddawa ed Beni Aros y su Extrano Rito* (Tetuan: Ediora Marroqui, 1955). All three works are of considerable intrinsic interest, even if not quite first-rank ethnographies.

6. Aubin and Doutté's *Morocco of Today* (London and New York: 1906).

7. For a full bibliography of Michaux-Bellaire, cf. R. Gerofi, "Michaux-Bellaire," Tinga, *Bulletin de la Société d'Histoire et d'Archéologie de Tanger,* **1** (1953) 79–85.

8. David M. Hart, "Clan, Lineage, Local Community and the Feud in a Rifian Tribe," in *Peoples and Cultures of the Middle East: An Anthropological Reader,* Vol. 2, Louise E. Sweet, ed., (New York: Natural History Press, 1970), pp. 3–75.

9. There are a number of worthwhile studies of Berber customary law in Morocco (even though the majority have not been written by professional anthropologists), notably: Marchy, "Le problème du droit coutumier Berbere," *La France Méditerrannéene et Africaine* (Paris: 1939, republished with preface by G. H. Bousquet in *Revue Algerienne, Tunisienne et Marocaine de legislation et de* jurisprudence (Algiers: 1954), pp. 127–170; Georges Marchy, *Le droit coutumier Zemmour, Publications de l'Institut des Hautes Etudes Marocaines,* Vol. 40 (Algiers: J. Carbonel, and Paris: Larose, 1949); a posthumous compilation of which the second volume on penal law was never published. Robert Aspinion, *Contribution a l'étude du droit coutumier Berbere Marocain: étude sur les coutumes des tribus Zayanes,* 2nd ed. (Casablanca: A. Moynier, 1946); G. H. Bousquet, "Le droit coutumier des Ait Haddidou des Assif Melloul et Isselaten," *Annales de l'Institut des Etudes Orientales* (Faculte des Lettres de l'Universite d'Alger), **14** (1956), 113–230; and in Spanish, for the Rifian tribes of what was Spanish Morocco, Emilio Blanco Izago, *El Rif,* 2a Parte—La Ley Rifena, II: *Los Canones Rifenos Comentados,* (Ceuta: Imprenta Imperio, 1939). In this case it was only the second volume of the work in question that was ever published. See also my ethnographically oriented critique of this last-mentioned work in David M. Hart, "Emilio Blano Izago and the Berbers of the Central Rif," *Tamuda,* **6**, 2 (1958), 171–237. And for an overall view, see G. H. Bousquet, *Les Berberes,* Collection "Que Sais-Je?" No. 718, 2nd ed. (Paris: Presses Universitaires de France, 1961). The subject of Berber custom may be an unpopular or even outdated one since Moroccan independence and the rescinding of the Berber Dahir of 1930, but it is nonetheless of great intrinsic interest, and a number of tribes have experienced real difficulties in various respects as a result of readjustment to the *sharîᶜa.*

10. There is, however, one excellent study of kinship and family structure in Arab Algeria, namely, Robert Descloitres and Laid Debzi, "Système de parenté et structures familiales en algerie," in *Annuaire de l'Afrique du Nord* (Paris: Centre National de la Recherche Scientifique, 1963).

11. There is a great deal of valuable material contained in the mass of unpublished North African tribal reports, mostly by French Army Officers, on file at the CHEAM (Comité des Hautes Etudes de l'Afrique Méditerrannenne), Paris, which was founded by Robert Montagne; and also evidently at the French Overseas Archives (Archives d'Outre-Mer) at Aix-en-Provence. In Spain the Garcia Figueras collection in the Africa Section (Section Africa) of the National Library (Biblioteca Nacional), Madrid, is very much worth consulting, and the same would seem to be true of the military archives at the Military Historical Service (Servicio Historico Militar), Madrid.

CHAPTER FIVE

Islamic Art and Archaeology

OLEG GRABAR

A fuller and more correct title of the "art" whose "state" is discussed here would be The History of Islamic Art and Islamic Archaeology. History of art and archaeology are related in that they both deal with man-made "things" as their raw material and that their primary or, at the very least, preliminary mode of operation is through visual observation. Beyond this generality the two disciplines diverge considerably, and their definition has given rise to any number of discussions. Without entering into the latter, I should like to propose the following working definitions for the purposes of this chapter.

DEFINITIONS

Archaeology can be understood in two ways. One is technical and refers to a procedure for the retrieval and ordering of "things"; in this sense it is akin to a field like statistics, which may have an exciting end in itself but which tends to be used most of the time for some other type of information. Archaeology in a broader sense is also an attempt to provide a complete description of the material culture of a time or place. It tends to be more effective synchronically than diachronically and, if utilizing proper techniques and done on a large-enough scale, it can come close to providing all available or possible information about its subject. Obviously enough, archaeology has been most successful and most developed in areas and times such as prehistory, where it is the only means to acquire any sort of information. When used in historical and highly literate periods like the Islamic Middle Ages, its functions have been modified and on the whole narrowed. At its most limited, it is a technique for the determination of an architectural monument's history; an excellent example of this type is the history of the Aqsa mosque worked out by Robert Hamilton, and similar enterprises are proceeding at the mausoleum of Oljaytu in Sultaniyah, at the Shah-Sindah sanctuary in

Samarkand, and in the Great Mosque of Isfahan. The ultimate value of the information received tends to depend on the importance of the monument.

At a somewhat broader stage, archaeology can provide the context, evolution, and contemporaneity of otherwise known features. For instance, we always knew that sugar existed in the Middle Ages but it is only through the discovery of a sugar factory in Susa that we know what an actual enterprise looked like; archaeology alone can provide the development of as typical a feature of medieval Islam as the bath. It is only through excavations that ceramics or glass, the most ubiquitous materials for objects of daily or unique use, can be seen both in their development and as contemporary groups. In all these instances the knowledge of the existence of sugar factories, ceramics, or baths precedes their archaeological investigation, but the latter makes knowledge more secure.

A third stage of archaeology is the discovery of new information. The most spectacular example of the sort in Islamic archaeology has been the revolution in our understanding of the Umayyad period that has come with the excavation and investigation of hitherto unknown and unsuspected princely establishments, and the concomitant disproof of the theory of the *badiya* developed by historians on the basis of texts alone is a striking legitimation of the activity as a whole. Though perhaps less striking, the Nishapur excavations did bring to light and into a reasonably assured chronological context a whole art of ceramics, until then little understood.

A last stage of archaeology is problem-oriented; i.e., it seeks to resolve through excavations or surveys questions raised through other means. For instance, archaeology can solve certain problems of trade by demonstrating the spread of traded objects and staples; it can delineate valid regional units at various times by showing the similarity of material culture between a variety of sites; or it can provide a physical setting for characteristic concerns of historians, such as urbanism or the expression of social differentiation. Although several archaeological enterprises such as the ones at Sirâf, Qasr al-Hayr, Balis, or Fusṭâṭ have some of the objectives in mind, the work itself is still not completed or not published, and it is too early to judge the results.

The first two kinds of archaeology are essential but in a way marginal to the existence of the monument and artifacts with which they deal, and the third one is frequently accidental; the last one, consisting as it does of the setting of problems and hypotheses to be resolved through the only technique that can do so, is obviously the most appealing and exciting. It presents one major danger, however. By being essentially quantitative, it can succeed only if it is done on a sufficiently large scale. Thus to know the urban structure of Fusṭâṭ does not solve the problem of Islamic urbanism, *unless* a large number of other cities are also investigated, and the spread of a certain kind of ceramic indicative of a discrete cultural entity can be assumed only with a large number of samples. Though reasonably well solved in such instances as Hellenistic or Roman cities or Bronze Age Palestine, these methodological questions have simply not been raised in Islamic archaeology, with the possible exception of northeastern Iranian ceramics, where at least the elements for solution do exist.

The history of art is a rather different discipline, although some of its material derives from archaeology and almost all of it can be given an archaeological context. It is based on the assumption that there are qualitative variations in the "things" made by man, and its primary concern is to determine the nature and development in time of these qualitative modifications. In other words, the history of art makes choices in existing documents. For the most part the choice is made according to the time of the document on the assumption that every period had a range of qualitative achievement. At times the choice is made by the taste of the contemporary observer, as different sensibilities lead to new or different interests. All sorts of means have been developed over the past century for visual analyses defining and explaining the nature of and the reasons for the creation of works of art. They range roughly from technique of manufacture, or other connotations, to style, with its definition of manners of treating a subject (composition, proportion, color, etc.), to mode, a complex combination of style and subject matter. As in archaeology, there is a tendency to consider most of these techniques of study as universally valid, and the end result of the art historian's job is threefold. First, it is to evaluate the quality of any one monument, as was done by Ettinghausen in a group of iconographic studies of paintings and ceramics, and by S. C. Welch in discussing the Houghton Shahnameh. Second, it is to provide a history of taste, i.e., of those elements which a culture, a time, or an area tended to consider as good or beautiful. No such work has yet been done in Islamic art except by inference, or in some particular cases of dating coherent groups of objects. Third, it is—or at least can be—a means either to demonstrate some broader relationship between man (of a time or universal) and his creation or to develop methods of visual analysis which, for one reason or another, can best be formulated through the art of a given culture. Thus Western art is probably best equipped for the study of the representation of man or of space and Islamic art for architectural ornament.

There is yet another level of dealing with a work of art, which is that of criticism. Its objective ranges from an attempt to explain to others the esthetic or qualitative point of a given monument all the way to a Ruskin-like personal, almost moral, statement inspired by looking at a work of art. Whether such criticism is really possible without a deep knowledge of the surrounding culture is a moot question, as can be shown in any number of ludicrous picture books with "personal" essays, but it can be assumed, at least as a methodological hypothesis, that something of value about a given monument can be said by considering it by itself.

SPECIFIC APPROACHES

There are instances or works by historians of Islamic art or by archaeologists dealing with Islam which illustrate characteristic procedures of either field, but such is not the case with all scholarship in Islamic art and archaeology. When compared to Italian or even Chinese art, the study of Islamic art is primitive and underdeveloped and certainly Islamic archaeology cannot be compared in achievement to classical archaeology. Part of the reason is its novelty, for as a definable concern it is hardly older than this century, and its practitioners have been and still are remarkably few. In addition, the field has been affected by the fact that it grew and still grows under the impact of a broad range of factors. Some of these are simply motivations, the reasons why an individual works in a field or a certain problem becomes studied; these are often unique to the field. Other factors are methods of work and can be shared by several areas of art history, but they are affected by peculiarities in the study of any one tradition. Still others are more personal preferences or even prejudices. In most scholarship more than one of these approaches or moods can be discerned, but they are interesting and important to identify, partly because they explain the growth of the field, its accomplishments, and its failures, and partly because they may best enable us to define what could and ought to be done. For each one of them has values and limitations. I should like to identify nine such factors, differing a great deal from each other in importance and impact, yet at times very much interrelated.

1. Without in any way acquiescing to the occasional pejorative aspects of the terms, I should like to call the first approach *antiquarian–scholarly*. Whether it started with collectors or with philologists, it was the first one formed, some time in the first half of the nineteenth century when Lanci, Reinaud, Coste, Dieulafoy, Khanikoff, and others began to study ruined or standing monuments all over the Muslim world and to notice Muslim objects in private and public collections. Although the first major monuments of this tradition were the pertinent volumes of Napoleon's expedition to Egypt, the tradition came into its own around the turn of the twentieth century, when Max van Berchem, Friedrich Sarre, Gaston Migeon, and Henri Saladin, to name only those whose works are best known, provided the first more general studies illustrating its point of view. The strength of this tradition was primarily its detached disciplinary rigor and secondarily its amazing spread of coverage. The knowledge of Oriental and Western languages or, alternatively, passionate collecting of objects, was essential to it, and Spain

and Central Asia as well as intermediary lands were felt to be understood together. It concentrated on making available and known monuments which were not in the normal circuit of educated men; it often tended to be descriptive, although the genius of Max van Berchem, for instance, did go much beyond the purely descriptive. The weakness of this tradition was first of all its very detachment; superbly proud in the quality and purity of its search for knowledge, it often failed to descend from its ivory tower and seemed at times arcane in its concerns, requiring a type of acquisitive, linguistic, and intellectual background which reduces its impact, as many of us have found as we confront modern students with its achievements. There was an elitist "clubbism" about this tradition, as there still is today among private collectors, "Orientalist" scholars, and world travelers. Another weakness is that it was a tradition that was very much aloof from the living culture of Islamic lands, even though one could argue that its high ideals made it independent of the relevant political and social contingencies. With the possible exception of Khalil Edhem in Istanbul, no Muslim or Near Easterner was involved in it in its early stages, and very few have been since then. In short, it serves as an example of the noble ideal of nineteenth-century scholarship, but as Herzfeld wrote so well in a sadly nostalgic obituary of Max van Berchem, there is some uncertainty about the likelihood of its value in today's world. Yet its successes, its dreams of large corpora, its ambition of making everything known and available, and its moral and intellectual rigor are permanent and will never be replaced.

2. The second point of view is of more recent vintage and, though it is not entirely correct to see it as a reflection of nationalism, there is little doubt that it was affected by nationalism and by the emergence of real or artificial nations all over the Muslim world. I should like to call this point of view *local*, and at times it has become parochial. Its sources are less in the elite universities of the Western world than in local initiatives, at times teachers in primary or secondary schools, at other times administrators, architects, or other professionals born in a certain place or sent there through some vagary of fate. Such were the French administrators of Algeria like General de Beylié, to whom we owe the first excavation of an Islamic site, or the British and Indian sponsors of the Archaeological Survey of India, or the Russian officials of the Society of Lovers of Archaeology in Turkistan, or Mubarak Pasha reporting on every street of Cairo with Maqrîzî's description at hand. At times inspired with tireless enthusiasm as in the case of A. U. Pope, who almost single-handed made Iranian art known to a wider public, it is a tradition that can be as dully descriptive as annual reports of local departments of antiquities or as ridiculously nationalist-parochial as some earlier works done in Turkey and more recently in Central Asia. Its main strength is that it examined one area in depth, through constant familiarity; it pro-

tected its own immediate heritage and collected objects in new museums whose frequently pitiful looks should not hide their importance. The works of Ayverdi in Turkey, of Irâj Afs̲h̲âr in Iran, of L. T. Bretanitski and others in Azerbaijan, and of Abû al-Farâj al-^{c}Us̲h̲ in Damascus are examples of this mode of activity at its most useful and, at times, its best.

By being local, this interest became supported by new governments, in ways that vary enormously from country to country but with the principle of a *national heritage* throughout. Much of its effort has been to preserve and to count. Thus one knows that there are nearly half a million objects of Islamic art registered in Turkey, and mechanisms for the repair of monuments exist. Bulletins, annuals, and annals are associated with this tradition in increasingly frightening numbers, but each issue brings to light something new and of value. It is also a tradition that involved Muslims in the understanding of art of the Muslim world, and in recent years it has adopted excavations and surveys as a useful way to increase knowledge about one's own patrimony. A striking achievement of these activities lies in the mass of usually unpublished archives on architectural monuments lying in archaeological and archival offices all over the Near East.

An approach to Islamic art and archaeology that can by extension be related to the local one is the approach of certain collectors and of a large body of literature issued from collecting. It involves concern with a single technique, regardless of its source of origin. Best known among students of carpets, it exists also among collectors of ceramics, glass, and coins, but its passion is not always matched by equal intellectual abilities.

The weaknesses of this tradition as a whole, however, are considerable. First the practical task of discovering, maintaining, and making available has almost throughout been beyond the financial, technical, and often intellectual possibilities of many countries. Whereas the Berlin Museum and the Metropolitan Museum can control their collections, the Cairo and Istanbul museums cannot, because their responsibility is national rather than selective and, though Western scholars may complain that the minarets of Herat are falling down, only the local administrators are obliged to do something about it. In theory this first weakness can easily be made up through funds and training, but of course matters are more complicated, for funds do not exist and personnel ready to be trained are even scarcer. A second weakness has been national compartmentalization, often of a ridiculous nature when combined with linguistic antagonisms. Books and knowledge do not move easily from Syria to Iraq, from Iran to Afghanistan, or from Soviet Central Asia to Iran. Much of this is the result of political realities that may change, but in addition there is inherent in this kind of concern the weakness of national distortion, which exists as well (or at least existed) in the study of French, German, or Italian art. Altogether, then, though the local approach is potentially highly desirable, it has not yet made its mark, for it has failed to meet some of the basic criteria of this field. It has not succeeded in generalizing, and it has not been able to define with adequate precision regional differentiations or else it has imposed improper ones. Some exceptions exist, as in North Africa and Spain or in Soviet Azerbaijan and Central Asia, partly also in Turkey, but in all cases, except possibly the city of Cairo, completeness of information has not been achieved in any accessible form and conclusions are often weakened by insufficient or improper knowledge of neighboring lands.

As one dreams of Dehio's work on German art, of Van Marle's on Italian painting, even of Siren's on Chinese painting, it is an approach that is still at an elementary level. However, in contrast to the preceding one, it is an approach that not only still exists but that is constantly growing.

3. A third approach is theoretically quite easy to define. It consists in starting from an accepted disciplinary problem or method of the history of art, and applying it to Islamic art. In this pure and simple form, as in attempts to identify the authorship of paintings, it has been rarely used, although the work of I. Stchoukine and S. C. Welch, among others, comes reasonably close to it. A series of iconographic studies by R. Ettinghausen can be used as examples of typical art historical methodology, and there are other examples as well. An important contribution to this approach has been made by scholars in other periods of the arts who sought in Islamic art some proof of or examples for a point raised elsewhere. E. Baldwin Smith in his *Architectural Symbolism* or Henri Stern and André Grabar in dealing with Christian art have utilized Islamic examples and have contributed to their understanding. But it is perhaps in the Vienna of the turn of the century that the formidable talents of Alois Riegl and of Joseph Strzygowski have sought to illustrate in the most interesting manner their own art historical theories through monuments of Islamic art. Although one still occasionally finds references to works of Islamic art in more recent manuals or theoretical works, such references are rare and usually limited to a few topics such as ornament or miniatures.

The strengths of an art historical approach are obvious. On the one hand, it removes the exoticism or parochialism attached to the first two points of view and furnishes a presumed universal system of investigation. On the other hand, it makes the knowledge of the Muslim world accessible to all who are interested in archaeology or in the arts. In theory it puts it on the same level of investigation and of value as any other artistic tradition. Perhaps most importantly, it introduces the Muslim world within the curriculum of all students rather than of a selected few, and almost all teaching commentators have pointed out that their audience consists much more frequently of students of other arts than of actual or potential specialists. The setting of monuments of Islamic art within generally accepted procedures and concepts of the history of art is thus a highly desirable goal.

The defects of this point of view are equally obvious. First of all, it tends to exclude those who belong to the Near Eastern world or to make them strangers within their own culture, for it is rarely realized how much the basic concepts of the history of art issue from a fundamentally European visual and intellectual tradition. A second defect is somewhat more insidious and applies particularly to the use of Islamic art for other traditions or for broadly theoretical purposes. It tends not only to abstract a monument from its setting but at times even to abstract a single feature in a monument for the demonstration of some general point. This has been very true, for instance, of the treatment of Islamic monuments by Strzygowski and by Baldwin Smith. Yet without denying the validity of any attempt at general patterns, an obvious objective of a historian, and a fortiori of an art historian, is to understand the uniqueness of a moment or of a single work of art. Finally, a defect of this approach concerns its practitioners. Ideally they should acquire mastery in two areas, as disciplinary specialists and as area specialists. In reality, one or the other tends to predominate in a frequently uneasy balance.

4. An ideal archaeological approach to Islamic "things" is easy enough to define, for it would simply consist in the gathering and analysis of the sum total of available information about a given place or time. Much of the acquisition of the information is to be made through excavation, but its interpretation requires other kinds of documents as well.

Up to World War II, excavations of Islamic sites were carried out by small teams, often only two or three staff members, and their objectives were the reconstruction of architectural settings (usually of a single monument) and the retrieval of complete or almost complete objects. Very few of these excavations were fully published, although their most notable finds were rapidly made available. In addition a very large number of excavations of pre-Islamic sites encountered perforce a lot of Islamic material. When not discarded altogether, these remains were only occasionally made public.

After World War II and especially in the past decade, archaeology has undergone extraordinary changes. It developed masses of new techniques of fieldwork and recording, and a large number of specialists became necessary for the proper evaluation and definition of its results. Staffs of 20 or more are no longer a rarity. Alternatively, survey techniques utilizing aerial photographs and a variety of sampling devices have made it possible, at least in theory, to provide reasonably accurate reconstructions of such features as town plans, canal systems, and other basic elements of traditional life. Furthermore, a whole branch of archaeology has become concerned with its own methods as an abstract phenomenon and seeks to use a site for the illustration of broad theoretical questions of knowledge and of interpretation.

Finally, mention should be made of an activity which is not archaeological in the sense that it is not carried out by professional archaeologists and that its excavation procedures are not systematic, yet is very common and has provided or can provide significant results for the understanding of an area's material culture. This activity is the restoration of major monuments, usually done by specialized architects with little or no training in the area.

Although the earlier, more artisanal, manner of operating still continues and will always exist (not necessarily with worthless results, though almost always without the expected completeness of results), and although the very latest methodological concerns have never yet been applied to an Islamic site, it is essentially the two methods of a large-scale operation with many specialists and of surveys as well as restorations that will affect the field. The best and almost unique example of the large-scale operation is the excavation of Sirâf in Iran. It is not yet possible to judge the results of the excavation from our present point of view in defining an approach, but two general points are worthy of note. One is that the preliminary publications of archaeological work tend to be overly technical and to avoid elements of hypothesis, speculation, or interpretation which are most likely to be of use to an area specialist. The other one is that the abstractly conceived technical process of recovery and recording occasionally hampers the elucidation of a particular site in its entirety, for only too often it is not or cannot be modified easily enough in order to adapt to the content being discovered. This need not be a criticism, if funds and time available for any excavation were unlimited. Since this is usually not the case, an archaeologist is compelled to make choices, and some of us feel that choices should be made on the basis of the site's likely significance for the culture investigated rather than for purely technical archaeological needs. It should be emphasized, however, that this is a point of view likely to be challenged by many, often with very valid arguments. Yet it seems altogether true that an archaeological approach of this sort tends to provide minute information which is difficult to relate to broader issues of the visually perceptible world of Islam. It may be added that this most objectively scientific method of gathering and analyzing documents is the only one pertaining to the arts that can be used only once, for it destroys the conditions in which it was used. None of the control devices that exist can entirely replace an assumption of honesty on the part of the investigator.

One by-product of this archaeology bears more immediate fruits. It consists in technical analyses of soils, mortars, glazes, metals, woods, and so forth. Although only in their infancy, analyses of minerals in ceramics, of gold residue in silver (a technique issued from other concerns but typologically relatable), and of sources for colors are likely to have significant results in such areas as identification of workshops, schools, and international trade.

Surveys have been done in a systematic way only in parts of Iraq, but the results have been quite fascinating, for it was possible, in R. M. Adams' work primarily, to provide fairly rapidly and at lesser cost than excavations an adequate picture of the use of land through history with all sorts of subsequent social and economic consequences. The main problem with surveys, of course, is that there is an accidental character to some of their evidence, especially in places of high occupational density, and therefore they must generally be followed by a coherent program of soundings and excavations. However, as preliminary hypotheses and as general indicators of an area's characteristics and likelihood for more precise work, they are essential.

Restorations appear at first glance to be no more than technical jobs of repair and consolidation. Their quality varies enormously from the admittedly superb work carried out in the Alhambra to controversial ones, like the restoration of the Dome of the Rock in Jerusalem, to sheer atrocities, both esthetic and historical, as in the mosaics of the mosque of Damascus. The problem is that most of the time these are generally expensive operations carried out either because of immediate necessity or for tourism. In most cases, the job is done under very loose scientific supervision and the results are rarely published. Thus there is a lack most of the time of adequate documentation of "before" and "after," and the justification for any one reconstruction is all too frequently unavailable. The objects or other remains found during the work are almost always unrecorded or thrown away. As a result, although restorations could become major archaeological sources, they have often become disasters, because for practical purposes they are irreversible. The remarkable exception of the work done by several Italian teams in Iran shows how invaluable restoration can be. Then, since all monuments cannot be preserved, there always remains the nagging question of which to preserve. Most commentators feel that all of them should be protected and old towns and new settlements should be developed in some meaningful relationship to older monuments; others argue that there are few monuments of demonstrable uniqueness and that they should not become frozen memorials to one time's esthetic choice.

To sum up the archaeological approach, one could say that it is a priori the most likely way to acquire a complete visual picture of a time or a place and that it has developed an important series of subfields of potential use. Moreover, because it is more abstract in its methodology, it can be adapted to many settings, and it is noteworthy that excellent archaeological work has been done by all Near Eastern countries, although few have dealt with the Muslim world except Iraq. The approach is weakened, however, by its cost, by the great variety of talents it requires, by an uncertainty about the degree of generality that can be derived from any one instance, and by a very spotty and unsatisfactory record of publications.

There is yet one aspect of archaeology that deserves mention, for even though it is a practical problem, it affects very strongly archaeology's actual and potential effectiveness. Although most other approaches can be used by a single scholar working alone, archaeology is an expensive activity usually funded by the country of the chief excavator (occasionally by international bodies like UNESCO for restorations) which depends for its success on the host country. The point is that there are enormous variations at this time in the kinds of facilities, help, and expectations to be found in the countries of the Middle East. These variations are not merely pleasant or unpleasant peculiarities of any one country but reflections of archaeological work still done predominantly by foreigners. Three questions appear to be constantly raised: what is the real use of excavations by foreigners, to develop a true national heritage or to provide documents for an alien concern? Should a host country control the choice of sites to be excavated as rigidly as most countries control the artifacts that are found? If so, how? Finally, is an excavation a privilege granted to a foreign investigator, whereby the purposes may be dictated in part by local needs, such as urban or agricultural planning (e.g., several instances of so-called "salvage" archaeology), or by touristic value, with implication of restoration and total uncovering of all remains usually not within the budget or competence of an archaeological team?

There are as yet no coherent answers to these questions, nor am I aware of meetings and consultations which could lead to answers valid for the whole area. It is rather unlikely in fact that this will happen, but the very fact that the questions are raised suggests that there will be an unsettled period in successful archaeological work. This is especially true for Islamic archaeology, which appeals enormously because it deals with the past of the area's present culture but which, precisely for the same reason, touches on practical problems and susceptibilities that rarely occur with more ancient archaeology. Although it is difficult to evaluate with certainty what will actually happen, it seems to many of us that a sort of official partnership with local institutions, with a built-in training program for young archaeologists, will become the rule for any kind of long-range and large-scale excavation and that the foreign mission will be required to undertake various tasks of preservation and restoration. On the other hand, surveys are likely to be more easily continued, although their requirement for detailed maps and aerial photographs often involves sensitive areas of national security. In general, it seems rather vain and foolish to consider an archaeological approach to the study of Islamic art from the exclusively theoretical point of view of a discipline, for its very nature as a team operating for many years as an employer of labor in investigating the past of a living culture compels its practical and intellectual integration in the concerns of each country.

5. The approach of the Islamist, i.e., of the scholar trained primarily in languages and in disciplines using language as the main source of data, to the

study of the arts and of archaeology has occurred in several different ways. At times, as in the case of J. Schacht, observations incidental to a scholar's main interest led to a group of archaeological studies. In a slightly more systematic way, the interests of L. Massignon and of A. Schimmel in mysticism and of Massignon in the setting of Muslim culture led them to esthetic or archaeological considerations. Most of the time these contributions illuminate a specific aspect of a monument but they never exhaust them, nor is their point of departure so much a visual one as a textual one. It is also fascinating to observe that quite frequently students of texts fail to notice the archaeological importance of their own discoveries; for example, this has frequently occurred in the publication and study of *waqf* documents which frequently refer to and can be made clearer by existing monuments.

Two other "Islamist" approaches have been far more fruitful and coherent. Although originating in many ways with Max van Berchem, the first one is best exemplified by the work of Sauvaget, who sought to find in the arts and in what he called archaeology (more a type of evidence than a methodological procedure) that "silent web of Islamic history," which Sauvaget defined in his inaugural lecture at the Collège de France. In this tradition visually perceptible and material remains are seen on a par with texts as necessary for an understanding of history; they are not an end in themselves, and Sauvaget was quite caustic about art historians, for he avoided and distrusted esthetic and value judgments as historical documents. Though he was the best exponent of this approach, it is one that has continued in the work of many younger scholars. J. and D. Sourdel's *Civilisation classique de l'Islam* is the first general book in which textual and visual information are closely bound together. A related approach, never expressed in theoretical form, appears in the work of L. Mayer, where texts are used to help the understanding of monuments but the two are not considered as totally parallel data to be sifted with the same philological or archaeological rigor, and usually the monument's analysis is more complete. However, it is worthwhile to point out that a large group of younger art historians began their careers as philologists or text-centered historians.

The other "Islamist" approach has dealt with those areas where writing and visual observation are intimately connected, epigraphy and numismatics. Although the latter is a field in itself that is not peculiar to the Islamic world but that has been strikingly advanced by the immense labor of G. Miles and of his school, the monumental writing studied by epigraphists has acquired in the Muslim world an unusually spectacular development. The reasons for this development are not important to our purposes, but it is important to point out that its investigation, which can illuminate the most varied aspects of Islamic culture, requires a knowledge of languages as well as an ability to define visually perceptible stylistic characteristics.

The key strength of an Islamist's approach to the visual world has been much more than the development of the two ancillary disciplines of numismatics and epigraphy. It involves, next to the sacrosanct text, a host of other documents, often more precise and more real in their own time than a chronicle. It can therefore be of much value to the historian, but it is an approach that is also essential to the art historian or to the archaeologist, for it compels him to put a monument in precisely defined historical, social, and human contexts. Seen theoretically, the weakness of the approach has been—but need not be—that it avoids the esthetic judgments which are almost necessary in the use of visual evidence and which were certainly an integral part of any cultural moment. Perhaps its practical weaknesses have been more important, however. One of them is that it has not really succeeded in developing the kind of partnership between text-centered and monument-centered scholarship which is necessary for its ultimate success. The best practitioners always knew both languages and at least rudiments of visual analysis (often technical rather than esthetic), but this combination, though useful, is not necessary a priori, and one can easily imagine a social historian or a historian of literature working out a number of problems together with an art historian or an archaeologist. However, such teams have simply never materialized, and at this time the double personality of the Islam-centered investigator is still the rule. The Islamic approach has been more successful with architecture and iconography than with other techniques or other art historical analyses. The reasons are easy to see, for architecture is most intimately tied to social life and subject matter is often dictated by literary references. Stylistic or modal analyses have been less frequently accepted by text-centered scholars, and art historians and archaeologists dealing with the *madrasa* have not quite been able to cope with the early literary evidence on the subject.

6. A sixth factor is a particularly delicate and difficult one to define properly, for it involves an important aspect of Islamic civilization. We may call it a presumed reluctance to the visual expression of esthetic feeling. The word "presumed" is used purposely, for it has not been established whether such a reluctance really existed and whether it was a continuous feature of the culture or only affected some segments in its history. The reasons for the existence of this feeling are several. One is the demonstrable fact of an absence of religious art with the representation of living beings. What is curious is that this absence and the existence of a number of iconoclastic texts led to the assumption that figures were absent in all arts, and as a result any example that did appear seemed to be an exception. It is interesting to recall how the discovery in the latter part of the nineteenth century of the paintings of Qusayr Amrah led to significant or ludicrous articles by almost every Orientalist of the time. It should also be recalled that many of the first academic Islamists

were Semitists who often sought in Islamic thought and practices an illustration of Semitic and, more specifically, Jewish ideas and modes of life. Another reason is that the Western and Hindu artistic traditions emphasized so much the representation of the human form that a tradition in which it was weaker seemed to be one without true artistic concepts. Then there appears to be a lack in Muslim writing of esthetic doctrines applicable to the visual arts; it is true that, as it became expressed in its eighteenth- and nineteenth-century forms, official Islam did not acknowledge visual beauty, representation, or symbols as particularly significant to its values, except in the area of calligraphy; the contrast with China or Japan is quite striking on this point. Finally, except in areas of artisanal creation such as carpets or brass objects, there had occurred a loss of immediate artistic creativity in the Muslim world by the time scientific enquiries began and a preconceived view of this creativity developed at a time when most mosques were closed to non-Muslims and the treasuries of palaces were inaccessible.

There may be other reasons as well, although in retrospect it is striking how much it is a West-centered view of what the arts ought to be that has colored the appreciation of Islamic art. In a manual of the history of architecture written in the early part of the century and still regularly reedited (Sir Bannister Fletcher), Islamic architecture is relegated to the "nonhistorical" styles, i.e., those without evolution or relationship to the grand Western tradition.

The consequence of all these factors was twofold. In the Muslim world itself it created for many decades an almost total lack of interest in Islamic monuments. Exceptions were few and usually limited to highly educated or Westernized individuals, often more concerned with Western art than with their own. But the most important result was that, as education developed at all levels, the visual world played almost no part in it. History books lack pictures, visits to museums or monuments are infrequent, and the history of art is almost nonexistent. Until the early 1960s Western art was taught at the universities of Istanbul and Ankara by Turks, but Islamic art was taught by Germans. Today Western art is taught by Iranians in Tehran, but not Islamic art; until very recently Westerners alone taught Islamic art in Beirut, and only in Cairo are Egyptians and Westerners involved. The most important consequence of this phenomenon appears as the situation in the Muslim world is compared with that of China or Japan, for in the latter many of the theoretical formulations for the study of the arts came out of the living culture. No such formulations or concepts came out of the Muslim world, not even at the artisanal level, where a whole vocabulary exists for forms; however, this has never been systematically collected.

Another consequence of this prevalent opinion of Islamic artistic creativity was that it affected the interest in it of Western scholarship. Seen almost exclusively in terms of surface ornament or of artisanal technique, Islamic art tended to be relegated to a secondary position in great artistic currents and considered interesting only as a source of possible influences or as an exoticism. Turqueries were known, but not the striking achievements of Ottoman architecture in Istanbul and Edirne, to use examples of cities which were accessible and fairly frequently visited in the nineteenth century. However, aside from the lack of concern with Islamic art, which is obvious in manuals, university curricula, and catalogs of book publishers, the subtler effect of this opinion has been that the world from Spain to India and from the seventh to the seventeenth centuries is thought of as one single world of esthetic sameness and that almost anyone can write about it. Although some changes in these feelings are beginning to appear for a variety of reasons, they are still easy to illustrate both in university appointments and in recent books.

7. The next two factors to be discussed are of an entirely different kind, for they really are methods of work rather than disciplinary approaches or historical and cultural limitations. In many ways they transcend most of the previous categories, but, partly because of the small number of practitioners in the field, they have very much affected the character of its scholarship. In many ways the most common methodological approach is *monographic* and consists in starting with a single object, painting, or monument of architecture and expanding from its description into as many questions as possible. The effectiveness of the method obviously depends on the quality and breadth of knowledge of the investigator, but it is an approach that is particularly characteristic of the art historian as a humanist, for its ultimate objective is the total understanding of an already existing entity; at its extreme it is applicable by the archaeologist who seeks to understand a particular site, but its greatest exponents have been the connoisseurs who identify and date the making of a work of art and the iconographers who explain its subject matter, its position in time, its impact on later times, and occasionally its belonging to a series.

The advantages of this method, which can be illustrated by several works of R. Ettinghausen on objects and miniatures and by L. Golombek's monograph on Gazur Gah, are obvious: a monument becomes as well delineated as information makes possible at any one time, and the only limitation lies in the author's abilities or knowledge. The weakness of the method is that, unless it is pursued over large numbers of examples or preceded by a theoretical explanation for any given choice, it runs the risk of making one building or object overly significant; hence a whole period may be misunderstood or wrongly focused.

8. The second methodological approach is problem-oriented or synthetic. Its purpose is generally to answer some broad question about the visual expression of a time or about characteristics that require partial information from many sources. An example of the first type would be O. Grabar's attempt to explain the formation of Islamic art; of the second type would be

Mayer's study of Mamluk costume. Although equally affected by the quality of the investigator, the major advantages of this method are that it responds to questions reflecting scholarly or other needs and that its answers tend either to become permanently valid as documents (for instance, Mamluk costume need no longer be investigated unless new evidence appears) or to be fruitful general statements or hypotheses for nonspecialists or students. The weaknesses of this approach are that it can easily lead to superficiality and that its necessary selectivity of information can also be misleading. In many ways its effectiveness depends either on intuition or on a lot of monographs.

9. It is important to point out that Islamic art is an area that is affected by the existence of an art market, although it is perhaps unfair to consider this a factor for the study of the whole of Islamic art. The acquisition of new objects or the transfer of older ones is a major activity which occupies much of the time and energy of the world's major museums and of a number of scholars and collectors. There are many ways of evaluating the impact of an active art market on any given field of study, especially after the recent controversies on the subject and the positions taken by archaeological and anthropological organizations. Without taking sides on these issues with ramifications that are not pertinent here, we could formulate the impact of the art market in the following way. The advantage is that collections can grow all the time if they wish to do so and are rich enough to afford it. As a result it is possible for any place in the world to develop a good collection, and the impact of and interest in Islamic art grow accordingly. There is little doubt that the sale and spread of objects is one of the most successful ways for a field to become better known, and this in turn generates, or at least can generate, the kind of enthusiasm which is useful for the growth of the field. A more limited sideline of an active market has been the development of all sorts of techniques for the detection of forgeries and thus technical study of metals has been much advanced. Even aside from this particular development, the context of a museum and the visual associations that can be made between different works of Islamic art and other traditions are intellectually and educationally fruitful, as the success of so many exhibitions clearly demonstrates.

There are, however, dangers in the existence of an art market. One such danger is that richer areas deplete poorer ones and it is striking that only the cities of Cairo and of Istanbul possess collections comparable in quality to the Islamic ones in the West. For science per se, this is not a significant defect. More serious is the fact that the energies and concerns of collectors or of museums are often unduly channeled toward the acquisition of a new piece rather than the study of an already existing one. But the most serious problem is that of occasionally limiting the availability of objects. Certain miniatures of extraordinary historical importance and esthetic merit have not been seen for almost 40 years, and some objects disappear for years without a trace. The secretiveness that surrounds some of the transactions concerning works of art is certainly not in a scholarly tradition and has on occasion been harmful to research.

It is not really possible to sum up in a simple series of statements the way in which the activities of the archaeologist and of the art historian seen in a broad and general way are affected by a variety of more uniquely Islamic factors or by actual methods of work. It can perhaps be suggested that, in the study of Islamic art, the expected disciplinary spectrum which ranges from cataloging to the elaboration of general theories has been and is still influenced by an unusual and uneasily matched variety of intellectual or practical interests, by a lack of intellectual direction from the culture itself, by the novelty of the field as a scientific enterprise, and by the paucity of its practitioners. As we see below its achievements are all the more remarkable, even if insufficient.

SUBFIELDS

Even if deans, departmental chairmen, center directors, and the general public tend to see a visual tradition of more than 1000 years from Spain to India as a proper field in which to exercise one's talents, in reality a breakdown into subfields has occurred, at least insofar as scholarly concerns and research are involved. Although acknowledging this fact and its necessary occurrence, several commentators have pointed out that some of the exciting aspects of the field are that it has not become overly specialized and that it is still possible, indeed necessary, to roam over vast spaces and chunks of time and to avoid the overspecialization of other areas. While agreeing with the excitement of this traditionally Orientalist view, one may question its value for an understanding of the past. To seek to know everything often means to end up knowing nothing, and a tendency to superficiality does occur unless generalization is based on a hierarchy of reasonably secure and digested information. Furthermore, if the categories of understanding are too broad, they fail to explain a given monument in the concreteness of its time of creation.

However, though the practitioner may expect pan-Islamic knowledge, scholarship and research have tended to divide into four clear types of subfields, and two others more difficult to define, which are unique to Islamic studies.

The clear fields are regional, technical, iconographic or stylistic cross-sections of areas and times, and period studies. Whether for linguistic, national, or other reasons, a great deal of the published work tends to be limited to certain areas: Spain, North Africa, Egypt, the Fertile Crescent (if not actually Syria as separate from Iraq), Turkey and the Ottoman empire, Iran, Soviet Central Asia, Soviet Azerbaijan, and India. Most of the strengths and weaknesses of what we have defined as the "local" approach apply to work done in this manner. Purely national approaches have been supplemented by broadly regional ones in a few cases, most successfully in western Islam. The second clear subfield is technical: the study of architecture, ceramics, glass, carpets, and so forth. Occasionally, especially with architecture, the two subfields become merged into one, most voluminously in recent years in the instances of Turkish and Central Asian architecture. Comparative studies of stylistic or iconographic motifs (e.g., the unicorn or the calyx as ornament) across techniques and regions are characteristic art historical concerns, requiring usually a particularly broad factual knowledge. Attempts to establish clearly the nature of a period's visual concerns are also typical endeavors, whether the periodization itself is based on historical definition (e.g., the art of a dynasty) or on a valid grouping of monuments.

The murkier but more uniquely Islamic subfields are the relationship between Islamic art and neighboring or earlier traditions and the question of a Muslim iconoclasm. Little has been written on the latter subject in very recent years; it is probable that neither new documents nor new ideas have occurred to anyone, and in all likelihood the traditional setting up of the problem in terms of a search for a coherent ideological position developed at a concrete time seems to have exhausted itself. Whether new ways of dealing with the matter are possible and desirable is very much an open question.

The relationship of Islamic art to earlier or neighboring arts has been the subject of much contemporary concern. The impetus for such studies came at times from other fields such as Byzantine studies or Western Christendom, and at times from the Near Eastern specialist who sought either to demonstrate certain external impacts and their nature or, perhaps more fruitfully, to seek the ways in which earlier artistic themes or ideas were adopted, rejected, or adapted by the new culture. The interesting feature of these investigations is that, when they are not simple catalogs or exercises in self-glory, they raise very important questions about the use and value of visual forms. For to borrow or to utilize a form created by another cultural setting implies a far greater (or at least different) consciousness of one's activity than to continue whatever is prevalent in one's own culture. Working independently Grabar and Ettinghausen have recently provided quite different examples of analyses of influences and impacts and the subfield is likely to be particularly fruitful, both methodologically and for its information.

ACHIEVEMENTS

In order to measure achievement, we must consider three kinds of features. One is whether monuments or other appropriate documents have been adequately studied and/or published, adequacy being measured by the satisfactoriness of substituting the studies for personal and direct contact with the monument. The second feature is whether these documents, if published, are reasonably accessible, for there is little value in knowing that certain groups of Fatimid ceramics have been discussed in detail in an Arab journal unavailable in most libraries of the world or that a very rare Russian book in honor of a Georgian poet contains the only coherent discussion of a very important piece of metalwork from the late twelfth century. But a third feature is equally important. It is essentially a synthetic one and can best be formulated through a series of questions: have general or partial syntheses been done? Are there general hypotheses or conclusions from which scholarship can grow or which can be presented to students as expressing a consensus of the profession? Are these hypotheses of primary significance to other art historians or to specialists in the Muslim world? In other words, how does the field compare with the Italian Renaissance, to use the example of a highly developed field, where complete works of major (and even minor) artists are available in several languages, with a constantly shifting range of hypotheses and generalities stretching from the brilliantly innovative to the chiché-ridden potboiler? Alternatively, is an interweaving of the visual and of the literary, which occurs in the works by Huizinga or Seznec for medieval Europe, possible from the results of Islamic art historians?

Basic Publications

If we take into consideration work in active stages of development as well as work that is known to have been done but that has not been published or exists only in restricted form, the following conclusions seem appropriate.

In architecture, Spain, North Africa, Egypt (until 1350), Anatolia, Azerbaijan, and Soviet Central Asia are reasonably well-known in the sense that the visible parts of standing monuments have been adequately recorded and for the most part published. For Palestine, Syria, and Iraq, the very early centuries are available in similar fashion, but the twelfth and later centuries are not. For Iran and Afghanistan, what is available is so minimal that it is almost impossible to teach an adequate course or to do any useful research without having traveled in the two countries, although much excellent information lies in the archives of various universities and especially in the offices of local departments of antiquities. But this overall conclusion on regions is valid only insofar as basic information is concerned, that is, plans and a fair number of photographs. When we turn to measured elevations, to systems of proportions, or to such features as brick or stone measurements, repairs, contemporary texts, inscriptions, later descriptions, and interpretations, matters are far less satisfactory. In effect it is only for Cairo that the combination of Creswell's measurements, of Max van Berchem's and Gaston Wiet's epigraphical and textual studies, and of a number of recent monographs may be considered satisfactory. Recent work in Central Asia and in Anatolia has been good for measurements but very weak on textual parallels and inscriptions. The occasional appropriate publication of the visible parts of a few Iranian monuments or of the Cordova mosque should not make us forget that for the Alhambra or for Isfahan in the seventeenth century, we still rely on publications of the middle of the nineteenth century. Finally, once again with the partial exception of Egypt and the more major one of Rempel's work on Central Asia, we have no coherent surveys of ornament, even though there is agreement on its importance, and we have only a minimal number of comparative studies or attempts at defining periods of architectural style. What there is of the latter is based exclusively on political history, not on monuments.

The situation in painting is almost worse. Preliminary surveys exist for Iran through Stchoukin's volumes, but their plates are insufficient. Only a handful of manuscripts has been published in complete form, often a long time ago and with uneven color reproductions. A few of the most famous Arabic manuscripts of the thirteenth century have been published, but not the celebrated albums from Istanbul, although a thorough search through dozens of books and articles does bring together a lot of information. Catalogs are adequate for the Chester Beatty Library, barely passable for the British Museum, the Bibliothèque Nationale, or the Leningrad public library, and practically unavailable for the richest collections in Istanbul or for most museums. Those commentators who dealt with painting have remarked with striking consistency on the inadequacy of much of the information provided even in the better catalogs; more is said about this later.

Thanks to the efforts of D. S. Rice, major works of inlaid metalwork of the twelfth to fourteenth centuries are reasonably accessible in superbly detailed form. Earlier or later objects are only intermittently available, and it is only very incidentally that the more expensive gold and silver objects or jewelry have been studied. Glass has been surveyed by Lamm and ivories are now ideally available through Kühnel's corpus. Rugs and carpets form the only area of Islamic decorative arts with a very extensive bibliography, some of which is only of commercial importance but excellent introductions and summaries do exist as well. Other textiles have been treated less systematically, although much information exists about them either in the form of Serjeant's studies of texts or in the publication of complete parts of single collections (Textile Museum, Boston), or through a number of studies devoted to individual textiles. Unfortunately there is hardly an instance where correlation could be established between a type of textile known through literary sources and a remaining artifact. If one recalls that thousands of fragments exist and that textiles were not only a major industry but also the most common honorific gifts throughout classical Islam, this lack of correlation is rather puzzling.

A relatable problem occurs with ceramics. Almost all existing studies, including the very valuable manuals written by A. Lane, deal with *la céramique d'art,* the more beautiful or technically more elaborate "museum pieces." Some success has been achieved in identifying major series and in explaining individual objects. On the other hand, none of these works has been of much use to archaeologists faced with the problem of defining and cataloging literally hundreds of thousands of shards. It may be more appropriate to say that, whereas the main types of artistic pottery from Spain, Egypt, Syria, Anatolia, and Iran have been identified, sometimes in considerable detail, the mass of medieval Islamic ceramics, against whose background the fancier pottery could better be understood, is still very much of an unknown quantity. In many ways this is also true of glass and of certain types of bronze objects, but in these areas the problems are less crucial because the objects do not lend themselves to the same kind of precise differentiation.

Although the record of availability by individual techniques is spotty and incomplete, the same is true for individual collections containing several techniques. The excellent catalogs of the Cairo Museum or the partial one of the Louvre are 40 or more years old and no longer correspond to the collections themselves. More recently a few reasonably complete simplified catalogs of public collections in Germany and of private ones in England were made, but too many of the most important collections are simply not available. Success has been achieved only in numismatics, mostly thanks to G. Miles, and in epigraphy, through the *Répertoire d'épigraphie Arabe.* In these cases, however, as in the case of all catalogs, there is always difficulty in bringing information up to date.

Attempts have been made over the years to create independent files of complete information, usually based on one private endeavor. Such files exist in Geneva for epigraphy (Max van Berchem archives), in Washington for Iranian architecture (M. B. Smith archives in the Smithsonian Institution), and in Jerusalem for all of Islamic art (L. A. Mayer Memorial Collection). The problems of all these depositories so far have been lack of personnel, sporadic funds, and uncertain direction over long periods of time. The newest one in Jerusalem is best equipped to solve these problems.

Accessibility

Access to Islamic art by the outsider or by anyone but the users of the richest and largest libraries is the weakest part of the field. None of the general surveys is even adequate and most are downright bad. With a handful of exceptions even more specialized manuals, such as existing ones on ceramics or on aspects of Islamic architecture, are spotty and insufficient, whereas the few existing coffee table books contain mediocre texts and usually arbitrarily chosen illustrations. The chapters in the *Cambridge History of Iran* are limited in scope, and the chapter in the *Cambridge History of Islam* is too short. Only one recent attempt has been made at defining the art of a period. Furthermore, it is almost impossible for anyone but the narrow specialist to keep up with recent work in the field, since most disciplinary journals hardly ever pay any attention to it and one must consult dozens of publications dealing with a wide variety of topics in order to find out what is going on.

Accessibility is somewhat less of a problem if one is willing and able to travel. Most monuments of architecture can be visited and most museum collections are open, although the storerooms are often closed and unorganized. Many museums (Freer Gallery, Victoria and Albert, Louvre, Berlin, Damascus) have short brochures highlighting their collections. Photographs can generally be obtained, at a constantly growing cost and with a degree of amiability related to the importance of the seeker, but there are no central files from which one could order them, and all but the largest and richest institutions are often reluctant or unable to satisfy a scholar's or a student's needs. Matters are far more complex when one deals with private collections, for which personal entries are generally needed. A further pernicious aspect of the field has been claims on rights of publication of certain monuments without time limit.

Finally one must consider accessibility through people, primarily university teaching. In this area changes have been considerable over the past few years. Some 14 institutions in the United States and Canada (Harvard, New York University, Hunter, University of Massachusetts, University of Pennsylvania, McGill, Toronto, Victoria, Michigan, Colorado, San Diego State, University of California, Los Angeles, Florida State, and Texas) have committed themselves in more or less permanent fashion to teaching the field. It is rather curious, however, that these do not include some of the best-known departments of art history or centers for Middle East studies. As a result, however well-trained and competent individuals may be, they are often hampered by lack of adequate libraries and photographs. Matters are less clear abroad. In England, Germany, and the Soviet Union, museums have tended to be better staffed than universities but in none of these countries is there any formal organization of training in Islamic art as such, although much can be learned, almost always with an "Islamic" rather than "art historical" or "archaeological" point of view. Such is the case with the School of Oriental Studies in London and now one of the Paris universities, which do provide organized teaching. Istanbul and Ankara are very active but tend to limit their efforts to Turkey only. The American University in Cairo has been a particularly strong center, perhaps more effective than Egyptian national universities. Some training is available in Iraq and in Israel, but none in Iran or in North Africa.

At the same time, it does seem that interest in the field has grown enormously over the past decade and a rather rough estimate is that some 300–400 students in American universities have been exposed to at least one semester course in Islamic art in 1971–1972; in 1960 the figure would have been around 50. No survey exists about the causes for the increase, but the experience of some of us would tend to suggest that students interested in the arts have become more involved in Islamic art than have area specialists. This seems clear from the success of Islamic exhibitions in large cities as well, as is demonstrated by the rapidity with which the Metropolitan Museum book on the Houghton Shahnameh became out of print. It is also true that there is much in contemporary art which bears at least superficial relationship to alleged values of Islamic art and that several prominent modern artists have claimed inspiration from the Near East. Finally, many of the more traditional fields and approaches of the history of art have lost some of their attractiveness, partly through overexposure and easy availability, and a new and ill-defined field seems exciting, at least initially. One of the commentators pointed out that in few other areas is it possible for a beginner to make major contributions about very well-known masterpieces.

But the means for effective teaching, be they good surveys or complete sets of photographic documents, are simply not there. The first result is that the gap between the few teachers in well-equipped centers and the many in less endowed ones tends to widen, and it is generally disheartening to read the pages written on the arts of Islam by historians or anthropologists, even though one realizes that the fault is not theirs. Another result of the enormity of the field and paucity of scholars is that too much of the learning and knowledge that exist come from privileged information. Tied at times to a secretiveness often associated with private collections, this need for personal contacts is dangerous, for it leads to cliques and to pettiness. We could give examples of both.

But in a deeper sense, we could argue that the field of Islamic art and archaeology is still at an artisanal level in which personal, almost family, contacts predominate for the dissemination of knowledge and ideas, whereas there is a reasonably demonstrable growth in interest on the part of potential art historians. There is a constant encounter with Islamic monuments on the part of all archaeologists (whereas they tended to dismiss the Muslim world in the not-so-remote past), and there seems to be an awareness on the part of the general public, whether the awareness is spurred by tourism, faddism, or simply an oversupply of information on Gothic cathedrals and baroque painting. It is more difficult to assess the changes that have taken place in the

Muslim world itself, as a highly Westernized generation is replaced by a new group of students, although not by better teachers. That interest in the arts as a whole has increased is clear enough, but it is far less clear whether this interest has carried over to an understanding of the artistic part of the culture. There are probably many reasons for this, but one is certainly the lack of accessible books. It is sufficient to see the works that have been translated into Arabic to realize the growing gap between the insufficiently productive and conscious "happy few" in half a dozen cities in the Western world and possibly four cities in the Near East (Istanbul, Cairo, Jerusalem, Shiraz) and the mass of young people seeking to know their own culture.

The final point about accessibility is linguistic. Works pertinent to Islamic art are available in 25 languages. No scholar or cultivated individual can possibly learn them all, nor is it likely that very rare and old books, which are frequently our only source of certain monuments, will be found in many libraries. The result is of course ignorance, for the arts cannot under any condition be nationalized according to contemporary or even linguistic frontiers. But it is not merely a question of unawareness of written words about the arts, for too often an unknown language has led to an automatic avoidance even of looking at pictures.

Beyond this level, however, there is the even more profound problem that it becomes increasingly difficult to control new material in whatever language it is published. A good knowledge of the 15,000 odd monuments of Islamic architecture in Turkey makes it impossible to know well the quarter of a million remaining Fatimid ceramics or some 10,000 illustrations of the Shahnameh. Even if it is true, as a commentator pointed out, that this mass of documents can be broken down into a manageable number of groups, the task of sifting the material in order to justify the groups has not been done. At this level, it is also a question of accessibility in the sense that the means are lacking to determine the originality or quality of any one monument.

One last point ought to be mentioned. One aspect of accessibility lies in an appropriate understanding of the manner in which a Muslim or, in a more general sense, a Near Easterner perceives the visual world surrounding him. Even if the patterns of today cannot necessarily be transferred to earlier times, it is still true that the intellectual or esthetic experience of contemporary man should or could have a bearing on the artistic production of the past. Some care should no doubt be exercised in using this evidence, for it is a priori foolish to think that a Parisian of today is more likely to understand a Gothic cathedral than an Italian or a Russian. Yet there are two ways in which contemporary Western esthetic habits are pertinent to an understanding of its past. One is that, in a variety of complex dialectic ways, the present is a product of the past; therefore, it is possible or could be possible to work backward from the better documented present into earlier times. However, the second way is more important. It is that, as any culture is surrounded by the monuments of its past—often still used, even if not always in their original form—it develops almost automatically visual associations, modes of esthetic judgments, and relationships between setting and activities which may change over the centuries but whose transformations are probably relatively slow. An awareness of these contemporary associations, judgments, and relationships as well as of contemporary creativity can well be utilized to make earlier monuments more accessible. The methods by which this awareness can be acquired belong to the social sciences, especially ethnography and psychology, much more than to the traditional humanities. Yet at this time no one has tackled these problems and we know next to nothing about contemporary attitudes toward the arts, judgments of quality about contemporary or older creations, or the nature of associations between the visually perceptible world of the Muslim and his activities or beliefs. Very little work has been done on folk art except occasionally on carpets, but without qualitative analyses. The few very general books of pictures and short texts on artificially revived or preserved local techniques of ceramics or metalwork (as in several Indian or Central Asian publications) are usually of very low intellectual caliber. A little more is known about techniques of manufacture and artisanal vocabulary, especially in Iran, where Wulff's book on traditional crafts is an invaluable source of information. As to contemporary art, its enormous development in all major countries of the Near East generally has been discussed only in a periodical literature limited to each country and totally unknown in the West. It is not assured, of course, that a thorough sifting and study of all this information will lead to a better understanding of the past, and it is important to repeat that there are many intellectual and emotional difficulties in explaining the past through the present. Fake romanticism and anachronisms are dangers indeed, but aside from the fact that the art historian and the ethnographer (who replaces the archaeologist for the contemporary world) of the Middle East are responsible for interpreting the contemporary artistic scene, it may also be that this understanding can contribute to a better explanation of the past.

Theory

The question here is whether elements of hypotheses, explanations, and theories peculiar to Islamic art and archaeology exist which can help to understand any newly discovered monument, which can be used by nonspecialists to demonstrate some artistic or archaeological process or to illustrate some aspect of Islamic culture at large, or which lend themselves to broader generalization either confirming some art historical paradigm and archaeological explanatory process or, at the highest possible level, creating such a paradigm.

Some such areas have been investigated. Thus much work has been devoted to the question of Muslim attitudes to images, to the early history of Iranian architecture, and to the subject matter of the twelfth- and thirteenth-century images in all media. In all these instances the Muslim example is important to such wider questions as iconoclasm, a phenomenon that is not unique to Islam, as the ways in which a strong artistic tradition adapts its forms to new needs, and as the reasons that a sudden explosion of representations occurs where few existed before. This is not to say that any of these possibilities were exploited, except perhaps iconoclasm, but the opportunity to do so certainly exists. Then there are the problems of decoration, i.e., of certain ways to treat the surface of objects or of architectural monuments, and of abstraction, i.e., of treating whatever subject one depicts in ways that are different from those of natural visual experience. In both these areas, especially the first one, the Muslim phenomenon is unique and could be significant in developing general theories about the artistic process altogether; in addition, there is an obligation to explain why it took place within the culture. Some work has been done on ornament, but the only book on the arabesque as such (by E. Kühnel) is found in only a few libraries.

All things put together, coherent statements and ideological systems comparable to what is known in the study of Renaissance or contemporary art simply do not exist. There is nothing on the esthetic of Persian painting and hardly anything on the symbolic values of Islamic visual expression. Calligraphy, acknowledged to be the highest form of visual expression in the Muslim world, has never been adequately studied. Only very recently have archaeologists realized that Islamic sites offer a wonderful opportunity for understanding such processes as urbanization and for matching excavated or other comparable evidence with literary sources, thus making it possible to evaluate archaeological methods and information. In a broader sense, however, what has not yet been achieved is a proper explanation of the epistemological significance of the visual arts in understanding the culture and a largely concomitant system of qualitative evaluation of individual monuments. Although it may be too much to hope that the field can acquire a Burckhardt, a Huizenga, or a Coomaraswamy, what can be expected is a series of generally accepted hypotheses about a tradition's character and a sense of their validity for the arts and for archaeology.

The key questions in dealing with these matters are whether such hypotheses must come from the field itself, whether they should consist primarily in attempts to fit into it theories established elsewhere, or whether this is a sort of investigation that should come from the Muslim world itself, somewhat in the manner in which native Chinese scholarship has sought to understand its own past and possibly in ways being developed by a group of Iranians, like N. Ardalan. On these particular issues commentators found themselves divided. Some argued that the field is much too young to lend itself to theoretical considerations, that catalogs and descriptions with occasional generalities are the maximum that can be expected. Others felt that the main solution lies in acquiring a thorough grounding in Western art before even seeking to understand the Muslim visual world, and that for better or worse the discipline is stuck with its European formulation. Still others indicated that theoretical considerations are individual preferences, secondary to the main objectives of the field. A fourth point of view was that, on the contrary, a new and ill-explored field lends itself particularly well to theoretical investigations because its very backwardness may make it possible to jump over certain stages of development demonstrable in other areas. Some objected quite violently to this thought. A strong opinion among a number of Turkish scholars, for instance, is that there is some fallacy in seeking any generally Islamic interpretation of the arts, because the possible bond between so many differentiated traditions is limited to a few practices and allegiances which are not pertinent to the technical possibilities and formal habits of the arts.

There is no clear consensus as to whether Islamic art is just an art to be studied and developed in traditional ways or whether, on the contrary, it can be an experimental area for the formation of art historical or other theories. Yet as one considers the variety of rather strong reactions which were received to an originally rather forceful assertion that by its own nature and by the nature of our knowledge of it, Islamic art lends itself particularly well to theoretical considerations, one wonders whether the variety of opinions expressed is not in itself conducive to theoretical elaboration. For one could argue that this very divergence implies an uneasy tension between the humanist's tendency to emphasize the unique and the different and a social scientist's search for patterns through which the unique can be explained but also dissolved. In part it is a tension between the history of art and archaeology. It occurs as well in the study of classical times or of the Middle Ages, and it may be comparable to the tension between linguistics and the history of literature. However, the fascinating point is that this tension occurs in a field that by common agreement is underdeveloped in information and that is part of a still living culture, even if its concentration is on the culture's earlier phases. It is therefore possible to suggest that it is an almost unique instance where traditional problems and questions can be resolved not simply in traditional ways but by the adjunction of ideas and methods from other fields, by the experience and self-analysis of the culture itself, and by the opportunity to concentrate on the subject matter with clearly defined hypotheses rather than with automatically acquired prejudices. We return in the following section to some concrete proposals for implementation, but it seems to us that the novelty of the field and the variety of its present directions can contribute in uniquely striking fashion to an understanding of both Islam and the arts or material culture in general.

PROJECTS AND PRIORITIES

The preceding observations can be summed up in the following manner. The directions of the field as a scholarly enterprise have been reasonably well mapped out (largely because they are dictated by the paradigms of two otherwise known disciplines or methods of inquiry), but the results have not always come up to the expectations, for it is still a highly personal field in which an individual's own knowledge of monuments and of his colleagues is more important than what can be acquired through readily accessible publications in a small number of languages. The field is weak in books and photographic tools for the beginner or the interested outsider, whether general art historian or Islamist. Although the more advanced student or scholar who has mastered four or five languages can find an enormous amount of written information in the better libraries of the world, he is also hampered by the lack of ready access to photographs, slides, and other basic means of work unless he gets them himself. The field is weak in hypotheses and theories, although the areas where these are likely to emerge most fruitfully can be outlined reasonably easily.

Where does one go from here? What sorts of projects and programs can be seen as useful to the field as a whole as well as to related fields and to intellectual and pedagogical endeavors? And what sort of ranking can be assigned to them?

First of all, we may agree that most work will still be done by individuals and that their interests and abilities do not lend themselves to external pressure or sponsorship, especially since most of them work far away from their most immediate colleagues. One could recruit into the field the most capable and promising students available. However, a deeper question is whether the rather striking improvement of recent years (one person teaching in the United States in 1955 and four curatorial appointments, compared with 13 teaching and seven curatorial appointments in 1972) is likely to continue. The answer does not lie within the objectives of this report, except to suggest that both the quality of the recruitment and the opportunities for jobs may well depend on the intellectual achievement that can be expected. If the field is seen less as an individual, artisanal activity than as a creative and fruitful enterprise with a strong promise of intellectual satisfaction, there is little doubt that it will attract students and compel the opening of jobs. It may even succeed in building teams working and teaching together in one institution, obviously progress over the present system of one person covering 1000 years over 10,000 miles.

A second area of need lies in what has been described as accessibility. One could suggest a many-pronged approach:

1. Publication of a series of manuals covering the field and identifying in each instance what is known, what is hypothetical, and what ought to be done: this suggestion met with considerable agreement on the part of all correspondents and commentators, and several felt that the very general picture books with incompetent texts ought to be simply banned. These manuals, whose need is particularly great in the Near East, would not be textbooks as much as teaching and research tools which could serve as blueprints for the work of at least a generation.

2. Creation of repositories of documents: this is not an original suggestion at all, and it has been mentioned that several such files have been started, usually around one individual's personal collection or through one man's initiative. Except for the new collection recently begun in Jerusalem, which may have been better planned than its predecessors, most of these repositories failed eventually for lack of continuous staff and funds. Although all commentators agreed about the need, there was much disagreement about the means of implementation, such as one center for everything, division by countries or by technique, or creation of a pilot project. Aside from the staggering expense of a well done job, two points were made. One is that many countries are planning repositories of national monuments and it may be more worthwhile to help them complete these tasks than to start new endeavors. The other is that the key obligation of such collections is to be easily accessible to all bona fide students. Finally, some felt that it may be simpler to begin with less ambitious projects, even if they are not complete, such as the repository of Qur'anic inscriptions being prepared in Beirut or the checklist of Shahnameh illustrations done at the University of Michigan. The field has been unusually slow to explore and utilize existing devices for the rapid and simple dissemination of visual materials, from movies to photographs or to surveying through photogrammetry; these are obvious means of better accessibility.

3. A journal that would be cheap enough for students to acquire in Egypt or in Pakistan, yet complete enough to transmit at regular intervals news of all latest occurrences in the field, from bibliographies to theses, museum acquisitions, or excavations: such a journal could also become the vehicle for the exchange of ideas and for discussions on a more informal basis than more common periodicals. The success of such enterprises in the social sciences seems a reasonable guarantee of usefulness and it may replace the personal and oral source of so much present knowledge.

4. A formal program of translations into English or French of major con-

temporary works or of sources in less well-known languages: this task ought to be done rapidly and in sufficiently large numbers to be really worthwhile; some commentators have questioned, however, whether this kind of exercise is worth the time and money needed for its successful completion, when any scholarship in depth would still require a knowledge of languages and thus a chasm would be maintained between the haves and the have-nots of the field.

Of these four suggestions, the first and the third are the most feasible and, initially at least, the most useful in removing some of the loneliness of each scholar and student and in forcing the field as a whole and its various subfields to define more specifically the "state of their art" than is possible here. These are also reasonably inexpensive enterprises which, after an initial push, could almost pay for themselves. The third suggestion is potentially the most fruitful one, but it is a little difficult to imagine how it could, without enormous resources in men and in funds, be properly staffed, operate with continuity over many years, and be accessible to all who need its information. Like the fourth suggestion, it may be left for the time being to individual initiatives with limited purposes, or, perhaps like the archaeological and monumental atlases suggested by several commentators, it could become a central concern of individual countries, as has happened in fact in most European countries.

The third area is scholarship itself, i.e., new knowledge and new interpretations, with or without the theoretical implications discussed earlier. This is an area where it is quite difficult to establish an order of priorities or even to identify all possible needs. For our purposes, we could identify three orders of needs, within each of which certain priorities could be established as each topic is discussed at greater length than is possible here. If more space is given to the third order, it is not that it is more important but that it has been less frequently discussed.

1. It is unlikely that complete corpora in the manner of Kühnel's work on ivories or Creswell's volumes on Egypt can find sponsors, even on the assumption that there are people to undertake them. Yet it is equally clear that the task of cataloging, ordering, and classifying the millions of remaining monuments of Islamic art must be continued, whether it is done through catalogs of museum collections, of archaeological remains already found, of libraries with manuscripts, or of the architectural monuments of a given city. New information must be acquired as well, primarily through excavations, provided these are properly funded and their results rapidly published. Two aspects of this task of classification and of cataloging documents seem to be particularly important to investigate. One is that it should seek to use more

efficient means of making itself known and available than the traditional and expensive "book" and that the information provided should be as complete as possible. The second one applies more particularly to archaeology and to restorations and consists in the particularly careful identification of the sites to be excavated or buildings to be repaired and of the reasons why. Perhaps in this particularly expensive side of the field, which has not yet demonstrated its ability to contribute as much as its technology leads one to expect, a coherent and collective effort on one task, a city, a province, or a period, could lead to methodologically and intellectually fruitful results.

Another aspect of basic information lies in vocabulary, i.e., in the establishment of a valid terminology for forms, techniques, or ideas. The main assumption here is that, whereas there are no doubt areas where neologisms issued from Western methods have to be used and artificially translated into Near Eastern languages, most of the morphology of Islamic "things" had and still has a native terminology. If it does not, the question is automatically raised whether the morphological distinctions are not themselves erroneous. There are two approaches to this question. One pertains in part to ethnography and to descriptive linguistics and requires simply collecting contemporary data, especially from artisans. The other one is more complex and demands a lexicographic study of older texts and especially of various technical manuals (when still existing in manuscripts) in order to develop a historical vocabulary of the arts. Although very little has been done in this area, some interesting results were reached by Rempel and others in dealing with architectural ornament with a local vocabulary.

2. Some areas of particular "underdevelopment" can be identified: Iranian architecture, complete publication of key manuscripts, iconographic systems, archaeologically discovered ceramics, periodization and period styles, patronage, and dozens of others as well. All these are basically "problems," in the sense that the raw data are available in reasonably sufficient form and that what is lacking is their correct or adequate interpretation. This is an area where it is particularly difficult to establish priorities, but it is also true that these are all questions that can be solved by traditional methods and that do not require uniquely special types of support. They are, so to speak, routine scholarship and their number or quality depends primarily on the scientists involved in them.

In terms of priorities, problem-oriented, interpretative, synthetic, or thematic subjects should take precedence over complete monographs, not because the latter are not needed but because the former have not been sufficiently developed. Furthermore, monographs of varying quality will continue to be done as Ph.D. theses or as the result of restorations or of other local activities. Many of them would be immensely improved and far more useful if they could be put in properly discussed and generally accepted categories and interpretations. Only then will it be possible to pursue the dialectic processes of understanding any monument in increasingly complex depth on the one hand and, on the other, of developing increasingly sophisticated concepts of esthetic and historical appreciation.

3. Several commentators pointed out that this report deals too much with cataloging and gathering of information and documents, at the expense of developing ideas and theories. This emphasis has several sources. In part, no doubt, it conforms to the humanist's natural feeling that ideas and theories are an individual activity which is only helped by the availability of information. Secondly, the humanist fears committing himself intellectually until he is sure of himself; he fears hypotheses, mental gambles, and discussions. Finally, there is his impression that he lacks sufficient information to make wider theories more than guesses, at best brilliant intuitions.

In order to check these debilitating tendencies, one can propose a number of more far-reaching topics, most of which require a series of preparatory conferences or discussions, all of which are essential to a coherent understanding of the field, demand the involvement of scholars and students with very varied technical and cultural backgrounds, and can serve the broader aims of general disciplinary theorists.

Such would be the question of the part played by the visual experience in traditional and contemporary Muslim culture. Is the latter purely verbal and is the visual secondary? If so, what is it that one learns about the culture when one studies its artifacts or its works of art? Is there something intrinsically different between a Muslim vision and a Christian or a Buddhist one? Are all Muslim experiences similar? A large number of ethnographic, social, and psychological inquiries are needed to answer these questions and others issued from them, for which to my knowledge there are no models available, although some work on the psychology of art and of perception does exist. It is the sort of inquiry which would, by necessity, compel a meeting of social scientific and humanistic minds. Its ultimate objective no doubt would tend to be that of identifying the unique component in artistic creativity, in this case the so far elusive Islamic or Middle Eastern element whose existence underlies our field but whose nature has never been studied in any detail. But the methods and procedures that would have been used in the process are likely to be of far broader significance.

One could also raise the question of archaeological information versus art historical judgment. How significant are the miserable remains of an early mosque in Iran for an understanding of the *Masjid-i Shah* in Isfahan? Or how does one distinguish between good and bad paintings in the fifteenth century? Although frequently formalized by intellectual habit or prejudices rather than by genuine intellectual effort, the more developed areas of the history of art tend to possess a number of techniques for qualitative judgment. It can be argued, however, that the very novelty of the field of Islamic art makes it particularly amenable to the elaboration of new and possibly more fruitful methods of qualitative and quantitative analysis and therefore that its investigation can progress faster rather than permanently lag behind other fields. It can serve for the development of models usable in other areas precisely because it is not burdened with established methods and theories. One example may suffice. By utilizing systematically the new techniques and concepts of communication theory or of transformational grammar, it may be possible to describe the arts of a period or of a technique of Islamic art through such terms as their redundant features (relatively meaningless in themselves but required to carry information) versus unique ones; stylistic change may be explained as transformations in the surface expression of "semantic structures"; the historical problem then becomes less that of describing changes and distinctions than of explaining them, for it is probably more sensible to explain changes of attitudes than changes of forms. There are other ways and other techniques, but it is striking that the immense and imaginative work done in recent years on language, on oral traditions, and on poetics has not been carried into visual communication. An underdeveloped field can be an excellent area for the investigation of such theories and methods.

As a final example one could give that of functional recognition and abstract design and thereby lead to questions that are central to an understanding of contemporary arts everywhere. Does one know from a facade whether a building is a mosque or a bath? Is it immaterial whether a certain ornament occurs on a ceramic or on a minaret? The initial point of departure of this example lies in a peculiarity of Islamic art that a small number of themes are used for a wide variety of purposes and in many media. The underlying assumption is that the nature of recognition and of visual pleasure may have occurred through means other than those of observable motifs. Was it color, geometry, size, or location that identified the purpose of a monument or of an object? For an answer one must once again turn to other areas, to social, intellectual, and psychological histories. Wherever one turns, however, the methods and the results are likely to be of broader importance than for the field of Islamic art alone.

Many other problems and questions can be raised for which it is obviously impossible to create an order of priorities, because in the final analysis this particular level of investigation will depend on the individuals working in the field far more than on the immediate requirements of the field itself.

Appendix

The elaboration of this report owes a great deal to the following: Richard Ettinghausen and Lisa Golombek, who attended the discussions, and Priscilla Soucek, Fay Frick, Erica Dodd, George C. Miles, Eleanor Sims, Marilyn Jenkins, John Shapley, Ed Binney, Donald Wilber, and Renata Holod, who wrote comments or made verbal remarks. All of them may recognize themselves in the "commentators" of the text.

Most bibliographical references can be found fairly easily in Creswell's bibliography for earlier works, in my own introduction in the *MESA Bulletin* (1968), in Pearson's *Index Islamicus*, or in the *Abstracta* of the *Revue des Etudes Islamiques*. What follows is a sample of such studies, mostly fairly recent, which seem best to illustrate the most fruitful and most useful recent investigations in the field and which have been quoted directly in the text.

1. For a history of the field, R. Ettinghausen, "Islamic Art and Archaeology," in *Near Eastern Culture and Society*, T. C. Young, ed. (Princeton: 1951).
2. For the archaeological history of monuments based on restorations, R. W. Hamilton, *The Structural History of the Aqsa Mosque* (Jerusalem: 1949); G. Zander, *Travaux de restauration* (Rome: 1968); and E. Galdieri, *Isfahan, Masjid-i Jumᶜa* (Rome: 1972–1974).
3. The Islamicist's approach has been best defined by Jean Sauvaget, "Comment étudier l'histoire du monde arabe," *Revue Africaine*, 1946.
4. Examples of art historical studies applied to and transformed by Islamic art are R. Ettinghausen, "The Emperor's Choice," *Essays in Honor of E. Panofsky* (New York: 1961) (iconography of painting); L. I. Rempel, *Arhitekturnyi Ornament Usbekistana* (Tashkent: 1961) (interpretation of designs); O. Grabar, "The Umayyad Dome of the Rock," *Ars Orientalis*, **3** (1959) (iconography of a building); S. C. Welch, *A King's Book of Kings* (New York: 1972) (connoisseurship of painting); R. Ettinghausen, "The Wade Cup," *Ars Orientalis*, **2** (1957) (style and iconography of an object).
5. Different methods and interpretations to reach comparable results occur in O. Grabar, *The Formation of Islamic Art* (New Haven: 1973) and R. Ettinghausen, *From Byzantium to Sasanian Iran and the Islamic World* (Leiden: 1972).
6. The best recent examples of monographs on individual architectural monuments are L. Golombek, *The Timurid Shrine at Gazur Gah* (Toronto: 1969) and S. Mustapha, *Kloster Ibn Barquq* (Blückstadt: 1968); the traditional masterpiece of the genre is K. A. C. Creswell, *Early Muslim Architecture*, 2nd ed. (Oxford: 1972), and *Muslim Architecture in Egypt* (Oxford: 1952, 1959).

7. Partial attempts at period styles occur in R. Ettinghausen, "The Flowering of Seljuq Art," *Metropolitan Museum Journal*, **3** (1970) and O. Grabar, "Les Arts Mineurs de l'Orient Musulman," *Cahiers de Civilisation Médiévale*, **11** (1968).

8. Broader attempts at interpretation occur in J. Sourdel-Thomine, "Art et société dans le monde de l'Islam," *Revue de Etudes Islamiques*, **36** (1968) and E. Dodd, "The Image of the Word," *Berytus*, **18** (1969).

9. Examples of excellent "local" investigations are the numerous works of G. A. Pugachenkova or L. Bretanitski; L. Hunarfar, *Ganjine-i Tarikhî-i Isfahân* (Isfahan: 1344); I. Afshar, *Yadgarhâ-i Yezd* (Tehran, 1348); T. Oz, *İstanbul Camileri* (Ankara: 1962).

CHAPTER SIX

Political Science

I. WILLIAM ZARTMAN

So little is agreed upon concerning the nature of political science that it would be possible to devote an entire review to the discipline itself without ever discussing the Middle East, or alternatively to discard the whole chapter for lack of an agreed subject, leaving the matter to boundary wars among history, law, philosophy, anthropology, and sociology (with their own identity problems). Neither drastic alternative is applied here, but rather (perhaps even more drastically) an attempt is made to grapple with the nature of the discipline and to relate current scholarship and future needs in Middle East studies to that nature.[1]

THE DISCIPLINE

It is important to remember, however, that political science itself is a newcomer to the organization of knowledge anywhere, not just in regard to the Middle East. It must therefore be evaluated in the context of time. Furthermore, the development of the discipline varies with geography as well. It is hopefully not an ethnocentric view that political science is most developed (in the sense defined below) in the United States and Britain, particularly in these countries' study of themselves, and that as an independent social scientific discipline it simply does not exist in many European, let alone Middle Eastern, universities. In its development the discipline has been strongly influenced, if not actually created, by the interaction of other disciplines, as the following discussion will show.

Yet even where no independent discipline exists, there is often much research and writing on politics, usually beginning with historians and participants, and only much later turning to the analysis of the society's own politics as an activity independent of the subject. The ability to reach this latter stage is a function of the development of social science but also of the capacity of a society to stand self-examination, and this is a point not all societies have reached. Yet it is ultimately the goal of social science (as of the humanities) to enable one to know oneself. The subject–object problem is not present in political studies in the same way as it is in religious studies and to some extent in philosophy. It is true that any writer has a position—some would say an ideology—that may have some relation to his perception of events, but the argument here is that eventually the nationality of the scholar need have no effect on the way political science is studied, in its methods, ontology, or epistemology. But we are not there yet.

Of the many categorical dichotomies that could be applied to the debate over the discipline (e.g., descriptive/prescriptive, macro/micro, institutional/functional, etc.), the one that seems primordial is the question whether it is the subject or the approach that makes a study political science. Most social sciences have declared their independence from the mother discipline of history over this issue and have spent their later lives trying to achieve self-realization and identity in their own terms. There is no likely end point in this process, but it should be evident logically that once one admits the existence of a discipline, the more independently developed it is—that is, the better it is able to explain its chosen kinds of phenomena or its chosen aspects of universal human experience in its chosen terms—the "better" it is. Thus it is a conjuncture of subject and approach that makes for a well-practiced discipline. Such, at least, is one of the bases for judgments expressed here.

In this view, the discipline of political science is something more than just modern history. It is not defined by time or other subject characteristics but by the way in which the subject is studied, through particular concepts, questions, and methods. As a result, a work must be more than simply about politics in order to be treated in this review. It needs to utilize political concepts more or less explicitly as its descriptive or explanatory terms—concepts relating to power, its use, and its users. Thus it has to provide explanations and descriptions that are not merely unique or internal to the event studied but are expressed in more general terms and constructs. This is not to say, however, that only self-styled political scientists write political science (so defined) or that political science is only what political scientists write. Conceptual frameworks are often visible in works about politics written by scholars who call themselves historians or members of other disciplines, and it would be unnecessarily restrictive—particularly given the state of development of the discipline—to exclude them from review here. Again, it is the approach applied to the subject that makes for the discipline.

This is, of course, not the only way in which the discipline could be characterized. One could adopt a more restrictive definition that would insist on fully explicit concepts and theories, hypothesis testing, and social scientific experimentation. The result would be that few of the works and little of the research currently devoted to Middle East politics would fall within the scope of this review. Such an overly narrow approach would exclude much of the important scholarship on the subject and would condemn the still-imperfect attempts at achieving disciplinary rigor. On the other hand, others might prefer to define the discipline purely by its subject matter and treat any work on politics, casting the net to include all political writings and most history and philosophy. Such a characterization would be so broad as to leave few criteria for evaluating accomplishments and trends and eventually for establishing future priorities.

Because the discipline itself, in the 1970s, is somewhere between the first and second of these latter alternatives, not having completely left its broad base but not having fully attained a narrow or rigorous paradigmatic stage, the basis for evaluation as initially outlined is maintained. This is appropriate because the focus of this entire review concerns the relation between discipline and the Middle East as a subject area, a relationship that can be plumbed through two questions: How has the discipline improved the understanding of the area? What have studies of the area contributed to the improvement (in the above terms) of the discipline? These questions are used as guidelines for judgments of past works, schools, themes, and debates. They also provide the guidelines used for a forward-looking discussion of new and unresolved tasks and opportunities for scholarship in the future.

Such questions about the relation between a discipline and an area phenomenon—between approach and subject—are natural concomitants of the general trend that differentiates specialized interpretations from general intellectual inquiry. Political scientists are seeking to develop appropriate concepts and methods for the study of politics as a discrete phenomenon, concepts and methods that are designed to provide better explanation and understanding of the subject. It follows, therefore, that it is appropriate to ask whether such attempts have indeed led to a fuller grasp of Middle East politics and whether they are suited to their subject, just as it is appropriate to ask whether attempts to grasp the subject have led to the generation or refinement of useful concepts for comprehending the phenomenon of politics in general. Ultimately, it matters little—or it should—whether the concern of the scholar is with the discipline or the area, that is, whether he cares about the study of the Middle East as an appropriate way of finding answers to disciplinary questions or about disciplinary questions as appropriate ways of finding out about Middle East politics. These are two sides of the same coin, and recognition of this fact should bring narrowly identified scholars together more than they perhaps have been in the past. If there is something distinctive about the Middle East, or parts of it, the testing of universal propositions should bring it out, and if there are universal characteristics of human action, their usefulness in explaining area events should in turn help make that fact plain.

Although the gap between students of Middle East politics and political scientists has been bridged by too few scholars to date, political science would be poorer without some of the work done on the area. In political science, unlike linguistics, the Middle East has not been rediscovered in any startlingly new disciplinary terms. But it has contributed to better understanding of some political phenomena that transcend the cultural area, phenomena such as the role of tradition in development, the dynamics of modernization movements, the nature of elites, and others that emerge from the following discussion. Although there have been few disciplinary experiments in the area and few tests of theory, research and writings in political science on the Middle East do employ the same concepts and ask the same questions as work in comparative politics (and to some extent, international relations) in general.

Nevertheless, the subject has dominated and reshaped these concepts and questions when it has met them and has determined the methodology, epistemology, and ontology used to study it. Political theory is bent to fit the subject, and the uniqueness of each level of analysis—area, component, country, subtopic—is exposed but rarely explained. The product is often a detailed and enlightened description of a strange object, made more explicit but no less different (strange) by the treatment. Yet if reasons for the gap between area and discipline are to be ventured, they may well be found in this very aspect: Middle East answers to common disciplinary questions often *are* unique because of the high degree of indigeneous development, the strength of tradition, the depth of a distinct body of political thought, and the complexity of Muslim society—characteristics of the Middle East which clash with similar ones in Asia and Europe and which do not find correspondence in Africa or Latin America.

The Middle East has occupied some important scholars of politics in the past, and political scientists are the second largest membership group (after historians) of organizations like the Middle East Studies Association. Yet it is not an area of study that attracts large numbers of the most innovative young (or old) practitioners of the discipline. Language barriers alone are one major factor: leaders of the Inter-University Consortium on Political Research, for example, have publicly belittled the time supposedly wasted in learning "languages like Chinese and Arabic that nobody speaks" and people well trained in the area usually have little time or interest for the new and changing methods of political science, which they term fads. Thus most of the political specialists in the area—and still a good deal of the writing and research—specialize in modern political history, current events, and description. It is interesting, too, that higher marks tend to be given to the current scholarship on Middle East politics by those whose commitment is to the political area studies side of this continuum than by those who identify disciplinarily.

Another way of placing the area within the discipline is by examining collections of leading works. Out of 13 recent anthologies dealing with comparative politics and development, only eight included one or more chapters on the Middle East.[2] However, the 17 chapters involved had important things to say to the discipline, primarily on pluralism and nationalism, religion and traditionalism, and civil–military relations, three topics on which the area can contribute rich insights. In another review of significant articles in international politics,[3] only two out of 168 cases were based on Middle East data; these concerned communications and conflict images, again problems of importance in the area. Perhaps the best preliminary conclusion to reach, then, is that there is a potential for fruitful area–disciplinary communication and that some important results can already be cited.

TRADITIONS AND LANDMARKS

The political science of the Middle East rose out of the traditions of religious law and political history and combined with political philosophy into the tradition of erudition known as the Orientalist school. It is as difficult to ignore the contribution of such important figures as Gibb, Goitein, von Grunebaum, Laoust, LeTourneau, and many others, or of their earlier predecessors in this century, as it is to see in their works an identifiable political science orientation. Their approach has been to comprehend the meaning of Muslim society through a broad acquaintance with culture and civilization, and political ideas and action have clearly been within their purview. To many of them, such actions and ideas were simply subjects among others for general intellectual inquiry; to others, clear concepts and analytical frameworks, even if implicit, underlie the study of political thought and action.

Thus Gibb's work on *Modern Trends in Islam* (1947) or the earlier collection on *Whither Islam* (1932) formulated the problem of modernization in religious terms, examining both the movements for change in Islamic doctrine and the limitations on their diverse responses. The study was important as a base for future work on the traditional responses to modernization, and specifically foreshadowed the later works of such diverse political historians and political scientists as Khadduri (1970), Kerr (1965), Safran (1961), and Binder (1964). Lord Lloyd's study of *Egypt Since Cromer* (1933, 1934) provided a careful historical narrative of 30 years of domestic and international politics in Egyptian government, with the empirical framework established on some very clear normative notions on politics: that welfare values should predominate over solidarity values, and hence that administration was more important than politics (which only got in its way). Such ideas went back to Bacon, Bagehot, and Mill and soon caused a reaction that would reorient the developing discipline. Ireland's *Study in Political Development: Iraq* (1937) was avant-garde not only in its title but also in its grasp of the politics of establishing an administration (a process that would later be termed "state-building"), the social bases of nationalism, and the welfare–administrative criteria of "good government." The work was succeeded by a series of important studies of Iraq in the same tradition (Khadduri, 1961, 1969; Rossi, 1966; Dann, 1969; and Vernier, 1962) and by political histories of other Middle Eastern countries undergoing governmental transformations. Montagne's study of *The Berbers and the Makhzen in the South of Morocco* (1930) and the smaller treatment of *The Social and Political Life of the Berbers* were sociological or anthropological works that were explicit in their analysis of political structures, processes, and change in Moroccan society, as a basis for more effective policies of modernization. They lay the basis not only for all later studies of North African politics (Waterbury, 1970, 1973; Gellner, 1970; Micaud and Gellner, 1973; Hermassi, 1972) but also for specific works of political science.

Many other works and authors could be cited, but these are typical of the best scholarship on politics in the pre-World War II decade. The period was dominated by European scholars, with as little contribution from the Middle East itself (except for participants' accounts) as from the United States or other areas. Scholars regarded their subject as part of religious thought and philosophy, of political and administrative history, or of a newer current of social organization and relations. Formal institutional aspects of each usually predominated, and past structures of thought and organization were treated as the predominant facts, which upon their breakdown were often regarded as either undesirable in theory or inadequate in practice.

Yet the modern Middle East has never been totally comfortable within the institutional paradigm. The dominant twentieth-century fact of the area, which brought it to the attention of political scientists and out of the hands of the legal and historical Orientalists, was the rise of a nationalism in response to Western imperialism, a very anti-institutional development indeed. In the words of the North African nationalists, the *pays légal* was not the *pays réel*, and scholarship had to be shaped to the reality. Events showed that descriptions of formal governmental institutions were not adequate to handle the subject matter of politics; both under colonial rule and then again under independence, formal structures often showed an annoying irrelevance to the overwhelming realities of noninstitutional politics. In addition, the institutional focus foundered on the problems of definition and equivalence, a matter of cultural relativity of concepts that continues to plague the study of the area. The reaction was therefore to disperse and search for other topics, or to regroup and hunt for a new paradigm that would encompass political reality. Both efforts have sometimes involved a search for new data, a need for new methods, a discovery of new concepts, in a word, a furthering of the discipline—a process in which the study of Middle East politics was very much involved.

At the risk of oversimplification inherent in any such overview, it may be said that the discipline began to form when the current of institutional history was joined by the newer stream of sociology which had its sources in Marx, Weber, Durkheim, and more recently, Parsons and which was also related to developments in the field of anthropology. This new approach brought a different concept of institutions, which it considered to be recurring but informal (as well as formal) patterns of behavior, and thus allowed a broader view of the structures of power in society. It also carried with it other notions of more mixed utility concerning functions (or inherent activities) and functionalism (or teleological causality). The first concept has permitted greater theoretical analysis by identifying performance characteristics, but the second has created some troubling problems of tautology and of ethnocentricity, particularly in accounting for the phenomena of development.

As in many other areas that fall within the scope of comparative politics, efforts to disperse and regroup began to crystallize in the late 1950s, some specifically directed toward the Middle East and others as part of a larger effort to revise the study of countries undergoing modernization and development. The major global work, in this as in other areas, was the collective effort on *The Politics of Developing Areas* (1960) organized by Almond and Coleman, with the chapter on the Middle East by Rustow, begun in 1955 under the sponsorship of the Social Science Research Council. Its major organizing concepts were political groups (primarily a typology of political parties), political functions (primarily input activities), and governmental structures analyzed according to the three classical branches of government renamed. The approach generally went well beyond the institutional descriptions previously presented, and provided the first conceptual setting that could come to terms with political modernization and integration. It brought to the fore the study of political parties as institutions and the study of political culture as a way around the pitfalls in the notion of national character.

Though it may be objected that the effort was merely a change in focus from irrelevant to relevant institutions and was essentially an exercise in reorganizing old data into new typologies, the change was nonetheless basic to a broader understanding of Middle East politics and its analysis in comparative terms. It raised important questions as to whether particular Middle Eastern regimes were "really" of one type or another, whether typologies were adequate and were properly exemplified by the particular data assigned to them, and whether more theoretical relations could be discerned to link categories and concepts, all matters with which later works grappled. It also gave rise to a series of works on political development which included chapters on Turkey and Egypt in the volumes on parties (Rustow, 1966; Binder, 1966) and elites (Rustow, 1965; Binder, 1965), the latter misleadingly called "political culture," and on Tunisia and Egypt in the volume on education (Brown, 1965; Kerr, 1965), and on some more analytical aspects of development in Iran and Turkey (Frey, 1963; McClelland, 1963). This important series shows well the tensions in the disciplinary study of the area. On the one hand, Middle East politics are included in a comparative attempt to apply common terms of analysis, but on the other hand, in each chapter the subject dominates the study and the rigor of parallel analysis is weakened.

Another important and controversial work that broke even further out of the formal institutional framework after a decade of research was Lerner's *Passing of Traditional Society* (1958). Although it focused on the Middle East alone, it was sponsored by the U.S. Information Agency in an attempt to improve American broadcasting to the entire Third World. It made an important impact on the discipline and the area, above all because of its use of survey methods, the first case of such extensive polling in the entire Third World. The book dealt very directly with modernization as a four-phase process of urbanization, literacy, media participation, and empathy. The latter concept was presented as the key to development, for it concerned the ability of an individual to relate to situations outside his immediate experience. The survey (after a pretest in Greece) was conducted in Turkey, Lebanon, Egypt, Syria, Jordan, and Iran, but the chapter on each country covered history and society as well as communications. Respondents were grouped into "moderns," "transitionals," and "traditionals," according to their survey responses, an overly neat classification (like any) that nevertheless brought the concept to the people and answered its questions by reference to individuals. The study brought out the identity problems that accompanied social change in the area and that were ultimately related to "the political problem of governance: Who shall govern, and in the name of what?" The survey questionnaire was criticized as naïve and foreign to its subjects, again bringing out problems of belief between those who consider the area to be unique and those who consider it comparable, and other surveys sampling mass opinion have been few and slow in coming. Yet in the subsequent decade and a half, Pascon and Bentahar (1972), Tessler and Keppel (1976), Klineberg (1976), and Entelis (1974) in North Africa;

Smock (1975), Dodd (1962), Hanf (1971), and Nasr and Palmer (1970) in Beirut; Berger (1957) and Moore (1974, 1975, 1976) in Egypt; and a few others elsewhere in the Arab world (not to speak of regular polling in Israel and some in Turkey) have conducted limited surveys among some groups (often students), successfully generating new data on attitudes toward modernization.

The third key work of the period also hung on the notion of modernization, but its break with formal institutional approaches took it in the direction of new social forces, rather than of behavioral analysis of individual attitudes. When Halpern published *The Politics of Social Change in the Middle East and North Africa* (1963), there was no advanced-level text on the area, but the study's value lies not only in its filling a classroom vacuum. The book introduced a number of important changes in the study of its subject. North Africa was treated as an integral part of the region. The study was organized topically rather than by country. Islamic philosophy and modern socio-political groups were juxtaposed. The work sought to encompass the revolution engulfing the area, a fivefold change in way of life, social system, range of value choices, array of political instruments, and worldwide political consequences. It utilized structural-functional concepts to provide criteria for evaluating institutions and their activities and "for drawing broad generalizations from incomplete data," but by the same token it recognized that the availability of only selective, often anecdotal data hampers the use of more universal or controlled methods. The most controversial contribution of this work was its identification of a new middle class, "a core of salaried civilian and military politicians, organizers, administrators, and experts . . . committed ideologically to nationalism and social reform." This new class, which grew out of a changing social system, has become the political instrument of further change: "only power which addresses itself to the problems of social change can hope to build enduring foundations for authority." Many scholars such as Polk (1965), Bill (1972), Rugh (1973,) and Hurewitz (1969) have studied the phenomenon further, and others have questioned whether there was in fact any commonality in these types of people and whether such people acted with any such ideological commitment or unity, important questions which were addressed only after Halpern's initial hypotheses.

COMPARATIVE POLITICS

Although one of the strengths of these landmark studies of the area lies in their comparison among or across component states of the region, the major impact of the new approaches in political science has been in the formulation of country studies. Here, comparison and control are achieved through the use of concepts and through evolution across time, rather than through the juxtaposition of cases, although it is rarer to find either application or testing of theory. Such studies have nevertheless provided authors with the occasion for the inductive development of new concepts, as well as for the critical use of others' terms. Binder's study of *Iran: Political Development in a Changing Society* (1962) is built on an elaborate conceptual framework that is basically structural-functional, although it begins with a reaction to Almond and Coleman and an emphasis on the concept of legitimacy. "The study of politics is the study of the legitimization of social power," somewhat of a reversal of Halpern's concern. At the same time, the study was very much a reflection of its subject; system maintenance became an important function because the pre-dominant feature of Iran was the fact that the system was being maintained; positive and negative system challenging entered the analytical vocabulary because the opposition was as much interested in simply entering the system as in overthrowing it; and rationalization was an important part of transition. The dynamic element in the system was found in the processes that characterized it, rather than in change among its component agents. An important part of Binder's initial argument was devoted to the defense of whole system analysis, studies of a national polity as an interrelated, interacting agglomeration of agents, processes, and policies. In this the work has had its followers, for the past decade has seen a wealth of significant single-country studies after a lapse in this type of work for nearly a quarter century. Now, however, such studies tend to focus less on formal institutions of government and more on institutions of political interaction—both formal bodies and informal groups—within a society-wide system.

But the adoption of a whole-system approach does not imply any particular units or terms through which the system is to be analyzed. Few studies have used the broadly conceived group approach which Binder or Halpern adopted in order to be able to cover all types of political forces within the system; instead they have generally tended to focus on one particular type of group perceived as the primary actor or the system studied. Usually this choice is dictated by the generally recognized nature of the country rather than by the preexisting ontological predilections of the author. Many of the units of analysis that have most frequently been adopted, such as ethnemes, classes, elites, parties, and associations, can be crudely grouped into two types: social groups that become political actors and specifically political groups with particular social compositions.

Considering the millet-system heritage of the Middle East and the importance of cultural minorities in many countries, it is surprising that the ethnic group has been so little used as the unit of systemic analysis. But it is not surprising that the one place where it has frequently been used in major studies is Lebanon. A symposium on *Politics in Lebanon* edited by Binder

(1966a) set the stage for the examination of the country as a multigroup system whose tensions hold it together. Two dissertations published in 1968, one on eighteenth- and early nineteenth-century Lebanon by Harik and the other on the postwar period by Hudson, used the confessional group as their primary unit of analysis and examined the system or intergroup relations in terms of conflict, tension, balance, and congruent relations. Interestingly, the systemic approach, which has often been criticized for an inability to handle change, was used by both studies to analyze systemic transformation in a country whose traditional nature is impressively persistent despite important signs of modernity. Only in the 1970s, as noted in the Smocks' work on *The Politics of Pluralism* (1975), does confessional convergence rise as an analytical theme.

Most of these studies make a point of noting that Lebanon is unique, and their terms of analysis reflect that characteristic. Other countries are usually not studied as a system of interacting cultural, ethnic, or confessional groups. It is easy to suggest explanations for this: efforts of developing countries such as those in the Middle East are ostensibly directed toward building national unity and overcoming cultural pluralism; praise of ethnic pluralism was often a colonial tactic of divide and rule and so tends to be suspect among scholars and subjects alike; disciplinary approaches include increasing attention to nation building and political socialization, which may press a study into focusing on unifying tendencies rather than diversified components. Spot examples of each effect are readily available. In Iran and Turkey, sensitive minorities are often disapproved subjects of research, so that studies like O'Ballance (1973), Eagleton (1963), and Arfa's (1966) of the Kurds are rare. In North Africa, political use of Berber separatism under colonial rule turned scholars away from explanations in ethnic terms, so that a long overdue reevaluation of the Berber role in society and politics such as the Micaud–Gellner (1973) collection could not be undertaken until well after North African independence. In Israel, where pluralism is written large and small across society, there are a number of carefully researched studies of the political behavior of Jewish immigrant (Weingrod, 1965; Deshen, 1970; Weintraub et al., 1971) and Arab resident (Cohen, 1965; Jiryis, 1968; Landau, 1969) communities, analyzing the difficulties of integration and the political reactions to these difficulties. However, the best whole-system studies, Safran (1963) and Fein (1967, under revision), less or more explicitly (respectively) adopted a political socialization approach which analyzed the polity in terms of efforts to create a political nation (out of a cultural nation) and a political culture (out of an ethnic culture), not in terms of tensions and relations among component groups. There are few other examples to add to illustrate an ethnopolitical approach to Middle East societies, a topic on which the existing works have made a contribution to political studies and where more useful work on an important dimension of political identity could be done.

Not only has ethnic, minority, and cultural politics been somewhat neglected but there has been remarkably little analysis of Middle East politics in terms of any other social units, categories, and strata. Class analysis is scarce, the only notable exceptions being a group of Marxist Egyptians who have critically examined their own society from home and from abroad and a number of Soviet scholars who sometimes seem more concerned with refining their own paradigm by matching it with local reality than with comprehending a Middle Eastern polity. In the first group, *The Class Struggle in Egypt from 1945 to 1968* as examined by Hussein (pseud. Rifa^{c}t and al-Nadî) (1969, 1975) is based on a number of "convictions" about class, mass, development, and outcomes in Maoist terms that invite some serious research rather than mere assumption; the work by Hassan Riad (pseud. Samîr Amîn) on *Nasser's Egypt* (1964) is a harsh condemnation of the meaningless of revolution as sociopolitical change; Abdel-Malek's study of *Egypt: Military Society* (1962, 1968) presents a less doctrinaire analysis but focuses on the bourgeois continuity in political leadership in the same period, and his work on *Ideology and National Renaissance* (1969) examines the development of political thought and culture as an expression of changes in the Egyptian social structure. Marxist Egyptians such as 'Amer (1958), Girgis (1958), and others have written in Arabic on class conflict in Egyptian history and society. Perhaps the most important Marxist writer on politics in Egypt has been Lutfî al-Khûlî, who often wrote as the ideologue of the Arab Socialist Union and critically analyzed both Egyptian society and Middle Eastern international relations in terms of class structure and conflict. Most of the few class studies done outside the area also focus on Egypt; for example, Ziegler's (1964) comparison of "revolutions" in Africa devotes a third of the work to a class analysis of Egypt, showing bourgeois continuity. However, non-Marxists like Berque (1965), Bill (1972b), and van Nieuwenhuijze (1965) provide a broader discussion of class in the Middle East, and Ashraf (1969, 1976) has used the concept in interpreting Iranian history. Some Russian scholars, among whom Fridman (1960, 1963) has shown thoroughness and imagination, have worked with Western or United Nations data to find objective indicators of class and then interpreted policy from inferences derived from the sociopolitical structure; others have depicted current politics in terms of class, as Rozaliev's (1966) study of the Turkish coup of 1960. There is also a much larger school of Russian historians of the Middle East who use class analysis.

Marxists of various degrees of deductive rigidity are present throughout the Middle East, in the universities as well as outside. Yet few indeed have conducted political analyses of their societies through class analysis. Even if one extends the notion of political science into the fringes of economics, sociology, and neighboring disciplines, or into journalism, the net would include only a few other Marxist works, such as Belal's analysis of *Investment in Morocco* (1968), Khallaf's (1962) account of social strata in *Egyptian Economic Revival*, Nirumand's (1969), study of *Iran: New Imperialism in Action* Steinhaus' (1969) *Sociology of the Turkish Revolution*, or critical analyses of bourgeois continuity in Algeria by Chaliand (1964), Bourges (1967), Lentin (1964), and Guerin (1964, 1965), or of class consciousness and self-management in Algeria by Clegg (1972), Laks (1970), and Blair (1970). Their information is often sound and new, but their concept of class is neither rigorous nor analytically powerful, a problem they share in fact with most class analyses. In a region where the existence of classes and class-dominated political systems—slavery, feudalism, capitalism—has traditionally been denied, it would seem important and fruitful to test whole-system studies with class as the unit of analysis but at the same time to be carefully explicit about the concept. The question whether class is a real group or a useful figment of analysis has not been conclusively answered anywhere, but at least there are enough attempts to grapple with the problem outside the area to provide impetus for similar studies on the Middle East.

Some might suggest that the Westerners' equivalent to class as a deductive concept is elite, although that would imply normative connotations that most elite analysts are eager to shed. If elite ideology is less well developed throughout the world than class ideology or Marxism, there is nevertheless a growing number of students of Middle East elites who are more self-conscious about their concept than class analysts have been about theirs. The pioneer in this direction was Berger (1957), whose work on *Bureaucracy and Society in Modern Egypt* bridged the concepts of class and elite by using historical and survey data to examine Westernization of bureaucratic behavior and to evaluate the role of the middle class in republican Egypt. The clear concern with Westernization, the early use of surveys and standard interviews (covering 249 top bureaucrats), and the focus on performance and bureaucracy were important contributions to the study of a developing elite. A decade passed before the study was repeated elsewhere, by Bent (1969) in Turkey. In the meantime, after long preparation, Frey's (1965) comprehensive analysis of *The Turkish Political Elite* appeared, showing the broader possibilities of background data for elite studies. Utilizing a computer technique which allowed him to handle 4387 incumbencies filled by 2210 deputies in parliament (including ministers) between 1920 and 1957, Frey analyzed educational and occupational characteristics of the deputies as a group, and then studied change over time in the evolution of the Turkish political elite. He also used his data to suggest stages of political development, in terms of the structure of power in the developing polity. Frey's work soon led to similar efforts in the area; within the decade, other elite studies were published by his students at Massachsetts Institute of Technology, further analyzing his data and conducting new surveys of their own.

The Rooses' (1971) published dissertation, *Managers of Modernization: Organizations and Elites in Turkey*, combined Berger's area of interest with additional panel survey data added to Frey's, and examined job satisfaction and mobility among political science graduates as a key to understanding the evolution of the political system. The work showed the usefulness of social scientific techniques of data generation and analysis for pinpointing phenomena which were previously ascertainable only through the "feelings" of experts. Zonis' (1971) published dissertation *Political Elite of Iran* combines a skillful ideographic portrayal of the Iranian system with a statistical analysis of the top "300" Iranians in terms of social background characteristics and also of factored attitudes interpreted along psychological dimensions. Analysis of a crucial period in the development of a new nation combined with an explanation of that development in terms of an explicit, verifiable model of political socialization is contained in a third published dissertation from MIT, Quandt's (1969) *Revolution and Political Leadership* on Algeria. The study analyzed social background data on 360 elite members, supplemented by interviews; the population was divided into experiential cohorts and it was shown that successive stages of nationalist protest arose because each cohort, living through a particular experience, reacted to the failure of the previous cohort to achieve its goal because of inadequate power (tactics plus resources). Once the rapid succession of different groups has ceased, with the achievement of independence or, more accurately, with the elimination of vestigial skills and attitudes after independence, this approach is less useful in explaining policy outputs and political interactions, but that very fact opens the way for greater refinements and adaptations of the model to other situations.

Such studies are important because they combine a theoretical framework with the generation or collection of new data; that is, they unite the discipline with the area. Other studies have also expanded the approach. Bill's (1972a) published dissertation on *The Politics of Iran* focuses most successfully on a conceptualization of some elite groups in the Irani system, and Dekmejian's (1971) published dissertation on *Egypt Under Nasir* is rich in data about the components of the Nasserite system. Waterbury's (1970) published dissertation on *The Moroccan Political Elite* shows great sensitivity in understanding and analyzing the Moroccan political system in terms of political groups and tactics, using a conceptual framework borrowed from the segmentary model of the anthropologists. Important work on social changes and continuities in Lebanese, Moroccan, and Tunisian ruling classes has been done by Harik (1972), Marais (1964), and deMontety (1939). Seligman's (1964) study of *Leadership in a New Nation* also made a significant contribution to the study of elites through the analysis of data gained by interviewing parliamentary members in Israel. But only recently have attempts been made to bring such materials together for comparison, theoretical refinement, and inductive generalization (Duchac, 1973; Tachau, 1975; Dekmejian, 1975; Lenczowski, 1975; Zartman, 1976).

In the absence of a predominant class, group, or elite approach to the analysis of whole systems, many students of the Middle East have modified an institutional approach to fit the political realities of the country. Instead of remaining within the formal institutions of government, they turned to the more important institutions of politics and focused on political parties as the primary unit of the political system or, on occasion, as the system itself. The pioneer work came from France, where Rezette (1955) applied Duverger's concept of party to the Moroccan nationalist movement, in an explicit attempt to refute French political attacks on the movement's legitimacy. The work is not only a new advance in the study of national liberation movements as parties but it also brings out a wealth of data on the emerging Moroccan political system. In the following years, a number of analyses of movement parties were undertaken under the twin impact of the invention of "political development" and the discovery of Africa. It is therefore not surprising that the first and best works on Middle Eastern party systems concern the Maghreb, although again the nature of the subject itself—where the party was a much more active and important aspect of postwar politics than in the eastern Mediterranean—also had its effect on the trend of scholarship. Ashford's (1961) published dissertation on *Political Change in Morocco* was among the first of the new wave of scholarship on the new nations in political science and the closest thing to a whole-system analysis to be found outside of Iran. In addition to its grasp of diverse political forces, it carried Rezette's analysis of the Istiqlal into the first years of the dominant-party period of Moroccan independence. It also utilized survey research techniques, not for purposes of testing a conceptual model, but as a standardized informational "interview" for gathering party data.

The most tightly crafted whole-system analysis based on the party was Moore's (1965) published dissertation on *Tunisia Since Independence* and his work with Micaud and Brown (1964). Coherence was as much a characteristic of the subject as of the treatment, but a number of other features distinguish the work. More than simply a full description of the party and its charismatic leader in Tunisian political life, the studies treated the two as agents of modernization and reorganization in a traditional, colonial society. Moore's book was also one of the very rare works to pay attention to policy making, by looking at two important cases. Again like the polity itself, the study stands as a model for its comprehension of single-party regimes. It is also to its credit that the thoroughness of Moore's work has not prevented further studies but has served as a basis for additional scholarship on related subjects. Thus Rudebeck (1969) and Bouhdiba (1968) conducted the surveys of local party officials that Moore could not do five years earlier and further developed an understanding of the party as the agent of modernization and mobilization. Abdallah's (1963) study of Neo Destour history and organization was a thorough work that preceded Moore's. A number of chapters on Tunisia, plus contributions on Egypt, Syria, Lebanon, and Iraq, are synthesized by Cherif (1971) in an attempt to find historical parallels and regularities and to examine the conflict between national and social causes in the rise of popular movements, Zagoria (1976) has analyzed the Algerian People's Party; and Halstead (1967, 1969) has made significant studies and comparisons of Moroccan and Egyptian nationalist movements.

Other studies of party systems have examined organization, recruitment, elections, and evolutions in multiparty systems, such as Suleiman's (1967a) published dissertation on the *Political Parties in Lebanon* or Karpat's (1959) on *Turkey's Politics: The Transition to a Multi-party System*, both thorough works that seek to describe the historical flow of events in terms of the social groups, ideas, organizations, and men that underlie the party divisions. Medding's (1972) published dissertation on the *Mapai in Israel* at long last provides a political biography of Israel's dominant party, whose organization, policy making, and leadership–followership functions are examined specifically in terms of competitive and noncompetitive patterns of penetration and control.

In addition to whole-system studies centered on the party, there have also been studies of political parties themselves, with little pretense at covering an entire polity. Almost by definition such studies would be expected to suffer from narrowness of scope, although there do exist smaller parties or parties that have only a minor role to play within their system and so could be properly treated in this way. The published dissertations of Abu Jaber (1966) and Rabinovich (1972) or the study of Safadi (1964) on the Syrian Ba'ath party are filled with detailed data, presented in conceptual categories in the first and in a historical flow in the second, but in neither study does the party appear life-sized. The Katâ'ib party of Lebanon and the Syrian Social Nationalist party, on the other hand, are manageable within the limits of a study that is conceptually structured but does not aspire to encompass the whole political system, as in Entelis (1974a) and Zuwiyya Yamak's (1966) published dissertations. Klinghofer (1965), Zidon (1967), Frank (1970), and Sayegh (1972) have analyzed the parties within the framework of Israel's parliamentary politics. Communist party strengths and weaknesses have been studied in terms of history, social composition, and issues in Iran by Zabih (1966) and Abrahamian (1970), in Turkey by Harris

(1967), in Palestine by Hen-Tov (1971), and in Israel by Czudnowski and Landau (1965), and throughout the area by Laqueur (1956, 1958); four studies have dealt seriously with the Muslim Brotherhood (Husseini, 1952; Zaki, 1954; Harris, 1965; and Mitchell, 1969). One Turkish party has been studied by Weiker (1973).

But now many other parties, whether "successful" or "unsuccessful", are there in the Middle East still awaiting a political scientist who will serve as their biographer! It is remarkable that such important—indeed famous—movement parties as the Algerian National Liberation Front or the Egyptian Wafd or the Turkish Republican People's Party have not been the principal focus of a single published work of political analysis (except for historical studies such as Klingmuller, 1937; Colombe, 1950; Zayid, 1965; Quraishi, 1967; or Ghali, 1969, on the Wafd); less striking examples of party activity such as Nasser's three experiments or the Sudanese sectarian parties have not yet been probed for lessons on the nature of parties and their successes despite some initial attempts by Heaphey (1966) and Harik (1973). Only Koury (1971) has attempted a synthesis of Arab movement parties, and the work is hardly definitive.

The generally plebiscitary nature of elections in the predominantly single-party systems of the area and their absence where parties are banned might suggest that there is little room for electoral studies. On the contrary, not only are there some thorough reports and analyses of results, but also there are attempts to test propositions and to relate to broader conceptual concerns on behavior and outcomes. What is more surprising, however, is the predominance of single election studies (such as Zuwiyya, 1972 on the 1968 Lebanese elections; Chehab, 1960, 1964, 1968 on three Lebanese elections; Karpat, 1961 on the 1957 Turkish elections; Abadan, 1966 on the 1965 Turkish election; Koç, 1969 on Turkish workers' voting in 1969; Özbudun and Tachau, 1975, on the 1973 Turkish elections), and at the same time the absence of a comprehensive study of the electoral sociology of such multi-party systems as Turkey, Lebanon, or Morocco. The closest thing to a complete ongoing analysis concerns Morocco, where the several studies of Leveau's team (1961, 1963, 1964, 1969, 1976) have focused on the relation of the nature of the candidates and the distribution of votes to the role of local winners within the political system. It is in the fourth multiparty system, Israel, that much work on electoral behavior has been done, notably by Arian (1972, 1973, 1975), Johnston (1968) and Guttman and Lissak (1974); the Institute of Applied Social Research has conducted regular surveys and pioneered in behavioral analysis; Arazi (1964) has also studied the rules of the electoral system. In addition, elections are also covered in multiparty systems as part of a study of parties or parliamentarians (Suleiman, 1967a; Frey, 1965; Seligman, 1964; Tachau, 1977).

Optimally, electoral studies analyze the relations between different features in the electorate and other variables with regard to candidatures and winners, seeking to establish correlations, regularities, and eventually projections and predictions. A number of studies have aimed at testing some general propositions: Czudnowski (1972) and Mavais (1972) show that national legislators in Israel and local councilmen in Morocco are recruited according to structural rather than local representative requirements; Suleiman (1967b) and Hudson (1966) examine hypotheses about the effect of elections on structural change in Lebanese society; and Tachau (1973) used Turkish events to test Huntington's (1968) idea of ruralizing elections. Even no-party and one-party systems can be studied usefully. Harik's (1974) analysis of the local electoral politics of single-party Egypt carries an important confrontation of reputational and effective power, and Zartman's (1970, 1977) work on winning chances among Algerian local candidates tests models of political promotion. Electoral data are not always easy to obtain, but they are present and important indicators of significant political phenomena deserving of even more study.

Though parties and associate processes in the Middle East continue to pose unresolved challenges to political analysts, the competing political institutions known as the military have drawn widespread attention. It is certainly attractive to study the armies, since that is where the action is, but the conceptual problems raised are not simple. An army is a miniature society rather than one of a set of groups (like parties, classes, or elites), although the moment it enters politics it also becomes something else that is not an army. Furthermore, political scientists have disagreed for some time over which governments qualify as military. Despite the important role of such military figures as ᶜUrabî and Atatürk, not to speak of Janissaries and various *mujâhidîn*, it was not until well after the end of hostilities in World War II that political scientists began to focus explicitly on the military as a political force.

The seminal treatments began with Khadduri's article (1953) tracing military intervention historically to the Arabs' "almost nostalgic longing . . . for a 'strong' regime" and Halpern's chapter (1962) treating the military as a form of the new modernizing middle class; these twin themes have remained the basic elements of military studies in the area ever since. The basic work on the process of military takeover and rule, scarcely improved to date, was contained in Rustow's chapter (1963) in Fisher's symposium on the subject. Berger's monograph (1960) on *Military Elite and Social Change: Egypt Since Napoleon* draws all these themes through a historical dimension. Since then, a number of major works have undertaken the job of fleshing out these parameters with historical detail and testing accepted interpretations. The most rigorous and detailed is Be'eri's study of *Army Officers in*

Arab Politics and Society (1970), but a broader area is also covered in depth in the work of Hurewitz (1969), which is notable as a series of comprehensive whole-system studies of Middle East politics centered on each country's military establishment, and of Vernier (1966).

Studies of military regimes are more plentiful than party studies, and they tend to be detailed portrayals of historical data that deal ideographically with such conceptual questions as: who are the military? Why did they take over? What did they do in power (that was specifically relatable to their military nature)? How did they get out of power, or alternatively, how did they stay in power and cease being military? Behind these questions generally lies a broader concern: is the political army, by ascription or by achievement, a modernizing force, and hence a "better" alternative than civilian rule? An unusually incisive whole-system study that necessarily used the military as its focus of analysis is Seale's work on *The Struggle for Syria* (1965), which grasps the dynamics of Syrian politics as interplay among local, regional, and global forces; but Vatikiotis' studies of *The Egyptian Army* (1961) and *Politics and the Military in Jordan* (1967) and the study of Syria by Torrey (1964) are other examples of detailed studies. First (1974) and Flory (1975) portray the Libyan military regime, but there is no solid political analysis of either military government in Sudan. In addition, any account of Nasser's Egypt—such as those by Dekmejian (1971), Abdel-Malek (1968), Wheelock (1960), Vatikiotis (1968), Vaucher (1959, 1960), Little (1967) or the Lacoutures (1958)—must necessarily focus primarily on the takeover and rule of the Free Officers and the Revolutionary Control Council. Frey (1960), Rustow (1959), Özbudun (1966), Harris (1968), Karpat (1970), and Lerner and Robinson (1960) among others have written on the Turkish military, and Weiker (1963) is the major work on the first postwar coup. The Moroccan and Algerian armies' different experiences have been analyzed politically in some detail in the works of Hamon (1966), Quandt (1969), Zartman (1964, 1970b, 1973), and Waterbury (1972). Luttwak and Horowitz (1975) and Perlmutter (1969b) have analyzed the role of the military in Israeli politics.

Although much material has been gathered and presented on a subject that is admittedly difficult to research, there are still many problems to be solved in the study of the Middle East military. Studies of military regimes are usually far from being whole-system studies; that is, it is hard to encompass the other forces in society which impinge, perhaps more strongly than openly, on politics. Despite some hypotheses and many diverse data there are still no established answers to the above questions. Doubtless the two problems are related: it is hard to find explanations for the army's political entrance, behavior, and exit when these activities are not placed within the full sociopolitical context.

The third element in the continuum of political processes, after the party election and the military coup, is the revolution. It may be surprising that there are practically no works on revolution in the Middle East, but the surprise is reduced when one realizes that, unless the term is stretched so out of shape as to encompass either all modernization or such diverse events as the Iranian land reform and the Sudanese coups, there have been few violent, transforming sociopolitical upheavals in the area. Stretching is commonplace, however, and is generally either literary (to underscore the seriousness of the slow changes occurring) or apologetic (to hide the absence of serious, rapid change), depending on whether the user is an analyst or a general. Even more frequently, works on "revolution" in the Middle East discuss mainly army coups and military regimes, which are not at all the same thing. Few studies have seriously grappled with the problem of revolution's causes and consequences, weighing events and their impact against conceptual criteria or process models. Such criteria and models abound in political scientific literature, but they have not penetrated into the area. Thus it would be useful to carry the study of the one unquestionable case of a violent political and social upheaval, the Algerian revolution of 1954–1962, even beyond the solid work of Quandt (1969), Chaliand (1964), Gordon (1966), Vatin and Leca (1975), and the Ottoways (1969). It will also be enlightening to follow the course of the Palestinian resistance, with its mixture of nationalism and revolution, beyond the growing literature that is already coming to grips with that dual nature, including Quandt, Jabber, and Lesch (1973), Sharabi (1969, 1970), Hudson (1969, 1972), Chaliand (1972), Allush (1963, 1970), Cooley (1973), Abu-Lughod (1971), Aruri (1970), Abu Yisr (1968), and Sayegh (1969). But it would also be instructive to analyze the events of 1906 in Iran, of 1919 and 1952 in Egypt, of 1922 in Turkey, and perhaps elsewhere, against explicit models of revolution and their outcomes to learn more about the nature of the political process. The collaborators of Vatikiotis (1972) on *Revolution in the Middle East* have taken a short step in this direction, but it is only a beginning.

Process can also be considered as an approach to the political study of a country, distinct from system (although of course the two can be disentangled only analytically, not really). Here much less work is done within the discipline to provide a background, and studies of the area reflect the same situation. The most important processual context is development, although to name it is not to identify it. The concept extends from a temporal notion of industrialization and scientific desacralization, through a cultural notion of Westernization, to a theoretical notion of self-sustained process expansion; it is further complicated when the restrictive term "political" is applied, where again it can refer to the use of inanimate sources of power, institutionalized democracy, or increased participation and problem solving. No one has followed any of these definitions very strictly in studying the Middle

East, but nearly all the works cited above have paid some attention to the general concept.

Rustow's contribution to the Almond and Coleman (1960) and the Ward and Macridis (1963) volumes got the work started, and the important comparison of *Political Modernization in Japan and Turkey* organized by Ward and Rustow (1964), although never fully integrated either within or between the two country chapters showed that the concept could be operationally applied in detail. Thereafter, Halpern, Binder, Moore, Ashford, Frey, Eisenstadt, Khallaf, Saab, and Rustow, to name a few important figures, have continued to debate the concept as a guide to the selection and use of data. To compare and analyze the definitions of each would be less than fruitful since they are ultimately only frameworks for a better description and explanation of events and changes within the area or countries. Suffice it to say that a focus on the developmental process has been more useful for investigating complex components within an era of open-ended change that is still not fully understood than for identifying a discrete reality (like a legislative process).

Many other units of focus identified above can be analyzed in terms of process (such as a legislative, electoral, or revolutionary process), but there is one, related to the notion of functional system itself, that requires special mention because of its neglect. One of the effects of the structural-functional analysis, combined with the attractiveness of nationalist movements, was that scholarship turned to "input" functions, with little concern either for "output" or for the institutions of conversion. Almond and Coleman were particularly unimaginative on output functions and the conversion baby generally went out the window with the institutional bath water in the study of developing nations (until Huntington [1968] reminded his audience that development could mean institutionalization). There have been few exceptions to this trend. Zartman's study of the *Problems of New Power: Morocco* (1964) examined decision making in five major areas of Moroccan government activity (economic, military, administrative, social, and sovereignty), from which a notion of developmental stages was elaborated. However, neither actors nor processes were typologized, nor were current theories of decisionmaking found to be of use for the study. Since then, with a few exceptions such as a section in Moore's work on Tunisia (1964) and an unusual book by Lapassat on *Justice in Algeria* (1968), output studies have continued to be wanting, and yet it is hard to pretend that a whole society is being analyzed without the study of its policies and policy making.

Policy areas, too, tend to be treated situationally or as self-contained studies, to the extent that they are dealt with at all, rather than being analyzed as part of a political process, either as an outcome or as a source of feedback on inputs and conversions. Thus industrialization, agricultural reform, social policy, infrastructural construction, fiscal and investment measures, and even legal codification have received scarcely any attention from political scientists within a processual framework. Rare exceptions such as Warriner's (1948, 1962) studies of land reform in the Middle East, Saab's (1967) work on Egyptian agrarian reform, and Lambton's (1953, 1969) study of land reform in Persia stand out because of their loneliness and their solid grasp of policy outputs and implications, but they are the work of people who would scarcely identify themselves as political scientists. The area coming closest to being an exception is education, whose key position in the development process has been identified (or overidentified). Brown (1965) has written about education and political development in Tunisia; Arasteh (1962, 1970) and Zonis (1971) in Iran; Başgöz and Wilson (1968), Kazamias (1966), Frey (1965), and Szyliowicz (1972, 1973) in Turkey; Mazouni (1969) in Algeria; and Kerr (1965) in Egypt. The impact of education on society and the types of educational systems have sometimes been well described, but few of these studies pay much attention to the process of making educational policy—the forces, choices, outcomes, and new forces created as a result. What policies Middle Eastern governments should adopt is of course a function of their own goals and resources. However, the implementation and implications of various policies are subjects that political science is equipped to analyze, and through which it could make itself more useful to the area.

The academic treatment of a society (or polity) usually evolves from an initial analysis of the national level and then, after some essays at grasping the whole system, turns to more detailed studies of component parts to test or verify the broad interpretation, before returning, at a third period of scholarship, to a reevaluation of the national system in light of the more detailed evidence. If this is indeed a normal pattern, the political science of the Middle East is only entering the second phase. The study of political components, either as politics at the local level or as groups "lower" than systemic units of analysis, is only beginning. Component groups are scarcely treated at all, despite some initial steps in that direction in such milestones as Fischer's (1955) collection on *Social Forces in the Middle East* or Halpern's (1963) focus on politics among social groups. "Voluntary political association," Vatikiotis (1961) tells us, "is perhaps a uniquely Western notion," although one highly indigeneous group, the *ᶜulamâ*, has been rather well handled in a political context by Keddie (1972), Binder (1962), and others. Ziadeh's (1968) work on lawyers, Moore's (1974–1976) on engineers, and Reid (1974) on professionals—all three on Egypt—are lonely examples of the analysis of other groups. Labor fares only slightly better: there is an excellent comparative study of *Labor Unions in North Africa* by Plum (1962), complementing studies of component countries by Salah Bey (1963), Beling

(1965), and Norman (1965), and one of the rare works on colonial Sudan is Fawzi's (1957) thorough study of labor politics and policy. A number of studies have been done on Israeli labor, including those by Preuss (1965) and Parker (1965). However, there is nothing specific on labor politics in Turkey or Iran, and almost nothing besides a monograph by Beling (1960) on the Arab East, in part because labor organization there was not a function of nationalism as it was in North Africa. Other associational groups fare no better in their academic treatment. Questions involving the internal structure and politics, the goals and goal-making processes, and the power bases and their use—in a word, the "personality" and "behavior"—of such collectivities, as well as their place in the larger polity, are still an open field for research.

Even more open is the whole field of local politics, in all its dimensions. On one hand there is the study of political interactions at the local level, including village and other communities' politics, local decisions and elites, local political cultures, and all the other concepts of political inquiry applied to the local level. On the other hand, there is the vertical dimension of national–local linkages which exist to some extent in any country but which vary widely according to system, stage, or culture. Finally, gathering the two together, there is the study of national politics as the emanation and aggregation of local politics, a whole system analysis from the bottom up. The third has not yet even been attempted, and it would require both a wealth of background studies in detail and a fully articulated political culture approach, neither of which exists to date.

The detailed background monographs along the first dimension are also rare, although the endless replication of ethnographies that has characterized anthropology is not a desirable alternative. Still, there have been some excellent exceptions. The studies of Moore in Tunisia (1965); Gubser in Jordan (1973a) and Lebanon (1973b); Bujra (1971) in Saudi Arabia; Harik in Egypt (1974); and Szyliowicz (1966), Weiker (1972), and the social science group organized by Şerif Mardin (1976) in Turkey have portrayed political attitudes and behaviors within a specific town or village framework, and in some cases have explored notions of structural and relational power along the vertical dimension as well. Antoun and Harik's (1972) *Rural Politics and Social Change* represents a unique attempt to bring together a number of related studies on structures, elites, and policies at the local level in the Middle East with an eye to establishing ideal types of national village life or to testing ideal types of political interaction. A particular subject of study in local politics exists in Israel in the kibbutzim and moshavim, where group relations, ideology, change, and structures have been the focus of works by Talmon (1972), Arian (1969), Perlmutter (1970), Willner (1968), and Weintraub et al (1971). Local–national linkages are a much more elusive subject. Ashford's *National Development and Local Reform* (1967) gave detailed attention to the process of mobilizing local participation in Morocco, Tunisia, and Pakistan, and Mayfield has treated *Rural Politics in Nasser's Egypt* (1971) in equal detail. So much more—even more of the same—remains to be done. Both the nature and the extent of local participation in local and national politics and the changes in these activities under successive regimes are still unknown quantities whose value is usually assumed, sometimes debated, and only rarely studied.

Of course, local politics is a subject, a level of analysis, but not a disciplinary concept or theory. It is an area where many approaches (both within and outside political science) can be applied. Ashford writes of cognitive change, Harik of power structures, and Perlmutter of institutionalization and mobilization. Indeed, many of the propositions and approaches which guide macrostudies can be fruitfully directed toward microstudies of national polities, in relation to both structures and processes. The local level of politics is a vast untilled field, and the studies undertaken show well enough that access to local politics is no more difficult than is data gathering on the perhaps more glamorous national level.

UNDERDEVELOPED STUDIES

In addition to those aspects of the Middle East that developed after landmark treatment in the early 1960s there were others that did not, despite an adequate disciplinary paradigm outside the area. Two striking gaps have been in the subjects of political philosophy and of law. Both topics of study were important in the Orientalist tradition but have fallen by the wayside as the study of politics develops as a social science. It has often been hard to separate law from political philosophy and political thought in the study of the Middle East; this fact reflects the oft-noticed characteristic of Islam as a pervasive sociopolitical system, but it also helps the subject defy the isolation of parameters and the comparison with other societies that a social scientific discipline demands. As a result, an important school of legal and philosophical studies is visibly more comfortable in dealing with the ideal organization of power as prescribed by the *Sharîʿa* than with modernizing movements that trouble the neatness of the classical subject.

Thus Gardet (1954) presented a comprehensive view of the ideal Muslim political order, synthesizing classical thought on the *khilâfa*, the *'umma*, Islamic humanism, and the disruption brought by modern democratic challenges and ideas. E. I. J. Rosenthal has summarized the evolution of political thought through major Islamic writers on the organization of the state, constitutionalism, and law in medieval Islam (1958) and, more impressionistically, in the modern national state (1965). Another reaction to the same problem within the same tradition, but from the Muslim side, is found in a work such as Zikria's (1958), which showed that democratic philosophy is embedded within traditional Islamic thought, or Saab's (1970), which grappled consciously with the notion of development as secularism and technology, and found a need to reconcile the high tradition of Islam and Western scientific thought within new Arab intellectual forms. Finally, Watt's study of *Islam and the Integration of Society* (1961) found in medieval Islam "the marriage of social discontent with appropriate ideas" and within this framework examined the integration of political structures, the transformation of mores, and the need for identical coherence.

Such works, and many others like them, present a comprehensive treatment of Islamic law and philosophy, usually dealing synthetically or evolutionarily with an ideal picture of the classical past, contrasted to the fragmenting, challenging plurality of modernism. Two works can be cited to characterize the "end points" of this trend of scholarship. Khadduri's intellectual history of *Political Trends in the Arab World* (1970) portrays the Arab search for a new ideology to replace the coherence of classical Islamic socio-political doctrine that Watt had identified. Binder's collection of related articles on *Ideological Revolution in the Middle East* (1964) approaches the subject as the sociology of thought, linking the evolution of values and ideology to changes in culture and society, and their relation to political events. The first represents the evolution of a tradition, now searching for a comfortable cast, the second the beginnings of a different approach that has still not found its organizing framework.

The comprehensive study of law and philosophy has fallen into splinters and disarray, partly under its own weight and partly in reflection of its subject. Some of the veins of scholarship have simply been mined out and exhausted by definitive studies, and are now awaiting the invention of new tools and extractive approaches or the discovery of new studies and sources. One of the oldest approaches to the study of Islamic law that can be termed higher criticism has enjoyed this fate. Following investigations in Europe into the authorship and authenticity of the books of the Bible, using internal and historic evidence, scholars undertook to study the traditions of the Prophet Muhammad, particularly those forming the basis of the law, and used the same process to examine them. After the pioneer work of Goldziher (1889, 1890), Schacht exhaustively studied *The Origins of Muhammedan Jurisprudence* (1950) to show that the sources of the legal traditions were to be found no earlier than the first Muslim century and that Umayyad administrative practice formed the basis of Islamic law. There has been little recent work to add to this approach and its findings.

Another approach to the study of law has been the collection, annotation, and synthesis of texts covering rules of governance. Practical manuals of government have descended primarily from the Persian tradition of rule where expediency has been the cardinal principle and practical politics dominates over legal ideals. Thus the *Siyâsat Nâma* of Niẓâm al-Mulk, vizier of the Seljuks, was translated first into the French by Schefer (1893) and later into English; the *Qabûs Nâma*, attributed to Kai Ka'us ibn Iskander, a Ziarid prince, was translated into English by Levy (1951); and the *Sharaf Nâma* of the Timurid ᶜAbdallah Marwarid was translated into German by Roemer (1952). A more modern example outside the Persian tradition concerns the prescriptions for political development by the nineteenth-century Tunisian reformist premier, Khayr al-Dîn al-Tunsi, translated by Brown (1967).

More directly related to law, a number of authors of legal schools or jurists who see the state and khilâfa as the fulfillment of God's design for the governance of his community have also been translated with commentary or summarized in legal studies. *Al-Mukhtaṣar* of al-Khalîl ibn Ishaq, a Malikî jurist, was translated into French by Perron (1848–1854); al-Mawardi's *al-Aḥkâm al-Sulṭâniyya* into English by Amedroz (1910–1911, 1916) and into French by Ostrorog (1906) and Fagnan (1915); and Aḥmad al-Baladhuri's *Kitâb Futuḥ al-Buldân* into English by Hitti and Murgotten (1916, 1924). More recently, Khadduri has translated Shafiᶜi's *Risâla* and Shaybanî's *Siyâr* into English (1961a, 1966), but he has also done important work of his own, particularly on Muslim conceptions of international law (1941, 1955, 1955a), on which so little other work has been done. In domestic law, a similar legal analysis, showing both the differences from Western practice and the internal tensions within various national legal systems, has, been undertaken by Chehata (1970, 1971) and by Coulson (1964, 1969, 1971), following Schacht (1964). But the subject is changing, as new codifications are undertaken and Western ideas of law are mixed with Islamic systems to form new national codes and practices. As a result, the study of classical Muslim rules for governance through legal texts either loses its appeal to the discipline or joins a different approach to the study of law.

The third—the developmental or applied—approach is not new; scholars have for a long time been aware of the dichotomy between "theory" and "practice" in Islamic law. Although the texts would make certain provisions, practice disregards them without repudiating their underlying theory; Islamic jurists continued to write about the theoretical state and its theoretical laws as if they were completely unaware of happenings around them. Their writing seemed like an exercise in piety whose aim was to describe an ideal state, not the actual state of affairs. This dichotomy fascinated many Western scholars who attempted to describe it in many fields of law and in many localities. One attraction lay in the practice in those localities, where ancient custom has not been superseded by a provision of the formal law. French scholars associated with the administration of North Africa have been prominent in the study of *ᶜurf* or customary law, with Bousquet (1956) Berque (1955), and Milliot (1922) reacting to or following the tradition of Salmon and Marcy. A very different type of study of the reconciliation of customary administrative practice and sacred law is the posthumous *Studies in Old Ottoman Criminal Law* of Heyd (1973) which combines critical text, annotated translation, and descriptions of four centuries of Ottoman justice. The current study of law is dominated by the University of London, where Anderson (as well as Coulson) has studied family law and Islamic legal history, examining law within the context of change, modernization, and development. Such studies are rare, however. The necessity that the colonial powers felt for dealing with a Muslim legal system no longer affects scholarship, and the current trends of disciplinary research do not seem to encourage attention to law. Legal reform, sociology of law, law making, legal philosophy, comparative law, and the application of law are all aspects of law that disciplinary scholarship now neglects and that could provide modern approaches consistent with current methods and substantive interests.

Not only has the study of law fallen into general inattention, however; in the process, other subjects that were formerly related to law and studied with it have been cut loose to search for their own frame of reference and have been no more successful than the study of law in that quest. Political thought and philosophy no longer carry their former legal and theological cast and so the study of thought, like the study of Middle East political action, is no longer comfortably encompassed within religion and jurisprudence. Just as the legal norms for political action have been scrambled, so the debate over both normative and normal standards has been secularized, pluralized, and revised by challenges and responses from international and national, and regional and external sources. Furthermore, just as Middle Eastern political thought has not yet found its frame of reference, so its study still searches for a comfortable frame of analysis; and just as the outsider may be surprised that one or another of the international value systems has not taken hold in the area, so the disciplinarian may also be surprised that recent developments in the study of political thought have not been utilized to give a sharper or more coherent analysis of the subject in the Middle East. There has been enough work done on ideology, cognitive systems, political and civic cultures, personal belief systems, and symbolic structures, among others, for such approaches to be useful in interpreting and explaining Middle East political thought. Yet despite some limited exceptions, treatment of the subject is still descriptive, restricted, and inadequate.

Most works on Middle Eastern politics feel obliged to take note of Arab (as well as Turkish, Persian, Israeli, and smaller units) nationalism and to grapple with the impact of modernism as a disruptive body of attitudes and values. Nationalism has been the basis of analyses of the area since the works of Toynbee (1927), Kohn (1929, 1932), and later, Antonius (1938). But the phenomenon (if the proper word is indeed singular) has defied a global comprehensive treatment, and Cottam's (1964) important work on *Nationalism in Iran* stands as a lone example in the analysis of the sources, components, and dimensions of even one country's nationalism and its critical role in modernization. One way of handling the problem has been through anthologies of nationalist writings, such as those prepared by Haim (1962) on Arab thought, by Sharabi (1966) on Arab revolutionary and nationalist writings, by Gendzier (1969) on Arab nationalism and Zionism, by Hertzberg (1964) on Zionism, by Vlavianos and Gross (1954) on Jewish political ideologies, and by Karpat (1968) on contemporary Arab and Turkish ideology. In each, an introductory essay synthesizes content under the notions of secularism and reformism, nationalism, and socialism. Despite the limitations of size and selectivity, such works can be eloquent in their examples and incisive in their introductory analyses, and more of them can be used.

A second approach is to treat the authors of political ideas as the subjects of analysis, through analyses that range from psychopolitical biography to philosophical treatises on a single man's ideas. Afghani, Abduh, and Rida have been the most frequent subjects of such study with Keddie's (1972) and Pakdaman's (1969) approaches closer to the psychological and Kerr's (1966) and Kedourie's (1966) more directly philosophical. But other scholars have shown the same range of approaches to other figures, as in Gendzier's (1972) work on Fanon, closer to the psychological side, in Heyd's (1950) work on Gökalp, on the conceptual analysis of ideas, and in Waterbury's (1973) work on al-Sûssi, bringing an anthropological approach to a typical figure. There have also been a number of biographies of Bourguiba, Atatürk, Ben Gurion, Dayan, Eshkol, Muḥammad V, Feiṣal, Zag͟hlûl, Nasser, al-Ḥusrî, and others, but most of them do not reach beyond simple historical narrative to the analytical level of the other scholars already cited. Since political biography is still an open area for innovative approach, much more could be done with Middle East figures, both with charismatic leaders and with more typical cases.

A third partial approach has been to study the development of political philosophy within one country and to relate it to the emergence of political action and organization, approaching the subject on a single-state basis much as Khadduri (1970) did for the area. Safran's (1961) published dissertation on *Egypt in Search of Political Community* bridges the traditional and modern study of intellectual political history, bringing together Islamic thought and social analyses of political movement, and Ahmed's (1960) study of *The Intellectual Origins of Egyptian Nationalism* covers much the same ground.

Mardin's (1962) published dissertation on *The Genesis of Young Ottoman Thought* and Ramsaur's (1957) and Ahmad's (1969) studies of political thought of *The Young Turks* do the same thing for the ideology of Turkish nationalism as Halpern (1969) does for Israeli nationalism. Arian's (1969) published dissertation on *Ideological Change in Israel* is a behavioral rather than a philosophical analysis. There are few other intellectual "biographies" of individual countries or of the region as a whole by political scientists that could provide a political and analytical equivalent, for example, to Albert Hourani's (1962) historical work on *Arabic Thought in the Liberal Age 1798–1939*. Even most of the studies that exist, while showing a sensitive awareness of nationalist language and thought within an evolving social context, have difficulty in transcending the subject's uniqueness, i.e., in explaining events in other than their own terms.

Finally, another way of writing about ideology is from within ideology itself, actually a position adopted by the very subjects of the above studies such as Abduh, al-Afghânî, Luṭfî al-Sayyid, Salâma Musâ, al-Fâssî, and many others. Most of this long wave of reformist-commentators have combined philosophy and politics, but a recent and important study by Laroui (1967) of *Contemporary Arab Ideology* combines political science and philosophy. As remarkable as the work itself, which offers a new ideological synthesis for modern Arabs, is the absence of competitors, unless one wishes to nominate such ideologues as ᶜAflâq, Fanon, Ḥarbî, al-Khûlî, or Haykal as honorary political scientists. Of these, Fanon (1964, 1966, 1967, 1969) probably comes closest to analyzing the political tendencies of emerging nations, desperately prescribing a peasant revolt against an unproductive bureaucratic bourgeoisie, whose eventual dominance he foresaw too clearly. Works of self-criticism are particularly prominent, whether within the Salafî tradition of al-Fâssî's *Self-Criticism* (1956) or his followers' *Istiqlâlism* (Ghallab, 1965; Awad, 1966), or from the secular socialist school of the Ba'th in such works as Ṣafadi's *Maᶜṣat al-Mawlis Maᶜṣat al-Nihaya* (1964b), and al-Razzâz' *al-Tajriba al-Murra* (1967); or from nationalists in the wake of defeat as in al-ᶜAzm (1969) or Bitar (1968) or Munâjjid (1968) or Naṣûr (1968). Their political assessments are both data for the study of the area and works of analysis about it. Many others could be mentioned and profitably assessed but they tend to fall outside the study of politics as a social science. They indicate, however, the already noted characteristic of both the subject of political philosophy and its study, that is, the search for a comfortable framework of expression and analysis, for a concordance of values and reality and for an acceptable standpoint from which to view the changing and incomprehensible world.

In sum, the study of system and process in Middle East politics has generally been pursued using the dominant political institution of the country—party, army—or social group—confessional group, elite, class—as the unit of analysis, with little concern about normative rules and debates relating to these systems and processes. In each case, a few works have wrestled consciously with theories and concepts of political science, and a larger number have made use of them in passing or have simply unearthed data of eventual use to comparativists. Yet analysts of Middle Eastern polities have taught the discipline some important things about stages in party evolution, elite socialization and recruitment, causative factors in military take-over, relations between protest and legitimacy, traditional and ideological reactions to change, and the relationship between modernization and Westernization, to name a few. In one sense, of course, there is not enough of this: the "interface" between area and discipline is still small, or ragged, or largely desert rather than a populated area. There are still many thorough, perspicacious, knowledgeable scholars in the area who maintain that the study of Middle East politics is part of a discipline of Middle East studies rather than politics, and who claim that placing the area in the latter context robs it of the cultural uniqueness which is the real explanatory factor. The reason "why they behave like Arabs" is that they *are* Arabs, not that they are people acting (for example) through parties, as elites, or in development processes. Beyond its basic tautology, however, this argument ignores the fact that its own best test would be an examination of Arabs, for example, within putatively universal political hypotheses to see if in fact they do behave differently, and then to ask why.

In the other direction, however, one can see that the study of politics in the Middle East has been "revolutionized"—even though there is a lot of *ancien régime* still around—if one considers the small amount of time the change of focus has taken and also the fact that the discipline itself is only getting started and finding its own identity along the way. Over a decade and a half of political studies of the Middle East, a number of features stand out which are useful as a background for establishing future directions and priorities.

First, the structural-functional development syndrome was crucial to the creation of disciplinary scholarship on the area, not because it imposed its paradigm on the field but because it shook the study of polities loose from the hands of historians. New kinds of politics (and politicians) that could not be handled within the previous institutional framework of political science arose in the area, bringing with them a shift from political history to political sociology and an emphasis on informal (or nongovernmental) institutions, social bases of politics, input analysis, sociopolitical change, and normative reevaluation.

As time passes, however, the corrective trend begins to develop its own limitations and no doubt eventually countertrends. The limitations are seen in a continued inattention to bureaucracy and administration, public policy and decision making, law and legal reform, and political thought and philosophy as major areas of serious study. Furthermore, scholars who (for all their interest in value-free social science) were attracted to the study of new nations as brave new experiments and who shared nationalist antipathies to colonialism and imperialism now often find that they were overly optimistic in their expectations and are sometimes sharply disenchanted by Middle East political forms. Solidarity values turn out to be an addition to, not a substitute for, welfare values and, scarcely to Lord Lloyd's surprise, not an unrelated addition at that. Marxists looking for Middle Eastern revolutions and liberals searching for modernizing middle classes have both undergone this reaction. On the other hand, the dialectical formation of paradigms, moving between structural descriptions and functional analysis of change, or between synchrony and diachrony, has not hit political science as sharply as it has anthropology or linguistics, for example. The reason is probably that political science has borrowed enough from such other disciplines to muddle sharp debates and correct extreme emphases, at least in regard to the study of the Middle East.

Second, there has been plenty of interaction among political scientists working on the Middle East, but remarkably little building of one study upon another. An exception is in the field of elite studies, where there has been some replication of research at different times and places, but even there theory building is not much further advanced than when Mosca and Pareto rediscovered elites. Neither replication nor the adoption of a common approach—not to speak of theorizing—has been characteristic of other studies. Indeed, despite the area isolation within the discipline, there is no "political science of the Middle East". Each polity is seen as an example of its particular characteristic, for example, Tunisia as the single-party regime, Pakistan as religious politics, Algeria as revolution, Turkey as multiparty dynamics, Lebanon as ethnic accommodation, and Egypt as a military and class polity; but there has been little attempt to examine that same characteristic in other states or to develop a comparative cross-national analysis. Thus debates that clarify and make explicit the content of analytical concepts and their applicability to a particular society are relatively muted or lost in the cultural woodwork, the debate on the new middle class being both an exception and a case in point, respectively.

The country studies that have appeared have been sensitive and skillful in grasping prominent features in the nature, and sometimes the dynamics, of national politics. To the extent it is used, however, disciplinary rigor is clearly at the service of cultural description and gives way before it as necessary. Not only are authors (except perhaps Lerner and the Rooses) more interested in presenting accurate portraits than in conducting rigorous experiments, but in addition, replicating experiments and collecting similar data in several countries are usually matters of real practical difficulty. Yet in the end the call for whole-system analysis has often been met with more vigor in form than in substance. There are many more country studies (denoting a level of analysis) than whole-system analyses (denoting a breadth of scope), so that almost none of the national polities in the area have been accorded a really comprehensive treatment.

Third, a sizable amount of data collection and even some significant data generation have been accomplished despite political instability and a research climate that is not always hospitable. Opinion surveys, reputational rankings, census data, biographical information, voting data, and content analyses are new types of aggregate and statistical data brought to light by scholars working on the area, along with detailed information on political events tapped by careful documentation and extensive interviewing. However, little more than some surface scratching has been done in any of these types of new data; the political scientist still depends on access to documents and to interviewees. To be effective in establishing a solid base for analysis, data collection needs to be exhaustive, systematic, and controlled. Present data sources are sporadic, incomplete, unstandardized, and unverifiable, yet fortunately the work of analysis goes on. Political scientists seem less concerned than others about their uneven data base, and it would be foolish to stop the studies until complete returns have come in, just as it would be foolish to confuse quantitative data with quality of results. Nevertheless, instead of giving exclusive credit to new and unique studies, political science needs also to encourage comprehensive data collection as an independent effort, just as it needs to encourage replication and "puzzle solving."

Even short of aggregate and statistical data, the expansion of continuous reporting and other data collection services in the postwar period has been remarkable. Where there was once only *Statesman's Yearbook*, *Cahiers de l'Orient Contemporain*, and *Oriento Moderno*, there is now a large number of careful sources including *Middle East Journal* chronology (Washington), *Middle East Annual Review* (Essex), *Travaux et Jours* (Beirut), *Arab Report and Record* (London), *Record of the Arab World*, *Middle East Record* (Tel Aviv), *Middle East Monitor* (Washington), *Middle East Intelligence Survey and Middle East Highlights* (Tel Aviv), and *Middle East and North Africa* (London). The North African area is covered most comprehensively of all, through the *Annuaire de l'Afrique du Nord* (Aix-en-Provence) and the bimonthly *Maghreb* (Paris), which give not only continuous chronologies, documents, statistics, and reports, but also articles that have become more and more scholarly in the decade of both publications' existence. In international relations, to be discussed more fully below, Hurewitz' (1956) four centuries of documents in *Near and Middle East Diplomacy*, revised for a second edition as *The Middle*

East and North Africa in World Politics (1975), constitute a rare example of collected source materials, and Mansoor's (1972) retrieval system for events in international area politics is a useful service made possible by use of the computer. Khalil's (1962) collection of constitutions and other documents is useful for internal politics, but journal and annual collections are more helpful because regularly renewable; that is why the early demise of the *Cahiers de l'Orient Contemporain* begun by Colombe and the *Arab Political Documents* of Khalid and Ibish is so regrettable. On the other hand, one of the results of the June War is an explosion of documentation from Europe, Israel, Egypt, and Lebanon and also from Palestinian organizations such as the Institute for Palestine Studies and the Research Center of the Palestine Liberation Organization.

Finally, although Middle Eastern scholarship in political science has been integrated without any special notation in the preceding review, there are some characteristics in the region's study of itself that stand out. Unlike local scholars in some of the other disciplines, Middle Eastern political scientists either join in current approaches to political inquiry as outlined above or they do not appear as political scientists at all. This observation, however, breaks down into several important distinctions: on one hand, most of the work done in the Middle East on Middle East politics is institutional, philosophical, or historical, with much less work in social scientific approaches as such. On the other hand, there is as yet no specifically Middle Eastern approach to the study of its own politics, as discussed in the section on political thought. Yet in addition to these facts is a third that fits with difficulty between the two: Middle East concerns and questions about politics often appear different in their form and emphasis from Western ones. To a large extent this is a result of a reaction to things Western, a suspicion of foreign attempts to find procrustean sameness and denigrating difference, and a search for identity and authenticity. But beyond this rejection of foreign forms of inquiry (reinforced by a fascination with them nonetheless), the question of real differences in content remains enigmatic.

Middle Eastern studies of politics remain largely institutional, philosophical and historical, partly because of differences in the stages of development in educational systems and partly because of related differences in the levels of self-study. For the most part, in Middle Eastern university systems, the premium labor lies in the translation of Western (including, where permitted, Marxist) works and in surveys of general disciplinary literature rather than in specific and applied study. With a few exceptions, the teaching of contemporary political systems of the area or the particular country is not provided, beyond rather formal institutional surveys that are often not very satisfying to university students. Such approaches leave the self-study of the polity to lawyers, journalists, and practitioners. Research may extend to sociology and history and to the description of administrative and legal systems, but "political" subjects are often "dangerous" subjects by definition. The fundamental dryness and often irrelevance of studies in the history of political thought, constitutional, administrative and international law, and diplomatic history push the pendulum of concern to headier philosophical questions of the Greatest Good and the Highest Value and a search for ideology in times of rapid change. In this search for a framework beyond institutional description, Marxist influences have been important in breaking away from traditional Islamic and European liberal patterns of thought. Yet the importance—like that of other structural-functional developmentists—has been greater precisely as a catalyst for the breakaway than as an alternative pattern, greater in opening new questions than in providing answers, and therefore greater in stimulating indigenous responses to large questions than in offering yet another ideology. In this form it is helpful to scholarship, probably in direct relation to the extent that it deviates from its own orthodoxy.

Although it is risky and not entirely accurate to characterize national scholarship by a particular theme, a rapid survey of some salient works by country can serve to illustrate the type of political inquiry undertaken. In Morocco, studies such as Lahbabi (1958), al-Fâssî (1954, 1956), Pascon and Bentahar (1972), and Laroui (1967, 1974) deal with the sources of political legitimacy. In Algeria, emphasis on administrative structures in the works of Remili (1968), Sbih (1968, 1972), and Mahieu (1969) predominates. In Tunisia, the structures of political participation are treated by Makhlouf (1968), ᶜAbdâllah (1963), Bouhdiba (1968), and Zghal (1971). In Lebanon, institutional structures are the focus of works by Rabbâṭ (1970), Salem (1973), Harik (1972), Maḥmasânî (1957), and al-Khatîb (1961). In Iran, Adamiyat (1961, 1967, 1970), Zarrinkub (1965a, 1965b, 1969), and Ashraf (1976) have studied the intellectual and social bases of politics in Iranian history. In Turkey there has been much attention to the study of political movements from various points of view, for example, philosophical, historical, and sociological, as seen in the works of Mardin (1962, 1965), Tunaya (1960, 1962), Akşin (1970), Özbudun (1970, 1975), Turan (1969), to name a few. In Israel, there is a wealth of scholarship on the social bases of politics, including works by Eisenstadt (1969), Segre (1971), Matras (1965), Arian (1968), Lissak (1969), and many others. In other countries, political inquiry tends to be less notable. This summary indicates, however grossly, both the direction and the limitation of current activity. It also suggests the effects of official views, such as that of the Algerian educator, that political science is of little practical value for development and is therefore an academic luxury, a judgment that is sobering if nothing else.

INTERNATIONAL POLITICS

The study of international relations in the Middle East shows many of the same characteristics as the study of comparative (domestic) politics but in starker focus. Endemic conflict in the area throughout the century has made it a natural subject of study, but at the same time has burned much of the scholarly detachment out of many of its students. As a discipline or subdiscipline, international relations is a residual grab bag even less developed than political science, and it has found no other discipline to turn to as a source of theory on relations between or among large groups. As a result, the study of Middle Eastern international politics has come straight out of political history, and more particularly, diplomatic history, without any of the leavening that the domestic study has received from sociology, anthropology, or even area studies. Lately, students of international politics have invented their own structuralism by focusing analytically on regional systems, but the concepts and methods are still tentative and sometimes seem to require more energy for their defense than for their testing. Balance of power, the dominant concept in international politics—and even national interest, the principal concept in foreign policy analysis—has had some distracting effects on the study of relations among Middle Eastern states. Taken literally, balance of power allows the area to be studied only as a pawn in European politics, a hangover of imperial times, and although it might be quite usefully applied directly as an analytical tool to intraregional relations, it has not been so used. As a result, international relations in the area have been studied either as an adjunct to Great Power politics or as an extension of domestic politics of the local states, two approaches that may well reflect reality but that leave little room to the study of regional interstate relations per se. This means, though, that linkage studies are the native, not the newcomer, to Middle East international relations, a situation from which many other areas and the subdiscipline in general could learn much.

Probably a review of this diplomatic history-cum-domestic politics tradition should begin with Toynbee's (1927) survey of *The Islamic World Since the Peace Settlement*, which brought the area up to date for inclusion in subsequent *Surveys of International Affairs*, but should also include Earle's *Study of Imperialism* (1923) and Howard's *The Partition of Turkey 1913–1923* (1931). Great Power interests in the Mediterranean were studied by Monroe (1938) and Boyeri (1938) before World War II, and by Kirk (1953, 1954) and Monroe (1963) over the wartime and early postwar periods. The American advent to the Mediterranean brought with it an important new geopolitical analysis by Reitzel (1948), which also identified a growing Russian interest, and deNovo (1963) later provided a background to *American Interests and*

Policies; Soviet policies in the area have been ably analyzed by Laqueur (1958, 1959, 1969) and more recently by a swarm of careful observers including Smolansky (1974), McLane (1973), Lenczowski (1972), Freedman (1975), Klieman (1970), Hunter (1969), Yodfat (1973), Penner (1973), Becker and Horelick (1970), Page (1972), and Confino and Shamir (1973), and Chinese policy by Khalili (1970). Outside the Mediterranean, Lenczowski's (1949) study of *Russia and the West in Iran* examines Iranian politics within the context of Great Power rivalry. Soviet and American interests, cutting across the security concerns of Egypt and Israel, form the elements of analysis for Whetten's (1975) detailed study of *The Canal War*.

A number of works have continued this tradition, often prepared collectively by study groups such as those of the Council on Foreign Relations. Campbell's *Defense of the Middle East* (1958) analyzed the effects of the post-colonial and cold war realignments on domestic politics; although an excellent historical survey of alliance diplomacy, it lacked conceptual structure. Cremeans' *The Arabs and the World* (1963) treated the same theme; neutralism had by then arisen as a central theme and much more attention was given to the influential role of domestic politics and Nasserite leadership. Badeau's study of *The American Approach to the Arab World* (1968) again reviews relations with the area. Another conference sponsored by the Academy of Political Science a decade after Campbell was the basis of Hurewitz' collection on *Soviet–American Rivalry in the Middle East* (1969). The symposium showed a greater effort at conceptualization through the use of model scenarios (cold war, limited détente, general détente) to examine relations between the dominant Great Power system of international relations and the subordinate or regional system. Another excellent treatment of the same specifically intraregional realignments since the formation of the United Arab Republic has been Kerr's *Arab Cold War*, which first appeared in 1965 and has been regularly reedited thereafter. Although its conceptual framework is only implicit, its well-organized narrative based on local sources is dispassionate and incisive, and useful alongside more theoretical studies as well. Seale's (1965) fine study of Syria is as much a work in international relations as in comparative politics, as befitting to its subject.

The major new element in the international politics of the area is oil, and the relations, interests, and diplomacy occasioned by it. Longrigg (1968), Mosley (1973), Shwadran (1970), and Lenczowski (1960) have dealt with the subject, but they have not provided a full analysis of the domestic–foreign political linkages that characterize the writing on other aspects of regional international relations. Again the study reflects political views of the subject; the West, and for that matter, maybe the Arab world, is just getting used to the fact that oil producers can manage their extractive industry for their own purposes, both economic and political. A thorough, detailed, conceptual study of oil politics and oil negotiation remains to be done.

Although the lines are more clearly drawn in the Arab–Israeli dispute, and the four-phase war contains a certain amount of inherent replication, the subject has not lent itself to disciplinary inquiry. Whereas there are some eloquent partisan statements and some dispassionate current events accounts, conceptual analysis is usually lacking. Hurewitz' published dissertation on *The Struggle for Palestine* (1950) was first among the historical background treatments relating community politics to international politics, and it is still the best place to begin. Among recent studies, Khouri's (1968) *The Arab–Israeli Dilemma*, Safran's (1969) *From War to War*, Evron's (1973) *The Middle East: Nations, Superpowers and Wars*, and Laqueur's (1974) *Confrontation* are generally regarded as the most scholarly and most comprehensive. Their quality lies in their grasp of complex events and their ability to avoid polemic and bias (although each has its favored side and strategy); in addition, they have diligently unearthed rare data and even imaginatively generated new types of data—notably in aggregate form—when less precise indicators are inadequate. But the approach remains the strategic study of power and interests. New concepts are not developed nor are explicit propositions tested, or even generated. Neither conflict nor attempts at conflict resolution in the Middle East have had the impact on the study of international politics that development in the area has had for comparative politics.

Structural analysis of Middle East international relations has provided fewer studies than has strategic and interactional analysis, but it has also led to some greater innovation. Despite the presence of some important formal structures there are few institutional studies of Middle East regional politics. MacDonald dissertation(1965) on *The League of Arab States* is the only full-length study of an international organization of the area, and although it fills the gap with a thorough well-organized description of Arab League activities, it has not preempted the field. A similarly entitled work by Beyssade (1968) is insightful diplomatic history, but not organizationally structured. Boutros Ghali (1954, 1959, 1961, 1969) has also described the diplomacy and international organizations of the Middle East states. Articles on the League and on the Arab bloc in the United Nations update these subjects from time to time but the study of the area's institutions has made no real contribution to conceptualization or theory or international organization, nor has it made much use of the disciplinary work for further understanding the area's institutional politics. Interest has risen in the Organization of Petroleum Exporting Countries (OPEC), as shown in the works of Mikdashi (1972) and Rouhani (1971), but is still on the descriptive level. Beling's (1960) study of the International Confederation of Arab Trade Unions gives a fuller treatment of a narrow segment of international organization in the Middle East than most other works do for larger and more active institutions in the area. Probably the only aspects of international organization that have received adequate study are some of the United Nations ventures in the area—peace-keeping by Higgins (1969), Rikhye et al. (1975), Forsythe (1972), and Frye (1957), UNRRWA by Buehrig (1971), and the United Nations itself by Lall (1968).

The one structural concept that has provided some political scientists with a theoretical framework that is particularly applicable to the peculiar mixture of domestic and international politics in the Middle East is the subordinate state system. The concept was introduced into the area by Binder (1958) and Brecher (1969) and extended into dynamic models by Harary (1961) and Thompson (1970); it has also been used occasionally to structure analysis and deal with alternative futures. It forms the underlying structure for many of the best descriptive analyses, such as Kerr (1965), Seale (1965), and Safran (1969). Etzioni (1964) and Nye (1971) included the Middle East as area cases in their important theoretical studies of regional integration. The regional system has also provided the setting for a new—and singularly controversial—method of data generation and analysis involving the use of aggregated event data, although the full systemic implications of the finding that the new data reveal have not yet been developed. Here the challenge of the area's political relations has attracted a number of political scientists who have had no previous brush with the Middle East, quite the reverse of previous procedures. Burrowes (1973), Azar (1972), Graber (1969, 1970), Ben-Dak (1975), and others have looked into the indicators of hostility and friendship in the area for patterns, trends, and correlates that can yield predictive signals for future events.

Within structures and interactions, the third focus of international political analysis is the study of individual states' foreign policy, providing the link between comparative and international politics. Brecher's (1972) *The Foreign Policy System of Israel* is a rare example that combines international systemic analysis and analysis of the political system as a policy process with decision-making analysis and elite analysis; although the author appears more interested in proving than in testing a framework for analysis, at least there is one, and a lot of data as well. Most other foreign policy analyses have been conducted for scattered countries, from Ramazani's (1966) study of 441 years of *The Foreign Policy of Iran* to Weisband's (1973) intensive investigation of two years of Turkish foreign policy, with such works as Vali (1971), Burke (1973), Colombe (1973), Chubin and Zabih (1975), Roberts (1974), and Ruf (1969) covering intermediate ranges of Turkish, Pakistani, Egyptian, Iranian, Israeli, and Tunisian foreign policy from the point of view of interactions, power and interests, and process.

Given the nature of the Middle East as a regional system with identifiable interactional and institutional structures, subject to influence to the point of intervention from the Great Powers, and animated by factions, coalitions, and issue alignments within its midst, it would be a mystery why more serious attention has not been given to the study of Middle East international politics, if the answer were not so obvious. The Arab–Israeli conflict has been debilitating to scholarship, along with everything else, in the area. It is a subject that overwhelms analysis with passion and uniqueness. There is no academic objectivity when findings and conclusions are inherently political, desanitizing even the most careful methods. Even objectivity itself becomes suspect when its implications become clear. Scholars then retreat into frank subjectivity or benevolent activism, as seen in its most academic form in the sincere and imaginative work of the American Friends Service Committee (1970), Reisman (1970), Tuma (1970), and Fisher (1963), among others. Or they simply study something else.

THE CHALLENGE

In conclusion, what do we know, understand, and explain in the Middle East in political scientific terms? What work needs to be done or, more modestly, what are the priority tasks given the present disciplinary state of concepts and theory and the area possibilities for research? There is no doubt that sensitive political scientists have been able to capture and portray essential characteristics of national communities in motion [to redo Cantwell Smith's (1957) phrase], explaining past events in terms of unique conjunctures of incidents and sometimes of conceptual themes and categories, and providing the background for an understanding of (usually similar) events in the future. But there is also no doubt that there are many other aspects of Middle Eastern politics that remain unknown and that could be the immediate and useful subject of disciplinary focus.

The enumeration of priority areas, however, requires the enumeration of criteria, even if the priorities are simply mentioned without being ranked, and criteria may appear to vary widely according to the nationality of the scholar. What is interesting to one group of scholars may not be so to another, and what is interesting to either is not always feasible. Middle Eastern writers on politics are often most concerned with questions about The Good Society or The Good Polity, which Western scholars, gun-shy from the battles of colonialism and neocolonialism, may treat as data but not as subjects of direct encounter. Often there is more affect than insight in the debate when a common issue is discussed; issues of cultural relativism and ethnocentrism have often crowded out fruitful debate on development rather than clarifying the phenomenon and its incidence (or alternatives to it). Yet at another level,

Middle Easterners are passionately concerned about development, the relation between tradition and new alternatives, the search for ideology in times of change, and the discovery of viable values under challenge. Thus the concerns and the criteria for priorities, and the need for further thought and research, may be more common than they first appear or than the surrounding debate may allow them to seem. The Western scholar, however, cannot enter into the debate directly; in a seeming reversal of role, *he* can only provide data, raw or analyzed, for the Middle Easterner who is in the business of doing politics as well as political science.

Criteria, therefore, can be very varied, in turn according to their referents and utilization. Theoretical interest, practical interest, feasibility, and newness are all research criteria whose importance may vary depending on whether one wants to solve problems, build paradigms, instruct schoolchildren, or explain area phenomena. (This variance should not be overdone, however; the same type of knowledge and even criteria for research can be justified by a desire to conquer a country or to defend it, by a wish to subvert a revolution or to achieve it. Much simplistic declamation and name-calling has arisen from a misleading—indeed, often willfully perverted—misunderstanding of this very problem.) It is therefore worth rating the criteria on this list before they are used, in turn, to designate research priorities.

Newness is scarcely a valid justification for research. There are no research areas in Middle East politics that are truly overpopulated, except relatively, but neither is the fact that a topic has not yet been studied sufficient reason for suggesting that it be given attention now. In fact, if anything, there is a need to overcome current academic prejudices in favor of new and unique studies and against testing and replication. We still need a good deal "more of the same"—studies that examine a second and third country or phenomenon on the same model and use the same terms as a previous work on one country, and studies that repeat the same research 5 or 10 years later.

Feasibility also is a necessary but not sufficient condition for research. Again the availability of data is important, but there are also studies worth doing even in the absence of perfect information. Israeli studies of Arab countries, like the American work over more than 25 years on China, shows how much can be accomplished without field research. Studies merely from abroad are not desirable, however, and Middle East governments must be aware of the importance of open inquiry and tolerance, above all for their own national scholars, just as visiting scholars must demonstrate concern for the value of academic diplomacy and collaboration.

Probably the greatest difference occurs when the criteria of academic interest and practical interest are confronted. The debate is not restricted to the Middle East; pure and applied researchers have been fighting it out for a long time. Common sense seems to give reason to each, in its own corner.

Many of the arguments for theoretical research—for academic concerns governing the course of priorities—are ultimately related to its usefulness for applied research, that is, utility and lead time. But these same arguments show that, at best, crisis-oriented research is likely to give results only when the theoretical basis for understanding has already been prepared. There is nothing wrong with the Middle East crisis, the population explosion, the revolution of rising expectations, or the Arab awakening motivating a surge of research, nor is the improvement of the research climate in a Middle East country or the reorientation of attention to the Persian Gulf to be scorned as an opportunity for studying problems of disciplinary interest there rather than elsewhere. However, such matters are only additional criteria for matters of academic interest.

For a subject to be one of research priority—in the following discussion, at least—it should lie in an area where a critical mass of scholarship and a chance for breakthrough are present. Such subjects can have benefited either from important theoretical work elsewhere that has not yet been tested in the Middle East or from a large amount of work in the Middle East that is ready to be aggregated and reevaluated. Beyond the use of this criterion, however, no particular order is implied in the following list of priorities.

To begin with, we know next to nothing about the political behavior (actions and attitudes) of *Homopoliticus mediorientalis* or his subspecies. A whole range of behavioral propositions generated in the West could be checked against the actions of Middle Easterners, a task by no means impossible under current research conditions. Topics such as the political socialization of children, motivations for voting, and the structure and diffusion of political culture are examples of ready research areas. It is time to begin some systematic study of the consequences for behavior of a number of important variables that have specific Middle Eastern meanings, such as nation, class (income and status), religion, and literacy. In this research area, the critical mass of work has been done outside the Middle East but data generation and analysis in the region remain to be done, in order to give some sound basis to continuing debates on universalistic generalizations, particularistic stereotypes, and appeals for authenticity.

The political anthropology of local politics is the next level of analysis, and one where the possibilities of neither of the two disciplines involved have been fully exploited. More descriptive political ethnographies are needed but are not enough; even more useful would be the investigation of linkages between local components (urban and village structures, styles, values, issues) and the national system. The amount of local power that flows upward, the amount of central authority that flows down, and the nature of the meeting points are in need of both detailed and synthesizing study. The parts of which the national polity is the sum (even if not only the sum), as well as the summing process, are poorly understood in every country in the area, and yet almost everywhere there are scattered studies which provide a beginning. Few political scientists have ventured into this topic.

For all the work done on elites, we have only begun to come to terms with the bubbling social stew[4] that brings self-conscious groups to the surface, coagulates new forces into cohesive bodies, disintegrates others, and supports different combinations of demands, actors, alliances, and policies in various countries. Beyond the invention of the New Man and the discovery of the Military Man, we need to develop concepts with which to identify and analyze the circulation of political elites, leading to a theoretical grasp of the process within the context of Middle East development; we also need ways of analyzing the bases of elite power, so as to understand shifts and continuities in the nature of the region's centralized political systems. Furthermore there is also a need for careful studies of such important groups and roles as technicians and businessmen, and for a systematic understanding of the relation between background characteristics and ultimate attitudes and behavior.

In an area that longs for revolution but instead finds only a few substantial evolutionary transformations and a rash of pale and noisy procedural imitations, there are scarcely any studies of revolution and its surrogates. Outside the Middle East there has been much comparative and theoretical treatment of the subject, so that applications of concepts and comparisons of processes could be fruitfully pursued in the area, and thus a fuller understanding of the process and its limitations in the Middle East can be achieved. Revolution is not the only concept that can be used as a lens to examine related events —war, social promotion, agrarian reform, and nationalization are some others—but it is a major topic where research could be used to replace nominalistic debate.

On another level, and again ironically, the whole process of nation and state building, in an area where "nation" is a contested concept and "state" a recent import, still defies effective grasp. The necessary ingredients in the formation of centralized and self-identifying polities and the relation this process in the Middle East bears to processes of the same name in Europe and on other continents are topics that political scientists have hesitated to deal with. The concept "class" is another that remains elusive, and its relation to nation and state bears examination. The disciplinary tools are doubtless not yet sharp enough to do these jobs deftly, but they can at least be whetted in the attempt, rather than being held aloof in ethnocentric declamations of a way to follow.

Enough work has now been done for two types of study to be undertaken on the national level. On one hand, a whole-system analysis of most countries still remains to be done. There have been country studies aplenty, but most of them focus on the dominant political force or institution; few of them try to encompass the whole spectrum of political forces, checking the findings of other country studies where another institution or force may be dominant. On the other hand, fully comparative study and evaluation of a particular unit of analysis across the area has yet to be done in almost every case, and the groundwork is frequently ready. Only in the case of the military has such comparative study been begun, and more can follow. Parties, the role of *ᶜulamâ* and businessmen, particular policies such as agrarian reform and planning, and political elites are ready for such study, even though other subjects such as bureaucracies or parliaments may still need more individual fieldwork.

For all the smoke that surrounds it, the subject of development is not yet exhausted. The polity in motion across time remains badly understood. Local debates on values and future goods need to be brought into the study more seriously, and the generation of alternative models and their open-minded testing against different national realities also need to be pursued. A real analysis of political culture and of the norms established for the developing system remains to be done for every country in the Middle East; the tools for analysis exist already in the discipline. Possibilities of comparison between different countries at different times are particularly attractive in an area where dates of independence were spread over four decades and two postwar periods and where the impact of the West took so many different forms (and elicited so many different responses).

A plea has already been entered for more output or policy studies. The policy-making process needs to be investigated and compared by subject across several countries and among several subjects within a single country, so that we may have a better grasp of the full political process. Such analysis should relate explicitly to power bases, and to relationships between "who" the decision makers are (in various terms) and "what" they do. The impact of particular policies in given areas also needs to be thought out and checked against "experimental data" provided by national governments. For comparative purposes and for comprehending the area and its component polities, some policies are more useful for study than others: agrarian reform, educational reforms, foreign policies on important issues such as trade terms or oil, foreign relations in special arenas such as the Arab League or OPEC, local investment measures, legal reform and codification policies, and intranational (ethnic) policies are important common areas of government action. They all open, in turn, into broader areas of research; the crucial and under-researched topic of language policy, in a region of bilingualism and diglossia combined with regional linguistic interdependence, is a fascinating and complex topic for political analysis.

There has already been some discussion about the need for new work in the field of law and of political thought. In both areas, the way is less clearly marked than in many of the previously mentioned topics. Instead there is more of a challenge to the scholar to find not only a topic but also an appropriate approach, but in the process a whole field of inquiry can be defined.

It is hard to maintain that work is not needed in the international field, both because of its importance to the well-being of so many and also because of the uneven quality and small quantity of works on related subjects in the area. But it is also hard to point to many topics in international politics where a critical mass of scholarship is gathering or where an intellectual breakthrough is likely. Probably the best combination of disciplinary concepts and detailed data from the area has been on the topic of alliance behavior and regional system patterns, where further refinement is still possible. At some point, however, this topic like many others blends into a global analysis of international politics and cannot be studied alone; yet the tools for a satisfactory study of a regional component of a global system need further refinement themselves. Unfortunately, the necessity of holding current events symposia tends to crowd out efforts at more insightful, rigorous, and long-range analysis.

There are other topics where work in the discipline or in other regions has laid the basis for good studies in the Middle East. Process (both policy-making and interaction) analyses of foreign policies, or interaction approaches to negotiations, or studies of politics within regional international organizations are three such areas where work can be pursued fruitfully. Probably the topic where both importance (both academic and practical) and neglect are the highest is oil politics. Although the subject suffers from some of the same problems as other subjects that are basically global in nature, there are many aspects that can be handled within a more limited framework. We know literally nothing about the dynamics of oil negotiations, the politics of producers' organizations, or the national processes of oil policy making. The challenges of the topic are not easily exhausted. Finally, for all the wearying verbiage already devoted to it, there are still many academic stones unturned in the Palestine problem. Analysis of unsuccessful negotiations, comparative studies of multinational communities, and continued work on the indicators of war are related topics of academic interest (and perhaps even of practical utility).

Finally, there is no reason why political science should fancy itself as merely a surfboard on the wave of time, subservient to publishers' criteria of updatedness. If its questions are relevant to universal human problems, its concepts important for understanding human actions, its methods useful for developing data, and its approach to inquiry helpful to explaining behavior, then it should begin to look at historic events for comparison and broader comprehensions and also for new phenomenan to study in their own right. Explicit concepts, generalized explanations, and other characteristics of social science are as applicable to past as to contemporary events. Limitations on data collection and generation are real, of course, but they do not make such work impossible. Examples exist, to be sure, but they are few and are often provided by scholars who do not consider themselves political scientists.

In a more procedural sense, there is another priority which cuts across all these topics. It is probably more difficult to organize collaborative research in political science than in most other disciplines. The problems of scarcity, interest, and sensitivity are all great, and it is probably the great importance of politics in developing countries which paradoxically places it beyond the limits where digging and debate by scholars of any nationality are welcome. Perhaps interdisciplinary collaborative research is one way around such problems. Perhaps, too, academics of all nationalities have a professional obligation to continue to explain and press for an understanding of the utility and intrinsic value of open inquiry and debate.

Ultimately analytical questions must relate to real questions. Pure research is a privileged terrain for finding explanations that are useful in the last analysis for understanding reality. No one can accuse Middle East political scientists of carrying out pure research, at least since scholarship in the area moved away from the hermeneutics of Islamic law. But how have political scientists used the insights of the discipline to understand the Middle East? The question is not how to make the Bedouin a Western man, but how does the Middle East political man act (differently or not from *Homopoliticus tout court*?), i.e., what is he and what is he becoming? Or where are authority and legitimacy in a changing polity? Or who wields power, derived from what sources, to what ends, as the criteria for deciding these questions shift within society? Such questions are the same as those political scientists are asking everywhere, and they are the guidelines for inquiry in current studies on the Middle East. They must be pursued; but in the process there must be a greater exchange of formulations and findings between scholars of the Middle East and others to avoid the tautologies of uniqueness that limit any subject's self-examination.

NOTES

1. In preparing this chapter, I am particularly grateful for the help of Gabriel Baer, Gabriel Ben-Dor, Robert Burrowes, Hamid Enayat, J. C. Hurewitz, Scott Johnston, Ergun Özbudun, Ayad al-Qazzaz, William Thompson, Michael Suleiman, Aristide Zolberg, Marvin Zonis, and Farhat Ziadeh, who provided detailed written comments; to Farhad Kazemi, Dankwart Rustow, Kalman Silvert, and Walter Weiker, who met to discuss an earlier draft in New York; and to Leonard Binder, Iliya Harik, and William B. Quandt, fellow political scientists in the Palo Alto discussions. Despite this collective expertise, judgments expressed in this chapter are my responsibility.

2. Almond and Coleman (1960); Claude Welch, ed., *Political Modernization*, 1st ed., (Wadsworth, 1967) contains Quint (1958) and Pfaff (1963), and the second edition (1971) contains Szyliowicz (1966b) and Wilcox (1968); Jason Finkle and Richard W. Gable, eds. *Political Development and Social Change*, 2nd ed. (New York: Wiley, 1971) contains Bellah (1958) and Perlmutter (1969a); Kalman H. Silvert, ed., *Expectant Peoples* (Random House, 1963) contains Dupree (1963), Nolte (1963), Gallagher (1963), and Bayne (1963); John Kautsky, ed., *Political Change in Underdeveloped Countries* (New York: Wiley, 1962) contains Carmichael (1959), David Apter and Harry Eckstein, eds., *Comparative Politics*, (Glencoe, Ill.: Free Press, 1963), contains Binder (1957) and Etzioni (1959); Frank Tachau, ed., *The Developing Nations*, (Dodd, Mead, 1972) contains selections from Halpern (1963) and Eberhard, Roy Macridis and Bernard Brown, eds., *Comparative Politics* (Homewood, Il: Dorsey, 1968, 3rd ed.) contains Braibanti (1959).

3. Susan Jones and J. David Singer, eds., *Beyond Conjecture* (Peacock, 1972) contains Graber (1969, 1970) and Sigler (1969). On a different conceptual level, Francis A. Beer, ed., *Alliances*, (New York: Holt, Rinehart & Winston, 1970) contains a selection from MacDonald (1965); Joseph Nye, ed., *International Regionalism* (Boston: Little, Brown, 1968) contains only a selection on Arab economic unification, and *International Political Communities: An Anthology* (New York: Doubleday, 1966) contains no Middle East selection at all.

4. Morroe Berger has kindly recalled that in social scientific terms this expression should properly be rendered as "the multidynamic interrelationship and dissonance between epiphenomenal behaviors of voluntaristic aggregations and goal-orientations of formal centralized influence concentrations."

BIBLIOGRAPHY

Abadan, N. *Anayasa Hukuku ve Siyasi Bilimler Açisindan* 1965 *Seçimlerinin Tahlili*. Ankara: Sevinç, 1966.

ᶜAbdallah, Ridah. "Le Neo-Destour," *Revue Juridique et Politique d'Outre-Mer.* **3** (1963), 358–428; and **4** (1963), 573–657.

ᶜAbdel-Malek, A. *Egypte: société militaire.* Paris: Seuil, 1962. English translation: *Egypt, Military Society.* New York: Random House, 1968.

———. *Idéologie et renaissance nationale.* Paris: Anthropos, 1969.

Abrahamian, Ervand. "Communism and Communalism in Iran: The Tudah and the Firqah-i Dimukrat," *International Journal of Middle East Studies.* **4** (1970), 291–316.

Abu Jaber, K. *The Arab Ba'th Socialist Party.* Syracuse: Syracuse Univ. Press, 1966.

Abu-Lughod, I., ed. *The Transformation of Palestine.* Evanston: Northwestern Univ. Press, 1971.

Abu-Yasir, S. M. *Jihâd Sha'b filisṭîn.* Beirut: Dar al-Fath, 1968.

Adamiyat, F. *Fikr-i Azadi va Muqaddamah-yi Nihzhat-i Mashrutiyat-i.* Tehran: 1961.

———. *Andishaha-yi-Mirza Âgâ Khan Kirmânî.* Tehran: Khwarezmi, 1967.

———. *Mirza Fatḥᶜ Alî Âkhûnd-Zadah.* Tehran: 1970.

Aflaq, M. *Fî sabîl al-ba'th.* Beirut: Dâr al-Ṭalîᶜa, 1959.

Ahmad, F. *The Young Turks.* Oxford: Clarendon Press, 1969.

Ahmed, J. *The Intellectual Origins of Egyptian Nationalism.* Oxford: Univ. Press, 1960.

Akşin, S. *31 Mart Olayi.* Ankara: Sevinc Matbaasi, 1972.

ᶜAllush, N. *al-thawra wal-jamâhîr.* Beirut: Dar al-Talîᶜa, 1962.

———. *al-thawra al-filisṭîniya.* Beirut: Dar al-Talîᶜa, 1970.

Almond, G., and J. Coleman. *The Politics of Developing Areas.* Princeton: Princeton Univ. Press, 1960.

Amedroz, H. F., "The Office of the Kadi in the Ahkam Sultaniyya of Mawardi," *Journal of the Royal Asiatic Society* (1910).

———. "The Mazalim Jurisdiction in the Ahkam Sultaniyya of Mawardi," *Journal of the Royal Asiatic Society* (1911).

———. "The Hisba Jurisdiction in the Ahkam Sultaniyya of Mawardi," *Journal of the Royal Asiatic Society* (1116).

ᶜAmer, I. *Thawrat Misr al-Qawmiyya.* Cairo : Dar al-Nadim, 1957.

———. *Al-ᶜArḍ wa al-fallaḥ: al-Mas'alah al-ziraᶜiyya fî misr.* N. P.: Daral-Misriyya lil-Kutub, Cairo 1958.

American Friends Service Committee. *Search for Peace in the Middle East.* Philadelphia: AFSC, 1970.

Anderson, J. D. N. ed. *Changing Family Law in Africa and Asia.* London: Allen & Unwin, 1968.

———. *Changing Law in Developing Countries.* London: Allen & Unwin, 1963.

Antonius, G., *The Arab Awakening.* New York: Putnam, 1938.

Antoun, R., and I. Harik. *Rural Politics and Social Change in the Middle East.* Bloomington: Indiana Univ. Press, 1972.

Arasteh, R. *Education and Social Awakening in Iran* 1850–1960. Leiden: Brill, 1962.

Arazi, A. *Le Système électoral israelien.* Geneva: Droz, 1964.

Arfa, H. *The Kurds: An Historical and Political Study.* London: Oxford Univ. Press, 1966.

Arian, A. *Ideological Change in Israel.* Cleveland: Case Western Reserve Univ. Press, 1968.

———. *The Elections in Israel* 1969. Jerusalem: Jerusalem Academic Press, 1972.

———. *The Choosing People.* Cleveland: Case Western Reserve Univ. Press, 1973.

———. ed. *The Elections in Israel* 1973. Jerusalem: Jerusalem Academic Press, 1975.

Aruri, N., ed. *The Palestinian Resistance to Israeli Occupation.* Medina: Medina Univ., 1970.

———. *Jordan: A Study in Political Development.* The Hague: Nijhoff, 1972.

Ashford, D. E. *Political Change in Morocco.* Princeton: Princeton Univ. Press, 1961.

———. *National Development and Local Reform.* Princeton: Univ. Press, 1947.

Ashraf, A. "Historical Obstacles to the Development of a Bourgeoisie in Nineteenth Century Iran." *Iranian Studies*, **2**, 1 (1969), 54–79.

———. with H. Hekmat. "The State of Traditional Bourgeoisie in Nineteenth Century Iran." In *Economic History in the Middle East.* A. Udovitch, ed.

Awad, A. *Al-istiqlaliyya.* Rabat: Maṭbaᶜat al-risâla, 1966.

Azar, E. "Conflict Escalation and Conflict Reduction in an International Crisis, Suez, 1956," *Journal of Conflict Resolution.* **16**, 2 (1972).

al-ᶜAzm, S. *Al-Naqd al-Dhatî baᶜd al-Hamza.* Beirut 1969.

Badeau, J. *The American Approach to the Arab World.* New York: Harper & Row, 1968.

Başgöz, I., and H. E. Wilson. *Educational Problems in Turkey* 1920–1940. Bloomington: Indiana Univ. Press, 1968.

Bayne, E. A. "Development and Cultural Reinforcement of Class." In *Expectant Peoples.* K. H. Silvert, ed. New York: Random House, 1963.

Becker, A. S., and A. L. Horelick. *Soviet Policy in the Middle East.* Santa Monica: Rand Corp., 1970.

Be'eri, E. *Army Officers in Arab Politics and Society.* New York: Praeger, 1970.

Beling, W. *PanArabism and Labor.* Cambridge: Harvard. Middle East Center, 1960.

———. *Modernization and African Labor.* New York: Praeger, 1965.

Belal, A. *L'Investissement au Maroc et ses enseignements en matière de développement économique.* The Hague: Mouton, 1968.

Bellah, Robert N. "Religious Aspects of Modernization in Turkey and Japan," *American Journal of Sociology,* **64** (1958), 1–5.

Ben-Dak, J. D., ed. *Methodologies in Search of Relevance: Assessing Arab-Israeli Relations.* London: Gordon & Breach, 1975.

Bent, F. T. "The Turkish Bureaucracy as an Agent of Change," *Journal of Comparative Administration* (1969).

Berger, M. *Bureaucracy and Society in Modern Egypt.* Princeton: Univ. Press, 1957.

———. *Military Elite and Social Change: Egypt since Napoleon.* Princeton: Univ. Center for International Studies, 1960.

Berque, J. *Structures sociales dans le Haut-Atlas.* Paris: Presses Universitaires de France, 1955.

———. "L'Idée de classe dans l'histoire contemporaine des Arabes," *Cahiers Internationaux de Sociologie,* **38** (1965), 169–184.

———. *Egypt: Imperialism and Revolution.* London: Faber, 1972.

Beyssade, P. *La ligue arabe.* Paris: Planete, 1968.

Bill, J. A. *The Politics of Iran: Groups, Classes and Modernization.* Columbus, Ohio: Merrill, 1972(a).

———. "Class Analysis and the Dialectics of Modernization in the Middle East," *International Journal of Middle East Studies,* **3** (1972b), 417–434.

Binder, L. "Prolegomena to the Comparative Study of Middle East Governments," *American Political Science Review,* **51**, 3 (1957), 651–669.

———. *Religion and Politics in Pakistan.* Berkeley: U. of California Press, 1961.

———. "The Middle East as a Subordinate International System," *World Politics,* **10**, 3 (1958), 403–429.

———. *Iran: Political Development in a Changing Society.* Berkeley: U. of California Press, 1962.

———. *The Ideological Revolution in the Middle East.* New York: Wiley, 1964.

———. "Egypt: The Integrative Revolution." In *Political Culture and Political Development.* L. Pye and S. Verba, eds. Princeton: Univ. Press, 1965.

———. ed. *Politics in Lebanon.* New York: Wiley, 1966 (a).

———. Political Recruitment and Participation in "Egypt." In *Political Parties and Political Development.* J. LaPalombara M. and Weiner, eds. Princeton: Univ. Press, 1966 (b).

Bitar, N. *Min al-naksa ila al-thawra.* Beirut: Dâr al-Ittiḥâd, 1968.

Blair, T. *The Land to Those Who Work It.* New York: Doubleday, 1970.

Bouhdiba, A. "Dialogue et politique," *Revue IBLA* (1968), 51–70.

Bourges, H. *L'Algérie a l'épreuve du pouvoir.* Paris: Grasset, 1967.

Bousquet, G. H. "Le Droit coutoumier des ait Hadidou," *Annalales de l'Institut des Etudes Orientales,* **14**, (1956).

Boutros, Ghali, B. *The Arab League* 1945–1955. Carnegie Endowment for International Peace, International Conciliation 498, 1954.

———. *al-Harakât al-afroasiyawiyya.* Cairo: Dâr al-Kitâb, 1959.

———. *Azmat al-diblumasiyya al-ᶜarabiyya.* Cairo: Dâr al-Kitâb, 1969.

———. *Dirâsât fî al-Siyâsa al-Dawliyya.* Cairo: Maktaba al Injahr al-Misriyya, 1961.

Boveri, M. *Mediterranean Cross-Currents.* London, New York: Oxford Univ. Press, 1938.

Braibanti, R. "The Civil Service of Pakistan: A Theoretical Analysis," *South Atlantic Quarterly,* **58**, 2 (1959).

Brecher, M. "The Middle East Subordinate System and its Impact on Israel's Foreign Policy," *International Studies Quarterly,* **13**, 2 (1969), 117—139.

———. *The Foreign Policy System of Israel.* New Haven: Yale Univ. Press, 1972.

Brown, L. C. "Tunisia." In *Education and Political Development.* J. Coleman, ed. Princeton: Univ. Press, 1965.

———. trans. *The Surest Path.* Cambridge: Harvard Middle East Center, 1967.

Buehrig, E. H. *The U.N. and the Palestinian Refugees.* Bloomington: Indiana Univ. Press, 1971.

Bujra, A. S. *The Politics of Stratification: A Study of Political Change in a South Arabian Town.* Oxford: Univ. Press, 1971.

Burke, S. M. *Pakistan's Foreign Policy.* Oxford: Univ. Press, 1973.

Burrowes, R., and B. Spector. "The Strength and Direction of Relationships Between Domestic and External Conflict and Cooperation: Syria 1961–1967." In *Conflict Behavior and Linkage Politics.* J. Wilkenfeld, ed. New York: McKay, 1973.

Campbell, J. C. *Defense of the Middle East.* New York: Harper, 1958.

Carmichael, J. "The Nationalist-Communist Symbiosis in the Middle East," *Problems of Communism,* **8**, 3 (1959), 35–41–.

Chaliand, G. *L'Algérie est-elle socialiste?* Paris: Maspero, 1964.

———. *The Palestinian Resistance.* London: Penguin, 1972.

Chambregeat, "Les élections communales marocaines." *Revue Française de Science Politique,* **11**, 1 (1961), 89–117.

———. "Le referendum constitutionel du 7 décembre au Maroc," *Annuaire de l'Afrique du Nord,* **1** (1962), 167–205.

———. "Les élections communales au Maroc," *Annuaires de l'Afrique du Nord,* **2** (1963), 119–128.

———. *Le role politique des élites locales dans le Maroc indépendant.* In press.

Chehab, C. *Les élections législatives de 1960, de 1964, de 1968.* Mimeo, 1960, 1964, 1968.

Chehata, Chafik. *Le Droit musulman: applications au Proche Orient.* Paris; Dalloz, 1970.

———. *Etudes de droit musulman.* Paris: Dalloz, 1971.

Cherif, Mohammed Hadi, ed. "Les pays arabes." In *Mouvements nationaux d'indépendance et classes populaires aux XIX et XX siècles en occident et en orient.* Vol. 1. Paris: Colin 1971.

Chubin, S. and S. Zabih. *The Foreign Relations of Iran.* Berkeley: Univ. of California Press, 1975.

Clawson, M. *The Agricultural Potential of the Middle East.* New York: American Elsevier, 1971.

Clegg, I. *Workers Self-Management in Algeria.* New York: Monthly Review Press, 1972.

Cohen, A. *Arab Border Villages in Israel.* Manchester: Manchester Univ. Press, 1965.

Colombe, M. *L'Evolution de l'Egypte.* Paris: Maisonneuve, 1950.

———. *Orient arabe et non-engagement.* 2 vols. Paris: Publications orientalistes de France, 1973.

Confino, M. and S. Shamir, eds. *The USSR and the Middle East.* New York: Wiley, 1973.

Cooley, J. *Green March, Black September.* London: Cass, 1973.

Cottam, R. W. *Nationalism in Iran.* Pittsburgh: Univ. of Pittsburgh, 1964.

Coulson, N. J. *A History of Islamic Law.* Chicago: Aldine, 1964.

———. *Conflict and Tensions in Islamic Jurisprudence.* Chicago: U. of Chicago Press, 1969.

———. *Succession in the Muslim Family.* Cambridge: Univ. Press, 1971.

Cremeans, C. *The Arabs and the World.* New York Praeger, 1963.

Czudnowski, M. M. "Sociocultural Variables and Legislative Recruitment," *Comparative Politics*, **4** (1972), 561–587.

———, and J. Landau. *The Israeli Communist Party and the Elections for the Fifth Knesset.* Stanford: Hoover Inst., 1965.

Dann, U. *Iraq under Qassem.* New York: Praeger, 1969.

Dekmejian, R. H. *Egypt under Nasir.* Albany: State Univ. of New York, 1971.

———. *Patterns of Political Leadership: Egypt, Israel, Lebanon.* Albany: State Univ. of New York, 1975.

DeNovo, J. *American Interests and Policies in the Middle East* 1900–1939. Minneapolis: Univ. of Minn. Press, 1962.

Deshen, S. *Immigrant Voters in Israel: Parties and Congregations in a Local Campaign.* Manchester: Manchester Univ. Press, 1970.

———, and M. Shokeid. *The Predicament of Homecoming.* Ithaca: Cornell Univ., 1975.

Duchac, R., ed. *La Formation des élites politiques maghrebines.* Paris: Centre National de la Recherche Scientifique, 1972.

Dupree, L. "Tribalism, Regionalism and National Oligarchy." In *Expectant Peoples.* K. H. Silvert, ed. New York: Random House, 1963.

Eagleton, W., Jr. *The Kurdish Republic of 1946.* London and New York: Oxford Univ. Press, 1963.

Earle, E. M. *Turkey, the Great Powers and the Baghdad Railway: A Study in Imperialism.* New York: Macmillan, 1923.

Eisenstadt, S. N. *Israeli Society.* New York; Basic Books, 1969.

Entelis, J. P. *Pluralism and Party Transformation in Lebanon.* Leiden: Brill, 1974 (a).

———. "Ideological Change and an Emerging Counter-Culture in Tunisian Politics," *Journal of Modern African Studies*, **4** (1974), 543–569. (b)

Etzioni, A. "Alternate Ways of Democracy: Israel," *Political Science Quarterly*, **74**, 2 (1959), 196–214.

———. *Political Unification.* New York: Rinehart & Winston, 1965.

Evron, Y. *The Middle East: Nations, Superpowers and Wars.* New York: Praeger, 1973.

Fagnon, M. E. *Les statuts gouvernementaux.* Algiers: Jourdan, 1915.

Fanon, F. *The Wretched of the Earth.* New York: Grove, 1964.

———. *Studies in a Dying Colonialism.* New York: Grove, 1966.

———. *Black Skin, White Masks.* New York: Grove, 1967.

———. *Toward the African Revolution.* New York: Grove, 1969.

al-Fassi, A. *The Independence Movement in Arab North Africa.* Washington, D.C.: American Council of Learned Societies, 1954.

———. *al-Naqd al-dhati.* Cairo: al-Maṭbaᶜa al-ᶜalamîyya, 1956.

Fawzi, Saad ed-Din. *The Labor Movement in the Sudan* 1944–1955. London and New York: Oxford Univ. Press, 1957.

Fein, L. *Politics in Israel.* Boston: Little Brown, 1967.

First, R. *Libya: The Elusive Revolution.* New York: Penguin, 1974.

Fisher, R. *Dear Israeli, Dear Arab.* New York: Harper & Row, 1973.

Fisher, S. N., ed. *Social Forces in the Middle East.* Columbus; Ohio State Univ. 1955.

———. ed. *The Military in the Middle East.* Columbus: Ohio State Univ., 1963.

Flory, M., ed. *La Libye nouvelle: rupture et continuité.* Paris: Centre National de la Recherche Scientifique, 1975.

Forsythe, D. P. *United Nations Peacemaking: The Conciliation Commision for Palestine.* Baltimore: Johns Hopkins, 1972.

Freedman, Robert O. *Soviet Policy toward the Middle East Since 1970.* New York: Praeger, 1975.

Frey, F. "Arms and the Man in Turkish Politics," *Land Reform,* **11** (1960), 13–14.

———. "Political Development, Power and Communcations in Turkey." *Communications and Political Development.* Lucian Pye, ed. Princeton: Univ. Press, 1963.

———. *The Turkish Political Elite.* Cambridge: MIT, 1965.

Fridman, L. A. *Capitalist Development of Egypt and the Position of the Working Masses* 1882–1939. Moscow: 1960. (in Russian).

———. and L. A. Gordon. "Particularities in the Composition and Structure of the Working Class (Examples of India and the UAR)." In *The Third World in Soviet Perspective.* T. P. Thornton, ed. Princeton: Univ. Press, 1963.

Frye, W. R. *A United Nations Peace Force.* New York: Oceana, 1957.

Gallagher, C. "Language, Culture and Ideology." In *Expectant Peoples.* K. H. Silvert, ed. New York: Random House, 1963.

Gardet, L. *La cité Musulmane.* Paris: Vrin, 1954.

Gellner, E. *Saints of the Atlas.* Chicago: U. of Chicago Press, 1970.

Gendzier, I. *A Middle East Reader.* New York: Pegasus, 1969.

———. *Frantz Fanon: A Critical Study.* New York: Grove, 1972.

Ghali, I. A. *L'Egypte nationaliste et libérale.* The Hague: Nijhoff, 1969.

Ghallab, A. *Al-istiqlâlîyya.* Casablanca: Maṭbaᶜa al-aṭlas, 1965.

Gibb, H. *Whither Islam.* London: Gollancz, 1932.

———. *Modern Trends in Islam.* Chicago: U. of Chicago Press, 1947.

Girgis, F. *Dirâsât fî târîkh miṣr al-siyâsî mundhu al-ᶜaṣr al-mâmlûki.* Cairo: Dâr al-miṣriyya lil-kitâb, 1958.

Goldziher, I. *Muhammedanische Studien.* Halle: Niemeyer, 1889–1890. C. R. Barber and S. M. Stern, trans. *Muslim Studies.* London: Allen & Unwin, 1967–1968.

Gordon, D. *The Passing of French Algeria.* New York: Oxford Univ. Press, 1966.

Graber, D. "Perceptions of Middle East Conflict in the U. N," *Journal of Conflict Resolution,* **12,** 4 (1969). 454–484.

———. "Conflict Images," *Journal of Politics,* **32,** 2 (1970), 339–378.

Gubser, P. *Politics and Change in al-Karak, Jordan.* London, New York: Oxford, 1973 (a).

———. "The Zu'ama of Zahlah," *Middle East Journal,* **27,** 2 (1973), 173–190. (b)

Guerin, D. *L'Algérie qui se cherche.* Paris: Presence Africaine, 1964.

———. *L'Algérie caporalisée.* Paris: Centrd d'etudes socialistes, 1965.

Guttman, E. and M. Lissak. *Political Processes in Israel.* Jerusalem: Acadamon. 1974.

Haim. Sylvia. *Arab Nationalism.* Berkeley: U. of California Press, 1962.

Halpern, B. *The Idea of the Jewish State.* Cambridge: Harvard U. Press, 1969.

Halpern, M. "Middle Eastern Armies and the New Middle Class." In *The Role of the Military in Underdeveloped Countries.* J. J. Johnson, ed. Princeton: Univ. Press, 1962.

———. *The Politics of Social Change in the Middle East and North Africa.* Princeton: Univ. Press, 1963.

Halstead, J. P. *Rebirth of a Nation: Origins and Rise of Moroccan Nationalism.* Cambridge: Harvard Middle East Center, 1967.

———. "Comparative Historical Study of Colonial Nationalism in Egypt and Morocco," *African Historical Studies*, **2**, 1 (1969), 85–100.

Hamon, L. *Le Rôle extra-militaire de l'armée dans le tiers monde.* Paris: Presses Universitaires de France, 1966.

Hanf, T. *Erziehung und Politik im Spiegel des Meingungen Libanesischer Studenten, Lehrkrafter und Politiker.* Freiburg: Arnold Bergstrasse Institut, 1971.

Harary, F. "A Structural Analysis of the Situation in the Middle East in 1956," *Journal of Conflict Resolution*, **5**, 2 (1961), 160–178.

Harik, I. *Politics and Change in a Traditional Society.* Princeton: Univ. Press, 1968.

———. *Mann yaḥkum Lubnân?* Beirut: Dar al-nahar lil-nashr, 1972.

———, "The Single Party as a subordinate Movement," *World Politics*, **26**, 1 (1973), 80–105.

———. *The Political Mobilization of Peasants.* Bloomington: Indiana Univ. Press, 1974.

Harris, C. *Nationalism and Revolution in Egypt.* The Hague: Mouton, 1965.

Harris, G. "The Role of the Military in Turkish Politics," *Middle East Journal*, **19**, 1 (1965), 54–61.

———. *The Origins of Communism in Turkey.* Palo Alto: Stanford, 1968.

Heaphey, J. "The Organization of Egypt," *World Politics*, **18**, 2 (1966), 177–193.

Hen-Tov, J. "The Communist International, The Palestine Communist Party, and Political Unrest in Palestine 1929." In *Forces of Change in the Middle East.* M. Roumani, ed. Worcester, Mass.: Worcester State, 1971.

Hermassi, E. *Leadership and National Development in North Africa.* Berkeley: U. of California Press, 1972.

Hertzberg, A. *The Zionist Idea.* Garden City, N.Y.: Doubleday, 1959.

Heyd, U. *Foundations of Turkish Nationalism.* London: Luzac: 1950.

———. *Studies in Old Ottoman Criminal Law.* V. L. Ménage, ed. Oxford: Clarendon Press, 1973.

Higgins, R., ed. *United Nations Peacekeeping: Documents and Commentary, the Middle East.* London, New York: Oxford U. Press, 1969.

Hitti, P. K. and F. C. Murgotten, trans. *The Origins of the Islamic State.* New York: Columbia Univ. Press, 1916, 1924.

Hourani, A. *Arabic Thought in the Liberal Age 1798–1939.* London, New York: Oxford Univ. Press, 1962.

Howard, H. N. *The Partition of Turkey* 1913–1923. Norman: Univ. of Oklahoma Press, 1931.

Hudson, M. "The Electoral Process and Political Development in Lebanon," *Middle East Journal.* **20**, 2 (1966), 173–186.

———. "A Case of Political Underdevelopment," *Journal of Politics*, **30**, 4 (1967), 821–37.

———. *The Precarious Republic: Political Modernization in Lebanon.* New York: Random House, 1968.

———. "The Palestine Arab Resistance Movement," *Middle East Journal*, **33**, 3 (1969), 291–307.

———. "The Palestine Resistance," *Journal of Palestine Studies*, **1**, 3 (1972).

Hunter, R. E. *The Soviet Dilemma in the Middle East.* London: Adelphi Papers, 59 & 60. Institute for Strategic Studies, 1967.

Huntington, S. P. *Political Order in Changing Societies.* New Haven: Yale, 1968.

Hurewitz, J. C. *The Struggle for Palestine.* New York: Norton, 1950.

———. ed. *Soviet-American Rivalry in the Middle East.* New York: by Praeger for the Academy of Political Science and Columbia Univ., 1969.

———. *Diplomacy in the Near and Middle East: A Documentary record.* New York: Octagon, 1956. Second ed.: *The Middle East and North Africa in World Politics.* New Haven: Yale, 1975.

Hussein, M. (pseud. Adel Rifa'a & Baghdad al-Nadi). *La Lutte des classes en Egypte de 1945 à 1968.* Paris: Maspero, 1969.

———. *L'Egypte II 1967–1973.* Paris: Maspero, 1975.

Husseini, I. M. *The Muslim Brethren.* Beirut: Khayat's, 1952.

Ireland, P. W. *Study in Political Development: Iraq.* London: Cape, 1937.

Jiryis, S. *The Arabs in Israel* 1948–1966. Beirut: Inst. for Palestine Studies, 1968.

Johnston, S. "Major Party Politics in a Multiparty System. The Mapai," *al Politico*, **30**, 2. (1965).

———. "Campaigns and Elections: The Case of Israel," *al Politico*, **33**, 4 (1968).

Karpat, L. *Turkey's Politics: The Transition to a Multi-Party System.* Princeton: Univ. Press, 1959.

———. "The Turkish Elections of 1957," *Western Political Quarterly*, **2** (1961).

———. *Political and Social Thought in the Middle East.* New York: Praeger, 1968.

———. "The Military and Politics in Turkey, 1960–1964," *American Historical Review*, **75** (1970), 1654–1683.

Kazamias, A. M. *Education and the Quest for Modernity in Turkey.* Chicago: U. of Chicago Press, 1966.

Keddie, Nikkie. *Sayyid Jamal ed-Din "al-Afghani": A Political Biography.* Berkeley: U. of California Press, 1972.

———, ed. *Scholars, Saints and Sufis.* Berkeley: U. of California Press, 1972.

Kedourie, E. *Afghani and Abduh: An Essay on Religious Belief and Political Activism.* London: Cass, 1966.

Kerr, M. "Egypt." In *Education and Political Development.* J. Coleman, ed. Princeton: Univ. Press, 1965.

———. *Islamic Reform.* Berkeley: U. of California Press, 1966.

———. *The Arab Cold War.* London and New York: Oxford Univ. Press, 1965.

Khadduri, M. *The Law of War and Peace in Islam.* London: Luzac, 1941.

———. "The Role of the Military in Middle East Politics," *American Political Science Review*, **46** (1953), 511–524.

———. *War and Peace in the Law of Islam.* Baltimore: Johns Hopkins, 1955. (a)

———, with H. J. Liebesny. *Law in the Middle East.* Washington: Middle East Institute, 1955. (b)

———. *Islamic Jurisprudence.* Baltimore: Johns Hopkins, 1961. (a)

———. *Independent Iraq.* New York: Oxford Univ. Press, 1961. (b)

———. *The Islamic Law of Nations.* Baltimore: Johns Hopkins, 1966.

———. *Republican Iraq.* London: Oxford Univ. Press, 1969.

———. *Political Trends in the Arab World.* Baltimore: Johns Hopkins, 1970.

Khalidi, W. and Y. Ibish. *Arab Political Documents.* AUB, 1963, 1964, 1965.

Khalil, M. *The Arab States and the Arab League.* Beirut: Khayat's, 1966.

Khalili, J. *Communist China's Interaction with the Arab Nationalists.* New York: Exposition, 1972.

Khallaf, H. *Al-tajdîd fî al-iqtiṣâd al-miṣri al-ḥadîth.* Cairo: Cairo Univ., 1962.

al-Khatib, A. *al-Usûl al-barlamâniyya.* Beirut: Dâr al-ᶜIlm, 1961.

Khouri, F. *The Arab-Israeli Dilemma.* Syracuse: Syracuse Univ. Press, 1968.

Khoury, E. *The Patterns of Mass Movements in Arab Revolutionary-Progressive States.* The Hague: Mouton, 1970.

Kirk, G. *The Middle East in the War.* Oxford: Univ, Press, 1953.

———. *The Middle East 1945-1950.* Oxford: Univ, Press, 1954.

Klieman, A. S. *Soviet Russia and the Middle East.* Baltimore: Johns Hopkins, 1970.

Klineberg, S. L. "Some Psychological Consequences of Social Change." In *Change in Tunisia.* R. Stone and J. Simmons, eds. New York: State Univ. of New York, 1976.

Klingmuller, E. *Geschichte der Wafdpartei.* Berlin: Springer, 1937.

Koç, A. N., et al. "Isciler Kime Neden Oy Veriyor?" *Milliyet,* **11** (October 1969).

Kohn, H. *A History of Nationalism in the East.* New York: Harcourt, 1929.

———. *Nationalism and Imperialism in the Hither East.* New York: Harcourt, 1932.

Lacouture, J. and S. *L'Egypte en Mouvement.* Paris: Seuil, 1956.

Lahbabi, M. *Le Gouvernement marocain à l'aube du XXe siècle.* Rabat: Editions Techniques Nord Africaines, 1958.

Laks, M. *Autogestion ouvrière et pouvoir politique en Algérie.* Paris: Etudes et Documentation Internationales, 1970.

Lall, A. *The United Nations and the Middle East Crisis.* New York: Columbia, 1968.

Lambton, A. K. S. *Landlord and Peasant in Persia.* London: Oxford Univ. Press, 1953.

———. *The Persian Land Reform.* Oxford: Clarendon Press, 1969.

Landau, J. *The Arabs in Israel.* London, New York: Oxford Univ. Press, 1969.

Lapassat, E. J. *La justice en Algérie.* Paris: Fondation Nationale des sciences politiques, 1968.

Laqueur, W. *Communism and Nationalism in the Middle East.* New York: Praeger, 1956.

———. *The Middle East in Transition.* New York: Praeger, 1958.

———. *The Soviet Union and the Middle East.* New York: Praeger, 1959.

———. *The Road to Jerusalem: The Origins of the Arab-Israeli Conflict* 1967. New York: MacMillan, 1968.

———. *The Struggle for the Middle East: The Soviet Union in the Mediterranean.* New York: Macmillan, 1969.

———. *Confrontation: The Middle East and World Politics.* New York: Quadrangle, 1974.

Laroui, A. *L'idéologie arabe contemporain.* Paris: Maspero, 1967.

———. *La crise des intellectuels arabes.* Paris: Maspero, 1974.

Lenczowski, G. *Russia and the West in Iran.* Ithaca: Cornell Univ., 1949.

———. *Oil and State in the Middle East.* Ithaca: Cornell Univ., 1960.

———. *Soviet Advances in the Middle East.* Washington, D. C.: American Enterprise Institute, 1972.

———, ed. *Political Elites in the Middle East.* Washington, D. C.: American Enterprise Institute, 1975.

Lentin, A. P. *Le dernier quart d'heure d'Algérie.* Paris: Juillard, 1964.

Lerner, D. *The Passing of Traditional Society.* Glencoe, Ill.: Free Press, 1958.

———, and R. R. Robinson, "Swords and Ploughshares: The Turkish Army as a Modernizing Force." *World Politics* **13**, 1 (1960), 19–44.

Levy, R. *A Mirror for Princes.* London: Cresset, 1951.

Lissak, M. *Social Mobility in Israeli Society.* Jerusalem: Israel Universities Press, 1969.

Little, T. *Egypt.* New York: Prager, 1967.

Lloyd, G. A. *Egypt since Cromer,* 2 vols. New York: Macmillan, 1933, 1934.

Longrigg, S. H. *Oil in the Middle East.* London: Oxford Univ., 1968.

Luttwak, E. and D. Horowitz. *The Israeli Army,* New York: Harper and Row, 1975.

MacDonald, R. *The League of Arab States.* Princeton: Univ. Press, 1965.

Mahieu, A. *L'avènement du parti unique en Afrique noire.* Paris: Libraire général de droit et de jurisprudence, 1969.

Mahmasani, S. *al-Awda' al-tashri*[c]*îyya fî al-Dûwwal al-*[c]*Arabiyya.* Beirut: 1957.

Makhlouf, E. *Structures agraires et modernisation de l'agriculture dans les plaines du Kef.* Tunis: CERES, 1968.

Mansoor, M. *Political and Diplomatic History of the Arab World 1900–1967.* Washington, D. C.: Microcard Editions, 1972.

Marais, O. "La Classe dirigeante au Maroc," *Revue Française de Science Politique,* **14**, 4 (1964); English trans. in *Man, State and Society in Contemporary Maghreb,* I. W. Zartman, ed. New York: Praeger, 1973.

———. "Elites intermédiaires, pouvoir et légitimité dans le Maroc indépendant," *Annuaire de l'Afrique du Nord,* **9** (1971).

Marais, O., and J. Waterbury. "Thèmes et vocabulaire de la propagande des élites au Maroc," *Annuaire de l'Afrique du Nord,* 1968.

Mardin, S. *The Genesis of Young Ottoman Thought.* Princeton: Univ. Press, 1962.

———. *Jön Türklerin Siyasi Fikirleri 1895–1908.* Ankara: Iş Bankasi kültur Yayinlari, 1964.

———, et al. *The Izmir Study.* In Press, 1976.

Matras, J. *Social Change in Israel.* Chicago: Aldine, 1965.

Mayfield, B. *Rural Politics in Nasser's Egypt.* Austin: U. of Texas, 1971.

Mazouni, A. *Culture et enseignement en Algérie et au Maghreb.* Paris: Maspero, 1964.

McClelland, D. "National Character and Economic Growth in Turkey and Iran." In *Communications and Political Development.* Princeton: Univ. Press, 1963.

Medding, P. Y. *Mapai in Israel: Political Organisation and Government in a New Society.* Cambridge: Univ. Press, 1972.

Meynaud, J. and A. Salah-Bey. *Le syndicalisme africain.* Paris: Payot, 1963.

Micaud, C. and E. Gellner, eds. *Arabs and Berbers.* Lexington: Lexington Books, D. C. Heath, 1973.

Mikdashi, Z. *The Community of Oil Exporting Countries.* Ithaca: Cornell Univ., 1972.

Milliot, L. *Les terres collectives: étude de législation marocaine.* Paris: Leroux, 1922.

———, and R. M. Avakov. "Class Structure in the Underdeveloped Countries." In *The Third World in Soviet Perspective.* T. P. Thornton, ed. Princeton: Univ. Press, 1964.

Mirskii, G. I. *Iraq in Troubled Times 1930–1941 (in Russian).* Moscow: 1961.

Mitchell, R. P. *The Society of Muslim Brothers.* London: Oxford Univ. Press, 1969.

Monroe, E. *The Mediterranean in Politics.* London: Oxford Univ. Press, 1938.

———. *Britain's Moment in the Middle East 1914–1956.* Baltimore: Johns Hopkins, 1963

Montagne, R. *Les berbers et le makhzen au sud du Maroc.* Paris: Alcan, 1930.

———. *La vie sociale et politique des berbers.* Paris: Societe de l'Afrique française, 1931. English trans. with introduction by D. Seddon: *The Berbers.* London: Cass, 1973.

de Montety, H. *Enquete sur les vieilles familles et nouvelles élites en Tunisie.* CHEAM mimeo, 1939. English trans. in *Man, State and Society in Contemporary Maghreb,* I. W. Zartman, ed. New York: Praeger, 1973.

———. "Le développement des classes moyennes en Tunisie." In *Développement d'une classe moyenne dans les pays tropicaux et subtropicaux.* Brussels: INCIDI, 1956.

Moore, C. H. "Politics in a Tunisian Village," *Middle East Journal,* **17**, 4 (1963), 527–540.

———. *Tunisia Since Independence.* Berkeley: Univ. of California, 1965.

———. "Class Origins of Egyptian Engineer-Technocrats." In Press, 1974.

———. "The New Egyptian Technocracy: Engineers at the Interstices of Power," *International Journal of Middle East Studies,* **6** (1975).

———, C. Micaud, and L. C. Brown. *Tunisia: The Politics of Modernization.* New York: Preager, 1964.

Mosley, L. *Power Play: Oil in the Middle East.* New York: Random House, 1973.

Nasr, N. and M. Palmer. "Some Social and Psychological Factors Relating to the Political Behavior of University Students in Lebanon and the Arab World." Paper presented to the Middle East Studies Association, 1970.

Nirumand, B. *Iran: New Imperialism in Action.* New York: Monthly Review, 1969.

Nolte, R. "From Nomad Society to New Nation." In *Expectant Peoples.* K. H. Silvert, ed. New York: Random House, 1963.

Norman, J. *Labor and Politics in Libya and Arab Africa.* New York: Bookman, 1965.

Nye, J. *Peace in Parts.* Boston: Little, Brown, 1971.

O'Ballance, E. *The Kurdish Revolt.* Hamden, Conn.: Anchor, 1973.

Ottoway, D. and M. *Algeria: The Politics of a Socialist Revolution.* Berkeley: U. of California Press, 1969.

Özbudun, E. *The Role of the Military in Recent Turkish Politics.* Cambridge: Harvard Center for International Studies, 1966.

———. "Established vs. Unfinished Revolution." In *Authoritarian Politics in Modern Society.* S. Huntington and C. H. Moore, eds. New York: Basic Books, 1970.

———. and F. Tachau. "Social Change and Electoral Behavior in Turkey." *Int. Journal of Middle East Studies*, **6**, 4 (1975), 460–480.

Page, S. *The U.S.S.R. in Arabia.* London: Central Asian Research Center, 1971.

Pakadaman, H. N. *Djamal ed-Dine Assad Abadi dit Afghani.* Paris: Maisonneuve & Larose, 1969.

Parker, T. *Die Histadrut.* Basel and Tübingen: Kyklos, 1965.

Pascon, P. and M. Bentahar. "Ce que disent 296 jeunes ruraux." In *Etudes sociologiques du Maroc.* Rabat: Société d'études économiques, sociales et statistiques, 1972. Originally in *Bulletin économique et social du Maroc*, **112/113** (1969).

Penner, J. *The USSR and the Arabs.* New York: Crane, Russak, 1973.

Perlmutter, A. "The Praetorian State and the Praetorian Army," *Comparative Politics*, **1**, 3 (1969), 382–404. (a)

———. *Military Politics in Israel.* London: Cass, 1969. (b)

——— *Anatomy of Political Institutionalization.* Cambridge: Harvard Center for International Affairs, 1970.

Pfaff, R. H. "Disengagement from Traditionalism in Turkey and Iran," *Western Political Quarterly*, **16**, 1 (1963), 79–98.

Plum, W. *Gewerkschaften im Maghreb.* Hannover: Verlag fur Litertataur und Zeitgeschehen, 1962.

Polk, W. *The United States and the Middle East.* Cambridge: Harvard Univ., 1965.

Preuss, W. *The Labor Movement in Israel.* Jerusalem: Arab World, 1965.

Quandt, W. B. *Revolution and Political Leadership: Algeria 1954–1968.* Cambridge: MIT, 1969.

———, F. Jabber, and A. M. Lesch. *The Politics of Palestinian Nationalism.* Berkeley: Univ. of California Press, 1973.

Quint, M. "The Idea of Progress in an Iraqi Village," *Middle East Journal*, **12**, 4 (1958), 369–384.

Quraishi, Z. *Liberal Nationalism in Egypt: Rise and Fall of the Wafd Party.* Allahabad: Kitab Makal, 1967.

Rabbat, E. *al-Wasît fî al-Qanûn al-Dustûrî al-Lubnânî.* Beirut: Dâr al-'ᶜIlm, 1970.

Rabinovich, I. *Syria Under the Ba'th.* New York: Halsted, 1972.

Ramazani, R. *The Foreign Policy of Iran.* Charlottesville: U. of Virginia, 1972.

Ramsaur, E. E. *The Young Turks: Prelude to the Revolution of 1908.* Princeton: Univ. Press, 1969.

al-Razzâz, M. *al-Tajriba al-Murra.* Beirut, 1967.

Reid, M. D. "The Rise of Professions and Professional Organization in Modern Egypt," *Comparative Studies in Society and History*, **16**, 1 (1974), 24–57.

Reitzel, W. *The Mediterranean: Its Role in America's Foreign Policy.* New York: Harcourt, 1948.

Remili, A. *Les institutions administrative algériennes*, Algiers: SNED, 1967.

Rezette, R. *Les partis politiques marocains.* Paris: Colin, 1955.

Riyad, H. (pseud. S. Amin). *L'Egypte nasserien.* Paris: Editions de minuit, 1964.

Rikhye, I. J., H. Michael, and E. Bjorn. *The Thin Blue Line.* New Haven: Yale, 1975.

Roberts, S. Survival or Hegemony: The Foundations of Israeli Foreign Policy. Baltimore: John Hopkins Univ., 1975.

Roemer, H. R., trans. *Staatsschreiben der Timuridzeit*. Wiesbaden: Steiner, 1952.

Roos, L. and N. *Managers of Modernization: Organizations and Elites in Turkey*. Cambridge: Harvard Univ., 1971.

Rosenthal, E. I. J. *Political Thought in Medieval Islam*. Cambridge: Univ. Press, 1965.

Rossi, P. *L'Irak des revoltes*. Paris: Seuil, 1966.

Rouhani, F. *A History of OPEC*. New York: Praeger, 1971.

Rozaliev, Y. N. *Classes and Class Struggle in Turkey*. Moscow Publishing, trans. Joint Publications Research Service, 1966.

Rudebeck, L. *Party and People*. New York: Preager, 1969.

Ruf, W. K. *Der Burgibismus und die aussenpolitik des unabhängigen Tunesien*. Bielefeld: Bertelsmann Universitätsverlag, 1969.

Rugh, W. A. "Emergence of a New Middle Class in Saudi Arabia," *Middle East Journal*, **27**, 1 (1973) 7–20.

Rustow, D. A. "The Army and the Founding of the Turkish Republic," *World Politics*, **11**, 4 (1959), 513–552.

———. "The Military in Middle Eastern Society and Politics." In *The Military in the Middle East*. S. N. Fisher, ed. Columbus: Ohio State Univ., 1963.

———. "Turkey." In *Political Culture and Political Development*. L. Pye and S. Verba, eds., Princeton: Univ. Press, 1965.

———. "Turkey." In *Political Parties and Political Development*. J. LaPalombara and M. Weiner, eds. Princeton: Univ. Press, 1966.

Saab, G. *The Egyptian Agrarian Reform 1952–1962*. London: Oxford Univ. Press, 1967.

Saab, H. *al-Mafhûm al-hadîth l'il-rajul al-dâwla*. Beirut: 1959.

———. *Taḥdîth al-ᶜaql al ᶜarabî*. Beirut: 1970.

Safadi, M. *Ḥizb al-baᶜth*. Beirut: Dâr al-Adab, 1964. (a)

———. *Maᶜṣat al-Mawlis, Maᶜṣat al-Nihâya*. Beirut: 1944. (b)

Safran, N. *Egypt in Search of Political Community*. Cambridge: Harvard Univ., 1961.

———. *The United States and Israel*. Cambridge: Harvard Univ. ,1963.

———. *From War to War*. New York: Pegasus, 1969.

Salah Bey, A. *Le syndicalisme algérien*. Paris: Payot, 1963.

Salem, E. *Modernization without Revolution*. Bloomington: Indiana Univ., 1973.

Sayegh, R. *Le système de partis politiques en Israel*. Paris: Librairie generale de droit et de jurisprudence, 1972.

Sayegh, Y. *Stratijiyyat al-tahrîr al-filistîniyya*. Beirut: Dâr al-ṭalîᶜa, 1969.

Sbih, M. *La fonction publique*. Paris: Hachette, 1968.

Schacht, J. *The Origins of Muhammedan Jurisprudence*. Oxford: Clarendon Press, 1950.

———. *An Introduction to Islamic Law*. Oxford: Clarendon Press, 1964.

Seale, P. *The Struggle for Syria*. London and New York: Oxford Univ., 1965.

Seligman, L. *Leadership in a New Nation*. New York: Atherton, 1964.

Sharabi, H. *Nationalism and Revolution in the Arab World*. Princeton: Univ. Press, 1966.

———. *Palestine and Israel*. New York: Pegasus, 1969.

———. *Palestine Guerrillas*. Washington, D. C.: Inst. for Strategic & International Studies, 1970.

Shwardran, B. *The Middle East, Oil, and the Great Powers.* New York: Wiley, 1970.

Sigler, J. "News Flow in the North African International System," *International Studies Quarterly,* **13,** 4 (1969), 381–397.

Smith, W. C. *Islam in Modern History.* Princeton: Univ. Press, 1957.

Smock, D. and A. *Politics of Pluralism: A Comparative Study of Lebanon and Ghana.* New York: Elsevier, 1975.

Smolansky, O. *The Soviet Union and the Arab East under Kruschchev.* Lewisburg: Bucknell Univ. Press, 1974.

Steinhaus, K. *Soziologie der turkischen Revolution.* Frankfurt am Main: Europaische Verlanganstalt, 1969.

Stone, R. and J. Simmons. *Change in Tunisia.* Albany: State Univ. of N. Y., 1976.

Suleiman, M. W. *Political Parties in Lebanon: The Challenge of a Fragmented Political Culture.* Ithaca: Cornell, 1967. (a)

———. "Elections in a Confessional Democracy," *Journal of Politics,* **29,** 1 (1967), 109–128. (b)

Szyliowicz, J. S. *Political Change in Rural Turkey: Erdemli.* The Hague: Mouton; 1966. (a)

———. "Political Participation and Modernization in Turkey," *Western Political Quarterly,* **19,** 2 (1966), 266–284. (b)

———. *A Political Analysis of Student Activism: The Turkish Case.* Beverly Hills: Sage Professional Paper in Comparative Politics 01-034, 1972.

———. *Education and Modernization in the Middle East.* Ithaca: Cornell Univ., 1973.

Tachau, F. with M. J. Good. "The Anatomy of Political and Social Change," *Comparative Politics,* **5,** 4 (1973), 551–573.

———, ed. *Political Elites and Political Development in the Middle East.* Cambridge, Mass.: Schenkman, 1975.

Tessler, M. and M. Keppel, "Political Generations." In *Change in Tunisia.* R. Stone and J. Simmons, eds. Albany: State U. of New York, 1976.

Thompson, W. R. "The Arab Sub-System and the Feudal Pattern of Interaction 1965," *Journal of Peace Research,* **7,** 2 (1970), 151–167.

Torrey, G. H. *Syrian Politics and the Military: 1945–1958.* Columbus: Ohio State Univ., 1964.

Toynbee, A. J. *The Islamic World Since the Peace Settlement.* London: Oxford Univ., 1927.

Tuma, E. *Peacemaking and the Immoral War.* New York: Harper and Row, 1970.

Tunaya, T. Z. *Türkiyenin Siyasî Hayatinda, bastililasma hareketkri.* Istanbul: Yedigün Matbaasi, 1960.

———. *Islamcelik Cereyani.* Istanbul: Baha Matbassi, 1962.

Turan, I. *Cumhuriet Tarihimiz.* Istanbul: Istanbul Matbassi, 1969.

Vali, F. *Bridge Across the Bosphorus.* Baltimore: Johns Hopkins, 1971.

Van Nieuwenhuijze, C. *Social Stratification and the Middle East.* Leiden: Brill, 1965.

Vatikiotis, P. J. *The Egyptian Army in Politics.* Bloomingon: Indiana Univ., 1961.

———. *Politics and the Military in Jordan.* New York: Praeger, 1967.

———, ed. *Egypt since the Revolution.* New York: Praeger, 1968.

———, ed. *Revolution in the Middle East.* London: Allen & Unwin, 1972.

Vatin, J.-C., and J. Leca. *L'Algérie Politique.* 2 vols. Paris: Colin, 1975.

Vaucher, G. *Gamal Abdel Nasser et son équipe*. 2 vols. Paris: Juillard, 1959, 1960.

Vernier, B. *L'Iraq d'aujourd'hui*. Paris: Colin, 1962.

———. *Armée et politique au Moyen Orient*. Paris: Payot, 1966.

Vlavianos, B. J. and F. Gross. *Struggle for Tommorrow: Modern Political Ideologies of the Jewish People*. New York: Arts, Inc., 1954.

Ward, R. and R. Macridis, eds. *Modern Political Systems: Asia*. Engelwood Cliffs: Prentiss-Hall, 1963.

Ward, R. and D. Rustow, eds. *Political Modernization in Japan and Turkey*. Princeton: Princeton Univ., 1964.

Warriner, D. *Land and Poverty in the Middle East*. London, New York: Royal Institute of International Affairs, 1948.

———. Land Reform and Development in the Middle East. London: Oxford, 1962.

Waterbury, J. *The Commander of the Faithful: The Moroccan Political Elite*. New York: Columbia, 1970.

———. *North for the Trade*. Berkeley: U. of California, 1973.

Watt, W. M. *Islam and the Integration of Society*. London: Routledge, Keegan & Paul, 1961.

Weiker, W. *The Turkish Revolution 1960–1961*. Washington, D. C.: Brookings Inst., 1963.

———. *Decentralizing Government in Modernizing Nations: Growth Center Potential of Turkish Provincial Cities*. Sage International Studies Series 02-007, 1972.

———. *Political Tulelage and Democracy in Turkey: The Free Party*. Leiden: Brill, 1972.

Weingrod, A. *Israel: Group Relations in a New Society*. New York: Praeger, 1965.

Weintraub, D., et al. *Moshava, Kibbutz and Moshav*. Ithaca: Cornell Univ., 1969.

———. *Immigration and Social Change*. New York: Humanities, 1971.

Weisband, E. *Turkish Foreign Policy 1943–1945: Small State Diplomacy and Great Power Politics*. Princeton: Princeton Univ., 1973.

Wheelock, K. *Nasser's New Egypt*. New York: Praeger, 1960.

Whetten, L. L. *The Canal War: Four-Power Conflict in the Middle East*. Cambridge: MIT, 1974.

Wilcox, W. "Political Change in Pakistan," *Pacific Affairs*, **41**, 3 (1968), 341–354.

Willner, D. *Nation-Building and Community in Israel*. Princeton: Princeton Univ. 1968.

Yodfat, A. *Arab Politics in the Soviet Mirror*. New York: Halsted, 1973.

Zabih, S. *The Communist Movement in Iran*. Berkeley: U. of California, 1966.

Zaki, M. S. *al-'ikhwân al-muslimûn fî al-Mujtama^{c} al-Miṣrî*. Cairo: 1954.

Zagoria, J. *The Rise and Fall of the Movement of Messali Hajj*. Pending.

Zarrin-Kub, A. *Dû qarn-i-Sukût*. Tehran: 1965a.

———. *Mirâth-i-Sufîyyah*. Tehran: 1965b.

———. *Bamdâd-i-Islâm*. Tehran: 1969.

Zartman, I. W. *Morocco: Problems of New Power*. New York: Atherton, 1964.

———. "Les élections départementales algériennes," *Annuaire de l'Afrique du Nord 1969*. Paris: CNRS, 1970. (a)

———. "The Algerian Army in Politics." In *Soldier and State in Africa*. C. Welch, ed. Evanston: Northwestern, 1970. (b)

———, ed. *Man, State and Society in the Contemporary Maghreb*. New York: Praeger, 1973.

———, and A. Rhazaoui. "Class, Status, and Party in Algerian Single-Party Elections," *American Political Science Review* Pending, 1977.

———, ed. *The Study of Elites in the Middle East.* Princeton: Univ. Press, 1976.

Zayid, M. Z. *Egypt's Struggle for Independence.* Beirut: Khayat's, 1965.

Zghal, A. "Nation-Building in the Maghreb," *International Social Science Journal*, **23**, 3 (1971), 435–452.

Ziadeh, F. *Lawyers, the Rule of Law, and Liberalism in Modern Egypt.* Stanford: Hoover Inst. 1968.

Zidon, A. *Knesset: The Parliament of Israel.* New York: Herzl, 1967.

Ziegler, J. *Sociologie de la nouvelle Afrique.* Paris: Gallimard, 1964.

Zikria, A. A. *Les principles de l'Islam et la democratie.* Paris: Nouvelles editions latines, 1958.

Zonis, M. *The Political Elite of Iran.* Princeton: Univ. Press, 1971.

Zuwiyya, J. *The Parliamentary Election of Lebanon 1968.* Leiden: Brill, 1972.

Zuwiyya, Yamak, L. *The Syrian Nationalist Party.* Cambridge: Harvard Univ., 1966.

CHAPTER SEVEN

Philosophy

SEYYED HOSSEIN NASR

The tradition of the study of Islamic philosophy in the West is nearly 1000 years old and can be divided into three phases, namely, the medieval period of translation, analysis, and study of Arabic texts; the second wave of translation and study in the Renaissance following the medieval effort, and finally a new attempt to study Islamic philosophy which began in the nineteenth century and continues to this day. Despite a certain continuity in this long history and connection between these three phases, it is essentially with the last period that we concern ourselves in this appraisal. Moreover, by "philosophy" we understand *al-falsafa* or *al-ḥikma al-ilahîyya* of the traditional Muslim sources and not the general meaning of the term philosophy as used in modern European languages, which would extend to many other traditional Islamic disciplines such as the principles of jurisprudence (*uṣûl al-fiqh*) and the sciences of language.

In the common parlance of European languages, "philosophy" evokes the idea of something having to do with the general principles, laws, definitions, origin, and end of things, and one speaks even of the philosophy of art or religion or science. In the classical Islamic languages, however, *al-falsafa* refers to a specific set of disciplines and to a number of distinct schools such as the *ma<u>sh</u>s<u>h</u>â'î* (Peripatetic) and *i<u>sh</u>râqî* (Illuminationist), not to just any school of thought which contains "philosophical" ideas. Moreover, in later Islamic history in the eastern lands of Islam the term *al-ḥikma al-ilâhîyya* became common and practically synonymous with *al-falsafa*, whereas in the western lands of Islam the older term *al-falsafa* continued to be used solely to denote the activity of the "philosophers." In both cases, however, these terms have always been used as the names for specific types of intellectual activity which Muslims came to identify with "philosophy" or rather, in the second case, "theosophy," whereas other disciplines cultivated within Islamic civilization and possessing notable philosophical dimensions in the Western sense of the term philosophy have not been categorized in the classical period of Islamic history as either *al-falsafa* or *al-ḥikma al-ilâhiyyah*. It must be added, however, that although we have limited ourselves to the discussion of *falsafa* in its traditional sense, it is necessary to discuss its relations to various fields such as Sufism, theology (*kalâm*), and the sciences. But we do not deal here with these disciplines in themselves or with the "philosophy" they contain in the general Occidental sense of philosophy.

Just as in the context of Islamic civilization, philosophy, though a very distinct discipline, has been closely related to the sciences on the one hand and Sufism and *kalâm* on the other, it has had ramifications in fields dealing with the practical aspects of human life, especially political science and jurisprudence. The classical division of the "intellectual sciences" and also philosophy by many Muslim authorities into the theoretical and the practical, the first comprised of metaphysics, physics, mathematics, and logic and the second of ethics, politics, and economics (in its traditional sense), reveals its relation to various fields and sciences which even embrace the religious sciences such as theology, Qur'anic commentary, and the principles of jurisprudence. Not only do these fields possess a "philosophy" of their own as philosophy is currently understood—the recent opus of Wolfson on the philosophy of the *kalâm* being an outstanding proof—but also *falsafa* as a separate discipline has been inextricably related to many aspects of their development. It is this second aspect that belongs to any integral treatment of the study of Islamic philosophy and that in fact calls for an interdisciplinary approach which should bear much fruit in the future.

* * *

Several schools can be distinguished in the history of the study of Islamic philosophy since the last century. They include first of all the Christian scholastic tradition cultivated mostly by Catholic scholars, who in a sense have continued the medieval study of Islamic philosophy within the matrix of Thomism or Neo-Thomism, some relying mostly on Latin translations and interested only in the role played by Islamic philosophy in Latin scholasticism such as Gilson and De Wulf, and others well acquainted with the Arabic material and the structure of Islamic thought in general, such as Massignon, Goichon, and Gardet. There is, moreover, a special school of Catholic scholars in Spain in whom a sense of "Spanish identity" and reliance upon Catholic theology are combined. This school has also produced scholars of repute, such as Asín Palacios, Cruz Hernandez, and Gonzales Palencia, who have made major contributions to the study of Islamic philosophy and related fields, but have been confined in their creative thought and research mostly to Spain and the Maghreb. The historians of Islamic science and thought,

Millás-Vallicrosa and J. Vernet are also in a sense related to this group in their Spanish orientation, although not closely identified with Catholic theology.

Another school that parallels the Catholic in its long history and that issued from the same scholastic background is that of Jewish scholarship, which had its roots in rabbinical training and also indirectly in medieval Jewish scholasticism, with which elements from the Western humanist school have sometimes been mixed. This school produced outstanding scholars in the nineteenth century, such as Steinschneider and Munk, and has continued to produce some of the most outstanding scholars of Islamic philosophy and of Islamic thought in general during this century, such as Goldziher, Wensinck, Horovitz, Wolfson, E. I. J. Rosenthal, Vajda, van der Bergh, Pines, and Walzer. The political turmoils of the past quarter century, however, have now changed the attitude of many, but not all, scholars of this type toward both Islamic philosophy and traditional Jewish thought itself, making many of them less sympathetic interpreters of traditional forms of Islamic thought.

Altogether the approaches of the scholars in the two groups already mentioned have been similar in that they have drawn from traditional Christian and Jewish philosophy and theology. Yet another group of scholars appeared on the scene in the nineteenth century; their background has been modern European philosophy and they have tried to understand the contents of Islamic philosophy in terms of different schools of thought prevalent in the modern West. From Renan, followed by L. Gauthier, who sought to make Ibn Rushd the father of rationalism, to Corbin, who has made use of the insights of phenomenology to penetrate into the inner meaning of Islamic philosophy, there has been a group of scholars who have approached Islamic philosophy as thinkers immersed in the current schools of Western philosophy rather than as scholars of texts or men with scholastic training in philosophy.

In contrast to these groups, there developed from the nineteenth century onward a large school of Orientalists with primarily a philological training who have studied Islamic philosophy textually and philologically without bringing, at least consciously, a philosophical or theological element into their study. This group has been responsible for the careful edition of many texts but has produced few meaningful interpretations. During the past decades training in the social sciences has supplemented that of philology, and a certain number of works have appeared on Islamic philosophy from the point of view of current theories of social science in the West, although these have been related mostly to political philosophy rather than pure philosophy.

Recently, with the extension in the West of the consciousness of the existence of several intellectual traditions in the world other than the Western, a school based on the comparative method has now come into being. With the success that this approach has had in the fields of Far Eastern and Indian metaphysics, a group of scholars has now turned to the study of Islamic philosophy in comparison with both Western and other Oriental intellectual traditions. The works of Izutsu, Ushida, Corbin, Gardet, and others mark a beginning in this potentially fecund field of study.

Finally, there has come into being, again only recently, a school which has begun to study Islamic philosophy as a living school of thought rather than as a matter of solely historical interest. The inner need of Western man for a new "existential" knowledge of the Oriental traditions has turned a number of men to seek within Islamic philosophy answers to questions posed by the modern world on the intellectual level. Such men as Corbin, Gardet, Durand, Nasr, and Arkoun have begun a new form of scholarship in Islamic philosophy which, without sacrificing in any way the scholarly aspect of such studies, has turned them directly into the service of the philosophical and metaphysical quest of those contemporary men who are aware of the profound intellectual crisis of Western civilization.

This new development, if pursued more extensively and in depth, could succeed in overcoming the excessive historicism of earlier works by treating Islamic metaphysical and philosophical ideas as something of innate value. Until now so much of the research in Islamic philosophy has been devoted to tracing historical influences that few have bothered to ask what a particular idea must have meant to those who held it and contemplated it, whatever might have been its apparent historical origin. Somehow the significance of the saying that truth has no history has rarely been realized in the case of Islamic philosophy with the result that, besides the exceptions already cited, few European thinkers of importance have been attracted to it in the same way that they have been pulled toward the intellectual traditions of the Indian world and the Far East. The combination of philosopher and Orientalist that one can find in a scholar like Corbin has only rarely appeared on the scene of Islamic philosophy, because this philosophy has been presented too often as nothing more than Greek philosophy in Arabic dress, without anything of innate value that could not be found in the Greek sources themselves. Only an extension of the activity of the group which considers Islamic philosophy as a living intellectual tradition worthy of study on its own basis can remedy the fault that has largely truncated a true appreciation of this subject in the West.

In addition to all the groups cited so far, who are mostly in touch or connected in one way or another with the Western intellectual scene, the past 50 years have produced numerous Muslim scholars, and a few non-Muslims from the Middle East such as Anawati and Fakhry, who have made many contributions to Islamic philosophy. They include scholars trained in modern methods of research, and writing often in both Islamic and Western languages, such as ᶜAbd al-Râziq, Madkour, Affifi, El-Ahwany, Abû Rîdah, Badawī, Mahdī, Fazlur Rahman, Nasr, Arkoun, and Sharif, some of whom also participate in the activities of the groups mentioned above. There are also those who continue the traditional method of cultivating and studying Islamic philosophy. This latter group is to be found especially in Persia, and includes such men as S. M. Ḥ. Ṭabâṭabâ'î, S. J. Âshtiyânî, J. Muṣliḥ, and many others whose activities during the past two decades have been studied in a recent monograph by Nasr (1972). But a great deal more effort must be made to make the works of Muslim scholars on Islamic philosophy known to the West and to facilitate genuine cooperation between Eastern scholars and those in the West whose field of interest is Islamic philosophy.

The various groups in the East and the West have naturally made numerous contributions during the past century. In the field of manuscripts, despite poor catalogs of many libraries even in the West, the holdings of most libraries that have material pertinent to Islamic philosophy have been cataloged in both the Occident and the Islamic world. Turkey and Iran remain as places of particular importance for the discovery of unknown collections which will certainly contain works of significance for Islamic philosophy and which will need to be cataloged. Collections in the Indo-Pakistani subcontinent are also certain to reveal many surprises especially for later Islamic philosophy. In certain special fields such as Ismâᶜîlî thought and Muᶜtazilite theology as it pertains to philosophy, the libraries of Yemen may also reveal some unknown riches.

Concerted work in the West as well as in the Islamic world itself has made available a number of texts of Islamic philosophy in scholarly editions, but distributed unevenly as far as historical periods are concerned. The few extant writings of al-Kindî have been edited by Abû Rîda; many of al-Fârâbî's works have seen the light of day, especially recently in carefully edited versions by Mahdî and others. Many of Ibn Sînâ's works have been edited by such men as von Mehren, Corbin, Dunyâ, Muᶜîn, Rahman, and most important of all, the group working under the direction of Madkour in editing the *Shifâ'*. As for Ibn Rushd, he has received a great deal of attention, one of the finest editions of Islamic philosophy being that of his commentary upon the metaphysics of Aristotle, by Bouyges. Badawî has also carried out an immense effort in this domain. Other Spanish philosophers have also been edited by Asín Palacios, Gomez Nogales, Fakhry, and others, but not as extensively as Ibn Rushd.

As far as later philosophy in the eastern lands of Islam is concerned, a major effort at editing the basic texts has been made, nearly completely in the East, but one can discern in the West a general rise of interest in the philosophy of Persia and other eastern lands of Islam which should make this effort more widespread in the near future. Suhrawardî has received much attention and most of his writings have now been edited by Corbin, Nasr, Abû Rayyân, Maᶜluf, and others. Ṣadr al-Dîn Shîrâzî has also been edited extensively, mostly during the past decade, by Ṭabâṭabâ'î, Âshtiyânî, Corbin, and Nasr. The works of Sabziwârî have been and continue to be edited by Izutsu and Mohaghegh. A few other works of the post-Avicennian period by such men as Naṣîr al-Dîn al-Ṭûsî and Quṭb al-Dîn al-Shîrâzî have also been printed, but mostly in editions which have not received sufficient scholarly care.

As for translations of basic texts of Islamic philosophy into European languages, there has been remarkably little done in comparison with either medieval Hebrew and Latin translations or contemporary translations from other Oriental traditions. There are, therefore, few of the original texts of Islamic philosophy that a student or scholar in the West can read if he does not possess a knowledge of Arabic or Persian. A few treatises of the earlier period of Islamic philosophy have been translated since the nineteenth century by such men as Dieterici, Horten, van den Bergh, Asín Palacios, and more recently, Goichon, G. Hourani, Filippani-Ranconi, and Rahman, and of later Islamic philosophy by Horten, Corbin, and Izutsu. However, taken together they represent a very small portion of existing texts of Islamic philosophy.

In the field of the history of Islamic philosophy, works have continued to appear since the first half of the nineteenth century by such men as Schmölders, followed by Dieterici, Munk, Dugat, Carra de Vaux, De Boer, Gauthier, Horten, Quadri, Cruz Hernandez, and others, and most recently Corbin and Fakhry. Muslim scholars such as Madkour, Ülken, Nasr, and Badawî have also written several works on the history of Islamic philosophy, the most extensive attempt being the two-volume opus edited by Sharif in which numerous Muslim scholars and several from the West collaborated, and in which an attempt has been made to cover the whole of Islamic philosophy for the first time.

In these histories and also in more limited histories of particular periods attention has nearly always been turned to the earlier centuries up to Ibn Rushd and excluding such schools as Ismâʿîlî philosophy and Shîʿite thought in general, Corbin's history of Islamic philosophy and also that of Sharif being exceptions. Also histories of particular branches of philosophy have been scarce; the works of Iqbal, Rescher, G. Hourani, and Pines in metaphysics, logic, ethics, and theories of atomism, respectively, are exceptions. Besides, even they are far from being exhaustive and do not treat all the periods of Islamic history thoroughly.

As far as the origin of Islamic philosophy is concerned, since Bergsträsser, followed in more recent times by such scholars as Walzer, Guidi, Badawî, and Georr, attempts have been made to study the textual relation of early works of Islamic philosophy with Greek sources and to establish a clear relationship between the two. In the case of some, such as Walzer, there has also been a keen interest in studying the continuity and also the transformation of the Greek philosophical heritage in the Islamic world. Several scholars have also edited existing Arabic translation of Greek works, among which the numerous editions of Badawî stand out. Moreover, the relationship between Islamic and Greek thought in the larger context of the two civilizations continues to be studied by F. Rosenthal, F. E. Peters, and others, basing themselves on the pioneering works of Steinschneider, Meyerhof and Bergsträsser, although a vast amount of work remains unfinished.

Some attention has also been paid to technical Islamic philosophy vocabulary by Wolfson, Bouyges, Goichon, Afnan, S. J. Sajjâdî, and others, but this is mostly of a fragmentary nature. The usual dictionaries of Arabic and Persian with English or French equivalents have included philosophical terms only accidentally, and no complete and systematic work has as yet been accomplished in this crucial field where Latin as well as modern European equivalents of Arabic and Persian terms are badly needed.

Investigations of Latin translations of Islamic philosophy continue by d'Alverny for Ibn Sînâ, and by the scholars working under the auspices of the Medieval Academy of America on the *Corpus Commentarum Averrois in Aristotelem* for Ibn Rushd. The work begun decades ago continues unabated, with much of the task still unaccomplished. Works on the influence of Islamic philosophy in the West have also been numerous, from those by Duhem and Dunlop, which deal mostly with the scientific aspect of Islamic philosophy, to those of Gilson, Asín Palacios, and Watt dealing with the more religious and theological dimensions of it.

Concerning the content of Islamic philosophy, those scholars who have themselves possessed a philosophical background and interest, such as Carra de Vaux, Wolfson, and Corbin, have brought out the main intellectual issues, mostly in metaphysics and epistemology with somewhat less attention paid to cosmology, except for a few works such as those of Burckhardt, Nasr, and Corbin. Much more attention has been paid to the earlier schools up to Ibn Rushd, and the serious analysis of the content of the works of Suhrawardî, Ṭûsî, Mîr Dâmâd, Ṣadr al-Dîn S͟hîrâzî, and other late figures is nearly limited to the writings of a small number of scholars including Horten, Corbin, Nasr, and Izutsu.

The relationship of Islamic philosophy to other aspects of Islamic studies has also received some attention, although not by any means sufficiently. As already mentioned, most Western scholars have refused to consider Islamic philosophy as anything more than an interim period between Greek and scholastic philosophy and as a kind of late survival of Greek thought. Few have bothered to view it in its integral relation with the rest of the Islamic intellectual tradition and Islamic civilization in general. The intrinsic relation between Islamic philosophy and the Islamic tradition itself has been explored by a few figures such as Schuon, Burckhardt, Nasr, and Corbin, and the relationship of Islamic philosophy to theology has received extensive attention from the time of Horovitz, L. Gauthier, and Goldziher to the present day studies of Gardet, Anawati, and especially Wolfson. But as far as the relation of philosophy to the background of Islamic society and also to various political and social forces is concerned, practically nothing has been done except some preliminary efforts by such men as Watt.

As far as the relation between Islamic philosophy and the sciences is concerned, the historians of Islamic science with interest in philosophy such as Duhem, Wiedemann, Meyerhof, Ruska, Kraus, Sarton, Pines, Plessner, and Nasr, as well as some of those dealing with philosophy per se such as Corbin, have dealt with at least some aspects of it. Practically nothing has been done concerning the philosophy of mathematics in Islam despite the vast amount of research that has been carried out on Islamic mathematics itself. But in the relation of Islamic philosophy to alchemy and astrology important studies have been made by Burckhardt, Kraus, and others and on medicine by Gruner and a group of eastern physicians connected with the Hamdard Institutes of both Karachi and Delhi.

The relation of Sufism to Islamic philosophy has also received some attention during the past few decades. The purely metaphysical doctrines of Sufism have been formulated for the first time in the West by Schuon, Guénon, Burckhardt, and Lings and their direct relationship to Islamic philosophy has been studied by Corbin, Nasr, and Izutsu. The recent rise of interest in later Islamic philosophy in which philosophy and gnosis, the intellectual aspect of Sufism, are closely interrelated has itself helped to intensify the study of the relation between Sufism, or more generally speaking Islamic esotericism, and Islamic philosophy, which in fact goes back to al-Fârâbî and the Ikhwân al-Ṣafâ', and which can be also seen clearly in the works of Ibn Sînâ.

* * *

Considering the present state of research, the task that remains to be accomplished in the field of Islamic philosophy is immense. But it can be outlined by concentrating upon several main categories and types of investigation that must be carried out. The first task is to make known all extant material on Islamic philosophy. Despite two centuries of cataloging libraries in the West and more recently in the East, and the work of such men as Brockelmann, Sezgin, Storey, Ritter, Ateš, Munajjid, and Daneshpazhuh in cataloging libraries and systematizing our knowledge of manuscript material, a major endeavour needs to be undertaken to make known the still unexplored collections. In Europe and America, except for a few holdings such as the Garrett collection in Princeton, which has not been studied fully, most of the existing philosophical manuscripts are known at least by name, but they need to be cataloged more carefully in many instances. In North Africa and Egypt private collections of great value as well as libraries of mosque schools of faraway regions are as yet unknown, although most likely they are richer in the fields of theology and Sufism than in philosophy.

In the Middle East, aside from private collections, the most important sources for new philosophical manuscripts are Turkey and Iran. In both countries many public or semipublic collections have not been fully cataloged as yet, not to speak of many manuscripts in various family collections. A city such as Shiraz is estimated to have over 10,000 manuscripts in private hands, a large number dealing with philosophy. Unfortunately there is the problem not only of these manuscripts remaining unknown, but of their being scattered and lost in many cases. There is an urgent need, first of all on the part of institutions in these countries and secondly on the part of international organizations, to provide funds to collect and preserve these manuscripts.

As far as philosophical works are concerned, outside of Turkey and Iran certain cities that were once centers of philosophic or scientific activity must also be scrutinized and investigated, for example, Mosul in Iraq and Aleppo in Syria. Casual research in these cities has already revealed remarkable manuscripts, for example, the correspondences (*Maktûbât*) of Suhrawardî discovered in Mosul a few years ago.

In the Indian subcontinent also many libraries, such as those of Rampur, Patna, Lucknow, and Hyderabad, have numerous philosophical manuscripts, many still not cataloged and almost all inaccessible. In certain parts of India, owing to a particular lack of interest in Arabic and Persian manuscripts during recent years, some notable collections such as one in Madras are deteriorating physically and may be beyond rescue if not stored properly soon. Considering the great interest of the Mogul kings in purchasing manuscripts dealing with the "intellectual sciences" (*al-ᶜulûm al-ᶜaqliyya*), a great deal remains to be discovered in the libraries of the subcontinent, especially as far as post-Avicennian philosophy is concerned.

The libraries of Central Asia are also relatively unknown, although suspected to be very rich in philosophy, again considering the importance of the role of this region in the history of Islamic thought. The work of some of the Russian scholars working in Islamic philosophy, such as Bertels, brings further proof of the role that the manuscript collections of Central Asia can play in our gaining a better knowledge of Islamic philosophy.

* * *

Parallel with discovering new material, there must be a concerted effort to edit in a critical fashion the major texts of Islamic philosophy, a thankless task that attracts fewer and fewer scholars every day, especially in the West. However, it remains, and will remain for some time to come, the most basic chore of scholars in this field.

As far as early Islamic philosophy is concerned, despite the work of Badawî, Walzer, Guidi, and many others, there remains the task of editing systematically the epigrammatic literature pertaining to the Greek and Alexandrian authors in Arabic which sets the background for the rise of Islamic philosophy. Of special interest is a critical edition of all the writings attributed to Aristotle and Hermes in Arabic.

As for Islamic philosophy properly speaking, what survives of al-Kindî has been edited, but the work of his students, such as Aḥmad ibn Ṭayyib al-Sarakhsî and Abû Ma^{c}shar, needs to be edited anew, considering the new material at hand since the pioneering efforts of Rosenthal and others. An urgent task is the critical edition of other newly discovered writings of al-Fârâbî following the work by Mahdi recently. Some of al-Fârâbî's earlier edited works are also in need of a critical edition; the *Madîna al-fâḍila*, which is perhaps the most important among them, is now being edited by Walzer.

A philosopher who has received much deserved attention recently is Abu Ḥasan al-^{c}Âmirī, the foremost philosophical figure between al-Fârâbî and Ibn Sînâ. But some of his works still remain unedited, especially his history of philosophy, *al-^{c}Amâd ^{c}ala al-abâd*. Also the history of philosophy of his contemporary, Abû Sulaymân al-Sijistânî, the *Ṣiwân al-ḥikma*, of which half survives, needs urgent attention.

Among Avicenna's writings the *Shifâ'* has finally been brought out in a critical edition, which should be finished soon. However, many of the other philosophical works such as the *Najât* still do not possess critical editions despite several impressions in commercial form. Considering his importance, Ibn Sînâ should perhaps be the first Islamic philosopher to have all his works edited critically in one series, in the form of the *Opera Omnia* of major Western thinkers. Likewise the writings of Ibn Sînâ's students such as Bahmanyâr, Ibn Zayla, al-Ma^{c}ṣûmî, and al-Juzjânî need to be assembled and edited in a collection.

A number of Ibn Sînâ's contemporaries, like Ibn Sînâ himself, were both philosophers and scientists. Such men as al-Bîrûnî, Ibn al-Haytham, and the like need to have their surviving philosophical works that are particularly important edited and studied. This holds true also for later philosopher-scientists such as Naṣîr al-Dîn al-Ṭûsî and Quṭb al-Dîn al-Shîrâzî.

Two schools of Islamic philosophy which need particular attention are the Pythagorean–Hermetic and Ismâ^{c}îlî, which in fact soon converged together and ran parallel to the better-known Peripatetic school. Despite the work of Kraus, Ivanow, Corbin, Mu^{c}în, Hamdânî, Kâmil Ḥusayn, and others, a great deal of material pertaining to such figures as Jâbir Ibn Ḥayyân, Abû

Ḥâtim al-Râzî, and Naṣir-i Khusraw must be edited so that this integral part of Islamic philosophy can be known fully at last. The writings of Nâṣir-i Khusraw, all in Persian, exist in print, but nearly all of them need a critical and carefully corrected edition which would be free from the numerous errors that mar the existing texts.

As far as Islamic philosophy in Spain is concerned, many works of Ibn Bâjja have been discovered recently and need to be edited. Also the edition of Ibn Rushd's works must be continued, especially along the lines established by Bouyges, Badawî, and G. Nogales. Also works dealing with Sufi metaphysics and related to certain facets of Islamic philosophy from Ibn Masarra and Ibn Qasyî to Ibn ʿArabî, much of which remains in manuscript form, await the hand of competent scholars to make them available to the world at large.

As for post-Avicennian philosophy in the East, Suhrawardî has been edited fairly extensively, although many of his Arabic works remain in manuscript form. However, after him the major figures spanning the very fecund but as yet little studied period leading to the Safavid renaissance remain nearly completely unedited. A few works of Sayyid Ḥaydar Âmulî and Ibn Turka have appeared in modern editions recently and a few appeared in lithographed form several decades ago. But literally hundreds of major texts remain to be unearthed and edited in scholarly fashion.

As a result of the concerted effort of the past decade the Safavid period has become better known, but nearly all the texts edited have concerned Mullâ Ṣadrâ (Ṣadr al-Dîn Shîrâzî), whereas so many other major figures, such as Mîr Dâmâd, Sayyid Aḥmad ʿAlawî, Lâhîjî, Kâshânî, Qâḍî Saʿîd Qummî, and the like continue to be known by the public at large only through a small number of their writings printed usually in a noncritical manner. The same holds true for the later period up to the present day. Except for Sabziwârî and M. Âshtiyânî, no other authors have been edited critically. The anthology of S. J. Âshtiyânî and Corbin is, however, providing at least a sample of this vast field that awaits to be explored more fully in the future.

The field of Islamic philosophy in India also has been sadly neglected. Manuscripts belonging to the philosophers of Farangi-mahal or the Khayrabadi school or those at the court of Akbar who cultivated Islamic philosophy have hardly ever been edited. The few works that have appeared usually have been in lithograph form.

Parallel to the edition of texts in Arabic and Persian there is an urgent need, as already mentioned, to expand the program of translation of Islamic philosophy. In this domain some treatises of al-Kindî have been translated by Rescher and others, and a few works of al-Fârâbî by Mahdi and Dunlop during the past few years, but there must be an effort to provide a scholarly translation of al-Fârâbî's major works, namely, the *Madîna al-faḍîla* and

Al-*jam*[c] *bayn ra'yay al-ḥakîmayn*. As for Ibn Sînâ, none of the major works exists in English in complete form. At least the *Ishârât wa al-tanbîhât*, which was rendered into French by Goichon, could be put into English, as could the *Najât*, which would provide an indispensable summary of Ibn Sînâ's Peripatetic philosophy in the absence of a translation of the *Shifâ'*, which is not possible at this time. Another helpful and much needed work would be an anthology of the writings of Ibn Sînâ prepared in such a way as to be a guide in his own words to the foundations of his thought, which is so central to the whole understanding of Islamic philosophy.

The full study of Islamic philosophy as well as the metaphysical needs of many philosophers in the West today also require the translation of works of later Islamic philosophy which in fact never reached the West through Latin translations. Foremost among these are the writings of Suhrawardî and Mullâ Ṣadrâ. Some of the shorter treatises of Suhrawardî have been rendered into French and English by Corbin and Spies and one major work of Mullâ Ṣadrâ into French, again by Corbin. Also certain selections have been made available in German by Horten. What is needed, however, is a clear English translation of the *Ḥikmat al-ishrâq* of Suhrawardî and a work of Mullâ Ṣadrâ, such as *al-Shawâhid al-rubûbiyya*, which contains the whole cycle of his philosophy in fairly synoptic form. Finally, there is need of a fairly extensive anthology in English embracing the whole of Islamic philosophy.

As far as the program of translation is concerned, it is essential to make widely known the propaedeutic importance of clear translations and the unique role they play in bringing the primary sources of Islamic philosophy back to life, making firsthand contact with the words and thoughts of Muslim intellectual figures possible for those who have not mastered the Islamic languages. It is also essential to establish a set of priorities and a program through some kind of international scholarly committee that might undertake the task of coordinating and directing the effort of translation. The principles upon which the priorities should be set would include the importance of the works in question for an understanding of various Islamic philosophical schools, the importance being determined either through the significance of the author, for example, the writings of al-Fārābī and Ibn Sînâ, or the popularity of the work itself in the Islamic world throughout the centuries, such as the *Kitâb al-hidâya* of Athîr al-Dîn al-Abharî. These principles would include also the innate profundity of the work and its ability to summarize the doctrines of a particular master or school. Finally, the influence of the work upon later Islamic schools and also upon the Western intellectual tradition and its role in explaining general developments in intellectual history could be considered. In setting priorities for translation, it is important to consider also the commentaries which in certain cases are absolutely necessary for the clarification of certain passages and ideas. For example, any one who would undertake to translate the *Ḥikmat al-ishrâq* of Suhrawardî could hardly succeed without referring to the commentaries of Shahrazûrî and Quṭb al-Dîn al-Shîrâzî, not to speak of the *Glosses* of Mullâ Ṣadrâ.

* * *

In the field of the history of Islamic philosophy there must be a concentration on special periods and areas and an effort to write monographs on as yet unexplored subjects before a full-fledged history of Islamic philosophy is even possible. As far as the early period is concerned, the interaction between Islam as a religion and the intellectual heritage of antiquity, an interaction which brought Islamic philosophy into being, must be studied further from the point of view of the spiritual genius and the inner structure of Islam and of Islamic civilization. In the field of Peripatetic philosophy ᶜAmirî and his students, such as Ibn Hindû, and other figures who stood between al-Fârâbî and Ibn Sînâ must be fully studied and the thought of al-Fârâbî himself reviewed once again in the light of his recently discovered works, especially the *Kitâb al-ḥurûf*.

Ibn Sînâ's commentaries upon the Qur'an and his relationship with Suhrawardî need full investigation in the light of his own writings as well as those of his students. Also the manner in which his influence reached the other spheres of Islamic thought including *kalâm* remains to be explored. A comparative study between al-Fârâbî and Ibn Sînâ on the one hand and the Andalusian philosophers, especially Ibn Rushd and Ibn Bâjja, on the other, would reveal much about the nature of the Andalusian school and its relation to the main tradition of Islamic philosophy in the East. Also a study of the manner in which Islamic philosophy disappeared in the Western part of Islam must be reinvestigated in the light of such figures as Ibn ᶜArabî and Ibn Sabᶜîn.

Despite numerous studies on the interaction between *kalâm* and philosophy, the significance of Islamic theologians other than al-Ghazzâlî has not been fully investigated. This is particularly true of Fakhr al-Dîn al-Râzî, whose philosophical significance has received much less attention than it deserves. A series of studies on the relation between *kalâm* and philosophy at this time, based on the writings of Râzî as well as such other important theologians as Sayyid Sharîf al-Jurjânî and Saᶜd al-Dîn al-Îjî, is essential for a better understanding of both *kalâm* and philosophy in later Islamic history. A similar study is also needed for the interaction between Sufism and philosophy, starting from al-Fârâbî and reaching the latest schools of Islamic philosophy, in which philosophy and Sufi metaphysics are in fact unified.

From Naṣîr al-Dîn al-Ṭûsî on, practically every philosopher needs to be studied separately and many scholarly monographs need to be written before this terra incognita becomes fully known. For centuries the West remained oblivious to the whole intellectual and spiritual life of Islam during the past 700–800 years. Thanks to the efforts of Corbin, Izutsu, Nasr, and others, this attitude is now changing slowly. However, there is such a vast field to cover that despite the newly created interest and effort in the subject much remains to be accomplished. Even the outstanding authorities of Islamic philosophy in the East know only the peaks, only such figures as Naṣîr al-Dîn al-Ṭûsî, Mîr Dâmâd, Mullâ Ṣadrâ, and Sabziwârî, but all the terrain that connects these peaks remains to be explored by scholars in both East and West.

Likewise there is need to delve fully into the history of schools of philosophy in the Ottoman empire and analyze the work of all the commentators of Suhrawardî and Ibn ᶜArabî in that region. The same holds true for the Indian subcontinent, where at least four centuries of Islamic philosophy, from Fatḥallâh Shîrâzî and Dârâ Shukûh to figures who survived into our own day, remain practically a closed book. This is because the main trunk from which this branch issued, namely, late Islamic philosophy in Persia, has only recently begun to attract intellectual and scholarly interest outside Persia.

Also a major lacuna in the historical study of Islamic philosophy is the lack of histories of different disciplines. Despite the work of Rescher there is no thorough history of Islamic logic, not to speak of ethics, political philosophy, philosophy of nature, philosophy of art, etc. Along with monographs on specific periods and figures which would prepare the way for the composition of a full-fledged general history of Islamic philosophy, it is necessary to devote considerable effort to writing the history of Islamic logic, Islamic ethics, metaphysics, the philosophy of art, etc., so that the tradition of the various disciplines which Islamic philosophy embraces becomes clear in its own light. There is, moreover, the necessity to deal with these disciplines separately in order to show the permanence of the Islamic intellectual tradition in which the historical unfolding of ideas occurs in relation to an ever-present immutable center.

There is also the need to produce general works on Islamic philosophy which would bring it out of the isolation in which it exists today in the West. At the moment treatises on Islamic philosophy are written in such a way that they attract the attention only of specialists in Islamic or in medieval European philosophy. If well-written general works on Islamic philosophy were produced, they would attract not only the above groups of students but also those interested in metaphysics and philosophy in general. A few well-written works on the Far Eastern and Indian intellectual traditions are already producing this very effect. There is no reason why such should not be the case with Islamic philosophy.

As far as the method used to study Islamic philosophy is concerned, there is need for a major reappraisal and reevaluation. On the one hand, simply philological methods cannot serve for philosophical studies; on the other hand, the mainstream of modern European philosophy flows in a direction so opposed to the Islamic that it is not possible to apply its categories and ways of seeing things as criteria for the evaluation of Islamic philosophy. There is need to master the necessary metaphysical concepts in order to study and comprehend Islamic metaphysical teachings. Such concepts, although not opposed to historical becoming, do not limit the truth to its temporal incarnation and are able to deal with the nontemporal teachings of Islamic metaphysics on its own terms. Without doubt the question of method and approach will occupy much attention in the future, especially as Islamic philosophy becomes of greater interest to contemporary thinkers and philosophers and reaches beyond the confines of textual scholarship. Most likely, in this process the comparative method is bound to be given a major role. In any case there is a need to study the appropriate method to study Islamic philosophy in the future, a method or a series of methods which will undoubtedly be related to what is being done in the fields of religion and mysticism.

* * *

To apply the methods that exist or will be developed and to pursue research in any of the fields or periods of Islamic philosophy, there is need of certain basic tools which unfortunately do not exist yet. There is first of all no one center in either the West or the East where all the primary and secondary sources for the study of Islamic philosophy as well as microfilms of the manuscript material could be assembled. A similar center is needed in the Islamic world. Secondly, there is no separate bibliography of an exhaustive nature for Islamic philosophy, despite the efforts of such men as De Menasce and Walzer. There is need for a regular bulletin devoted solely to the bibliography of Islamic philosophy, as one finds for Western philosophy. This could be complemented by a work like the *Index Islamicus* but devoted to only Islamic philosophy and related fields and including articles in Oriental languages and books in the languages of both East and West.

Another urgent need is a veritable lexicon of philosophical vocabulary in Arabic (and also Persian), Greek, possibly Syriac, Latin, and a modern European language. Afnan, Goichon, Bouyges, and a few Eastern scholars have made a beginning but the task of composing a complete work of a reliable nature remains unaccomplished. Considering the technical nature of philosophical terminology in Islam the lack of such a lexicon remains one of the greatest impediments to research and teaching in this field.

Along with the lexicon it is necessary to have an encyclopedia of Islamic philosophy similar to the recently published *Encyclopedia of Philosophy*, or along the lines of the *Encyclopaedia Universalis* but on a smaller scale, which would be devoted completely to the doctrines, schools, and figures of Islamic philosophy treated in the manner in which the few articles on Islamic thought found in existing encyclopedias approach their subject in the limited space allotted to them.

With these tools at hand research in Islamic philosophy would certainly be facilitated, but the creative aspect of this research must come not from a simple imitation of what has gone on already but from charting new directions which are in fact old in that they reflect the traditional structure of Islamic philosophy itself.

One of these new directions is the application of the interdisciplinary approach to Islamic philosophy, without forgetting of course the basic necessity of studying pure Islamic philosophy in itself. Islamic philosophy has played a major role throughout Islamic history in many other domains of Islamic civilization such as Sufism, art, science, theology, anthropology, sociology, political thought, and literature. Many facets of Islamic studies cannot be understood without this interaction in mind. How little has the philosophy of Islamic art been studied in the West, or the philosophy of Islamic science, or the interaction between philosophy and literature. Even in fields such as theology and political science where some studies have been made by such men as Horovitz, Wolfson, and Gardet for theology, and Strauss, Mahdi, E. I. J. Rosenthal, and Binder for political science, much remains to be done. In the field of sociology the intimate link between this discipline and philosophy has rarely been investigated except in the case of Ibn Khaldûn, where the nexus is too evident to be ignored. A great deal of more advanced study as well as future research is bound to rely on an interdisciplinary basis in order to enable the student or scholar to develop means of better understanding both philosophy and the facets of Islamic civilization with which it has had creative interaction.

Another important way to chart a new course in Islamic studies is to study its content as living wisdom and knowledge rather than as ideas of solely historical interest. The breakdown of so much of modern philosophy and its inability to play a meaningful role in the intellectual quest of so many people in the West today is turning a number of today's most intelligent students toward the study of Oriental metaphysics as a source of living wisdom rather than as surviving samples of the ideas of a bygone species belonging to earlier stages of the so-called "evolution" of man. Future success in cultivating Islamic philosophy in the West will depend to a large extent on the degree to which scholars can succeed in presenting it as a living intellectual tradition. In fact, in the Islamic world itself the main task is to expound Islamic philosophy as a way of thinking about perennial questions in a manner that is of permanent interest. Without such a transformation it will become even more difficult to attract good students to the field. And without good students, who are the future scholars, no project can be carried out.

Of course the problem exists as to where such students should be trained. Should Islamic philosophy be taught in the philosophy departments or departments of Islamic studies? Until now a paralyzing compartmentalization has separated the two; in most places one group of students is trained in the necessary linguistic tools and another in the needed philosophical background. This particular problem does not exist for the most part in Muslim countries, but in the West, where Arabic and Persian are completely unknown before students enter college, it is essential to create interdepartmental programs between philosophy and Middle Eastern languages even at the undergraduate level, offering to students the possibility of training in Arabic and philosophy, in the same way that some study Greek or Latin and philosophy together.

For many centuries and until very recently interest in Islamic philosophy in the West was closely allied to interest in scholasticism and especially Thomism, which was the dominant theology of the Catholic Church, and even now this relationship survives to a certain extent. However, with the gradual diminishing today of the importance of Thomistic theology and the rise of the revolutionary pseudotheology of Teilhard de Chardin in so many circles, and also with the remarkable thirst of the young for spiritual experience and vision, the best way to attract outstanding students to the field of Islamic philosophy is not to present only its Peripatetic half with the message locked in syllogistic form, which many of the best minds eschew and seek to avoid. Islamic philosophy must also present its other half, its Oriental half as reflected in such figures as Suhrawardî and Ṣadr al-Dîn Shîrazî, for whom true philosophy is inseparable from spiritual experience and vision of the supernal world. Moreover, the ultimate unity of the Islamic philosophical tradition, both Eastern and Western, must always be kept in mind. Fortunately the immense richness of Islamic philosophy is such that despite the change of the past decade or two in the intellectual interests of Western man and from a certain point of view because of it, this philosophy can still attract men into its fold, and in fact much more so than before. But this is possible provided Islamic philosophy is studied in the West on its own terms, not only as a chapter of Western intellectual history, but as an authentic intellectual tradition with branches spreading to the East and the West and stretching from the rigor of rational analysis to the joy of spiritual vision and beatitude.

BIBLIOGRAPHY

Afnan, S. *Avicenna: His Life and Works.* London: Allen & Unwin, 1958.

Alonso, M. *Teologia de Averroes.* Madrid and Granada: Maestre, 1947.

Anawati, G. C., and L. Gardet. *Introduction à la théologie musulmane.* Paris: J. Vrin, 1948.

Asín Palacios, M. *La escatologia Musulmana en la Divina Comedia*, 2nd ed. Madrid: Masetre, 1943.

Badawî, A. *al-Aflâṭûniyya al-muḥdathat ᶜind al-ᶜarab: Neoplatonici apud Arabes*. Cairo: 1947.

———. *Aristû ᶜind al-ᶜarab*. Cairo: al-Nahḍah, 1947.

———. *La Transmission de la philosophie grecque au monde arabe*. Paris: Vrin, 1968.

Burckhardt, T. *Moorish Culture in Spain*. A. Jaffa, trans. London: Allen & Unwin, 1972.

Carra de Vaux, B. *Les Penseurs de l'Islam*. 5 vols. Paris: Geuthner, 1929–1926.

Corbin, H. *Avicenna and the Visionary Recital*. W. Trask, trans. New York: Pantheon Books, 1960.

———. *En Islam iranien*. 4 vols. Paris: Gallimard, 1971–1972.

——— (with the collaboration of S. H. Nasr and O. Yahya). *Histoire de la philosophie islamique*. Vol. 1. Paris: Gallinard, 1964.

———. *Terre céleste et corps de résurrection*. Paris: Corrêa, Buchet, Chastel, 1961.

Cruz Hernandez, M. *La filosofia arabe*. Madrid: Revista de Occidente, 1963.

———. *Historia de la filosofia hispano-musulmana*. 2 vols. Madrid: Asociasión Española para el Progresso de las Ciencias, 1957.

De Boer, T. J. *Geschichte der Philosophie in Islam*. Stuttgart: 1901. English ed: *The History of Philosophy in Islam*, E. R. Jones, trans. London: Luzac, 1903.

Duhem, P. *Le Système du monde*. 10 vols. Paris: A. Hermann et fils, 1913–1917, 1954, and 1964.

Fakhry, M. *History of Islamic Philosophy*. New York: Columbia Univ. Press, 1970.

Gabrieli, F. *Alfarabius compendium legum Platonis*. London: institutii Walburgiani, 1952.

Gauthier, L. *Ibn Roshd (Averroes)*. Paris: Presses universitaires de France, 1948.

Georr, K. H. *Les Catégories d'Aristote dans leur versions syro-arabes*. Beirut: Institut français de Damas, 1948.

Gilson, E. "Les Sources gréco-arabes de l'Augustinisme Avicénnissant," *Archives d'histoire doctrinale et littéraire du moyen Âge*, **4** (1929), 1–149.

Goichon, A. M. *La Distinction de l'essence et de l'existence d'aprés Ibn Sina*. Paris: Desclée de Brouwer, 1937.

Horten, M. *Die Philosophie des Islam*. Leipzig: Reinhardt, 1924.

Hourani, G. *Agreement of Philosophy and Religion* (trans. of *Faṣl al-maqāl of Ibn Rushd*). London: Luzac, 1961.

Ibn Rushd, A. *Tafsîr mâ baᶜd al-tabîᶜa*. With Introduction by M. Bouyges, ed. Beirut: Impr. Catolique, 1967.

Iqbal, M. *The Development of Metaphysics in Persia*. London: Luzac, 1908.

Izutzu, T. *A Comparative Study of the Key Philosophical Concepts in Sufism and Taoism*. 2 vols. Tokyo: Keio Institute of Cultural and Linguistic Studies, 1966.

———. *The Concept and Reality of Existence*. Tokyo: Keio Inst. of Cultural and Linguistic Studies, 1966.

Kraus, P. *Jâbir Ibn Ḥayyân*. Cairo: El-Khargi, 1942–1943.

Madkour, I. *L'Organon d'Aristote dans le monde arabe*. Paris: Vrin, 1934 and 1969.

———. *La place d'al-Fârâbî dans l'école philosophique musalmane*. Paris: Maisonneuve, 1934.

Mahdi, M. *al-Fârâbî's Philosophy of Plato and Aristotle*. Glencoe, Ill: the Free Press, 1962.

———. *Ibn Khaldûn's Philosophy of History*. London: Allen & Unwin, 1957.

Massignon, L. *La Passion d'al-Hallaj*. Paris: Geuthner, 1922.

Munk, S. *Mélanges de philosophie juive et arabe*. Paris: Franck, 1859.

Naṣîr-i, Khusraw. *Jâmi^c al-ḥikmatain*. H. Corbin and M. Mo^cin, eds. French prolegomena by H. Corbin. Tehran-Paris: Bibliothèque Iranienne, 1953.

Nasr, S. H. *An Introduction to Islamic Cosmological Doctrines*. Cambridge: Belknap Press of Harvard U. Press, 1964.

———. *Islamic Studies*. Beirut: Librairie du Liban, 1966.

———. *Islamic Philosophy in Contemporary Persia: A Survey of Activity during the Past Two Decades*. Utah: University of Utah, Research Monograph No. 3, 1972.

———. *Science and Civilization in Islam*. Cambridge: Harvard U. Press, 1970.

———. *Three Muslim Sages*. Cambridge: Harvard U. Press, 1968.

Pines, S. *Beiträge zur islamischen Atomenlehre*. Berlin: Gräfenhainichen, 1936.

Quadri, G. *La filosofia degli arabi nel suo fiore*. Firenze: 1930. French trans. by R. Huret, *La Philosophie arabe dans l'Europe médiéval*. Paris: Payot, 1947 and 1960.

Rahman, F. *Avicenna's Psychology*. London: Oxford U. Press, 1952.

Renan, E. *Âverroes et l'averroïsme*. Paris: Levy, 1882.

Rescher, N. *The Development of Arab Logic*. Pittsburgh: U. of Pittsburgh Press, 1964.

Rosenthal, F. *Ahmad b. al-Ṭayyib as-Sarak̲h̲sî*. New Haven: American Oriental Society, 1943.

Schuon, F. *Dimensions of Islam*. P. Townsend, trans. London: Allen & Unwin, 1970.

———. *Logic and Transcendence*. P. Townsend, trans. New York: 1975. French original: Paris: Editions traditionnelles, 1972.

———. *Understanding Islam*. D. M. Matheson, trans. London: Allen & Unwin, 1963.

Sharif, M. M., ed. *A History of Muslim Philosophy*. 2 vols. Wiesbaden: O. Harrassowitz, 1963–1966.

Spies, O. and S. Khatak. *Three Treatises on Mysticism*. Stuttgart: Kohlhammer, 1935.

Steinschneider, M. *Die Arabische Übersetzungen aus dem Griechischen*. Graz: Akademische Druck u-Verlagsanstalt, 1960.

Suhrawardî. *Opera Metaphysica et Mystica*. Vol. 1. H. Corbin, ed., with French prolegomena. Istanbul: Maarif Matbaası, 1945. Vol. 2, H. Corbin, ed., with French prolegomena. Tehran-Paris: Institut Franco-Iranien, 1952. Vol. 3, S. H. Nasr, ed., with intro. and French prolegomena by H. Corbin. Tehran-Paris: Bibliothèque Iranienne, 1970.

Walzer, R. *Greek into Arabic*. Cambridge: Harvard U. Press, 1962.

Watt, W. M. *Islamic Philosophy and Theology*. Edinburgh: Univ. Press, 1962.

CHAPTER EIGHT

Linguistics

GERNOT L. WINDFUHR

Having withstood or at least passed through the grinding interrogations by my fellow authors–compilers, the Research and Training Committee of MESA, and a few specialist colleagues, I acknowledge a certain feeling of relief in presenting this survey. In a way the essential problem, or rather challenge, in writing this chapter is epitomized by the pun implicit in the task set forward, to compose an orientation paper on one Orientalistic discipline.

For centuries the Orient has been the object of fascination, and of the search for "origins" and deeper truth. Thus the "language" of the Bible, the Qur'an, and Muslim philosophy, were the first and main targets of Orientalistic scholarship. The extraordinarily high hopes toward the end of the eighteenth century of learning about ancient wisdom from the first translation of Zarathushtra's Gathas, and the disappointment thereafter demonstrate best that the innate basic difficulty in understanding the Orient is the difficulty in properly understanding its "language," i.e., its grammars as well as the higher linguistic levels of "semantics" and "Oriental logic."

It seems that most, if not all, of us "Orientalists" have been drawn to this area by our conscious or subconscious empathy for it. Yet today we are faced with at least two crucial changes; first, the Orient is no longer the center of the humanistic universe, and second, the all-out humanistic approach which attempted to understand the area in all its aspects has given way to a more skeptical approach. Although the ultimate objective may still be a universal insight in the area (certain suggestions are made below), there is neither a theoretical nor methodological framework yet for such a global approach. Thus Orientalistic research has arrived at a phase where guidance and orientation are sought from individual humanistic and social disciplines. There is little wonder that linguistics, probably earlier and to a greater extent than any other humanistic science, has contributed to, and is subject to, this process toward reorientation and theoretization. Also, more than in other disciplines, one observes new linguistic theories or variants of theories following each other in ever-increasing acceleration, patterns in a kaleidoscope changing with ever more frantic turns. The fascination with the Orient is giving way to the fascination with patterns, the "paradigms" of the disciplines, and the new insights made possible. But perhaps the most crucial development in linguistics is that for the first time in recent history questions are asked about itself as a discipline, its interrelationship with other disciplines, and its position and justification in relation to higher levels of human thought. Accordingly, a good part of this paper is an attempt to ask questions about linguistics in Middle Eastern studies.

The challenge facing the linguist of Middle Eastern languages, and possibly his most important contribution, is to find a way to uphold his double orientation, to the discipline and to the area.

So far there are not very many Middle Eastern linguists who have adopted the guideline of linguistic theory, and even fewer who have contributed to the further development of the general discipline. A new paradigm, or paradigms, not only requires the acquisition of a new language, the "linguese" of today, but more importantly, it implies radical shifts of viewpoint, and the equally radical selection of subjects "worth studying." This in turn affects to a considerable degree research in, as well as the teaching of, Middle Eastern languages and linguistics. Even more, it affects communication between scholars in the field and, on a different level, the job market and funding.

Approach

Major efforts are being made to cover and summarize the linguistics of the world, including of course the Middle East, by such series as *Handbuch der Orientalistik*, *Current Trends in Linguistics*, and the new *Janua Linguarum. Series Critica*. This survey cannot be as detailed as those, nor is it intended to be. Instead, the emphasis here is on some aspects that have been less highlighted: first, the identification of main trends and problems common to the various areas of Middle Eastern linguistics, and second, suggestions for future directions of scholarship.

It should be recognized that I do not feel like the high priest of Stonehenge, far ahead, far from, and far above, the folks of my age. In fact, this survey does not represent entirely my own opinion. Rather, it is based on the analysis of the more or less detailed observations of those 40 scholars from all walks of Middle Eastern linguistics who answered a questionnaire that I sent out. This inquiry was followed by a workshop of 10 American Middle Eastern linguists held at Ann Arbor. Since most answers were received from American and, less so, German scholars, and very few from other countries, including

Middle Eastern countries, there may be a certain preponderance of the American outlook.

The most interesting revelation emanating from this preparatory investigation was that for the majority of the respondents one of the most important problems, besides the level of achievement in the various subareas of Middle Eastern linguistics, was a matter of professional "setting" and communication between scholars: between those in the various languages within Near or Middle East departments and, most importantly, between linguists and nonlinguists who deal with Middle Eastern languages.

In order to provide the proper framework, the discussion of the present state of Middle Eastern linguistics, as well as suggestions for future research, is preceded by an outline of the area and scope of Middle Eastern languages, a brief statement of the concerns of linguistics as a general discipline, and some major theoretical approaches.

Those outlines and statements, like the chapter in general, attempt to achieve a balance of description for the insider as well as for the interested outsider with regard to both the general discipline of linguistics and Middle Eastern linguistics. At the same time, there is an attempt to represent the many and various opinions of specialist colleagues. I acknowledge that such a delicate task is all but impossible to accomplish to the satisfaction of all, and I ask the reader to accept my quite personal interpretation as a stimulus for discussion rather than as a final and finite set of postulates and rules.

Finally, I apologize to those of my colleagues who so kindly answered my questionnaire for not identifying each of their observations, mainly because many observations were reflected in several, if not most, of the letters or communications received. Indeed, this very fact stresses our common concern. It was decided that direct citations be made only where a particular, longer paragraph from a letter fits directly into the context of this survey. All respondents whose observations were particularly helpful are acknowledged by name.

Area and Scope of Middle Eastern Languages

The Middle East is the area of intersection of three main culturally, ethnically, and linguistically definable groups: Afro-Asiatic (Hamito-Semitic), Indo-European, and Altaic, each represented there by dominant subgroups: Semitic, Iranic, and Turkic, and in turn, by the dominant languages of these subgroups, Arabic, Persian, and Turkish. Each of these three languages reflects the successive political domination of the Islamic Middle East up to the beginning of this century.

However, even though the advent of Islam resulted in several changes in the sociopolitical superstructure, these changes did not break the linguistic continuum in terms of dialectology. Although it resulted in the establishment of these three languages as new *Hochsprachen*, among others, they are but members of unbroken systems that existed long before Islam. Middle Eastern linguistics therefore cannot be confined to Islamic times only. In fact, linguists working in this area have an advantage over specialists in most other areas: they can study linguistic dynamics over a period of some 5000 years.

MAJOR LANGUAGE FAMILIES. The following is only a brief survey of the scope in time and space of the three major language families participating in the Middle Eastern *Kultur- und Sprachbund.*

The emphasis is on the main members of the Semitic, Iranic, and Turkic families and, again, within the subgroups on Arabic, Persian, and Turkish.

Unlike the Indo-European family, which is mostly located outside the Middle East proper, the *Afro-Asiatic* family is localized in the Middle East itself. Its members are Semitic, Egyptian, Cushitic (from which "West Cushitic" or "Omotic" is probably to be distinguished), Chadic, and Berber. The oldest records, Egyptian and Semitic (represented by Akkadian) date back some 5000 years. The records of the other Afro-Asiatic members begin only in the last couple of centuries. The largest branch is Semitic, which is spread over the entire area of Afro-Asiatic; it is subgrouped into a Northeast group, Mesopotamian (represented by long-extinct Akkadian); a Northwest group in Syria–Palestine [Canaanite (Hebrew and extinct Phoenician-Punic), extinct Ugaritic, and Aramaic-Syriac (with exclaves in Iraq, Iran, etc.)]; and a Southwest group consisting of North Arabian (Arabic), South Arabian, and Ethiopic.

Arabic, in turn, is spread from the Arabian Peninsula west over North Africa to the Atlantic Ocean, north along the Levant to Iraq, with exclaves in the Caucasus, Iran, Afghanistan, and Central Asia (Uzbekistan), on Cyprus, as well as in colonies on islands in the Indian Ocean. At one time it had spread into Spain, and an Arabic superstrate has resulted in Maltese.

Although the Arabs were mentioned by the Assyrians as early as the ninth century BC, the earliest Arabic inscriptions date back to the first centuries of the Christian era. There was a highly developed literary koine in pre-Islamic Arabic, which ultimately served as the basis for Qur'anic and Classical Arabic. One line of scholarship assumes that sedentary Arabic dialects are based on a military koine developed by the intermingling Arabs during their military campaigns in the spread of Islam; Bedouin tribes later spread over the desert areas of the Arab world, implanting a Bedouin type of Arabic which is easily distinguishable from sedentary Arabic.

Semitic languages such as Akkadian, later Aramaic, and, after Islam, Arabic were official languages and lingua francas in the Middle East.

The *Indo-European* (-Hittite) group in the Middle East is represented by extinct Hittite, the Indo-European languages of Anatolia, Armenian, and Aryan. The latter is represented by the Iranic, the Dardic-Kafir, and the Indo-Aryan groups. Although the latter is mainly located on the Indian subcontinent, a minor Indo-Aryan group, Gypsy, has spread throughout the Middle East and the world.

The split of the Aryans into a western group, which moved into Iran, and an eastern group, which moved into India, made Northwest India a cultural border area between the Middle East and Southeast Asia. Indo-Aryan on the Indian subcontinent, Dardic-Kafir in the Pamir-Hindukush, and Armenian in the Caucasus may be regarded as bordering the Middle East, but Iranian constitutes an integral part of it.

The record of the diachronic and dialectical development of *Iranic* stretches over some 2500 years. Three main stages can be distinguished, beginning with *Old Iranic*: Old Persian is recorded since the establishment of the Empire of the Achaemenids in the sixth century BC; Avestan, the language of the first Zoroastrian religious texts, goes back to about the same time. *Middle Iranic* developed between the fourth and third centuries BC. Seven Middle Iranic languages are known: two West Iranic, Middle Persian and Parthian; and five East Iranic, Sogdian, Saka, Khwarezmian, Bactrian (known only since the last decade), and Kushan-Hephthalite. The *modern* stage of Iranic languages dates from the advent of Islam in the seventh century AD. The West Iranic languages are Persian, Kurdish, and Baluchi; another large group, the so-called Median and Central dialects; and smaller groups. The East Iranic languages are Pashto (one of the two major languages of Afghanistan) and several other smaller groups in that country and the Pamir; Yaghnobi (in Soviet Tajikistan, the only survivor of Sogdian); and Ossetic in the Caucasus.

West Iranic languages, i.e., Achaemenid Old Persian, Parthian, and then Sasanian Persian, were the official languages of the respective pre-Islamic empires of the Middle East. Modern Persian has been the lingua franca for the northeastern part of the Middle East and Central Asia for more than 1000 years and was the official language of the Mogul empire in India until the advent of the British. This West Iranic language, Persian, developed three main variants: Persian in Iran, Dari in Afghanistan, and Tajiki in Soviet Tajikistan. Persian thus overlaid most of the Iranic speaking territory.

The range of recorded Iranic stretches from Mesopotamia (some exclaves are found in Oman), Anatolia, and the Caucasus through Iran into Central Asia and India. At one time, Iranic languages were found deep in Chinese Turkistan and north of the Caucasus.

Iranic overlaps with Turkic over much of its area, and it borders on Semitic in the northern half of the fertile crescent.

Like Indo-European, most of the *Altaic* languages are located outside the

Middle East proper, in Central Asia and Siberia. Its main members are Turkic, the oldest record of which dates from the seventh century AD, Mongol, and Tungus. Turkic is the largest group, with seven members: Chuvash, Oghuz (SW), Qipchaq (NW), Uighur-Chaghatai (SE), South Siberian (NE), Yakut, and Khalaj. Of these, Khalaj is located in the center of Iran and Uighur in Southwestern Central Asia. But the most important Altaic languages of the Middle East are the members of the Oghuz subgroup. According to Doerfer, this group is divided into a western group consisting of Osman Turkish (i.e., *the* Turkish) and Azerbaijani and Qashqai in western and northern Iran and in the eastern Caucasus; and an eastern group, Khorasani and Turkmen in Northeastern Iran, Afghanistan, and Uzbekistan; it is also spread into Southwestern Central Asia. For 900 years, Turkic and Mongolian dynasties were dominant in Iran and India, in Iran until 50 years ago. Turks once ruled the Balkans, as well as Egypt and part of North Africa.

Turkish is thus the southwesternmost projection of Altaic, and the population center of Altaic is still the southern and central steppes of the USSR. Over large parts of their extension, i.e., eastern Anatolia, Iran, Afghanistan, and Southwestern Central Asia, Altaic languages have been in symbiotic contact with Iranic languages for some 1000 years as well as with Slavic languages in the Balkans. There are some remaining settlements in Afghanistan speaking a Mongolian–Persian dialect.

OTHER LANGUAGE FAMILIES. The aforementioned language families represent successive waves of Semitization, Iranization, and Turkization of the Middle East. It is worthwhile to at least note here that there are other, mostly extinct, languages; there is Sumerian, which profoundly influenced Akkadian; Urartaean, in the later Armenian area; and Elamite, which was an official language before and during the time of the Old Persian Achaemenids. The family affiliations of these languages are unknown, although very recent comparative studies link up Elamite with the Dravidian language family now in India.

Brahui in Southeastern Iran is the only survivor of Dravidian in the Middle East proper (the remaining Dravidian speakers moved into central and south India). Finally, there are the Caucasian languages, such as Georgian, and their splinter settlements in Turkey, Iran, and other Middle East countries.

Linguistics and Some Adjacent Disciplines

Thus one of the basic phenomena of Middle Eastern linguistics is the complex pattern of intersecting languages and language groups in time and space; and dialectology has been an important discipline in Middle Eastern linguistics.

At the same time language is a social phenomenon, a fact that has not always been recognized in Middle Eastern studies (or elsewhere). Languages do not exist in the abstract but are part of the dynamics of social groups. *Sociolinguistics* is one of the interdisciplinary approaches that only recently has regained the focus of attention. It studies linguistic groups, and the social/geographic conditions of linguistic change and/or consolidation; thus, it studies among others, the causes and courses of the development of regional standards and national languages; diglossia; pidginization and creolization; and code-switching, that is, the change of language and linguistic behavior depending on the person addressed.

The actual locus of those interference patterns is the individual psyche. Again, *psycholinguistic studies* are rare or absent in Middle Eastern linguistics, that is, studies such as speech and perception, speech-act phenomena, language acquisition, disruption of speech such as aphasia and so forth.

Of all the disciplines intersecting with linguistics it is *literature* as verbal art and craft that has been studied fairly intensively, even though the linguistic aspect of this interrelationship has not sufficiently been elucidated. The reason for this attention to literature is found in the medieval trivium of grammar, rhetoric, and dialectics, as well as in the contemporary theory of texts. The intimate connection between the two disciplines is further evident in *stylistics*, which studies the peculiarities of linguistic features of individual works, authors, and periods.

Similarly, the *philosophical* approach to language is founded on medieval tradition as well as on modern *Sprachphilosophie* and semasiology, semiotics and semantics which investigate the correlation between language as a system of signs and reality, content, and context.

For the last ten years or so until recently the discussion of the logical, formal-abstract theoretical problems of linguistics has overshadowed other aspects of linguistic studies, the main cause for the antagonism of many linguists, as will be briefly shown below.

LEVELS AND ASPECTS OF LINGUISTIC STUDY. Not unlike other disciplines, linguistic research can be described as marked by the dialectic cycle of observation, hypothesizing, verification, or modification of the theorems by renewed focused observation. Ideally, theorems or hypotheses are first set up for individual languages, resulting in the establishment of the "grammars" of those languages; these may be called their theories. Next, general linguistics derives general theorems and hypotheses from insights based on such individual grammars and attempts to establish a general theory of linguistics.

It need not be particularly stressed that actual linguistic research is a process of interaction between these levels, and that in terms of scholarship there are linguists who concentrate on research on the higher abstract level of general linguistic theory as well as linguists who concentrate on research on individual languages. Thus the latter are "specialists" investigating individual languages to the utmost detail, and the former are less interested in every detail of individual languages than in particular features or rules in more than one language. Ideally, language specialists are also general linguists, either applying insights of general linguistics to their languages or utilizing features of their languages to contribute to general linguistic theory.

GRAMMATICAL LEVELS. Linguistic theories vary as to the number and interrelationship of grammatical levels. The following is a brief list of such levels (their "definition" here is to be understood as a rough approximation only): *phonetics*, the study of the acoustic and articulatory properties of sounds; *phonology*, the study of the language's specific system of sounds, e.g., the pharyngeals (or emphatics) of Arabic; *morphology*, the study of the structure of words and of word classes, such as the root and pattern system of Semitic; *syntax*, the study of the structure of phrases, clauses, and sentences, such as word order or subject–verb agreement, or subordination; *discourse analysis*, the study that addresses itself to the problems of structures larger than the sentence, e.g., the transition between paragraphs, or plot structure; *lexicon*, the study of words as units of meaning; and *semantics*, the study of the interrelationship between language and meaning on all levels.

These levels are studied either within the system of a language at one point in time, i.e., synchronically, or in comparison with earlier stages of that language, i.e., diachronically. Besides, dialectology studies these levels in comparison with dialects belonging to the same language or language group spread over geographical space, or dialects distinguishing socially definable groups; an important subfield of Middle East linguistics such as etymology may thus be defined as combining the study of lexicon, semantics, the diachronic aspect, and cultural history.

SOME MAJOR THEORIES. It should be understood that although much insight has been gained during the last 100 years or so, linguistics is still in an early stage of development. Historically speaking, there has been a series of major new "theories," each of which is based on the insights of its predecessors. There can be observed an interesting dialectical process which may be briefly outlined here (not all theories can be discussed here, such as Hjelmslev's glossematics or Pike's tagmemics, etc.). "Traditional" or "Latin" grammar was the first in the medieval trivium of the liberal arts, i.e., grammar, rhetoric, and dialectics. It described languages according to a preconceived, "logical" system of language, for which, for all practical purposes, Latin grammar provided the model. (Similarly, Arabic grammar provided the model for traditional Middle East grammars.) As such, traditional grammar was largely prescriptive and normative, and concerned with correct speech.

Perhaps the major revolutionary change introduced by Western linguistics was the Humboldtian insight that languages are not static, but are organisms that change. Comparative–historical grammar developed this new concept, its objective being to identify and specify the "genetic" relationship between languages and language families, and to reconstruct the common ancestor from which the individual languages and dialects could be shown to have developed through a series of sound changes. This led to the great pioneering work in Indo-European linguistics.

The major subsequent breakthrough was largely due to Saussure, about the turn of the century, when he introduced the notion of synchrony, implying that languages are complex systems which function at one point in time, i.e., are "synchronic" systems at any of their stages, and should be studied as such. Diachronic linguistics then studies the interrelationship and the systematic changes that occur between these stages.

Structural linguistics can be identified as the systematization and solidification of the methodology and theory of synchronic linguistics, epitomized in the United States by Bloomfield's *Language* (1933). Structural linguistics developed the notion of the phoneme and morpheme, the phoneme being determined as the minimal unit of sound that suffices to distinguish one morpheme from other morphemes in a given language (such as English *b*it vs. *p*it) and which is defined bi-uniquely against every other phoneme of that language; the morpheme is defined as the minimal meaningful sequence of phonemes, and may be a word or part of a word (e.g., case endings).

It was these two levels of linguistics that attracted the main emphasis of structural grammar and that were further developed; for the levels of syntax and semantics, and for the diachronic aspect, no methodology or theoretical model were developed, but were left for future development. The subsequent major step based on the insights of structural grammar was brought forth by *transformational grammar*, which addressed itself to the very problem of syntax and the interrelationship between "surface" structure and "deep" structure, i.e., between the "underlying" or implicit syntax and the actual utterance. As an example, one may cite the by now famous sentence, "Flying planes can be dangerous," a sentence which has two readings, "To fly planes can be dangerous," and "Planes that fly can be dangerous"; i.e., here two different underlying sentences are "transformed" into identical sequences on the "surface."

The process by which "underlying" sentences are "surfaced," i.e., the sequence and order of the set of rules that are applied to the underlying forms, is understood as the "transformational" "generative" process. Transformational linguistics rapidly developed its theoretical and methodological basis. One of the most important contributions is that it devised a model by which it was possible clearly to describe and explain such differences as exemplified above, differences which were always understood but for which no way had ever been developed to investigate and to describe them in a systematic, precise, nonintuitive fashion, to cite an observation by Hetzron.

Transformational grammar generally did not consider semantics; the "semantic component" of grammar is considered to be simply inserted into the well-formed syntactic chain. Syntax is the creative component; it interprets the sentence. *Generative semantics* (a cover term for a multiplicity of approaches including transformational) attempts to overcome interpretative syntax and to demonstrate the priority of interpretative semantics. Syntax is predetermined by the "natural logic" of the semantic input. It can be derived directly from the selectional and cooccurrence properties of semantic classes. This allows for generalizations about those properties. For example, since the semantic predicate KNOW is implied in "forget," the latter shows the same selectional restrictions as KNOW itself; this implication explains the fact that a sentence like "*he forgot that America was discovered in 1950" is wrong just as "*he knows that America was discovered in 1950" is wrong, since their shared semantic predicate KNOW requires that its complement be true (asterisk indicates "wrong sentence"). In practice most studies of generative semantics focus on very small semantic sets; yet even though fragmentary, the semantic explanations for a multitude of syntactic irregularities hitherto unexplainable are of the highest value, especially for the "specialist," not only for applying the insights to his own linguistic research but, perhaps more importantly, also for teaching his language.

Transformational-generative grammar can be viewed as representing the final stages in the full cycle from the logical approach to language in classical and medieval times to similar concepts in our days. It cannot be denied that it gave the study of linguistics an impetus it rarely had before. At the same time it can now be considered a dialectically essential episode in linguistic thinking that is fast turning to aspects of language which transformational-generative theories neglected.

GLOTTODYNAMICS. Generativists, perhaps more concretely than others, have begun to recognize the basic problem in linguistics—the fact that language is non-discrete. Binary and other distinctions are embedded, so to speak, in a mesh of continua. The new search for a theory of speech-act and its "presuppositions" is only part of what appears to me, among others, to be a major reorientation in linguistics toward a new comprehensive vista which may be called "glottodynamics." It could be circumscribed as an approach to cope with the nondiscreteness of language in terms of variables of quantitative tendencies and the correlations of continua rather than in terms of the correlation of discrete units. This new development is already visible in many studies by sociolinguists. As one of the first pioneering "dynamic" studies in dialectology one may cite Herzog (1965). In fact glottodynamics, as the study of systematic variations and change, will integrate the study of genetic relationships and dialect geography with sociolinguistics. In general terms, it would be an integrated study of the function of language in geographical, temporal, and social space and interaction, and the conditions of changes and the reflections thereof in grammatical space.

Of course, the approaches of sociolinguistics and diglossia studies are only now beginning to be discussed on a larger level, even in the well explored languages of the West. Obviously, such a "grand total" approach to glottodynamics and the development of a unified theory are still far from reality, but they pose an extraordinary challenge. The 1973 Linguistic Institute of the Linguistic Society of America, under the significant motto "Language in Society," and the 1974 meeting of Societas Linguistica Europaea under the motto "Intralingual Variety and Interlinguistic Contrast" are the visible mark of the reassertion in linguistics of theoretical approaches that turn attention away from the narrow "structural"-formal consideration of much of recent linguistics toward the function of language in complex social groups (Hymes, 1974). As probably the most revolutionary articles toward the understanding of language and linguistic change one may cite Weinreich, Labov, and Herzog (1968) and Chen and Wang (1975). It is with the larger aim in mind that the various contributing aspects just mentioned deserve priority in research.

PHILOLOGY AND LINGUISTICS. At this point, one may at least try to delineate philology as opposed to linguistics. The connotations of philology vary considerably. In the most general usage, it implies all studies of the "texts" of cultures, and their history, as exemplified in the *Grundriss der Iranischen Philologie* and *Philologiae Turcicae Fundamenta*, only the first volumes are devoted to language studies. Philology is thus much more comprehensive than linguistics, and not a discipline as such, but an overall approach of research in the humanities.

With regard to the linguistic aspects of philological research, it is fair to say that philology has as its main objective the extraction and affirmation of linguistic data from texts in most scrupulous detail, and its exhaustive codification and compilation. This recovery procedure thus provides the basic data for further analytical and descriptive studies.

As J. Malone has observed, linguists have often overlooked the fact that the data provided by philological groundwork must be regarded as analogous to the data gathered by the linguist during fieldwork or working with an informant. Modern linguistic attitudes, especially as concern area studies, have to date overemphasized one aspect of data soliciting and collecting, namely, the synchronic aspect of fieldwork on spoken languages. They have virtually neglected the other aspect, namely, the "diachronic" aspect of "fieldwork" involving centuries of written materials. And this means, essentially, philological research. This neglect is, of course, an excellent example of the way in which the goals of a particular theory, or of a stage of it, condition the direction and scope of basic research, not unlike the way in which comparative-historical theory tended to neglect research on contemporary spoken languages. As long as linguistics is not to be limited to contemporary languages, a primary prerequisite for the linguist is not only "field methods" but a thorough competence in the methodologies of philology, as well as, among others, paleography and textual criticism. Middle Eastern linguistics appears to be one of the first fields where this is beginning to be realized, and precisely by theoretically oriented scholars (but many philologically oriented scholars have yet to realize the inverse, i.e., the prerequisite of modern theoretical skills).

The basic situation has required that the by far largest part of Middle Eastern linguistics has been devoted to philological groundwork, given the vast amount of written material, but it should be added that for many Orientalists, work has not stopped at observation, that is, with philological groundwork; rather, they have gone on to the second, descriptive stage and have produced descriptions of their findings, i.e., complete or partial grammars of the individual languages of their area. And in many instances, their descriptive achievements have reached an admirable level of sophistication (just as Orientalists, as scholars of an area, have reached equal levels in other disciplines). There is little wonder why it is that descriptions like Reckendorf's *Arabische Syntax* or Wright's *A Grammar of the Arabic Language* are still unsurpassed and have to be used for any general theoretical research. The increasing number of reprints of grammars and dictionaries even from the middle of the preceding century is clear evidence of the importance and appreciation of earlier Orientalists' research.

STATE OF MIDDLE EASTERN LINGUISTICS

Disciplinary Problems

The introduction of theoretical approaches in Middle Eastern studies has brought with it the gradual diversification of general "Oriental" studies into discipline-oriented studies, to be observed most prominently in the study of Middle Eastern languages. As an example of the diversification one may mention the increasing attention of many Orientalists to the main religions; thus Hebrew studies became divorced from Semitics, many Arabists became Islamists, and Ethiopic and Syrian studies turned to Christian literatures, leaving the "new" linguists with their interest in the modern languages.

The problem of linguistics in establishing itself within Middle Eastern studies lies in the very central position of languages in this field and its own affiliation with virtually all other disciplines. As a consequence, the domain of linguistics has not always been clearly identified. On the other hand, it must be understood that linguistics is only one discipline among many. Middle Eastern linguistics does not differ much from other areas of linguistics such as Romance and Germanic, at least with regard to the fact that traditionally little effort has been made to recognize the objectives and scope of the discipline of linguistics as such, i.e., to advance the theory as opposed to practice.

Whereas Near or Middle East departments reflect the notion of the Middle East as a culturally unified system, Middle Eastern linguistics (like literature) has not followed this old insight. Instead, linguistic research was and still is largely divided according to the model of the genetic language family tree. Consequently, surveys have usually reflected this approach. This chapter, however, is an attempt to review Middle Eastern linguistics as a whole, as the linguistics of an area; we attempt to deal holistically with linguistics as a discipline rather than limit ourselves to any particular phase of it.

DICHOTOMY IN MIDDLE EASTERN LINGUISTICS. Middle Eastern linguistics, like any area-defined linguistics, has to live with a built-in dichotomy. The observations made earlier imply a certain identification of linguists and linguistics with linguistic theory. This is in line with the disciplinary development which is also reflected by the format of this chapter. In a way, it posits the implicit priority of the theoretician over the practitioner, and has caused considerable emotional arguments on all sides. However, not everybody who considers himself a linguist is necessarily theoretically oriented, or accepts the primacy of theory. Such is especially true with linguistic research in areas like the Middle East that are less well-known than the areas where the theories have originally been developed. In such research, the theory is often felt to be of secondary importance, if important at all. Thus besides linguistics for linguistics' sake, which constitutes a relatively small section of Middle Eastern linguistics, the major part of the study of Middle Eastern languages is "special" linguistics (with three major language groups involved: Afro-Asiatic, Indo-European, and Altaic), not general theoretical linguistics. Special linguistics is invariably based on some general linguistic assumptions, though it is not always the case that these are consciously recognized and tested. Yet it is precisely the testing of postulates of general theoretical linguistics that can lead to better insights into both general and special linguistic issues.

Inversely, only the thorough knowledge of specific details will lead to reasonable theoretical conclusions. Understanding these basic premises and their mutual dependency is necessary to overcome the dichotomy that has developed in Middle Eastern linguistics. Linguistic theory cannot make up for incomplete and/or incompetent understanding of the data, nor can detail make up for incompetence in linguistic theory.

A near ideal coordination of theoretical and special research is often found at times of major changes in theoretical paradigms.

Similar to the way in which urbanization studies by archaeological anthropologists highlight the area of the Middle East today, the detailed study of the modern as well as the ancient Indo-European of the Middle East contributed decisively to the establishment of comparative-historical linguistics, and many scholars of that era were ideal examples of combined special and theoretical linguistics.

THEORETICAL PROBLEMS OF RESEARCH AND COMMUNICATION. With the advent of comparative-historical linguistics, a relatively small number of scholars had overcome the limitations of area studies and had combined the study of their individual languages and language groups with general linguistics and linguistic theory. However, as a result there developed a certain separation and loss of communication between this group—which acknowledged the priority of the discipline of linguistics—and the larger group, which continued to give priority to the linguistic-cultural context in their research. Thus, though the discipline-oriented scholars did not generally overcome the limitations of their genetic language area, as mentioned above, they did take the step onto the higher level, i.e., the discipline.

For the sake of convenience the theoretically oriented scholar of Middle Eastern languages is henceforth referred to as the "linguist," as opposed to the "Orientalist."

Although comparative-historical linguistics separated from the ways of traditional grammatical studies of Middle Eastern languages, linguistics developed new theories which in turn resulted in the separation of the new school of linguists from comparative-historical linguists and in the increasing difficulty in communication with each other. Within Middle Eastern linguistics the parting of ways began to show in the 1950s. That was the period when contemporary structural linguistic approaches, which had been neglected in most language areas for many years, began to be more widely utilized in Middle Eastern studies. Great importance must also be given to developments in the Soviet Union about the same time, where Stalin's recognition of the independence of language from "historical dialectics" instigated a revival of linguistics. There, too, the particular Soviet variant of descriptive-structural grammar began to be applied to Middle Eastern linguistics. Unlike the Soviet approach, however, the approaches by structuralist and especially by transformational-generative grammarians, which are theoretically much stricter, gave rise to severe objections. The rift appears thus to be mainly found in the West, especially in North America. It is related to basic theoretical assumptions and their limitations.

As indicated earlier, the most important innovative concept of structuralist linguistics was synchrony, i.e., the recognition that languages function as intricate and integral systems at any one point in time; consequently, the main task of linguists is to analyze and describe that working system, the synchronic structure of a language. By the 1950s, a rigorous and scrupulous methodology of analysis had been developed, when it was introduced on a larger scale into Middle Eastern linguistics. This new methodology abolished the superimposition of the "universal" system of traditional "Latin" grammar, and arranged grammars according to the system inherent in the individual languages. Illustrative of this are the many textbooks, for both literary Arabic and the dialects, produced in the United States since World War II. No wonder that many "traditionalists" did not see the radical departure, and failed to find anything new in "rearranging known data" and were appalled by the "formalism." But more importantly for the drifting apart of the two groups, the introduction of the synchronic approach soon led many linguists, given the limits to their energies and time, to the neglect of diachronic research, i.e., comparative-historical linguistics.

Another self-imposed limitation of structural linguistics which antagonized area specialists was the neglect of semantics, which was even considered by some extremists to be outside the realm of linguistics proper. Thus again much of the research Middle Eastern scholars were interested in was pushed aside.

Finally, a limitation that was not as implicit in structuralistic theory itself was that the structuralists dealt almost exclusively with modern spoken languages which they could investigate with the help of a native speaker, their "informant." As a consequence, research on earlier classical and ancient languages and with it the painstaking philological preparatory work for such research fell into neglect, often with the excuse that it was ultimately incomplete data which could not be checked by informants.

This exclusion of diachrony can nowadays be regarded as an unfortunately "antithetic" but, dialectically speaking, necessary step which was overcome in the late 1950s (especially since Weinreich) but not in Middle Eastern linguistics. Fortunately, the rigor of analysis and the necessity of basing diachronic research on sound synchronic statements has now been accepted by a good many Middle Eastern linguists.

There remain, however, many who by either their predilection or their education continue to be prestructural, and who consider structuralistic statements "horrible distortions." This is justified to some extent by all-too-quick or simplified structural statements, which mark not a few structuralistic attempts. This does not speak against the approach. However, opposition must be voiced against the tendency of many structuralists to reduce the data to "phonemic" and "morphemic" descriptions and to omit data believed to be not essential or not "emic."

The neglect of diachrony, of semantics, of classical, medieval, and ancient languages, the disregard of painstaking philological groundwork, and oversimplification all contributed to antagonizing the Orientalist. Moreover, there often emerged an unnecessary vanity on the part of the "exact linguistic theoretician" which made it difficult for others to separate the constructive advantages of the structuralist approach from its self-imposed limitations.

In counterbalance, it is in place here to recall the main objections of the structuralists to earlier approaches: the preoccupation of linguistic studies with diachronic, comparative-historical objectives; the preoccupation with the written letter and lack of distinction between letter, sound, and phoneme; the overattention to the prestigious classical literary languages combined with the notion that they were somehow monolithic and never changed; the neglect of modern spoken languages; the disregard for language-specific structure in favor of the distortion by the Procrustean bed of "traditional" grammar; moreover, the tendency to see the value of linguistic studies in the very detail rather than in broader aspects and insights, resulting in overcomplication and a good amount of trivial scholarship; and the often unnecessary vanity of the erudite insider in the esoteric niche of the special field and subfield of Middle Eastern philology-linguistics.

The objectives of structuralists can be summarized as follows. Take first things first: first analyze the modern languages in the greatest detail possible, since they can be checked with the help of informants; first learn about the synchronic structure before you compare various stages of it; first learn about the "grammar" before you tackle semantics; and first know linguistic theory and its strict and rigorous analytical methodologies.

These intradisciplinary—and resulting personal—antagonisms were passed on to transformational-generative grammar which is historically based on and utilizes structuralist concepts. One of the assumptions of that approach should be specifically mentioned here since it deeply affected linguistic research in language areas like the Middle East; it is the notion of the "competent speaker" and the claim in the earlier phases of transformational-generative grammar that insight in the grammar of a language can be achieved correctly only if the linguist is himself the native speaker, and vice versa. This untenable extreme position which has been since discarded practically rejected all research by nonnatives, and thus would declare unreliable that work which is done by most linguists of the world, including Middle Eastern scholars, namely, the study of other languages. The antagonism among linguists themselves, i.e., between structuralists and transformational-generativists, however, has more fundamental causes which, as J. Malone observed, lie in the very transformational-generative approach that was briefly sketched above. Structuralists generally fail to recognize, among other things, that the transformational-generative approach is in principle—not necessarily always in practice—considerably more "integral" than structuralism; that irrespective of other facets of the generative theory and practices, the methodology of this theory is a priori much more likely to discover linguistic *correlations*. In that sense it can be considered superior to structuralistics, since in the present state of linguistics correlations are all-important.

It is only fair to mention here Pike's (1967) tagmemic-matrix theory, which is explicitly all-inclusive in its approach and forces the linguist to consider every logically possible theoretical permutation and correlation. However, little if anything has been done on Middle Eastern languages on the basis of this theory. Another attempt to group correlations is Shaumjan's (1965) model of "applicational-generative linguistics." Doerfer used it as a basis for his own version developed on material from Altaic languages.

As of now, the generative model is still the most widely used by American linguists. In fact, it can provide an important tool in fieldwork, in that through the formulation of transformational-generative rules based on the elicited data it assists in detecting overlooked, unexplored areas as Hetzron rightly remarked. Such oversights in the field have limited the work at home for many scholars, especially in doctoral dissertations.

On the other hand, it cannot be denied that in a "reductionist" attitude similar to that of the structuralists, many generativists have a tendency to reduce their descriptions of field data to formulaic exercises, leaving the reader without the possibility of checking the inclusiveness, accuracy, and correctness of these data or of their conclusions.

Several of the major shortcomings of transformational-generative grammar have been or are being corrected to such an extent that the present stage can be regarded as a new breakthrough. One should mention, for example, the abolition of the notion of "deep structure" and the investigation of "deep semantics," which was motivated by the renewed study of the relationship between language and logic. It must be noted, however, that generative semantics has little to do with etymology. Instead, it is part of the achronic aspect of language study; in fact, this logicogrammatical vista of generative semantics probably best epitomizes the distance between the philological-linguistic and the theoretical-linguistic researcher, and at the same time makes understandable the inherent difficulties in communication between them.

Though generative grammar constitutes an undeniable advance in linguistics toward achronic, universal grammar, it has the limitations it shares with structuralist grammar as well as its own limitations, most of which concern aspects in which Middle East linguists were and are interested, and which *are* of "universal" importance. Among those is what may be summarized as the dynamic aspect of language as mentioned above. Thus the aspects of diachrony and dialectology have hardly been reconsidered, but, for phonology, with Jakobson-Halle's distinctive feature analysis and the subsequent generative phonology, a powerful descriptive tool has been developed to investigate "deeper" correlations. The understandable consternation of Middle East scholars about such limitations of view continues.

TOWARD A MEETING OF THE "PARADIGMS." The most essential problem, obviously, is which scientific paradigm should scholars accept? The Orientalist is not usually inclined to accept the priorities of the next higher level of abstractness—in this case of the discipline of linguistics—over his area specialization, although he may in fact be implicitly theoretically oriented. Moreover, in the eyes of many, Middle Eastern linguistics is still very much in the developing stage, so that it is seen as still quite remote from quarrels over theoretical problems.

Therefore, except for the major languages of the Middle East and some other occasional dialects and languages, the various subareas are for the most part philological provinces. The origin of Orientalists from a broad overall humanistic approach makes the inclination to continue this tradition quite understandable. But not only the Orientalist is to blame; the linguist is as of now still little inclined to go beyond the limitations of his school and theory.

However, it seems that, generally speaking, the "setting" of Middle Eastern linguistics has resulted in a situation conducive to maturation now, and further that the bridge between Orientalist and linguist is gradually being crossed

A good many Orientalists have adopted the analytical and descriptive methodologies of contemporary linguistics without necessarily embracing the theory behind them uncritically. Other scholars have described the widening of their view from strict area specialization through the adoption of linguistic concepts to becoming theoretical linguists. Inversely, linguists acknowledge their development toward an increasing recognition of area specialization. There have been several attempts to demonstrate the possibilities not only with contemporary, but also with historical material. Good work has been done with this objective, but much more needs to be done to be convincing. Phonology has always been ahead in this respect, long ago in comparative-historical, then in structural, and now in generative linguistics; one may cite here the work by Malone (1971, 1972), Sharifi (1971), Lees (1961), and Zimmer (1969).

As to higher levels, there are Hetzron's (1970) contribution to a deeper understanding of case theory and deep predication (with Ethiopic material), Hodge's (1970) research also in deep predication and the "linguistic cycle" (with Afro-Asiatic material), Brame's (1973) advocacy of cyclic application of stress rules in Maltese and Palestinian Arabic, Bashiri's (1973) dissertation on semantics of Persian utilizing among other concepts some of Avicenna's, or Doerfer's (unpublished) new concept of grammatical theory derived from his knowledge of Altaic languages, a concept similar to but more refined than Shaumjan's (1965) model of "applicative linguistics."

One should cite here those few brave general linguists, not Middle East specialists, who have adduced evidence from Middle Eastern languages as well as from languages of other areas for their hypotheses. One such is Herdan (1964, 1966), who used statistical material provided by Iranists for his studies on mathematical linguistics. Likewise, Turkic vocalic harmony and stress placement in Maltese Arabic have been used for studies in "cyclical rules," the pharyngeals of Arabic in phonetics or even Indo-European laryngeal theory, and several similar contributions. As few as these have been and still are, they offer proof for the potential importance of Middle Eastern languages for "general" theoretical issues and thus offer hope for *intra*disciplinary dialogue.

The widening scope of linguistics will very likely contribute to the narrowing of the gap. It must be noted, however, that although there would seem to be a "return" of the linguist to the bosom of Orientalistic studies, this is simply not so. Contemporary linguistics is accompanied by a much more powerful analytic and descriptive framework than Middle Eastern linguistics had available before on all levels of language, in phonology as well as syntax and semantics. It is up to the Orientalist and the linguist to jointly explore the possibilities of the study of linguistic "dynamics," and the potentials of the 5000-year record of Middle East languages. If there has been any change in the study of Middle East linguistics, it is the beginning of a new vivacity in theoretical thinking as an integral part of this areal study.

Professional Problems

PAUCITY OF SCHOLARS. There still are relatively few scholars of Middle East studies; there are fewer who are philologist-linguists; there are still fewer who are linguists narrowly defined, i.e., mainly theoretically oriented. These are thinly spread over the breathtaking variety of languages in time and space, with Arabic, Persian, and Turkish as the main *Hochsprachen* attracting the lion's share of attention by the few, while the remaining languages are shortchanged in various degrees. There are, relatively speaking, more Semitists than Iranists than Turkologists. Being members of a relatively small group,

Middle Eastern linguists are faced from the outset of their careers with the task of what may be called an uphill fight, quite different from their colleagues in the mainstream academic fields. They have to do research in a much broader spectrum, in a field that has perhaps the largest amount of data in terms of time and scope but that is much less investigated in detail. They may enjoy the excitement of being able to tackle so many unsolved problems; at the same time the "exotic" languages themselves seem to inspire a certain awe in their specialist colleagues.

The scarcity of scholars is one of the main causes of Middle Eastern linguistics (similar to other "exotic" areas) being the poor relative not only within the humanities but also within linguistics, except during the heyday of Indo-European studies. One should add, with McCarus, that these few face the problems of keeping up not only with rapidly changing linguistic theory but also with their own specialities, not to mention Middle East history, anthropology, art, religion, literature, etc., together with new research in languages adjacent to their study; thus Iranists should keep up with Turkology, and so forth.

The number of scholars is a problem that lies outside the capabilities of the scholars themselves to change. It has, however, direct consequences for the academic standing of the field: a small number is less able to bring their field to heights equal to other fields; they are less able to establish adequate communication and exchange of their research with other fields. Even more so, it is difficult to make their research understood or appreciated by their administrative superiors. It is possible at least at times to demonstrate their expertise and "value" directly by turning their attention and efforts to applied linguistics. Thus, following observations by Killean, the high tide of Middle Eastern linguistics in North America was during the 1950s and early 1960s, when Near and Middle East Centers were blooming, and when the increased interest in international studies counted on Middle Eastern linguistics and their cooperation with work on *applied* linguistics. In that period, when social scientists needed to acquire language skills as quickly and as accurately as possible, the crying need for useful, up-to-date pedagogical materials made applied linguistics the primary activity of Middle Eastern linguistics in the States. The ensuing flood of textbooks of both standard and colloquial languages of the Middle East demonstrated our field's response to this demand. Now that the impact of national funds and other sources has ebbed, there is of course still need for applied research carried out for practical and immediately relevant purposes, although it may not be as urgent as before.

It is quite inconceivable that the number of scholars and chairs for this field will not increase, especially in the present United States; the ever-growing importance of the Persian Gulf alone should encourage efforts at an ever better understanding of the Middle East area.

The basic problem of manpower is ultimately conditioned by political factors. Thus the Middle Eastern linguist in North America, and all the Western world for that matter, this shortchanged exotic unicum within the context of the humanistic academic background, observes with frustration that his colleagues in the Soviet Union are responsible for an amount of research and study that perhaps equals that of all the rest of the world. As to the USSR, there is little need to detail the reasons why that country has never ceased to sponsor Middle East studies in the most generous manner. It is such efforts which allow the continuation of not only the huge amount of scholarship but also the high quality of much of Soviet research, especially in Middle Eastern linguistics.

As of now, the ideal of "jack of all trades" still has high priority within the humanistic concept of the present-day university, especially with regard to its area-defined departments. This is to the detriment of both interdisciplinary and interarea studies, although there are exceptions.

The situation in Europe is not much different. The most significant difference, it seems, is the fact that in Europe there are even fewer chairs in Iranistics, Semitics, or Turkology occupied by linguists than there are in North America.

OVERSPECIALIZATION. Returning to our immediate academic setting and our field, a few observations may be added that concern certain scholarly attitudes of communication. Unfortunately, communication is often hampered by what may be called specialist's blinds among Middle East scholars themselves, who have done their share in exaggerating the notion of esotericism in Middle East studies and who even tend to pride themselves on it. Outside nonspecialists noticing such "overspecialization" can hardly be blamed for little utilizing the insights of Middle Eastern linguistics. As an extreme example, one may mention the inclinations of many of the scholars who specialized in Middle Iranic until only a few years ago. Although one must admire their brilliant pioneering work in this most intricate field of Middle Eastern linguistics and their many contributions to the languages, cultures, religions, and the history of Iran and Central Asia, this subfield remains very much closed for the uninitiated. Most specialists were and are disinclined to provide even basic tools like introductions and intelligible surveys. Thus even fellow researchers in Iranic, unless they follow the traditional learning process between master and apprentice, are virtually kept away and are often disenchanted by the combination of philological erudition and a certain linguistic naïveté which marks many of the publications on Middle Iranic.

This "insiderdom" among practitioners in the same language field is paralleled on the next higher level by "insiderdom" of one field against the other; namely, one seldom finds a Semiticist talking productively with an Iranist or

Turkologist! This fact has to do not only with erudition in each of these three fields, but more significantly with the perpetration of the genetic aspects of linguistics within area-defined studies; i.e., the area of individual interest is in fact still the area covered by the respective "genetic" *Stammbaum*, not the Middle East. Interestingly enough, this has not changed much even with most of those scholars who are generalists, i.e., mainly structuralist or transformational-generative linguists.

Linguistic theoreticians are hardly free from similar attitudes. Perhaps the thing most detrimental to the field, said Hetzron, was and still is the often supercilious ingroupishness and dogmatic party line of the theoretical schools, which declare a truth today only to attack it vehemently the next day; the transformational generativists, realizing obvious shortcomings of their predecessors, decided to ignore everything before them. Instead of trying to integrate their theory with the other trends of linguistics, they made it an independent schism. Interestingly enough, they adopted an unnecessarily esoteric terminology, as if to cut off communication with others. One should also note the scarcity of introductory books to transformational-generative linguistics until fairly recently. One often has the impression that these people do not want "outsiders" to understand their theory. Now, of course, since there are many of them, the whole field is becoming more open.

Thus the extremist Orientalists and extremist linguists both joined hands in creating schisms which were bound to alienate even their nearest of kin.

Mary Levy and others from the Center for Applied Linguistics, Washington D.C., conducted a study of communication between professional linguists and scholars in related fields (unpublished). The results are extremely illuminating: communication between linguistics departments and those departments to which Middle Eastern linguists belong is poor or nonexistent (there are exceptions). Further, there is often overt hostility between the linguistically oriented and the humanistically oriented. Again, the communication among linguists varies with their theoretical orientation and training. Structuralists often have nothing to say to transformational generativists; both communicate better and more frequently with structuralists or transformational generativists of other fields. Most important is the observation that the linguists specializing in an area often lead a *dual existence*, as theoretical linguists and as area-oriented specialists.

The statement that linguists of the same school communicate with each other appears to be somewhat optimistic. It is not always so; most frustrating may well be the fact that even the Middle Eastern linguist who has learned to speak modern generative *linguese* and contributes new ideas to general linguistics sometimes finds his research neglected or rejected outright by general linguists. This is due, at least in part, to the image of exoticism which still shrouds Middle East studies, and which is still perpetrated by our academic system and many Orientalists. It should be noted here that much of the program for the September 1975 meeting of the German Oriental Society is devoted to "Oriental Studies in the Humanities."

Summary of Common Trends and Achievements

The following is a brief survey of the main common trends and achievements since the flourishing of structural grammar in the 1950s and 1960s and, more recently, transformational-generative grammar. The details are well outlined in *Current Trends in Linguistics*, Volume 6; anyone who takes the time to read those surveys will acknowledge that as a whole they offer excellent, thought-provoking insights into the problems and the advances of the postwar period in the various fields and subfields.

The survey of the major achievements of Middle Eastern linguistics (as a kind of projection onto the present "surface" of Middle Eastern linguistics of those works that constitute the most adequate or best available literature for present research) shows that some of those works date back more than 70 years! That presently used research material is of such age not only reflects the excellence of some of the earlier scholarship but also the poor state of much of contemporary Middle Eastern linguistics.

Certain generalizations can be made: philological-linguistic research is most prominent with medieval and ancient languages; strictly linguistic work is mainly conducted on modern *Hochsprachen* and to some extent on modern dialects, but also ancient languages, especially Akkadian, but the study of medieval languages is neglected throughout and constitutes largely a disaster area.

In terms of linguistic levels and aspects, experimental phonetic studies are the best represented, both synchronic and diachronic; morphological studies are acceptable, if still largely on the word and phrase levels; syntactic studies cry for more research; the extremely few studies on text theory are still essentially literature-oriented, as are studies of stylistics; semantics is perhaps the best researched in terms of lexical diachrony, i.e., etymology; achronic (generative) semantics has been tackled by one or two studies only; dialectology is plentiful but utterly fragmented; studies of *Sprachbund* and sociolinguistics, except for one or two attempts, are impressionistic at best; and finally, statistical studies are good but extremely rare.

The overall picture that evolves is one of a collection of works with an extremely varied degree of sophistication and completeness, and marked by successive layers of theory, among which the diachronic-historical approach is still the most widely represented, and the descriptive-structural approach is well accepted, whereas recent approaches such as generative theory or sociolinguistics constitute but a trickle.

Perhaps the two most striking observations that deserve emphatic mention are first, that the progress in Middle Eastern linguistics was made to a large extent through doctoral dissertations or *Habilschriften*, many of which have not been published yet, and second, that a good number of those dissertations were written by young native scholars from the Middle East who were educated in the West and East. The impact of those scholars not only within the context of Western academia but, more importantly, in their own academic communities is bound to be extraordinary.

One of those dissertations now published deserves a special note, it seems to me, because it not only highlights the breadth and width which some of these young scholars have achieved, but at the same time represents a striking argument for the power of contemporary linguistics in our field: the dissertation by Abdel-Massih on Tamazight Berber. A native Egyptian trained at the University of Michigan, he endeavored to apply generative methodology to Berber. With his one master stroke, the study of Berber was brought to the highest level of linguistic research. For the first time he discovered and described exhaustively the sets of discrete morphophonological rules that predictably generate the intricate surface forms of the verb system in Berber, including its ablaut and metathetic systems which, unrecognized, had presented insurmountable problems for Berberologists for a century. The purpose, and probably most important insight, of his study concerns the ability of the native speaker of Tamazight to freely "generate" a great number of morphologically complex verb forms! (He thus took up a point that usually has been pushed aside by generativists, whose eyes are generally fixed on syntax.)

In general, remarkable progress has been made and new ideas and methodologies have permeated practically all fields of linguistics to various degrees. Common to all is the attention to experimental phonetics, phonology, syntax, dialectology, and research in the origin and development of *Hoch-* and *Schriftsprachen.* Moreover, for most major languages and national or ethnic standards there now exist textbooks, such as for Azerbaijani and Uzbek; Egyptian, Moroccan, Iraqi, and Syrian and other Arabic dialects; Baluchi; Kurdish; for many languages excellent dictionaries are either in progress or have been published.

Many contemporary approaches have been tried, from structuralist grammar in its American and European versions, to transformational-generative grammar, to contrastive analysis, statistics, and glottochronology, on all levels of grammar.

One observes a distinct difference of approach between European and American structural descriptivists: as noted by Abboud (1970), the European scholars, mostly on the path of the earlier Prague School, are still much more careful and often exhaustive with detail, but often also do not attempt or dare to draw important generalizing conclusions. Moreover, diachronic points are usually inserted liberally throughout. The American approach, on the other hand, is marked by an obvious rigidity of description and the love of elegant patterns and clear rules, but there is a certain dislike of detail.

It is the generality and rigidity of the American schools that have won over many of the young scholars in the United States and, increasingly, in Europe. Yet so far, following Abboud, one has to acknowledge they have had uneven success in the reanalysis, restructuring, reclassification, and new analysis of the data.

It seems appropriate to cite here some observations by A. Bloch, since they capture *in nuce* the basic caveats with regard to the current study of much of Middle Eastern linguistics in North America. According to him, "Syntactic studies on Arabic which have been produced in this country in recent years are, with very few exceptions, narrow in outlook and of limited usefulness. . . . They are really more exercises in transformational methodology than contributions to the understanding of the language. As a result their insights are often uninspired to the point of banality." Again linguists and Orientalists join hands, this time in producing banalities: here the Orientalist with his overestimation of the very detail of his language, there the linguist with his overestimation of the theory, both overestimating their respective methodologies.

Several linguists have carefully tried to avoid extremes and to combine earlier with contemporary approaches, such as Erica Reiner (1966) "*A* Linguistic Analysis of Akkadian," the first nonhistorical one for that language, in which she applies the generative approach to some sections but still within the traditional presentational framework. Other examples of these efforts are various articles on Aramaic and Hebrew by Joseph Malone (1971, 1972), Karl Zimmer (1969) on Turkish, and Moyne (1971) on Persian.

Significant, if not voluminous, progress has been made in phonetics and phonology (which for Persian and Hebrew, e.g., began about 1939). Here especially native Middle Eastern scholars trained in the West and East represent some of the brightest hopes. Most important for phonological studies is the increased research on Middle Eastern language data in different writing systems, such as Latin, Greek, Indic, and Hebrew orthography for Judeo-Arabic, Judeo-Iranic, Turkish, etc.

In terms of grammatical level, another most significant trend is the rising interest in syntactic studies, including ancient languages, such as Akkadian, the level mostly neglected before. This trend is concomitant with transformational grammar (most conspicuous in doctoral dissertations) but it has inspired also syntactic research by scholars of other training. It is obvious that much of it is still in a pioneering stage, for the very reason that syntax had been relatively neglected until now.

In terms of which language types are the focus of research, another most significant step forward is that the earlier predominance of research on the literary languages, *Schriftsprachen*, e.g., Classical Arabic and Classical Persian, has ended. For the first time, the study of those languages has been recognized as a separate field; they are no longer considered monolithic; for example, the some 1500 years of Arabic has been divided into definable segments and stages. Moreover, the regional standards, the "colloquials" (as opposed to local variants) have now been recognized in their own right.

As to historical dialectology, the main thrust, according to Killean, has focused on three questions: (1) the dialect situation at the time of the formation of the classical languages; (2) the origins of the classical languages, e.g., Classical Arabic, Classical Persian, Turkish, and Hebrew; and (3) the stages of the internal developments in the literary languages.

As to contemporary dialectology, some of the most intricate and interesting aspects are now being recognized: the development of regional standards, such as Moroccan, Egyptian, Syrian, and Iraqi Arabic; or Iranian, Afghani, and Tajiki Persian.

Besides the question of diachronic and synchronic regional standardization, good progress has been made in dialectology in all geographical areas as well as in pre-Islamic language groups. There is a remarkable increase in the writing of grammars, dictionaries, and textbooks. New dialect areas, little or not at all known before, have been and are being covered: Ethiopia, the Arabian Peninsula, North Africa, Turkish dialects in Anatolia and Rumelia, Northwest and Central Iran, Central Asia, and most recently, Afghanistan.

But quite exciting, one must say, is that since 1968 one of the last blank spots in Middle East dialectology, the Turkish and Mongolian dialects of Iran and Afghanistan, has begun to be investigated by Doerfer (1970) and others. This study has brought to light a heretofore unknown seventh Turkish language group, the Khalaj, in West Central Iran. The study of Irano-Altaistica is immensely important because of the fact that those Altaic languages have been in contact with Iranian for more than 1000 years and that the greater part of Altaic/Turkic speakers in the Middle East are bi- or multilingual.

An important trend, very likely the most important for the future, has been the study of diglossia and its higher level, sociolinguistics, such as the studies by Ferguson (1969), who compared the Arabic situation with that of Greek, Swiss German, and Haitian Creole communities, or the excellent study of the Arabic dialects of the various religious communities in Baghdad by Blanc (1964).

Studies of substrate languages in relation to dialectology have been flourishing in the context of ancient languages. The many problems of the theory are well-known, however. One may mention the study of MacKenzie (1961), who tries to show that the difference between the three main Kurdish dialects is directly related to the local non-Kurdish Iranian substrate.

Studies in borrowings are intensive but still mostly lexically oriented and tentative. The theoretical basis of the investigation has never been worked out, as has been noted. One of the most comprehensive recent studies in this field is undoubtedly Doerfer's mammoth multivolume work on the Turkish and Mongolian elements in Persian (1963–1967).

Glottochronology, i.e., the study of the rate of change of vocabulary in related languages, has been tested mainly on Afro-Asiatic. Moreover, statistical studies, mostly French, it seems, have been conducted for diachronic and synchronic research in many of the Middle Eastern languages, both modern and ancient. The computer has been utilized for the analysis of Hebrew morphology by Shapiro and Shvika (1963–1964), and the ongoing analysis of Modern Standard Arabic syntax conducted at the University of Michigan under the direction of McCarus and Rammuny.

There is one interesting observation that should be inserted here. It appears that there has been not only a general common direction of research but also the preference for certain selective problems in ancient as well as modern languages, e.g., stress and syllable structure, emphatics, laryngeals, the verb system and its tenses, and such syntactic problems as topic-comment and cleft clauses, noun-phrase embedding including relative clauses, attributive subordination, and apposition, the nominal sentence types, and nominalization.

This section on achievements concludes with some remarks on large-scale surveys, published or in process.

The first monumental survey in Middle Eastern linguistics was the *Grundriss der Iranischen Philologie*, 2 vols. (1895–1904) covering the knowledge of Iranic until that time. It still has not been replaced, in spite of overwhelming new data. Similarly, Bartholomae's *Altiranisches Wörterbuch* (1904) remains the only comprehensive dictionary for Old Iranic, and indeed, it seems to be almost unsurpassable. Semitics is indebted forever to Brockelmann's *Grundriss der vergleichenden Grammatik der Semitischen Sprachen*, 2 vols. (1908, 1913). Turkology is the most recent to have reached a period of its first major recapitulation with the *Philologiae Turcicae Fundamenta*, 2 vols. (1959–1964) (vol. 3 in progress). Redard's *Atlas Linguistique d'Iran et Afghanistan*, initiated in 1957, will soon publish its first volume on Afghanistan.

The new *Janua Linguarum. Series Critica* (Mouton) plans a number of volumes on Middle Eastern languages, among them 10 on Turkology alone.

The Conseil International d'Etudes Turques headed by Hazai is working on large-scale documentation of texts in non-Arabic orthographic traditions. Similar efforts are being made by some of the language academies and the series *Corpus Inscriptionum Semiticarum*, *Iranicarum*, etc.

The ongoing monumental efforts of the Chicago Akkadian Dictionary and the historical dictionary projects of the Turkish and Hebrew language Academies, the Iranian Culture Foundation, and the Iranian Language Academy should be mentioned.

Middle Eastern Countries

The following discussion can only be very brief. Excellent detailed discussions are found in *Current Trends in Linguistics*, vol. 6, pp. 665–758.

Linguistics has certainly other connotations in the Middle Eastern countries than it has in the West. This fact is clearly reflected in the structure of the university: linguistics departments are either very recently instituted or nonexistent.

The study of languages still constitutes a politically sensitive issue in all countries; priorities are determined not on abstract theoretical grounds but by reference to national priorities. Middle Eastern countries naturally give the dominant language groups top priority in philological work, even more than do foreigners. To various degrees a good part of linguistic study is tinged by certain apologetic views, in which these native scholars are joined by sympathetic Orientalists who have earlier expressed, and to some extent still express, similar ideas, with the unavoidable distortions, exaggerations, and selectivity of topics. One may mention enthusiasm about archaic or rare words, notions of this or that dialect being "practically Middle Persian," etc.

One may insert here some notes on language politics. This can be described as organized conscious efforts to channel the "natural" course of language standardization. Virtually all countries have been or are being faced with this problem, including Middle Eastern countries.

The methodologies and approaches are as varied as the countries involved. One basic prerequisite, however, is a thorough language census, which exists only for Iran and Algeria (both with considerable shortcomings). The problems of standardization require likewise extensive grammatical studies, the most basic, and generally first to be tackled, of which are writing reform and lexical reform. Whereas the former can be decreed relatively easily, the latter generally cannot, or only partially. Even more difficult are conscious attempts at the standardization on higher levels of grammar, such as morphology and syntax.

Since decrees have generally failed, other ways are tried, mainly through education, i.e., in schools, as well as through audiovisual media. Evidently these are much more effective, especially with regard to the propagation of the official language over areas speaking other related or nonrelated languages.

On the negative side, there are the inevitable increasing rate of extinction of dialects, and the likelihood of a break with the native-local cultural tradition. Language politics is marked by a built-in dichotomy: on the one hand, the record of dialects and local culture serves the end of correlating the present with the past (marked by the search for archaic words, etc.); on the other hand, dialectical diversification and the study of dialects is frequently believed to impede and counteract efforts at standardization.

The most visible vehicles of language studies have, of course, been the national language academies and similar institutions, such as the Ha-aqademiyyah ha-leshon ha-^{c}ivrit in Israel, the Majma^{c} al-lugha al-^{c}arabiyya in Egypt, the Farhangestân-e Zabân-e Irân and the Bonyâd-e Farhang in Iran, the Pashto Ṭolena in Kabul and Peshavar, and the Türk Dil Kurumu in Turkey. Not too different from their French model, the Academie Française, the institution of most of them was politically motivated. Nowhere has this been more overt than in Turkey, where Atatürk made language and writing reform one of the primary national targets, the first branch of science. Thus their first main task is the establishment of the national prestige language: its standardization, modernization and purification, and nationalization.

It should be noted, however, that although this approach appears to be a direct offshoot of European nationalism, such efforts have an age-old tradition in one of the countries, Iran. The reawakening of Iran after the Muslim conquest was accompanied not only by the reinstitution of Persian as the main language of writing, but also by a strong movement toward language standardization and purification, i.e., Persianization. As a most prominent personality in this movement one can cite here none other than Avicenna. Those efforts are certainly neglected—if not ridiculed—by some linguists as language engineering, although they should be considered in earnest as a viable facet of linguistic study, one where fruitful cooperation with the Middle Eastern countries seems very promising.

The efforts of the academies and foundations have brought forth a group which increasingly contributes to the knowledge of Middle Eastern linguistics: the linguistically interested native speakers of a local dialect. Their work, mostly published in local journals and magazines, must be highly appreciated; more often than not it can be utilized by the initiated specialist. In some instances, a solid linguistic education or cooperation with a linguistically trained scholar has produced excellent research.

Several of these academies have begun to broaden their perspective and to engage in extraordinarily long-range efforts at full-scale and detailed collection and documentation of all linguistic data, standard or nonstandard, historic or contemporary, such as the *Farhangestân-e Zabân-e Irân*. This is in marked contrast to the remarks of the secretary-general of one of the other language academies, in answering the questionnaire on which this survey is based: "The subject we deal with is solely the . . . language . . . its origin, its history, stages of development, its local dialects, its defense against foreign incursion, its reform, and secondarily the . . . languages and dialects . . .," and further, "We recur to general linguistics only incidentally, as a general guide."

A good part of linguistic research in the Middle East may be described as a combination of European-style philology with the traditional model of Muslim grammarians. Thus much is still oriented toward a normative and stylistically correct grammar.

Given these premises, it is understandable that Middle Eastern linguistic research has only recently been able to absorb the initiatives from modern Western linguistics. However, several countries have made conscious efforts at broadening the linguistic approach. Not only have increasing numbers of young scholars been trained in the West in Western linguistics, but there have appeared some linguistic journals, there have been instituted linguistic departments, and language-linguistic societies have been established.

General linguistic topics are slowly gaining importance at congresses and meetings. Some countries such as Iran make conscious efforts to sponsor local, national, and international congresses devoted to linguistics and philology pertinent to that country, and to invite foreign scholars as well as many local scholars from universities as well as high schools, in an effort to broaden the basis of such studies. It is very likely that sooner or later the activation of local resources will make the Middle Eastern countries themselves increasingly important centers for Middle East studies and linguistics.

It is true that work done in the Middle East is often not accepted by Western scholars. The fundamental reason is the traditional Middle Eastern "paradigm" of scholarly approach which still partially follows the pre-philological "paradigm." The problems that Middle Eastern native innovators face are similar to those which their colleagues faced in the West: a new "paradigm" invariably involves the introduction of a new terminology, but more important is the very break with a whole tradition and cultural humanistic outlook. Moreover, many of the first attempts to introduce the new ideas are little more than the superimposition of the new models and even of details of certain "standard" works on English grammar in the "new linguistics"; this Procrustean bed rarely leads to new insights into Middle Eastern languages.

Yet is must be recognized that the first task is to prepare colleagues and the field for the radical departure. Some Middle Eastern scholars were very much aware of this task and referred to the difficult choice they had to make: to prepare introductory material for their field in their country, and to postpone and even neglect basic research, as bitter a choice as it may be.

As of now, there are still considerable problems with regard to scholarly communication. Some object to the fact that, like the earlier political stance,

Western scholarship perpetrates a kind of scientific imperialism, and that the acceptance of the particular Western view of scholarship with its particular selection of topics including linguistics is the precondition for scholarly communication, whereas it need not necessarily be fit for the Middle East. (As an extreme example, one may cite the observation that Indo-Europeanists are chauvinists by trying to find a most remote Indo-European root rather than accepting a loan from non-Indo-European languages.) Communication between Western and Middle Eastern linguists has been largely on a personal basis. And it has often been the Middle Eastern scholars themselves who kept the contact alive by sending literature. Again, one must cite here the efforts of Iranian institutions, which have begun in a most generous fashion to distribute their publications to interested scholars worldwide. In general, Middle Eastern scholars have begun to recognize the need to cooperate with their Western colleagues and to learn modern methodology in order to apply it to their own problems.

SUGGESTED PRIORITIES FOR FUTURE RESEARCH

Any attempt to stake out the range of priorities for future research in Middle Eastern linguistics should not be marred by possible threats of "accountability" from outside the field. Middle Eastern linguistics has shown its potential by assisting in remedying outside needs by the preparation of textbooks and readers in the 1950s and early 1960s, which were an easy—perhaps the only—way for outsiders to appreciate and justify Middle Eastern linguistic research.

Nevertheless, this very intensive work on applied linguistics has demonstrated more clearly than ever before that there is a real need for an increase in our basic knowledge and supply of data. Only by satisfying these needs will we be ready to respond to similar or more advanced pedagogical needs in the future with the solid background preparation. We thus need much more basic research to be carried out for both practical needs and for the purely theoretical goals of the future.

The acknowledgment of the need for basic, experimental research does not at all imply the failure of this field up to now. In fact much of the work to date is excellent; the textbooks and readers have been extremely helpful and successful, and, being based on more than a century of often brilliant work, they constitute only the most widely visible surface of this work.

The following outline of future needs, tasks, and priorities attempts to cover Middle Eastern linguistics as a whole. Although there are certain differences as to specific geographic or historical areas within Semitics, Iranistics, and Turkology, it is interesting to note that there is general agreement of Middle

Eastern linguists with regard to those objectives. It must be borne in mind that in suggesting priorities we do not commit ourselves to the same mistake as administrations tend to do; i.e., we must not prescribe priorities for the moment's benefit.

There are many needs and suggestions for future research. The major areas for priorities are as follows: in terms of glottodynamic studies, all studies of bilingualism and social dialectology, including the study of dialect areas most threatened with extinction, e.g., South Arabic dialects; in terms of grammar, syntactic studies and studies of text theory; in terms of applied linguistics, studies of language acquisition; in terms of "tools," comprehensive dictionaries as well as topical dictionaries; and in terms of organizational aspects, a clearinghouse for current research.

Following is a more detailed list of priorities and needs, first in terms of linguistic level and aspect and second in terms of individual language family. These are followed by suggestions involving the academic setting.

The suggestions reflect both the priorities of the discipline of linguistics and the priorities for individual language areas, and identify only the most urgent objectives. Thus when South Arabic dialects are singled out, it does not mean that other dialect areas should be neglected. Rather it means that a disciplinary priority is the study of dialects threatened by extinction, particularly those South Arabic dialects where the least is being done; other dialect areas are being investigated, if only by very few.

Glottodynamics

The suggestions for priorities should justly begin with the direction of research that may be the most likely to contribute to the cooperation between the Orientalist and the linguist, since it concerns aspects of research in which many Orientalists have been interested and since it has regained increasing interest for linguists. At the same time, it appears to be the potentially most innovative and promising, so that just as the study of Indo-European languages of the Middle East contributed decisively to new vistas in linguistics, so it is likely that Middle East linguistics can again contribute significantly to a developing new vista in linguistics: a dynamic integrated systems approach which has tentatively been called here "glottodynamics," that is, the linguistic aspect of "human dynamics," which implies the theory of linguistic diffusion and interference in temporal, geographic, and social space. The potential for real Middle Eastern contributions to this kind of research lies in the very fact mentioned earlier; the huge area of the age-old Middle Eastern *Kulturbund* is the area of intersection of three major language groups: Afro-

Asiatic, Indo-European, and Altaic. Together with their Middle Eastern member languages they are better and longer recorded and researched than any similar constellation in the world. Although the Middle East as a whole constitutes one large ideal field for glottodynamic studies, such multilingual, multiethnic metropolitan cities as Cairo, Beirut, Jerusalem, Tehran, and Istanbul are ideal and convenient laboratories for direct focused studies of these phenomena.

In somewhat more detail the following tasks are ahead of us. In terms of the three main language groups, research needs to be done in the successive waves of dominance: first the Semiticization, then the Iranization, and since about 1000 AD, the Turkicization of distinct parts of the Middle East and their overlapping patterns. As to the contemporary evidence, census studies are recommended to provide important basic data. Only greater India on the margins of the Middle East and to some extent, the first (not the recent, second) census of Iran and the census of 1966 in Algeria offer such basic data. They have not been coupled yet in any systematic way with dialectal-comparative linguistics.

In addition to the linguistic turbulence in the center of the Middle East resulting from these waves, the turbulence on the margins needs to be more carefully investigated, especially in such areas as Central Asia, Ethiopia, and the Balkans, to which should be added the Caucasus and the Pamir- Hindukush areas.

On a different level, the study of prestigious lingua francas in the Middle East and their influence on other languages can contribute much to the understanding of linguistic interference, and has to be carefully investigated; i.e., Aramaic until Muslim times, Arabic thereafter, Persian in the entirety of the northeastern part of the Middle East including Central Asia and Mogul India until modern times, and more recently to some extent, European languages.

The sociolinguistic dynamics of *standardization* and *regionalization* cries for investigation: e.g., the phenomenon of the development of three major variants of Persian, as official regional *Hochsprachen* in Iran, Afghanistan, and Soviet Tajikistan evidently conditioned by political separation, or the recent development of a Standard Kurdish and Standard Baluchi which have never existed before.

It is here that linguists can contribute much to combat such simplistic myths as that dialectological isoglosses lie along political borders, myths perpetuated by our own talk of, e.g., "Iraqi Arabic," "Egyptian Arabic," and "Moroccan Arabic." These notions show clearly that we need a much better understanding of the hierarchical dynamics between regional standards and national *Hochsprachen*.

We need continuing investigation of the effects of higher education and audiovisual media on diglossia, standardization phenomena, etc. We need studies of code switching, especially switching to different languages and communicative style, a field that is still marked by the relative theoretical naïveté of researchers; similarly required are paralanguage and semantic-semiotic studies, which have as yet hardly been tackled.

Studies of code switching in sociolinguistics must be investigated as part of a continuum that also includes literary stylistics and thus directly relates to the linguistic "rhetoric" study of literature.

The study of genetic relationships will clearly play an important part in a better understanding of the large-scale diachronic and geographic dynamics throughout the millenia. This study is especially important for the ancient languages as well as the margins of the modern Middle East.

We need first a clear understanding of and proof for the genetic relationships within major groups themselves. Even this task of comparative-historical linguistics has not been fulfilled yet. Thus most groups of Afro-Asiatic languages need clarification, such as the Semitic and Cushitic languages of Ethiopia, Berber, and Old Egyptian. Similarly, the interrelationships in Altaic and the problem of ethnogenesis as a result of migrations are still open to debate because of the lack not so much of data as of scholarship. But even within the center of the Middle East there is utter lack yet of sufficient data for a clear picture of genetic relationships even with modern languages and dialects. Thus Arabic, Iranic, and Turkic dialects are too little recorded and known yet to draw conclusions even within the same subgroup, let alone to begin studies of linguistic interference.

It must be stressed here that although genetic-dialectological studies are a basic necessity for dynamic studies, they constitute but one dimension among several. It is necessary to rid oneself of unidimensional genetic dialectology for its own sake, especially since interferential phenomena are not restricted to unrelated languages but occur between all symbiotic languages, be they related dialects or not. Another problem that has still not been eradicated is the tendency to take one language, such as Classical Arabic, as the standard reference for rules of historical and dialectological change. A similar problem is the postulation of rules on the basis of some standard reconstructed proto-forms, with the result that there remains a great number of unexplained exceptions.

Ultimately, studies in linguistic dynamics may lead to insights into the way languages function, operate, and change in their environment and to the understanding of the mechanics of nuclei and margins, communication channels and barriers between speech communities in temporal, geographic, and social space and their reflexes in grammatical space.

The challenge is great, the more so because this multi-aspect research invariably requires the cooperation of specialists in many disciplines. It is for this reason that most scholars expressed a warning with regard to interdisciplinary studies such as required by glottodynamics: first know your discipline and its limits well. It is not possible to continue the "jack of all trades" approach of much of Orientalistics so far, nor should one accept a new version of it, as begins to be shown by some linguists, unless he develops competence also in the other disciplines he employs.

Middle Eastern linguistics in the first place has to be linguistics, and its different objectives must be clearly distinguished, especially from disciplines near it. Inversely, the urgent interdisciplinary approach must clearly outline the common issues between disciplines. Thus an interdisciplinary approach between linguistics and its close sister, literature, in terms of text theory must be carefully distinguished from literary criticism here and grammatical analysis there, and so on.

DIALECT STUDIES. It is worth adding a few suggestions concerning the conduct of dialect studies, covering not only geographical but also social dialects.

First of all, the "descriptions" of dialects should not be in fact eclectic listings of differences deemed interesting with regard to other dialects or with regard to a vague notion of the "grammar" of the particular dialect area, as is the case with most dialect descriptions so far.

In general, dialect studies, at least for some major areas, are good but frequently difficult to interpret. Based on different linguistic systems of notation, the actual phonetic material is difficult to reconstruct and use for comparative studies. Therefore, general descriptions of the dialect picture are still very hard to draw up. There is thus first the need of surveying the available material; much of it will require reconfirmation by renewed fieldwork.

It is with dialects that the need for recording and preservation of rapidly extinguishing languages is most justified, such as the South Arabic dialects, the Aramaic dialects of Ma^{c}lula and Turoya, or the totality of Iranic dialects in West Iran as well as in Afghanistan. An important suggestion by Killean should be added here: dialect studies of the future must be published in a unique new way with accompanying tapes of the data on which the analysis is based. Without this preserved audio material to justify phonological decisions in the linear, written representation of the sound system, no accurate comparative studies in dialectology can be carried out. Each generation of linguists must repeat the work of their predecessors. With the kind of publication proposed here, chronological comparative studies of dialects as well as *Sprachbund* will be possible in the future. One should try to build up a library of tapes.

Badly needed are dialect atlases, as has been started for Iranic (of Afghanistan); Semitic and Turkic have nothing similar to offer.

Grammar

Before any studies of dynamic aspects are possible, it is necessary to study the "static" synchronic aspects of the participating languages. The available data are not bad for the more important languages but quite scanty for the rest. Moreover, the data are analyzed and described by adherents of many schools and vary considerably in detail, comprehensiveness, and degree of insight.

What we need is an ever better and deeper understanding of the modern, classical, and ancient languages of the Middle East. This implies the application of new analytical as well as descriptive methodology. The entire field must be updated. As J. Malone remarked, we need a torrent of activity on all languages and linguistics levels. A first major research priority is a thorough survey, a synthesis of the results of more than a century of philological-linguistic investigation, in order to rectify the complementary distribution of "Orientalist" and the "linguist."

The reanalysis of this vast amount of data is not simply compiler's work; if conducted in the manner suggested, it will constitute a major innovative approach to Middle Eastern linguistics, and will require much original new analytical research in order to fill in the many oversights and gaps in the available data. This has never been clearer than during the efforts at producing textbooks of Middle Eastern languages in the 1950s and early 1960s. Then, in the words of Killean, "fortunately, for the preparation of teaching materials, basic phonological and morphological facts about the major ME languages were already known so that tables of forms for nouns, verbs, etc., were easily copied or converted to linguistic diagrams. These were readily available in older textbooks of the classical languages, but what was sorely needed were drills to teach these forms in the lexicon of modern written usage. Therefore, stress in linguistic research was placed on statements of morphological derivation of forms and modern developments in the lexicon, thus in fact perpetrating the traditional reduction of a language to paradigms. However, in writing these textbooks the weak point in our knowledge of the modern languages was revealed—syntax. Merely knowing what potentially can occur in Arabic, Persian, Turkish, etc., did not help if our knowledge did not include quantitative studies of what actually does occur in present syntactic usage. Studies of this type, such as the computerized research on Arabic syntax conducted at Michigan, continue to be badly needed in all major languages of the ME."

There is unanimous agreement that of all levels of grammar, studies in syntax deserve the highest priority. Although this holds for all languages and dialects, for reasons of manpower and financial prospects, access to and/or availability of data as well as degree of need, the syntax of the major languages of the Middle East in their modern and earlier stages should be the primary object of study.

Unlike syntax, other levels of grammar have been relatively well served, but this observation here does not imply that levels such as phonology or experimental studies should not be intensively supported. It is not only to facilitate the writing of textbooks and drills, as mentioned above, that syntax urgently needs to be investigated; it is rather the recognition that syntax holds a central position in grammar. One should recall here that "syntax" implies the hierarchy from "surface" syntax over "deep" syntax to "deep" semantics and natural logic.

The study of syntax is thus intimately connected with studies in linguistic theory. There are good indications that the knowledge of Middle Eastern languages, as a counterpart to English and the European languages, can decisively contribute to general linguistics, as indicated.

Moreover, there are highly important levels of grammar which have become the focus of linguistics only recently, such as text theory. The long tradition of rhetorics and dialectics in the Middle East offers exciting possibilities for such innovative studies.

As to the analytical and descriptive methodology for these studies, some version of the generative approach is suggested for the simple reason that generative methodology is more concise and concrete and more likely to explain correlations in space and time than other approaches.

However, it was noted by some that the careful description of the surface data (and, if possible, a tape recording) should accompany those descriptions in order not to make impossible the control of the particular analysis. The disasters occurring if the material is attuned to any one theory are not exclusively modern, as evidenced, according to J. Malone, by the distortion of the Masoretic ideas by later Jewish grammarians trained in Arabic linguistics.

We still have only intuitive ideas of how to write a grammar, what format and what technical parlance are required. Therefore, it was felt necessary by most to urge our colleagues to avoid notational and terminological fads in linguistic research in writing up basic research. With such a tiny handful of researchers, it is imperative that we communicate rapidly and well with each other, and above all, that our written work endure to inspire students and ease their entry into the field.

With regard to language teaching, basic research in contrastive grammar, i.e., Middle East languages versus English, may prove to be extremely helpful.

Native Middle Eastern Linguistic Theory

With the advent of modern linguistic theory in Middle East studies, one observes with interest the efforts at reviewing and explicating the grammatical theories of the classical Muslim grammarians and philosophers such as Avicenna, and their epistemological ramifications. For assisting this research, a complete glossary of the traditional terminology of Arabic, Ethiopic, Persian, Turkish, etc., grammarians is very much needed.

Moreover, the studies in the sources of medieval linguistic thinking such as the Syrian and Greek tradition, or Indian and probably pre-Islamic Iranian linguistics, are important for our entire field.

Applied Linguistics

Another important contribution of Middle Eastern linguistics should be in applied linguistics, not so much in writing textbooks as in studies in language learning, especially of a second language, which still is largely a matter of intuition. Since such research has been largely restricted to Western languages, learning studies with Middle Eastern languages are likely to provide new insights into both practice and theory. Interestingly enough, this is presently the type of research government agencies appear to be most interested in funding rather than new or revised textbooks.

Irrespective of these financial opportunities, every advance in linguistics should be taken into consideration as far as practicable, to alleviate frustration and to shorten the seemingly endless time it takes to learn certain Middle Eastern languages, to the benefit of the general humanities.

A further aspect of applied linguistics that deserves priority is language engineering, i.e., that aspect that involves research in written, oral, and visual media approaches to language teaching and standarization. Such studies appear to be the most promising for cooperation between foreign and native scholars and are likely to provide dividends not only for purely theoretical linguistics but for the theoretical and methological basis of applied linguistic and language engineering as well.

Preparatory Research and "Tools"

The course of Middle Eastern linguistics suggested here must be accompanied by intensive work on basic learning "tools" and preparatory work in order to facilitate access to the field, both for the initiated researcher and the uninitiated student or the outside scholar interested in Middle East problems.

This research must not be misunderstood as being of secondary importance. Much of it constitutes orginal research in its own right, and is a "tool" and preparatory only with respect to the research suggested above.

DICTIONARIES. Linguists join all Arabists, Iranists, Turkologists, etc., in pleading for more and better dictionaries. Although intensive efforts are being made there is comparatively little that is adequate. There is great need for a comprehensive dictionary of Classical Arabic, as well as for contemporary dictionaries, and even more so, for areal (dialect/*Mundarten*) and period dictionaries, dictionaries of synonyms and antonyms, topical dictionaries, comparative-historical dictionaries, as well as etymological dictionaries; most of the few existing ones are long outdated.

Obviously, such efforts need the revival of a whole classical philogical tradition (widely unfashionable these days, especially in North America). The high costs involved may well be reduced not only by cheap reproductive methods but also by the application of technology, such as utilized for the computerized dictionaries of Berber by Abdel-Massih (1971), the Iranic dialect of Sangesari by Azami and Windfuhr (1972), and the ongoing Arabic Lexicography Program on Cairene Arabic directed by Hinds and Badawi in Cairo.

CONCORDANCES AND TEXT EDITIONS. Many of these dictionaries require the prior preparation of concordances of representative works and authors. Again the computer will allow for considerable reduction of costs. In turn, concordances have as prerequisites text editions.

It may be most reasonable for linguists themselves to undertake the urgent edition and reedition of selected texts. Unfortunately, in most editions so far, interesting linguistic problems and insights do not appear in independent articles which could help in identifying the general grammatical features, but instead are "buried" in "philological commentaries" and footnotes.

REFERENCE GRAMMARS. There is great need for adequate reference grammars even for the major languages, but especially for the lesser known languages and dialects. Accepting the fact that much is yet unknown, it is urgently suggested that such grammatical surveys be prepared, possibly in the form of a series of medium-length monographs like the *Narodny Azii i Afriki* series.

Though such grammars will mainly serve the student and nonspecialist, a necessary step towards specialists' work on grammar is detailed collations of grammatical evidence for various stages of the languages involved. Such an outstanding mammoth work as Lazard's on early modern Persian (1963) may be cited as a guideline.

Similarly, the grammatical features of individual authors and important individual works should be collated.

In writing grammatical statements, loose statements like "often," "almost always," etc., should be avoided, since they evidence that the rule has simply not been sorted out; as Reiner observed, such should be clearly identified as open problems. This is especially detrimental in a number of concise grammars where one observes a mixture of solid data with conjectures not identified as such for the noninitiate.

WRITING SYSTEMS. In this context one should stress the need for a linguistic study and survey of the bewildering number of different Middle Eastern writing systems from antiquity up to today and their correlation with the phonological systems.

Highly important to this end is the study of orthographic traditions of Middle Eastern languages written in alphabets other than the Arabic script, such as Persian or Turkish texts written in Hebrew, Latin, Greek, or Georgian etc.

The problems of paleography are intimately related to this point. Ideally, this branch of study would be an important auxiliary to historical dialectology and chronology if it were not so badly in need of a solid foundation. There have been only a few studies in this field which have succeeded in showing the advantages of an overall view over piecemeal notes.

Writing systems have not yet lost their aura as enigmatic "runes" of forbidding complexity. But as Reiner (1973) has shown so beautifully, the ambiguity of alphabets is largely a fiction perpetrated by certain insiders.

TRANSLATIONS. There is common agreement about the need for good, annotated translations of basic Middle Eastern texts important to linguists, such as works of Muslim grammarians and rhetoricians, as well as annotated translations of Muslim philosophy as far as it pertains to linguistics. Though generally frowned upon by the research community as a whole as not innovative or creative enough to warrant serious consideration, they are in fact badly needed as sources to speed up teaching, to encourage students and help them to see the possibilities of research in the field of Middle Eastern linguistics. In addition, they are needed as high-level evidence in the history and philosophy of language, especially in view of the present trends in general linguistics. Such work would benefit general linguists and improve communication between linguistic traditions. Such translations are valid dissertation topics.

A first step would be to prepare a list of the high-priority works to be translated into English. This effort should include not only resources in Middle Eastern languages, i.e., mainly Arabic, but also some basic texts on Middle Eastern linguistic history in other languages. Language barriers often hamper teaching as well as research. Thus not everybody is able to utilize important contributions written in Georgian. Even Russian is not yet well known in the West, although nearly half the research on the Middle East is conducted in the Soviet Union. Although Russian scholars have begun to add English résumés to their works, many of their contributions need to be translated, especially the many excellent surveys and introductions such as Oransky's introduction to Iranic linguistics (1960) or the five volumes of *Jazyki Narodov SSSR* (Moscow, 1966–1968).

A particular problem for North America is not only Russian works, but also the extraordinary amount of scholarship in German, including surveys, introductions, and dictionaries. They are not always easily utilized and should be translated, as has been done with Wehr's Arabic dictionary (1961). Lack of such translations constitutes a problem in teaching Middle Eastern linguistics as well as in utilizing the material for general linguistics courses, not only in North America. (It may be remarked that this need for translations from Western languages has to do not so much with the decreasing standard of education as with the common trend in all sciences toward English as the language of communication.)

EVALUATIVE SURVEYS: GENERAL AND CURRENT. As indicated in the beginning, there has been no lack of recent surveys. However, once published they are no longer current. And most have a graver drawback: rather than offering a critical, evaluative apparatus with indication of prominent contributions, they have a tendency to treat everybody as equal and to take the printed word as truth. This defect makes more sophisticated surveys urgently needed. Some of the volumes of the *Series Critica* may partially fill this gap.

More urgent yet is the need for reviews that include and offer an evaluative *synthesis* of *current* research. The number of scholars in this field should be small enough for specialists to keep up with them, but scholars and students alike even in related fields in the same language area generally find it difficult to evaluate contributions. Such reviews as Sobelman's bibliography on Arabic dialectology (1962) are helpful beginnings, where a few scholars review and evaluate the contributions and indicate gaps. There is great hope that the planned register of current research and the monographic journal of Near Eastern linguistics by Hetzron and Buccelati will remedy this gap.

Since even a cursory glance at most existing surveys makes it obvious that some of their articles will last whereas others are even now of little value, such expensive publications should, as Hodge suggests, be supplanted by a series of separate fascicles, to be replaced as soon as felt necessary by the editorial board, reproduced cheaply, and made available by subscription to all or any part of them.

Finally, much has been said against huge, all-encompassing surveys. Yet the example of the *Grundriss der Iranischen Philologie*, much of which still is of basic value today even if limited in terms of linguistic levels and views, is ample proof that such surveys are worthwhile and desirable ultimate goals, if prepared thoroughly and published at crucial points in a particular field. Iranistics and Semitics appear to be at such a point, and Turkology is already publishing its *Philologiae Turcicae Fundamenta*.

BIBLIOGRAPHIES: GENERAL AND CURRENT. Full bibliographies, especially including research done in the Middle East, could be attached to such fascicles as mentioned in the preceding section or issued separately in a similar, cheap fashion. One should mention here as an example the short-lived project of a computerized bibliography of Iranic studies at the Center for Near Eastern and North African Studies at the University of Michigan, directed by K. Allin Luther. The use of the computer allows for inexpensive printouts of literature on any particular combination of topics.

The issues of the *Linguistic Bibliography* appear much too far behind the year of publication of most entries. One may suggest a clearinghouse, perhaps one for Semitics, Iranistics, and Turkology each, and one for the remaining languages, each of which can produce cheap computer printouts. The bibliographical books take much too long, are too expensive, and are often too selective. Special need is indicated with regard to publication in the Middle East itself; thus communications with prominent journals or libraries in the Middle East, such as the *Rāhnemā-ye Ketāb* in Tehran, should be established or improved for quick exchange of information.

A note of critique may be added. The length of bibliographies listing works on Middle Eastern linguistics is often misleading; there is actually very little specifically linguistic literature. Moreover, there are marked differences in the standards of the various compilers. At least some system or code should be devised to identify the linguistic relevance or the relevant points.

Individual Language Families and Areas

In terms of particular families and areas the various needs are quite similar to those general needs mentioned above.

Berber needs most a comparative reference grammar and comparative dictionary of North African Berber dialectology.

Cushitic needs studies at all levels. (The observations on Cushitic, Ethiopian, Semitic, and South Arabic are based on a letter by Gragg and on Leslau, 1970.) Not even the largest language, Gala, has a reliable dictionary. The possibility of so-called West Cushitic or "Omotic" languages being a sixth Afro-Asiatic language family needs to be investigated by sober reconstruction work in Cushitic and Chadic, subfamily by subfamily, until it is possible to make responsible statements.

Semitic: there is a wealth of data available for Semitic; what is urgently needed is the application of modern linguistic theory and methodology for the reconstruction of Proto-Semitic. The first major attempt at this, Louis H. Gray's *Introduction to Semitic Comparative Linguistics* (1934), was rejected by Semiticists as too hypothetical! Large-scale efforts to reconstruct the source of the Semitic languages and to clarify their position within Afro-Asiatic is a prime desideratum.

Semitic in *Ethiopia*: it has been said that, more than any other area of Semitics, the study of Ethiopian languages has married the best of contemporary linguistic methods to raw material of remarkable variety and age. But basic morphological information needs to be gathered even for *Tigre.* Needed are text editions of *Ge'ez* with grammatical appendices, a *Ge'ez* reference grammar with present-day pronunciation, textbooks, and a comparative-etymological dictionary. Ethiopia deserves tremendous attention for two reasons. (1) It is the best instance in Semitic of changes undergone by language groups in contact, i.e., Semitic and Cushitic; and (2) it is a laboratory for Semitic historical linguistics where a well attested protolanguage, or a close relative of it, namely, Ge'ez, splits into 9 or 10 clearly distinguished languages or dialect clusters. Once Tigre and some other dialects are better investigated, a genuine historical grammar of Ethiopic Semitic can be attempted. It should be as revealing for Semitic as the analogous Romance historical grammar is for Indo-European, and as destructive of long-ingrained myths about the organization, drift, and diachronic changes undergone by the Semitic languages.

South Arabic needs renewed basic fieldwork since the Vienna expedition at the turn of the century, because much of the material from that expedition has not yet been published; grammars, including phonology and morphology, e.g., for Soqotri, and more complete dictionaries of most dialects, as well as a comparative-etymological dictionary are needed. This important Semitic language group should be given *highest priority* for field research since it is most threatened with extinction and may be replaced by neighboring Arabic dialects.

Arabic needs research in syntax, an overview of the dialects, including fieldwork on the neglected dialects of Saudi Arabia itself, new field research, and atlases to complement the only great publication of this sort, that on greater Syria by Bergsträsser (1915). Social dialectology should be stressed and the diachrony of modern Standard Arabic and its regional standards investigated. There is a basic need for good historical, period, etymological, and topical dictionaries.

A completely blank spot on the map of Arabic appears to be Arabic spoken in southwestern and northeastern Iran; but a little has been published on Afghani and Central Asian Arabic enclaves, only some on Khuzistani.

Maltese and *Cypriotic* Arabic are ideal cases for bilingual studies. Maltese is almost single-handedly researched by Aquilina, the holder of the only chair of Maltese studies. This field needs more researchers.

Extinct Spanish *Mozarabic* is still a literary-philological province.

Aramaic and *Hebrew* still have to rely on the masterpiece of Rosenthal (1939), Bauer and Leander (1927), and Leander (1928). All levels need intensive renewed research. Hebrew linguistics has gained considerable momentum in Israel, especially Israeli Hebrew; for earlier stages the philological aspects have to be kept distinct from the linguistic aspects. Most important appear to be syntactic studies and diachronic dialectology, especially with regard to Aramaic-Hebrew *Sprachbund* features. Aramaic needs reedition of texts with grammatical appendices, descriptive, historical, comparative grammars, and comparative-etymological dictionaries; *Mandaic* especially deserves better attention. Important studies are those of ancient Achaemenian *Reichsaramäisch* as a lingua franca and its influence on other languages.

Extinct *Ugaritic* and also *Phoenician* and *Punic* need intensive philological work before an adequate summary can be drawn.

Akkadian reached a turning point with von Soden's *Grundriss der Akkadischen Grammatik* (1952) and his *Syllabar* (2nd ed., 1967). With the ongoing publication of the *Chicago Akkadian Dictionary*, Akkadian studies are ahead of many other areas. Needed are period, dialectal, historical, and comparative grammars, and syntactic research.

Iranic: Old Iranic urgently needs syntactic studies. Middle Iranic is largely a philological province; West Middle Iranic, i.e., Parthian and Middle Persian, needs comprehensive descriptive, comparative, and historical grammars and dictionaries which, as prerequisite, need grammars and dictionaries of individual major works, periods, and religious traditions, i.e., Zoroastrian, Buddhist, Christian, and Manichaean.

Among East Middle Iranic, Khwarezmian, Bactrian, and Kushan-Hephthalite are still so little known and so recently discovered that the basic need is philological groundwork in cooperation with linguists. Sogdian, however, better known now, urgently needs a good comparative reference grammar and a comparative-historical etymological dictionary.

All Middle Iranic languages need syntactic studies and thorough phonological analyses.

Modern Iranic: Modern Standard Persian has not yet been described adequately. Syntax must be the major object of studies—some everyday constructions have been discovered only recently. Period grammars [(of the caliber of Lazard's on early modern Persian (1963)] are badly needed. Up-to-date comparative-historical and etymological dictionaries are lacking in spite of plenty of available research data. The study of the Persian koines and the processes that led to the development of Iranian, Afghani, and Tajiki Persian, and in general the entire question of Persian dialectology today and in diachrony have hardly been investigated.

West Iranic languages besides Persian have been relatively well served, e.g., Kurdish and Baluchi. But much in Iran itself is little known, or unknown. Kumzari, known only from one little monograph (1922) and some other unrecorded Iranic dialects on the Arabic side of the Persian Gulf in

Oman, should offer exciting insights into bilingual studies. Similarly, the Persian pidgin ^{c}*Ajami* in the Persian Gulf has never been studied.

East Iranic languages in the Soviet Union, such as Ossetic and the Pamir languages, are well covered but there is a lack everywhere of comparative grammars and comparative etymological dictionaries. Pashto, the second most important East Iranic language, needs thorough syntactic studies as well as period grammars, dictionaries, and dialect studies.

Armenian is relatively well served. Most important are period grammars and, for the Western reader, a comprehensive reference grammar for Old Armenian as well as modern Armenian. Historical dialectology presents one of the most complicated problems in the Middle East.

Dardic-Kafir languages are poorly covered except for such single-handed efforts of Morgenstierne (1944; 1956). Work on all levels needs to be done. It is evidently too early to expect a comprehensive reference grammar.

Gypsy in the various countries of the Middle East has been little studied. Of all Middle Eastern languages, it is probably the most intricate subject for sociolinguistics and *Sprachbund* studies.

Of the *Altaic* languages, *Mongolian*, represented by a few remaining villages in Afghanistan, needs study on all levels.

Turkish, as the largest group of Turkic languages, has the same needs as Persian and Arabic: diachronic and synchronic phonology and syntax, the development of Ottoman as a *Schriftsprache*, thorough editions of selected historical texts in Khwarezmian-Chagatai, Mamluk-Qipchak, the recording of Balkan-Rumelian and Anatolian dialects, and that blank spot mentioned above, the Turkish dialects in Iran and Afghanistan, as begun by Doerfer. Further desiderata are *Sprachbund* studies of Turkic with Slavic and a host of Iranic languages, descriptive grammars for all historical and modern dialects. Most important especially for phonology are the Turkish documents in non-Arabic orthography.

A dialect atlas is badly needed, as are comprehensive comparative-etymological dictionaries.

Academic Setting and Communication

The preceding survey attempts to demonstrate two points: first, the overriding importance of Middle Eastern linguistics for the analysis and theory of the linguistic aspect of human dynamics; second, the great efforts and the renewed vivacity in Middle Eastern linguistics.

It is the task of the departments, the universities, and the academic community to recognize these hopeful developments, and to support them. The situation in which linguists feel forced into a kind of dual existence depending on their audience, here as linguists, there as area specialists, must be avoided.

Similarly, linguists' feelings of frustration caused by the conflict between their teaching obligations and their actual research should be lessened. Such obligations, imposed by the academic environment, are not conducive to creative communication, especially with regard to the rapid changes within linguistics: even the most creative mind is bound to be overwhelmed by duties once out of and away from the centers of the field, as well remarked by Killean.

It must not be forgotten that the huge amount of scholarship has been accomplished by a minimal number of scholars. The very first priority, therefore, could well be to increase this number substantially. More data than in any other area have to be covered, data stretching over 5000 years of recorded human history, longer than anywhere else.

Some colleagues expressed certain doubts as to the implementation of suggestions for the future, and argued that the availability of basic textbooks, the introduction of the self-instructional method, the lack of funding of material development, and the lessening interest of the administrations in international studies all indicate that the number of (employed) linguists of the Middle East will remain the same, if not decrease; job openings are less likely to occur, because linguists tend not to retire as fast as graduates are available.

This need not be so. The reorientation of Middle Eastern linguistics, which is only part of a general reorientation in the humanities as a whole, and the renewed attention to interdisciplinary studies may well bring about new approaches in the academic setting, and implement such an appealing suggestion with regard to "glottodynamics" studies as was made by Doerfer: to form new departments in order to study the problems of the correlation between (such long-lasting symbiotic language familes as) Altaic-Turkic and Iranic languages and their cultures; this would not simply mean correlating the two fields but a close junction, a completely new approach within the humanities and social sciences.

One may cite here a note by Polotsky (see Reiner 1970, p. 282), referring to "Semitic philology," but which applies to all Middle Eastern philology, "In a field where both workers and academic posts are relatively few, there are practical reasons against carrying the distinction between linguistics and philology to the full length demanded by theoretical considerations." Nevertheless, although extremes should be avoided, the suggested course for Middle Eastern linguistics requires, as Killean pointed out, that students of this field be exposed to a heavy dose of linguistic theory, learn the language of the theorists in all its shifts and nuances, and write in "linguese," in order to be valued by other members of the linguistic profession and to open communication channels. In the same way, more native speakers must be trained in theory and methodology to apply it to their own and/or neighboring dialects and languages. Not only will Middle Eastern linguistics thus establish wide communication but also offer sensible and significant data for future studies in syntax, semantics, and other aspects of language. It is suggested that scholars in this field not be ashamed of taking refresher courses, and attend summer linguistic institutes and linguistic society meetings, to keep Middle Eastern linguistics up-to-date, known, and recognized.

With the aim of better communication it is recommended that scholars initiate correspondence on a large scale, send offprints and especially preprints to colleagues not only in America, but also in Europe, the Soviet Union, and the Middle East, and increase publications in oriental and linguistics journals.

On the university level, linguists of the Middle East should increase their effort in contributing Middle Eastern examples to general basic linguistic courses, and offer seminars and higher-level courses in Middle Eastern linguistics.

In short, Middle Eastern linguists, in spite of the fact and exactly because of the fact that they are so few in number, should try to overcome the odor of esoteric erudition still widely connected with Middle East studies; they must create interest in the unparalleled potentials of the Middle East as a linguistic research area by increased communication as well as by providing adequate tools.

The question of how to implement all this may be answered by Ferguson's suggestion that an agency or an institute be created to direct specific long-range projects; such an agency could be attached to universities or other institutions. One may cite here again the concerted efforts within the USSR.

Moreover, he suggests that such projects need not be confined to one country. Thus the basic and most important work on dictionaries could well be commissioned to scholars or groups in those countries where the art of dictionary writing is most alive, with English as the language of reference, for the simple reason that English is increasingly becoming the language of science.

With regard to general linguistic study in Middle Eastern countries, one should think about the possibility of cooperating on a regular basis, such as by the exchange of scholars and publications.

ACKNOWLEDGMENTS

I thank all those who contributed in various ways to this report. Of the many scholars who so kindly answered the original questionnaire, the following submitted responses that were particularly useful:

Ömer Asim Aksoy, General Secretary, Turkish Language Academy, Ankara.
J. Aquilina, Malta (Maltese).
Faridun Badre'i, Tehran (Persian).
Iraj Bashiri, Minneapolis (Persian).
Catherine Bateson, Tehran (Arabic).
Haim Blanc, Jerusalem (Arabic).
Ariel Bloch, Berkeley (Arabic, Semitics).
A. J. E. Bodroligeti, Los Angeles (Persian, Turkish).
Gerhard Doerfer, Göttingen (Turkology, Altaic).
Charles Ferguson, Stanford (general Middle East, general linguistics).
Tahir Necat Gencan, Istanbul (Turkish).
Gene Gragg, Chicago (Ethiopic, Akkadian, general Semitics).
G. Hazai, Berlin GDR (Turkish, Altaic).
Robert Hetzron, Santa Barbara (Ethiopic, Semitics).
Carleton T. Hodge, Indiana (Afro-Asiatic).
Parviz N. Khânlari, General Secretary, Iranian Culture Foundation, Tehran.
Sâdeq Kiâ, President, Iranian Language Academy, Tehran.
Carolyn Killean, Chicago (Arabic).
George Krotkoff, Baltimore (Arabic).
Wolfgang Lentz, Marburg (Iranistics).
Mary M. Levy, Washington, D.C., LSA Committee on the Manpower Survey.
Joseph Malone, New York (Semitics).
Ernest McCarus, Michigan (Kurdish, Arabic).
Karle Menges, New York (Turkology, Altaic).
Hormoez Milâniân, Tehran (Persian).
Don Nilsen, Cedar Falls, Iowa (Afghanistan).
Habibullah Tegey, Illinois, Kabul (Afghanistan).
Ehsan Yarshater, New York (Iranistics).
Karl Zimmer, Berkeley (Turkology).

In addition to the above, I offer special thanks to those members of the faculty at the University of Michigan with whom I have discussed this report and who have helped clarify my thinking. Besides Ernest McCarus, some comments came from the following:

Ernest T. Abdel-Massih.
Edna Coffin.
Herbert Paper.
Gene Schramm.
Sabahat Tura.

I am most grateful to Ernest McCarus, who kindly went over the manuscript repeatedly and made many suggestions toward its improvement.

It should be unnecessary to add that none of the above are responsible for any of the shortcomings which, given the nature of the undertaking, will almost certainly be detected.

BIBLIOGRAPHY

Abboud, P. F. "Spoken Arabic." In: *Current Trends in Linguistics.* Vol. 6. T. A. Sebeok, ed. The Hague: Mouton & Co., 1970, 439–66.

Abdel-Massih, E. T. *Tamazight Verb Structure: A Generative Approach.* (*African Series,* Vol. 2.) Bloomington, Indiana: Indiana University Press, 1968. (Originally University of Michigan Ph.D. thesis).

———. *A Computerized Lexicon of Tamazight: A Berber Dialect of the Ayt Seghrouchen.* Ann Arbor: Center for Near Eastern and North African Studies, 1971.

Azami, Ch. A. and G. L. Windfuhr. *A Dictionary of Sangesari. With a Grammatical Outline.* Tehran: Franklin Book Programs, 1972.

Bartholomae, Ch. *Altiranisches Wörterbuch.* Strassburg: Trübner, 1904.

Bashiri, I. *BE as the Origin of Syntax: A Persian Framework.* (Bibliotheca Islamica. Middle Eastern Languages and Linguistics, number 2.) Minneapolis, 1973. (Originally University of Michigan Ph.D. thesis).

Bauer, H. and P. Leander. *Grammatik des Biblisch-Aramäischen.* Halle/Saale, 1927.

Bergsträsser, G. "Sprachatlas von Syrien und Palästina," *Zeitschrift des Deutschen Palästina-Vereins,* **38** (1915), 169–222.

Blanc, H. *Communal Dialects in Baghdad.* (*Harvard Monographs,* Vol. 10.) Cambridge, Massachusetts: Harvard University Press, 1964.

Bloomfield, L. *Language.* New York: H. Holt & Co., 1933.

Brame, M. "On stress assignment in two Arabic dialects." In *A Festschrift for Morri's Halle.* S. R. Anderson and P. Kiparsky, eds. New York: Holt-Rinehart-Winston, 1973, pp. 14–25.

Brockelmann, C. *Grundriss der vergleichenden Grammatik der semitischen Sprachen.* Berlin: Lemcke & Buechner; New York: Reuther & Reichard, 1908–1913.

Chen, M. Y. and W. S.-Y. Wang. "Sound change: actuation and implementation," *Language,* **51.2** (1965), 255–281.

Current Trends in Linguistics. Vol. 6. *Linguistics in South West Asia and North Africa.* T. A. Sebeok, ed.; Ch. A. Ferguson, C. T. Hodge and H. H. Paper, associate eds. The Hague-Paris: Mouton & Co., 1970.

Doerfer, G. *Türkische und mongolische Elemente im Neupersischen,* Vols. 1-3. (*Veröffentlichungen der Orientalischen Kommission,* Vols. 16, 19, 20). Wiesbaden: F. Steiner, 1963–1967.

———. "Irano-Altaistica: Turkish and Mongolian Languages of Persia and Afghanistan." In: *Current Trends in Linguistics,* Vol. 6. T. A. Sebeok, ed. The Hague: Mouton & Co. 1970, pp. 216–234.

———. with W. Hesche, H. Scheinhardt, and S. Tezcan. *Khalaj Materials.* (*Uralic and Altaic Series,* Vol. 115). Bloomington, Indiana: University of Indiana Press, 1971.

Ferguson, Ch. "Diglossia," *Word,* **15** (1959), 325–340.

Fishman, J. A., ed. *Advances in Language Planning.* (*Contributions to the Sociology of Language*, Vol. 5). The Hague-Paris: Mouton & Co. 1974.

Gelb, I. et al. *The Assyrian Dictionary of the Oriental Institute of the University of Chicago.* Chicago: Oriental Institute, 1964 sqq.

Gray, L. *Introduction to Semitic Comparative Linguistics.* New York: Columbia University Press, 1934.

Grundriss der Iranischen Philologie. W. Geiger and E. Kuhn, eds. Strassburg: Trübner, 1895–1904.

Handbuch der Orientalistik. Bertold Spuler, ed. Leiden-Köln: Brill, 1952 sqq.

Herdan, G. *Quantitative Linguistics.* London: Butterworths, 1964.

———. "Haeckels biogenetisches Grundgesetz in der Sprachwissenschaft," *Zeitschrift für Phonetik*, **19** (1966), 321–338.

Herzog, M. *The Yiddish Language in Northern Poland: Its Geography and History.* Bloomington: Indiana Univ., the Hague: Mouton & Co., 1965.

Hetzron, R. "Toward an Amharic case-grammar," *Studies in African Linguistics*, **1** (1970), 301–354.

———. "Presentative function and presentative movement," *Studies in African Linguistics*, **2** (1971), 79–105.

Hodge, C. T. "The linguistic cycle," *Language Sciences*, **13** (1970), 1–7.

Hymes, D. *Foundations in Sociolinguistics.* Philadelphia: University of Pennsylvania Press, 1974.

Lazard, G. *La langue des plus anciens monuments de la prose persane.* Paris: Klienksieck, 1963.

Lees, R. B. *The Phonology of Modern Standard Turkish.* (*Ural-Altaic Series*, Vol. 6). Bloomington, Indiana: University of Indiana Press, 1961.

Leslau, W. "Ethiopic and South Arabian." In: *Current Trends in Linguistics*, Vol. 6. T. A. Sebeok, ed. The Hague: Mouton & Co., 1970, pp. 467–527.

MacKenzie, D. N. "The origins of Kurdish." In *Transactions of the Philological Society.* Oxford: Blackwell, 1961, pp. 69–86.

Malone, J. "Wave theory, rule ordering, and Hebrew-Aramaic segolation," *Journal of the American Oriental Society*, **91** (1971), 44–66.

———. "A Hebrew flip-flop rule and its historical origins," *Lingua*, **30** (1972), 422–448.

Morgenstierne, G. *Indo-Iranian Frontier Languages.* 3.2 and 3.3 *The Pashai Language.* (*Instituttet for Sammenlignedne Kulturforskning*, Series B, Vol. 40). Oslo: Ascheboug; Leipzig: Harrassowitz, 1944; 1956.

———. *Irano-Dardica.* (*Beiträge zur Iranistik*, Vol. 5). Wiesbaden: Reichert, 1973.

Moyne, J. A. "Reflexive and emphatic," *Language*, **47.1** (1971), 141–163.

Oranskij, I. M. *Vvedenie v iranskuju filologiju.* Moscow: Izd. Vostočnoj Literatury, 1960.

Philologiae Turkicae Fundamenta. J. Deny et al., eds. Wiesbaden: F. Steiner, 1959–1964.

Pike, K. L. *Language in Relation to a Unified Theory of the Structure of Human Behavior.* (*Janua Linguarum. Series Major*, Vol. 241.) The Hague: Mouton & Co. (2nd revised ed.) 1967.

———. *Tagmemics and Matrix Linguistics Applied to Selected African Languages.* Ann Arbor: Center for Research in Language and Language Behavior, 1966.

Reckendorf, H. *Arabische Syntax.* Heidelberg: C. Winter, 1921.

Reiner, E. *A Linguistic Analysis of Akkadian.* (*Janua Linguarum. Series Practica*, Vol. 21.) The Hague: Mouton & Co., 1966.

———. "Akkadian." In: *Current Trends in Linguistics*. Thomas A. Sebeok, ed. The Hague: Mouton & Co., 1970, pp. 275–303.

———. "How we read Cuneiform Texts?" *Journal of Cuneiform Studies*, **25** (1973), 3–58.

Rosenthal, F. *Die aramäistische Forschung seit Th. Nöldekes Veröffentlichungen*. Leiden: Brill, 1939.

Shapiro, M. and Y. Shvika. "Nittuaḥ mekanografi s̱hel hamorfologia ha-ᶜivrit," *Las̱honenu* **27–28** (1963–1964), 354–372.

Sharifi, H. *A Generative Approach to the Development of Avestan and Old Persian Consonants*. Ph.D. thesis. Ann Arbor: University of Michigan, 1971.

Šaumjan, S. K. "Outline of the applicational generative model for the description of language," *Foundations of Language*, **1.3** (1965), 189–222.

Sobelman, H., ed. *Arabic Dialect Studies. A Selected Bibliography*. Washington, D.C.: Center for Applied Linguistics, 1962.

Soden, W. von. *Grundriss der akkadischen Grammatik*. (*Analecta Orientalia*, Vol. 33.) Rome: Pontificium Institutum Biblicum, 1952.

———. and W. Röllig. *Das akkadische Syllabar*. 2nd ed. (*Analecta Orientalia*, Vol. 42.) Rome: Pontificium Institutum Biblicum, 1967.

Thomas, B. *The Kumzari Dialect of the Shihuh Tribe, Arabia*. (*Asiatic Society Monographs*, Vol. 21.) London: Royal Asiatic Society, 1930.

Wehr, H. *A Dictionary of Modern Written Arabic*. English ed. by J. M. Cowan. Ithaca, New York: Cornell University Press, 1961.

Weinreich, U., W. Labov, and M. L. Herzog. "Empirical foundations for a theory of language change." In: *Directions for Historical Linguistics*. W. P. Lehmann and Y. Malkiel, eds. Austin, Texas: University of Texas Press, 1968, pp. 97–145.

Wright, W. *A Grammar of the Arabic Language*. Cambridge: Cambridge University Press, 1859–1862.

Zimmer, K. "Psychological correlates of some Turkish morpheme structure conditions," *Language*, **45** (1969), 309–321.

CHAPTER NINE

Literature

ROGER ALLEN

It is much harder to obtain statements about poetry than expressions of feelings towards it and towards the author.

I. A. Richards, *Practical Criticism*

What university criticism is disposed to admit is, paradoxically, the very principle of interpretive criticism, or, if one prefers (although the word still frightens), of ideological criticism; but what it will not admit is that this interpretation and this ideology should decide to operate in a purely internal field of the work; everything is acceptable provided the work can be connected to *something other* than itself, that is to say something other than literature.

Roland Barthes, *Modern Language Notes*, December, 1963

INTRODUCTION

Of all the disciplines to be discussed and analyzed in this book, perhaps none admits of so many different definitions and interpretations as that of literature. As a humanity, literature is less prone to analysis on the basis of statistical data or other easily identifiable criteria than some of the other disciplines under discussion. For example, it would be a rash person who would try to provide a general definition of a novel, bearing in mind the works of Richardson, France, Tolstoi, Joyce, and Beckett. Many of our correspondents, probably with all this in mind, have simply suggested that any attempt to set terms of reference for the discipline of literature should be avoided. This view is indeed tempting in that it permits a good deal of flexibility and latitude in both conception and approach, which are desirable where artistic and aesthetic criteria are involved. As will be seen, however, this has often led in the past to the emphasis of some aspects of literature at the expense of others, and further to the confusion of certain nonliterary activities (such as philology) with purely literary ones. Although it is undeniably true that the scholar in literature owes the availability of many of the tools for his research to work carried out in companion disciplines such as philology and lexicography, these and other kindred subjects can be considered as part of "literature" only in the widest possible sense, and they are touched upon within the context of this chapter only where they are relevant to the narrower concept of literature now to be outlined.

In order to avoid any confusion concerning our basic boundaries, it should be explained that the general conception within which literature is discussed here is that of *belles-lettres*. The dictionary definitions of the word "literature" talk of "writings whose value lies in beauty of form or emotional effect" (Oxford English Dictionary, s.v. "literature"), and "written works collectively, especially those of enduring importance exhibiting creative imagination and artistic skill" (Standard College Dictionary, s.v. "literature").

Such boundaries as these have been suggested by a significant number of respondents to our requests for information; they also represent the views of the literature scholars who have met to discuss the preparation of this Chapter and to assess some of the implications of its conclusions. It should immediately be pointed out that, in comparison with other disciplines represented at the conference, respondents on the subject of literature were few in number, a fact that aptly demonstrates the paucity of scholars engaged in the field. Thus one of the potentially largest subjects of all may be reflected in the views of a comparatively small number of specialists.

* * *

In analyzing the discipline of literary study as discussed in the above preamble it is possible to identify three modes of approach basic to literary study in general: the *literary historical*, which sees literature as a chronological sequence of works bound integrally to the historical process; the *literary critical*, which deals analytically with concrete works, and the *literary theoretical*, which treats the fundamental principles, categories, and criteria of literature.

Literary historical (diachronic) studies would include literary histories, period studies (the study of a more limited temporal segment of a literature), genre studies (the historical study of a literary form), literary biography, and any one of the possible combinations of the above.

Literary critical studies are primarily, though not exclusively, synchronic and cover a broad range of analytical work based on criteria intrinsic and/or extrinsic to the literary object itself. Under this rubric would fall psychological and social interpretations, stylistic analysis, lexical analysis (study of the use of literary language), formal analysis (rhyme, meter, etc.), structural analysis (the shaping and organization of literary utterances), figure analysis (the use of simile, metaphor, etc.), and many other analytical approaches to works of literature.

Literary theory deals not with concrete works but with the formulation of literary principles which find their application in historical or critical study. Such study would include work on prosody, aesthetics, text theory, and the like.

These various activities of the literary scholar are in a very real sense mutually dependent to the extent that deficiencies in one area of study are inevitably detrimental to work in other areas.

Beyond these categories lies the collection of materials for literary study, and the task of editing and translating texts. These are labors which demand not only philological and lexical tools but the integrated use of theoretical, analytical, and historical data from the study of literature. Text edition, translation, and the literary implications thereof, though relegated somewhat to the periphery of European and American literary study, are areas in which students of Middle Eastern literature do and most certainly should feel great concern.

Within the sphere of the study of Middle Eastern literatures, the Orientalist tradition grew out of a general intellectual milieu in which classical and Biblical studies were combined in a Christian context with a curiosity about and defensive stance toward Islam. Within such a framework, it is hardly surprising that much of the early research on Middle Eastern literature has been philological and historical in nature rather than critical or theoretical. Initially at least, such an order of priorities may have been the logical one, but unfortunately too few scholars seem subsequently to have been prepared to break away from the "classical" tradition and lay the foundations of a study of Middle Eastern literature which will conform more closely to that of other world literatures.

The view of literature as "written works in general" is also to be found in a number of anthologies of literature available in English. A few examples will suffice. James Kritzeck's *Anthology of Islamic Literature* contains extracts from Ibn Isḥaq's *Life of the Prophet*, Nizâm al-Mulk's *Siyâsat-Nâma*, Ibn Baṭṭûṭa's *Travels*, and (of course!) Ibn Khaldûn's *Muqaddima*. The same compiler's anthology of *Modern Islamic Literature* includes works by Al-Jabartî, Ziya Gökalp, King Abdallâh, Jamâl ᶜAbd al-Nâṣir, and Mohammed Reza Shah Pahlavi. Another such work (by Najib Ullah) contains sections on historical literature and geography, science, juridical literature, and commentaries on the Qur'ân within a work entitled *Islamic Literature*. Such works as these are listed here not so much to criticize their compilers as to point out that, like much previous research in Middle Eastern literatures, they fall within a much wider conception of literature than is envisaged in this chapter, and have contributed to a certain lack of focus in the discipline of literature studies within the Middle Eastern area in general. Notwithstanding such comments, previous generations of writers within this scholarly tradition, both Middle Eastern and Western, have produced works of lasting value without which a more exact discipline, which we would wish to advocate here, could not be undertaken.

There is, then, a tension existing between the conscious and rigorous approach advocated here and the consciously generalist approach of the Orientalist tradition. Implications of this tension become apparent in the work produced from within both traditions. Specifically, modern disciplinary literary work is carried out on the basis of articulated literary theory, whereas the more traditional, generalist work was often performed without the benefit of a theoretical orientation, or when it did have such an orientation, it may or may not have been literary-theoretical. A result of this situation is that the corpus of literary work produced from within the Orientalist tradition was by and large literary-historical with scarcely any analytical-critical efforts being made. In addition, the scope of "literature" was considerably broadened to include kinds of material (such as history, geography, and science) which were amenable to study without reference to strictly literary criteria.

It should be pointed out immediately that the tension thus described is probably more apparent than real. In stating the situation in these terms, there is no intention of declaring invalid work on materials other than literary materials within the definition above. What *is* intended is to remove literary-historical work from the general context of work done on the basis of a non-literary or quasi-literary theoretical orientation, and to set it within the total context of work done on the basis of literary theory.

* * *

Previous studies on the literature of the Middle East discussed here have been periodized along lines following political events. An attempt at categorization based on the kind of literary criteria which have been outlined above would subdivide along lines of literary schools and even genres. It is an accurate reflection of the "state of the art" that, in the absence of sufficient competent studies which treat these literatures along such lines, such an approach would at the moment be a risky and undesirable undertaking. In the surveys which follow, therefore, periodization based on external historical and/or political criteria will be deemphasized, as will geographical categorizations. Although a general chronological framework is implicit in the surveys, it is hoped that the lack of explicit emphasis on such boundaries will enable us to concentrate on the problems of literary study rather than on purely historical concerns within the literature itself.

The following sections are surveys of the study of individual Middle Eastern literatures with reference to types of and approaches to literary activity as mentioned above. In this connection, two points should immediately be emphasized. Firstly, only the literatures of Arabic, Persian, and Turkish have been chosen for examination, and thus major literary traditions such as that of Hebrew and Armenian are not covered; neither are the literatures of other Middle Eastern languages such as Urdu and Pashto. Secondly, the surveys are neither surveys of the literatures themselves nor bibliographical guides to the literatures or to studies on the literatures. Instead, they are selective analyses of literary studies of various kinds which attempt to show the kind of research which has been conducted on the literatures of the Middle East. In these surveys, attention is paid, as far as is possible and practical, to agreements and divergences between the Western and Middle Eastern traditions of literary study as reflected in the surveys. Finally, there is a categorization and evaluation of the studies mentioned, in order to indicate areas in which further literary study is needed.

The individual surveys are followed by a general conclusion which indicates problems facing the scholar today and priorities for future research in the field of Middle Eastern literature as a whole.

Arabic Literature

ROGER ALLEN

The literature written in Arabic which is known to us spans a period of approximately 14 centuries. The Arabs themselves were interested in the recording and collation of such works from a very early date (in this they seem to differ from the Persian tradition, as emerges from the section on Persian literature), and thus the tradition of literary study in the Arab world is scarcely less ancient than the literature itself. With regard to the Western tradition, one may perhaps record the school of Toledo as one of its first centers. There in the twelfth century, a group of translators under the guidance of Archbishop Raymond worked on a number of treatises in Arabic and passed to European culture some of the major achievements of Greek and Arab science and culture. Thus by any gauge that one cares to use, the scope of the survey that follows is enormous. It is therefore as well to emphasize at the outset that no attempt is made here to cover either all of the literature or all of the studies on the literature. The present writer's aim is merely to highlight certain approaches to the study of literature by quoting the works of scholars within the context of a survey of the major trends in the literature itself.

A number of works have been consulted in the process of writing this survey; some of them have been of major assistance in identifying attitudes to literature (and specifically to Arabic literature) and trends within the scholarly tradition, and others of a more bibliographic nature have helped to identify works which illustrate literary approaches. From lexica of world literature such as Kindler's, one gains the impression of a token gesture being made towards a major literature such as that of Arabic, and yet the material is mostly historical and descriptive and does not equal either in quantity or detail the entries for the Western and even Oriental literatures. With reference to Arabic, Brockelmann's monumental bio-bibliographical work, *Geschichte der arabischen Literatur,* uses a definition of "literature" more general than the ones which we are applying here, but in the sections devoted to *belles-lettres* can be found copious information concerning authors, works, and studies on works within a framework which is basically chronological but which manages to subdivide styles and schools by category This process is being continued and elaborated in the work of Fuat Sezgin, *Geschichte des arabischen Schriftums*; the volume in this series devoted to artistic prose has yet to appear. Meanwhile, a book which can provide information on recent publications is the "bibliographical introduction," *Middle East and Islam,* edited by Hopwood and Grimwood-Jones, in particular, the sections on "Classical Arabic Literature" by Derek Latham and "Representative Writers of Modern Arabic Literature" by Muṣṭafâ Badawî provide the student of literature with a useful short list of works which treat literature within the belles-lettrist context which we have adopted for this chapter.

To parallel these bibliographical sources in Western languages, mention should be made of a work of tremendous value published recently in Beirut. *Al-Adab al-ᶜArabî fî Âthâr al-Dârisîn* (Arabic Literature in the Writings of Scholars) [Al-ᶜAlî et al., 1971] represents the collective bibliographical wisdom of a group of Arabic literary scholars. The traditional periodization of Arabic literature (pre-Islamic, Umayyad, Abbasid, etc.), is followed, and each period is covered in a separate chapter; the last is devoted to a comprehensive survey of literary studies in which genres, schools, and approaches are dealt with in separate sections. The value of this work in assessing the state of the art as it has developed in the Middle East cannot be overestimated.

With regard to studies of Arabic literature available in Western languages, it should be pointed out that a relative lack of knowledge of and interest in Middle Eastern literatures among Western readers (when compared with European literatures) is reflected in the small number of publications in book form. That is a topic to which we return later in this section. As a result of this situation, it happens that much, if not most, research in the field of Arabic literature—particularly at present—appears for the first (and often the only) time in article form. In gathering and assessing this corpus of literary research, the *Index Islamicus*, prepared by Pearson in London, is and will no doubt continue to be an indispensable tool for the researcher. In order to reflect as much current research as possible in this paper, the author has relied heavily on the latest supplement to this series (up till 1973), and such information has been augmented by details kindly provided by colleagues in literature in the Near East and West. It is also worthy of mention at this point that the series entitled *Handbuch der Orientalistik*, which is in the process of publication, will also be of value to the scholar in Arabic literature. One volume already provides useful information on chronology and papyrology, and forthcoming volumes will doubtless furnish information which will add further dimensions to the reference tools available for literary study.

In the introduction to this Chapter, some specific guidelines with regard to approach and selection have been outlined. To conclude this brief preface to the section on Arabic literature, it should be mentioned that a good example exists of the kind of approach to the history of Arabic literature which is advocated here: the article "ᶜArabiyya" in the new edition of *The Encyclopaedia of Islam*, in which Sir Hamilton Gibb sets out within a literary framework the major schools and trends in both prose and poetry while deemphasizing aspects of politics, period, and geography. Although we would not wish to include, as he does, works of history and other nonliterary subjects, the article nevertheless represents one of the first attempts in the West—if not the first—to produce a survey of Arabic literature which discusses trends in and approaches to the literature to the same extent as it discusses the littérateurs themselves. It is within this framework that this section proceeds, while bearing in mind the caveat provided for us by I. A. Richards, quoted at the beginning of this chapter.

THE CLASSICAL PERIOD

Poetry

In the period preceding the birth of Muhammad and the rise of Islam, there was in the Arabian peninsula a tradition of oral poetry which the Arabs regard as the beginning of their literature. The origins of this tradition have not come down to us, and indeed it is unlikely that they were ever recorded in writing. However, several aspects of the developmental stage are available to us through a variety of poems preserved in collections recorded in the Islamic period. To this tradition belongs the *qaṣîda* (which may originally have carried the significance of "poem with a purpose," but which is usually rendered as "ode"). In particular, a group of poems composed by some of the most famous poets of this period were singled out by later compilers because of their length and poetic excellence in form, language, and of the imagery, and are known as the *Muᶜallaqât*. It is an unfortunate consequence of the singling out of these poems, however, that with a few exceptions literary scholars, both Arab and Western, have tended to devote their attention to them to the exclusion of the other poetry of the period, and also to generalize about the entire tradition on the basis of these poems, which are only one aspect of a many-sided tradition.

Stories about Muhammad's opposition to poetry and poets seem to have been exaggerated. Whatever the truth of the matter, poets such as Ḥassân ibn Thâbit wrote during the Prophet's lifetime, and the tradition continued with renewed vigor after his death. The *qaṣîda* form flourished at the hands of al-Akhṭal (d. 710), Jarîr (d. 728), and al-Farazdaq (d. ca. 728); the famous *Al-Naqâ'iḍ* (polemics) in which these three poets flung insults at each other were, to quote Nicholson, "redeemed from vulgarity by their literary excellence and by the marvellous skill which the satirists display in manipulating all the vituperative resources of the Arabic language."

In the Arabian peninsula, a group of poets began to devote their attention to erotic poetry and the development of the *ghazal* (love poem). The acknowledged master of this form is ᶜUmar ibn Abî Rabîᶜa (d. ca. 719), who dispensed with the conventions of the amatory prelude found in many earlier *qaṣîdas* and presented a more personal and unified picture of his own. The tradition of the detached lover pining for his absent beloved is represented by Jamîl al-ᶜUdhrî (who writes about his beloved Buthayna) and Majnûn (who languishes for love of Laylâ).

Mention must be made here of another category of poetry which has generally been overlooked by literary scholars, namely, the religious poetry of the Khârijites and also the Shîᶜites. Both these groups produced poets who expressed in their poetry attitudes to Islam from within their own tenets; Khârijite poetry in particular is noteworthy for its severe religious fervor and the stirring words with which the poet attempts to rouse his listeners to action.

It was a scholar of al-Baṣra, al-Khalîl ibn Aḥmad (d. 791), who examined much of the poetry described thus far, and by formalizing its rhythmic patterns, laid the basis for the literary theoretical study of *ᶜarūḍ* (prosody). The system which he devised, whereby the meters were divided up into initially 15, and later 16, different patterns on the basis of rhythmic combinations of vocalized and quiescent letters, has been retained almost unchallenged until the present day.

With the shift of focus of Islamic rule from the Arabian peninsula to Damascus and thence to Baghdad, the function of poetry and the milieu within which the poet would produce his work changed. In particular, the meeting of Arab and Iranian cultures and their mutual assimilation had a profound effect on both; this is visible in the development of Arabic poetry and prose.

During the latter half of the eighth century, two poets of Iranian extraction began to produce poetry which showed a tendency towards a greater simplicity of expression, Bashshâr ibn Burd (d. 784) and al-Ḥasan ibn Hâni', usually known as Abû Nuwâs (d. 803). From the point of view of the attitude of the poet to his art, Abû Nuwâs is remembered for his distaste for the conventions of the *qaṣîda* as expressed in his parody of the *nasîb* (amatory prelude) of the older tradition. Similar to these two poets in use of language but different in the content of his poetry is Abû al-Atâhiya (d. 826), who wrote poems with a pious and moralistic content.

The challenge to the old tradition exemplified by Abû Nuwâs' attitude, coupled with the development of the schools of philosophy centered on the cities of al-Kûfa and al-Baṣra in al-ᶜIrâq, led to the appearance of a "new school," in which the manifold resources of the Arabic language with regard to antithesis and other forms of word play were exploited to the full through a new facet of poetry which became known as *badîᶜ*, a reasonable translation of which might be "conceit." In the poetry of Abû Tammâm (d. 846) and al-Buḥturî (d. 897), this new trend is combined with a studied imitation of the poetry of the earliest period. In this connection, it is not insignificant that both poets produced anthologies of earlier poetry entitled *Kitâb al-Ḥamâsa* (Book of Bravery). Ibn al-Muᶜtazz (d. 907), the caliph of one day, not only wrote poetry himself but also supplied a theoretical study of the tenets of this new school in his *Kitâb al-badîᶜ* (Book on Poetic Conceits).

Among the great centers of literary patronage which emerged in the tenth century as a result of the decentralization of political control and the rise of local dynasties was the court of the Ḥamdânid prince, Sayf al-Dawla (d. 967). To it were attracted writers in many fields of learning [including the philosopher al-Fârâbî (d. 950)], and among the poets who flourished in its midst was Sayf al-Dawla's own cousin, Abû Firâs (d. 967). However, it is Abû al-Ṭayyib al-Mutanabbî (d. 965) who is generally considered to be the greatest poet of this age and, some would claim, of any age. His poetry represents a combination of the more studied and retrospective aspects of the works of earlier poets and the most skillful use of all the artifices provided by the *badîᶜ* style. The tradition of "court poetry" (traceable earlier in Abû Tammâm's famous ode celebrating the victory over the Byzantines at

Amoreum in 838, and in al-Mutanabbî's works, in poems written for or against various rulers) is also noticeable in the works of Ibn ᶜAbd Rabbihi (d. 940) and Ibn Hâni' (d. 973). The former was court poet of the Umayyads at Cordoba in al-Andalus (as the Arabs term Spain) and is the author of the famous *Kitâb al-ᶜIqd al-Farîd* (The Unique Necklace), an anthology on a variety of subjects divided into 25 books. Ibn Hâni', known as al-Andalusî (the Spaniard), led a somewhat checkered career in that he left Cordoba under a cloud and spent much of his life writing panegyrics for the Fâṭimid caliph, al-Muᶜizz, in a style imitative of that of Abû Tammâm.

Much different from al-Mutanabbî, although an admirer of his in earlier years, is Abû al-ᶜAlâ' al-Maᶜarrî (d. 1057). In his first collection entitled *Siqṭ al-Zand* (Spark of the Flint), he follows the tradition set by al-Mutanabbî in eschewing the studied classicisms of earlier poets, but in the *Luzûmiyyât* a title almost impossible to translate but implying that the poet imposes on himself rules of prosody not demanded by al-Khalîl's system), he produces a series of poems which discuss in the most pessimistic and critical terms the social and moral ills of his times and often scoff at the outward signs of Islamic devotion and practice.

Within the context of this period, three poets from al-Andalus are worthy of mention, Ibn Shuhayd (d. 1035), Ibn Ḥazm (d. 1063), and Ibn Zaidûn (d. 1070). While the third is probably the finest poet, the other two are significant for their contributions to poetic theory in general and courtly love in particular through their prose works, *Risâlat al-Tawâbiᶜ wa al-Zawâbiᶜ* and *Ṭawq al-Ḥamâma* (The Treatise of Familiar Spirits and Demons and The Dove Neckring, respectively). In the former work, Ibn Shuhayd suggests that the soul of the poet is responsible for the beauty of his writings and not his mastery of language and rhetoric, and in the latter Ibn Ḥazm analyzes the psycholology of love and includes some of his own verses.

All the poets mentioned thus far composed their poetry within the framework of the prosodic structure elaborated by al-Khalîl. Two innovations which occurred in the Arabic poetic tradition during this period were the development of the *muwashshaḥ* and the *zajal*, both of which first appear in al-Andalus. The origins of both these genres are obscure, and the history of their study in the West is a comparatively recent development in Arabic literary studies. With regard to the *muwashshaḥ* (a strophic poem ending in a colloquial *kharja* or "envoi"), we are fortunate in having not only some splendid examples transcribed and edited by a few dedicated Western scholars but also a work of poetic theory on the genre by Ibn Sanâ' al-Mulk (d. 1211), an Egyptian poet and critic. Whereas only the *kharja* of a *muwashshaḥa* is in the colloquial language, the *zajal* is composed entirely in it. Of this genre, the acknowledged master is Ibn Quzmân (d. 1160), and we are again fortunate in that Ṣafî al-dîn al-Ḥillî (d. 1349) has devoted a chapter of his work on colloquial poetry to the *zajal*.

The emergence of the *muwashshah* and *zajal* is symptomatic of the increasing role which folk literature began to play throughout the Arabic-speaking world. As the use of *badîᶜ* encouraged more and more artificiality in the output of poets, so did the imaginative and aesthetic aspects of the art become less important. To be sure, a few poets of great ability were able to avoid this tendency, but they are exceptional. The great mystic, Ibn al-ᶜArabî (d. 1240), for example, wrote some poetry of great beauty, and the Egyptian ᶜUmar ibn al-Fâriḍ (d. 1235) also wrote mystic poetry which has long been admired for its poetic qualities and the subtlety of its many-leveled significances. Finally, the poetry of another Egyptian, Bahâ' al-dîn Zuhayr (d. 1258), may perhaps be regarded as a kind of swan song for the "classical" period of Arabic poetry which revivalists were to imitate some six centuries later.

Within the field of Arabic poetry, literary activity was first focused on the task of compiling collections of the poems of earlier periods; this activity in itself was part of a growing interest in philology (itself an outgrowth of study of the Qur'an text), together with the needs of the urban secretarial class for works which could both divert and inform. The collection known as the *Muᶜallaqât* has already been mentioned. Another collection which included a number of shorter poems was compiled in the eighth century and named *Al-Mufaḍḍaliyyât* after its compiler, al-Mufaḍḍal (d. 787). In addition to the *Ḥamâsa* collections of Abû Tammâm and al-Buḥturî, the great littérateur al-Jâḥiẓ (who will be mentioned again in connection with prose literature) compiled among other works his *Kitâb al-Ḥayawân* (Book of Animals). The culmination of this activity was the *Kitâb al-Aghânî* (Book of Songs) by Abû al-Faraj al-Iṣfahânî, which is not only a collection of poems by a number of poets but also an invaluable source of literary biographical detail serving to remind us of the continuing oral aspect of the poetry and the connection of the poetic art with that of music.

Other writers at a slightly later period endeavored to place poets in classes (*ṭabaqât*) and thus inevitably found themselves drawn into making critical and analytical judgments. In particular, Ibn Sallâm al-Jumaḥî (d. 845) was apparently the first person to raise a question concerning the authenticity of some of the lines in the poetry written before Muhammad's birth. Bearing in mind the oral nature of the transmission of this poetry through the *râwî* or narrator (who was himself often a poet), such a question seems entirely reasonable. It was raised again in much more forceful and detailed fashion during the 1920s when two scholars, D. S. Margoliouth, (1925) and Ṭâḥâ Ḥusayn (1926) separately but simultaneously analyzed the poems and came to the conclusion that much of it was written in the Islamic period. The arguments advanced by these two eminent scholars, together with the objections of the many who objected to them, have recently been conveniently summarized by Monroe (1972) in an important article in which he points out that, in many ways, a stalemate has now been reached between the two sides and that a new approach seems warranted. By applying the Parry-Lord theory of the formulaic nature of oral poetry (originally tested on Homeric and Yugoslavian examples and used within the context of Arabic poetry in earlier dissertations by Hyde at Princeton and Zwettler at Berkeley), Monroe shows that exact textual niceties cannot be a part of a discussion of oral poetry and that, with some allowances for minor variations and memory lapses, the poetry which has been recorded is an accurate reflection of the tradition.

As the scope of philology and the study of the text of the Qur'ân expanded, a number of writers attempted to set down criteria for the assessment of poetry based on literary theoretical principles. Ibn Qutayba (d. 889), for example, suggested in the introduction to his *Kitâb al-Shi^{c}r wa al-Shu^{c}arâ* (Poetry and Poets) that a poem should be assessed on its own merits and not on the basis of the period in which it was written. In a more theoretical level, al-Jâḥiẓ (d. 869) produced an important work on rhetoric, *Kitâb al-Bayân wa at-Tabyîn* (Clearness and Elucidation), and Ibn al-Mu^{c}tazz set terms of reference for the "new" style in his *Kitâb al-Badî^{c}* (Conceits). Such early endeavors in literary analysis were brought to even greater heights in the tenth and eleventh centuries. al-Âmidî (d. 981) compares the poetry of Abû Tammâm and al-Buḥturî in his *al-Muwâzana* (Comparison) and proceeds to discuss the relative merits of individual lines of each poet. al-Qâḍî al-Jurjânî (d. either 977 or 1005) analyzes the poems of al-Mutanabbî in his *al-Wasâṭa* and considers the objections of his opponents. This movement reaches its culminating point in work of ^{c}Abd al-Qâhir al-Jurjânî (d. 1078—not to be confused with the former figure). al-Jurjânî stresses the importance of the whole context of the poem and not merely its formal aspect; ideas and structure cannot be considered separately. Furthermore, this theory of poetic imagery is unique in the Arab tradition in that it offers a comprehensive view of the psychological origin and impact of the image and of its nature and function in the work of art. A final figure whose name should be cited in this brief survey of the development of a tradition of poetics in Arabic is Ḥâzim al-Qarṭâjannī (d. 1285), who examined the implications of Aristotle's *Poetics* in a penetrating study entitled *Kitâb Sirâj al-Bulaghâ wa Minhâj al-Udabâ* (Guide for the Eloquent and the Way for the Littérateur).

The above paragraph shows clearly that the study of Arabic poetry and the principles underlying it are a tradition of long standing. The literature scholar is also fortunate in that a good deal of research has been carried out on the theories developed by this tradition, perhaps the more so in recent times when a number of scholars have begun to take a greater interest in the applications and implications of literary theory. A number of excellent editions and translations of the works of criticism briefly described above have been published, including de Goeje's text of Ibn Qutayba's *Kitâb al-Shi^c^r wa al-Shu^c^arâ* (1947) (the important introduction to which has also been translated into French by Gaudefroy-Demombynes), Kratchkovsky's edition of Ibn al-Mu^c^tazz *Kitâb al-Badî^c^* (1947) Bonebakker's edition of *Naqd al-Shi^c^r* by Qudâma ibn Ja^c^far, (1956) and Ritter's edition and German translation of al-Jurjânî's *Asrâr al-Balâgha* (1954, 1959). Gustave von Grunbaum devoted a great deal of work early in his career to a study of al-Bâqillânî and to numerous articles on the subject. The student of Arabic poetics is also fortunate in that there is a good analytical history of this interesting period in the development of criticism, namely, the study of Amjad Trabulsi, *La critique poétique des Arabes*, in which can be found details on critics, the different conceptions of poetry and of the function of the poet, and the genres and motifs found within the art.

In a paper presented at a recent conference on "Logic in Classical Islamic Culture," Bonebakker (1970) has traced the early development of Western interest in some of the earlier philologists and critics. Ignaz Goldziher (1896) was apparently the first to notice the change in attitude to the poetry of previous generations personified by Ibn Qutayba (in his *Abhandlungen zur arabischen Philologie*). Subsequent research by Gibb and others has led to a revision of certain points of Goldziher's, and Bonebakker's own careful work (as mirrored in the paper mentioned above and in other works) has shown that a close analysis of the works of these early Arab literary scholars can still reveal valuable insights into the development and nature of Arabic poetic criticism and theory. One example of such a close analysis has recently been published, Raymond Scheindlin's excellent study (1974) of Ibn Qutayba's theories in the light of the works of one particular poet, *Form and Structure in Arabic Poetry: The Poems of al-Mu^c^tamid ibn ^c^Abbād*. The important figure of ^c^Abd al-Qâhir al-Jurjânî has been the object of research by a number of scholars. In addition to the work of Ritter described above, mention should also be made of A. A. Badawî, who has written a complete work on al-Jurjânî, and of Muḥammad Mandûr, who stresses the importance of this early literary theorist in his *Fî al-Mîzân al-Jadîd* (In the New Balance). Among works in English, pride of place must be given to the Oxford thesis (soon to be published) of Kamal Abu Deeb in which al-Jurjânî's ideas and theories are examined and discussed within the context of modern literary theory.

We turn from those who may be termed the earliest scholars in Arabic literature and those who have studied their writings to the poetry itself and those who have investigated the texts and poets and analyzed their history and approach to the art. Scholars in both East and West have long been engaged in the process of editing the *Dîwâns* of poets; many of those published in both areas were printed in the nineteenth century, and the process of producing new editions with the dual benefits of better printing and modern scholarship continues in the major publishing centers of the Middle East. Among European scholars who undertook the arduous task of copying and collating manuscripts and producing early editions were Germans such as Nöldeke and Rückert. Sir Charles Lyall was an early champion of the lesser-known collections such as the *Mufaḍḍaliyyât* (1918), although he ascribes the first endeavors with that particular collection to Thorbecke of Heidelberg. Lyall also produced some of the finest translations of this poetry, a distinction he shares with Wilfrid and Lady Anne Blunt and Nicholson. The following is the unusual verdict of Nöldeke (1899–1901, introduction) on this poetic tradition:

> It is questionable whether the aesthetic pleasure provided by the study of ancient Arabic poetry is worth the great pains required even to approach an understanding of the same.

One can say only that many other attempts at translating this poetry seem rather to show the labor involved in the process than a particular awareness of the aesthetic pleasure to be had in appreciating the results; an interesting study in such a process of appreciation is to be found in the first volume of the *Journal of Arabic Literature* under the title "And Heard Great Argument."

Mention was made above of the need for further research on religious and political poetry, represented in the summary by that of the Shîᶜites and Khârijites. Within that context, a beginning has been made with regard to the latter group with the publication by Iḥsân ᶜAbbâs in 1963 of a collection of Khârijite poetry, a collection which shows convincingly how important such literary expression is in the assessment of the beliefs of such groups within the compass of Islam.

A few select scholars in recent times have devoted their attentions to the poetry of Spain; among Spaniards, Garcia Gomez and Ribera, and among other Western nationalities, Stern, Nykl, and most recently Monroe. In spite of the efforts of these scholars and others to publish texts, editions, and translations, there remains a need to make much of the poetry of lesser-known poets available in good editions so that scholars may base their verdicts on the poetry and its influence on a wider sample than is generally accessible at the moment.

In assessing works in which the poetry and poets are discussed and analyzed, we are confronted with a great wealth of material. Among histories that deal specifically with a particular period or area, we would single out for mention *Ta'rîkh al-Shiᶜr al-Arabî ḥattâ Âkhir al-Qarn al-Thâlith al-Hijrî* (History of Arabic Poetry Till the End of the Third Century A.H.), by Najîb al-Bahbîtî. This work, in spite of the historical tone of its title, succeeds in discussing genres and theories in a convincing literary fashion. A similar work on one period of Spanish literature (with heavy emphasis on poetry) is *Ta'rîkh al-Adab al-Andalusî*: *ᶜAṣr Siyâdat Qurṭuba* (History of Spanish Literature: The period of Cordoba's Ascendancy) by Iḥsân ᶜAbbâs. Broader in scope but equally valuable is Jawdat al-Rikâbî's *Fî al-Adab al-Andalusî* (On Spanish Literature). A more general and less detailed work on the development of poetry and poetics in the East is a chapter by von Grunebaum (1944) in *The Arab Heritage*, edited by N. A. Faris.

On a more theoretical level, von Grunebaum's studies published in the 1940s should also be cited. In *Die Wirklichkeitweite der früharabischen Dichtung* (The Range of Reality in Early Arabic Poetry), he discusses the various classes of poetry (satire, elegy, etc.) in the early period described above and then addresses the question as to how far reality entered the range of poetry and was sublimated by the poet's own creativity. In the general thrust of his works published at this time, he seems to be anticipating many of the remarks made in the introduction to this chapter, in that he stresses the need to identify belles lettres as an object of study in and of itself, to ascertain its historical development, and then to foster a sense of artistic and aesthetic appreciation.

A number of critics in the Arab world had of course been following this approach already. Prime among these was Ṭâhâ Ḥusayn, with such works as his controversial study of pre-Islamic poetry, *Fî al-Shiᶜr al-Jâhilî* [later revised and republished as *Fî al-Adab al-Jâhilî* (On Pre-Islamic Literature)], and *Ḥadîth al-Arbiᶜa* (Wednesday Talk), in the three volumes of which he discusses a number of poets mentioned in the above survey. Muhammad Mandûr has already been mentioned in connection with his study of al-Jurjânî in *Fî al-Mîzân al-Jadîd*, and he too has contributed a great deal to the development of literary criticism and theory in the modern Arab world. In connection with the appreciation of poetry (and perhaps as a partial response to the negative comment of Nöldeke noted above), we should mention the important work of Muhammad al-Nuwayhī, *al-Shiᶜr al-Jâhilî: Manhaj fî Dirâsatihi wa Taqwîmihi* (Pre-Islamic Poetry: A Way of Studying and Appreciating It).

Some of the critics mentioned in the preceding paragraph have also contributed valuable studies to the corpus of biographical writings. There is an enormous list of works which simply use the literary histories and *ṭabaqât* works to produce a study of an individual poet, but several books stand out from this list by virtue of the penetration with which their authors interpret, both artistically and psychologically, the writings of the poet himself in order to present us with new insights. Among these works are Ṭâhâ Ḥusayn's various studies on al-Maᶜarrî (1936, 1937, 1944) in addition to one of al-Mutanabbî, (1936), those of al-ᶜAqqâd on Abû Nuwâs (a psychological study) and Ibn al-Rûmî, those of al-Nuwayhî on Bashshâr and Abû Nuwâs, and that of al-Bahbîtî on Abû Tammâm. To these should be added a recent work by Wagner on Abû Nuwâs.

Several genres within Arabic poetry have been the subject of individual studies. Shawqî Ḍayf has written on the elegy and Muhammad Ḥusayn on the satire. In his study of the love poem (*ghazal*), Shukrî Fayṣal provides a fine example of the many kinds of insight (social, political, psychological, etc.), that emerge from an analytical survey of a number of poets who write in a single genre.

A few isolated works are available in European languages which treat an aspect, genre, or motif of poetry in detail. A fine study of the love poem (*ghazal*) as a genre, to be placed alongside that of Shukrî Fayṣal in quality, is *The Development of the Ghazal in Arabic Literature* by A. Kh. al-Kinany, a Syrian who had the work published in English in Damascus. The author traces the emergence of the *ghazal* itself, quoting examples of aspects of it in the *qaṣîda* tradition, and then goes on to analyze the concept of courtly love as seen in the poetry itself and to investigate the structure and imagery of the poetry before giving examples in translation from a selection of poets. In a recent work by Andras Hamori, *On the Art of Medieval Arabic Literature*, a section is devoted to the study of genres and their transformation, provoking in the process some interesting ideas which demonstrate both the value of this kind of detailed study and the need for further efforts in the same direction.

Two modern studies of the poetry written before the rise of Islam deserve special mention because of the way in which they open new horizons for research. The first is *Structural Continuity in Poetry* by Mary Catherine Bateson, in which the author uses the techniques of modern structural linguistic analysis to examine five *qaṣîdas*. Employing phonological and morphological statistics, she suggests some far-reaching ideas not only about the form of the poems and the poet's attitude to his art, but also about ways in which this method of study may produce still more results in the future. The second is *Studien zur Poetik der altarabischen Qaside* by the German scholar, Renata Jacobi. In this work, there is a systematic investigation of the simile and metaphor within the *qaṣîda* found in Ahlwardt's *Diwans of Six Arabian Poets*. Jacobi joins Bonebakker and others in urging caution before accepting Ibn Qutayba's analysis of the *qaṣîda*. Under Jacobi's analysis the *qaṣîda* emerges as an organic unity in the mind of the Arabs of the time, and it seems appropriate that von Grunebaum himself is the reviewer who declares this work to be "a great leap forward . . . [making] skillful use of the advances in stylistic theory and analysis made during the last decades in more fully developed fields of literary research" (*IJMES*, **3**, 2, 223).

Some of the most significant advances in our understanding of the influences of and on Arabic literature are occurring in the field of Hispano-

Arabic studies. Pioneering work of an essentially philological nature has been done by Garcia Gomez, Nykl, and Stern, thus making many texts available to us. Stern, following the lead of M. Hartmann in his *Das arabische Strophengedicht*, conducted studies of a more theoretical nature in analyzing the structure and form of the *muwashshaḥ* and *zajal*. *Les chansons mozarabes*, "Les vers finaux . . .," "Studies on Ibn Quzman," and "Two Anthologies of *muwashshaḥ* Poetry" are good examples of the careful work of this outstanding scholar. All students of Hispano-Arabic literature will be grateful for the recent publication of most of Stern's materials on the subject in book form under the title *Hispano-Arabic Strophic Poetry*. This tradition of careful textual interpretation and analysis is being continued by James Monroe in his *Risālat al-Tawābi^c wa al-Zawābi^c: The Treatise of Familiar Spirits and Demons by Abū ^cÂmir ibn Shuhaid al-Ashja^ci al-Andalusī*, "The Historical Arjūza . . .," and other works.

An attempt has been made by some scholars (Nykl, Pérès, and von Grunebaum) to enter the vast field of comparative literature and identify influences of Hispano-Arabic literature on the troubadour tradition. However, the entire question of the effect of one culture or literature on another is a subject which would seem to require more concrete information than is currently available to the scholar in Romance and Hispano-Arabic literatures. Scholars are broaching the question from both sides, and one of the more interesting aspects is that of Aljamiado literature (Romance written in Arabic characters). For the purpose of this chapter, it is sufficient to note that current research carried out by scholars such as L. P. Harvey tend to suggest that the theory that Hispano-Arabic literature influenced the Romance tradition may have to be revised.

To conclude this survey of studies on the poetry and poetics of the "classical" period, we return to one of the very bases of the poetry itself, namely prosody. The system of al-Khalîl, whereby poetry was classified into 16 meters in which rhyme and syllabic quantity were the criteria, was followed by the majority of poets in the Arab world until the twentieth century when, as will be noted later in this chapter, experiments such as blank and free verse were tried. The German scholar Weil, after prolonged research on the subject, suggested in 1954 that *stress* may have been the principal factor involved in the quantification of the line of Arabic poetry as conceived by al-Khalîl. In 1967, Shukrî ^cAyyâd published his *Mûsîqâ al-Shi^cr al-^cArabî*, in which he delved further into this subject, and in a recent article Kamal Abu Deeb, a young Syrian scholar, has carried this a stage further by analyzing a number of al-Khalîl's "meters" according to a completely different system based on stress. The title of this article talks of "A Radical Alternative to al-Khalîl's Prosody," and this attempt to question one of the very bases of classical Arabic literary theory is perhaps the best example one could wish for to illustrate ways in which new studies based on modern literary techniques may alter some of our approaches to Arabic poetry and poetics.

Prose

As with poetry, so with prose any study of the earliest period with respect to the emergence of a prose tradition is hampered by the lack of texts. From a variety of sources it is possible to glean examples of gnomic sayings, and aphorisms and proverbs which were frequently composed by *kuhhân* (soothsayers) in *saj*^{c} or rhyming prose, a stylistic device whereby the morphological resources of the Arabic language are used to build up series of phrases or sentences, the final syllables of which rhyme. However, these materials can give us only a sketchy idea of a tradition at that time.

The Qur'an itself remains the first recorded manifestation of an Arabic prose style, and from the outset it has been regarded as the masterpiece of all Arabic writing, being possessed of the quality of *i*^{c}*jâz* or "inimitability." This concept has been discussed in a number of works written in different periods; al-Bâqillânî, ^{c}Abd al-Qâhir al-Jurjânî, and Muṣṭafâ Ṣâdiq al-Râfi^{c}î (d. 1937) are a few of the many authors who have expressed views on this subject. In these works discussion has touched on the question of the style of the Qur'an, and that in turn has had considerable effect on the development of criteria for the analysis of both poetry and prose. The Qur'anic text itself has had a pervasive influence on prose writing in Arabic, and indeed, in its earlier *Sûras* (chapters), the use of *saj*^{c} heralds the appearance of a new prose genre in the tenth century and a stylistic phenomenon which was to have a profound effect on the development of Arabic prose literature in the ensuing centuries.

Among the first figures associated with the development of an artistic prose tradition is ^{c}Abd al-Ḥamîd al-Kâtib (d. 750). The description "al-Kâtib" (secretary, scribe) seems significant since much activity in the sphere of early prose writing centered around the ethics and manners of the "secretarial" school (which we have already mentioned in connection with the compilation of early anthologies of poetry). Urbane works began to appear in which modes of conduct for the emerging secretarial class and court officials were suggested, and from this environment the literary politesses of Arabic prose began to emerge. The fact that the Arabic word for belles-lettres is *adab*, which also implies "good manners," is no accident. Another prose writer of this early period is a pupil of ^{c}Abd al-Ḥamîd, the Persian Rûzbih, who assumed the Arab name of Ibn al-Muqaffa^{c} (d. 757). He translated the Sanskrit *Fables of Bidpai* into Arabic as *Kalîla wa Dimna*, and as often happens in the process of translation, he found himself constrained to produce a refined and elegant prose style in Arabic which would be suitable for these tales while avoiding the rhyming conventions of earlier times.

The scholar whose erudition and sense of style single him out from this general tradition is Abû ᶜUt͟hmân ᶜAmr ibn Baḥr, usually known by his nickname al-Jâḥiẓ. ("the goggle-eyed," d. 869). One of the greatest polymaths in the corpus of Arabic writings, he produced detailed and witty compendia of earlier literature in his *Kitâb al-Ḥayawân* (Book of Animals) and *Kitâb al-Buk͟halâ'* (Book of Misers), an important work on rhetoric, *Kitâb al-Bayân wa al-Tabyîn*, and numerous essays on a variety of subjects, religious, philosophical, and cultural. Through all these he developed a prose style which is uniquely his own, one in which a sense of variety and, at the same time, balance was combined with a conciseness which often seems almost Tacitean to produce a distinctive and highly polished literary style. A younger contemporary of al-Jâḥiẓ, Ibn Qutayba (whose work on poetry and poets has already been mentioned) contributed a great deal to the development of a secretarial prose style on a rather less exalted level than that of al-Jâḥiẓ. *Adab al-Kâtib* (The Manners of the Secretary) and *ᶜUyûn al-Ak͟hbâr* (Choice Stories) both illustrate the pedagogical function of many of his writings and his concern with providing his readers with entertaining materials written in a clear and concise style. Compendia of stories such as *ᶜUyûn al-Ak͟hbâr* were also produced by Ibn ᶜAbd Rabbihi (whose *al-ᶜIqd al-Farîd* has already been discussed) and by Abû Manṣûr al-T͟haᶜâlibî (d. 1037), who in addition to collecting stories in works such as *Laṭâ'if al-Maᶜârif* (Fascinating Pieces of Knowledge), also produced a valuable anthology of poetry entitled *Yatîmat al-Dahr* (Solitaire of the Age).

While this process of compilation continued in different parts of the Arabic-speaking world, another prose writer followed the lead of al-Jâḥiẓ more consciously in devoting his attention to the development of an artistic prose style, namely, Abû Ḥayyân al-Tawḥîdî (d. 1023). By all accounts a rather unsavory personality with an acid tongue, he was a great admirer of al-Jâḥiẓ, and in his own works such as *Kitâb Mathâlib al-Wazîrayn* (Faults of the Two Ministers) he displays both his splendid prose style and his own bitter personality through some pithy comments on the faults of two prominent Buyid *wazîrs* of the period.

One of the greatest poets of the era also wrote prose works of some importance, Abû al-ᶜAlâ' al-Maᶜarrî. In his *Risâlat al-G͟hufrân* (Treatise on Forgiveness) he portrays a *shayk͟h* as visiting a group of poets from the pre-Islamic period in Paradise, finding that they have been forgiven their heathen practices, arguing with them about their poetry, and generally observing their antics in the hereafter.

Al-Tawḥîdî and al-Maᶜarrî both wrote their prose works at a time when the stylistic element of *saj*ᶜ (rhyming prose), present in the Qur'an and, in a sense, inherent in the morphological potentialities of the Arabic language itself, became a major element in an entirely new prose form. There are a number of suggestions concerning the origins of the *maqâma*, as the new form was termed, but most critics are prepared to give the credit for being the originator to Aḥmad al-Hamadhânî (d. 1007), usually known as *Badî*ᶜ *al-Zamân* (Wonder of the Era). In his *maqâmât*, a narrator, ᶜÎsâ ibn Hishâm, describes the wiles of a hero, Abû al-Fatḥ al-Iskandarî, who uses his eloquence and wit to win the admiration and money of his unsuspecting audience. This framework not only gave the author the opportunity to display his virtuosity in the use of the Arabic language, but also permitted him to portray aspects of society in a most accurate and penetrating fashion, a fact which seems to have escaped the attention of most historians of the period. This highly successful fomula was taken up a century later by one of the greatest masters of the Arabic language, al-Ḥarîrî (d. 1121), whose writings in this genre lack the spontaneity and narrative content of those of al-Hamadhânî but constitute closely wrought masterpieces of incredible complexity and virtuosity. Many commentators admired this virtuoso aspect of al-Ḥarîrî's *maqâmât*, and yet it began a process the results of which had a profound effect on prose writing, namely, that his successors produced works which tried to emulate this verbal jugglery at the expense of any particular interest in content. The increasing incursion of *saj*ᶜ into almost every aspect of Arabic prose writing, from book titles to official documents, led to a general trend which is closely mirrored in the emphasis on *badî*ᶜ in poetry. For several centuries, as much, if not more, emphasis was placed on the style in which a work was written as on its contents, something which almost automatically produced a stereotyping and stylization of most forms of literary expression. The major exception to this trend was the folk literature tradition.

* * *

"If technical writings are excluded, Arabic literature consists predominantly of poetry." Thus does Charles Pellat speak of the balance between literature in poetry and prose during the period of which we are speaking (*Life and Works of Jahiz*, p. xiii), and the comparative brevity of the survey of prose literature just essayed demonstrates clearly the lack of both texts and studies of the prose works which are extant. In studying these works and setting them in a developmental perspective, we have available two works of a general nature. The first is *La Prose Arabe au IVme siècle de l'hégire* by Zakî Mubârak (also published in Arabic), a dissertation completed in Paris in which this

Egyptian writer surveys most of the prose authors up to and including the fourth century A.H., places them in their historical setting, and gives translations of some of their works. A more analytical work is that of Anîs al-Maqdisî, *Taṭawwur al-Asâlîb al-Nathriyya fî al-Adab al-^{c}Arabî* (The Development of Prose Styles in Arabic Literature), which, as its title implies, takes a more penetrating look at the period from a literary critical viewpoint. The author gives a good survey of the precedents to the development of an artistic prose tradition and then treats each major writer in turn, quoting extracts from his works and analyzing the facets of his style. In addition to these two works, mention should be made of those writings of Ṭâhâ Ḥusayn which are concerned with the development of prose writing; the seventh chapter of his *Fî al-Adab al-Jâhilî* (Pre-Islamic Literature) is devoted to the prose writing of that period, and in *Min Ḥadîth al-Shi^{c}r wa al-Nathr* (Talking of Poetry and Prose), he devotes several chapters to a study of prose which is both historical (in his treatment of various periods) and analytical (in his studies of various important figures such as ^{c}Abd al-Ḥamîd al-Kâtib, Ibn al-Muqaffa^{c} and al-Jâḥiẓ).

The shortage of more detailed studies of individual aspects of the art of prose writing may help to account for the small number of general introductory surveys; this applies particularly insofar as Western languages are concerned. A number of scholars have devoted their attention to producing translations of famous works of prose. al-Jâḥiẓ has been translated by Pellat, al-Tha^{c}âlibî by Bosworth, and al-Tanukhî (d. 994) by Margoliouth. The tremendous difficulties involved in producing readable translations of the *maqâmât* have been met by Blachère, Nicholson, Prendergast, Chenery, Steingass, and others. In spite of all these efforts, no attempt has been made thus far to produce a *literary* study of the prose writers mentioned above, either as a group or as individuals. Those studies that do treat one author or one work are usually a combination of translation and analysis of the implications of the contents of the work rather than an analysis of its intrinsic qualities. The situation seems little improved when works written in Arabic are added to those of Western scholars.

Concerning Ibn al-Muqaffa^{c}, we have a short biographical study by ^{c}Abd al-Laṭîf Hamza and a long article (also descriptive rather than analytical) by Gabrieli. Of a similar nature is Ishaq Musa al-Huseini's study written in English, *The Life and Works of Ibn Qutaiba.* As one might expect, the figure of al-Jâḥiẓ has attracted several scholars, prime amongst whom is Charles Pellat. In a number of works (e.g., *Le Milieu basrien . . .*, *The Life and Works of Jahiz*), he has provided the literature scholar with useful information concerning the author's life and environment as well as examples of his art. A short but useful study of the storytelling art and style of al-Jâḥiẓ is *Fann al-Qiṣaṣ fî Kitâb al-Bukhalâ*" (The Story-Telling Art in the Book of Misers) by Muhammad al-Mubârak. Another famous writer who has been studied in several works by one scholar is al-Maᶜarrî. In the many studies on the blind writer by the blind scholar Ṭâhâ Ḥusayn, we are given a penetrating psychological analysis of this versatile writer along with many insights into his life and intellectual development. Finally in this list of studies on artistic prose, mention should be made of a short work by Iḥsân ᶜAbbâs, *Abû Ḥayyân al-Tawḥîdî*. This writer obviously deserves a much broader treatment than this small study can provide, but the lack of any larger work makes it a useful contribution to the study of this important stylist.

In dealing with the *maqâma* genre, the scholar is marginally more fortunate. Shawqî Ḍayf has written a short study in which he lists the characteristics of the genre and its style and gives the names of the most important authors who wrote *maqâmât*. Also useful are the introductions to the translations of Blachère and Masnou, Chenery, and Prendergast; to these can be added Crussard's study of Ḥarîrî, *En lisant Harīrī*, and a recent article by Beeston in which he suggests a possible source for the origin of the genre in a segment of al-Tanûkhî's *Al-Faraj baᶜda al-Shidda* (Escape After Hardship).

In the discussion of poetry and its study, it was noted that many philologists and literary critics wrote works in which they analyzed the craft of writing and eloquence (*balâgha*) and the facets of the various genres in which works of literature could be composed. Many of these analytical studies contained direct advice to the secretarial class and were quite practical in their approach (containing sections on correct pleasantries, lists of animals, and the like); two deserve to be mentioned in the particular context of prose. Ibn Wahb's work, *Naqd al-Nathr* (Prose Criticism), was attributed (apparently wrongly) to Qudâma ibn Jaᶜfar. In view of the fact that the latter wrote a work entitled *Naqd al-Shiᶜr* (Poetic Criticism) and both writers were generally thought to have been strongly influenced by Aristotle, the confusion is perhaps understandable. The second work, Abû Hilâl al-ᶜAskarî's *Kitâb al-Ṣinâᶜatayn* (The Two Arts), is an extremely practical and well organized manual on both poetry and prose (the two arts). It discusses good and bad examples of usage, composition, conciseness, plagiarism, simile, and rhyming prose. No less than 35 chapters are devoted to *badîᶜ*, thus weighing the balance of contents heavily in favor of poetry.

One final aspect of prose writing which merits further study is that of the Sufis. Syed Hussein Nasr has given us a general biographical introduction to Shihâb al-dîn al-Suhrawardî (d. 1234) in *Three Muslim Sages*, and both Arberry and Adûnîs have written on Muhammad al-Niffarî. Although almost every aspect of prose is in need of further study on a more literary basis, research into such authors seems certain to add new dimensions to our understanding and appreciation of Arabic literature in general.

BETWEEN THE CLASSICAL AND MODERN PERIODS

The final chapter of Goldziher's *A Short History of Classical Arabic Literature* has as its title (in translation) "The Period of Decadence." Most surveys of Arabic literature, whether in Arabic or Western languages, discuss the period of six centuries or so before the *nahḍa* (renaissance) in the nineteenth century as "the Age of the Mamlukes" (Gibb), "From the Mongol Invasion till the Present Day" (Nicholson), or *ᶜAṣr al-Inḥiṭât*, the Arabic equivalent of Goldziher's title above. In the chapter in *Al-Adab al-ᶜArabî fî Âthâr al-Dârisîn* (discussed in the beginning of this section) which is devoted to "Arabic literature from the fall of Baghdad till the beginnings of the renaissance," Shukrî Fayṣal spends much time in trying to trace the origins of this attitude to six centuries of Arabic literature and the reasons for it. It is indeed significant that he declines to give a bibliography at the end of his chapter to match the copious lists of references provided for every other chapter in the book; it aptly reflects the unfortunate truth that little or no serious literary study has been devoted to this period.

In more recent times, there have been signs of a change in this situation and the attitudes which led to it. Research by anthropologists and specialists in folklore is leading to an increasing interest in folk literature; in particular, the focus of the structuralist school, with Levi-Strauss as its foremost exponent, on the question of myth and folktales has already produced some remarkable results in treating other world areas. Furthermore, the theories of Parry and Lord (already mentioned with regard to research on pre-Islamic poetry) are demonstrating wide areas of application within the oral, folk literature field. As a recent writer has expressed it:

> Long cast into that critical netherland of Middle Arabic and dialect "non-literature", the vast body of tales termed *al-sîra* becomes newly interesting, comprehensible, and even respectable *as a literary problem*. . . . [italics mine]

The *sîra* consists of collections of tales which recount the exploits of various heroic figures, the pre-Islamic cavalier ᶜAntar, Abû Zayd, and the Banî Hilâl, Sulṭân Baybars (who defeated the Mongols in 1260), and Sayf ibn Dhî Yazan. The tradition of recounting these tales in cafes and private houses is graphically recorded for us in Edward Lane's *Manners and Customs of the Modern Egyptians* (Chapters 21–23), and an equally vivid impression of their impact and importance can be gained from a reading of the first volume of Ṭâhâ Ḥusayn's famous autobiographical work, *al-Ayyâm* (The Days, or, in its English version, *An Egyptian Childhood*, translated by E. H. Paxton). Most famous of all, of course, is the collection *Alf Layla wa Layla* (A Thousand and One Nights), which has been known in the West in translation since at least the seventeeth century and in the Near East since the tenth.

An attempt will be made here to do what Shukrî Fayṣal was not prepared to do in his above-mentioned article, namely, to list some of the works written on the subject of this folk literature. One could mention Suhayr al-Qalamâwî's topical study of *Alf Layla wa Layla*, the series of articles by D. B. McDonald on the same collection, and the work of Paret and others on individual *sîras*. However, some recent studies seem to demonstrate ways in which modern literary theory may be used to good advantage (alongside literary critical techniques). The first is Mia Gerhardt's *The Art of Story-Telling*, in which she not only supplies interesting information about the compilation and sources of *Alf Layla wa Layla*, but also subjects the stories to literary analysis according to terms which she lays down at the beginning of the book. Some stories from this collection are also analyzed in Hamori's work, *On the Art of Medieval Arabic Literature*, mentioned above. In addition to these two, we should cite a recent article from which the quotation above was taken, Bridget Connelly's "The Structure of Four Banī Hilāl Tales," in which a structuralist approach is taken to a collection of tales from a particular area and many problems connected with a purely textual analysis no longer apply. The implications of this article would seem to be that the study of folktales of this type will add a further dimension to our knowledge of Arabic literature, and that such research is a nascent field in which the skills of the anthropologist, linguist, and literature scholar can be combined with benefit to all three disciplines.

THE MODERN PERIOD

It was renewed or increased contact with the West which served to stimulate the renaissance in literature or the reexamination of attitudes and approaches, which is known in the Arab world as the *nahḍa*. This contact was of a different nature in the various parts of the Near East. In Syria and Lebanon, for example, there had been contact between the Christian community and France since the eighteenth century, and there was a Maronite college in Rome. Thus in the nineteenth century, we can find members of a number of Syrian families—those of Yâzijî, Shidyâq, and Bustânî, for instance—turning their attention to the writings of the classical period, examining the nature of their language, and pointing out alien interpolations in its vocabulary and structure, while at the same time illustrating their point of view through the literature of the classical period and works of their own composition. Nâṣîf al-Yâzijî (d. 1871), for example, edited the *dîwân* of Al-Mutanabbî and also read the *maqâmât* of al-Ḥarîrî in the French edition of De Sacy before producing his own work in rhyming prose, *Majma^{c} al-Baḥrayn* (Meeting Place of the Two Seas). On the other hand, there were also other writers who traveled in Europe and then returned to their homeland where they attempted to reproduce new forms—the novel and drama, for instance —in the Arabic language. The families of Marrâsh and Naqqâsh are examples of this latter trend. However, a historical factor intervened in this process during the 1850s when, in a period of civil strife, many of these families found it necessary to flee to Egypt where the regime of the Khedive Ismâcîl provided an atmosphere which was very receptive to Western culture and where censorship seemed less capricious.

Egypt's encounter with the West was a good deal more abrupt, taking the form of Napoleon's invasion of 1798. In its aftermath, Muḥammad cAlî was able to seize control of the country and proceeded to remodel the army along the lines of the French one which he had seen defeat his own. Missions of young men were sent initially to Italy and then to France, and on their return they were set to work in army schools translating and teaching. Eventually and inevitably some of these young men, in particular Al-Ṭahṭâwî and his pupils, turned their attention to translating works of European literature. Soon readers of Arabic were able to study Fenelon's *Télémaque*, La Fontaine's *Fables*, and some of the novels of Alexandre Dumas, to name just a few. Thus began the long process of assimilation, translation, imitation, and finally individual and indigenous creation whereby the original and independent literature of the modern Arab world has emerged.

The historian of this early period in the history of modern Arabic literature is Louis Cheikho, who in two works which represent amalgamations of articles originally published in the periodical *al-Mashriq* lists most of the major figures in the nineteenth and early twentieth centuries. A work in English which provides a most penetrating study of the development of Arabic thought during this period is Albert Hourani's *Arabic Thought in the Liberal Age*, in which the ideas of most of the major thinkers of the early period of the *nahḍa* and the influences exerted on them are summarized and analyzed in great detail. The works of many writers who traveled to Europe at the earliest stage in the process of assimilation are described in the work of Ibrahim Abu Lughod, *The Arab Rediscovery of Europe*.

Poetry

In the sphere of poetry, writers aimed initially at a revival of the style and spirit of the great poets of the classical period which we have described above. Poets such as Maḥmûd Sâmî al-Bârûdî (d. 1904), Ḥâfiẓ Ibrâhîm (d. 1932), and Aḥmad Shawqî (d. 1932) wrote ceremonial odes praising rulers and politicians and lamenting their deaths; in such poems can be found all the devices of the *badîc* style found in the works of Abû Tammâm and al-Mutanabbî centuries earlier. In addition to such traditional themes expressed in classical form and style, these poets also turned their attention to new themes, including nationalism, the position of woman in society, and education. This trend toward the treatment of modern social and even scientific topics is also to be found in the poetry of two Iraqis, al-Zahâwî (d. 1936) and al-Ruṣṣâfî (d. 1945). In more personal utterances, Shawqî described scenes of nature, ballrooms and the like, all this in a poetic language of great beauty and musicality. A third poet who is often associated with Ḥâfiẓ and Shawqî is Khalîl Muṭrân (d. 1949) who also wrote ceremonial and official poems, but who has been recognized as a precursor of romanticism in modern Arabic poetry.

The poetry of Shawqî and Ḥâfiẓ was the subject of a great deal of debate and criticism involving such important literary figures as Muḥammad al-Muwaylihî (d. 1930), Muṣṭafâ al-Manfalûṭî (d. 1924), and, at a later stage, al-^{c}Aqqâd (d. 1964). With the poet often confined within the rigid boundaries of such criticism, it is perhaps not surprising that the next major development in the tradition of modern Arabic poetry occurred at a distance from the Arab world itself, namely, in the United States. It was the so-called *mahjar* (émigré) school of poets who fully and unequivocally introduced romanticism in Arabic poetry, and who began to conduct experiments with such forms as the prose poem. Out of the range of the Arab world's conservative critics, the *mahjar* poets [such as Jubrân, Ilyâ Abû Mâḍî (d. 1957), and Naṣîb ^{c}Arîḍa (d. 1946)] could give almost free rein to their romantic ideas, with only their colleagues to criticize them or spur them on. In spite of the distance separating them from the Near East, copies of their periodical *Al-Sâ'iḥ* (The Traveler) reached the area and its effect was profound.

In Egypt, however, the process of change was rather more measured than was the case in the Americas. One of the major reasons for this is that, between the poetry of Muṭrân and the emergence of a romantic school, there stand another group of poets known as the "*Dîwân*" school [named after the blistering piece of criticism published under that title by two of them, al-^{c}Aqqâd and al-Mâzinî (d. 1949) in 1921]. Joined in this group by ^{c}Abd al-Raḥmân Shukrî (d. 1958), these poets abhorred the occasion pieces written by poets such as Shawqî and, strongly influenced by the English romantics, stressed the importance of emotion in the composition of a poem. However, though they also believed in the organic unity of the poem, they were not prepared to countenance any changes in either form or versification, and thus it was within these terms of reference that the romantic poets of the Arab world itself began to compose. Among prominent poets of this school are Abû Shâdî (d. 1955), Ibrâhîm Nâgî (d. 1953), ^{c}Alî Maḥmûd Ṭâhâ (d. 1949), and the young Tunisian poet al-Shâbbî (d. 1934), whose stirring calls to the Arab people are given even more poignancy by the tragedy of his death at a very early age.

The last three decades have witnessed enormous changes in both the structure of Arabic poetry and in the general approach to the form as a whole. Poetry of great complexity and subtlety is now being written, and experiments are being conducted in the prose poem and "*Al-shiʿr al-Ḥurr*" (a misunderstanding of the concept of the European term "vers libre"). Space does not permit us here to discuss all the poets or the various "schools" to which they have adhered at different periods; indeed it is a sign of the vigor of the modern Arabic poetic tradition that probably every literary critic could choose a different list of poets to form a representative selection. Among early symbolists, Saʿîd ʿAql may be mentioned, and he has been followed at various stages by Badr Shâkir al-Sayyâb, Yûsuf al-Khâl, and Adûnîs. ʿAbd al-Wahhâb al-Bayyâtî in al-ʿIrâq and Ṣalâḥ ʿAbd al-Sabûr in Egypt have been concerned with social realism, and race and the problems of Africa have been the subject of many poems by Muḥammad al-Faytûrî. Early proponents of change in the form of poetry were the Iraqis Nâzik al-Malâ'ika and Al-Sayyâb (although mention should also be made in this context of the efforts of Lewis ʿAwaḍ in Egypt in his collection *Plutoland*). One of the major aims of these poets was to vary the length of lines by making the *tafʿila* (foot) the basic unit instead of the complete *bayt* (line). Even more radical than this has been the development of the prose poem as seen in the works of Tawfîq Ṣâyigh (d. (1971), Jabrâ Ibrâhîm Jabrâ, and Muhammad al-Mâghûṭ.

A group whose works have a great impact in the Arab world today are the Palestinian poets who express in their verse the frustrations, anger, and anguish of their people. Writing both inside and outside of Israel, their poetry makes a powerful use of symbolism and imagery—often with a very practical purpose added to the artistic one, namely, of avoiding censorship, and the works of such poets as Maḥmûd Darwîsh, Samîḥ al-Qâsim, Fadwâ Ṭûqân, and Râshid Ḥusayn are read and admired throughout the Arab world.

The foregoing brief survey of modern Arabic poetry may be sufficient to show that poetry in the Arab world reflects both the artistic aspirations of those who write it and their political and social concerns. The poems which have been published in such Beirut journals as *Shiʿr* (Poetry—now defunct) and continue to appear in *al-Âdâb* (Literature) and *Mawâqif* (the publication of Adûnîs) are the subject of almost instantaneous analysis in the cafes, newspapers, and journals of Lebanon and Syria. It is thus hardly surprising that there are a large number of studies written on modern Arabic poetry which explore the subject from a variety of points of view.

To begin with general surveys, the two which are most detailed are known to the present writer but have yet to be published. The huge work of Salmâ al-Jayyûsî is soon to be published, but its importance and detail can be gauged from her long article, "Al-Shiʿr al-ʿArabî al-Muʿâṣir: Taṭawwuruhu wa Mustaqbaluhu" (Modern Arabic Poetry: Its Development and Future). Another work soon to be published, the general value of which can be gauged from previous articles, is that of Moreh. Less detailed but valuable as introductions to the subject are the prefaces to two anthologies, Muṣṭafâ Badawî's (in English) to his *An Anthology of Modern Arabic Verse*, and that of Norin and Tarabay (in French) to their *Anthologie de la littérature arabe contemporaine*. More particular in either subject or treatment are S̲h̲awqî Dayf's *Dirâsât fî al-S̲h̲iᶜr al-ᶜArabî al-Muᶜâsir* (Studies on Modern Arabic Poetry), Muhammad Mandûr's *Al-S̲h̲iᶜr al-Miṣrî baᶜda S̲h̲awqî* (Egyptian Poetry After Shawqi), and al-Aqqâd's *S̲h̲uᶜarâʾ Miṣr* (Egyptian Poets). In a recently published study, *Poetry and the Making of Modern Egypt*, Mounah Khoury has shown convincingly the important role which the works of many of the poets in Egypt (such as Bârûdî, S̲h̲awqî, and Ḥâfiẓ Ibrâhîm) played in both reflecting and influencing the social and political conditions of the time. To these works should be added studies on the *mahjar* school such as *Al-S̲h̲iᶜr al-ᶜArabî fî al-Mahjar* (Arabic Poetry in America) by Iḥsān ᶜAbbâs and Muhammad Najm, an excellent analysis of the poetic principles and poets of this school, and Nâdira Sarrâj's study, *S̲h̲uᶜarâʾ al-Râbiṭa al-Qalamiyya* (Poets of the Bond of the Pen), which, in spite of its title, is a general survey of the cultural milieu in which these poets lived as well as being a study of individual poets. It is surprising that, in spite of the importance of this school and the obvious connections with the literatures and societies of the West, no serious study has yet appeared in a Western language to compare with the above-mentioned works in Arabic. The selection of articles on individual figures is useful but insufficient.

There are innumerable studies of individual poets within the modern period; we list only a few of the more significant ones here. Among detailed treatments, mention must be made of al-Malâ'ika's *Dirâsât fî S̲h̲iᶜr ᶜAlî Mahmûd Ṭâhâ* (Studies on ᶜAlî Mahmûd Ṭâhâ's Poetry), two studies by Iḥsân ᶜAbbâs *ᶜAbd al-Wahhâb al-Bayâtî* and *Badr S̲h̲âkir al-Sayyâb*, and another work on the latter poet, Issa Boullata's *Badr S̲h̲âkir al-Sayyâb: Ḥayâtuhu wa S̲h̲iᶜruhu* (Al-Sayyâb: His Life and Poetry, a title, incidentally, which is exactly the same as that of an earlier study of the poet by Nabîla al-Lajmî). Ṭâhâ Ḥusayn has provided a useful comparative study, *Ḥâfiẓ wa S̲h̲awqî*, in which he gives his views on the merits and faults of each poet and assesses their work in relationship to other poets such as Muṭrân, who is himself the subject of a study by Muhammad Mandûr. Studies such as these in book form can be supplemented by a large number of articles. Boullata has written several on Al-Sayyâb in English and also a recent estimation of the poetic genius of Tawfîq Ṣâyig̲h̲. Muṣṭafâ Badawî has provided a useful study of some of the poetry of al-Bârûdî, and Robin Ostle has written on Muṭrân and the members of the *Dîwân* school.

With so much poetic activity in the modern Arab world, it is not surprising that it has been accompanied by an equal expansion in the realm of writings about poetry, poetics, and criticism. We noticed that the poems of Shawqî were subjected to severe attack at an early stage in the development of modern Arabic literature by Muḥammad al-Muwayliḥî, and it is not without significance that among the latter's pupils was ᶜAbbâs Maḥmûd al-Aqqâd, who was later (1921) to acknowledge a debt to his mentor in his fierce attack on Shawqî in *Al-Dîwân*. In *Four Egyptian Literary Critics*, David Semah has studied and analyzed the works and attitudes of four Egyptian critics, Ṭâhâ Ḥusayn, al-ᶜAqqâd, Muhammad Ḥusayn Haykal, and Muhammad Mandûr; in a recent article, Semah has discussed the approach of the last of these critics to the question of the "new poetry." Another important work of criticism is Mikhâ'îl Nuᶜayma's *al-ghurbâl* (The Sieve) in which he discusses a wide variety of literary topics, including dramatic language, and the poetry of Shawqî, Muṭrân, and Al-Rîḥânî. Samples of the many other studies in article form on individual poets, critics of poetry, as well as "schools" can be found in Muhammad Najm's excellent article on the subject in *al-Adab al-ᶜArabî fî Âthâr al-Dârisîn*.

The activities of al-ᶜAqqâd, Shukrî, and al-Mâzinî are indicative of a trend among modern Arab poets whereby many of them write works about poetry as well as composing poetry itself. Two poets, Abû Shâdî and al-Malâ'ika have written studies of the problems of modern Arabic poetry with almost identical titles in which they discuss the different types of poetry, questions of form, meter, and content. Muhammad al-Nuwayhî has also produced an important study on the subject while in another work ᶜIzz al-Dîn Ismâᶜîl discusses the musicality, imagery, language, symbolism, and committedness of modern poetry. This analysis of the "problem(s)" of modern poetry is further reflected in the title of Ghâlî Shukrî's contribution to this subject, *Shiᶜrunâ al-Muᶜâṣir: Ilâ Aina?* (Whither Our Modern Poetry?), in which he discusses the directions in which the modern poets seem to be heading, analyzes some of the implicit contradictions involved, suggests methods of criticism, and talks about the "ideology" of modern poetry. All these studies discuss modern poetry, its direction and problems, under a number of rubrics. Among studies which focus on a particular aspect of poetry, mention should be made of Ibrâhîm al-Samârrâ'î's study *Lugha al-Shiᶜr Bayna Jîlayn* (The Language of Poetry Between Two Generations), in which the poetic language of a number of Iraqi poets is analyzed and discussed. On the question of form and meter, we are indebted to a number of detailed articles by Moreh in which he describes the various experiments which have been made in "poetry in prose," blank verse and free verse. Lastly, we should list the important article by Adûnîs on the prose poem (1960). In works such as *Zaman al-Shiᶜr* (The Time of Poetry), this poet discards many of the conventions of the past, and, setting his own terms of reference, seems to be looking to the future. The implications of this attitude are obviously profound and are analyzed at the conclusion of this survey.

The Short Story and the Novel

The witty anecdotal collections of al-Jâḥiẓ, the *maqâma* genre with its vignettes depicting the society of the times, the folktale literature as seen in *Alf Layla wa Layla* (1001 Nights), in which many series of tales contain a narrative thread, however tenuous: all these may be considered as precedents for the development of a fictional literature in prose during the modern period.

At the end of the nineteenth century, a number of different types of fictional writing began to appear, all of them sponsored by the growing press tradition, which were to contribute to the emergence of the modern novel and short story forms. In the first place, there was Muḥammad al-Muwayliḥî's *Ḥadîth ᶜÎsâ ibn Hishâm*, in which the author brilliantly combines facets of the *maqâma* tradition (separate episodes involving two main "characters" and the use of rhyming prose at the beginning of each episode) and closely observed portraits of the stereotypes of Egyptian society in a work which has a clear social-reformist purpose. More popular than al-Muwayliḥî's masterpiece (the language of which restricted its audience to the well educated) were the historical novels of Jurjî Zaydân, who also published histories of Islamic civilization and of Arabic literature. Another prose writer of the times whose works were extremely popular on account of their uncomplicated style was Muṣṭafâ Lutfî al-Manfalûṭî (d. 1924). His fictional essays which appeared under the title *Al-Naẓârât* (Views) and *al-ᶜAbarât* (Tears) are loaded down with simplistic platitudes which tend to give them a merely stylistic interest in the light of subsequent developments in fiction.

The first work in Arabic which can be termed a novel appeared in 1914, Muḥammad Ḥusayn Haykal's *Ẓaynab*. Extremely romantic in its treatment of characters, overloaded with description of countryside, and suffering from some psychological falsehoods, *Ẓaynab* nevertheless represents a significant advance in the development of the novel. During the 1920s a group of writers, of whom the most famous is Maḥmûd Taymûr, began to write short stories on the model of European writers such as de Maupassant in which increasing emphasis was put on situation and character delineation. The publication of such short stories, together with that of Ṭâhâ Ḥusayn's gently ironic autobiographical work, *al-Ayyâm* (The Days), had a profound effect on the corresponding aspects of the novelistic tradition and also aroused a great interest in prose fiction. A competition in novel writing was organized and was won by Ibrâhîm al-Mâzinî with *Ibrâhîm al-Kâtib* (Ibrahim the Author), a work which seems at least partly autobiographical in spite of the author's insistence that it is not. The publication of this work in 1931 marked the beginning of a decade in which the Arabic novel reached new levels of sophistication. In 1933, Tawfîq al-Ḥakîm published *ᶜAwdat al-Rûh* (Return of the Spirit), and within four years followed it with two other fictional works, *Yawmiyyât Nâ'ib fî al-Aryâf* (Diary of a Provincial Prosecutor) and *ᶜUṣfûr min al-Sharq* (Bird from the East). Ṭâhâ Ḥusayn published *Adîb*, which, like the last work of al-Ḥakîm mentioned above, describes the life of an Egyptian in Paris and followed this in the 1940s with *Duᶜâ al-Karawân* (Call of the Plover) and *Shajarat al-Bu's* (Tree of Misery). In 1938, Al-ᶜAqqâd published his only novel, *Sâra*, which consists of a psychological study of the breakdown of a love affair. Maḥmûd Taymûr (whom we have already mentioned as one of the leading figures in the emergence of the short story) also produced a novel in the 1930s, *Nidâ' al-Majhûl* (Call of the Unknown), set in the mountains of Lebanon. 1938 also saw the publication of a collection of short stories by a young Egyptian writer, Najîb Maḥfûẓ, and in 1939 he produced a historical novel set in ancient Egypt entitled *ᶜAbath al-Aqdâr* (Fates' Mockery). These works represent the first publications of the prose writer who is acknowledged as having brought both the novel and the short story to a very high level. Over the past three decades, he has written over 20 novels and produced seven collections of short stories.

The works of Maḥfûẓ bring us to the modern period in which he and many other writers of novels and short stories have been contributing excellent works of art to the corpus of modern Arabic prose fiction. Among such writers, mention should be made of Egyptians such as Yaḥyâ Ḥaqqî, ᶜAbd al-Raḥmân al-Sharqâwî, and Yûsuf Idrîs; of representatives of Syria, Lebanon, and Palestine such as Ḥalîm Barakât, Zakarîa Tâmir, and Jabrâ Ibrâhîm Jabrâ; among Algerians, Mawlûd Maᶜmarî and Kâtib Yâsîn; and of the Sudanese novelist and writer of short stories, al-Ṭayyib Ṣâliḥ. Some of these writres share with Maḥfûẓ a concern to portray in fictional form the role of the individual in his society and to use symbolism to inculcate some often unpleasant truths in the minds of his readers. Others are experimenting with a more synchronic approach to the novel form itself and producing works of great artistic value and popularity which are read throughout the Arab world.

The Drama

The family name of Naqqâsh has already been mentioned in connection with those who traveled to European countries in the nineteenth century and then returned to the Near East where they attempted to adapt new literary forms in the Arabic languages. In the person of Mârûn Naqqâsh we have a pioneer in the sphere of Arabic drama. Returning to Lebanon from Italy, he proceeded to write and produce a series of plays in the family home beginning in 1847. Apart from Shî^{c}ite passion plays and shadow puppet performances, the Arab world knew little of drama until its importation from the West, and thus this incipient tradition in Syro-Lebanon (many of the members of which moved to Egypt in the wake of the civil disorders of the 1860s) may be considered as the beginning of the modern Arabic drama, although contemporary accounts suggest that some kind of theatrical tradition was already in existence in Egypt as well.

As imitation and translation led gradually to the production of original works, the production of plays raised several dilemmas. In the first place, the role of the actor in society and more particularly the attitudes to the appearance of women in public acting out amorous situations caused the art to gain a rather seedy reputation and led it initially down the path of vaudeville. At a later stage, Najîb al-Rîhânî brought this form to a higher level of sophistication with his famous plays involving the character of Kishkish Bey, the provincial tyrant who is duped by the inhabitants of the cosmopolitan city.

In the 1890s, Aḥmad Shawqî was sent to France by the Egyptian Khedive Tawfîq, and while there he came into contact with a number of French writers and saw a number of French plays. In 1893, he sent back to Egypt the manuscript of a verse play entitled *^{c}Alî Bey al-Kabîr*; this was the first attempt at producing verse drama, and it was not until the late 1920s that Shawqî again turned his talents to writing other works in this form (such as *Maṣra^{c} Kliûbâtra*, *Majnûn Laylâ*, and *^{c}Antara*). He also revised *^{c}Alî Bey al-Kabîr* during this period and thus republished at the very end of his long and illustrous career one of his earliest works in this genre.

Another Egyptian, Tawfîq al-Ḥakîm, was similarly influenced by French drama when he spent some years in the French capital during the 1920s. He had been writing plays for the ^{c}Ukâsha troupe before his departure, wrote a play in French while in Paris, and then returned to publish a whole series of works which gave the genre new impetus and respectability. Each of these plays published in the 1930s and 1940s takes its theme and background from a different historical period and source, as the titles indicate: *Ahl al-Kahf* (People of the Cave), *Shahrazâd*, *Pygmâliyûn*, *Sulaymân al-Ḥakîm* (Solomon the Wise), and *Ūdīb* (Oedipus), to name just a few. Over the years, al-Ḥakîm has continued to experiment with new ideas, forms, and schools within the dramatic milieu; in *Al-Ṣafqa* (The Deal) he uses the colloquial language, and in *Yâ Ṭâli^{c} al-Shajara* (O Tree Climber, or in English translation, *The Tree Climber*), he experiments with the theater of the absurd following models of Ionesco and Adamov; *al-Aydî al-Nâᶜima* (Soft Hands) enters the realm of politics and society in the post-revolution period of 1954, in that a prince has to adapt to the exigencies of the new socialist society.

Other playwrights such as Maḥmûd Taymûr have also written dramas, and one in particular, *al-Makhba' Raqm Thalâthata ᶜAshara* (Shelter Number 13), is of interest because the author endeavored to write it in such a way that it could be performed in either written or colloquial Arabic. The question of the use of language in modern Arabic drama is something which has kept many pens busy; indeed the problem also concerns the writers of novels and short stories in which there is dialogue. Expressed succinctly, is it possible for Arab characters to address each other in the *written* language, or alternatively, can the colloquial dialects in a written form be considered as literature? Views on this subject have varied widely; among the most lucid expositions of the problem is that of Mikha'îl Nuᶜayma in the Introduction to his play *al-Âbâ' wa al-Banûn* (Fathers and Sons). Today the situation with regard to the use of language is quite open. The colloquial language has certainly been accepted as a medium for dramatic expression; the highly successful plays of Nuᶜmân ᶜÂshûr in Egyptian colloquial, *An-Nâs illi Fo'* (The People Upstairs), *An-Nâs illi Taht* (The People Downstairs), and *al-ᶜÂ'ilat al-Dughrî* (The Middle-of-the-Road Family), along with the enormously successful and controversial *Farâfîr* (1964) by Yûsuf Idrîs, are evidence enough of that. Meanwhile other dramatists continue to produce plays in the written language, and these too are acted on the stages of the theaters of the Arab world with equal success. Of recent plays, one in particular is very striking because of both its setting and technique, *Ḥafla Samr Min Ajl Khamsa Ḥazîrân* (A Party for the 5th of June) by Saᶜd Allâh Wannûs, which appeared originally in *Mawâqif* in 1968. In its treatment of the problems of the Arab world today and in its experiments with the dynamics of theatrical performance, this play is a splendid example of the vigor of the contemporary dramatic scene in the Arab world.

* * *

In attempting a brief survey of works on fiction and the drama, we begin with some studies which try to set terms of reference for the genre. In a work which demonstrates its author's wide reading in the world literature, Muhammad Najm discusses various aspects of the art of fiction in his *Fann al-Qiṣṣa* (The Art of the Story); he analyzes the elements in a story as well as such aspects as structure, style, and presentation. The same author has also written a similar work entitled *Fann al-Maqâla* (The Art of the Essay), and we refer later to another of his works in this same series concerning the play. An Egyptian writer, Abdel Meguid, has provided a useful work in English (a University of Manchester dissertation published in Cairo) in which he analyzes the various Arabic words used to represent works of fiction, and thereafter provides the Arabic text of some examples of short stories in the developmental stage along with a certain amount of content and structural analysis. This generalist approach to the genre can also be seen in *Dirâsât fî al-Qiṣṣa wa al-Masraḥ* (Studies on the Story and Drama) by Maḥmûd Taymûr; although the author does refer to specific (and mostly Egyptian) works, he is chiefly concerned with the nature of the art, the role of the writer, and the practical application of literature in society.

In discussing particular works in both area and approach, we begin with Egypt, whose writers have been covered in most detail. Pioneering work on the novel in Egypt was done by Ignaz Kratchkovsky, who published an article on the historical novels of Zaydân (translated into German in 1930) and also by Gibb, whose famous series of articles published in the early 1930s contains quite detailed information on many of the early figures and movements in the *nahḍa*. Among works in Arabic which present a historical approach to the development of the novelistic tradition, mention should be made of Yaḥyâ Ḥaqqî's short work, *Fajr al-Qiṣṣa al-Miṣriyya* (Dawn of the Egyptian Short Story), which provides an excellent summary of the subject. The most detailed and useful source on the subject, however, is ᶜAbd al-Muḥsin Ṭâhâ Badr's perceptive work, *Taṭawwur al-Riwâya al-ᶜArabiyya al-Ḥadîtha* (Development of the Modern Arabic Novel), in which the author provides an analysis of the most significant novels of the developmental stage (1870–1938) from a both historical and critical point of view. A similar approach is also adopted by Maḥmûd Shawkat in his *Al-Fann al-Qaṣaṣî fî al-Adab al-ᶜArabî al-Ḥadīth* (The Art of the Story in Modern Arabic Literature), in which, after sketching the precedents to the development of a modern fictional tradition, Shawkat gives a brief discussion of a number of novels, from the early works of Zaydân up to the period of the 1940s and Najîb Maḥfûẓ. Essentially the same novelists are covered in a more analytical and less historical work by ᶜAlî al-Râᶜî, *Dirâsât fî al-Riwâya al-Miṣriyya* (Studies on the Egyptian Novel), in which each novelist is represented by a single work which is studied from the point of view of characterization, structure, and style. In a work published in English, the young Egyptian scholar Ḥamdî Sakkût has divided the works of many of these same novelists into three groups, the "romantic" trend, the "historical," and the "realistic" in a work entitled *The Egyptian Novel and Its Main Trends, 1913–1952*. More recently, Hilary Kilpatrick (1974) has addressed herself to the same subject, although her treatment is more topical and discusses several recent works. Another work which takes a particular period as a term of reference is Muhammad Najm's *al-Qiṣṣa fî al-Adab al-ᶜArabî al-Ḥadîth*, in which he describes the works of a number of Syro-Lebanese writers (such as Bustânî, Yâzijî, Shidyâq,

Zaydan, and Faraḥ Anṭûn) and their contribution to the development of the modern Arabic tradition of fiction between 1870 and 1914. A final work which must be mentioned in connection with studies on the novel is the recent article by Shukrī ᶜAyyâd, "Al-Riwâya al-ᶜArabiyya al-Muᶜâṣira wa Azmat al-Ḍamîr al-ᶜArabî" (The Contemporary Arabic Novel and the Crisis of Arab Conscience), in which this distinguished Arab critic, after a brief introduction in which he sets his terms of reference, proceeds to analyze a number of contemporary Arabic novels (by such writers as al-Ṭayyib Ṣâliḥ, Ghassân Kanafânî, Jabrâ Ibrâhîm Jabrâ, and Lailâ Baᶜalbakkî) according to four stances on the part of the authors: Shift from Past to Future, the Individual Presence, the Critical Stance, and Metaphysical Self-Questioning. With its lack of emphasis on the writers or novels of a particular country and its use of literary critical analysis to categorize the works discussed, this article seems to represent a worthwhile line of research for scholars interested in the modern Arabic novel.

Turning to the short story, we are again faced with a preponderance of works on Egypt. A very useful index of stories published up till 1961 has recently appeared, *Dalîl al-Qiṣṣa al-Miṣriyya al-Qaṣîra 1910–1961* (Guide to the Egyptian Short Story) by Sayyid al-Nassâj, who has also written a study of the development of the short story in Egypt, *Taṭawwur Fann al-Qiṣṣa al-Qaṣîra fî Miṣr min Sana 1910 ilā Sana 1933.* We are again indebted to the scholarship of Shukrî Ayyâd (himself a writer of short stories, incidentally) for his *al-Qiṣṣa al-Qaṣîra fî Miṣr*, in which he discusses the precedents in classical Arabic literature, examples from European literature, the resurrection of the *maqâma* genre, the literary essay, and finally the emergence of the "artistic" short story at the hands of Taymûr and others in the 1920's. A work with an identical title by ᶜAbbâs Khiḍr covers the period up to 1930, mentioning more Arab writers but with less reference to sources of influence, Arab or Western. Other parts of the Arabic-speaking world are less well represented in studies on fiction in general (although the present writer must admit that this may be a consequence of the holdings in Western libraries). A Cambridge thesis on the Syrian story by H. al-Khateeb has not as yet been published, but an article in the *Journal of Arabic Literature* on a story by Zakarîa Tâmir suggests that the larger work will be a valuable contribution to studies on the modern Arabic short story. Among works already published are *Adab al-Qiṣṣa fî Sûriyâ* (Story Literature in Syria) by ᶜAdnān ibn Dhurayl, *Fî al-Qaṣaṣ al-ᶜIrâqî al-Muᶜâṣir* (On the Contemporary Iraqi Story) by ᶜAlî Jawâd al-Ṭâhir, and *Al-Qiṣṣa al-Maghribiyya al-Ḥadîtha* (The Modern Maghrebi Story) by Muhammad ᶜAfîfî.

This last title brings up an area of the Arab world the literature of which has been generally neglected by scholars in Arabic literature, the Maghreb. Although many writers in the area produce novels and stories in French, there is a significant and expanding literature written in Arabic. Good general studies of the historical background, society, and literature of the region have been provided by Su^{c}âd Khiḍr, Abû l-Qâsim Sa^{c}dallâh, and ^{c}Abdallâh Kânûn, but more detailed research in this area of modern Arabic literature remains slight.

Although a number of societies in the Middle East have produced writers in a European language, only in the Maghreb has such literature reached a magnitude large enough to attract comprehensive critical studies and expressed ideas close enough to local experience to be called national literature.* North Africa has indeed created some literature in Arabic, but up to the present North African literature is above all in French. Morocco, Algeria, and Tunisia use the Western language imposed on them as an arm to combat colonization and as the vehicle through which to express the tearing of their soul between two cultures. Henri Krea wrote, "Revolution and poetry are the same thing."

This literature is contemporary; there is little of it that antedates World War II. It takes the form of short stories, novels, and poetry, and themes are above all built on the conflict within two dualities: the political dyarchy of colonialism and anticolonialism, and the social strains of biculturalism. The complexities of these two dichotomies have been exacerbated after independence, when some of the writers, including some of the most talented, have found that their critical approach is not appreciated by the newly independent regimes. And so they continue to write from abroad, where the problems of acculturation are accentuated. In all these aspects, this literature is typically expressive of the situation of the marginal, alienated intellectual that often accompanies a revolution.

It is therefore not surprising that works of literary criticism study North Africa's French-language literature above all from a social—or even sociological—point of view, and indeed many of them are sociologists rather than specialists in the field of literature. Plum, Gordon, and Khatibi are within the first category, whereas Memmi, Dejeux, Senac, Levi-Valensi, Bencheikh, and Pantucek are in the second. Most of these students of the literature are themselves bilingual, and can therefore perceive the influence of both language traditions on North African writings. They have noted the stronger influence of French writers such as Hugo, Eluard, Prevert, Aragon, and Apollonaire, whose attachment to similar themes underlie other similarities in style and language, but they have been slow to pick up elements of cadence and litany, particularly in North African French-language poetry, that may be closer to Arabic literary notions. It is particularly in the presenta-

*The following section on North-African literature in French is the work of Professor I. William Zartman.

tions of Levi-Valensi and Bencheikh that one finds a literary appreciation of structures and vocabulary, and in the many studies of Dejeux a concern with images and symbols.

For the most part, however, the studies of Dejeux and Khatibi and more recent theses of Tramier and Yetiv are concerned with thematic analysis and the sources of themes, rather than with the study of language. Most frequently the themes are found in the traditional life and land of the three countries, in the combat against the colonizer, and in the confused state of cultural schizophrenia in which the Westernized intelligentsia finds itself. More recently, there has also arisen a literature, similar to that in Arabic in Egypt, which criticizes the inefficient impersonality of the bureaucracy. Finally, there is a growing body of works on the condition of the women in North Africa, often the most rebellious theme of all. Perhaps an even broader dichotomy in the themes would be found in a literature of righteousness (folk and nature themes, but above all the literature of rebellion and combat) and a literature of quandary (sexual and cultural problems).

* * *

Bearing in mind the popularity of Maḥfûẓ, it is perhaps not surprising that a large number of studies have been devoted to his works. Many of his stories have been translated into European languages, and a recently published work in English, *God's World* by Abadir and Allen, contains over 20 short stories in translation. Among works which analyze his novels and short stories, mention should be made of G͟hâlî S͟hukrî's *al-Muntamî* (The Insider), in which Maḥfûẓ' output is discussed under a number of general rubrics, and then individual works are described and analyzed according to criteria of intrinsic analysis (involving characterization, etc.) and external factors are illustrated by the rubrics (defeat, revolution, etc.). Another work concerning Maḥfûẓ, on a smaller scale and dealing with more recent works, is *Ta'ammulât fî ᶜÂlam Najîb Maḥfûẓ* (Meditations on the World of Najîb Maḥfûẓ) by Maḥmûd Amîn al-ᶜÂlim. A work in which several of Maḥfûẓ' novels are subjected to a literary analysis (on the basis of characterization, plot, etc.) has recently been published, *The Changing Rhythm*, by Sasson Somekh. With its survey of the development of the novel genre, the biographical details of the author's life, and especially the treatment of the novels themselves, this work provides a very useful introduction in English to the works of the most renowned novelist in the Arab world today. Somekh's study includes material from an earlier article which he wrote on one of Maḥfûẓ' most interesting works, *Awlâd Ḥâratnâ* (Children of Our Quarter); this work was the subject of a study published in 1965, *Een moderne ârabische Vertelling* by L. O. Schuman.

Among other works on individual writers, we should list two works on al-Mâzinî, *Ibrâhîm al-Mâzinî* by Muhammad Mandûr and *Adab al-Mâzinî* (Mâzinî's Literary Works) by Ni^c^mat Fu'âd. We are indeed fortunate to have a detailed study in English on Ṭâhâ Ḥusayn, one of the most important figures in the whole of modern Arabic literature. Dr. Pierre Cachia's study of him analyzes the various aspects of his output from a number of points of view and provides us with a subtle and penetrating insight into the works of this great littérateur. To these studies can be added a large number of unpublished works and shorter essays in article form. Worthy of mention are Allen's studies on al-Muwayliḥî, Le Gassick's on a number of writers including Maḥfûẓ, ^c^Abd al-Quddûs, and Barakât, and Muṣṭafâ Badawî's valuable contributions on works by Yaḥyâ Ḥaqqî and al-Mâzinî.

In any attempt to undertake a literary study of works of fiction in the modern Arab world, an awareness of the developments that have occurred in the language itself are of course essential. A remarkable work by Jaroslav Stetkevych, *The Modern Arabic Literary Language*, quotes from sources such as the journals of the Arab Language Academies, the novels of Najîb Maḥfûẓ, the verses of al-Malâ'ika, as well as from the *Kitâb* of the famous eighth-century grammarian Sîbawayh and the works of the classical philologists, to show the ways in which lexical and stylistic changes have occurred in the Arabic language to produce the "modern standard Arabic" used by the writers of today.

* * *

Bearing in mind the quantity and quality of dramatic literature being produced in the Arabic-speaking world today, the close scrutiny which such works undergo in the newspaper columns of the various countries and the political and social topicality of many of the situations which they treat (e.g. Wannûs' play described above), it is surprising that so little attention has been paid to this important new medium by Western scholars. Indeed, even in dealing with studies by Arab writers, we are chiefly indebted to a few prominent critics who have laid the foundations for a more profound study of the genre.

An initial problem has been the unavailability of the texts of the plays themselves, except, of course, with such famous figures as Tawfîq al-Ḥakīm. We lacked accurate texts of plays from the early period until in the 1960s Muhammad Najm began to publish his important series of volumes, *Al-Masraḥ al-^c^Arabî* (The Arab Theater), in which he treats in turn the works of Mârûn al-Naqqâsh, Shaykh Al-Qabbânî, Ya^c^qûb Ṣanû^c^, ^c^Uthmân Jalâl, Salîm al-Naqqâsh, and Najîb Ḥaddâd; in each case, we are provided with a useful biography as well as the texts of several of the playwrights' most important works. However, many other important plays are still published in series or periodicals (one thinks of *Farâfîr* by Idrîs, and again the Wannûs play) and are thereafter extraordinarily difficult to obtain.

Such problems aside, there are some good studies in Arabic on this young literary tradition. Muhammad Mandûr has produced a short but extremely useful study on the development of the genre, tracing it from ancient Egyptian times up to the present and discussing in the process the works of some of the more significant playwrights. Among these are Shawqî and Tawfîq al-Ḥakîm, who are both the subject of individual works in which this eminent critic analyzes several of their plays and places them in an artistic and intellectual frame of reference. In another book, *Al-Masraḥ al-Nathrî* (Prose Drama), Mandûr discusses the beginnings of the form in Lebanon and then devotes most of the remainder of the work to a study of its development in Egypt. In a work with a similar title, *Fi al-Nathr al-Masraḥî* (On Dramatic Prose), Fu'âd Duwwâra collects a series of articles previously published in newspapers and magazines to provide a survey of some prominent plays produced in Egypt in recent years and of problems faced by theatrical producers. The newspaper article format does not of course allow for much elaboration, and yet, with a shortage of works on this genre, Duwwâra's collection remains a useful source of background information.

In turning to Western works on Arabic drama, the situation is a sorry one. There is a solitary introductory work to the genre, Jacob Landau's *Studies in the Arabic Theater and Cinema*, in which he describes precedents in the passion play and *karagöz* puppet performances, and then gives brief descriptions of some of the major plays of Shawqî, al-Ḥakîm, and Maḥmûd Taymûr (with reference also to his brother Muḥammad). Not least among the virtues of this book is the list of over 600 plays and 200 translated plays which can be found at the end of the work. Among European scholars, it is the French who have taken the most interest in Arabic drama. In addition to several volumes of translations published by *Nouvelles éditions latines* (particularly of al-Ḥakîm's plays, which have been performed with great success in France, there is also a collection of lectures delivered at a UNESCO conference and published under the title *Le théatre arabe*. Edited by Nada Tomiche, this work includes introductory surveys by Jacques Berque and ᶜAlî al-Râᶜî followed by a number of interesting articles on the situation in several Arab countries, including some not usually discussed within the general milieu of modern Arabic literature, Saudi Arabia, Sudan, and the Maghreb. Much of the material covered in Landau's work mentioned above is discussed in slightly more detail in a series of three articles by Nevill Barbour published in 1935 and 1937. The date of publication, however, points up the fact that they cover only the early period in the development of the genre. Most recently, we are indebted to Matti Moosa for an article decribing and analyzing the dramatic oeuvres and productions of Mârûn an-Naqqâsh, and another discussing the works of Ya^cqûb Ṣanû^c. In addition to these studies, there are of course a number of dissertations on the modern Arab theater in general and on several of its major figures, but none of them have been published in book form.

PAST AND PRESENT

At the beginning of the section on modern Arabic literature, we pointed out that it was the impact of Western culture that provided much of the stimulus to revive old forms and experiment with new ones in the period of the *nahḍa* (renaissance). In a recent article, Jabrâ Ibrâhîm Jabrâ has published a very perceptive analysis (showing, incidentally, his own wide acquaintance with Western literatures) in which he outlines many of the tensions which this situation has produced. For example, we can see at several different periods revivalists of the old classical tradition resurrecting the language and style of earlier periods, while at the same time "modernists" are translating European works into Arabic and producing their own attempts in the same genre. Thus al-Yâzijî writes his *Majma^c al-Baḥrayn* in direct imitation of the *maqâmât* of al-Ḥarîrî while his contemporaries translate and perform the plays of Molière. Other writers are accused of being too modern early in their career, only to see their views overtaken by the opinions of younger littérateurs at a later date. Shawqî, for example, is castigated by al-Muwayliḥî for writing "modern" poetry under the influence of Western concepts and suffers the same fate at the hands of al-^cAqqâd some 20 years later for writing stilted occasional poetry. Ṭâhâ Ḥusayn begins his career as the hero of the modernists for his stand against the religious establishment over the authenticity of pre-Islamic poetry and later comes under attack by Salâma Mûsâ on account of his refusal to consider the colloquial language a suitable medium for literary expression in fiction and drama.

The rapidity with which Middle Eastern littérateurs have had to absorb the ideas of schools such as expressionism, surrealism, and symbolism, as well as to experiment with new forms, has not always led to satisfactory results in the works of literature themselves. An attempt to introduce blank verse, for example, ended in failure. However, a number of writers in the Near East have taken the time and effort to make a profound study of the very bases of the Western movements, and it is interesting to note (as Jabrâ does) that the list of commentators and translators who have, for example, applied themselves to the poetry of T. S. Eliot are among the most famous poets of the contemporary Arab world. One of the major contemporary figures among these poets, and one who has read widely in European literature and literary theory, is Adûnîs, who not only writes poetry of great beauty and profundity but also publishes works *about* poetry. His most recent book, *Zaman al-Shi^{c}r* (The Time of Poetry) contains a statement which aptly summarizes this approach to his art:

> New poetry . . . is a vision, and vision by its very nature represents a leap outside of normal concepts. So it is a change in the order of things and in the way of looking at them. Modern poetry, then, is a revolt against old poetic forms and methods, a rejection of attitudes and styles whose aims are no longer to be found.

Adûnîs' journal, *Mawâqif*, which provides an outlet for some of the most radical young writers in the modern Arab world, has as its motto, "For Freedom, Creativity, Change," a triad which illustrates the literary and supraliterary role envisaged for the modern Arab writer in his society. This stance has been well captured for us by Muṣṭafâ Badawî in the introduction to his *Anthology of Modern Arabic Verse*:

> The Arab poet or writer is no longer regarded as a mere craftsman. As a result of a growing sense of individuality, both politically and pyschologically, and an increasing awareness of his place in society, he is now expected to have a message, to maintain his artistic integrity and not to sell his poetic or prose wares to the highest bidder, or to serve a cause in which he does not believe, sincerity being now regarded as the prime consideration. The quest for identity in a fast moving world culture, the heart searching and at times agonising self-analysis, to which the Arabs are driven through their dealings with Western culture, are all reflected in the questions and preoccupations, the themes and motifs of their literature, prose and poetry alike.

While contemporary Arab littérateurs and literary scholars discuss new works and new literary attitudes and approaches, it is interesting to note that many of them are at the same time reexamining the literature of the classical period according to new criteria. Adûnîs himself has published an anthology of Arabic poetry from the classical period and examples of the writings of the Sufi, al-Niffarî. Shukrî Fayṣal has devoted much time to a study of the "period of decadence," which seems likely to lead to a reassessment of that neglected era. Furthermore, a large number of critics and commentators have published works in which they analyze the general concepts of art, literature, and criticism in great detail and thus attempt to lay the theoretical bases on which future generations may study their contemporary literature and that of previous eras; Iḥsân ^{c}Abbâs, Shukrî Ayyâd, Shawqî Ḍayf, Shukrî Fayṣal, Muhammad Mandûr, and Muhammad al-Nuwayḥî are a few of the more famous scholars who have discussed these topics in general terms, and the list can be considerably lengthened by consulting Muhammad Najm's article in *Al-Adab al-^{c}Arabî fî Âthâr al-Dârisîn*.

CATEGORIZATION

In the introduction to this Chapter on Middle Eastern literatures, the discipline of literature itself was analyzed and subdivided into a number of fields: literary historical, literary critical, and literary theoretical, as well as the ancillary activity of text preparation and edition. These activities, along with others such as translation, were identified as being the main concerns of the literature scholar. On the basis of our survey of studies on Arabic literature, we will now attempt to categorize research by quality, quantity, and emphasis, so that we may be able to identify those areas in which further research is desirable.

A general statement which may be made at the beginning of such a section as this is that the total amount of materials available to the researcher in most periods of Arabic literature is relatively small (a reflection, needless to say, of the small number of scholars who have devoted themselves to this particular discipline). Thus a *Hauptwerk* on a particular subject or period may exist, but there remain large periods (that between the thirteenth and eighteenth centuries, for example) about which almost nothing is known. In previous generations, some scholars have attempted to provide the Western scholarly world with introductory works which survey the field of Arabic literature in broad sweeps. Their knowledge of particular periods or genres was broad and profound, and yet at several points they too had to rely on secondary materials which proved unreliable. When such points of erroneous fact or interpretation were included in a work which remained for perhaps several generations the only work on a particular field or genre, they became canonized into fact by time and footnotes. This point is made here purely to illustrate one of the dangers inherent in a discipline where for certain kinds of information scholars have to rely on a single source.

Literary Historical

At the beginning of the survey on Arabic literature, we noted some of the motives which lay behind the study of the Arabic language and its literature in earlier days. Against the background of such a "classical" approach to the works of literature, it is perhaps hardly surprising that much of the research conducted in the West has tended to conform with the tendencies described by Roland Barthes in the quotation cited at the beginning of this Chapter. With very few exceptions, scholars seem to have been interested in finding out facts about the literature and littérateurs and also in gleaning facts from the literature to use in other connections (Arab history, Islamic dogma, Near Eastern societies, etc.). All this is aptly reflected in the numerical preponderance of literary historical research evident in this survey.

To begin with, there are numerous histories of the literature, although with few exceptions the concept of literature is much wider than is advocated here. Gibb's excellent article in the new *Encyclopaedia of Islam* (Arabiyya) has already been cited as an example of the type of "literary" literary history which is needed. Among works in book form which should be cited for their attention to literary criteria are those of Blachère (in three volumes), Nicholson (including numerous examples in translation), a revised and updated version in German of Gibb's short history of the literature prepared by Landau under the title *Arabische Literaturgeschichte*, and an excellent survey in Spanish, *Literatura arabe* by Juan Vernet Gines. The histories currently available in Arabic (for example, those of Zaydân and al-Zayyât) suffer from being essentially compendia of dates, authors, and works, as do the studies of shorter periods by Cheikho. However, Shawqî Ḍayf has now embarked on a massive project to write a comprehensive analytical history of Arabic literature under the title *Târîkh al-Adab al-*^{c}*Arabî*; the series of works began in the 1960s, and at least four volumes have now been published.

In the field of literary biography, too, there has been a good deal of activity, and the scholar in Arabic literature has a number of useful sources at his disposal from which he can find the necessary facts about authors and works. Among the most brilliant examples of this type of research are the volumes of Brockelmann and now of Sezgin, in both of which there is copious information about authors and their works as well as general introductions to periods and genres. European scholars now owe a debt of gratitude to Bayard Dodge for his annotated translation of the famous *Fihrist* (Index) of Muhammad al-Nadîm (d. 995), in which are to be found not only details of authors and works up till the end of the tenth century (A.D.) but also titles of numerous works which have not come down to us. Using sources such as these and general biographical dictionaries like those of Ibn Khallikân (*Wafayât al-A*^{c}*yân*), al-Ziriklî (*al-A*^{c}*lâm*), Zaydân (*Tarâjim Mashâhîr al-Sharq*), and Zakî Muhammad Mujâhid (*al-A*^{c}*lâm al-Sharqiyya*), many writers have produced biographies of the famous figures in Arabic literary history. For both the classical and modern periods, the list is a long one. Examples which stand out from the usual summary of facts about the author's life and writings (usually with examples from the latter) are Pellat's work on al-Jâḥiẓ, ^{c}Abbâs' studies of al-Tawḥîdî and al-Bayyâtî, and Ṭâhâ Ḥusayn's studies of al-Ma^{c}arrî (although these latter are in fact more than simply biographical).

Studies which deal with individual genres or periods are less common than either history or biography, although paucity of numbers is generally compensated for by a more uniform quality. For example, al-Bahbîtî's study of the first three centuries of Arabic poetry is an excellent contribution to research on this difficult period, and so too is Nallino's study on early poetry called *La littérature arabe* (in its French translation by Pellat). Iḥsân ᶜAbbâs has also provided us with a fine study of the literature of al-Andalus during the heyday of Cordoba. It seems fair to state that a more accurate history of Arabic literature will emerge from a whole series of studies such as these which examine a particular period in some depth, rather than from vague generalizations based on scanty evidence.

With regard to genres, the modern period seems particularly well-served, the classical period less so. In the latter case, this seems especially true of the prose tradition, in which the works of Mubârak and al-Maqdisî emerge as essentially introductory surveys of a field which needs much more research and analysis. Of the poetic genres, it is the *ghazal* (love poem) which seems to have fared best at the hands of Shukrî Fayṣal and A. Kh. Kinany, both of whose works lend genuine insight into the genre, its writers, and their environment.

Thus we may perhaps summarize this short resume on the literary historical approach by suggesting that more research is necessary in both period and genre studies in order that the more general categories of this subfield of literature studies may have more precise information on which to base their works of reference.

Literary Critical

As the preceding survey has shown, a tradition of literary analysis and criticism was developed very early among the Arabs, and in particular the theories of such a figure as al-Jurjânî are remarkable for their "modernity." A modern history of Arabic literary criticism would probably begin with Orientalists such as Goldziher, Nöldeke, and Rückert, and then proceed to mention some of the Near Eastern scholars whose critical acumen was sharpened through study in Europe, mainly in France. That certainly was where the great Ṭâhâ Ḥusayn acquired much of his training which he proceeded to put into practice in his works on pre-Islamic poetry and other topics, and also in his instruction of a generation of literature scholars among whom Muhammad Mandûr and Suhayr al-Qalamâwî are merely two of the more famous names. Many of Mandûr's studies have been mentioned in the survey, and his name leads us to the present day when a number of excellent Arab critics are addressing themselves to Arabic literature of all periods. Among these, we would single out in particular Shukrî ᶜAyyâd Iḥsân ᶜAbbâs, Muhammad al-Nuwayḥî, Shukrî Fayṣal, and Muhammad Yûsuf Najm.

On the subfields within the literary critical approach, the psychological, social, and formal aspects seems to have attracted the most attention; studies such as those of al-Nuwayḥî and al-ᶜAqqâd on the psychological makeup of Abû Nuwâs and Ba<u>sh</u>sh<u>â</u>r, together with numerous good studies on a variety of forms, are symptomatic of this trend. Much less well represented are the stylistic and figure aspects, and for this reason the excellent works of Stetkevych on modern literary language and style and Jacobi on figures in pre-Islamic poetry are most welcome addition to the scholarly literature in this subfield of literary studies. In general, articles such as those on poems of <u>Sh</u>awqī and al-Maᶜarrî which have appeared in the *Journal of Arabic Literature* (Vols. 2 and 4) show that there is still a great need for research into criticism at a very primary level, namely, that of analyzing the language, imagery, and structure of individual works of literature. Only when such basic skills have been mastered and practiced on a wider scale can we expect to be able to discuss the terms of reference of criticism with any conviction.

In the West, a small number of scholars seem to be laying the basis for a critical study of Arabic literature within its various subfields, and it is to be hoped that the efforts of such scholars as Bateson, Hamori, Jacobi, Moreh, Stetkevych, and others will help to attract interest in Arabic literature as a worthy subject of intrinsic literary study according to those criteria which have been and are being practiced with other world literatures.

Literary Theoretical

A rapid reading of our survey shows that, of the three literary approaches mentioned in the introduction to this chapter, the literary theoretical is the least well represented in the studies which have been treated. Yet here, too, developments are taking place in a number of different areas. Worthy of particular mention are the researches of Weil, ᶜAyyâd, and Abu Deeb on the very bases of Arabic prosody, the experiments with the Parry-Lord theory of oral poetry essayed by Hyde, Zwettler, and most recently Monroe, and the structuralist approaches of Bateson (in poetry) and Connelly (in folk literature).

These researches, coupled with an ever-increasing concern among literature scholars in the Near East and West with the fundamental criteria of art in general and literature in particular, lead the present writer to characterize the "state of the art" in Arabic literature as being at a very important crossroads. At this juncture, the road of the Orientalist and generalist tradition has met that of the literature scholar who has frequently been trained in the disciplines of Western literatures, and a new tradition of literary scholarship seems to be emerging based on a solid philological foundation, but also using the criteria and methods of these latter literature disciplines.

In addition, the long-standing tradition of literature scholarship and criticism in the Near East has been revived, has come into contact with Western schools of literature, and is now broaching Arabic literature of both ancient and modern periods with renewed vigor and acumen. Increased contact between Near Eastern and Western scholars in this field will no doubt serve to resolve some of the tensions inherent in this meeting of different cultures and scholarly attitudes, and it is hoped that the resultant exchange and fusion of ideas will enhance this scholarly discipline till it comes to be placed alongside that of other world literatures.

BIBLIOGRAPHY

Note. Limitations of time and space and problems of communication have made it impossible to include here reference to or discussion of works written in the Slavic languages or those of the Far East.

Key to Categorization

(*a*) Literary historical.
(*b*) Literary critical.
(*c*) Literary theoretical.
(*d*) Philological, lexicographical.
(*e*) Texts, diwans, anthologies.
(*f*) Translations.
(*g*) Bibliographical, biobibliographical.

Abadir, Akef and Roger Allen. *God's World*. Minneapolis: Bibliotheca Islamica, 1973. (f)

^{c}Abbâs, Iḥsân. *^{c}Abd al-Wahhâb al-Bayyâti*. Beirut: Dâr Bayrût, 1955. (a,b)

———. *Abu Ḥayyân al-Tawḥîdî*. Beirut: Dâr Bayrût Lil-Ṭibâ^{c}a wa al-Nashr, 1956. (a,b)

———. *Badr Shâkir al-Sayyâb*. Beirut: Dâr al-Thaqâfa, 1969. (a,b)

———. *Dîwân ibn Sahl al-Isrâ^{c}îlî*. Beirut: Dâr Ṣâdir, 1967. (e)

———. *Fann al-Shi^{c}r*. Beirut: Dâr Bayrût, 1959. (c)

———. *Shi^{c}r al-Khawârij*. Beirut: Dâr al-Thaqâfa, 1963. (e)

———. *Târîkh al-Naqd al-Adabî ^{c}ind al-^{c}Arab*. Beirut: Dâr al-Amâna, 1971. (a,b)

———. and Muḥammad Y. Najm. *al-Shi^{c}r al-^{c}Arabî fî al-Mahjar*. Beirut: Dâr Ṣâdir, 1957; 2nd ed. 1967. (a,b)

Abdel Meguid, Abdel Aziz. *The Modern Arabic Short Story*. Cairo: al-Ma^{c}ârif Press, (ca. 1954).

Abu Deeb, Kamal. "Al-Jurjani's Classification of *Isti^{c}âra*." *Journal of Arabic Literature*, **2** (1971), 48ff. (c)

———. "Fî Îqâ^{c} al-Shi^{c}r al-^{c}Arabî: Naḥwa Badîl Jidhrî Li-^{c}Arûḍ al-Khalîl." *Mawâqif*, **22** (Aug. 1972), 17ff. (c)

Abu Lughod, Ibrahim. *The Arab Rediscovery of Europe*. Princeton: Univ. Press, 1963. (a)

Abû Shâdî, Aḥmad Zakî. *Qadâya al-Shi^{c}r al-Mu^{c}âṣir*. Cairo: al-Sharika al-^{c}Arabiyya Lil-Ṭiba^{c}a wa al-Nashr, 1959. (c)

Adûnîs. "Ta'sîs Kitâba Jadîda." *Mawâqif*, **3**, 17/18 (1971). (b)

———. "Fî Qaṣîdat al-Nathr." *Shi^cr*, **14** (Spr. 1960). (b)

———. *Zaman al-Shi^cr*. Beirut: Dâr al-^cAwda, 1972. (c)

^cAfîfî, Muḥammad. *al-Qiṣṣa al-Maghribiyya al-Ḥadîtha*. Casablanca: Maktabat al-Waḥda al-^cArabiyya, 1961. (a)

al-^cAlî, Ṣâliḥ Aḥmad, et al. *al-Adab al-^cArabî fî Âthâr al-Dârisîn*. Beirut: 1971. (g)

al-^cÂlim, Maḥmûd Amîn. *Ta'ammulât fî ^cÂlam Najîb Maḥfuẓ*. Cairo: al-Hay'a al-Miṣriyya al^cAmma Lil-Ta'lîf wa al-Nashr, 1970. (b)

al-Âmidî, al-Ḥasan ibn Bishr. *al-Muwâzana*. Cairo: Dâr al-Ma^cârif, 1961. (b)

Anthologie de la Littérature Arabe Contemporaine. Preface by Jacques Berque, Trans. by Raoul and Laura Makarius. Paris: Editions du Seuil, 1964.

al-^cAqqâd, ^cAbbâs Maḥmûd. *Abû Nuwâs al-Ḥasan ibn Hâni'—Dirâsa fî al-Taḥlîl al-Nafsânî wa al-Târîkhî*. Cairo: al-Anjlû, 1954. (b)

———. *Ibn al-Rûmî: Ḥayâtuhu min Shi^crihi*. Cairo: Maṭba^cat Ḥijâzî, 1938. (a,b)

———. *Shâ^cir al-Ghazal*. Cairo: Maṭba^cat al-Ma^cârif wa-Maktabatuha, 1943. (a,b)

———. *Shu^carâ' Miṣr*, 3rd ed. Cairo: Maktabat al-Nahḍa al-Miṣriyya, 1965. (a)

———, and Ibrahîm al-Mâzinî. *al-Dîwân*, 2nd ed., 2 parts. Cairo: Maktabat al-Sa^câda, 1921. (b)

Arberry, A. J. *Anthology of Moorish Poetry*. Cambridge: Univ. Press, 1953. (e)

———. *The Mawâqif and Mukhâtabât of Muḥammad Ibn Abd al-Jabbâr al-Niffarî*, Gibb Memorial. Cambridge: Univ. Press, 1935. (e)

al-^cAskarî, Abû Hilâl. *Kitâb al-Ṣinâ^catayn*. Cairo: ^cÎsâ al-Bâbî al-Ḥalabî.

Ayyâd, Shukrî. *Kitâb Arisṭûṭâlîs fî al-Shi^cr*. Cairo: 1967. (c)

———. *Mûsîqâ al-Shi^cr al-^cArabî*. Cairo: 1968. (c)

———. *al-Qiṣṣa al-Qaṣîra fî Miṣr: Dirâsa fî Ta'ṣîl Fann Adabî*. Cairo: Jâmi^cat al-Duwal al-^cArabiyya, 1968. (b,c)

———. "al-Riwâya al-^cArabiyya al-Mu^câṣira wa Azmat al-Ḍamîr al-^cArabî." *Majallat ^cÂlam al-Fikr*, **3** (Oct.–Dec., 1972), 9ff. (b)

———. *Tajârib fî al-Adab wa al-Naqd*. Cairo: Dâr al-Kâtib al-^cArabî Lil-Ṭibâ^ca wa al-Nashr, 1967. (b)

Badawî, A. A. *^cAbd al-Qâhir al-Jurjânî*. Cairo: al-Mu'assasa al-Miṣriyya al-^cÂmma Lil-Ta'lîf wa al-Tarjama wa al-Ṭibâ^ca wa al-Nashr, 1962. (a,c)

———. *Ḥâzim al-Qarṭajannî wa Naẓariyyat Arisṭû fî al-Balâgha wa al-Shi^cr*. Cairo: Ayn Shams University, 1961. (a,c)

Badawî, Muṣṭafâ. *An Anthology of Modern Arabic Verse*. Oxford: Univ. Press, 1970. (e)

———. "Al-Bārūdī, Precursor of the Modern Arabic Poetic Revival." *Die Welt des Islams*, N.S. **12** (1969), 288ff. (a,b)

———. "The Lamp of Umm Hashim: The Egyptian Intellectual Between East and West." *Journal of Arabic Literature*, **1** (1970). 145ff. (f).

———. "Al-Māzinī the Novelist." *Journal of Arabic Literature*, **4** (1973). 122ff. (a,b)

Badr, ^cAbd al-Muḥsin Ṭâhâ. *Taṭawwur al-Riwâya al-^cArabiyya al-Ḥadîtha*. Cairo: Dâr al-Ma^cârif, 1963. (a,b)

al-Bahbîtî, Najîb. *Abû Tammâm al-Ṭâ'î*. Cairo: Maṭba^cat Dâr al-Kutub, 1945. (a)

———. *Târîkh al-Shi^cr al-^cArabî ḥattâ Akhir al-Qarn al-Thâlith al-Hijrî*. Cairo: Dâr al-Kutub 1950. (a,b)

Barbour, Nevill. "The Arabic Theatre in Egypt." *Bulletin of the School of Oriental Studies,* (1935–1937), 173ff, 991ff, (a)

Bateson, Mary Catherine. *Structural Continuity in Poetry: A Linguistic Study of Five Preislamic Arabic Odes.* The Hague: Mouton, 1970. (b,c)

Beeston, A. F. L. "The Genesis of the Maqāmāt Genre." *Journal of Arabic Literature,* **2** (1971). (a)

Blachère, Régis. *Histoire de la Littérature Arabe,* 3 vols. Paris: Maisonneuve, 1952–1956. (a)

———, and Pierre Masnou. *Al-Hamadhānī: Choix de maqāmāt.* Paris: Klincksieck, 1957. (a,f)

Bonebakker, Seeger, A. "Poets and critics of the 3rd Century A.H." In *Logic in Classical Arabic Culture.* Wiesbaden: Harrassowitz, 1970. (b,c)

———. "Reflections on the *Kitab al-Badi*ᶜ of Ibn al Muᶜtazz." In *Atti 3 Cong. studi arabi e islamici* (Ravello 1966–1967), 191–209. Naples: Instituto Universitario Orientale, 1967. (b,c)

Boullata, Issa (Bullâṭa, ᶜÎsâ Y.) *Badr S̲h̲âkir al-Sayyâb: Ḥayâtuhu wa S̲h̲iᶜruhu.* Beirut: Dâr al-Nahâr li'l-Nas̲h̲r, 1971. (a,b)

———. "Badr Shākir al-Sayyāb and the Free Verse Movement." *International Journal of Middle East Studies,* **1** (1970), 248ff. (b)

———. "Badr Shākir al-Sayyāb: A Life of Vision and Agony." *Middle East Forum,* **46** (2–6), 73ff. (a)

———. "The Beleaguered Unicorn: A Study of Tawfiq Sayigh." *Journal of Arabic Literature,* **4** (1937), 69ff. (b)

———. "The Poetic Technique of Badr Shākir al-Sayyāb." *Journal of Arabic Literature,* **2** (1971), 104ff. (b)

Brockelmann, Carl. *Geschichte der arabischen Literatur,* 2 vols. Berlin: Felber, 1898–1902. (a,g)

Cachia, Pierre. *Taha Husayn: His Place in the Egyptian Literary Renaissance.* London: Luzac, 1956. (a,b)

Cheikho, Louis, (*S̲h̲aik̲h̲û Lûwîs*). *al-Âdâb al-ᶜArabiyya fî al-Qarn al-Tâsiᶜ ᶜAs̲h̲ar.* Beirut: al-Maṭbaᶜa al-Kâthûlîkiyya, 1924–1926. (a)

———. *Târîk̲h̲ al-Âdâb al-ᶜArabiyya fî al-Rubᶜ al-Awwal min al-Qarn al-ᶜIs̲h̲rîn.* Beirut: al-Maṭbaᶜa al-Kâthûlikiyya, 1926 (a)

Chenery, Thomas. *The Assemblies of al-Harīrī.* London: Williams and Norgate, 1867–1899. (f)

Connelly, Bridget. "The Structure of Four Banī Hilāl Tales." *Journal of Arabic Literature,* **4** (1973), 18ff. (c)

Crussard, E. *En lisant Harīrī.* Tunis: Guénard and Franchi, 1923. (b)

Ḍayf, S̲h̲awqî. *al-Adab al-ᶜArabî al-Muᶜâṣir fî Miṣr.* Cairo: Dâr al-Maᶜârif, 1957. (a)

———. *Dirâsât fî al-Shiᶜr al-ᶜArabî al-Muᶜâṣir.* Cairo: Dâr al-Ma ârif, 1959. (b)

———. *al-Fann wa Mad̲h̲ahibuhu fî al-S̲h̲iᶜr al-ᶜArabî.* Cairo: Dâr al-Maᶜârif, 1960 (c).

———. *Fî al-Naqd al-Adabî.* Cairo: Dâr al-Maᶜarif, 1966. (b)

———. *al-Maqâma.* Cairo: Dâr al-Maᶜarif, 1954 and 1955. (a)

———. *al-Rit̲h̲â' fî al-Adab al-ᶜArabî.* Cairo: Dâr al-Maᶜârif, 1955. (a)

Dozy, Reinhart. *Supplément aux dictionnaires arabes.* Leiden: Brill, 1881, 1927, 1967. (d)

Duwwâra, Fu'âd. *Fî al-Nat̲h̲r al-Masraḥî.* Cairo: 1963. (b)

Encyclopaedia of Islam, 1st ed., 4 vols. Leiden: Brill, 1913–1936. Supplement, 1913–1938. 2nd ed., 3 vols. published. Leiden: Brill, 1954. (a,g)

Fayṣal, S̲h̲ukrî. *Abû al-ᶜAtâhiya.* Damascus: Maṭbaᶜat Jâmiᶜat Dimas̲h̲q, 1965. (a,b)

———. *Manâhij al-Dirâsa al-Adabiyya fî al-Adab al-ᶜArabî.* Cairo: Maktabat al-Khânjî, 1953. (c)

———. *Taṭawwur al-Ghazal Bayn al-Jâhiliyya wa al-Islâm.* Damascus: Maṭbaᶜat Jâmiᶜat Dimashq, 1959 and 1964. (a,b)

Fu'âd, Niᶜmat. *Adab al-Mâzinî,* 2nd ed. Cairo: Mu'assasat al-Khânjî, 1961. (a,b)

Gabrieli, F. "L'opera di Ibn al-Muqaffaᶜ." *Rivista degli Studi Orientali,* **13** (1931–1932), 197ff. (a)

———. *Storia della litteratura araba.* Milan: Academia, 1951. (a)

Gerhardt, Mia. *The Art of Story-Telling.* Leiden: Brill, 1963. (a,b)

Gibb, H. A. R. *Arabic Literature.* Oxford: Univ. Press, 1926, 1963. (a)

———. "Arabiyya." In *Encyclopaedia of Islam,* 2nd ed. Leiden: Brill, 1954. (a)

———. "Literature." In *The Legacy of Islam,* T. Arnold, ed. Oxford: Univ. Press, 1931. (a)

———. "Studies in Contemporary Arabic Literature." (i) The Nineteenth Century, (ii) Manfaluti and the new style, (iii) Egyptian Modernists, (iv) the Egyptian Novel. In *Studies on the Civilisation of Islam.* London: Routledge and Kegan Paul, 1962, 245ff. (a)

———, and Jacob Landau. *Arabische Literaturgeschichte.* Zurich: Artemis, 1968. (a)

Goldziher, Ignaz. *Abhandlungen zur arabischen Philogie.* Leiden: Brill, 1896. (d)

———. *Ein orientalischer Ritterroman.* Pr. Lloyd, 1891. (a)

———. *A Short History of Classical Arabic Literature.* Joseph de Somogyi, trans. Hildesheim: Olms Verlagsbuchhandlung, 1966. (a)

Gomez, Garcia. *Poemas arabigo-andaluces.* Madrid: Espasa-Calpe, 1943. (e)

———. *Poesĩa arabigoandaluca, breve sintesis historica.* Madrid: Maᶜhad al-Dirâsât al-Islâmiyya, 1952 (a).

Grohmann, Adolf. *Handbuch der Orientalistik: Arabische Chronologie—Arabische Papyruskunde.* Leiden: Brill, 1966. (g)

Von Grunebaum, Gustave. "The Aesthetic Foundation of Arabic Literature." *Comparative Literature,* **4** (Fall, 1952). (c)

———. "The Arab Contribution to Troubadour Poetry." *Bulletin of The Iran Institute,* **6** (1946), 138ff. (a)

———. "Arabic Literature in the 10th Century." *Journal of the American Oriental Society,* **61** (1941), 51ff. (a,b)

———. "Growth and Structure of Arabic Poetry A.D. 500–1000." In *The Arab Heritage,* N. A. Faris, ed. Princeton: Univ. Press, 1944. (a)

———. *Medieval Islam.* Chicago: Univ. Press, 1946, 1954. (a)

———. *Modern Islam.* New York: Vintage Books, 1964. (a)

———. *Die Wirklichkeitweite der Früharabischen Dichtung.* Vienna: Selbstverlag des Orientalischen Institutes der Universität, 1937. (c)

al-Hamadhânî, Badîᶜ al-Zamân. *The Maqâmât.* W. J. Prendergast, trans. London: Luzac, 1915.

Hamori, Andras. *On the Art of Medieval Arabic Literature.* Princeton: Univ. Press, 1974. (b,c)

Hamza, ᶜAbd al-Laṭîf. *Ibn al-Muqaffaᶜ,* 3rd ed. Cairo: Dâr al-Fikr al-ᶜArabî, 1965. (a)

Ḥaqqî, Yaḥyâ. *Fajr al-Qiṣṣa al-Miṣriyya.* Cairo: Dâr al-Qalam, 1960. (a)

Hartmann, M. *Das arabische Strophengedicht. I: Das Muwaššaḥ.* Weimar: 1897. (a)

Harvey, L. P. "Aljamiada." In *The Encyclopaedia of Islam,* 2nd ed. Leiden: Brill, 1954. (a)

Hopwood, Derek and Diana Grimwood-Jones, eds. *Middle East and Islam.* Zug, Switzerland: Interdocumentation Co., 1970. (g)

Hourani, Albert. *Arabic Thought in the Liberal Age.* London: Oxford Univ. Press, 1962, 1967. (a)

Huart, Clement. *A History of Arabic Literature.* New York: D. Appleton, 1903. (a)

Ḥusayn, Muḥammad. *Al-Hijâ' wa al-Hajjâ'ûn fî Ṣadr al-Islam.* Cairo: Maktabat al-Âdâb bil-Jamâmîz, 1947. (a)

Ḥusayn, Ṭâhâ. *Al-Ayyâm,* Vol. 1. Cairo: Maṭbaᶜat al-Maᶜârif wa Maktabatuhâ, 1944–1945. English trans: *An Egyptian Childhood.* E. H. Paxton, trans. London: Routledge and Sons, 1932. Also, *The Stream of Days.* Hilary Wayment, trans. Cairo: al-Maaref, 1943.

———. "Al-Bayân al-ᶜArabî min al-Jâḥiẓ ilâ ᶜAbd al-Qâhir." *Introduction to Qudâma ibn Jaᶜfar's Naqd al-Nathr.* Cairo: Maṭbaᶜat Dâr al-Kutub al-Miṣriyya, 1926. (a)

———. *Fî al-Shiᶜr al-Jâhilî.* Cairo: Maṭbaᶜat Dâr al-Kutub al-Miṣriyya, 1926. (b)

———. *Fuṣul fî al-Adab waal-Naqd,* 4th ed. Cairo: Maṭbaᶜat al-Maᶜarif wa Maktabatuhâ, 1945. (b)

———. *Ḥadîth al-Arbiᶜâ'.* Cairo: Dâr al-Maᶜârif, 1925–1945. (a,b)

———. *Ḥâfiẓ wa Shawqî.* Cairo: Maktabat al-Khanjî, 1932. (a,b)

———. *Maᶜa Abî al-ᶜAlâ' fî Sijnihi.* Cairo: Dâr al-Maᶜârif, 1936. (a,b)

———. *Maᶜa al-Mutanabbî.* Cairo: Dâr al-Maᶜârif. 1936. (a,b)

———. *Min Ḥadîth al-Shiᶜr waal-Nathr.* Cairo: Dâr al-Maᶜârif, 1936. (b)

———. *Ṣawt Abî al-ᶜAlâ'.* Cairo: Dâr al-Maᶜârif, 1944. (a,b)

———. *Tâjdîd Dhikrâ Abî al-ᶜAlâ'.* Cairo: Maṭbaᶜat al-Maᶜârif, 1937. (a,b)

Huseini, Ishaq Musa. *The Life and Works of Ibn Qutayba.* Beirut: the American Press, 1950. (a)

Ibn ᶜAbd Rabbih, Aḥmad ibn Muḥammad. *al-ᶜIqd al-Farîd.* Cairo: Lajnat al-Ta'lîf wa al-Tarjama wa al-Nashr, 1940–1953. (e)

Ibn Dhurayl, ᶜAdnân. *Adab al-Qiṣṣa fî Sûriya.* Damascus: 1966. (a)

Ibn Khallikân, Shams al-Dîn. *Wafayât al-Aᶜyân.* Cairo: Maktabat al-Nahḍa al-Miṣriyya, 1948, 1964; and Beirut: Dâr Ṣâdir, 1968. English trans.: *Ibn Khallikan's Biographical Dictionary,* 4 vols. Bn. MacGuckin de Slane, trans. Paris: Printed for the Oriental translation fund of Great Britain and Ireland, 1843–1871. (a)

Ibn al-Muᶜtazz. *Kitâb al-Badîᶜ.* Ignatius Kratchkovsky, ed. London: Luzac, 1935. (b)

Ibn Qutayba, ᶜAbd Allâh ibn Muslim. *Kitâb Adab al-Kâtib.* Miṣr: Maṭbaᶜat al-Waṭan, 1882, 4th ed. Cairo: al-Maktaba al-Tijâriyya al-Kubrâ, 1963. (b)

———. *Kitâb al-Shiᶜr wa al Shuᶜarâ.* Leiden: Brill, 1875. (b)

———. *ᶜUyûn al-Akhbâr.* Cairo: Egyptian National Library Press, 1925–1930. (e)

———. *Introduction au Livre de la poésie et des poètes.* Gaudefroy-Demombynes, ed. and trans. Paris: Société d'Edition "Les Belles Lettres." 1947. (e,f)

Ibn Sanâ' al-Mulk. *Dâr al-Ṭirâz fî ᶜAmal al-Muwashshaḥât.* Jawdat al-Rikâbî, ed. Damascus: Rikâbî, 1949. (b)

Ismâᶜîl, ᶜIzz al-Dîn. *al-Shiᶜr al-ᶜArabî al-Muᶜâṣir: Qaḍâyâhu wa Ẓawâhiruhu al-Fanniyya waal-Maᶜnawiyya.* Cairo: Dâr al-Kâtib al-ᶜArabî, 1967. (c)

Jacobi, Renata. *Studien zur Poetik der altarabischen Qaside.* Wiesbaden: Steiner, 1971. (b)

al-Jâḥiẓ, ᶜAmr ibn Baḥr. *al-Bayân waal-Tabyîn,* 3rd ed. Cairo: al-Maktaba al-Tijâriyya al-Kubrâ, 1947. (b)

———. *Le Livre des Avares.* Claude Pellat, trans. Paris: Maisonneuve, 1951.

al-Jayyûsî, Salmâ. "al-Shi^c^r al-^c^Arabî al-Mu^c^âṣir: Taṭawwuruhu wa Mustaqbaluhu." *Majallat ^c^Âlam al-Fikr*, **4** (July–Sept. 1973), 11ff. (a,b)

al-Jurjânî, ^c^Abd al-Qâhir. *Asrâr al-Balâgha*. H. Ritter, ed. Istanbul: Istanbul Üniversitesi, Şarkiyat Enstitüsü, 1954; Cairo: Maktabat al-Qâhira, 1972. German trans: H. Ritter, *Die Geheimnisse der Wortkunst*. Wiesbaden: Steiner, 1959. (b,c)

———. *Dalâ'il al-I^c^jâz*. Rashîd Riḍâ, ed. Cairo: Maṭba^c^at al-Manâr, 1911–1912; and Maktabat al-Qâhira, 1970. (c)

al-Jurjânî, al-Qaḍî ^c^Alî ibn ^c^Abd al-^c^Azîz. *al-Waṣâṭa bayn al-Mutanabbî wa Khuṣûmihi*. Sidon: Maṭba^c^ at al-^c^Irfân; and Cairo: ^c^Îsâ al-Bâbî al-Ḥalabî, 1945. (c)

Kânûn, Abdallâh. *Aḥâdîth ^c^an al-Adab al-Maghribî al-Ḥadîth*. Cairo: Jâmi^c^at al-Duwal al-^c^Arabiyya: Ma^c^had al-Dirâsât al-^c^Arabiyya al-^c^Âliya, 1964. (a)

Khalafallâh, M. "^c^Abd al-Qahir's Theory in his *Secrets of Eloquence*: a Psychological Approach." *Journal of Near Eastern Studies*, **14** (1955). (c)

Al-Khateeb, H. "A Modern Syrian Short Story: Wajh al-Qamar." *Journal of Arabic Literature*, **3** (1972), 96ff. (b,f)

Khiḍr, ^c^Abbâs. *al-Qiṣṣa al-Qaṣîra fî Miṣr min Nash'atihâ ḥattâ Sana* 1930. Cairo: al-Dâr al-Qawmiyya Lil-Ṭibâ^c^a wa al-Nashr, 1966. (a)

Khiḍr, Su^c^âd. *al-Adab al-Jazâ'irî al-Mu^c^âṣir*. Sidon: al-Maktaba al-^c^Aṣriyya. 1967. (a)

Khouri, Mounah. *Poetry and the Making of Modern Egypt*. Leiden: Brill, 1971. (a,b)

Kilpatrick, Hilary. *The Modern Egyptian Novel*. London: Ithaca Press, 1974.

Kinany, A. Kh. *The Development of the Ghazal in Arabic Literature*. Damascus: Syrian Univ. Press, 1951. (a,b)

Klein-Franke, F. "The *hamāsa* of Abū Tammām." *Journal of Arabic Literature*, **2** (1971), 13ff. **3**(1972), 142ff. (a,b)

Kratchkovsky, Ignaz. "Der historische Roman in der neueren arabischen Literatur." *Die Welt des Islams*, **12** (1930–1931), 51ff. (a)

Kritzeck, James. *Anthology of Islamic Literature*. London: Penguin, 1964. (e)

———. *Modern Islamic Literature*. New York: Rinehart & Winston, 1970. (e)

Landau, Jacob. *Studies in the Arabic Theater and Cinema*. Philadelphia: Univ. of Penn. Press, 1958. (a)

Lane, E. W. *Arabic-English Lexicon*, 8 parts. London: Williams & Norgate, 1863–1893; and Beirut: Librairie du Liban, 1968. (d)

———. *Manners and Customs of the Modern Egyptians*. London: 1836. London: Everyman, 1908, and many reprints.

Le Gassick, Trevor. "A Malaise in Cairo." *Middle East Journal* (Winter 1967), 35ff. (a,b)

Lyall, C. J. *Ancient Arabian Poetry*. New York: Columbia Univ. Press, 1930. (e)

———. "Four Poems of Ta'abbata Sharra, the Brigand Poet." *Journal of the Royal Asiatic Society* (1918), 211ff. (b)

———. "Some Aspects of Ancient Arabic Poetry as illustrated by a Little Known Anthology." *Proceedings of the British Academy* (1917–1918), 365ff. (b)

———. *The Mufaddaliyyat, an Anthology of Ancient Arabian Odes*. Oxford: Clarendon Press, 1918. (e,f)

———. "The Pictorial Aspects of Ancient Arabian Poetry." *Journal of The Royal Asiatic Society* (1912), 133ff. (b)

Al-Maydânî. *Arabum Proverbia*, 3 vols. G. W. F. Freytag, ed. Bonn: A. Marcum, 1838–1843. (d) al-Malâ'ika, Nâzik. *Muḥâḍarât fî Shi^{c}r ^{c}Alî Maḥmûd Ṭâhâ.* Cairo: Jâmi^{c}at al-Duwal al-^{c}Arabiyya: Ma^{c}had al-Dirâsât al-^{c}Arabiyya al-^{c}Âliya, 1965. (b)

———. *Qaḍâyâ al-Shi^{c}r al-Mu^{c}âṣir.* Baghdad: Maktabat al-Nahḍa, 1965. (c)

Mandûr, Muḥammad. *al-Adab wa Madhâhibuhu.* Cairo: Dâr Nahḍat Miṣr, 1968. (c)

———. *Fî al-Mîzân al-Jadîd.* Cairo: Maṭba^{c}at Lajnat al-Ta'lîf waal-Tarjama waal-Nashr, 1944. (b,c)

———. *Ibrâhîm al-Mâzinî.* Cairo: Maktabat Nahḍat Miṣr, 1954. (a,b)

———. *al-Masraḥ.* Cairo: Dâr al-Ma^{c}ârif, 1963. (a,b)

———. *al-Masraḥ al-Nathrî.* Cairo: Jâmi^{c}at al-Duwal al-Arabiyya: Ma^{c}had al-Dirâsât al-^{c}Arabiyya al-^{c}Âliya, 1959–1960. (a,b)

———. *Masraḥiyyât Shawqî,* 3rd ed. Cairo: Maktabat Nahḍat Miṣr, 1963, (a,b)

———. *Masraḥ Tawfîq al-Ḥakîm,* 2nd ed. Cairo: Dâr Nahḍat Miṣr Lil-Ṭibâ^{c}a waal-Nashr, 1966. (a,b)

———. *Muḥâḍarât ^{c}an Khalîl Muṭrân.* Cairo: Dâr Nahḍat Miṣr Lil-Ṭibâ^{c}a waal Nashr, 1972. (a,b)

———. *al-Shi^{c}r al-Miṣrî ba^{c}da Shawqî.* Cairo: Maktabat Nahḍat Miṣr, 1963. (a,b)

al-Maqdisî, Anîs. *Taṭawwur al-Asâlîb al-Nathriyya fî al-Adab al-^{c}Arabî,* 3rd ed. Beirut: Dâr al-^{c}Ilm lil-Malâyîn, 1965. (a,b)

———. *Umarâ' al-Shi^{c}r al-^{c}Arabî fî al-^{c}Aṣr al-Abbâsî,* 7th ed. Beirut: Dâr al-^{c}Ilm lil-Malâyîn, 1967. (a,b)

Margoliouth, D. S. "The Origins of Arabic Poetry." *Journal of the Royal Asiatic Society* (1925), 417–419. (b)

McDonald, D. B. "A Bibliographical and Literary Study of the First Appearance of the Arabian Nights in Europe." *The Library Quarterly,* **2** (1932), 387–420.

———. "Alf Laila wa-Laila." In *Enzyklopaedie des Islâm.* Ergänzungsband, 1938.

———. "From the Arabian Night to Spirit." *The Moslem World,* **9** (1919), 336–348.

———. "The Earlier History of the Arabian Nights." *Journal of the Royal Asiatic Society* (1924), 353–397.

———. "Thousand and One Nights." In *Encyclopaedia Britannica.* 14th ed., 1929.

Monroe, James. *Hispano-Arabic Poetry.* Berkeley: Univ. of California Press, 1975. (e)

———. "The historical *Arjūza* of Ibn ^{c}Abd Rabbihi, a Tenth Century Hispano-Arabic Epic Poem," *Journal of the American Oriental Society,* **91** (1971) 67ff. (a,b,f)

———. "The muwashshahāt." *Collected Studies in Honour of Americo Castro's Eightieth Year.* Oxford: Univ. Press, 1965, 335ff. (b)

———. "Oral Composition in Pre-Islamic Poetry." *Journal of Arabic Literature,* **3** (1972).

———. *Risalāt al-Tawābi^{c} wa al-Zawābi^{c}: The Treatise of Familiar Spirits and Demons by Abū ^{c}Āmir ibn Shuhaid al-Ashjā^{c}ī al-Andalusī.* Berkeley: Univ. of California Press, 1971. (b)

Moosa, Matti. "Naqqāsh and the Rise of the Native Theatre in Syria." *Journal of Arabic Literature,* **3** (1972), 106ff. (a)

———. "Ya^{c}qūb Ṣanū^{c} and the Rise of Arab Drama in Egypt." *International Journal of Middle East Studies,* **4** (1974), 401ff. (a)

Moreh, S. "Blank Verse in Modern Arabic Literature." *Bulletin of the School of Oriental and African Studies* **29**, (1966), 483ff. (a)

———. "Free Verse in Modern Arabic Literature: Abū Shādī and His School 1926–1945." *Bulletin of the School of Oriental and African Studies* **31** (1968), 28ff. (a,b)

———. "Poetry in Prose (Shi^{c}r Manthūr) in Modern Arabic Literature." *Middle East Studies*, **4**, (1967), 330ff. (a,b)

al-Mubârak, Muḥammad. *Fann al-Qiṣaṣ fî Kitâb al-Bukhalâ' lil-Jâḥiẓ*, 2nd ed. Damascus: Dâr al-Fikr, 1965. (b)

Mubârak, Zakî. *La Prose Arabe au IVme siècle de l'hégire*. Paris: Maisonneuve, 1931; Arabic version, Cairo: al-Maktaba al-Tijâriyya al-Kubrâ, 1957. (a)

al-Muwayliḥī, Muhammad. *A Study of Hadīth ^{c}Īsā ibn Hishām*. Introduction, study and translation by Roger Allen. Albany: State Univ. of New York, 1974. (a,b)

al-Nadîm, Muḥammad ibn Isḥâq. *al-Fihrist*. Gustav Fluegel, ed. Leipzig: Vogel, 1871–1872; and Beirut: Maktabat Khayyaṭ, 1966. English translation by Bayard Dodge. *The Fihrist of al-Nadim: A Tenth Century-Survey of Muslim Culture*, 2 vols. New York: Columbia Univ. Press, 1970. (g)

Najm, Muḥammad Yûsuf. *Fann al-Maqâla*, 3rd ed. Beirut: Dâr al-Thaqâfa, 1963. (b)

———. *Fann al-Qiṣṣa*. Beirut: Dâr Bayrût lil-Ṭibâ^{c}a wa-al Nashr, 1955. (b)

———. *al-Masraḥ al-^{c}Arabî*. 6 vols. Beirut: Dâr al-Thaqâfa, 1961. (e)

———. *al-Qiṣṣa fî al-Adab al-^{c}Arabî al-Ḥadîth* (1870–1914), 3rd ed. Beirut: Dâr al-Thaqâfa, 1966. (a,b)

Nallino, C. A. *La Littérature arabe*. C. Pellat, trans. Paris: 1950. (a)

Nasr, Syed Hussein. *Three Muslim Sages: Avicenna, Suhrawardi, Ibn ^{c}Arabi*. Cambridge: Harvard Univ. Press, 1964. (a)

al-Nassâj, Sayyid Ḥâmid. *Dalîl al-Qiṣṣa al-Miṣriyya al-Qaṣîra 1910–1961*. Cairo: al-Hay'a al-Miṣriyya al-^{c}Amma Lil-Kitâb, 1972. (g)

———. *Taṭawwur Fann al-Qiṣṣa al-Qaṣîra fî Miṣr min sana 1910 ilâ sana 1933*. Cairo: Dâr al-Kâtib al-^{c}Arabî, 1968. (a)

Nicholson, R. A. *A Literary History of the Arabs*. Cambridge: Univ. Press, 1930; several reprints, 1962. (a)

Nöldeke, Th. *Fünf Mo'allaqat übersetzt und erklärt*. Vienna: Akademie der Wissenschaften, Philosophisch-historische Klasse, Sitzungsberichte. Vol. 140, No. 7, 1899. (e)

Nu^{c}ayma, Mikhâ^{c}îl. *al-Ghurbâl*, 7th ed. Beirut: Dâr Ṣâdir, 1964. (b)

al-Nuwayhî, Muhammad. *Nafsiyyat Abî Nuwâs*. Cairo: Maktabat al-Nahḍa al-Miṣriyya, 1953. (b)

———. *Shakhṣiyyat Bashshâr*. Cairo: Maktabat al-Nahḍa al-Miṣriyya, 1951. (b)

———. *Qaḍiyyat al-Shi^{c}r al-Jadîd*. Cairo: Jâmi^{c}at al-Duwal al-^{c}Arabiyya: Ma^{c}had al-Dirâsât al-^{c}Arabiyya al-^{c}Âliya, 1964. (c)

———. *al-Shi^{c}r al-Jâhilî, Manhaj fî Dirâsatihi wa-Taqwîmihi*. Cairo: al-Dâr al-Qawmiyya lil-Ṭibâ^{c}a wa al-Nashr, 1966. (b)

———. *Thaqâfat al-Nâqid al-Adabî*. Cairo: Maṭba^{c}at Lajnat al-Ta'lîf waal-Tarjama waal-Nashr, 1949; 2nd ed. Beirut: Maktabat al-Khânjî, 1969. (b)

Nykl, A. R. *Hispano-Arabic Poetry*. Baltimore: J. H. Furst, Co., 1946. (a)

Ostle, Robin. "Khalil Mutran, the Precursor of Lyrical Poetry in Modern Arabic." *Journal of Arabic Literature*, **2** (1971), 116ff. (a,b)

———. "Three Egyptian Poets of 'Westernization,' Abd ar-Rahmān Shukrī, Ibrāhīm Abd al-Qādir al-Māzinī and Abbās Mahmūd al-Aqqād." *Comparative Literature Studies*, **7** (1970), 354ff. (a,b)

Paret, Rudi. *Sirat Saif ibn Dhi Jazan: ein arabischer Volksroman*. Hannover: Orient-Buchhandlung, H. Lafaire, 1924. (a)

Pearson, J. D., ed. *Index Islamicus* (original volume 1906–1955, with three supplements). Cambridge: Heffer, 1958– . (g)

Pellat, Charles. *The Life and Works of Jahiz.* D. M. Hawke, trans. Berkeley: Univ. of California Press, 1969. (a)

———. *Le Livre des avares de Ǧāḥiẓ.* Paris: Maisonneuve, 1951. (f)

———. *Le Milieu baṣrien et la formation de Ǧaḥiẓ.* Paris: Adrien-Maisonneuve, 1952. (a)

al-Qalamâwî, Suhayr. *Alf Laylâ wa Laylâ.* Cairo: Maṭbaᶜat al-Maᶜârif, 1943. (b)

Qudâma ibn Jaᶜfar. *Naqd al-Shiᶜr.* S. Bonebakker, ed. Leiden: Brill, 1956. (b)

al-Râᶜî, ᶜAlî. *Dirâsât fî al-Riwâya al-Miṣriyya.* Cairo: al-Mu'assasa al-Miṣriyya al-ᶜÂmma lil-Ta'lîf waal-Tarjama waal-Ṭibâᶜa waal-Nashr, 1964. (b)

Rosenthal, Franz. "Literature." In *The Legacy of Islam*, 2nd ed. Schacht and Bosworth, eds. Oxford: Univ. Press, 1974. (a)

Rückert, Friedrich. *Hamasa oder die ältesten arabischen Volkslieder übersetzt und erläutert*, 2 vols. Stuttgart: 1846. (e)

Saᶜdallah, Abû al-Qâsim. *Dirâsât fî al-Adab al-Jazâ'irî al-Ḥadîth.* Beirut: Dâr al-Âdâb, 1966. (a)

Sakkût, Hamdî. *The Egyptian Novel and Its Main Trends 1913–1952.* Cairo: American Univ. in Cairo Press, 1971. (a,b)

al-Samarrâ'î, Ibrâhîm. *Lughat al-Shiᶜr bayna Jîlayn.* Beirut: Dâr al-Thaqâfa, n.d. (b)

Sarrâj, Nâdira. *Shuᶜarâ' al-Râbiṭa al-Qalamiyya.* Cairo: Dâr al-Maᶜârif, 1964. (a,b)

Scheindlin, Raymond P. *Form and Structure in Arabic Poetry: The Poems of al-Muᶜtamid ibn ᶜAbbād.* Leiden: Brill, 1974. (b,c)

———. "Poetic Structure in Arabic: Three Poems by Al-Muᶜtamid ibn ᶜAbbâd." *Humaniora Islamica*, **1** (1973), 173ff. (a,b)

Schuman, L. O. *Een moderne arabische Vertelling.* Leiden: Brill, 1965. (b)

Semah, David. *Four Egyptian Literary Critics.* Leiden: Brill, 1974. (b)

———. "Muhammad Mandūr and the New Poetry." *Journal of Arabic Literature*, **2** (1971), 143ff. (b)

Sezgin, Fuat. *Geschichte des arabischen Schriftums.* Leiden: Brill, 1967, 1970, 1971, in progress. (a,g)

Shawkat, Maḥmûd. *al-Fann al-Qaṣaṣî fî al-Adab al-ᶜArabî al-Ḥadîth.* Cairo: Dâr al-Fikr, 1963. (a,b)

Shukrî, Ghâlî. *Shiᶜrunâ al-Muᶜaṣir: Ilâ Ayna?* Cairo: Dâr al-Maᶜârif, 1967. (c)

———. *al-Muntamî.* Cairo: Dâr al-Maᶜârif, 1969. (a,b)

Somekh, Sasson. *The Changing Rhythm.* Leiden: Brill, 1973.

Stern, Samuel. *Les chansons mozarabes.* Palermo: Universita di Palermo (Instituto di filologia), 1953. (e)

———. *Hispano-Arabic Strophic Poetry.* L. P. Harvey, ed. Oxford: Univ. Press, 1974. (a,c)

———. "Studies on Ibn Quzman." *Al-Andalus*, **16** (1951), 379ff. (a,b)

———. "Les Vers finaux in espagnol dans les muwaššahs hispano-hebraiques." *Al-Andalus*, **13** (1948), 299ff. (a,b)

Stetkevych, Jaroslav. *The Modern Arabic Literary Language.* Chicago: Univ. of Chicago Press. 1970. (b)

———. "Some Observations on Arabic Poetry." *Journal of Near East Studies*, **26** (1967), 1ff. (b) al-Ṭâhir, ᶜAlî Jawâd. *Fî al-Qaṣaṣ al-ᶜIraqî al-Muᶜâṣir.* Sidon: al-Maktaba al-ᶜAṣriyya, 1967. (a)

Taymûr, Maḥmûd. *Dirâsât fî al-Qiṣṣa waal-Masraḥ.* Cairo: al-Maṭbaᶜa al-Namûdhajiyya, n.d. (a,b)

al-Tanûkhî, al-Muḥassin ibn ᶜAlî. *Table-Talk of a Mesopotamian Judge.* D. S. Margoliouth, trans. London: Royal Asiatic Society, 1921–1922.

al-Thaᶜâlibî, Abû Manṣûr. *Laṭâ'if al-Maᶜârif* (The Book of Curious and Entertaining Information); trans. and with introduction and notes by C. E. Bosworth. Edinburgh: Univ. Press, 1968.

———. *Yatîmat al-Dahr.* Cairo: Maktabat al-Ḥusayniyya, 1934.

Tomiche, Nada, ed. *Le théatre arabe.* Paris: 1969. (a)

Trabulsi, Amjad. *La critique poétique des arabes.* Damascus: Institut Français de Damas, 1955. (b)

Ullah, Najib. *Islamic Literature.* New York: Washington Square Books, 1963. (e)

Vernet Gines, Juan. *Literatura arabe.* Barcelona: Editorial Labor, 1968. (a)

Wagner, Ewald. *Abu Nuwas: Eine Studie zur arabischen Literatur der frühen Abbasidenzeit.* Wiesbaden: Steiner, 1965. (a,b)

Weil, Gotthold. "Das metrische System des Al-Xalil und der Iktus in den Altarabischen Versus." *Oriens,* **7** (1954), 304ff. (c)

Zaydân, Jurjî. *Târîkh Âdâb al-Lugha al-ᶜArabiyya,* 4 vols. Cairo: Maṭbaᶜat al-Hilâl, 1912–1924, and 1957. (a)

——— *Tarâjim Mashâhîr al-Sharq.* Cairo: Maṭbaᶜat al-Hilâl, 1902; and Beirut: Dâr Maktabat al-Ḥayâ, 1969. (a)

al-Zayyât, Aḥmad Ḥasan. *Târîkh al-Adab al-ᶜArabî.* 5th ed. Cairo: Lajnat al-Ta'lîf waal-Tarjama, waal-Nashr, 1930. (a)

al-Ziriklî, Khayr al-Dîn. *al-Aᶜlâm.* Cairo: Maṭbaᶜat Kustâtsûmâs wa-Shurakâh, 1954–1959. (a)

Persian Literature

WILLIAM L. HANAWAY, JR.

The Persian literature to be considered in this chapter is that literature written in the Persian language within the Iranian cultural area, and thus includes literary works from such regions as Transoxiana, Afghanistan, and India, which today are outside of Iran proper. The literary studies to be discussed fall under the general rubrics of literary history, literary criticism, literary theory, and comparative literature. This section presents an overall picture of the state of the study of Persian literature. The history of that literature is not discussed, nor is the history of the study of it. As a survey of studies on Persian literature, it does not attempt to be comprehensive, but rather it aims to identify and characterize the most important examples within the above-mentioned categories. It also indicates where studies are inadequate or entirely lacking.

Thus two kinds of material are discussed in this paper: literary works and studies of literature. The criteria for inclusion are different for each of these categories. The reasons for mentioning any given work or body of literature are its value as literature, its importance in the history of Persian literature, and the existence of significant studies of it. Some important literary works are mentioned about which adequate studies do not exist, in an effort to identify gaps in the total panorama of literary study. Studies of literature are included on the basis of their critical perceptiveness, scholarly soundness, or value to the Western scholar of Persian literature, or because they are typical examples.

Islamic Persian literature covers a span of over 1000 years. Besides scattered fragments from earlier periods, major examples survive from the early tenth century. These are the earliest remains of a highly productive literary tradition which started long before the tenth century and still flourishes today. The literature of these 10 centuries, mainly poetry but including a cultivated prose tradition as well, is broad in its extent and rich in its variety. Works about this literature are correspondingly abundant. A paper such as this can convey no idea of this richness and abundance and must necessarily confine itself to the highest of the high points, leaving the remainder unmentioned but not unacknowledged.

BIBLIOGRAPHICAL SOURCES

The task of bringing this large body of literature and literary study under bibliographical control is formidable. The first major step in this direction has been taken by the recently published Russian edition of Storey's *Persian Literature*. Although it does not deal directly with literature in the restricted sense of this section, this edition of an earlier work in English provides a large amount of data on manuscripts and related printed works useful for literary study. Y. E. Bregel and Y. E. Borshchevsky, the editors of *Persian Literature*, have proposed a worldwide biobibliographical survey of Persian literature (in its broadest sense), which if carried to completion with the care and thoroughness of the reedition of Storey, would provide the most solid foundation possible for the future study of Persian literature.

The need for a catalog of Persian printed books has been largely met by the second edition of Khân Bâbâ Mushâr's *Fihrist-i Kitâbhâ-i Châpî-i Fârsî*. A current national bibliography was begun in 1954 by Īraj Afshâr as *Kitâbhâ-i Irân*, and has been continued since 1964 as the *Kitâbshinâsî-i Millî*, published by the National Library in Tehran. Afshâr's *Kitâbhâ-i Dah Sâla*, covering the decade 1954–1963, provides admirably thorough coverage for the period. The current publishing output is reported in the bimonthly journal *Râhnimâ-i Kitâb* and the newly founded *As͟hnâ'î bâ Kitâb*.

The challenge of organizing and recording studies of Persian literature published in journals has been better met. Pearson's general reference work *Index Islamicus* lists articles on the Persian language and Persian literature in all Western languages. Similar material published in Persian is recorded in Afshâr's *Index Iranicus*. In addition to the above, general bibliographical sources for books and articles published in Russian in the Soviet Union are Sverchevskaya's *Bibliografiya Irana*, and Kukhtina's *Bibliografiya Afganistana*, the first of which has over 1800 entries for literature alone. Both need to be updated. In general it can be said that the bibliographical coverage of Persian literature is uneven but improving. Some areas such as manuscript resources are not at all well covered, whereas other areas such as the current output of books and articles are much better under control. As is true with most other literatures, the indexes are considerably behind in recording the publishing output. There is also a dearth of subject bibliographies. There is an awareness of these problems, however, and efforts are being made to correct them.

STUDIES OF INDIVIDUAL AUTHORS AND WORKS

Within a literary tradition spanning as many centuries as does that of the Persians, there is bound to be a continuity which will remain unbroken despite changes in the political or religious situation. Although we know little about pre-Islamic Persian belles lettres, largely because so little of it has survived, some idea of this continuity may be gained from the two most extensive surviving examples, the *Kârnâmag î Ardas͟hîr* and the *Ayâdgâr î Zarêrân*. The former is a romance about the youth of Ardashir I and the founding of the Sasanian dynasty, and the latter is a fragment of an epic poem from the national legend. It has been pointed out by Mary Boyce in a survey article in the *Handbuch der Orientalistik* that the *Ayâdgâr î Zarêrân* contains a number of characteristics of oral epic poetry such as fixed epithets, repetitions, and hyperbole, and that it represents an old epic tradition which continued well into the Islamic era; but there is not yet a detailed analytical study on these pieces that attempts to specify their place in the larger literary continuity. Excellent background work along these lines has been done by Boyce in her article on the Parthian minstrels and the tradition in which they worked. This research will be one of the foundations of any future study of the literary continuity from Middle Iranian to Islamic Persian.

After the Arabic conquest of Persia in the mid-seventh century, there followed a period of some 300 years from which only the barest fragments of writing in the New Persian language have survived. Lazard has assembled, edited, and translated the surviving works of poets through 980 AD, with the exception of Rûdakî of Samarkand (d. 940), and portions of the works of Daqîqî and Maysarî.

Rûdakî is the earliest major poet whose works have come down to us in any quantity. Qasidas, generic ghazals or taghazzuls, and extended narrative poems flowed from his pen, and judging from the indirect evidence, much more of his poetry has been lost than has survived. The sources for Rûdakî's poetry and for information about his life are widely scattered, and the first systematic attempt to bring together this material and sort out the poetry of Rûdakî from that of Qatrân of Tabriz, with which it had been thoroughly mixed by inept editors, was made by Sa^cîd Nafîsî in his three-volume work *Aḥvâl va Ash^câr-i Rûdakî-i Samarqandî* which appeared over the decade 1931–1941. The work contains a vast amount of information, a great part of it having only the most tenuous connection, if any at all, with Rûdakî and his poetry. This work may be taken as an exemplar of the traditional mode of literary study in Persia, being a mammoth collection of antiquarian facts, source and parallel hunting, opinions of others, geographical data, etc., all presented systematically but not synthetically. Nafîsî's critical judgment is exercised in identifying the poetry of Rûdakî, but not in elucidating or evaluating it, nor in the judicious selection of biographical or historical information pertaining to Rûdakî. A second, one-volume edition of this work was completed in 1958, and although it corrects errors of the first edition and eliminates much of the nonessential or totally irrelevant historical information, it still shows no critical development. Three quarters of the book is devoted to a history of Samarkand and Bukhara, and the remaining quarter is about evenly divided between a description of the poetry and the poetry itself. In spite of these shortcomings, Nafîsî did bring together a great deal of material about Rûdakî, and the book is important from this point of view.

A more tightly knit and closely focused work is Mirzoyev's *Abû ^cAbd Allâh Rûdakî*, also published in 1958. Mirzoyev, a Tajik scholar, surveys the age of Rûdakî, his literary heritage, the poet's thought, and his place in the literary tradition. Furthermore, the author provides a detailed historical and critical survey of the study of Rûdakî's poetry by both Iranian and Western scholars. This is one of the very few critical surveys of the scholarly work done on any Persian poet. Mirzoyev stays closer to his subject than does Nafîsî, and he provides us with a great deal of literary history but he also gives an analysis of Rûdakî's thought from a Marxist point of view, thus giving an evaluation of the poetry itself as well.

These two works have been discussed at somewhat greater length than are other works because they represent quite well the traditional approach to literary study within the Persian tradition. In this context the ideology of the writer is not important. Nafîsî's work is a good product of the older school of literary study, and Mirzoyev's is a good example of the same tradition modernized, but not essentially redirected.

Abû al-Qâsim Firdawsî (d. ca. 1025) is considered by many to be Persia's greatest poet by virtue of his *Shâhnâma*, a part of the Persian national legend cast into epic poetry. Because of its literary quality and national appeal, the *Shâhnâma* has inspired more scholarship, good and bad, than has any other single Persian work. A useful guide to this body of material, both Persian and foreign, is Iraj Afshâr's *Kitâbshinâsî-i Firdawsî*, which lists editions, translations, and studies of the *Shâhnâma*, and works about Firdawsî. The scholarship on the *Shâhnâma* is of such a varied nature that only examples representing specific types can be mentioned here.

The main problem facing modern scholars of the *Shâhnâma* is the lack of a reliable edition of the text. The closest to a reliable text so far produced is the nine-volume Moscow edition completed in 1971. An entirely new edition of *Shâhnâma* to be edited by Mujtabâ Mînuvî has been announced, and the first portion of this, the story of Rustam and Suhrâb, has recently appeared in print. In addition, the first issue of *Sîmurgh*, a journal devoted to studies of *Shâhnâma* and related subjects, has been published by the Foundation for Firdawsî's *Shâhnâma* of the Ministry of Culture and Arts.

The basis for the modern study of the *Shâhnâma* and the Persian national legend was laid by Nöldeke with his *Das iranische Nationalepos*. This landmark of scholarship discusses the origins and development of the Iranian national epic, various manifestations of it, and finally, the *Shâhnâma* itself, in a learned and dispassionate manner. Although some of Nöldeke's conclusions are no longer valid in the light of more recent scholarship, the work is still basically sound and cannot be ignored. Other historical studies of great importance are those on Firdawsî and the *Shâhnâma* by Taqîzâda, collected in the *Hazâra-i Firdawsî*.

The language of the *Shâhnâma* has received much attention, from the standpoint of both lexicon and grammar. Wolff's *Glossar zur Firdosis Schahname* is a highly accurate concordance with brief indications of meanings. Although it was based on older editions of the epic, it is still extremely useful. To complement, partially at least, Wolff's concordance, are the dictionaries of the *Shâhnâma* by Shafaq and Nûshîn. Shafaq's dictionary has recently appeared in a second, expanded edition that must be used together with the first edition, however, because it is not basically improved, merely changed. More scholarly is Nûshîn's work, but this too is not comprehensive and should be used together with Shafaq. One advantage of Nûshîn's dictionary over those of Shafaq is that Nûshîn's is based on the Moscow edition of the *Shâhnâma*, whereas Shafaq's are based on older editions. The Arabic vocabulary of the epic has been repeatedly studied, but there too the final conclusion must await a completely reliable edition of the text.

The grammar and syntax of *Shâhnâma* have been examined very thoroughly but in a traditional manner by Shafî^cî in his *Shâhnâma va Dastûr*. In order to use this book efficiently, a familiarity with traditional Persian grammatical categories and approaches is necessary. This study is based mainly on older editions, and Volumes 1 and 2 of the Moscow edition.

There are many studies of *Shâhnâma* which attempt to set it in a larger context. Recently psychological and comparative studies have begun to appear. In this respect, two books of Miskûb must be mentioned for their excellence. In these essays, Miskûb discusses the personalities of Rustam, Isfandiyâr, and Siyâvush in an extremely sensitive fashion from the psychological and comparative point of view. The author is widely read in Western literature, and these works represent one of the forefronts of literary study today in Iran. Along with a small number of others to be mentioned later, these studies indicate that the long needed change of direction away from historicism and antiquarianism toward broader and deeper literary study is starting to take place.

From before the time of Firdawsî until the end of the thirteenth century AD the qasida was the dominant poetic form, and during this period it reached its highest peak of development. Of all the poets of the Turkistânî or Khurâsânî style, which prevailed until the decline of the qasida in the thirteenth century, only three have been accorded full-length studies deserving of mention. The most traditional is Yûsufî's study of Farrukhî of Sîstân (d. 1047). Farrukhî was a poet in the court of Mahmûd of Ghazna, and Yûsufî's book is a study of the life, times, and poetry of Farrukhî, with a good deal of attention focused on Sultan Mahmûd, his court, and the life and role of a poet in those surroundings. The information which the author provides on these subjects is well selected, and can be of use in studying the situation of other poets of the time. Yûsufî presents Farrukhî's poetry descriptively and analytically, and demonstrates a clear awareness of the critical problems and pitfalls which have beset some of his colleagues, such as ethical criticism and the Intentional Fallacy.

Manûchihrî (d. 1040), another Ghaznavid court poet, was first examined comprehensively by Kazimirsky, and has been treated in an up-to-date manner by Clinton. Using modern critical concepts, Clinton has analyzed Manûchihrî's poetry and discussed its formal and thematic integrity, the patterning of its images, and the poet's metaphors. He emphasizes Manûchihrî's creative originality and vigor.

The third poet so treated is Khâqânî (d. 1199). The German scholar Reinert, in his monograph *Ḥâqânî als Dichter*, has analyzed the poet's figurative language using a methodology based on predicative logic. Further study is needed to determine whether this approach will be truly productive for future literary study.

Court poets were expected to be well-versed in the entire range of knowledge of their time, and the wider the range of learning they could display in their poetry, the more they were admired. This display of learning must have strained the understanding of readers in the past just as it strains ours today. Because of this, annotating, explaining, and explicating difficult poetry have been respectable literary activities in Iran for centuries. Three commentaries are mentioned here as examples of this activity, and others will be cited later.

One of the traditional commentaries, the *Sharḥ-i Mushkilât-i Dîvân-i Anvarî* of Abû al-Ḥasan Farâhânî (d. 1630) has been published in Tehran. This is a rather unsystematic commentary, explaining some whole qasidas, individual lines of others, and single words of still others. It is useful as far as it goes, but there are many difficulties in Anvārī's poetry that it does not touch upon, and one of the fuller but still unpublished commentaries would be of more practical use. Two excellent modern works are Mudarris Rizavî's commentary on Sanâ'î's (d. 1130) *Ḥadîqat al-Ḥaqîqat*, and Humâ'î's edition of and commentary on the divan of ᶜUthmân Mukhtârî (d. before 1153). Both these commentaries provide a wealth of information for the reader, and their usefulness extends well beyond the individual texts to which they are devoted.

Corresponding approximately to the heyday of the qasida is the great period of extended narrative poetry, epic, romantic, didactic, and mystical. The first and most important epic poem, *Shâhnâma*, has been discussed. Though not the earliest surviving romantic narrative, Fakhr al-Dîn Gurgânî's (d. after 1074) *Vîs u Râmîn* is an old Iranian romance. Minorsky's lengthy and detailed study of it seeks to demonstrate the Parthian background of the poem with a careful and convincing argument, but other scholars such as Molé and Zarrînkûb have interpreted the evidence in an entirely different manner.

The romantic epic reached its apex of refinement in the *Khamsa* or Five Poems of Niẓâmî (d. 1209). Only four of the five, *Khusraw va Shîrîn*, *Laylî va Majnûn*, *Haft Paykar*, and *Sharaf Nâma/Iqbâl Nâma*, are actually romances, while the fifth, *Makhzan al-Asrâr* is an ethical philosophical narrative. Many studies of these poems, individually and as a unit, have been made, and again only selected examples can be mentioned here. From among the various editions of the *Khamsa*, Vaḥîd Dastgirdî's, though not as reliable textually as later editions by Russian scholars, is useful because of its annotations. H. Duda's *Ferhâd und Shîrîn* is a valuable work of *Stoffgeschichte* on the theme of these two lovers. Muᶜîn's *Taḥlîl-i Haft Paykar-i Niẓâmî*, apparently unfinished, discusses at length the symbolism of the number seven in this romance. Nafîsî has written a biography of the poet to accompany an edition of his nonnarrative poetry. Finally, Ritter's *Über die Bildersprache Niẓâmîs* must be mentioned as a useful study of Niẓâmî's figurative language.

With regard to didactic and mystical narratives, Sanâ'î has already been mentioned. In this connection, Bo Utas' *Tarîq al-taḥqîq* is a carefully executed critical edition, commentary, and textual history of a Sufi *mas̱navî* traditionally ascribed to Sanâ'î, but as Utas demonstrates, probably written by another author. We must be extremely grateful for critical editions of even minor works such as this.

Another narrative poet is ^{c}Aṭṭâr (d. ca. 1230) who wrote a number of allegorical and mystical *mas̱navîs*, the best known of which are *Manṭiq al-Ṭayr* and *Ilâhî Nâma.* Furûzânfar's *S̲h̲arḥ-i Aḥvâl-i . . . ^{c}Aṭṭâr* gives a biographical sketch of the poet, and an analysis and commentary on the above poems plus *Musîbat Nâma* and a famous section of the *Manṭiq al-Ṭayr* entitled "Shaykh Ṣan^{c}ân." For all of these, Furûzânfar discusses the structure of the entire work, analyzes the various sections and divisions of each, and identifies the sources of anecdotes and individual lines. This is traditional Persian literary work at its best, done by a scholar of great learning and devotion to his material. In a different vein is Ritter's *Das Meer der Seele.* This large work is a comprehensive study of ^{c}Aṭṭâr's mystical vision, and goes a long way toward explaining much of ^{c}Aṭṭâr's symbolism. It is valuable for the study of the poet's literary technique as well as his mystical thought.

Jalâl al-Dîn Muhammad Rûmî (d. 1273) is considered by most critics to be Persia's greatest mystical poet. In addition to his enormous *Mas̱navî-i Ma^{c}navî,* he left a voluminous collection of g̲h̲azals, and both have inspired large quantities of study and commentary. As in the case of Firdawsî, ^{c}Aṭṭâr, Sa^{c}dî, and Ḥâfiẓ, the works on Rûmî to be mentioned here do not reflect a proportionate selection of the total number of studies which have been produced. Scores of articles, monographs, and full-length books have been written about all these poets and their works, but limitations of scope require that only a highly selected sample be presented here. It must be added that of these numerous studies, few are the result of disciplined literary scholarship.

The major work on Rûmî to date is Nicholson's edition, translation, and commentary on the *Mas̱navî.* This eight-volume work is the fundamental source to which students of the *Mas̱navî* must turn, both because of Nicholson's care and accuracy, and because of the richness of his commentary owing to his wide knowledge of Persian and Arabic mystical writings. Since this edition was published new manuscripts have come to light and have provided Furûzânfar with the material for an entirely new commentary on the *Mas̱navî.* When this scholar died in 1970 he had published only two or three sections of his projected multivolume commentary, but his work is being carried on by his collaborators in Tehran.

During his long career, which was devoted largely to the study of Rûmî, Furûzânfar produced a biography of the great mystic, a work on the sources of the anecdotes in the *Mas̱navî*, and another book on references to the Qur'an and Hadith in the same work. In addition to these, he edited Rûmî's ghazals in eight volumes. In a similar vein. Gawharîn has compiled a dictionary of words and expressions in the *Mas̱navî*. Schimmel's *Die Bildersprache Dschelāladdīn Rūmīs* is an exception to the normal course of historical, lexical, and exegetic studies of Rûmî, being an examination of the poet's figurative language and its relation to his mystical beliefs.

The only other poet to receive considerable attention, scholarly and otherwise, before the period of the dominance of the ghazal, was ^{c}Umar Khayyâm (d. 1122). The amount of precise information available on the life and works of Khayyâm is amazingly scant in spite of the number of works written about him. The main problems concerning Khayyâm's nonscientific writings are (1) did he actually write any quatrains, and (2) if so, have any survived? From the early fourteenth century on, more and more quatrains were ascribed to him, some collections containing over 1000 of these poems. No scholarly attention was paid to Khayyâm the poet before FitzGerald published his *Rubáiyát of Omar Khayyám* in 1859. Since that time the situation has become both better and worse. It has improved owing to the studies of Christensen, S. Hidâyat, and Furûghî, because these scholars painstakingly attempted to separate the oldest quatrains appearing in the most reliable texts from the numerous later accretions. Something over 50 quatrains are common to these three selections, and have been accepted as probably authentic. Approximately 150 others are considered as probable or likely, although these three scholars (and others as well) do not agree in all cases.

Because of the uncertainty about the authenticity of the quatrains ascribed to Khayyâm, and for other reasons, forgers and charlatans have entered the field and have achieved more than modest success, thus worsening the whole situation of scholarship on Khayyâm. In recent years manuscripts of Khayyâm's quatrains have been published in London and Moscow, which later research by Mînuvî and Minorsky has shown to be forgeries. A similar fiasco occurred with the publication by Robert Graves of a "translation" of an apparently nonexistent Khayyâm manuscript. A brief account of research on Khayyâm may be found in Elwell-Sutton's translation of Dashtî's *Damî bâ Khayyâm*, which is a discussion and appreciation of Khayyâm's quatrains by a sensitive and cultivated Persian, and represents the culmination of earlier efforts of Furûghî, Hidâyat, Christensen, and others.

Prose, not only during this period but indeed until the end of World War I, was considered a distant second to poetry as an artistic medium, and consequently prose works of belles lettres were very few. Consistent with our definition of literature, some famous prose works of this era such as *Târîkh-i*

Bayhaqî, *Qâbûs Nâma*, and *Siyâr al-Mulûk* are not discussed here. This is no reflection on their quality as works of prose, but merely an effort to separate the literary from the nonliterary within our frame of reference. Belletristic prose tends to fall into four general categories: the didactic tale, often in the form of a framed story; the collection of anecdotes; the *maqâma*; and the traditional romance.

The earliest major example of belletristic prose surviving in Persian is Naṣr Allâh's *Kalîla va Dimna*, his version of the old Indian collection known generally as the *Fables of Bidpay*. This didactic collection of animal fables had appeared in a number of Persian versions, now all lost, before Naṣr Allâh rewrote it in 1143–1145. It has been excellently edited by Mînuvî, and an extensive history and analysis of it has been published by Maḥjûb.

Of the same type is the *Sindbâd Nâma* in the version of Muḥammad ibn ᶜAlî al-Ẓahîrî al-Samarqandî, of 1161. Like *Kalîla va Dimna*, *Sindbâd Nâma* is known to have existed in several Persian versions, all of which have disappeared. There is a scholarly edition of the text by Ateş, and a major study of its history and the relationship of its various versions and redactions by Perry, a scholar of folklore and comparative literature. The other major work of this genre, the *Marzbân Nâma* of Saᶜd al-Dîn Varâvînî (fl. 1210–1225), has been the subject of no significant scholarship other than a critical edition made in 1909 by Qazvînî.

Of three important early collections of anecdotes, only the *C͟hahâr Maqâla* of Niẓâmî ᶜArûẓî (written 1155–1156) is available in a reliable text. Edited first by Qazvînî and later reedited with an extensive commentary by Muᶜîn, it has been translated into English by Browne in 1921, and into French by de Gastines in 1968. The Persian adaptation by ᶜAwfî (d. 1232) of al-Tanûk͟hî's *al-Faraj baᶜd al-S͟hidda* has been published but not critically edited, and ᶜAwfî's *Javâm*ᶜ *al-Ḥikâyât* has never been published in its entirety.

The *maqâmât* are elegant, highly rhetorical collections of stories, verses, aphorisms, and the like, created to display a writer's verbal dexterity. The principal Persian writer of *maqâmât* in this period was Ḥamîd al-Dîn Abû Bakr of Balkh (d. 1164), who modeled his essays on those of his more famous Arabic predecessor al-Ḥarîrî (d. 1122). Other writers tried their hand at writing *maqâmât*, but the genre reached its culmination in the *Gulistân* of Saᶜdî. Fâris Ibrâhîmî Ḥarîrî has published a thorough historical and descriptive study of this genre in Persian and its Arabic background.

The traditional romances form the last of the prose genres during this period. *Samak-i ᶜAyyâr*, *Fîrûz S͟hâh Nâma*, *Ḍârâb Nâma*, *Iskandar Nâma*, *Abû Muslim Nâma*, and others all originated before the sixteenth century, although their oldest surviving manuscripts are generally from a later date. Long oral tales written down for, or by, storytellers, these romances are just now beginning to receive scholarly attention. Episodes from the *Fîrûz S͟hâh Nâma* of Bîghamî have been translated into English as *Love and War* by Hanaway. Maḥjûb and Khānlarī have dealt with certain aspects of the romances in two series of articles in the journal *Sukhan*. Hanaway's forthcoming study will treat these romances in a more comprehensive manner.

During the period from the end of the twelfth to the end of the fourteenth century the ghazal reached its peak of development with Ṣaᶜdî (d. 1292) and Ḥafiẓ (d. 1390). Given the fact that these two poets are and have been universally known and admired in Persia, and are known in the West through translations of their works, it is astonishing that they have been served so inadequately by both Persian and Western literary scholars.

The greatest service to students of Saᶜdî has been rendered by Aliyev, who has published reliable critical texts of the *Gulistân* and the *Saᶜdî Nâma*, or *Bûstân*. Earlier editors such as Garakânî and Furûghî have laid the basis for a critical edition of his divan, although until now no such edition has been undertaken. These editors, and others such as Qazvînî and Iqbāl, have also contributed much to our understanding of Saᶜdî's literary and social milieu. Other than this, the majority of the work on Saᶜdî has been confined to commentaries on *Gulistân* and *Bûstân*. With Aliyev's editions, the ground has been prepared for serious study of the *Gulistân* and *Bûstân*. There is a great need for a critical edition of the divan.

Ḥâfiẓ has fared scarcely better than Ṣaᶜdî, the more surprising because Ḥâfiẓ is considered by many as the greatest of the medieval lyric poets. With regard to a critical edition of his divan, however, the problems seem quite intractable. A series of editions by Khalkhâlî, Qazvînî and Ghanî, Khânlarî, Afshâr, and Farzâd, and basic research by Rehder and Hillmann have brought us inch by inch closer to a reliable text, but the situation is still far from satisfactory. In fact, the question of editing Ḥâfiẓ's divan raises a host of fundamental theoretical problems which face the modern scholar of Persian literature. For example, how does one edit the divan of Ḥâfiẓ, or of any other poet, when there are so few competent critical studies available of Ḥâfiẓ, of other poets, and of Persian poetic language and structure? On the other hand, how can one make critical studies without reliably edited texts on which to base them? Furthermore, how can one either write critical studies or edit divans without a coherent theory of Persian literature?

Background information for the study of the history, politics, and religious thought of Ḥâfiẓ's era is supplied in Ghanî's two-volume *Baḥs dar Âsâr va Afkâr va Aḥvâl-i Ḥâfiẓ*. Here Ghanî supplies a mass of external detail and helps us to identify contemporary references in Ḥâfiẓ's ghazals, but he contributes little to a literary understanding of the poet. A discussion of Ḥâfiẓ's language, thought, and art may be found in Dashtî's *Naqshî az Ḥâfiẓ*. Dashtî has set down his thoughts and feelings about Ḥâfiẓ and other medieval poets in a series of books that reflect the kind of study and appreciation of literature characteristic of the older generation of educated and cultured Persians.

Arberry made a new start with his article "Orient Pearls at Random Strung," in which he argues for the artistic unity of the individual ghazal of Ḥâfiẓ despite its thematic diversity. Rehder has replied at length to these arguments. Lescot attempted a chronological ordering of the ghazals on the basis of their subject matter. Islâmî investigated closely the structure of a ghazal in an article reprinted in his *Jâm-i Jahân-Bîn* and translated in Hillmann's "Sound and Sense in a *Ghazal* of Ḥâfiẓ," and Hillmann investigated the metrical and rhythmical structure of the same ghazal and its relation to overall structure and meaning in his "Hâfez and Poetic Unity through Verse Rhythms." Each of these articles takes a different path, but all are going in substantially the same direction. A general awareness of the nature and magnitude of these theoretical problems should help clear the air, still badly smogged by the often well-meant but irrelevant vaporings of scholars and amateurs of both the East and the West.

Jâmî (d. 1492), the last of the great pre-Safavid poets, has been largely ignored outside the Soviet Union as a subject of extensive study. The only poet between Jâmî and the nineteenth century to be treated at length in a modern manner is Bedil (d. 1720), a leading representative of the so-called Indian style. Bedil's poetry, though not popular in Iran, was widely admired, studied, and imitated in both India and Transoxiana, and indeed he is still studied today in Tajikistan and in the West. The Tajik critic Sadriddin Ayni's *Mirzo Abdulqodir Bedil* is a major study of this poet's works, and Bausani's articles discuss the problems of Bedil's complicated style and his conception of nature.

The last poet before the Persian Revolution of 1906 to receive the attention of a Western critic is Qâ'ânî (d. 1854). On the centenary of his death, Kubíčkova published a monograph on Qâ'ânî which deals with his life and times, largely ignores his divan, and concentrates on his *Kitâb-i Parîshân*, an imitation of Sa^cdî's *Gulistân*. Kubíčková examines Qa^cânî's presentation of reality and its artistic value.

Finally, three studies of twentieth century authors are cited. Nîmâ Yûshîj (d. 1960) is considered to be the "father" of modern Persian poetry in that it was he who first broke with the forms and subjects of the classical tradition. His followers and imitators are many, and there is a growing body of studies on him, mostly in Persian. ^cAbd al-^cAlî Dast Ghayb has written a wide-ranging discussion of his poetry in the light of contemporary intellectual currents, European and Persian. As in his other works, the critic's emphasis here is on the social content of literature. Bahman Shâriq's *Nîmâ va Sh^cir-i Pârsî* examines Nîmâ's poetic techniques, and the poet's success in terms of his literary aims.

Another study of Dast Ghayb's is that on the prominent dramatist and writer Ghûlâm Ḥusayn Sâᶜidî, pseudonymously Gawhar-i Murâd. This book is an analysis of Sâᶜidî's stories and plays, defining their current and historical context within Persian literature. Dast Ghayb's emphasis is on the social and psychological aspects of Sâᶜidî's works, and in the case of the plays, this aspect is stressed over criticism of them as dramas.

In sum, this review of studies on individual authors and works reveals three significant facts. First, the major studies of both Western and Persian scholars cluster around only a few individual poets and their works, leaving many other poets and prose writers to be studied. Broadening the field of study would surely result in the revision, possibly in a major way, of the history of Persian literature. Second, the majority of works produced, including most of those not mentioned, are literary-historical and antiquarian in approach. This means that almost the entire body of Persian literature, including the major writers already widely written about, is virgin territory for critical study. Third, it is apparent that reliable editions of texts, both prose and poetry, are essential for future study.

GENERAL HISTORIES OF LITERATURE, THEORY AND CRITICISM, GENRE STUDIES, *STOFFGESCHICHTE*

General histories of Persian literature are numerous, in Persian as well as in Western languages. In format and approach they have their roots in the long *tazkira*, or critical anthology, tradition in Persia, a tradition which goes back at least to the early thirteenth century.

A convenient starting point for the development of historical studies of Persian literature is the year 1878 when Hidâyat published his *Majmaᶜ al-Fuṣaḥâ*, a *tazkira* which summarized many earlier *tazkiras*. In the West, the *tazkira* tradition is best represented by Browne's *A Literary History of Persia*. This is a straight chronological history of poetry and prose (with no restriction to belles lettres), organized and closely tied to dynastic history. Browne expands on earlier *tazkiras* by adding a great deal of political history, but follows the lead of Persian scholars in his choice of poets and how he presents their work. Though now superseded in some respects, Browne's classic still remains a reference work of major importance. Ṣafâ's *Tarîkh-i Adabiyyāt dar Irân* resembles Browne's *Literary History* in organization, in scope, and approach, but is much broader and contains a wealth of new material.

The *tazkira* tradition is still thriving in Persia, and a modern example which deserves mention is Furûzânfar's *Sukhan va Sukhanvarân*. In its second, largely revised edition it covers poets only through Khâqânî. Though the work must be used with some caution with regard to its factual material, the author's judgments of the poets included are intelligent and independent, and make the book worthwhile.

There are also histories of literature organized not by ruling dynasty but by literary genre. These tend to remain closer to the Western concept of belles lettres and do not include such a wide range of non-belletristic prose, while still depending on Persian tradition for the selection of writers to include. Pizzi's *Storia,* dealing strictly with poetry, is an early example of this type. Ethé's "Neupersische Literatur" includes prose and thus covers a wider scope than Pizzi. In the same category is Pagliaro and Bausani's excellent *Storia della letteratura persiana,* which is the first history of Persian literature attempting to be analytical and critical rather than merely descriptive. The latest of this type is Rypka's *History of Iranian Literature.* The title is misleading because the book does not deal with literature in Iranian languages other than Persian and Tajik, but this is somewhat compensated for by the breadth of its scope within these languages and its excellent bibliographical coverage. It is a composite work, and contains, for example, chapters on Persian literature in India and Tajikistan. In approach it combines traditional literary history with a certain amount of analysis and criticism, but in the uneven fashion which is often characteristic of composite works.

Finally, mention must be made of de Bruijn's contribution entitled Literature in the article, "Iran," in the new edition of the *Encyclopaedia of Islam.* In this lengthy review the author discusses the origin, general nature, and forms of Persian literature understood in its broadest sense, and then gives a historical survey of it from the tenth century until today. His treatment of literature through the nineteenth century is a useful summary, but his section on twentieth-century literature is weak and incomplete.

Regional histories of Persian literature exist but are generally of low quality. Muḥammad ^{c}Abd al-Ghanî's *A History of Persian . . . Literature at the Mughal Court* is very uncritical and impressionistic, and is of little use. Khusrawshâhî's *Sh^{c}ir va Adab-i Fârsî dar Âsyâ-i Ṣaghîr* brings together useful information about Persian literature in Asia Minor but devotes too much space to diplomatic correspondence, and displays a strong national bias. Neither of these regional histories makes any effort to define the differences between the literature of their region and that of Persia proper, and neither displays a critical spirit. Tikku's *Persian Poetry in Kashmir* is a decided improvement in regional histories. It is a literary history in the traditional style, organized dynastically, and filled with interesting information. Unfortunately the book is marred by a seemingly total lack of editorial attention. Of a different sort is Schimmel's *Islamic Literatures of India,* in which she discusses the major works in Arabic, Persian, and Turkish written on the subcontinent. The author defines literature in its widest sense, and because of the relatively small space allotted to her, has produced what is in effect a useful bibliographical essay.

Period histories are in general better than the regional histories. One of the first to deal with the literature of a period in a critical manner was Yar Shater in his *Sh^cir-i Fârsî dar ^cAhd-i Shâhrukh*. For the literature of the late eighteenth to the early twentieth centuries, Âryanpûr's *Az Ṣabâ tâ Nîmâ* is a detailed and copiously documented study. Political history is kept to a bare minimum and the focus remains clearly on the literature, understood in the traditional sense of belles lettres and all serious prose writing. The author avoids many of the defects of earlier histories of literature such as excessively broad and superficial coverage, tedious and conventional expressions of praise and respect, and a dependence upon political history to explain literary history. His discussions of the development of journalism are especially useful as they show the rapid spread and influence of newspapers and journals, and the effect that these had on literature, its language, and its relation to society. A lengthy essay on this book was published by Zarrînkûb, who discusses Âryanpûr's critical stand and historical perspective.

A work dealing with literature in the second half of the nineteenth and the early twentieth centuries in what is now Tajikistan is Hodizoda's *Adabiyoti Tojik dar Nimai Duvvûmi Asri XIX*. Though it covers some of the same time span as Âryanpûr's *Az Ṣabâ tâ Nîmâ*, it does so in a much different fashion. The book begins with a detailed discussion of the manuscript and printed sources for the period, and an account of how the study of this period has developed, especially since World War II. Then follows a discussion of changing intellectual currents in Central Asia after the middle of the nineteenth century, as they affected and were reflected in the literature. Finally the author examines thoroughly the works of two leading poets of the era. Hodizoda tries to strike a balance between literary history and criticism, and although the weight falls on the side of history, he does examine the poetry in detail and with a critical eye. In his discussion of poetry he does not link it directly to political history but more often adopts the approach of a biographical critic. He also discusses the individual qualities of each poet's style in a sensitive manner. This is a well documented book by a scholar thoroughly steeped in the period about which he is writing.

Machalski's *La Littérature de l'Iran contemporain* covers only poetry during the period 1880–1941, although a section on prose has been announced. Though largely historical and descriptive in his approach, Machalski does give some analysis and criticism of the poetry. He is less critical than Âryanpûr, but like him gives generous selections from the poets whom he discusses.

The prose of approximately the same period has been discussed by Kamshad in his *Modern Persian Prose Literature*, in which he describes its background and development. In surveying the scene for the past 100 years, he concentrates the greater weight of his attention on Ṣâdiq Hidāyat; while according to Hidâyat his proper place in the evolution of modern prose fiction, this serves to unbalance the book. Kamshad's approach to most of the novelists is descriptive, but in his treatment of Hidâyat he becomes more analytical and discusses Hidâyat's works from a social and psychological point of view. Like Âryanpûr and Machalski, Kamshad provides useful biographical information about modern writers. Kamshad has departed from the usual practice of giving selections from various writers in his text, and has published a *Reader* as a companion volume to his *History*. The *Reader* contains substantial selections from the prose of major writers, plus a Persian–English vocabulary, thus making it useful to students as well as to those seeking an overview of the prose writing of this period.

The last of the period histories to be mentioned is ᶜAlavî's history of modern Persian literature. The author, a Marxist critic, adheres to the conventional periodization of twentieth-century literature in terms of political events, and discusses both poetry and prose. ᶜAlavî is a novelist and short-story writer of acknowledged stature, and has been involved in the Persian literary scene for many years. He thus brings to bear insights into the literature and politics of the period which give his work an authority that must be respected.

More period studies are badly needed, but their development is hampered by the problems of periodization. Braginsky's suggested scheme for periodizing Persian literature, though not ideal, is the best produced so far because it is not tied directly to political, economic, or dynastic changes. Nineteenth- and twentieth-century literature is easier to periodize because its intrinsic nature as well as its relation to the social and intellectual currents of the time cause it to fall into almost natural divisions. Medieval literature presents more problems, and until they are solved it will be difficult to write good period histories. This is an obvious theoretical gap that needs to be filled.

A number of genre studies have been written, but the theoretical problem of genre definition in Persian literature has scarcely been touched on except by Scott for the peripheral genre of riddles. The two main areas of genre study have been epic poetry and the *taᶜziya*. Persian epic poetry has received a good deal of attention in both Iran and the West. Following Nöldeke's lead is Ṣafâ, with his *Ḥamâsa Sarâ'î dar Îrân*. Unlike most other genre studies in Persian, *Ḥamâsa Sarâ'î* has a theoretical basis for its descriptive studies of Persian epic poems. Though Ṣafâ depends heavily on European scholarship for his theoretical and historical material, he himself has read widely and critically in Persian epic literature, and has managed to integrate a large amount of information into a unified whole.

Although lyric poetry has received considerable attention, few studies of it as a genre exist. Heinz's *Der indische Stil in der persischen Literatur* is an important work which, in spite of its title, deals exclusively with poetry. In it the author examines the vocabulary and rhetorical structure of Indian style poetry, largely the ghazal, and lays the groundwork for future research in this area.

The other major group of genre studies concentrates on the *ta^{c}ziya*, an indigenous Persian dramatic form. The *ta^{c}ziya*, a Shî^{c}î passion play performed in all seasons but mainly during the month of *Muḥarram*, has received considerable scholarly attention in recent years. Interest in these plays has gone hand in hand with the interest in Western style drama which has grown at a very rapid rate in Persia since World War II. The interest of Persian literary scholars in the drama has produced a number of works on the theater in Iran, all of which include a section on the *ta^{c}ziya*.

Fundamental to any study of the *ta^{c}ziya* is Rossi and Bombaci's *Elenco di drammi religiosi persiani*, which includes an informative introduction and a description of over 1000 *ta^{c}ziya* manuscripts in the Cerulli collection in the Vatican library. One of the first to study, rather than merely describe, the *ta^{c}ziya* is Virolleaud, who discusses a number of these plays in his *Le Théâtre persan*, and places them in their historical setting of religious drama in Iran and Mesopotamia. Rezvani, a professional dancer, compiled his *Le Théâtre et la danse en Iran* from a wide variety of sources which he used uncritically. Nevertheless he writes from the point of view of one intimately involved in the theater and dance, and this adds a dimension to his work that most other books on the theater do not have. He discusses the *ta^{c}ziya* historically and technically, and translates the text of one into French. A more scholarly treatment is that of Bayẓâ'î in his *Namâyish dar Îrân*. This is a general history of the theater in its broadest sense from pre-Islamic Persia to the mid-twentieth century. It is a more thoughtful and critical book than Rezvani's; and Bayẓâ'î's discussion of the *ta^{c}ziya* is based on a more discriminating use of historical sources. The most recent Iranian work on this subject is by Humâyûnî, who discusses the recent history and current situation of the *ta^{c}ziya* in some depth, and gives the texts of three plays.

Three recent works devoted exclusively to the *ta^{c}ziya* are of interest because although they all cover common ground, each in its own way takes the study of these plays farther than it has been taken before. Mamnoun's *Ta'zija* concentrates on the technical aspects of the *ta^{c}ziya*, such as the production and direction of the plays, and scenery and costumes, subjects covered also by Bayẓâ'î. Monchi-Zadeh's *Ta^{c}ziya* concentrates on the plays themselves and their subject matter. Basing his work heavily on Litten's facsimiles of manuscript *ta^{c}ziyas*, Monchi-Zadeh summarizes and translates parts of 15 plays. Müller's *Studien zum persischen Passionsspiel* focuses more on the religio historical and mythological status of *ta^{c}ziyas*, and gives the text and translation of one play. There is little purely literary discussion of these dramas in any of these books, and it is a subject that needs to be explored.

In the area of *Stoffgeschichte*, Duda's *Ferhâd und Shîrîn* has been mentioned. A more recent contribution is de Fouchécour's book on the description of nature in eleventh-century poetry. He has given us an enormously detailed work, citing thousands of references to various aspects of nature in this early poetry. With it he has laid the groundwork for more detailed studies of the evolving conceptions of nature and the changes in poetic language that accompanied them.

A modest number of comparative studies have been produced, and have tended to cluster around three focuses: Firdawsî-Arnold, Khayyâm-FitzGerald, and Ḥâfiẓ-Goethe. Articles by Javadi, Yohannan, and Rose on these subjects may be found in a recent issue of the *Review of National Literatures.* Another popular area of inquiry is exemplified in Saffari's interesting study of Persian stories and tales in eighteenth- and nineteenth-century English literature. In Persian, Islâmî Nudûshan's essays and Amīrī's recently revised study of Matthew Arnold's "Sohrab and Rustum" are examples of a small but growing interest in comparative literature in Iran. It is, however, an area that needs a great deal more attention.

In theory and criticism, there are signs of serious interest and intent in some of the thoughtful works that have recently appeared. For example, the history of literary criticism is discussed at length by Zarrînkûb in his *Naqd-i Adabî.* He begins with an examination of critical schools and theories in the West, and proceeds to concentrate on the history of Persian criticism. Because the author has read widely and critically in medieval Persian literature he is able to offer the scholar an authoritative survey of how Persian poets, writers, and critics have viewed their own literature.

The history of literary theory and criticism in Persia is long but rather one-dimensional. From the eleventh century *Tarjumân al-Balâgha* of Râdûyânî, through the most important medieval work, Shams-i Qays's *al-Muᶜjam,* to Maḥjûb's recent analysis of the Khurâsânî style, criticism has been prescriptive and has focused solely on meter, rhyme, and rhetorical devices, that is, on the external form of the poetry. Traditional criticism in Persia was not based on a clearly formulated theory of literature, and did not deal with the internal structure of works, imagery, symbolism, or any of the other concerns of modern criticism. Literary scholarship was largely concerned with the biographical study of authors, parallel hunting, and other antiquarian pursuits. Since World War II the situation has changed much for the better. Bahâr worked out a complete analysis of prose style in his *Sabk Shinâsî,* a work that is somewhat distorted by faulty periodization, but which nevertheless deserves praise for its scope and ambition. Literary theories are being advanced, as will be discussed below.

Modern poetry, now that it has become firmly established, need no longer be defended against the conservatives, but can now be the object of serious theoretical and critical study. As in the West, strongly opposing views of the nature and function of poetry are current. For example, Pûrqumî in his *Shᶜir va Siyâsat* argues that poetry is a political act and that the languishing state of poetry in Iran today is due to the failure of poetic language to be comprehensible to the masses of the people. Today's poetry is not of its age, he argues. Dast Ghayb takes another view in his *Sâya Rawshan*. This critic, partly under the influence of Eliot, argues that the poet must strive to be an integral part of his whole poetic tradition, but at the same time he must be a part of his own society and speak for it. He must be engaged, but not be a propagandist.

The last three books to be discussed all begin with a theory of poetry, and then apply this theory to the works of several poets. These books represent serious attempts to spell out theories of poetry with specific references to Persian poetry. The authors are familiar with Western theory and criticism, and with the Western and Persian literary traditions. Each book has its special strengths and weaknesses.

Barâhinî's *Ṭilâ dar Mis* of 1968 is the earliest of the three. The author begins with what is more of a manifesto than an introduction, which in its shrill tone, blatant nationalism, and preoccupation with "Westoxication" sounds somewhat naïve and out of place today. He then presents his theory of poetry, worked out intelligently and in great detail. In the final section are the author's essays on individual modern poets. Barâhinî takes a strongly realist stand and even calls for a poetry of engagement. For the most part, the essays are sensitive and penetrating, but they are sometimes marred by the author's strong anti-romantic prejudice. Unfortunately a self-serving tone emerges from time to time when the author reviews or continues his personal literary battles.

Contrasting with Barâhinî's strong and very personal book is Nûrî ᶜAlâ'î's *Ṣuvvar va Asbâb*. Nûrî ᶜAlâ'î too is a realist critic, but his personal position is less clearly articulated, and his theoretical section has the quality of a general manual of poetry, with various aspects of the major critical problems being discussed. The book, because of the way it is printed, gives more the impression of a collection of notes and jottings than of a fully integrated text. In the essays on individual modern poets, the author tends to classify or pigeonhole the poets rather too neatly. He does state his own views of the poets, however, and this along with quotes from other poets and critics gives an insight into currents of literary thought in Iran.

Shafîᶜî Kadkanî's *Ṣuvar-i Khiyâl* is of a different nature. In this book, the author deals solely with the problem of imagery, which he takes to be the central element of poetry. In his theoretical section he discusses imagery from many points of view, and reviews critically the statements of traditional Persian and Arabic critics with regard to this subject. He then examines the imagery of a number of early medieval poets in the light of his theoretical position. He does not engage in the extremely close readings of the New Critics since he is concerned with only one aspect of poetry. Of these three books, this is the deepest and narrowest. It is a sensitive and thoughtful work, unique in Persian criticism.

In concluding this section, certain points should be mentioned. It is clear that much theoretical work needs to be done in the areas of periodization, the study and definition of genres, the nature and structure of narrative in prose and poetry, and indeed in all other branches of literary theory. Persia has produced a great deal of narrative poetry, and it is conceivable that a close study of Persian narrative could advance the general theory of narrative in literature. On the other hand, the time seems to have come to cease writing large histories, or even small ones, until the manuscript sources for this literature are better known, and until more critical and theoretical work has been done. Regional histories have generally suffered from the lack of a critical approach, and from obtrusive nationalism. More and better regional and period studies are badly needed. Finally, studies of themes and motifs which are more than mere compilations of examples would be useful. A more general awareness of modern literary methods would be of immense help in redirecting the currents of literary study in the West as well as in Persia.

SUMMARY

In summary it is useful to indicate the points of agreement and divergence between the Persian and Western traditions of studying Persian literature. In Persia, as we have seen, no general theory of literature was ever developed, and attempts at such began in earnest only after World War II. There were detailed books on the art of poetry written all through the medieval period, but they were practical rather than theoretical, and were concerned with the external forms of poetry. On the basis of this approach to poetry, *taẕkira* writers and poets criticized poetry by asserting, on the whole, their personal taste. The writers of *taẕkiras* in selecting authors and works for inclusion were guided again by educated personal taste. These attitudes toward literature prevailed until the twentieth century.

In the early twentieth century, Persian and Western scholars and literary men began to mix more frequently, and ideas of Western literary theory and critical practice were taken up by Persian literary scholars. It is at this point that the Western and Persian scholarly traditions begin to merge. The West brought the Orientalist tradition to the study of Persian literature, and from the Persian *taẕkira* writers it learned which poets were admired within the Persian tradition. Two early examples of this symbiosis were Qazvînî, who was the first Persian scholar to produce meticulously edited texts according to Western Orientalist tradition, and Browne, whose *Literary History* derives ultimately from the *taẕkira* tradition. It so happened that these two were also long-time friends and collaborators.

Both traditions supplied their share of antiquarianism. It had long been an accepted literary activity in Europe, and in Persia it was part of the *tazkira* tradition. Scholars from East and West gloried in petty historical minutiae, neither tradition being able to erect from this mass of facts and parallels a general and comprehensive structure. This school of literary study flourishes vigorously in Iran, especially among the older scholars and in the universities. Nor is it dead in the West, but here it has, for the most part, retired to the sidelines.

Comparative studies have only recently become an important part of the Persian literary scene. Arabic language and literature have been studied for centuries in Persia, and the Arabic influence on Persian literature has long been a concern of Persian scholars. This is not comparative literature in the modern Western sense, however.

The situation of literary theory and criticism is similar to that of comparative literature. After World War I Western literary theories and critical methods began to gain a foothold in Persia, but it is only books from recent years like those of Barâhinî and Shafîᶜî Kadkanî that demonstrate that these theories and methods can be applied successfully to the study of Persian literature. At the same time, Westerners are beginning to use their own methods to study the literature of Iran. Clinton's study of Manūchihrī, Windfuhr's use of advanced linguistic methods for the analysis and criticism of poetry in his "A Linguist's Criticism of Persian Literature," Reinert's use of logical and mathematical theories to examine Khâqânî's figurative language, and Bausani's and Heinz's treatment of Indian style poetry all point in the same direction. The two traditions are drawing closer together, and one hopes that this cross-fertilization will produce a greater understanding and appreciation of the rich literature of Persia.

BIBLIOGRAPHY

Key to Categorization

(*a*) Literary historical.
(*b*) Literary critical.
(*c*) Literary theoretical.
(*d*) Philological, lexicographical.
(*e*) Texts, divans, anthologies.
(*f*) Translations.
(*g*) Bibliographical, biobibliographical.

Abû al-Maᶜâlî Naṣr Allâh. *Kalîla va Dimna*. Mujtabâ Mînuvî, ed. Tehran: University of Tehran, 1964. (e)

Afshâr, Iraj. *Index Iranicus*, Vol, 1, 1910–1958, Tehran: University of Tehran, 1961. (g)

———. *Index Iranicus*. Vol. II, 1959–1966. Tehran: University of Tehran, 1969. (g)

———. *Kitâbhâ-i Dah Sâla*. Tehran: Anjuman-i Kitâb, 1967. (g)

———. *Kitâb-shinâsi-i Firdawsî*. Tehran: Anjuman-i Âsâr-i Millî, 1968. (g)

ᶜAlavî, Buzurg. *Geschichte und Entwicklung der modernen persischen Literatur*. Berlin: Akademie-Verlag, 1964. (a)

Amîrî, Manûchihr. *Mâthyu Ârnuld: Suhrâb va Rustam*. Shiraz: Pahlavi University, 1975. (a)

Arberry, A. J. "Orient Pearls at Random Strung," *BSOAS*, **11** (1943–1946), 699–712. (b, c)

Âryanpûr, Yaḥyâ. *Az Ṣabâ tâ Nîmâ*. 2 vols. Tehran: Kitâbhâ-i Jîbî, 1971. (a, b)

Ayni, Sadriddin. *Mirzo Abdulgodir Bedil*. Stalinabad: Tadshikskoe gos. izd-vo, 1954. (a, b)

Bahâr, Muḥammad Taqî. *Sabk Shinâsī*. 3 vols. Tehran: Amîr Kabîr, 1958. (b)

Barâhinî, Riżâ. *Ṭilâ dar Mis*. Tehran: Zamân, 1968. (b, c)

Bausani, Alessandro. "Contributo a una definizione dello 'Stile indiano' della poesia persiana," *Annali dell'Instituto universitario orientale di Napoli*, N.S. **7** (1958), 167–178. (b, c)

———. "Note su Mirza Bedil," ibid. N.S. **6** (1957), 163–191. (a)

———. "Note sulla natura in Bēdil," ibid., N.S. **15** (1965), 215–228. (b)

———. "Bēdil as a Narrator," *Yâdnâma-i Jan Rypka*. Prague: Academia, 1967, 227–235. (b)

Bayżâ'i, Bahrâm. *Namâyish dar Îrân*. Tehran: Châp-i Kâviyân, 1965. (a)

Bîghamî, Muḥammad. *Love and War: Adventures from the Firuz Shāh Nāma*. William L. Hanaway, Jr., trans. Delmar, New York: Scholars' Facsimiles and Reprints, 1974. (f)

Borshchevski, Yu. E., and Yu. E. Bregel. "The Preparation of a Bio-bibliographical Survey of Persian Literature,," *IJMES*, **3** (1972), 169–186. (g)

Boyce, Mary. "Middle Persian Literature." In Spuler, B., ed., *Handbuch der Orientalistik*, I, IV, ii, i. Leiden: Brill, 1968, 31–66. (a)

———. "The Parthian Gōsān and the Iranian Minstrel Tradition," *JRAS* (1957), 10–45. (a)

Braginsky, I. S. "Periodization in Persian Literature," *Central Asian Review*, **12** (1964), 132–139. (c)

Browne, Edward G. *A Literary History of Persia*. 4 vols. Cambridge: University Press, 1902–1924. (a)

De Bruijn, J. T. P. "Literature." In *Encyclopaedia of Islam*, 2nd ed., Vol. 4, pp. 52–75. (a)

Christensen, Arthur. *Recherches sur les Rubâᶜiyât de 'Omar Hayyâm*. Heidelberg: Winter, 1905. (a, b)

———. *Critical Studies in the Rubá'iyát of ᶜUmar-i Khayyám*. Copenhagen: Kongelige danske videnskabernes selskab, 1927. (b)

Clinton, Jerome W. *The Divan of Manūchihrī Dāmghānī*. Minneapolis, Minn: Bibliotheca Islamica, 1972. (b)

Dashtî, ᶜAlî. *In Search of Omar Khayyam*. L. P. Elwell-Sutton, trans. London: Allen & Unwin, 1971. (b, f)

———. *Naqshî az Ḥâfiẓ*. Tehran: Amîr Kabîr, 1963. (b)

Dast Ghayb, ᶜAbd al-ᶜAlî. *Naqd-i Âsâr-i Ghulâm Ḥusayn Sâᶜidî*. Tehran: Mîrâ, 1973. (b)

———. *Nîmâ Yûshîj*. Tehran: Farzîn, 1972. (b)

———. *Sâya Rawshan-i Shi^c r-i Naw-i Pârsî.* Tehran: Farhang, 1969. (a, b)

Duda, Herbert W. *Ferhâd und Shîrîn.* Prague: Orientální ústav, 1933. (a)

Ethé, Hermann. "Neupersische Literatur." *In Gundriss der iranischen Philologie,* Vol. 2, Wilhelm Geiger and Ernst Kuhn, eds., 2 vols. Strassburg: Trübner, 1895–1904, pp. 212–368.

Fakhr al-Dîn Gurgânî. *Vîs u Râmîn.* M. Todua, and A. Gwakharia, eds. Tehran: Bunyâd-i Farhang-i Irân, 1970. (e)

Farâhânî, Abû al-Ḥasan Ḥusaynî. *Sharḥ-i Mushkilât-i Dîvân-i Anvarî.* Mudarris Riẓavî, ed. Tehran: University of Tehran, 1961. (d, e).

Firdawsî. *Dâstân-i Rustam va Suhrâb.* Mujtabâ Mînuvî, ed. Tehran: Bunyâd-i Shahnâma-i Firdawsî, 1973. (e)

———. *Shâhnâma.* E. A. Bertels, ed., 9 vols. Moscow: Akademiya Nauk, 1966–1971. (e)

Fouchécour, C.-H. de. *La Description de la nature dans la poésie lyrique persane du XIe siècle.* Paris: Klincksieck, 1969. (b, c)

Furûzânfar, Badî^c al-Zamân. *Aḥâdîs-i Masnavî.* Tehran: Univ. of Tehran, 1955. (a, b)

———. *Ma'khaz-i Qiṣaṣ va Tamsîlât-i Masnavî.* Tehran: Univ. of Tehran, 1954. (a, b)

———. *Risâla dar Taḥqîq-i Aḥvâl va Zindigânî-i Mawlânâ Jalâl al-Dîn Muḥammad.* Tehran: Zavvâr, 1936. (a)

———. *Sharḥ-i Masnavî-i Sharîf.* Vol. 1. Tehran: Univ. of Tehran, 1967. (b)

———. *Sharḥ-i Aḥvâl va Naqd va Taḥlîl-i Âsâr-i ^c Aṭṭâr.* Tehran: Anjuman-i Âsâr-i Millî, 1960–1961. (a, b)

———. *Sukhan va Sukhanvarân.* Tehran: Khvârazmî, 1971. (a)

Gawharîn, Ṣâdiq. *Farhang-i Lughât va Ta^c bîrât-i Masnavî.* Vol. 1. Tehran: Univ. of Tehran, 1958. (d)

Ghanî, Qâsim. *Baḥs dar Âsâr va Afkâr va Aḥvâl-i Ḥâfiẓ.* 2 vols. Tehran: Zavvâr, 1961. (a)

Ḥafiẓ. *Dîvân.* ^c Abd al-Raḥmân Khal Khâlî, ed. Tehran: Kâvâ, 1927. (e)

———. *Dîvân.* Muhammed Qazînî and Qâsim Ghanî, ed. Tehran: Zavvâr, 1941. (e)

———. *Ghazalhâ.* P. N. Khânlarî, ed. Tehran: Sukhan, 1958. (e).

———. *Jâma^c -i Nusakh-i Ḥâfiẓ.* Mas^c ûd Farzâd, ed. Shiraz: Pahlavi University, 1968. (d)

———. *Ṣiḥḥat-i Kalamât.* Mas^c ûd Farzâd, ed. Shiraz: Pahlavi Univ., 1970. (d)

Ḥamîd al-Dîn Abû Bakr. *Maqâmât.* ^c Alî Akbar Abarqûyî, ed. Isfahan: Univ. of Isfahan, 1960. (e)

Heinz, Wilhelm. *Der indische Stil in der persischen Literatur.* Wiesbaden: Steiner, 1973. (c)

Hidâyat, Riẓâqulî. *Majma^c al-Fuṣaḥâ.* 2 vols. in 6. Tehran: Amîr Kabîr, 1957–1961. (a)

Hidâyat, Ṣâdiq. *Tarânahâ-i Khayyâm.* Tehran: Châpkhâna-i Rawshanâ'î, 1934. (b)

Hillmann, Michael C. "Sound and Sense in a *Ghazal* of Ḥâfiẓ," *The Muslim World,* **61** (1971), 111–121. (b)

———. "Hāfez and Poetic Unity through Verse Rhythms," *JNES,* **31** (1972), 1–10. (b)

———. " The Text of Ḥâfiẓ: Addenda," *JAOS,* 95 (1975), 719–720.

Hodizoda, Rasul. *Adabiyoti Tojik dar Nimai Dūvvumi Asri XIX.* Vol. 1. Dushanbe: Donish, 1968. (a, b)

Humâyûnî, Ṣâdiq. *Ta^c ziya va Ta^c ziya-Khânî.* Shiraz: Jashn-i Hunar, 1974. (a)

Ibrâhîmî Ḥarîrî, Fâris. *Maqâla Nivîsî dar Adabiyyât-i Fârsî.* Tehran: Univ. of Tehran, 1967. (a, b)

Islâmî Nawdûshan, Muḥammad ^c Alî. *Jâm-i Jahân-Bîn.* Tehran: Irânmihr, 1967. (a, b)

Jalâl al-Dîn Muḥammad Rûmî. *Kulliyyât-i Shams.* 8 vols. B. Furûzânfar, ed. Tehran: Univ. of Tehran, 1957–1963. (e)

———. *The Mathnawí.* 8 vols. R. A. Nicholson, ed. and trans. London: Luzac, 1925–1940. (d, e, f)

Javadi, Hasan. "Matthew Arnold's 'Sohrab and Rustum' and its Persian Original," *Review of National Literatures*, **2** (1971), 61–73. (b)

Kamshad, Hasan. *Modern Persian Prose Literature.* Cambridge: Univ. Press, 1966. (a, b)

———. *A Modern Persian Prose Reader.* Cambridge: Univ. Press, 1968. (e)

Khânlarî, Parvîz N. "Â'în-i ^{c}Ayyârî," *Sukhan*, **18** (1968), 1071–1077; **19** (1969), 19–26, 113–122, 263–267, 477–480. (a)

Khusrawshâhî, Riżâ. *Shi^{c}r va Adab-i Fârsî dar Âsyâ-i Ṣaghîr.* Tehran: Dânishsarâ-i ^{c}Âlî, 1971. (a)

Kitâbshinâsî-i Millî. Tehran: Kitâbkâna-i Millî, 1964. (g)

Kubíčková, Vera. *Qāānī.* Prague: Akademie Věd, 1954. (a, b)

Kukhtina, T. I. *Bibliografiya Afganistana.* Moscow: Akademiya Nauk, 1965. (g)

Lazard, Gilbert, *Les Premiers Poètes persans.* 2 vols. Tehran and Paris: Maisonneuve, 1964. (e, f)

Lescot, Roger. "Essai d'une chronologie de l'oeuvre de Hafiz," *Bulletin d'études orientales* (*Damascus*), **10** (1944), 57–100. (b, c)

Litten Wilhelm. *Das Drama in Persien.* Berlin: de Gruyter, 1929. (e)

Machalski, Fr. *La Littérature de l'Iran contemporain.* 2 vols. Warsaw: Akademie Nauk, 1965–1967. (a, b)

Maḥjûb, Muḥammad Ja^{c}far. "Â'în-i ^{c}Ayyârî." *Sukhan*, **19** (1969), 869–883, 1059–1073, 1182–1195; **20** (1970), 38–51, 173–199, 301–311. (a)

———. *Dar Bâra-i Kalîla va Dimna.* Tehran: Khvârazmî, 1970. (a)

———. *Sabk-i Khurâsânî dar Shi^{c}r-i Fârsî.* Tehran: Sâzmân-i Tarbiyat-i Mu^{c}allim, 1966. (b)

Mamnoun, Parviz. *Ta'zija: Schi'itisch-persisches Passionsspiel.* Vienna: Notring, 1967. (a)

Manûchihrî. *Menoutchehri, poète persan. Texte, traduction, notes et introduction par A. de Biberstein Kazimirski.* Paris: Klincksieck, 1886. (d, e, f)

Minorsky, Vladimir. "The Earliest Collections of O. Khayyam." In *Yâdnâme-ye Jan Rypka.* Prague: Academia, 1967, pp. 107–118. (a)

———. "Vîs u Râmîn." In his *Iranica.* Tehran: Univ. of Tehran, 1964, pp. 151–199. (a, b)

Mînuvî, Mujtabâ. "Khayyâmhâ-i Sâkhtigî: Tawżîḥ," *Rahnema-ye Ketab*, **6** (1963), 238–240. (b)

Mirzoyev, ^{c}Abdulghanî. *Abû ^{c}Abd-Allâh Rûdakî.* Stalinabad: Nashriyot-i Davlatî-i Tâjîkistân, 1958. (a, b)

Miskûb, Shâhrukh. *Muqaddima bar Rustam va Isfandiyâr*, 2nd ed. Tehran: Amîr Kabîr, 1969. (b)

———. *Sûg-i Siyâvush.* Tehran: Kvârazmî, 1971. (b)

Monchi-Zadeh, Davoud. *Ta^{c}ziya: Das persische Passionsspiel.* Stockholm: Almqvist & Wiksell, 1967. (a, f)

Mudarris Rižavî, Muḥammad Taqî. *Ta^{c}lîqât-i Ḥadîqât al-Ḥaqîqât.* Tehran: ^{c}Ilmî, 1966. (d)

Muḥammad ^{c}Abd al-Ghanî. *A History of Persian Language and Literature at the Mughal Court*, 3 vols. Allahabad: Indian Press, 1929–1930. (a)

Muḥammad Ibn ᶜAlî al-Ẓahîrî al-Samarqandî. *Sindbâd Nâma*. Ahmed Ateş, ed. Istanbul: Istanbul University, 1948. (e)

Muḥammad Ibn ᶜUmar al-Râdûyânî. *Tarjumân al-Balâg̲h̲a*. Ahmed Ateş, ed. Istanbul: Istanbul University, 1949. (e)

Muᶜîn, Muḥammad. *Taḥlîl-i Haft Paykar-i Niẓâmî*, Vol. 1. Tehran: Univ of. Tehran, 1959. (b)

Müller, Hildegard. *Studien zum persischen Passionsspiel*. Freiburg i. Br., 1966. (a)

Mushâr, Khân Bâbâ. *Fihrist-i Kitâbhâ-i C̲h̲âpî-i Fârsî*, 2nd ed., 3 vols. Tehran: Bungâh-i Tarjuma va Nashr-i Kitâb, 1971–1973. (g)

Nafîsî, Saᶜîd. *Aḥvâl va As̲h̲ᶜâr-i Rûdakî-i Samarqandî*. Tehran: Taraqqî, 1931–1941. (a, b)

———. *Dîvân-i Qaṣâ'id va G̲h̲azaliyyât-i Niẓâmî*. Tehran: Furûg̲h̲î, 1959. (a, e)

———. *Muḥît-i Zindigânî va Aḥvâl va As̲h̲ᶜâr-i Rûdakî*. Tehran: Ibn Sînâ, 1963. (a)

Niẓâmî, ᶜArûẓî Samarqandî. *C̲h̲ahâr Maqâla*. Muḥammad Muᶜîn, ed. Tehran: Zavvâr, 1955. (e)

Nöldeke, Theodor. *Das iranische Nationalepos*. 2nd ed. Berlin: de Gruyter, 1920. (a, b)

Nûrî ᶜAlâ'î, Ismâᶜîl. *Ṣuvar va Asbâb dar S̲h̲iᶜr-i Imrûz*. Tehran: Bâmdâd, 1969. (b, c)

Nûs̲h̲în, ᶜAbd al-Ḥusayn. *Vâzha Nâmak dar bâra-i Vâzhahâ-i Dus̲h̲vâr-i S̲h̲âhnâma*. Tehran: Bunyâd-i Farhang-i Irân, 1972. (d)

Pagliaro, A., and A. Bausani. *Storia della letteratura persiana*. Milan: Nuova Accademia, 1960. (a, b)

Pearson, J. D. *Index Islamicus*, 1906–1955. Cambridge: Heffer, 1958. Supplements 1962, 1967, 1972. (g)

Perry, B. E. *The Origin of the Book of Sindbad*. Berlin: de Gruyter, 1960. (a)

Pizzi, Italo. *Storia della poesia persiana*. 2 vols. Turin: Clausen, 1894. (a)

Pûrqumî, Nâṣir. *S̲h̲iᶜr va Siyâsât*. Tehran: Numûna, 1972. (c)

Rehder, Robert M. "New Material for the Text of Ḥâfiẓ," *Iran*, **3** (1965), 109–119. (a)

———. "The Text of Ḥâfiẓ," *JAOS*, **94** (1974), 145–156. (a)

———. "The Unity of the Ghazals of Ḥâfiẓ," *Der Islam*, **51** (1974), 55–96. (a)

Reinert, Benedikt. *Ḫāqānī als Dichter: Poetische Logik und Phantasie*. Berlin: de Gruyter, 1972. (b, c)

Rezvani, Medjid. *Le Théâtre et la danse en Iran*. Paris: Maisonneuve, 1962. (a)

Ritter, Helmut. *Das Meer der Seele*. Leiden: Brill, 1955. (a, b)

———. *Über die Bildersprache Niẓāmīs*. Berlin: de Gruyter, 1927. (b)

Rose, Ernst. "Persian Mysticism in Goethe's 'West-Östlicher Divan'," *Review of National Literatures*, **2** (1971), 92–111. (b)

Rossi, E. and A. Bombaci. *Elenco di drammi religiosi persiani*. Vatican: Biblioteca Apostolica Vaticana, 1961. (g)

Rypka, Jan. *History of Iranian Literature*. Dordrecht: Reidel, 1968. (a)

Saᶜd al-Dîn Varâvînî. *Marzbân Nâma*. Muḥammad Qazvînî, ed. Leiden: Brill, 1909. (e)

Saᶜdî. *Gulistân*. Rustam ᶜAliyev, ed. Moscow: Akademia Nauk, 1959. (e)

———. *Saᶜdî Nâmâ, yâ Bûstân*. Rustam Aliyev, ed. Tehran: Kitâbhâna-i Pahlavî, 1968. (e)

Ṣafâ, Zabîḥallâh. *Ḥamâsa Sarâ'î dar Îrân*. Tehran: Amîr Kabîr, 1954. (a)

———. *Târîk̲h̲-i Adabiyyât dar Îrân*. 3 Vols. to date. Tehran: Ibn Sînâ, 1953. (a, b)

Saffari, Kokab. *Les Legendes et contes persans dans la littérature anglaise des XVIIIe et XIXe siècles, jusqu'en 1859.* Paris: Les Presses du Palais-Royal, 1972. (a)

Schimmel, Annemarie. *Die Bildersprache Dschelāladdīn Rūmīs.* Walldorf-Hessen: Vorndran, 1950. (b)

———. *Islamic Literatures of India.* Wiesbaden: Harrassowitz, 1973. (a)

Scott, Charles T. *Persian and Arabic Riddles: A Language-centered Approach to Genre Definition.* Bloomington: Indiana University, 1965. (c)

Shafaq, Rizâẓâda. *Farhang-i Shâhnâma.* Tehran: Majma^{c}-i Nâshir-i Kitâb, 1941. (d)

———. *Farhang-i Shâhnâma,* 2nd ed. Muṣtafâ Shahâbî, ed. Tehran: Anjuman-i Âsâr-i Millî, 1971. (d)

Shafî^{c}î, Maḥmud. *Shâhnâmâ va Dastûr.* Tehran: Nîl, 1964, (d)

Shafî^{c}î Kadkanî, Muḥammad Riżâ. *Suṣvar-i Khiyyâl dar Shi^{c}r-i Fârsî.* Tehran: Nîl, 1971. (b, c)

Shams al-Dîn Muḥammad Ibn Qays al-Râẓî. *al-Mu^{c}jam.* Muḥammad Qazvînî, ed., revised by M. Riẓavî. Tehran: Tehran, 1959. (e)

Shâriq, Bahman. *Nîmâ va Sh^{c}ir-i Pârsî.* Tehran: Tahûrî, 1971. (b)

Storey, C. A. *Persian Literature: A Bio-bibliographical survey,* 3 vols. Translated into Russian and revised with additions and corrections by Yu. E. Bregel, Yu. E. Borshchevsky, ed. Moscow: Akademiya Nauk, 1972. (g)

Sverchevskaya, A. K. *Bibliografiya Irana.* Moscow: Akademiya Nauk, 1967. (g)

al-Tanûkhî, al-Muḥassin Ibn ^{c}Alî. *Al-Faraj ba^{c}d al-shidda.* Ḥusayn ibn As^{c}ad al-Dihistânî, trans., M. Mudîr, ed. Tehran: ^{c}Ilmiya-i Islâmiya, 1954. (e, f)

Tikku, G. L. *Persian Poetry in Kashmir, 1339–1846.* Berkeley: Univ. of California Press, 1971. (a, b)

^{c}Umar Khayyâm. *Rubâ^{c}iyyât.* Muḥammad ^{c}Alî Furûhgî and Qâsim Ghanî, eds. Tehran: Zavvâr, 1942. (e)

———. *The Rubáiyát of Omar Khayyám.* Edward FitzGerald, trans. London: Quaritch, 1859. (f)

———. *The Rubaiyat of Omar Khayaam.* Robert Graves, trans. London: Cassell, 1967. (f)

^{c}Umân Mukhtârî. *Dîvân.* Jalâl al-Dîn Humâ'î, ed. Tehran: Bungâh-i Tarjuma va Nashr-i Kitâb, 1962. (d, e)

Utas, Bo. *Ṭarīq ut-taḥqīq: A Sufi Mathnavi.* Lund: Studentlitteratur, 1973. (d, e)

Virolleaud, Charles. *Le Théâtre persan.* Paris: Maisonneuve, 1950. (a)

Windfuhr, Gernot. "A Linguist's Criticism of Persian Literature." In Richard N. Frye, ed., *Neue Methodologie in der Iranistik.* Wiesbaden: Harrassowitz, 1974, pp. 331–352. (b, c)

Wolff, Fritz. *Glossar zu Firdosis Schahname.* Berlin: Reichsdruckerei, 1935. (d)

Yâr Shâter, Iḥsân. *Sh^{c}ir-i Fârsî dar ^{c}Ahd-i Shâhrukh.* Tehran: Univ. of Tehran, 1956. (a)

Yohannan, John D. "The Fin de Siècle Cult of FitzGerald's 'Rubaiyat' of Omar Khayyam," *Review of National Literatures,* **2** (1971), 74–91. (b)

Yûsufî, Ghulâm Ḥusayn. *Farrukhî Sîstânî.* Meshed: Bâstân, 1962. (a, b)

Zarrînkûb, ^{c}Abd al-Ḥusayn. *Naqd-i Adabî.* Tehran: Andîsha, 1959. (b, c)

Turkish Literature

WALTER ANDREWS

Turkish literature from the earliest inscriptions to the present was produced over a period of some 1300 years in geographical areas from Eastern Central Asia to Egypt and the Balkans. Even the Islamic–Turkic literatures which are the subject of this survey have some 900 years of history and emerged in such diverse areas as India, Transoxiana, and the Crimea as well as the better known lands of Ottoman Turkish domination. The Ottoman tradition, in particular, produced a vast number of literary works for the most part rather well preserved, and the Turkic peoples posssess an equally vast folk literature that is only now being collected and studied. As is the case with the other literatures discussed in this survey, the amount of material worthy of mention is enormous and the limitations on the size of the paper are severe. Therefore, there is no attempt here to provide a comprehensive bibliography of literary study, but rather the emphasis is on surveying basic trends and the available *types* of literary study. The knowledgeable reader will, for example, find one or two works of a certain type cited and be dismayed to find many excellent works omitted when possibly inferior works of a different *type* receive a citation. It is hoped that such inequities will be understandable in view of the purposes of this survey and that neither the expert nor the neophyte will view this chapter as anything but a comment on the general nature of literary study. Moreover, it is worth pointing out that one criterion for the selection of works cited was general availability; thus work in progress, dissertations, etc., are seldom if ever mentioned because limited availability severely restricts their influence on the state of the art as a whole.

There are several works used for this paper which provide the detailed background of the following survey. Beyond the standard general sources for the Islamic literatures (*Index Islamicus, Handbuch der Orientalistik*) there are several excellent bibliographical tools. The *Philologiae Turcicae Fundamenta*, Volume 2 (*PTF II*) contains historical outlines and bibliography for all the Turkic literatures, monographs on popular forms, classical prosody, an interesting introduction, etc. The Turks have also produced the *Türkiye Bibliyografyası*, which cites by subject all books published in Turkey, and the *Türkiye Makaleler Bibliyografyası*, which lists selected periodical articles. The problem of dealing adequately with Turkish periodicals is, however, a basic problem of the field and virtually insoluable within the scope of this paper.

For example, one researcher engaged in the study of a modern Turkish poet located relevant articles in 76 Turkish periodicals, many of which are quite difficult to locate even in Turkey, except, perhaps, at the National Library in Ankara. Such factors, combined with less than satisfactory access to very significant work being done in the Soviet Union, again restrict the scope of this paper to the identification and evaluation of major currents in literary study—all of which restriction and limitation reflects one very obvious aspect of the state of the art.

INTRODUCTION

Prefatory to the rather more detailed survey of the literary scholarship, it is necessary to make a few remarks concerning the development of writing about Turkic literature.

The Islamic literary tradition, as adopted by the Turks, was not at all conducive to *writing* about literature. The basic texts of literary theory or "poetics" were more or less immutably established and although they underwent translation, recension, précis, and commentary at the hands of Persians and Turks, very little was added. Even in cases of wide divergence from Arab theory (in prosody, for example) the application of the theory changed while its articulation remained essentially the same.

Perhaps the most fertile field for recorded discussion of literature was literary biography (the *Teẕkire-i şşuᶜarâ* genre), which was widely practiced from the end of the fifteenth century on. (See James Stewart-Robinson, "The Tezkere Genre in Islam," and "The Ottoman Biographies of Poets.") Literary critical or analytical work, however, is virtually nonexistent. More properly it seems clear that criticism and analysis were widely practiced at gatherings of littérateurs—the judgments are recorded in the biographical works—but the tradition was oral and only the barest traces of it have survived.

In the latter half of the nineteenth century, when Ottoman Turkey underwent fundamental political and social changes, there occurred a similar upheaval on the literary scene which had repercussions throughout the Turkic world. Changing views about literature and the search for new directions necessitated the establishment and promulgation of a radically altered set of literary principles and criteria. As a result, literary artists and scholars, newly aware of European practices, began to produce a large number of works about literature. An outstanding example of these several trends is Nâmıḳ Kemāl's series of articles (*Tahrîb-i Harâbât, Taᶜḳîb*) criticizing Ziya Paşa's traditional anthology of Islamic literature (*Harâbât*, 1874). In subsequent decades there appeared many books and articles of criticism, theory, and literary history heavily influenced by European theories and the need to reshape the received tradition. (The article by Kenan Akyüz, "La Littérature moderne de Turquie" in *PTF II* contains sections entitled "La Critique littéraire" and "L'Histoire littéraire" for each period up to 1925; these give an excellent picture of the development of Turkish writing about literature since the *Tanẓîmât.*)

In the area of literary scholarship, the influences of European historicism, evolutionary theories of literature, and a growing tendency (in Europe) to separate literary criticism from "Literaturwissenschaft" left an indelible mark on Turkish writing about literature. M. F. Köprülü's "Türk Edebiyatı Tarihinde Usul" (The Principles of Turkish Literary History), first published in 1913, set the stage for the careful and orderly development of literary history in Turkey. Though it added scholarly methodologies and a broader social and historical view to the preexisting biographical tradition, Köprülü's theory, like its European counterparts, left little room for more synchronic critical/analytical approaches. In general, the wave of interest in the close analysis of individual works which swept Europe and the United States (as "the new criticism") has had little effect on most areas of Turkish literary study in both Turkey and the West. Moreover, historical and evolutionary literary approaches in Turkey and the West have been dominated by emphasis on revealing the "national spirit" (*Volksgeist*) of the Turkic people as expressed through their literature—an approach that tends to see the "national spirit" as dormant during the "Islamic period," carried on only by the folk literature to reawaken during the "national revival" in the nineteenth and twentieth centuries. Such a view, strained somewhat to fit a nationalist model for French, German, and British literary history, has tended to concentrate interest on the earliest and latest periods of Islamic-Turkic literature, on the folk literature and on obvious manifestations of Turkic proto-nationalism.

In general, scholarship on literature in Turkey can be divided into three basic groups: (1) the literary historical, which places heavy emphasis on the broad awareness of periods, genres, collections of works, and characterizations of a poet's "thought," milieu, influences, etc.; (2) the traditional school of text commentary and the elucidation of difficult passages and vocabulary; and (3) those scholars with analytical approaches to concrete works. Of these, the first is by far the largest and most active, and the last is most heavily represented by scholars working on modern and folk literature, in which areas the influences of worldwide trends are most immediately felt. There remain, however, strong tendencies toward relegating the study of traditional literature to traditional approaches and toward limiting the evaluative, critical side of literary study to a literary subgenre of educated impressions of works or groups of works. (See, for example, the collection of various popular articles by A. H. Tanpınar, *Edebiyat Üzerine Makaleler*, a collection that well represents the subgenre mentioned but is only a minor offshoot of Tanpınar's outstanding scholarly work.)

KARAHANID LITERATURE

The earliest substantial monuments of Islamic-Turkic literature come to us from the Empire of the Karahanids who supplanted the Samanids in Transoxania in the eleventh and twelfth centuries. Among the few surviving works of this era, the *Ḳutadgu Bilig* of Yûsuf Ḫâṣṣ Ḥâcib, a mirror for princes presented to the Karahanid Tafgaç Buğra Han in 1069 AD, is perhaps the most studied. There exist editions by Radloff (1890–1891 and 1900–1910) and R. R. Arat (1941) and several studies on various of its literary aspects such as Bertel's "Uygurskaya Poema 'Kutadgu Bilig' . . ." on the meaning of the poem; Hartmann's "Zur metrische Forme des Kutadgu Bilik"; Valitova on folklore motives ("Voprosy u Folklornekh Motivakh . . ."), Bombaci's "Kutadgu Bilig hakkında bazı mülâhazalar," and the work of Robert Dankoff.

A less significant didactic work, the *Atabet al-Ḥaḳâyıḳ* by Edîb Aḥmed Yüknekî has been edited by R. R. Arat but is so far the subject of little literary interest.

In the popular-mystic tradition, the *Dîvân-ı Ḥikmet* of Aḥmed Yesevî, the eponymous ancestor of the Yesevî order of dervishes, has not yet been the subject of intensive study, perhaps for lack of an adequate and authenticated text. There exist the historical and literary historical studies of Gordlevskiy and M. F. Köprülü's valuable "*Türk Edebiyatında* Ilk *Mutasavvıflar*"; however, little significant literary work is available on this important figure who is the direct ancestor of the flourishing popular dervish literature of Anatolia.

The *Divanü Lugat û-it-Türk*, a dictionary of Turkish composed in Arabic by Maḥmûd of Kashgar between 1071 and 1077 AD is worthy of mention here because it contains a large number of Turkish verses and verse fragments otherwise unrecorded. The Türk Dil Kurumu has done a facsimile edition (1941) of the unique 1265 AD manuscript, and an English translation and edition is being prepared (by Professors Kelly and Dankoff), but the job of analyzing and presenting the literary material (as Lazard has done for early Persian poetry) has not been competed (although the poetry has been collected by Brocklemann in "Alttürkistanische Volkspoesie I and II").

In general, the literary historical significance of this important transitional period has been recognized and discussed (see Köprülü, *İlk Mutasavvıflar*, *Türk Dili Ve Edebiyatı Hakkında Araştırmalar*, Z. V. Togan in *Handbuch*, R. R. Arat, *Eski Türk Şiiri* etc.). The lack of any critical mass of other types of literary study for this period, however, is a serious weak point in our understanding of the origins of Turkic literature.

EARLY ANATOLIAN LITERATURE

The Turkish literature of Anatolia before the rise of the Ottomans has attracted considerable interest both in Turkey and the West. Although Mevlana Celaleddin Rumi belongs more properly to the realm of Persian literature, the *Meṣnevî* has been translated into Turkish and commented upon by Turks since medieval times, and new translations and studies such as Mansuroğlu's "Celaluddin Rumi's Türkische Verse" continue to appear in both Turkish and Western publications. It is the followers of Rumi and his spiritual descendants, however, who bring mysticism properly into the area of Turkish literature. His son, Sultan Veled, was recognized at the outset of interest in Turkish literature as one of the earliest poets to attempt classical Islamic verse in the dialect of Anatolia. From von Hammer-Purgstall's article on the *Rebâbnâme* (1829) to studies of Kunos (1892) and Martinovic (1917) there was considerable early interest in Sultan Veled as the representative of an important transitional period in the development of Turkish literature. Perhaps because of the limited and primitive nature of Sultan Veled's work, and as a result of the discovery and study of several other important poets of the Selcuk period, there has been little recent interest in expanding the scope of literary study on his early figure.

The development of the study of Turkish literature in the Seljuk period owes much to M. F. Köprülü, who made scholars aware of such poets as Aḥmed Faḳîh, Şeyyâd Ḥamza, and H̱oca Dehhânî (e.g., "Anatolische Dichter in der Seldschukenzeit"). Köprülü's work has also been followed by a series of studies by Mecdut Mansuroğlu (e.g., "Anadolu Metinleri"). The primary thrust of work in the Selcuk period, however, has been on the discovery of texts and the literary historical background.

The dervish literature of pre-Ottoman Anatolia has, for various reasons, been a source of great interest. Firstly, the poetry of the Anatolian dervishes, most notably of Yûnus Emre, is couched in a simple but powerful Turkish, and is philosophically and stylistically the precursor of a mystical-minstrel tradition which endures today and provides a direct link between modern Turks and their ancient past. As such, Yûnus Emre's poetry is considered an example *par excellence* of the "Turkish national spirit." This feeling is attested to by a plethora of popular articles and books appearing in Turkey and such Western articles as Birge's "Yunus Emre: Turkey's Great Poet of the People." The popularity of Yûnus Emre has brought with it serious scholarly interest. A. Gölpınarlı, the outstanding Turkish student of mysticism, has several important studies of Yûnus Emre as do Rossi, A. Schimmel, Walsh (*Numen*, **7**, 1960) and others. An international Yunus Emre seminar was held in Istanbul in 1971 and produced 25 papers which were collected and published by a Turkish bank (Akbank). Talât Halman has also published a volume of translations in English entitled *The Humanist Poetry of Yunus Emre* (1972).

The number and scope of studies on Yûnus Emre contrast sharply with the state of work on other pre-Ottoman mystics (and indeed on almost all Turkish literature). There exist literary historical studies on Pîr Sultan Abdâl (Cevdet Kudret, Öztelli), Gülşehrî (Taeschner), and 'Âşıḳ Paşa (Babinger, Gölpınarlı) and several works locating unknown works or manuscripts (e.g. Levend, on 'Âşıḳ Paşa), but the range and number of purely litrary studies are severely limited.

The case is essentially the same for those poets, Aḥmedî and Şeyḫî, who can be considered the direct precursors of the Ottoman tradition. Aḥmedî has been studied, for the most part, as the author of a verse history of the early Ottomans which is only a minor part of *İskendernâme*, and his significant literary stature has yet to be explored (cf. Aslanov, "Ahmedi i ego 'Iskender-nāme'.")

The poet Şeyḫî has been given rather more attention, primarily as a result of the efforts of A. N. Tarlan, who has produced an analytical study of his divan (also there exists a TDK facsimile edition of his divan; and F. K. Timurtaş produced editions and studies of his *Ḫusrev ü Şîrîn* and *Ḫarnâme*). It is a sorry commentary on the state of the art that Tarlan's attempt to devise literary analytical tools for Ottoman poetry (*Şehyî Divanı'nı Tetkik*, 1934–1936) has received little critical attention. It represents a pioneering effort which might have benefited greatly by testing through application to specific literary problems (see below on Necatî).

The early literature of eastern Anatolia, a direct ancestor of the Azeri tradition, has received sparse attention. Some of the poetry of Kadı Burhaneddin, the ruler of Sivas, was edited as early as 1922 (Goodsell) and later the whole divan was done in facsimile by the Türk Dil Kurumu (1943). Individual literary studies are difficult to find, however, although A. N. Tarlan's article "Kadı Burhaneddin'de Tasavvuf" is worthy of mention.

The *ḥurûfî* poet and martyr, Nesîmî, although he received some attention from both Turkish and Azeri scholars (e.g., the latter, Araslı, *Fedakâr Şair*), has been the subject of very little study, primarily for lack of access to his work. This situation has been rectified somewhat by the work of Burrill (1972) which should provide a sound basis for further work.

KIPÇAK LITERATURE

During the period (thirteenth and fourteenth centuries) when an Islamic literature in Turkish was developing in Anatolia, lands from Khwarezm to the Crimea and Egypt saw a similar literary growth in the Kıpçak dialect.

This literature, a forerunner of the Çağatay tradition, has attracted considerable interest in Eastern Europe, Turkey, and the Soviet Union. General literary historical interest began early (e.g., Thúry, *Török Nyelvemlekek* . . ., 1903), and was built upon by such scholars as Köprülü (*Türk Edebiyatı Tarihi*, "Çağatay Edebiyatı" in *IA*, etc.) and Malov (e.g., his anthology and studies in *Pamyatniki Drevneturkskoy Pismennosti* . . ., 1951). Individual studies, though generally philological in nature, join with extensive work on locating and publishing texts to provide a workable background for further literary work.

Ḳuṭb's Turkic rendition of Niẓâmî's *H̠üsrev ü Şîrîn* has been the subject of several important studies by Abdülkadir İnan and A. Zajaçzkowski. Zajaçzkowski's literary studies (e.g., "Studia nad Stylistyka i Poetyka . . ." and many others) concentrating on Ḳuṭb are outstanding examples of the type of work possible on early literature. It is unfortunate, however, that such studies are not translated as a matter of course into more widely read languages.

Literary work, beyond the important areas of text edition and translation, is relatively rare for such works as the *Muḥabbet-nâme* of Khwârezmî (cf. Nadzhip, *Khwarezmi, Muhabbet-name* for text, commentary, and Russian translation and the work of Gandjei) and prose works such as the *Nahj al-Farâdis* (cf. Karahan, . . . *Kırk hadîs Toplama, Tercüme ve Şerhleri*) or the Ki*ṣṣaṣ al-Enbiyâ* of Rabguzî (of which there are several Russian translations).

The Kıpçak literature of the Mamluk court of Egypt is also worthy of mention in that there exist significant scholarly studies such as Zajaçzkowski's work on Barka Fakih's appendix to Ḳuṭb's *H̠üsrev ü Şîrîn* and A. Bodrogligeti's studies on Sayf of Saray (e.g., "Note on the Turkish Literature at the Mamluke Court," his edition of the "Gulistân bi't-türkî," and "A Collection of Turkish Poems from the 14th Century," *Acta Or. Hung.* **16** (1963), 245–311).

ÇAĞATAY LITERATURE

It is in the literary language, Çağatay, that Eastern Turkic literature achieves its most brilliant flowering within the Islamic tradition. Although there are indications that Çağatay literature had its roots in the thirteenth and fourteenth centuries (for this and following see Köprülü, "Çağatay edebiyatı" in *İslam Ansiklopedisi*; and Eckmann, "Die Tschaghataische Literatur," in *PTF II*), literary record begins in the fifteenth century, in the last half of which it reached its height in the work of Nevâ'î. Any discussion of Çağatay literature, whether of the literature itself or of literary scholarship, presumes an awareness of Mîr ᶜAlî Şîr Nevâ'î. Himself a poet, literary biographer (*Mecâlis ân-Nefâ'is*), literary theoretician (*Mîzân al-Evzân*), and apologist for

Turkic literature (*Muḥâkemet al-Lugateyn*), Nevâ'î is at once the touchstone of Çağatay literary achievement and the initiator of a scholarly tradition.

Modern scholarship has produced several useful general literary historical works on Çağatay literature beginning with Thúry in Hungary (1904) and including the work of Köprülü (see above and "Dokuzuncu ve onuncu asırlardaki Çağatay şairleri"), E. R. Rustamov's (1963) study on the first half of the fifteenth century, and the wealth of material covered in Bertel's *Navoi*. Individual studies of the littérateurs who precede Nevâ'î appear to be rather few in number. There exist editions of portions of the divan of Sekkâkî [e.g., Eckmann, "Çağatay dili örnekleri III . . .," and *Sakkakiy, Tanlangan Asarlar* (selected works in transcription)], but no outstanding literary study. The poet Lüṭfî has been edited (Ertaylan, *Lûtfi Divanı*); Erkinov has done a brief study of his *meṣnevî* "Gül ü Nevruz" and Samojlovich has studied his *tuyugs*. There are also a few other interesting works on this period and its literature including Rustamov's study of folk elements in the literature (Narodniye Elementi . . .) and articles such as İz's "Yaḳīnī's 'Contest of the Bow and Arrow'."

The bulk of work on Çağatay literature, however, radiates in all directions from the figure of Neva'î, touching, through questions of influences, sources, etc., on most of the other major figures of the literary tradition. The range of influence of the court of Ḥuseyn Bayḳara in Herat gives a strong impetus to far-reaching comparative study insofar as it counted among its frequenters such noted littérateurs as the Persian poet Jâmî and the peripatetic founder of the Mogul Empire, Bâbur. Perhaps the most important factor, however, in the study of Nevâ'î is the national hero status which he enjoys among Uzbeks, including Uzbek scholars, and the high level of support given to research on him in the Uzbek SSR. The Uzbek SSR Fanlar Akademiyasi supports an impressive museum devoted to Nevâ'i, his works and memorabilia, a large number of scholars (*Navoişinos*) devoted to Nevâ'î scholarship, and extensive publication of both texts and studies. It would be impossible to list even a representative sample of Uzbek works on Nevâ'î, though the interested reader might refer to a recent collection of articles (*Navoî va Adabî Ta'sir Masalalari*) for some indication of the quality of Uzbek scholarship.

This great interest has been echoed outside Uzbekistan by some very important literary work. In Turkey, A. S. Levend has published a three-volume edition of Neva'î's literary works with extensive literary, historical, analytical, and bibliographical introductions. There have been studies of Neva'i's literary theory (Samoilovich, "Izvlecheniya iz Traktata po Prosodii," T. Gandjei, "Nava'î on Rhyme . . ."), on Nevâ'î as a critic (Engelke), and an English translation of the *Muḥâkamat al-Lughatain* (Devereaux). Moreover, the above-mentioned works represent only a sample of the available scholarship. (For further reference see the bibliography by Eckmann, *PTF II*, 352–357.)

It is rather more difficult to assess the state of scholarship on Neva'î's contemporaries and successors since the bulk of such work is directly tied to the study of Nevâ'î (see, e.g., Ghanieva, "Navoi va Husain Boikaro," in *Navoî va Adabî Ta'sir Masalari*). Ḥuseyn Bayḳara's *Dîvân* has been published in facsimile by Ertaylan, but there exist no outstanding literary studies dealing solely with his work. There are several translations of the *Bâburnâme* beginning with Pavet deCourteille (1871: French) and including Beveridge (1922: English) and Arat (1943: Turkish). The text, however, is in need of a definitive edition and its value as an example of Çağatay prose has been less than adequately explored (see V. Zahidov, "Babirning faaliyati va adabiy, ilmiy merasi haqida," which appears as an introduction to the new edition of Z. M. Babir, *Babirnâma*).

For the rest of Çağatay literature up to the emergence of modern Uzbek literature there is no body of purely literary scholarship on which to base a general discussion (for text editions, manuscript studies, etc., see *PTF II*). In addition to the general sources cited above, literary historical information for the later period can be found in Mallaev (1955), and Eckmann (1960).

In general, progress in the literary scholarship on Çağatay literature may be described as being as decreasingly concentrated and intense as it is removed in time or place from a center about Nevâ'î. Even the efforts of such outstanding scholars as Ertaylan and Eckmann seem to be no substitute for the interaction of a large body of scholars with similar interests. Such a concerted effort is a rare phenomenon in the study of the Turkic literatures, but one that has produced valuable results.

OTTOMAN LITERATURE

The high literature of the Ottoman period (which for purposes of this section we assume runs from the mid-fifteenth to the mid-nineteenth centuries) is perhaps the most complete and certainly the most prolific outpouring of Islamic-Turkic literature. A broad range of literary documents has been preserved; Turkey is and has been relatively open to literary scholars and yet, for reasons touched upon in the introductory remarks, literary scholarship in this important area is extremely uneven and scarce in proportion to the available materials for study.

Literary historical interest in the Ottoman Empire began rather early. As part of his massive recording of Ottoman history and culture, von Hammer-Purgstall (in 1834–1838) compiled translations from the Ottoman *tezkires* (biographies of poets) into a four-volume history of Ottoman poetry. By the end of the nineteenth century, Smirnov had done similar work in

Russia and soon afterward, E. J. W. Gibb's *History of Ottoman Poetry* appeared in English. Gibb's massive study in many ways typifies the problems of this early literary historical work. The author was a sensitive literary scholar possessed of keen insights into Ottoman poetry, but his work is a first attempt, filled with unfounded judgments, errors of fact, and colored by a very real anti-Ottoman bias fostered by the specter of a floundering empire and the view of Turkish literary reformers. Gibb himself was by no means unaware of the preliminary nature of his work, but it was left to Köprülü to take up the task of improving the accuracy of our literary historical perspective. Köprülü's *Türk Edebiyatı Tarihi* and numerous other studies do indeed resolve innumerable problems of historical fact; however, significantly less progress has been made toward expanding our knowledge of *literary* fact. This literary historical tradition has produced some general works which give a rather clear and up-to-date picture of Turkish literary history such as Banarlı's expansion and popularization of Köprülü's work (*Resimli Türk Edebiyatı Tarihi*), which recently underwent expansion and revision, and Bombaci's *Storia della Letteratura Turca* (1956) revised for the French translation (by I. Melikoff, 1968) and being further expanded for a forthcoming English edition. Moreover, mini-studies of individual poets (studies of the "Life, Art, and Works" variety) can be found in Turkish in such publications as the "Türk Klâsikleri" series (e.g., Karahan, *Nef*ᶜ*î*), which gives a rather broad though superficial literary historical background. The fundamental narrowness and incompleteness of our view of Ottoman literature, however, can be seen only with reference to the state of the art in the nonhistorical areas of literary scholarship.

The study of Ottoman literature is approaching a point at which a significant number of major works are available to scholars in adequate, if in many cases far less than ideal, editions. Such editors as Tarlan (Ahmet Paşa, Necatî, Hayalî, Zatî, Fuzulî), Gölpınarlı (Nedim, Şeyh Galip), Karahan (Figanî), Mashtakova (Mihrî Hatun), and Meredith–Owens (the *tezkire* of ᶜÂşıḳ Çelebî) have made considerable progress in providing a usable corpus of literary works. There still remain serious gaps: for example, editions of the divans of Nefᶜî, Nâbî, Neşâtî, Taşlıcalı Yaḥyâ, etc., a redoing of Bâḳî, editions of several *tezkires*, and many, many other important tasks remain to be done, not to mention previous work which needs redoing. Anthologies (such as İz's *Eski Türk Edebiyatında Nazım* and *Nesir*) make a broader range of works available but are limited both in the size and in the amount of editorial work that can be expected of a compiler who must deal with a large number of unedited manuscripts.

However, edition, like literary history, demands a certain amount of input from other branches of literary study. The edition of Ottoman manuscripts, often numerous, complex, and confused for any single work, necessitates selection, correction, and reconstruction, all of which in turn requires a thorough understanding of the background and theoretical principles underlying the individual, concrete literary work. It is at this level that the relative scarcity of scholarly work is most urgently felt. It is usual that, as a part of the task of editing a work of literature, the editor will do his own literary historical and critical analysis (see, e.g., the Gölpınarlı edition of *Hüsn ü Aşk*, Mashtakova's introduction to *Mikhri Khatun: Divan*, or Timurtaş' edition of Şeyhî's *Hüsrev ü Şirin*. There are serious limitations on such studies, if only that very often our knowledge of an author or work is determined by the point of view of one scholar. In very few cases does there exist a "critical mass" of scholarly work which could provide the editor, literary historian, or student with adequate background material or an insight into literary and comparative literary problems.

As examples of the type of material that does exist, although in insufficient quantity, one might cite Rypka's studies on Bâḳî (e.g., *Baki als Ghazeldichter*; see also Timurtaş on the "Kanunî Mersiyesi") and S̱âbit, or the analyses of Tarlan (Şeyhî, cf. above) and his student Çavuşoğlu (Necatî). There also exist a few studies of genres such as Levend's work on the *şehrengiz*; Tietze's studies on early prose fiction ("Aziz Efendi's Muhayyelât" and "Kerkermeister-Kapitan"); Tarlan on *Tevhid* and *Mucamma*; Tietze and Rossi's work on the literature of Turkish seafarers and James Stewart-Robinson on the *teẕkire*; some thematic studies (e.g., Levend on Leyla and Mecnun, I. Melikoff on themes in epic literatures, T. Halman on poetry and society); a few tentative attempts at formal analysis (e.g., Veselá-Přenosilova on Fuzuli and W. Andrews on Bakî); very few usable works on "poetics" (e.g., Köprülü on *aruz* in *PTF*, Rymkiewicz on rhyme, Banarlı in *Resimli Türk Edebiyatı Tarihi*, new edition); and some recent translations (e.g., Sofi Huri's English translation of Fuzûlî's *Leylâ ve Mejnûn*). In none of these areas, however, is there either a body of work or a producing group of scholars with interacting interests, in some part a reflection of the vastness of the field and the relatively small number of active scholars.

In only one case, that of the sixteenth-century poet, Fuzûlî, who spans the Ottoman and Azeri traditions, is there an adequate and developing body of scholarly study. As in the case of Nevâ'î, Fuzûlî is recognized by Turks in Turkey and especially in Azerî-speaking lands as a (perhaps, *the*) national literary master, somewhat of a rallying point of cultural pride and identity. Thus the efforts of Azeri scholars combined with the work of Turkish and European scholars such as Tarlan, Gölpınarlı, and Bombaci have produced a rather impressive bibliography of literary studies. It is not possible to cite even a sample of the literary work on Fuzûlî here, but the number and range of works on this single figure provide an interesting contrast to the state of the rest of the field and are an indication of what can be done given concentrated scholarly interest. For those interested in specific works, see the bibliography in *PTF* (Caferoğlu, "Die Azerbeischanische Literatur"), the *Fuzûlî Bibliyografyası*, and for a sample of the types of work being done, the collection of articles in *Mehemmed Fuzûlî.*

Beyond the impressive range of studies on Fuzûlî, literary scholarship on the rest of Azeri literature appears to fit the pattern observed elsewhere. There exists a long-standing literary historical tradition including the general works cited above (Smirnov, Krimskiy), as well as work by Köprülü (e.g., *Azeri edebiyatına ait tetkikler*), Hamid Araslı (e.g., *Qadim Edebiyat*), Ahmet Caferoğlu (e.g., *Azerbeycan Dil ve Edebiyatının Dönüm Noktaları*), Minorski ("The Poetry of Shâh İsmâᶜîl"), etc. All other types of literary work, except in the case of Fuzûlî, if they exist at all, are so rare as to be totally inaccessible to the nonspecialist in Azeri literature. (In this regard it is again necessary to point out that my access to work being done in the Soviet Union and especially in Azerbaijan is quite limited.)

FOLK LITERATURE

The high culture Islamic literature of the Turks represents only a part of the literary production of the Turkic peoples. There exists a vast and varied popular tradition with firm roots in pre-Islamic Turkic culture, a tradition that was and is the literary world for millions of Turks, whereas the high culture was the province of a relatively small educated elite.

It is with many trepidations that one approaches the question of the study of Turkic folk literature in a paper of such limited length. On one hand, even a cursory glance at any general bibliography for the study of Turkic folklore (e.g., *PTF II*: the series of articles by P. N. Boratav, İlhan Başgöz, and Helga Anhegger) suggests that doing justice to folk-literary study would demand a paper substantially longer than is contemplated for this whole survey. On the other hand, the study of folk literature is today a somewhat distinct and self-sufficient branch of literary study with its own methodologies, journals, etc., bearing much the same relationship to traditional literary study as ethnomusicology to music, or perhaps political science to history. In the area of Turkish literary study, however, the study of popular literature holds a rather special place. Ignored by the literary elite, overshadowed by the highly sophisticated Islamic tradition, the popular literature of the Turks was not an object of serious scholarly attention until the nineteenth and twentieth centuries. Following the *tanzîmât* period and the subsequent search for national Turkish identity, the folk literature was, in a sense, "discovered" by Turkish littérateurs and scholars as a model for the language, forms, and substance of the "new" Turkish literature. This discovery was in some part precipitated and reinforced by European attitudes and prejudices which tended to see the Turkish adoption of Islamic culture as a sign of national decadence and inferiority. Thus the folk literature became at once a source for the reaffirmation of Turkish national pride and a subject of scholarly study immediately accessible to Westerners and Western methodologies.

At the turn of the century, when Turkish literature began to attract the attention of a body of European scholars, Radloff's work on the folk literature of the Turks of South Siberia (1866–1904) was already available as a model for the study of the popular literature of the Turks in the Near East. Such scholars as Georg Jacob (e.g., *Das Türkische Schattentheater*, 1900; *Türkische Volksliteratur*, 1901), F. Giese (e.g., *Erzahlungen und Lieder aus dem Vilajet Konjah*, 1907) Gordlevskiy (*Obrazts'i Osmanskogo Narodnogo Tvorchestva*, 1916) and Ignacz Kunos (e.g., *Türk Halq Edebiyatı*, 1925) laid the groundwork for serious scholarly consideration of Turkish folk literature. In Turkey itself, the greatest impetus toward the "legitimization" of folk literature derived from the work of Köprülü (for his general theory see "Türk edebiyatı tarihinde usul," and for folk literature, *Türk Saz Şairleri*). Köprülü's many and varied publications were instrumental in opening the question of Turkish contributions to Near Eastern literature and in demonstrating the value of literary research on the popular literature. The accessibility of popular literature to Turkish audiences and its amenability to translation for non-Turks has since resulted in a considerable body of scholarly publications covering a wide range of folk literary forms. Examples of Western studies might include the work of Hellmut Ritter (*Karagös*), Martinovich (*Turkish Theater*), and A. Bombaci ("Ortaoyunu") on Turkish theater, as well as that of Otto Spies (*Volksbücher*), I. Melikoff (*Melik Danişmend*), and Andreas Tietze (*Aziz Efendi*). In Turkey there exist several special periodicals devoted entirely or in part to folklore (*Türk Folklor Araştırmaları, Türk Etnografya Dergisi*) and other periodicals which have given special attention to folk literature. Moreover, it is Turkish scholars who have rightfully taken the lead in the study of folk literature. Certainly the outstanding scholar in the field has been Pertev Naili Boratav, who has published a large number of works in Turkish (e.g., *Folklor ve Edebiyat*) and in French (e.g., "Les recits populaires . . ."). The range of work coming out of Turkey includes studies of individual authors such as those by S. N. Ergun (Karacaoğlan, Hengâmî, etc.), Öztelli (Köroğlu, Dadaloğlu), Gölpınarlı (Kaygusuz Abdal); studies of special forms and genres such as Metin And's outstanding work on the Turkish theater (e.g *Geleneksel Türk Tiyatrosu*, and the English edition, *A History of Theatre and Popular Entertainment in Turkey*, Ankara, 1963–1964), S. N. Gerçek, *Türk Temaşası*, A. Caferoğlu, *Toplamalar*, etc., E. B. Şapolyo, *Türk Efsaneleri*, E. G. Güney, *Halk Türküleri*, and T. Alangu, . . . *Külhanbey edebityatı*; and analytical studies such as those by S. E. Siyavuşgil (*Karagöz, Psikolojik bir Deneme*), M. Kaplan ("Türk destanında Alp tipi"), and A. Caferoğlu ("Dede

Korkut hikâyelerinin antroponim yapısı"). Moreover, the international community of interest in folklore and general agreement on purposes and methodologies has resulted in outstanding work by Turks working outside of Turkey (e.g., İlhan Başgöz and P. N. Boratav) and also in some outstanding examples of scholarly cooperation such as Zhirmunskiy and Zarifov on the Uzbek epic; N. K. Chadwick and Zhirmunskiy (Oral Epics of Central Asia); F. Sümer, A. E. Uysal, and W. S. Walker (The Book of Dede Korkut); and Uysal and Walker (Tales Alive in Turkey).

This brief and incomplete sampling of work done on Turkish folk literature by no means gives more than an indication of the quality and quantity of work being produced in this area. For example, substantial work being done on Azeri and Uzbek folk literature has not been mentioned. The general picture given, however, appears to be reasonably accurate. There exists considerable interest and, because this field of scholarly study is a rather recent phenomenon, there seem to be few obstacles (in the form of traditional approaches) to wide-ranging comparative study, new methodologies, and creative approaches. Thus folk literary study is one of the areas in which the study of the Turkic literatures is making substantial and satisfactory progress.

MODERN TURKISH LITERATURE

Turkish literature, like Turkish history itself, has been marked by upheaval and transformation since the mid-nineteenth century. Halycon periods and continuities notwithstanding, Turkey has witnessed, since the *Tanẓimat*, vast political changes (from absolute monarchy to constitutional government, from multiracial and multinational theocratic empire to more homogeneous, unitary nation-state and republic, from one-party rule to parliamentary democracy) as well as evolutionary and revolutionary cultural changes from Islamic Ottoman to nationalism and Westernization. The literature of the same period has been a corollary, a catalyst, and an embodiment of all these changes in addition to its own internal transformation.

The impact of European culture and literature has given modern Turkey new genres, forms, values, norms, styles, philosophical and ideological concepts, aesthetic principles, methods, and myths. Consequently, a heavily Westernized Turkish literature with a new *Weltanschauung* has evolved. As Turkey enters its second half-century as a republic, many of its literary works may be compared favorably with their European or American counterparts, although much of its output is still in a developing stage. Among the genres adopted from the West are drama, the novel, and journalism, as well as such forms of literary scholarhip and criticism as general histories, critical anthologies, thematic studies, period surveys, and critical monographs on authors and works. The body of scholarly and critical surveys has gained size, momentum, and stature from the *Tanzimat* to the present day. After centuries of "critical vacuum" except for the *tezkeres*, Turkish literature is finally beginning to acquire critical tools based primarily on a systematic survey of Turkish literary history in its entirety and on a broad appreciation of world literature. As of now, however, this development is only in a rather rudimentary stage—paralleled, one might add, by the development of study of this literature throughout the world.

The outgrowth of a recent Turkish literature on generally European models not only resulted in an explosion of literary scholarship in Turkey but facilitated the burgeoning of study in Europe as well. Political as well as literary interests made Germany an early and continuing source of work on recent Turkish literature. Early literary historical studies by authors such as Otto Hachtmann ("Die türkische Literatur des zwanzigsten Jahrhunderts," 1916) and Paul Horn (*Geschichte der türkische Moderne*, 1902) were followed by a large number of studies such as the translations and studies of Hartmann (e.g., "Ja'kub Kadri," 1918), A. Fischer ("Übersetzungen und Texte aus der neuosmanischen Literatur," 1921), and Otto Spies (e.g., the translations in *Das Blutgeld* . . . 1942, and the literary historical survey, *Die türkische Prosaliteratur der Gegenwart*). This rather intense German interest was echoed, to a somewhat lesser degree, in the rest of Europe by such works as those of Saussey (e.g., *Prosateurs Turcs Contemporains*, 1935) and E. Rossi (e.g., "Odierne tendenzi letterarie e politiche . . .," 1929).

In form and content the study of Turkish literature in Europe continues, in general, to follow earlier models. Translation, especially into German, continues to be popular (see, e.g., Yüksel Pazarkaya's recent anthology of German translations of modern Turkish lyrics), as do studies of the work of individual authors (such as V. Dinescu-Szekely's study on the satire of Aziz Nesin). The Soviet Union has also begun to produce an important body of work on modern Turkish literature, perhaps best exemplified by the work of L. O. Al'kaeva (e.g., on Tevfik Fikret and Ömer Seyfettin).

In English the development of interest in modern Turkish literature is rather more recent—retarded perhaps by the untimely death of Gibb before he could complete his work on the more recent period of Turkish literary history. However, a growing body of translated works has become available. In England Derek Patmore published a short anthology of pre-1945 poetry entitled *The Star and the Crescent*, and the monthly *Modern Poetry in Translation* devoted its Spring 1971 issue to Turkish poetry. In the United States, *The Literary Review* published two special issues (1960 and 1972) featuring a generous sampling of modern Turkish literature. There also exist occasional translations of Turkish literature in such journals as *Literature East and West*, *Stand*, etc., and translations are regularly reviewed in *Books Abroad*. Some novels such as Mahmut Makal's *Bizim Köy* (trans. Sir Wyndham Deedes, *A Village in Anatolia*), Reşat Nuri Güntekin's *Çalıkuşu* (trans. Deedes, *The Autobiography of a Turkish Girl*), and Yaşar Kemal's *İnce Memet* (trans. Edouard Roditi, *Memed, my Hawk*) and several others (e.g., *Wind from the Plain*, trans. Thilda Kemal, and *They Burn the Thistles*, trans. M. Platon) have been translated. Moreover, there are also several translations of poetry available in book form, such as Talat Sait Halman's translations of Fazıl Hüsnü Dağlarca's *Selected Poems* and Orhan Veli Kanık's *I am Listening to Instanbul*, or Taner Baybars' translation of Nazım Hikmet (e.g., *The Moscow Symphony*).

Critical studies in English are, as elsewhere, rather limited. One might cite such studies as Kemal Karpat's "Social Themes in Contemporary Turkish Literature," Carole Rathbun's book, *The Village in the Turkish Novel and Short Story 1920–1955*, and Halman's long article, "Poetry and Society: The Turkish Experience."

In the West interest in recent Turkish literature has only taken a few basic steps toward the development of broad-ranging study. Beyond the types of work mentioned, there exists little as yet, especially in the area of critical analysis on the basis of modern literary theory. Correspondence with scholars and students in the field, however, indicates that there is considerable work taking place in exactly those areas that have been hitherto negleced.

The greatest volume of work on Turkish literature is, of course, being done in Turkey and it is the development of native Turkish scholarship that will, in the end, have the largest influence both on our understanding of recent Turkish literature and on the development of the literature itself.

In the area of biography and bibliography the early contributions of Bursalı Mehmet Tahir (*Osmanlı Müellifleri*) and İnal on Ottoman literature have given rise to such works as the useful literary "Who's Who" of Behçet Necatigil. Moreover, the number of bibliographical surveys of periods, authors, schools, and themes has increased substantially in recent years. There is, however, no comprehensive encyclopedia of Turkish literature. Turkish scholars have also expended a vast effort to compile anthologies, collections, compendia, etc. There is virtually an industry of anthologies in Turkey. Innumerable collections from different periods, selections from individual authors, anthologies devoted to specific themes, etc., have inundated the market. In the tradition of early post-*Tanẓîmât* anthologies of Ottoman and transitional literature such as Ebüzziya Tevfîk's *Nümûne-i Edebiyyât-i 'Os̱mâniyye*, more recent works give a good picture of the best of modern literature (see, e.g., Orhan Burian's influential annotated anthology of twentieth-century poetry and Ümit Yaşar Oğuzcan's recent anthology of modern poetry). Among the best critical anthologies are Kenan Akyüz' *Batı Tesirinde Türk Şiiri* (Turkish Poetry Under Western Influence), the anthologies of modern fiction by

Tahir Alangu and Cevdet Kudret, and İsmail Habib Sevük's works on Turkish literature since the *Tanzîmât* (e.g., *Tanzimattan beri Türk Edebiyatı tarihi*).

In the area of general surveys of period and genre the outstanding example is Ahmet Hamdi Tanpınar's superb *Ondokuzuncu Asır Türk Edebiyatı Tarihi*, perhaps the best literary historical analysis of any period of Turkish literature. Nonetheless, solid literary historical work is evidenced as well in numerous monographs and essays on individual poets. Tanpınar's study of the neo-classical poet Yahya Kemal Beyatlı and Mehmet Kaplan's book on Tanpınar's poetry are oustanding examples of a genre of scholarship in which there is a plethora of useful works (see also Mustafa Kutlu, *Sabahattin Ali*, Kaplan, *Namık Kemal*, and for further reference see *PTF II*).

The *Tanzîmât and Servet-i Fünûn* periods in the nineteenth century, striving to introduce innovation in Turkish literature, produced a substantial body of critical writing, discussion of aesthetic principles, and argument about the function of literature. Most of this type of writing was influenced by French critics and at times sounded like direct translation or seemed to endeavor to reinvent what had already been invented elsewhere. Yet, particularly in terms of the challenge posed to traditional aesthetics and the new intellectual dimensions it introduced, the literary cricitism of such littérateurs as Namık Kemal, Şinasî, Ziya Paşa, and Recaizade Ekrem, served an effective function. This significant phenomenon has not yet been the subject of any systematic study, perhaps because the material is scattered insofar as it appeared not in book form but in magazines, newspapers, correspondence, etc. It is indeed regrettable that no one has made even a preliminary study of the development of Turkish literary criticism.

The dominant mode of criticism in Turkey is the essay form and the brief article, primarily because critical analysis as a *scholarly* methodology is no more widely recognized in Turkey than it is by the bulk of Western scholars of Turkish literature. Nonetheless, virtually all major literary figures and many outstanding scholars have utilized this type of criticism. Its most effective practitioners, however, have been the professional critics led by Nurullah Ataç, perhaps the most influential Turkish critic who dominated the literary scene in the 1940s and 1950s. Orhan Burian, a professor of English literature, held the promise of becoming the Turkish literary critic *par excellence*, but his death at the age of 39 terminated a brilliant and promising career. The critical essay, however, remains a highly popular genre in the hands of such competent critics as Yaşar Nabi Nayır and the poet-critic Melih Cevdet Anday. Tanpınar (e.g., *Edebiyat Üzerine Makaleler*) was a master of this form whose insights were strengthened by a vast knowledge of classical Turkish and French literature. The movement toward methodological soundness is exemplified by Asım Bezirci, who stresses textual analysis and concrete criteria, as well as by his sometime collaborator Hüseyin Cöntürk, who emphasizes "scientific methodology" in literary evaluation.

The single outstanding example of a major scholarly critical analysis of concrete works is the two-volume *Şiir Tahlilleri* of Mehmet Kaplan in which the author presents close critical readings of individual poems by leading poets of the nineteenth and twentieth centuries. In many ways this work represents a solitary step in a direction which still lies in the future for Turkish literary study. Competent methodological approaches in the area of criticism must be located and applied if the study of Turkish literature is to progress.

In general, impressionistic criticism continues to hold sway, although other approaches are being tried (see, e.g., Tatarlı and Mollof, *Marksist Açıdan Türk Romanı*). It is felt, however, that the language still lacks sophisticated critical terminology and most of the critics seem unable to deal with fundamental aesthetic matters on a sound methodological basis.

In this section, no attempt has been made to represent anything but a very general impression of the work on and in recent Turkish literature. In fact, the generous comments, analyses, and references provided by Professor Halman for the production of this section have been considerably cut and altered to fit both the scope of the paper as a whole and my own views. In no way is Professor Halman to be held accountable for anything but those valuable points of information which I allowed to remain. Moreover, it is with some deep regret that there is insufficient space to provide a similar discussion of the recent literatures of the Uzbeks, Azeri Turks, etc. These literatures and their recent development are so far out of my area of competence and so deserving of serious scrutiny that they are omitted altogether, with the hope that this intentional oversight will stimulate some qualified scholar to remedy the deficiency.

CONCLUSIONS

Literary Historical

As can be seen throughout the survey, the bulk of work on the Turkic literatures has been literary historical in nature. In many areas, however, even our literary historical tools show serious weak points. In most literary historical works, careful attention to historical/biographical detail contrasts sharply with a very loose, impressionistic approach to the literature. Quite often the only critical judgments rendered are in the form of direct quotations from *tez̲kere* writers; otherwise the evaluation seldom goes beyond one or two general characterizations based not on penetrating analysis or comparative study, but on long since canonized judgments of hazy provenance. Both in the Near East and the West the study of the Turkic literatures *qua* literature is living some 50–75 years in the past; the basic tools, methodologies, and training are philological rather than literary, and the prospects for attracting and/or training students interested in literature are only fair.

The above comments are not intended to discredit or deny the value of literary history. If the non-Turkic world is to be made aware of Turkic literature, if the unfounded, invidious comparisons to Persian and Arabic literatures are to be replaced by some semblance of fact, and if Turkic literature is rightfully to be recognized as one of the world's broadest-ranging and most interesting literatures, then the totality of specialized scholarly work must from time to time be summed up in its historical context and be made publicly available. In this regard the Burrill translation of Bombaci, forth-coming works by Fahir İz and Talat Halman, and such publications as the recent (Spring, 1973) *Review of National Literatures* should fill a yawning gap in English language histories of Turkic literature. Moreover, Turkey has produced some excellent literary histories (e.g., Kocatürk, Tanpınar, etc.)—all of which will help to provide both the scholar and the general reader with an up-to-date background for literary appreciation. Up-to-date, however, is a long step or a journey of many steps from complete or definitive, and insofar as literary history, especially general literary history, represents a summing up of many aspects of literary study it cannot truly progress until there is development of the field over a broad front. Thus the most deleterious gaps in literary historical study are the result not so much of failures on the part of literary historians but of the failure of the field both to develop interests beyond the philological/historical and to keep up with the growth of literary study in general over the past several decades.

Critical, Analytical

It is in the area of literary criticism and analysis that the gap between literary study in general and the study of the Turkic literatures is the greatest. One would expect this area to show the largest disparity between the work of Western and Near Eastern scholars, assuming that Western scholars have more direct and almost unavoidable contacts with recent developments in criticism, analysis, and the interesting questions raised by modern linguistics. With the exception of a few isolated (hence as yet unimportant) instances, however, this is not generally the case. If many Turkish scholars have understandably shown little awareness of recent developments, the number of Turkic literature specialists in the West who have an interest in the work of, let us say, Richards, Frye, Burke, Eliot, or even Levi-Strauss is likewise extremely small. How many advanced degrees in Turkic literature, after all, require any knowledge whatsoever of modern literary criticism and analysis?

A hard look at the future of the study of the Turkic literatures in the West must inevitably face the question: What can the nonnative bring by way of valuable contributions to the study of this literature? What he obviously cannot bring is an intuitive appreciation in terms of a hazy aesthetics, that is, of the type: The work is beautiful, moving, excites the spirit of the Turk, etc. . . . Nor can he count upon being in the forefront in many areas such as philology, text edition, and linguistic analysis, for these areas will and should become the strongest points of native scholarship. One thing that the Western scholar can offer is direct contact between the rapidly expanding field of literary criticism and theory and the study of Turkic literature.

Many aspects of Turkic literature, especially the art, poetry, and prose of the Islamic period, would benefit from new and, perhaps, innovative scrutiny —if for no other reason than to test the validity of the many pejorative and unproven axioms which make Turkic literature a far less than equal component of the study of Near Eastern literatures in general. It is certainly well past time for Turkic literature to cease being a backwater within a backwater as far as Western scholarship is concerned. The answer, however, would seem to lie not in more concentrated intellectual inbreeding, but in an attempt by scholars to reach out into the world of literary study and make other scholars aware of the unique and interesting challenges offered by the Turkic experience. If the methodologies of modern literary criticism and analysis are applicable to Turkic literature (which is undoubtedly the case with post-Tanzimat and folk literature), then they should be learned and applied. If not, the criticism and analysis are lacking in some fundamental way and it is the duty of literary scholars to point out and remedy the deficiencies. It is neither necessary nor desirable for the world of Turkic literary scholarship to remain limited and restricted. If specialists in the literature of the Turks are urged to speak to a broad audience of literary scholars, comparativists, and students interested in literature, and can show some familiarity with generally interesting problems, then the field cannot help but benefit, both intrinsically and in terms of expanded enrollments, more employment opportunities, and a more appropriate level of interest in Turkic literature.

Literary Theoretical

What has been said in the preceding paragraphs is equally relevant to work on literary theory. In fact, a very striking lack of literary theoretical work has been a real and formidable obstacle to progress in the study of many aspects of Turkic literature. For example, Köprülü has made several interesting observations on Islamic-Turkish prosody. (cf. *PTF II*, "Aruz") but there has since been little if any creative thought given to the significance of Köprülü's data. Likewise the problems of "poetics," of metaphor, simile, etc., are dealt with in a very traditional way, ignoring very powerful indications that the Perso-Arab tradition was only nominally related to the facts of Turkic literature in any case. Moreover, even the views of Turkish theoreticians of the more recent era (e.g., Muallim Naci, Ahmet Cevdet, Recaizade Ekrem, etc.), have not been the subjects of major scholarly inquiry. In short, specialists are generally aware of the tenuousness of the relationship between Perso-Arab theory and the facts of Turkic literature, but there has been no concentrated effort to explore or discuss the differences and consequently no clear picture has emerged of the distinctively Turkic contribution to Islamic literature.

Other Areas

The problems involved in producing materials for literary study must also be mentioned. Reliable, scholarly editions of major works have always been and remain among the prime desiderata of the field. At present, the major obstacles to such work appear to be excessive cost and limited facilities for the production of texts in Arabic script. In Turkey and the rest of the Turkic world, the needs of a relatively large reading public result in almost exclusive publication of transliterated texts with minimal scholarly annotation and critical apparatus. In the West, scholars wait years for the appearance of editions which are in the end almost prohibitively expensive—if indeed the scholar can find someone to publish his text. Several scholars have indicated that they have manuscripts ready to publish but cannot find any reasonable means to do so. It would seem that some concerted effort is needed on the part of Turkish literature specialists to explore the possibilities for the funding and production of text editions. Such organized effort could also be directed toward the production of a journal or journals devoted to literary study and the exploration of critical and theoretical problems.

Outside the Near East the field of Turkic literature is, and will likely continue to be, relatively small; if dissipated, the work of individual scholars has only minimal effect. Whereas some areas (Eastern Europe and the Soviet Union, for example) have centralized institutes which bring together scholars and library resources, such concerted effort on a national scale is rare in the West and especially in the United States and Canada. If progress is to be made, at least some consideration should be given to organizing a body of literature specialists, perhaps about a series of long- and short-term projects (e.g., a text edition series, a journal, or a volume or volumes of collected articles), with the intention of increasing productivity in the field and stimulating contacts and cooperation within a widely scattered scholarly community. The needs of the field are many and the number of producing scholars are few and widely diverging in their priorities. However, if some sense of general purpose and urgency can be aroused in the scholarly community, it is quite conceivable that substantial progress will be made and the Turkic literatures will achieve the recognition and honest appraisal that they deserve.

ACKNOWLEDGMENT

Special appreciation is herewith rendered to those scholars who responded to requests for information with their valuable comments and criticisms, to James Stewart-Robinson and William Hickman for their additional assistance, and especially to Talat Halman, who put together the post-Tanzimat section and gave generously of his time and knowledge during the preparation of the rest of the survey. The author assumes sole responsibility for the many omissions and for any critical commentary.

BIBLIOGRAPHY

Key to Categorization

(*a*) Literary historical.
(*b*) Literary critical.
(*c*) Literary theoretical.
(*d*) Philological, lexicographical.
(*e*) Texts, divans, anthologies.
(*f*) Translations.
(*g*) Bibliographical, biobibliographical.

Akyüz, K. *Batı Tesirinde Türk Şiiri.* Ankara: Güney, 1953. (2nd ed. 1970). (e)

Alangu, T. *Cumhuriyetten Sonra Hikâye ve Roman I-III.* Istanbul: Istanbul, 1959–1965. (e)

Al'Kaeva, L. O. "Tevfik Fikret," *KSIV*, **22** (1956), 45–55. (a)

And, M. *Geleneksel Türk Tiyatrosu.* Ankara: Bilgi, 1969. (a)

Andrews, W. G. "A critical interpretive approach to the Ottoman Turkish gazel," *IJMES*, **4** (1973), 97–110. (b)

Araslı, H. *Fedakâr Sair* (*Imadeddin Nesimi*). Baku: Azeb. filial AN, 1942. (a)

———. *Qadim Edebiyyat.* Baku: Azeb. filial AN, 1937. (a)

Arat, R. R. *Eski Türk Şiiri.* Ankara: Türk Tarih Kurumu, 1965. (a)

———, ed. *Kutadgu Bilig:* I, Text. Istanbul: Millî Eğitim, 1947. II, Translation. Ankara: Türk Tarih Kurumu, 1959. (e)

———, ed. *Vekayi: Babür'ün Hatıratı I & II.* Ankara: Türk Tarih Kurumu, 1943–1946. (e)

Aslanov, V. I. "Ahmedi i ego 'Iskender-name'," *NAA*, **4** (1966), 161–175. (a)

Babinger, F. "Ašyq Pašas Gharîb-name," *MSOS*, **31** (1928), 91–97. (a)

Babir, Z. M. *Babirnama*, new ed. Tashkent: Izd-vo, 1960. (e)

Banarlı, N. S. *Resimli Türk Edebiyatı Tarihi.* Istanbul: Yedigün, nd. New ed. (fasc. 1–6). Istanbul: M. E. B. Devlet Kitapları, 1971. (a)

Baybars, T., trans. *The Moscow Symphony and Other Poems by Nazım Hikmet.* Chicago: Swallow, 1970. (f)

Bertel's, E. *Navoi.* Moscow-Leningrad: Izd-vo Akademiîa nauk sssr, 1948. (a)

———. "Uygurskaya Poema 'Kutadgu Bilig' i ee Znachenye," *Şark Hakkikatı*, **1–2**. Tashkent: NYPL, 1949. (d)

Beveridge, A. S. *The Bābur-nāme in English.* London: Luzac, 1922. (f)

Bezirci, A. *Nurullah Ataç.* Istanbul: Ak, 1965. (b)

Birge, J. K. "Yunus Emre, Turkey's great poet of the People." In *Macdonald Presentation Volume.* Princeton: Univ. Press, 1933, pp. 43–60. (a)

Bodrogligeti, A. "Notes on the Turkish Literature at the Mameluk Court," *Act. Orient. Hung.*, **14** (1962), 273–282. (a)

———. *Sayf-i Sarāyī's Gulistān bi't-türkī.* Bloomington: Indiana, 1969. (e)

Bombaci, A. "Il poema turco 'Leila e Mejnun' di Fuzūlī," *OM*, **23** (1943), 337–356. (a)

———. "Kutadgu Bilig hakkında bazı Mülâhazalar." In *Fuad Köprülü Armağanı.* Istanbul: O. Yalçın, 1953, pp. 65–75. (a)

———. "Ortaoyunu," *Wiener Zeitschrift für die Kunde des Morgenlandes*, **56** (1960), 285–297. (a)

———. *Storia della Letteratura Turca.* Milan: Nuova accademia editrice, ca. 1956. French trans.: *Histoire de la Littérature Turque.* I. Mélikoff, trans. Paris: C. Klincksieck, 1968. (a)

Boratav, P. N. *Folklor ve Edebiyat.* Vol. I. Istanbul: R. Ulusoğlu, 1939. Vol. II. Ankara: R. Ulusoğlu, 1945. (a)

———. "Les récits populaires turcs (hikâye) et les 'Mille et une Nuits,'" *Oriens*, **1** (1948), 63–73. (a)

Brocklemann, C. "Alttürkestanische Volkspoesie," Vols. I and II. *Asia Major Probeband (Hirth Anniversary Volume).* 1924, pp. 3–24, 24–34. (e)

Burian, O. *Denemeler-Eleştiriler.* Istanbul: Can, 1964. (b)

———. *Kurtuluştan Sonrakiler.* Istanbul: Yücel, 1946. (e)

Burrill, K. R. F. *The Quatrains of Nesimi.* Paris-The Hague: Mouton, 1972. (e)

Caferoğlu, A. *Anadolu Ağızlarından Toplamalar.* Istanbul: Bürhaneddin, 1943. (a, e)

———. *Azerbaycan Dil ve Edebiyatının Dönüm Noktaları.* Ankara: Yeni Cezaevi, 1953. (a)

———. "Dede Korkut hikâyelerinin antroponim yapısı," *TDAY* (1959), 58–80. (b)

Çavuşoğlu, M. *Necâti Bey Dîvânı'nin Tahlili.* Istanbul: Millî Eğitim, 1971. (b)

Chadwick, N. K. and V. Zhirmunskiy. *Oral Epics of Central Asia.* London: Cambridge U. P., 1969. (a, f)

Cöntürk, H. and A. Bezirci. *Günlerin Götürdüğü-Getirdiği.* Istanbul: Ataç, 1962. (b)

Deedes, Sir W., trans. *A Village in Anatolia* (by Mahmut Makal). London: Vallentine, Mitchel, 1954. (f)

Devereaux. R., trans. *Muḥākamat al-lughatain* (by Nevâ'î). Leiden: Brill, 1966. (f)

Dinescu-Szekely, V. "La prose satirique d'Aziz Nesin," *Studia et acta or.*, **5–6** (1967), 138–204. (b)

Edib Ahmed b. Mahmud Yükneki. *Atabetü 'l-Hakayık.* R. R. Arat, ed. Istanbul: Ateş, 1951. (e)

Eckmann, J. "Çağatay dili örnekleri III, Sekkâkî divanından parçalar," *TDED*, **12** (1963), 157–174. (e)

———. "Çağatay edebiyatının son devri," *TDAY.* (1960), 59–62. (a)

Engelke, I. "ᶜAli Sir Nava'i als Kritiker der Verse des Sultans Ḥusain Bāiqarā.," *UAJ* (1970), 91–113. (a)

Ergun, S. N. *Karacaoğlan. Hayatı ve Şiirleri.* Istanbul: İkbal, 1933. (a)

———. *Beşiktaşlı Gedâyî.* Istanbul: Sühulet, 1933. (a)

Erkinov, S. "Lutfiy va unig 'Gul va Navruz' dastani," *Şark Yulduzi*, **25**, 2 (1957), 99–113; **25**, 3 (1957), 78–99. (a)

Ertaylan, İ. H., ed. *Litfû Divanı.* Istanbul: Edebiyat Fakültesi, 1960. (e)

———, ed. *Türk Edebiyatı Örnekleri V. Divan-i Sultan Hüseyn Mirza Baykara "Hüseyini"* (facs.). Istanbul: Burhaneddin Erenler, 1946. (e)

Fischer, A. "Übersetzungen und Texte aus der neuosmanischen Literatur. I: Die Dichtungen Mehmed Emins." In *Morgenländische Texte und Forschungen I*, vol. 3, Leipzig: Pfeiffer, 1921. (e, f)

Fuzûlî Bibliyografyası. Ankara: Maarif, n.d. (g)

Gandjei, T. "Il Muhabbat-nāme di Hōrazmi," *Ann. Inst. Or. Napoli*, **6** (1954–1956), 131–161; Part II (trans.), *AION*, **7** (1957), 135–166. (a)

Gerçek, S. N. *Türk Temaşası. Meddah, Karagöz, Ortaoyunu.* Istanbul: Kannaat, 1942. (a)

Gibb, E. J. W. *A History of Ottoman Poetry I-VI.* London: Luzac, 1900–1909. (a)

Giese, F. *Materialien zur Kenntnis des anatolischen Turkisch. I: Erzählungen und Lieder aus dem Vilajet Konjah.* New York: Halle, 1907. (e)

Goodsell, F., ed. *Ḳādī Burhāneddin'in Gazel ve Rubâ'iyyātından bir Ḳısmı ve Tuyugları.* Istanbul: Matbaa-i Âmire, 1922. (e)

Gölpınarlı, A. "Aşık Paşanın Şiirleri," *TM*, **5** (1935), 87–100. (a)

———. *Kaygusuz Abdal, Hatayi, Kul Himmet.* Istanbul: Varlık, 1953. (a)

———, ed. *Nedim: Divan.* Istanbul: Inkilâp, 1951. (2nd ed., 1972.) (e)

———, ed. *Seyh Galip: Hüsn ü Aşk.* Istanbul: As, 1968. (e)

———, ed. *Yunus Emre: Risâlat al-Nushiyya ve Divan.* Istanbul: S. Garan, 1965. (e)

Gordlevskiy, V. *Obrzts'i Osmanskogo Narodnogo Tvorchestva.* Moscow: Tip. "Krestnago kalendaria," 1916. (a)

Güntekin, Reşat Nuri. *The Autobiography of a Turkish Girl.* Sir W. Deedes, trans. London: Allen & Unwin, 1949. (f)

Güney, E. C. *Halk Türküleri.* Vol. I, 2nd ed. Istanbul: Yeni, 1956. Vol. II. Istanbul: Yeni, 1956. (a)

Hachtmann, O. "Die Türkische Literatur des zwanzigsten Jahrhunderts." In *Die Literatur des Ostens in Einzeldarstellungen IV.* Leipzig: C. F. Amelangs, 1916. (a)

Halman, T. S., trans. *Fazıl Hüsnü Dağlarca: Selected Poems.* Pittsburgh: Univ. of Pittsburgh Press, 1969. (f)

———, trans. *I am listening to Istanbul: Selected Poems of Orhan Veli Kanık.* New York: Corinth, 1971. (f)

———, trans. *The Humanist Poetry of Yunus Emre.* Istanbul: Matbaasi, 1972. (f)

———. "Poetry and Society: The Turkish Experience." In *Modern Near East: Literature and Society.* New York: Center for Near Eastern Studies, N.Y.U., 1971. (a)

Hammer-Purgstall, J. von. *Geschichte der osmanischen Dichtkunst bis auf unsere Zeit.* Vols. I-IV. Perth: C. A. Hartleben, 1836–1838. (a)

———. (On the "Rebabname"), *Jahrbücher der Literatur,* **48** (1829), 103–120. (a)

Hartmann, R. "Ja'kub kadri. Ein moderner türkischer Erzähler," *WI,* **5** (1918), 254–282. (a)

Hartmann, M. "Zur metrische Formen des Kutadgu Bilik," *KSZ,* **3** (1902), 141–153. (b)

Horn, Paul. *Geschichte der türkischen Moderne.* Leipzig: C. F. Amelangs, 1902. (a)

Huri, S. *Leylā and Mejnūn* (trans. from Fuzūli). London: Allen & Unwin, 1970. (f)

İnal, İbnülemin Mahmud Kemal. *Son Asır Türk Şairleri.* Vols. 1-12. Istanbul: Orhaniyye, 1930–1942. (a)

İnan, A. "Kutub'un Husrev ve Şirin'inden örnekler," *TDB,* **3** (1951), 14–15. (e)

İz, F. *Eski Türk Edebiyatında Nazım I-II.* Istanbul: Küçükaydın, 1966–1967. (e).

———. *Eski Türk Edebiyatında Nesir I.* Istanbul: Osman Yalçın, 1964. (e)

———. "Yaḳīnī's 'Contest of the Arrow and the Bow'." In *Nemeth Armağani.* Ankara: Türk Tarih Kurumu, 1962, pp. 267–287. (a)

Jacob, G. *Das türkische Schattentheater.* Berlin: Mayer & Müller, 1900. (a)

———. *Türkische Volksliteratur.* Berlin: Mayer & Müller, 1901. (a)

Kaplan, M. *Namık Kemal.* Istanbul: I. Horoz, 1948. (a)

———. *Tanpınarın Şiir Dünyası.* Istanbul: Baha, 1963. (a, b)

———. "Türk destanında Alp tipi." *Zeki Velidi Toğan'a Armağan* (1950–1955), 204–213. (b)

Karahan, A. *Figânîve Divançesi.* Istanbul: Edebiyat Fakütesi, 1966. (e)

———. *Nef'i.* Istanbul: Varlık, 1954. (a, e)

———. *Islâm-Türk Edebiyatında Kırk Hadîs Toplama, Tercüme ve Şerhleri.* Istanbul: I. Horoz, 1954. (a)

Karpat, K. H. "Social Themes in Contemporary Turkish Literature," *MEJ,* **14** (1960), 29–44; 153–168. (a, b)

Kemal, Thilda, trans. *Wind from the Plain* (by Y. Kemal). London: Collins and Harvill, 1963. (f)

Kocatürk, V. M. *Türk Edebiyatı Tarihi.* Ankara: Edebiyat *Yayınevi,* 1964. (a)

Köprülü (Zâde), M. F. "Anatolische Dichter in der Seldschukenzeit. i. Sejjad Hamza. ii. Ahmed Faqīh," *KCA,* **1** (1921–1925), 183–190; **2** (1926–1932), 20–38. (a)

———. *Azerî Edebiyatına ait Tetkikler.* Baku, 1926. (a)

———. *Türk Edebiyatında İlk Mutasavvıflar.* Istanbul: Matbaa-i Âmire, 1918. (a)

———. *Türk Edebiyatı Tarihi.* Istanbul: Millî, 1926–1928. (a)

———. "Türk Edebiyatı Tarihinde Usul." In *Edebiyat Araştırmaları.* Ankara: Türk Tarih Kurumu, 1966. (a)

———. *Türk Dili Ve Edebiyatı Hakkında Araştırmalar.* Istanbul: Kanaat, 1934. (a)

———. *Türk Saz Şairleri.* Vols. 1–5, 2nd ed. Ankara: Güven, 1962–1965. (a, e)

Kudret, C. *Pir Sultan Abdal.* Istanbul: Yeni, 1965. (a)

———. *Türk Edebiyatında Hikâye ve Roman.* Vols. I-II, 2nd ed. Ankara: Varlık, 1965–1968. (e)

Kunos, I. *Türk Halq Edebiyatı.* Istanbul: Ikbal, 1925. (a)

———. "Egy török nyelvemlekek," *Nyelvtud. Közlem.*, **22** (1892), 480–497. (a)

Levend, A. S. *Ali Şir Nevaî.* Vol. 1. Ankara: Türk Tarih Karumu, 1965. *Divanlar.* Vol. 2. Ankara: Türk Tarih Karumu, 1966. *Hamse.* Vol. 3. Ankara: Türk Tarih Karumu, 1967. (e)

———. *Arap, Fars ve Türk Edebiyatında Leyla ve Mecnun Hikâyesi.* Ankara: Türk Tarih Kurumu, 1959. (b)

———. "Aşık Paşa'nın bilinmiyen iki mesnevisi. Fakrname ve Vasf-i hal," *TDB* (1953), 205–255. (a)

———. *Türk Edebiyatında Şehr-engizler ve Şehr-engizlerde Istanbul.* Istanbul: Baha, 1958. (b)

The Literary Review (Turkish Issue) **4**, 2 (Winter 1960–1961); **15**, 4 (Summer 1972). (f)

Mahmud Kaşgarî. *Divanü Lûgat-it-Türk* (facs. ed.). Ankara: Türk Dil Kurumu, 1941. (e)

Mallaev. *Uzbek adabiyati tarikhi.* Tashkent: Uchitel', 1955. (a)

Malov, S. E. *Pamyatniki Drevnoturkskoy Pismennosti, Teksti i Issledovaniya.* Moscow-Leningrad: Izd-vo, 1951. (a, e)

Mansuroğlu, M. "Celâluddin Rumi's türkische Verse," *Ural-Altaische Jahrbücher* (1952), 106–115. (a)

———. "Anadolu Metinleri," *TM*, **7-8** (1940–1942), 95–104. (e)

Martinovich, N. *The Turkish Theater.* New York: Theatre Arts, 1933. (a)

———. "On the Ibtidānāme." *Zapiski*, **26** (1917), 205–232. (a)

Mashtakova, E. I., ed. (and intro.). *Mikhri Khatun: Divan.* Moscow: Nauka, 1967. (a, b, e)

Mehemmed Fuzuli. Baku: Azerbaidzhanskoe gos. izd-vo, 1958.

Melikoff, I. *La Geste de Melik Danişmend.* Vols. 1 and 2. Paris: Maisonneuve, 1960. (a)

———. "Nobres symboliques dans la littèrature epico-religieuse des Turcs d'Anatolie," *JA*, **250** (1962), 435–445. (b)

Meredith-Owens, G. M., ed. *Meşāᶜir üş-Şuᶜarā* (by ᶜÂşık Çelebi). London: Luzac, 1971. (e)

Minorski, V. "The Poetry of Shāh Ismāᶜīl," *BSOAS*, **10**, 4 (1942), 1006ª–1053ª. (a)

Nadzhip, E. N. *Khorezmi, Muhabbet-name.* Moscow: Izd-vo, 1961. (e)

Navoî va Adabî Ta'sir Masalalari (collection of articles). Tashkent: Fan, 1968.

Necatigil, B. *Edebiyatımızda İsimler Sözlüğü.* 2nd ed. Istanbul: Varlik, 1964. (a)

Öztelli, C. *Köroğlu ve Dadaloğlu.* Istanbul: Varlık, 1953. (a)

Pavet de Courteille, M., trans. *Memoires de Baber* (by Babur). Paris: Maisonneuve, 1871. (f)

Philologiae Turcicae Fundamenta. L. Bazin et al., eds. Wiesbaden: Steiner, 1965. (a, g)

Platon, M., trans. *They Burn the Thistles* (by Y. Kemal). London: Collins, Harvill, 1973. (f)

Radloff, W. *Das Kutadgu Bilik des Jusuf Chass-hadschib aus Balasaghun.* Vols. 1 and 2. St. Petersburgh: Kaiserliche akademie der wissenschaften, 1891, 1900–1910. (e)

———. *Proben der Volksliteratur der türkischen Stämme Sud-Siberiens.* Vols. 1–10. St. Petersburgh: Eggers, 1866–1904. (d, e)

Rathburn, C. *The Village in the Turkish Novel and Short Story, 1920–1955.* The Hague: Mouton, 1972. (b)

Ritter, H. *Karagös. Türkische Schattenspiele.* Vol. 1.

Roditi, E., trans. *Memed, my Hawk* (by Y. Kemal). London: Collins and Harvill, 1961. (f)

Rossi, E. "Due canti di marinai turchi del secolo XVI," *RSO*, **29** (1954). (a)

——. "Il poeta mistico turco Yunus Emre (secoli XIII-XIV)," *OM*, **20** (1940), 75–86. (a)

——. "Odierne tendenze letteraire e politiche in Turchia," *OM*, **9** (1929). (a)

Rustamov, E. R. "Narodniye Elementi v Uzbekskoya Poeziy Pervoy Poloviny XV Veka." In *Vosprosi Uzbekskoy Literaturi. Literaturnokriticheskie Stat'i.* Tashkent: Goslitizdat, 1959. (a, b)

——. *Uzbekskaya Poeziya v Perovoy Poloviny XV Veka.* Moscow: Izd-vo, 1963.

Rymekiwicz, S. "Beitrage zur Entwicklung des Reims in der türkischen Kunstliteratur," *RO*, **27** (1963), 45–101. (c)

Rypka, J. *Baki als Ghazeldichter.* Prague: Rivnáče, 1926. (b)

——. "Les müfredat de Sabit," *Arch. Or.*, **18**, i-ii (1950), 444–478. (b)

Sapolyo, E. B. *Türk Efsaneleri.* Istanbul: Rafet Zaimler, n.d. (a)

Samoylovich, A. "Chetverostishiya Tuyugi Lutfi," *DAN* (1926), 78–80. (a)

——. "Izvlecheniya iz traktata po prosodii Mir Ali Shira Nevayi 'Mizanu-l'avsan'," *Vostochnuiy Sbornik* (1962), Moscow: s.n. 105–114. (b, c)

Sakkakiy, Tanlangan Asarlar. Tashkent: Goslitizdat, 1958. (e)

Saussey, E. *Prosateurs Turcs Contemporains.* Paris: de Baccard, 1935. (a)

Schimmel, A. "Yunus Emre," *Numen*, **8** (1961), 12–33. (a)

Sevük, I. H. *Tanzimattan beri Türk Edebiyatı Tarihi.* Vols. 1 and 2. Istanbul: Remzi, 1944. (a)

Siyavuşgil, S. E. *Karagöz. Psikososyolojik bir Deneme.* Istanbul: Maarif, 1941. (b)

Spies, O. *Das Blutgeld und andere türkische Novellen.* Leipzig: Meiner, 1942. (a, f)

——. *Die türkische Prosaliteratur der Gegenwart.* Leipzig: Harrassowitz, 1942. (a)

——. *Türkische Volksbücher.* Leipzig: Eichblatt, 1929. (a)

Stewart-Robinson, J. "The Ottoman Biographies of Poets," *JNES*, **24**, 1 and 2 (Jan.-Apr., 1965), 57–73. (a)

Sumer, F. A. Uysal, and W. S. Walker, eds. *The Book of Dede Korkut: A Turkish Epic.* Austin: Texas, 1973. (f)

Taeschner, F. "Des altrumtürkischen Dichters Gülşehri Werk 'Mantık ut-tayr' und seine Vorlage das gleichnamige Werk des persischen Dichters Fariduddin 'Attar," *Nemeth Armağanı* (1962), pp. 350–371. (a, d)

Ṭâhir, Bursalı Mehmet. *ᶜOşmânlı Mü'ellifleri.* Vols. 1–3. Istanbul: Matbaa-i Âmire, 1914–1923. (a)

Tanpınar, A. H. *Edebiyat Üzerine Makaleler.* Istanbul: M. E. B. Devlet Kitaplari, 1969. (b)

——. *Ondokuzuncu Asır Türk Edebiyatı Tarihi.* 2nd ed. Istanbul: I. Horoz, 1956. (a)

——. *Yahya Kemal.* Istanbul: Berksoy, 1962. (a, b)

Tarlan, A. N. *Ahmet Paşa Divanı.* Istanbul: Millî Eğitim, 1966. (e)

——. *Divan Edebiyatında Tevhidler.* Istanbul: Burhaneddin, 1936. (b, d)

——, ed. *Fuzûlî Divanı. Gazel, Musammat, Mukattaᶜ ve Ruba'i Kısmı.* Istanbul: Üçler, 1950. (e)

——. *"Kadı Burhaneddin'de Tasavvuf,"* *TDED*, **8** (1958), 8–15. (a)

———. *Şeyhî Divanı'nı Tetkik.* Istanbul: Edebiyat Fakültesi, 1964. (b)

Tevfik, Ebüzziya. *Nümûne-i Edebiyyât-i ᶜOsmôniyye,* 6th ed. Istanbul: Matbaa-i Ebüzziya, 1913. (e)

Thury, J. *A Közép-ázsiai Török Irodalom.* Budapest, 1904. (a)

———. *Töröl Nyelvemlék a XIV Század Végéig.* Budapest, 1903. (a)

Tietze, A. "Aziz Efendi's Muhayyelat," *Oriens,* **1** (1948), 248–329. (a)

———. "Die Geschichte von Kerkermeister-Kapitan. Ein türkischer Seerauberroman aus dem 17. Jahrhundert," *Act. Or.* **19** (1942), 152–210. (a)

———. "XVI asir Türk şiirinde gemici dili: Agehî kasidesine nazireler," *Zeki Velidi Toğan'a Armağan* (1950-1955), 451–467. (a)

Timurtaş, F. "Bâkî'nin Kanunî Mersiyesi'nin dil bakımından izahı," *TDED,* **12** (Dec. 1962), 219–232. (d)

———. *Şeyhî'nin Husrev ü Şîrin'i.* Istanbul: Edebiyat Fakültesi, 1963. (a, e)

Türk Dil Kurumu. *Kadı Burhaneddin Divanı* (facs.). Istanbul: Alâeddin Kıral, 1943. (e)

Türkiye Bibliyografyası. Istanbul: Millî Eğitim, (continuing publication). (g)

Türkiye Makaleler Bibliyografyası. Istanbul: Millî Eğitim, (continuing publication) (g)

Valitova, A. A. "Voprosy o Folklornekh Motivakh v Poeme 'Kutadgu Bilig'," *SV* (1958), 89–102. (b)

Veselá-Prenosilova, Z. "Quelques remarques sur l'analyse formale des vers de Mehemed Fuzuli," *Arch. Or.,* **35** (1967), 378–382. (b)

Zajaçzkowski, A. "Studia nad stylistyka i poetyka tureckiej wesji 'Hüsräv u Şirin Quṭba'," *RO,* **25** (1961), 31–82; **27** (1963), 7–44.

———. *Najstarsza wersja turecka 'Hüsräv u Şirin Quṭba.'* Warsaw: Pánswawe Wydawn. Naukowe, 1958. (d)

Zhirmunskiy, V. M. and H. T. Zarifov. *Uzbekskiy Narodn'iy Geroicheskiy Epos.* Moscow: Ogiz, Goslitizdat, 1947. (a)

An Ancillary Comment

ROGER ALLEN

The preceding surveys have underlined the fact that these literatures suffer from a paucity in two major areas, publication and scholars. This factor is of course not exactly germane to the present survey of the state of the *art,* and yet it inevitably has an effect on the discipline as a whole. A few words on the subject therefore seem in order.

As regards *publication,* many works mentioned in the preceding survey have been published once and are now unobtainable (although various reprint organizations are now republishing the more important studies). Another factor is that most current research in literature has to be published in article form (frequently in obscure journals) since the publishing industry does not regard works on Near Eastern literatures as marketable. The section on Arabic literature illustrates well how much good material has already been published in the *Journal of Arabic Literature* (along with its offshoot series of *Studies* and *Translations*), and my colleagues and I can no doubt think of countless basic studies of the literatures under discussion—textual editions, translations, and critical studies—that have not been published in any form apart from that of a dissertation.

It seems entirely unrealistic to expect research in literature of any kind to thrive or even continue at its present level when there is scant chance of its ever seeing the light of day in print. A continuation of the kind of research being advocated here will occur only if it is encouraged by a vigorously supported program such as the late lamented ACLS series of translations. The market for such productions is admittedly very small at the moment and the costs are high, but new developments such as microfiche and computerized Arabic text production should help to keep costs down. One thing that does seem clear is that the market will remain small until the vicious circle of ignorance and commercial expediency is pierced by a publishing program sponsored by some enlightened funding agency.

Scholars who are working in the literatures of the Near East do not need to be told that their colleagues are few in number. Most of this small group also realize that few of them do not spend a great deal of their available time on an essentially nonliterary activity, namely, teaching language. This subject draws us into the pedagogical area, and yet, when such activity diverts the attention of so many members of such a small group from their research work, it has a direct effect on the state of the art. It must be emphasized here that language teaching is an honorable academic activity, particularly where these languages are concerned, but that language and literature are two separate entities which are often tied together for administrative convenience at Western institutions at which research in literature is possible. Too often, literature scholars are also the language teachers in university departments. When they cannot find time or are not afforded the opportunity to practice research in their specialized field, there seems to be little incentive to continue their work in such a vacuum. At this point, the somewhat cynical comments of Stetkevych in describing the incipient literature scholar and his inability or unwillingness to use the skills he has acquired seem peculiarly appropriate:

> With a lifetime career of conferences ahead of him, he rides comfortably on the crest of the wave of success into academia or anywhere. The old dreams of aesthetic discovery he now terms youthful fancy merely. He is not ashamed of them, however. Like a flower in the lapel of a well-pressed dinner jacket, they are good to wear. [*JNES*, **26**, 1967]

CONCLUSIONS

Desiderata

Bearing in mind the fact that much past research in "literature" has been shown by this survey to be devoted to purely philological and literary historical activities, perhaps the first desideratum which might be identified is that of strengthening the disciplinary focus and consciousness of scholars of literature so that both they and their colleagues in kindred disciplines may be aware of *all* the aspects of the study of literature. A corollary of the above statement would of course also involve the training of specialists in literature according to the criteria we have outlined in the preceding pages, specialists who would provide the basis for the development of a future tradition of study and research in Near Eastern literatures, the standards and terms of reference of which would match those of other world literary traditions.

Another fact to emerge from the above surveys or, more accurately, from the preliminaries to them, is the generally poor contact between literature scholars in the West and the Near East itself. That this is unfortunate is too obvious to need elaboration. Every effort should be made officially and personally to foster contacts with both littérateurs and literature scholars in the Near East. Among obvious benefits of such contacts are immediate acquaintance with current trends in both literature itself and literary studies in the area, and valuable information on research opportunities in countries which often regard any requests from aliens to work in libraries and archives with suspicion. Such contacts might also encourage Western scholars to publish their research in the appropriate language in journals of the area itself, thus bringing their work to the attention of a much wider audience than is generally afforded by Western publications.

Means

The preceding pages have shown that, in varying degrees, a basis for the study of Near Eastern literatures does exist, but that in all cases there is a shortage of works of almost every kind. We would obviously not wish to suggest any priorities here among theoretical, critical, and text studies, but merely to point out that all are needed in order that disciplines of Arabic, Persian and Turkish literature may be undertaken according to the criteria which were outlined at the beginning of this chapter. Furthermore, since one of the major functions of the *present* generation of literature scholars seems to be to train a fully competent generation to follow it, we must conclude by recommending that attention also be focused on the preparation of such basic tools as bibliographies of articles in the languages themselves arranged topically or theoretically, edited and annotated texts to serve as means of approach to the study of the literatures, and finally, introductory works of all kinds which will treat forms, genres, styles, and every other aspect of the literary discipline.

ACKNOWLEDGMENT

The coordinator would like to acknowledge the valuable advice and assistance of the following colleagues: Kamal Abu Deeb, Fahir Iz, Talat Halman, James Monroe, Muhammad al-Nuwayhî, and Jeanette Wakin.

CHAPTER TEN

Sociology

GEORGES SABAGH

I am particularly indebted to Professors Elbaki Hermassi, Department of Sociology, University of California, Berkeley; and Ayad al-Qazzaz, Department of Sociology, California State University, Northridge for the papers which they prepared for this review. Elbaki Hermassi's paper is on "A Note on the State of Sociology in the Maghrib" and that of Ayad al-Qazzaz is on "Some Impressions about the Status of Sociology in Iraq." I am also greatly indebted to the many and extensive comments, suggestions, and criticisms by Professors Elbaki Hermassi; Ayad al-Qazzaz; Morroe Berger, Department of Sociology, Princeton University; Samir Khalaf, Department of Sociology, American University in Beirut; Abdelkader Zghal, University of Tunis; Nader Afshar Naderi, University of Tehran; Ilhan Tekeli of Middle Eastern Technical University in Ankara; Mahmut Tezcan of Ankara University; and Ahmad Abou Zeid, Alexandria University. I would also like to express my appreciation for the comments, suggestions, and criticisms by Professors Fuad Baali, Department of Sociology and Anthropology, Western Kentucky University; George H. Gardner, Department of Sociology, Alfred University; Ronald E. Krahenbuhl, Department of Sociology, California State University, Northridge, Russell A. Stone, Department of Sociology, State University of New York; and George H. Weightman, Department of Sociology, Herbert H. Lehman College of the City University of New York; and by Mr. Justin McCarthy and Miss Andrew Ball of the University of California at Los Angeles.

INTRODUCTION

In any review and assessment of the state of sociology of the Middle East it would seem that we should first specify what we mean by sociology and how we can distinguish contributions to this field from those in other social sciences. Unfortunately, as suggested by the following appraisal by Neil Smelser, this is no simple task (1969, p. 5):

> Sociology, by comparison with some other sciences, lacks a single accepted conceptual framework. The field is difficult to distinguish from others because it contains a diversity of frameworks, some of which it shares with other fields such

> as psychology and social anthropology. If anything, then, sociology is too comprehensive, diffuse, soft in the center, and fuzzy around the edges.

Needless to say, there are some sociologists who would disagree violently with this appraisal. Radical sociologists would argue that Marx and Marxist scholars such as Lukacs and Lefebvre do provide a single conceptual framework as well as a methodology. Other sociologists view the structural-functional framework as well as the work of Parsons on the social action system as providing a unitary though complex theoretical orientation. Most American sociologists, while recognizing the pluralistic nature of their discipline, both with respect to theory and methods, would argue that there are some central themes and common concerns. Indeed, Smelser has attempted to delineate as follows, "five aspects of social life that constitute the major perspectives of sociology" (1969, p. 32):

> The subject matter of sociology, then is found in the demographic-ecological, social-psychological, collective, structural, and cultural aspects of social life. The sociological enterprise is to explain regularities, variations and interdependencies among these aspects. This enterprise has both static and dynamic aspects. Sometimes sociologists ask why patterns of organized social life persist, but equally often they are concerned with processes of social change, which destroy old social forms and create new ones.

Although Smelser's statement seems to provide a good working definition of the sociological enterprise, it represents essentially an American perspective. We also need to consider how Middle Eastern scholars themselves view and delineate the sociological enterprise. Though the influence and impact of American, French, and English sociology is still noticeable, many of these scholars have been striving in recent years to develop a distinctively Middle Eastern orientation.

For many Middle Eastern sociologists, particularly those from the Maghreb, this field must be defined and delineated in a sociohistorical context. For example, both Hermassi (1973) and Khatibi (1967) interpret the nature and development of sociology in terms of the colonial and postcolonial experiences. Hermassi defines as follows three phases in Maghrebi sociology (1973, pp. 1–2):

> In addition to (the) colonial school, there are two other major moments of intellectual effervescence: namely, sociological studies published during the formation of national liberation movements; and contemporary post-independence studies. Distinguishable already by the historical period in which they appear, these three schools or moments of sociology in the Maghrib employ different approaches and modes of analysis as well. The colonial school was predominantly anthropological, concentrating on small, simple social units such as tribes and villages, using the case-study method in which the investigator actually immerses

> himself in the single culture to be studied. The second productive moment focused on the urban society and used a Marxist paradigm with an emphasis on social classes. Finally, recent sociology, though most difficult to describe except schematically, has drifted toward empirical research while remaining theoretically open and fundamentally eclectic.

Another Maghrebi sociologist, Stambouli, expressed his views most succinctly by saying that "the sociology of decolonization must above all involve a decolonization of sociology" (1967, p. 192).

In the search for original and precolonial sources of insights and bases of legitimization of their discipline, Middle Eastern sociologists have naturally turned to the work of Ibn Khaldûn (1958), a brilliant and earliest precursor of sociology. From the Arab East to the Arab West he has been hailed as the founder of sociology. According to Ayad al-Qazzaz, Ibn Khaldûn's *Muqaddima* not only legitimizes sociology as part of the "Arab world culture," but also presents theories that "are still more pertinent and in many ways more appropriate to understanding the social questions and the problems of Arab societies, including Iraq, than the theories of many western writers on the Arab world" (1972, p. 95). Hassan el-Ṣaaty states that "Egypt is the first country in the world where Sociology was ever studied! The first teacher of the new science was its first originator and classifier, the historian and philosopher ᶜAbd al-Raḥmân Ibn Khaldûn" (1964, p. 146; cf. Dunham and Lutfiyya, 1971). Samir Khalaf begins his assessment of the development of sociology in Lebanon by reviewing Ibn Khaldûn's major principles of social analysis and suggests that many Arab social scientists have neglected these important principles (1965). Ibn Khaldûn's *ᶜilm al-ᶜUmrân* is echoed in Bouhdiba's call for a sociology of development and forms the basis of analysis of traditional Maghrebi society by Zghal and Stambouli (Bouhdiba, 1970; Zghal, 1970; Stambouli, 1970). Finally, for Hermassi, Maghrebi sociology can look both backward and forward in drawing inspirations from the "breadth, the passion and the vision of a profoundly maghribi and cosmopolitan 13th century theorist, Ibn Khaldun" (1973, p. 10).

Unlike most of their American colleagues, Middle Eastern sociologists have tended to be more interdisciplinary in their perspectives. This poses a real problem in any attempt to summarize and evaluate "sociological" studies of the Middle East. In a personal communication, Zghal, a Tunisian sociologist, has clearly delineated the nature of the dilemma faced in such an evaluation (Zghal, 1973b):

> You have in the United States autonomous Departments of Sociology, Anthropology and Political Science, not to mention History, Economics, and Psychology. In addition, you have Middle East Centers with research scholars with different disciplinary training. These scholars try to elucidate certain theoretical problems

> of their disciplines by utilizing "material" drawn from Middle Eastern societies. It is true that these scholars have in common some understanding of Muslim–Arab civilization and that some of them try to go beyond the narrow framework of their disciplines in utilizing concepts and propositions from other disciplines. But one must admit that, in general, the research of these scholars is basically guided by hypotheses from their own disciplines. In this case, should one consider only as "sociological" the work of scholars trained in Departments of Sociology, or should one include also anthropologists and political scientists who have been interested in the Middle East?

The situation may be quite different in the Middle East, where, for example in Tunisia, "in the last few years American political scientists and British anthropologists have had some impact on Tunisian sociologists familiar with English" (Zghal and Karoui, 1973, p. 15). The difficult decision to exclude from this review many important and sociologically relevant contributions by anthropologists and political scientists was guided mainly by the fact that they are discussed and evaluated elsewhere in this volume by Richard T. Antoun and I. William Zartman. Similarly, no attempt was made to review the many significant and pertinent studies of the socioeconomic history of the Middle East, such as studies of Egypt or Turkey in the nineteenth century. The chapter by Hourani provides a synthesis of the major contributions in this field.

Finally, it should be noted that many Middle Eastern sociologists have been particularly concerned with the relevance of their theories and research in helping them understand the nature of their societies in terms of the legacy of the past and the current social developments, dislocations and experiments. As suggested by Khalaf, this perspective of Middle Eastern sociologists with an emphasis on the need to "strike a balance between rediscovery and institutional transformation, between continuity and change" has many implications that should be explored (Khalaf, 1973).

This essay is too brief to allow a systematic review of all the important sociological studies about or in the Middle East. The few that were selected for discussion are those that have important implications for an understanding of the field as well as those that illustrate types of research, topics of major interest, and types of orientations. Furthermore, these studies pertain to only some of the Arab countries of the Middle East, although sociological studies of both Iran and Turkey were explicitly included. On the other hand, no attempt was made to review the vast and growing sociological literature on Israel. Since Weller (1974) recently published an extensive survey of this literature and a synthesis of its major findings about the nature of Israeli society, there is no need for a duplication of effort. It should be noted, however, that Weller's review excludes studies of Arabs in Israel or of Middle Eastern societies by Israeli anthropologists such as Marx (1957) or Rosenfeld

(1969) or by Israeli social historians such as Baer (1969). His lengthy bibliography includes no references to articles published by *Hamizraḥ Heḥadash* (the New East), the journal of the Israel Oriental Society. Although Eisenstadt has some references to the Middle East in his general theoretical work (1966), there seem to be few Israeli sociologists who have studied either Arabs in Israel or Middle Eastern societies. On the other hand, some Israeli demographers such as Schmelz (1973) have analyzed Arab population structure and change.

Following the lead of Hermassi, Khatibi, and others, a brief sketch is presented of some of the sociohistorical factors that could explain the development of the sociology of the Middle East. We then turn to an examination of the current status and major accomplishments of this discipline. A third and final section is devoted to an assessment of future needs.

SOCIOHISTORICAL CONTEXT IN THE DEVELOPMENT OF THE SOCIOLOGY OF THE MIDDLE EAST

If we are to understand why and where the sociology of the Middle East experienced the most or least rapid growth, why certain theories and methods were more popular than others, and why certain topics were emphasized whereas others were neglected, we must consider the sociohistorical context in the development of this field. Unfortunately, there have been only few and limited attempts to analyze sociologically the development of the sociology of the Middle East. The kind of insight that such a study could provide is *illustrated* by considering in some detail the experience of Morocco, which is somewhat comparable to that of Algeria and Tunisia. It must be emphasized, however, that we cannot generalize from such an analysis to the rest of the Middle East. As is indicated later, a separate sociological analysis of the growth of sociology would have to be carried out for each of the major regions or countries of the Middle East.

Both Maghrebi and French sociologists have described the development of sociology in the Maghreb in terms of its relationship to French colonial policies (Hermassi, 1973; Khatibi, 1967; Pascon, 1962, 1963; Berque, 1956; Nicolas, 1968). Starting in Algeria and continuing in Morocco, the objective of ethnographic and sociological field work was to document the pre-Islamic heritage of the Maghreb and to focus on the studies of the Berbers and on the "discovery" of distinctions between Arabs and Berbers. As stated by Hermassi, "the colonial school was overshadowed by one predominant ideological preoccupation: how to assimilate politically and intellectually the rural and especially the Berber populations. . . . There is no doubt that sociology at this stage was a tool of conquest first for 'pacification' and later for domination"

(1973, p. 2). The role played by sociology during the colonial period in the Maghreb can be described in greater detail for Morocco.

Sociology was introduced in Morocco from the very beginning of French colonial control and achieved official recognition as an essential part of this process of control. In 1904, a few years before the establishment of the protectorate, a *Scientific Mission* was founded in Tangiers by le Chatelier, a professor of Muslim sociology in the College de France. Michaux-Bellaire, who became its director in 1907, expressed as follows the aim of this *Mission* (Khatibi, 1967, p. 10):

> The object of this *mission* . . . was (to initiate) sociological studies. . . . It was necessary to make an inventory of Morocco, its tribes, its cities, its brotherhoods, to find their origins, their ramifications, their wars and alliances, to trace their history in various dynasties, to study its institutions and customs, in other words, to understand as much as possible the area where, one day we might be called upon to take some action. . . .

This *Mission* was officially recognized in 1913, a year after the protectorate, and in 1920 was incorporated in the Sociological Section of the *Résidence Générale*. Lyautey, the *Résident Général* of Morocco, supported this sociological enterprise because he saw in it ways of implementing his policies of indirect rule and preservation of traditional institutions and customs. It should be noted that sociology was defined in a rather general way and included ethnographic studies and social history. Furthermore, its practitioners were historians and Orientalists rather than sociologists by training, and some of them had a military background.

The alliance between colonial authority and "official" sociology had a number of important consequences for this field in Morocco. First of all, sociological studies were essentially practical in nature with the objective of providing needed information to the colonial administrators. Secondly, all these studies were carried out by Frenchmen. Thirdly, the theoretical basis of these studies had clear political implications. Thus Michaux-Bellaire (1927) argued for the need to distinguish a Moroccan sociology from a *makhzan* and Islamic sociology, with the clear implications that a Moroccan sociology would try to identify the pre-Islamic and non-Arab elements in Moroccan society. He expressed himself as follows in 1927: "after being hypnotized for a long time by the appearances of an official Morocco (solely Arab and Muslim), we realize now that the sociological studies of the country which would make it possible to understand its true structure must also be focused on Berber tribes, and more particularly on those that have most completely preserved their language and institutions" (p. 295). A few years later Robert Montagne, who was to replace Michaux-Bellaire as the most prominet sociologist of the colonial period, published his study on *The Berbers and the Maghzen*.

As Khatibi (1967) suggests, a distinction should be made between the period 1912–1925, when Lyautey was in control, and the later period. The scientific policy of the earlier period was based on a "desire to understand the internal dynamics of Moroccan society" in order to foster a better comprehension of the colonized by the colonizers. But "the departure of Lyautey in 1925 put an end to the relative ambiguity of the colonial system, and opened the field to a separatist (Arabs and Berbers) and racist colonial policy that inflamed the national sentiment and provoked indignation in the Arab world" (Khatibi, 1967, p. 14). The culmination of this policy was the *Dahir Berbère* of 1930, which inaugurated a judicial system for Berber areas.

In all fairness to the work of sociologists such as Le Coeur, Berque, and others, Khatibi notes that there was a more academic sociology that kept its distance from official colonial policies. Indeed, the work of Berque can be considered to be the beginning of the decolonization of Moroccan sociology. Nevertheless, the sting of "official" sociology was still felt by Moroccan intellectuals who participated in the fight for independence. As a consequence, sociology in independent Morocco had to be critical and had to reject the old models and theories if it was to gain some degree of legitimacy. But it can also become critical of existing political arrangements and economic structure.

Seddon, Stauder, and others have suggested a similar interrelationship between British colonial policy and the development of British social anthropology during the 1930s and 1940s. The scientific counterpart to the principle of indirect rule in Africa is to be found in the structural-functional approach with its emphasis on the analysis of the interrelations and functioning of the key social and political institutions.

The detailed discussion of the colonial context in the emergence of sociology in the Maghreb and Morocco should not lead us to assume, however, that it also describes the situation in other countries of the Middle East. Thus the links between French and English colonial policies in the Arab East and the development of sociology in that region are somewhat more tenuous. It would be difficult or even impossible to trace the impact of these policies on the work of such forerunners of modern sociological study of the Middle East as Weulersse (1946), Chatila (1934), and Tannous (1943) in Syria and Lebanon, Granqvist (1947) in Palestine and Kremer (1863), Clerget (1934), Blackman (1927), Ayrout (1938), and Ammar (1954) in Egypt. It is clear, however, that French and English control or influence in this region increased the likelihood that scholars would visit and study this region. The motives of these scholars were undoubtedly quite varied and ranged from romantic longing for the past to a scholarly interest in Biblical origins and in antiquity. As suggested by Sweet (1969, p. 232), however, "far more systematic and professional study was carried out by French scholars in their sphere of control (Morocco, Algeria, Tunisia, Syria and Lebanon) than by the British in theirs (Egypt, the Sudan, Palestine, Jordan, Iraq, and the Persian Gulf and South Arabian Emirates), with the exception of Evans-Pritchard's work in Libya and the Sudan."

In Turkey the ebb and flow of interest and work in sociology is closely related to the political, social, and intellectual revolutions experienced by that country in the twentieth century. In a personal discussion, Ilhan Tekeli has suggested that one may identify the following stages in the development of sociology in Turkey:

1. After the revolution of 1908 and until the 1920s, sociological thought played an important and prestigious role in the political and intellectual life of Turkey. Gökalp occupied a "pivotal role" during this "formative period of Turkey's national development" (Kazamias, 1966, p. 108). Gökalp saw sociology, particularly the sociology of Durkheim and the concept of collective representation, as paving "the way for the establishment of modern national culture" (Ülken, 1950a, p. 141). The influence of Durkheim is still strong in Turkey and is to be noted in the sociology curriculum of high schools and some universities. Another influence is that of Le Play and his school whose approach emphasizing field studies was introduced in Turkey by Prince Sabahattin (Tezcan, 1975).

2. The period of the 1930s was marked by increasing emphasis on an economic orientation and a consequent decline in the dominance of sociology.

3. The formation of the Village Institutes between 1939 and 1946 provided a real impetus for village studies and rural sociology (Ülken, 1950b; Planck, 1972). Boran, Berkes, and Sherif returned from the United States and established a strong Department of Sociology at the University of Ankara with an emphasis on village studies. Both Boran and Berkes carried out sociological studies of villages (Planck, 1972, p. 193). In Istanbul University, Ülken and Findikoğlu strengthened their Department of Sociology and also carried out village studies. It should be noted that many Turkish sociologists, including Tanyol, Kurtkan, Tütengil, Yasa, Kıray, and Türkdoğan, are still engaged in research on villages (Tezcan, 1975, Beeley, 1969).

4. The years 1950–1960 witnessed the nearly total eclipse of sociology. This was a period marked by the dominance of the conservative Democratic party which relied for its support first on "small landowners, merchants, craftsmen, and families with established social status in the local community" and subsequently on "new leaders whose claims to status were based on wealth" (Karpat, 1973b, p. 58).

5. The revolution of 1960 ushered in a new era in the political, social, and economic life of Turkey. The period 1960 to the present is marked by a

vigorous growth of sociology and sociological research. Thus, writing in 1971, Janowitz could assert that "it is no accident that for the Middle East, scholarship on Turkey has been the locus of some of the best systematic research on societal processes" (1971, p. 304).

Although an interest in sociology emerged much later in Iran than in Turkey, that interest was also awakened by the rapid social change experienced by Iran starting in the 1950s (Naraghi, 1967). Because much of this change is directed from the "top," there has been increasing need for the kind of sociological knowledge that could guide "the formulation and execution" of policies (Naraghi, 1967; Enayat, 1974). It should also be noted that starting in the 1950s there were some "limited possibilities of self-expression and meaningful discussion of social problems" (Enayat, 1974, p. 8).

Though it is clear that rapid social, political, and economic change is likely to have an impact on the development of sociology, much more work needs to be done to identify the particular changes that are most or least favorable to the rapid growth of this field, in terms of its methods, its theories, and its subject matter. More should be known on the relationship between the development of this field and the nature of the political regime, the type of economic or social structure. The experience of Turkey suggests the importance of assessing the impact of revolutions, changes in political regime, and movements of national liberation and independence on the state of sociology.

CURRENT STATE OF THE SOCIOLOGY OF THE MIDDLE EAST

In those regions of the Middle East under colonial control, each country or region was in some way the "private domain" of social scientists from the colonial power. As a result of independence, these social scientists lost their privileged position, but this did not necessarily mean the end of involvement of Western sociologists in the Middle East. André Adam has interpreted the situation as follows (1972, p. 32):

> During the colonial period, North Africa hardly attracted any foreign scholars. It seems that the French "stronghold" was no less scientific than political. . . . Things have changed since independence: from Agadir to Gabes, hordes of anglo-saxon scholars have swooped on the Maghrib. Why? Is it because of greater freedom, now that it is no longer the "preserve" of Frenchmen? Is it because of an underlying political and economic interest in this region?

Western sociologists who study Middle Eastern societies are essentially "outside" observers who, no matter how insightful, are guided in their research by the perspective and problems of their disciplines rather than by the problems faced by these societies. Thus as Zghal and Karoui suggest, during the colonial period "such research confronted non-European cultures with questions which did not necessarily interest them, questions which were destined instead to facilitate the expansion of Europe and to reduce the resistance of native cultures" (1973, p. 12). With independence, the first Middle Eastern sociologists, particularly in the Maghreb, rejected the "colonial research tradition" and sought to study and understand their societies from "within" and to search for new perspectives. Yet many of them had received their formal training in Western universities and were most familiar with Western sociological theory and methods. As a consequence, their work reflects both this training and their concern for developing theories and methods which are appropriate to their society. For example, the work of Tunisian sociologists, most of whom were trained in France, "results from an attempt to reconcile the Marxist orientation of Gurvitch and the phenomenology of Berque with their own need to throw light on the problems of post-colonial Tunisia" (Zghal and Karoui, 1973, p. 15).

In Iran the founders of the Institute of Social Studies and Research, who were all trained in French or Swiss universities, "have often expressed the desire that social science in Iran would lead, not to an imitation of Western sociology, but to the discovery of concepts and methods peculiar to Iranian society" (Enayat, 1974, p. 10).

It is clear from the preceding discussion that although some interesting comparisons could be made between the perspectives of Western and Middle Eastern sociologists, it would be difficult if not impossible to make a separate assessment of the contributions of sociologists by their regions of origin or residence. There is a distinct difference, however, in the nature and extent of support for and acceptance of sociological study of the Middle East both in the West and in the Middle East.

Current Acceptance of and Support for Sociological Studies of the Middle East

THE WEST (MAINLY THE UNITED STATES). As suggested by Van Nieuwenhuijze (1971) and Richard Lambert (1973), many American sociologists have been doubtful about the usefulness or even the validity of an *area* approach in the study of society. But for a discipline whose main objective is to develop theoretical insights and propositions which are of *universal* validity, an area approach appears to be somewhat marginal to its central concerns. Clearly, however, the "universal" validity of any sociological principle is problematic unless *tested* in a variety of societal and cultural contexts. Comparative sociology has rapidly emerged as an important subdiscipline in the United States in the last 20–30 years not only as a result of the increasingly felt need to test sociological theories and methods in a cross-cultural setting but also as a result of the expanding role of the United States in world affairs. The presence of many foreign students working for higher degrees in sociology in American universities has also had its impact on the discipline. As might be expected, the major objective of comparative sociology in the United States has been the use or collection of data from foreign countries to test hypotheses. For example, Melvin Seeman (1972), who has developed and tested a number of hypotheses about the determinants of alienation in the United States, has also tested these hypotheses with comparable data which he collected in Sweden and France. The focus is not so much on Sweden or France as such, but on the extent to which the determinants of alienation vary from one industrial society to another.

The task of assessing the growth of American sociological studies of the Middle East is not an easy one, even if it were limited to a cursory review of all pertinent articles in professional journals. Such a review would have to include not only the general and specialized sociological journals in the United States, such as the *American Sociological Review* and the *Sociology of Education*, but also foreign or international sociological periodicals in the English language such as *British Journal of Sociology* and interdisciplinary American journals such as *Comparative Studies in Society and History* and *Economic Development and Cultural Change*. Furthermore, the results of sociological research on the Middle East are also likely to be published in "area" journals as the *Journal of Asian and African Studies*. Nevertheless, in view of the importance of such a review it was decided to carry out an analysis of the content of one specialized and three general American sociological journals for the period 1963–1973 and the two major American journals on the Middle East for the years 1970–1974.

A count was made of articles in the sociological journals presenting an analysis of data for all countries outside of the United States and Canada and for all Arab countries of the Middle East, Israel, Iran, and Turkey. For the years 1963–1973, there are approximately 50 articles on foreign countries in the *American Sociological Review*, the official journal of the American Sociological Association published six times a year. Of these there are only six on the Middle East, of which five were on Israel (Katz and Danet, 1966; Katz et al., 1973; Shuval, 1963; Talmon, 1964; Yuchtman, 1972) and one on Egypt (Abu-Lughod, 1969). As suggested by their titles, all these articles are mainly concerned with a theoretical or methodological problem and the Middle East is merely a vehicle to test hypotheses. Indeed, three of the articles do not identify the country in their titles. For the same period there are also about 50 articles on foreign countries in the *American Journal of Sociology*, the oldest in the United States and also published six times a year. Of these, there are three articles on Israel (Matras, 1964; Peres, 1971; Weintraub and

Bernstein, 1966), two on Egypt (Abu-Lughod, 1964; Petersen, 1971), and one on Turkey (Schnaiberg, 1970). In addition, in both journals there are a few articles in which Middle Eastern countries appear among a number of countries in a general quantitative analysis. Although there are not many more articles on the Middle East in *Sociology and Social Research*, a quarterly, they are somewhat more evenly distributed by countries. Of a total of about 45 articles on foreign countries, two are on Israel (Shoham and Shaskolsky, 1969; and Shoham and Hovar, 1963), two on Turkey (Davis, 1972 and 1973), two on Iraq (Baali, 1967; Alzobaie, 1968), and one on Israel and Jordan (Brown, 1969). The picture changes markedly when we turn to *Demography*, an official quarterly of the Population Association of America. Of the approximately 160 articles on foreign countries, five are on Turkey (Adlakha, 1972; Fişek and Shorter, 1968; Schnaiberg, 1970; Stycos and Weller, 1967; and Treadway, 1972), two on Israel (Ben-Porath, 1973; and Klaff, 1973), two on Morocco (Brown, 1968; and Sabagh and Scott, 1967), two on Tunisia (Lapham, 1970; and Povey and Brown, 1968), one on Egypt (Toppozada, 1968), and one on Iran (Sardari and Keyhan, 1968). In addition, in a lengthy article El-Badry (1965) compared the demographic characteristics of Egypt, Lebanon, Syria, Jordan, Iraq, and Kuwait, and Youssef (1971) compared the patterns of female labor force participation in the Middle East and Latin America. Finally, there were 11 articles in which Middle Eastern countries appeared among other foreign countries in a general analysis.

The two major American "area" journals selected for analysis were the *International Journal of Middle East Studies*, the official quarterly of the Middle East Studies Association, and *The Middle East Journal*, a quarterly published by the Middle East Institute. Since the first issue of the former journal appeared in 1970, it was decided to select the period 1970–1974. The task of identifying articles that can be classified as contributions to the sociology of the Middle East is not an easy one. Obviously, the simplest but narrowest solution would be to consider only those articles authored by persons with advanced training in departments of sociology. As might be expected, the results of such an analysis are somewhat disappointing. Only three sociologists (Dodd, 1973; Mardin, 1971; and Stone, 1974) had articles in the *International Journal of Middle East Studies* but a somewhat greater number, five (Barakat, 1973; Bean, 1974; Lapham, 1972; Nagi, 1974; and Srikantan, 1973), authored articles in *The Middle East Journal*. Interestingly, four of these five sociologists are either demographers or writing on a demographic subject. There are, however, a number of other articles in both journals that are sociological in their orientation or conceptualization, although they were authored by nonsociologists. A tentative analysis yielded 12 other articles in the *International Journal of Middle East Studies* (Albaum and Davies, 1973;

Ashford, 1973; Bill, 1972; Divine, 1973; Fahim, 1973; Goldberg, 1971; Eickelman, 1974; Keddie, 1971; Ramazani, 1974; Rahman, 1970; Rosen, 1972; and Sayigh, 1971), and an additional 16 papers in *The Middle East Journal* (Awad, 1971; Bill, 1973; Entelis, 1973; Gubser, 1973; Issawi, 1971; Kuroda, 1972; Magnarella, 1970; Mitchell, 1971; Moore, Asayesh, and Montague, 1974; Nachmias, 1973; Nakhleh, 1971; Oren, 1973; Rugh, 1973; Saltzman, 1971; Stookey, 1974; and Tuma, 1974). Although this list excludes most historical studies it includes many contributions by anthropologists and political scientists. Of all articles published in the *International Journal of Middle East Studies* for this period approximately 14% are "sociological," and the comparable figure for *The Middle East Journal* is 25%.

The preceding analysis of the content of journals suggests the following tentative conclusions. If we exclude *Demography*, there appears to be a greater tendency for sociologists of the Middle East to publish their work in Middle Eastern journals rather than in the journals of their discipline. As suggested by al-Qazzaz in a personal communication, this may be more a consequence of editorial policies of sociological journals than of the wishes of the authors. It seems that, with the possible exception of demographers, the scholarly output of American sociologists on the Middle East is still very modest. On the other hand, it appears that other social scientists have recognized the value and importance of sociological conceptualization.

How can this situation be explained? First of all, as suggested by Table 1, there are few departments of sociology in the United States and Canada with specialized courses on the Middle East. This situation reflects the low priority that American sociologists attach to area studies, particularly of the Middle East, as well as the lack of strong institutional support. Secondly, as long as research findings tend to be descriptive and area-oriented rather than hypothesis-oriented, they are not likely to be published in American sociological journals. Thirdly, American sociologists may find it hard to locate appropriate data on the Middle East. For example, when Janowitz was preparing his book on *The Military in the Political Development of New Nations* he "found the greatest difficulty in assembling material on the Middle East" (1971, pp. 304–305). Finally, those who would consider fieldwork in this region are discouraged from doing so by real or imagined difficulties, one of which, of course, is the language problem.

The situation is not all that dismal, however, and there are some hopeful developments concerning American sociological studies of the Middle East. As was indicated earlier, a number of American demographers have been engaged in research on this area and have published their results either in *Demography* or in *The Middle East Journal*. Table 1 documents the scarcity of sociology courses on the Middle East in American universities, but it also shows that there are at least 20 departments of sociology, or sociology and

TABLE I

Departments of Sociology in Universities and Colleges in the United States and Canada with Courses on the Middle East and/or Faculty Members with Specialization or Research Interest in the Middle East, 1974

University or College	Courses	Faculty Members
United States		
Alfred*		George H. Gardner‡
American*		Samih Farsoun‡ Karen Petersen
Bowling Green†		Mustafa Nagi Aida K. Tomeh
Calif. State Univ. Hayward†		Peter Geiser
Calif. State Univ. Northridge*		Ronald E. Krahenbuhl‡
Calif. State Univ. Sacramento†	ME (Middle East) Society and Culture	Ayad al-Qazzaz‡
Miss. State Univ.		Mohamed El Attar
Univ. of N. C.		Ali Paydarfar
Northern Illinois Univ.*	Societies of the ME	Abdo Elkholy‡
Northwestern*		Janet Abu-Lughod
Ohio State*		Saad Nagi
Princeton*	Contemporary Social Institutions of NE (Near East); Study in the Contemporary NE	Morroe Berger‡
Simmons College†		Elaine Hagopian‡
State Univ. of N.Y. Binghamton*		David Makovsky
State Univ. of N.Y. Buffalo*	NE Society	Russell Stone‡
Univ. of Calif. Berkeley*	Modern NE Social Structure	Elbaki Hermassi‡
Univ. of Calif. Los Angeles*	Population and Society in the ME Comparative Sociology of ME	Georges Sabagh‡
Univ. of Southern Calif.†		Nadia Haggag Youssef
Univ. of Utah*	Family, kinship, and social order (ME); Regional sociology (ME)	L. L. Bean Jalil Mahmoudi‡
Western Kentucky Univ.†		Fuad Baali‡

Table I (contd.)

University or College	Courses	Faculty Members
Canada		
Univ. of Alberta†		Baha Abu-Laban
Univ. of Manitoba*		A. Lutfiyya
		A. H. Latif

* From *Middle East Studies Association Bulletin*, Special Issue, 1974, p. 8.
† From the American Sociological Association, *Graduate Guide to Sociology Departments*, 1974, and other sources.
‡ Fellow of the Middle East Studies Association, 1974.

anthropology, with one or more faculty members with a research interest in the Middle East. The majority of these faculty members belong to both the American Sociological Association and the Middle East Studies Association. There is no doubt that the founding of the latter association in 1966 has provided a strong impetus to the sociology of the Middle East. Sociologist members of this association increased from 12 in 1968 to 25 in 1972 and its annual meetings have provided an increasing number of sessions and papers on sociological topics. Since the study of many facets of Middle Eastern societies should be interdisciplinary, this association provides a forum for a dialogue between sociologists and other social scientists. The Association of Arab–American University Graduates, which was founded in 1967, has also provided impetus to sociological studies of the Middle East. Its president in 1973 was the sociologist Baha Abu-Laban and the sociologists Ayad al-Qazzaz, Fuad Baali, Abdo el-Kholy, Rashid Bashur, Elia Zureik, and Elaine Hagopian have presented papers at its annual conventions (cf. Abu-Lughod and Abu-Laban, 1974).

There have been a few, though too few, but noteworthy attempts by American sociologists to integrate research findings from the Middle East in general reviews of knowledge in their fields of specialization. Goode (1963) has done this for the family and Janowitz (1971) for military institutions, and neither are area specialists. Berger (1962) and Van Nieuwenhuijze (1971) have summarized and integrated a number of sociological studies of the Middle East, but unlike Goode and Janowitz, they are both specialists on the Middle East. Also, some sociologists such as Inkeles (1969) have included Middle Eastern countries in their comparative research to test sociological hypotheses.

Finally, the most promising development in the past 20 years has been the initiation of collaborative and interdisciplinary research projects involving sociologists as well as other social scientists in both the United States and the

Middle East. Among these projects we should mention the cross-cultural study of college and secondary school students in the United States, Egypt, Iraq, Jordan, Lebanon, and Syria which was completed in 1956 (Hudson, Barakat, and Laforge, 1959), the 1959 survey of Turkish high-school students, and the 1962 survey of Turkish peasants by Frey and his American and Turkish associates (Frey, 1963), and a planned cross-national study of the sociopsychological impact of modernization by sociologists from the University of Pittsburgh as well as from other countries, including Morocco (anonymous, 1973). The new Social Science Research Council program of grants for collaborative research should provide a strong impetus for this type of sociological research on the Middle East. The projects supported for 1972–1973 include one by an American anthropologist (Nicholas S. Hopkins) and a Tunisian sociologist (Abdelkader Zghal) that will involve a comparative study of modernization in two Tunisian rural communities within the national context (SSRC, 1972).

THE MIDDLE EAST. If we use as indicators the number of universities with departments of sociology, the number of professors and undergraduate students of sociology, and the range of undergraduate courses, there is no doubt that this discipline has been rapidly gaining wide acceptance throughout most of the Middle East. As suggested by Hermassi (1973) for the Maghreb and al-Qazzaz (1973) for Iraq, however, the establishment of these departments was not always an easy matter and met with some resistance from other disciplines. Furthermore, there is the problem of placing graduates in sociology and related fields as well as the question of acceptance by governments of social science training and research (Zghal, 1973b). Even in countries such as Egypt and Turkey that had university programs in sociology prior to the 1940s, most of the growth of sociology occurred along with the rapid expansion of existing Middle Eastern universities and the founding of new ones in the 1950s and the 1960s. Nevertheless, growth during this period was impressive. Thus the number of faculty members of the departments of sociology and social work (which were combined in 1969) of the University of Baghdad increased from 5 to 20 in this period, and there were 500 students in these departments in the late 1960s (al-Qazzaz, 1973).

Growth of undergraduate education, although desirable, is not sufficient to promote the scholarly development of a discipline such as sociology. There are a number of conditions that need to be considered. They include the scope and quality of graduate education, the pattern of training and recruitment of sociologists and their professional self-image, and the conditions that foster or hamper sociological research and scholarly work including the availability of funds. The few reviews of these conditions that are available suggest that the present situation is far from satisfactory for most of the Middle East, but they also indicate that there are a few promising trends.

It is well beyond the scope of this essay to assess the scope and quality of sociology graduate education in Middle Eastern universities. It should be noted that although most of these universities have master's programs in sociology, a much smaller number have doctoral programs. And where they do have such programs, as in Cairo, Alexandria, and ᶜAyn Shams universities in Egypt, only a small number of doctoral degrees have been granted (de Jong, 1971). What hampers the development of these programs is in part the continuing tendency among Middle Eastern graduate students to seek foreign doctorates in sociology, mainly in the United States, France, England, and Western Germany.

Some Middle Eastern Universities, such as the American University of Beirut, have departments of sociology whose faculty members are heavily involved in their individual research projects. In other institutions, institutes have been established to facilitate research, particularly interdisciplinary, by sociologists and other social scientists. These include the Center for Social Studies at the Lebanese University, the Center for the Study of Modern Arab Society at St. Joseph University in Beirut, the Center for Social and Economic Studies and Research of the University of Tunis, the Social Research Center of the American University in Cairo, the Institute of Population Studies of Hacettepe University, and Tehran's University Institute for Social Studies and Research. These institutes are funded either by the respective national governments or by such outside agencies as the Ford Foundation. As noted for the program of Tehran's University Institute, government financing favors research projects that have immediate practical applications or that try to find solutions for social problems of concern to the government. Conditions in many other Middle Eastern universities are much less favorable to sociological research. For example, al-Qazzaz gives the following reasons for the "heavy emphasis on general sociology" in the writings of Iraqi sociologists (1973):

> (When these sociologists return from their training abroad they) are pressed to publish books in sociology to fill the empty library in Arabic in this field. . . . Secondly, writing books on sociology and its fields is easier than doing original research which needs a good deal of devotion, energy and patience. Thirdly, funds for original research are lacking. . . . Lastly, original research within the framework of Iraqi society is very difficult and beset with many problems that discourage researchers. . . .

Egyptian national universities are interested mainly in teaching and do not have funds to support research by their professors. In Egypt as well as in other Middle Eastern countries, however, there are research projects carried out by sociologists and other social scientists in the various ministries of the national government or in research institutes established within or by these ministries outside of the universities. For example, a Center for Demographic Studies and Research is attached to the Moroccan Division of Statistics (C.E.R.E.D.), and the Algerian Ministry of Economics has an Association for demographic, economic, and social studies (A.A.R.D.E.S.). A National Institute for Criminology was established in Egypt in 1955, and in 1959 its name was changed to the National Center for Social and Criminological Research to reflect its expanded scope. According to Ahmed Abou Zeid (1973) this center is "the only Egyptian national institute which takes a real interest in sociological studies." Following the Egyptian model the Iraqi Ministry of Social Affairs established a comparable center in 1970. Most of the research projects carried out by these centers are social problem-oriented and include such topics as penal institutions, juvenile delinquency, drug addiction, bribery, divorce and adultery, prostitution, and traffic problems. Since some of these studies are "meant to be used by the appropriate governmental agency" they have not been published (de Jong, 1971; el-Saaty, 1964).

Most of the current generation of university professors of sociology have been trained in the West, mainly in the United States and Western Europe. For example, all the resident professors of the Department of Sociology at the American University of Beirut received their Ph.D.'s in the United States (American Sociological Association, 1974). Almost all the sociologists at the University of Tehran and the University of Tunis were trained in France or Switzerland (Enayat, 1974; Zghal and Karoui, 1973). In some cases, as in Egypt and Turkey, the older generation of sociologists was trained in Western Europe before World War II, when the emphasis was on social theory, but the younger generation received a more empirical and quantitative training in the United States after World War II (Weiker, 1971). This means, of course, that in these two countries there are sharp distinctions in the type of sociological work that is published. This pattern of training facilitates the dialogue between Western and Middle Eastern sociologists, but it does have some negative implications for Middle Eastern sociologists. Maghrebi sociologists who were trained mostly in France tend to have more professional contacts with French-speaking sociologists than with their colleagues in the *Mashriq*, many of whom have doctorates from the United States. Sociologists in the Maghreb participate actively in the meetings of the International Association of French-speaking Sociologists and tend to publish in French or in French journals, whereas those in the Mashriq tend to publish in English and Arabic or in American journals. This situation is, of course, a consequence of the colonial period which still affects the professional and scientific status of Middle Eastern sociologists. Hermassi has somewhat pessimistically summarized as follows the consequences of Western training for Maghrebi sociologists (1973):

> Maghribi sociologists are French trained when in France, itself, the discipline is in utter confusion. The ego-ideals, the maîtres, live beyond national frontiers and are mostly either retired colonial officials or high-school teachers converted to sociology late in life. They have projects of their own and sponsor the native primarily to the extent that he fits in their own work. Their familiarity with the Maghrib is, of course, beyond doubt, but they were trained themselves, in the colonial school back in the 1940's, and they have nothing to contribute in terms of theoretical or methodological substance. Young maghribis, having apprenticed themselves in this alienating labor, find that they are completely at loss to tackle the overwhelming demands of University teaching and research in their own societies.

There are some hopeful signs, however, throughout the Middle East. There is increasing professional consciousness among Middle Eastern sociologists and social scientists as evidenced by the formation of the Turkish Social Science Association in 1967, the Iraqi Sociological Association in 1969, the Egyptian Sociological Association in 1971, and the Moroccan Sociological Association in 1973. The Turkish Social Science Association held a conference in 1970 to assess the state of the social science disciplines in Turkey and to discuss the problems faced by Turkish social scientists. The Moroccan Sociological Association is preparing a state of the discipline report in Morocco. The Egyptian Sociological Association is publishing its first annual volume to be devoted to the main trends in Egyptian sociology and anthropology, with particular emphasis on methodological problems.

Current State of Sociological Studies of Middle Eastern Societies

The preceding discussion might lead one to expect that there would not be a very large number of published sociological studies of the Middle East. The opposite seems to be true, however, if we consider the scope of available bibliographies. Thus Mahmut Tezcan's bibliography of Turkish publications in sociology from 1928 to 1968 includes a staggering 6255 items, while Peter Suzuki's bibliography, which is limited to studies of social change in Turkey from 1950 to 1969 has 866 entries (Weiker, 1971). In a survey of the literature pertaining to the study of Lebanese society, Samir Khalaf found approximately 250 publications in Arabic, English, and French from the 1900s to 1965 (1965). An annotated bibliography prepared by Jean T. Burke and focusing on sociology, social anthropology and psychology, and education lists 1453 items in English for the Arab East for a mere 10 years 1945–1954 (1956).

A more recent and inclusive bibliography of books and articles in English, French, German, and Italian on *Arab Culture and Society in Change* includes 4954 titles (Center for the Study of the Modern Arab World, 1973). Another bibliography published in 1975 and covering the period 1948–1973 contains 6314 annotated references in the Social Sciences (Atiyeh, 1975). While most of these references are in Western European languages, there are a number of them in Arabic, Turkish, and Persian. Finally, a third recent bibliography limited to social science publications (after 1960), mostly in English and French, on the family in Arab states contains 354 items (Allman, Ben Achour, and Stone, 1974). There is no doubt that equally lengthy bibliographies could be found in other languages and on other parts of the Middle East.

How is this vast literature to be assessed? The task seems almost hopeless. But as we start perusing some of the items in these bibliographies it is immediately clear that many of them are brief, journalistic, or not very analytical or sociological in their conceptualization.

A systematic assessment of this literature would have to be done in two steps. First, all pertinent references for a given period would have to be classified on the basis of some selected criterion. For example, Weiker proposed the following criterion to evaluate the relevant Turkish literature (1971):

> By "social research" in this article I mean studies of all aspects of Turkish society, data usually developed by the researcher through field work or other appropriate use of primary sources and also involving some attempts to use scientific research methods (not necessarily only quantitative) and to test hypotheses and make generalizations.

On the basis of this criterion, Weiker suggests that "a large proportion of the entries in a new bibliography by Mahmut Tezcan . . . must be excluded." But, as Tezcan suggests in a personal communication, Weiker is stressing only empirical research in sociology. Tezcan's objectives in preparing his bibliography were to include theoretical contributions, general discussions, as well as empirical studies and to cover not only sociology but also social psychology and cultural anthropology (1975). The second phase of the assessment would be a systematic review of all or a sample of the items that "passed" the preliminary test. These items could be analyzed both quantitatively and qualitatively to bring out the main theoretical orientations, the main themes and hypotheses, the range of methods used, the aspects of society studied, the major conclusions, and the theoretical and practical implications of the findings. It seems that only two sociologists, Armstrong and Khalaf, have come close to this way of assessing the literature, although they limited themselves to a quantitative analysis (Khalaf, 1965; and Armstrong, 1958a and 1958b). Armstrong used Burke's bibliography for the Arab East, 1945–1954, and

Khalaf established his own bibliography for Lebanon. Unfortunately, it is well beyond the scope of this essay to replicate their analysis for other parts of the Middle East or other periods. Before a presentation of some of the achievements of the sociology of the Middle East, it would be of some interest to discuss briefly the quantitative assessment of Armstrong and Khalaf as well as a few other less extensive surveys.

Armstrong classified 1115 out of the 1453 items appearing in Burke's annotated bibliography in terms of a criterion of "scientific rigorousness" which favors quantitatively oriented studies. His categories as well as the number of items in each category are as follows (1958a):

1. Experimental or Quantitative Field Studies involving systematic data collection, census or sample; test of a hypothesis; scientific analysis; and use of controls if possible or applicable.................................. 31
2. Less rigorous than (1) statistically but excellent theoretically and methodologically . . . rigorous content analysis; superior case study and participant observation 100
3. Semi-scientific descriptive studies, limited in quantification but based on intensive case study or observation or exhaustive library research...... 277
4. Scholarly but nonobjective, nonquantitative description.............. 242
5. Poor journalism, propaganda, social reformism and opinion 242

In addition to these five scaled categories, Armstrong had a sixth category of "scientific theoretical analysis and discussions" with 54 items, and a residual category of 167 items which could not be included in the scale (e.g., biographies and bibliographies). If we agree with Armstrong's criterion and consider all the items in categories 1, 2, and 6, then approximately 20% of the classifiable items in Burke's bibliography would be considered to be "scientifically rigorous." Unfortunately, Armstrong does not provide us with an assessment of the theoretical relevance or importance of these studies, or with a sense of what are some of their major findings. He does present, however, a quantitative classification of the topics or subfields of these studies as well as a brief and general assessment of some of the major studies and an indication of some of the gaps. As might be expected, demography, ecology, and social psychology rank highest in terms of "scientific quality." Other subfields with significant and high-quality studies include family and kinship, urban-industrial, social control and communication, rural sociology, and social structure. But Armstrong notes the paucity of such studies in many of these subfields.

Samir Khalaf (1965), in a similar quantitative analysis of studies of Lebanese society, classified them in the following four types: (1) analytical (26 studies, half of which were M.A. theses at the American University of Beirut); (2) descriptive (75 items); (3) general theoretical studies (79); and

(4) popular writings (35). These studies were also analyzed in terms of subjects and subfields, language, type of author, and place and form of publication. The most frequent topics or subfields for each type were as follows: social psychology and industrial sociology in (1); social structure, rural sociology, national heritage, and the family in (2); civilization, social and economic change, and political science in (3); and social problems and women's status in (4). It is also interesting to note that almost all analytical studies were in English and all popular writings in Arabic.

An analysis by André Adam of current research, including dissertations, on the sociology of the Maghreb provides an overview of the frequency of various research themes (1972). There were approximately 20 projects for each of the following topics: cultural and educational sociology, sociology of women, the family and kinship, and sociology of development. Adam comments that the emphasis on these topics is not surprising since it reflects the primary concerns of the Maghreb with problems of education, development, the family, and women. Next in importance, with about 10–14 studies, were the areas of oral literature, social structure and class, rural sociology, political sociology, demography, social history, and urban sociology. The themes that were least popular included sociology of religion and minorities. Adam notes the absence of any studies in such subfields as formal organization, industrial sociology, and the sociology of mass media. The absence of research projects on industrial sociology and the small frequency of sociopsychological studies in the sociology of the Maghreb stand in contrast to the importance of these subfields in the literature on Lebanon.

In a recent article Zghal and Karoui (1973) present a tabulation of the topics and fields of articles and books written by Tunisians and published in the *Revue Tunisienne de Sciences Sociales* or as the *Cahiers du CERES* since 1964. Interdisciplinary topics of research by geographers, economists, sociologists, and demographers include, in order of decreasing frequency, reform of agrarian structures and agricultural cooperatives (1 book, 18 articles), urbanization and urban relations (16 articles), demographic studies (3 books, 11 articles), regular and adult education (1 book, 12 articles), migration and rural exodus (8 articles), industrialization and employment (8 articles), and tourism (2 articles). Zghal and Karoui also give the following breakdown of themes for demographic and sociological studies: family planning (10 articles), political traditions and new elites (8 articles), family (3 articles), Islamic studies (3 articles), and juvenile delinquency (1 book, 1 article).

Finally, a preliminary review of articles on the *National Review of Social Sciences* published by the Egyptian National Center of Social and Criminological Research (from 1964 to 1969) revealed a strong social problem orientation in sociological or sociopsychological articles. This orientation is suggested by the following titles: "Study of Housing Conditions of Rural Areas: Giza Governorate" (Zaki and Fahmy, 1965), "Analysis of the Employment Situation Among the Educated Classes in the U.A.R." (Hamza, 1967), "Social Adaptation of Old People" (Fahmy, 1967), and "The Marriage and Fertility of Neurotics" (El-Islam and Shaalan, 1969). Fields, subfields, or topics of study of articles in this journal were, in decreasing order of frequency, psychology, education, social psychology, mental and physical health, rural sociology, and formal organization.

We now turn to a more qualitative assessment of studies of Middle Eastern societies, with particular emphasis on the work of sociologists. The preceding discussion suggests that there are various types of sociological work. Some sociologists are concerned with the development of a theory, a set of concepts, or a theoretical perspective that would help in the understanding of Middle Eastern societies and would guide empirical research. Other sociologists are engaged in qualitative or quantitative description of some aspects of Middle Eastern societies, such as the social origins of industrial workers and the academic or occupational aspirations of young people. Still other sociologists are engaged in the empirical test of selected hypotheses.

THEORETICAL WORK AND THEORETICAL ORIENTATION. As has already been indicated, the first sociological theory to emerge out of the Middle Eastern experience is that of Ibn Khaldûn's *Muqaddima,* which has been a source of theoretical inspiration as well as a model for many Middle Eastern sociologists. A few, such as al-Wardi (1966, and 1972), have also developed theories which are focused on an analysis of Middle Eastern societies. Thus according to Baali (1973), "al-Wardi's theory and explanation of the socialization process (including political socialization)" is based on the experience of Iraqi society as well as of other Arab societies. In spite of the pioneering work of Ibn Khaldûn, al-Wardi, and others, Western sociological theories have had a much greater impact on the development of the field in the Middle East. As indicated by Ahmed Abou-Zeid (1973), the first Egyptians who taught sociology at Cairo and Alexandria universities received their doctoral degrees in France and studied under Mauss and Fauconnet, two sociologists of the Durkheim school. The Durkheim influence was reinforced by Radcliffe-Brown, who introduced anthropology at Alexandria University in 1947. The French tradition is still noticeable in Cairo University, where the interest is mainly on theoretical problems such as solidarity, socialization, and social control. The French influence is also strong among the French-trained sociologists at St. Joseph and Lebanese Universities in Beirut (Khalaf, 1973), at the University of Tunis (Zghal and Karoui, 1973), and at the University of Tehran (Naderi, 1973; Enayat, 1973). On the other hand, in Alexandria University there is an attempt to integrate the French sociological approach with anthropological research techniques. Young Egyptian sociologists, particularly at ᶜAyn Shams University, favor a Marxist sociology and focus on the study of such topics as class struggle and class consciousness. There is no doubt that, partly because of its strong anti-colonial and anti-imperialistic perspective, Marxist theory is appealing to many young sociologists not only in Egypt but throughout the Middle East. Marxist theory has provided the impetus for some excellent research on ghettos, proletariat, rural and urban workers, and land tenure systems by such Maghrebi sociologists as Sebag, Pascon, and Hermassi. The emphasis on modes of production that is to be found in the work of Zghal, Karoui, and others suggests a Marxist influence.

As was indicated earlier, there is a very large number of speculative essays and books on various facets of Middle Eastern societies, such as nationalism, the status of women, and the effects of modernism, but most of these do not constitute sociological theory. Furthermore, a number of Middle Eastern sociologists have written textbooks on general sociology or essays in Arabic, Turkish, or Persian to acquaint their students and the general public with Western sociology. From the following evaluation by al-Qazzaz it is clear that these can hardly be considered to be valuable contributions to sociological theory (1973, p. 9):

> The writings . . . in addition to being theoretical and general, are not very systematic in presentation. Indeed, some are very confused. It offers the reader a shallow treatment of subject matter. Furthermore, although these writings are not direct translations of English sociology textbooks, close examination reveals that a good many of them are indirect translations with some modification, adaptation and summarization here and there from English textbooks, particularly the standard ones.

Although the aim of general speculative arguments and general sociological theory may be the same, mainly an explanation of general societal processes, their structure differs. A systematic sociological theory is made up of a set of formally defined concepts and a set of axioms, postulates, propositions, and hypotheses which incorporate these concepts and which are logically interrelated. It has been argued, however, that the lack of such a grand theory in the sociology of the Middle East is not to be deplored at this stage of the development of the discipline. Thus Hermassi suggests that "contemporary sociologists avoid the route of grand theory" (1973, p. 5). Lilia Ben Salem goes even further and argues that no solid theory could be developed without prior intimate knowledge of one's society (1968). Though Enayat regrets the "heavy utilitarian slant to most research projects" of Irani sociologists and their negligible "contribution to basic research," he sees these projects as playing "a major part in laying the foundation of a future, comprehensive sociology of Iran" (1973, p. 12).

Hermassi as well as other sociologists would argue in favor of "middle range" theory that is less ambitious and somewhat less systematic than grand theory. The focus of such a theory is not society as a whole, but one of its aspects such as the distribution of power or socialization. The advantage of this theory is that it is more flexible, provides a better guide to empirical research, and can be more easily reformulated in the light of pertinent evidence. It may be fair to assert that although there is a large number of tested and untested hypotheses about various aspects of Middle Eastern societies, few of these hypotheses have been integrated into "middle range" theories. Indeed, it could be argued that this is the next most important step in the development of the sociology of the Middle East.

MAJOR THEMES IN SOCIOLOGICAL RESEARCH ON THE MIDDLE EAST. As suggested by Hermassi, one of the major themes of sociological research on the Middle East has been the analysis of the nature, sources, and consequences of social change. Thus a few years ago, when the Turkish Social Science Association decided to launch an interdisciplinary project, the focus of this project was on social change in Izmir. The main objective of the research was to look "at the process of change as an interaction of fostered and spontaneous elements" in all phases of the social structure of Izmir. The decision to focus on the "study of social change on urban centers" was guided by the fact that it is in these centers "where the institutionalization of the new values of the Republic was most successful" and where "the influence of 'spontaneous' change already in motion at the time of the establishment of the Republic have been most visible" (anonymous, undated). The process of industrialization in Adaqazari, the major city in the province of Sakarya near Istanbul, is the focus of another interdisciplinary research project sponsored by the Faculty of Economics of Istanbul University. A Center of Sakarya Social Research was established for this purpose (Tezcan, 1975). Similarly, many interdisciplinary research projects of the Tehran Institute of Social Studies and Research had as their main objective the study of the various aspects of economic development including urbanization, changes in rural and tribal communities, industrial growth, social stratification, and changes in family structure (Enayat, 1973; Naraghi, 1967; Naderi, 1973).

A review of the abstracts of MESA annual meeting papers (1972) which deal with contemporary Middle Eastern societies reveals an overwhelming concern with social change. Indeed, this is suggested by the titles of such papers as "Modernization Theory and Family Change in Lebanon" (Samih K. Farsoun), "Industrialization and its Impact on Kinship Organization in an Egyptian Village" (Hani Fakhouri), "Modernization and the Liberation of Women in Tunisia, Algeria and Egypt" (Kathryn Boals), "Social Change and Political Participation in Turkey" (Ergun Ozbudun), and "Social Change in the Qazvin (Iran) Bazaar" (Howard J. Rotblat). Such an interest in the process of social change is, of course, not limited to Middle Eastern sociologists. For example, a number of sociologists from the United States, Finland, Yugoslavia, Rumania, Poland, Hungary, West Germany, and Morocco have recently devised a cross-national project of the sociopsychological impact of modernization, with an emphasis on the effects of the "different forms of development, which constitute the development process, in societies with various cultural backgrounds and different social and economic systems" (anonymous, 1973, p. 9).

There is a number of contrasting theoretical perspectives in the analysis of social change in Middle Eastern societies. Some social scientists such as Lerner (1964), McClelland (1963), and Halpern (1963) have favored an essentially Western model of modernization which is presumed to have universal application. As Lerner expressed it, "modernization . . . is a secular trend unilateral in direction—from traditional to participant lifeways" (1964, p. 89). Modernization involves both structural changes—urbanization, industrialization, expansion of mass media and literacy—as well as sociopsychological changes—increase in need-achievement, empathy, and psychological mobility. Modernism and traditionalism stand at opposite poles, linked only by Lerner's "transitionals." This view of social change has been challenged by a number of Western and Middle Eastern sociologists. Thus Karpat has argued that "Daniel Lerner's theory . . . is ethnocentric, for it accepts Western development as a unique model of modernization" and that "its major shortcoming lies in the fact that his theory of stages of modernization based on the correlation between industrialization, urbanization, literacy, and mass exposure is not historically correct" for the Middle East (1973, pp. 22–23). Duvignaud (1963) uses a Southern Tunisian village he studied to show that there is no necessary conflict between tradition and progress, and that traditional communities can undergo change partly because of their strong cohesion. Khalaf (1972) has used available data on family firms, kinship association, and company unions in Lebanon to show that traditional values and structure can generate change and facilitate an adaptation to modernization. For example, he states that "at Lebanon's present stage of industrialization, the family has proved to be a source not only of talent and service, but of initial capital for investment as well" and that "the kinship association in Lebanon is another, perhaps unique, institution that supports the hypothesis that extended kinship relations need not be inconsistent with urban and industrial requirements" (1972, p. 576). Khalaf is at present completing a book on the "convergence of tradition and modernity in Lebanon" in which he "examines critically some Western models of modernization (Lerner, Halpern, Eisenstadt, etc.) and suggests a few viable and relevant alternatives" (Khalaf, 1973). Farsoun has also documented the continued strength of the Lebanese extended family in the most urban and modern sectors of Lebanese society (1970). Janet Abu-Lughod has used demographic and ecological data on Egypt, and particularly Cairo, to challenge the views of some American sociologists on the nature and consequences of urbanization (1964). It is clear that this emerging theoretical perspective on the nature of modernization and its impact on traditional social structure is likely to influence research in many subfields of sociology such as the family, formal organization and bureaucracy, and social stratification.

In recent years sociological research in or on the Middle East has been focused on the following subfields: demography, the family, urban and rural communities, and social stratification. The main themes and some of the findings of this research are presented in the following discussion. This discussion also indicates the current status of sociological studies of formal organization, religion, deviant behavior, education, and youth.

Sociological Aspects of Population. There is no doubt that an increasing awareness of the social and economic implications of population growth and redistribution as well as the adoption of explicit population policies by a number of Middle Eastern countries has provided a real impetus to demographic analysis and to population studies by sociologists, economists, and other social scientists in this world region (anonymous, 1974a). This review is limited to sociological studies of population, with particular reference to fertility and rural–urban migration. The first systematic and sociologically oriented fertility surveys were carried out under the direction of Rizk in Egypt (1957) and Yaukey in Lebanon (1959). Since 1960 the following surveys of fertility and family planning have been completed: Algeria 1967–1968, rural Iran 1965, Tehran 1965 and 1971, Jordan 1972, Lebanon 1973, Morocco 1966–1967, urban Tunisia 1964, and Turkey 1963 and 1968 (Baum, Dopkowski, Duncan, and Gardiner, 1974a and 1974b). More limited information on fertility is available from censuses and demographic surveys (Sabagh, 1970). As might be expected, there are many analyses of data from these various sources, and although most of them are fairly descriptive some have attempted to test hypotheses about the relative impact on fertility and family planning of such social structural variables as urbanization, education, occupation, and female labor force participation (Lapham, 1971; von Allmen-Joray, 1971; AARDES, 1972; Cairo Demographic Center, 1971; Stycos and Weller, 1967; Paydarfar, 1974; and Rizk, 1972). The recent work of Leila el Hamamsy and her colleagues at the Social Science Research Center in Cairo has focused on an analysis of women's roles and self-concepts.

In the words of Youssef one should consider the effects on fertility of "the interplay between prohibitions imposed informally by males, which restrict women to marital and motherhood related roles, and the volitional resistance of women to claim the ability to exercise their 'rights' in the supra familial world" (1974, p. 44).

In view of the rapid urbanization and increase in rural–urban migration in the Middle East (Ibrahim, 1974; Clarke and Fisher, 1972), one would expect many more sociological studies of this process. The hypotheses of Abu-Lughod (1961) about the nature of peasant adjustment to life in Cairo are well-known in the American sociological literature, but seem to have been tested systematically only by Petersen (1971). Using data on a cluster of migrants from five villages living in Cairo, Petersen concludes as follows (1971, p. 575):

> The limited interview data reviewed here offer strong support, although qualified, to Abu-Lughod's assertions about where migrants settle in Cairo, their working conditions, and the role of formal and informal institutions in their adjustment. More important, this analysis points to the need for more rigorous inquiry into rural-urban migration in Egypt and comparable societies and into the dynamics of underlying adjustments of villagers to life in the city.

In another paper, Janet Abu-Lughod (1972) has argued that the extent of selectivity in migration is related to the politicization of rural migrants in urban areas. This is another hypothesis that should be tested with systematic data on Cairo or some other Middle Eastern city. An interesting attempt to study rural–urban migration from the place of origin is provided by Fuad Khuri's paper on migration from two Lebanese villages (1967). Other aspects of rural–urban migration have been analyzed by sociologists such as Baali (1966), Geiser (1967), Nagi (1974), and Yasa (1973).

As suggested by the work of Makhlouf (1972), B'chir (1972), Attia (1970), Seklani (1970), Picouet (1971), and the volume edited by Clarke and Fisher (1972), the work of demographers and human geographers on internal migration complements that of sociologists. Demographers tend to analyze internal migration in terms of its effects on population changes in areas of origin and destination as well as in terms of age and sex differentials. This perspective has revealed, for example, the importance of natural increase in the growth of many Middle Eastern cities. Geographers tend to emphasize the spatial aspect of migration. In a detailed monograph, Daniel Noin (1970) has documented the different migration streams between rural regions and urban areas. But he also describes the characteristics of these streams and the determinants of rural–urban migration.

Although the international migration of workers from both the Maghreb and more recently from Turkey to Western Europe has attracted the attention of many social scientists (MESA, 1972; Talha, 1974; Gokalp, 1973; Krane, 1975; and Michel, 1974), there have been too few studies by sociologists of the exodus of Palestinian Arabs (Dodd and Barakat, 1969).

Urban and Rural Communities. In spite of increasing urbanization, the Middle East is still predominantly rural; this in part explains the preponderance of studies of villages and nomads (Planck, 1972; Enayat, 1973; Harik, 1974). There may also be methodological and theoretical reasons for such an emphasis on rural communities. If the objective of the research is to comprehend the total social structure of a community and the methods are essentially those of field observations, then the village or nomadic group is a logical choice. However, the recent work of a number of American sociologists suggests that if one were willing to give up this objective, it would be possible to use qualitative field observations for an understanding of segments of the social and ecological structure of a city. On the other hand, studies of the overall social or ecological structure of a city would require the use of quantitative methods.

Unfortunately, there are too few studies of rural and urban communities by sociologists. Sociologists who have studied rural areas have tended to focus on the structural consequences of such changes as farm mechanization, land redistribution, the initiation of cooperatives, and land reform programs (Enayat, 1973; Zghal and Karoui, 1973; Harik, 1974; Karpat, 1960; Yasa, 1969–1970). The comparative and quantitative research on four Turkish villages by Hinderink and Kıray (1970) provides a good example of a sociological approach. Another good example is given by Gadalla's (1962) analysis of the effects of land reform on Egyptian rural communities and families and based on a survey carried out in three land reform estates and three matched waqf estates.

The kind of contribution that sociologists can make to the study of Middle Eastern cities is well illustrated by Khuri's work on Beirut (1974), Kıray's analysis of work life and settlement patterns in Izmir (1972), Khalaf and Kongstad's analysis of urbanism and urbanization in Beirut (1973), Abu-Lughod's monograph on Cairo (1971), and Adam's extensive study of the changing social structure of Casablanca (1968). There have been a large number of studies of Turkish urban slums (gecekondu) carried out by Turkish sociologists such as Yasa, Geray, Keleş, Kongar, and Saran (Tezcan, 1975). In recent years a few sociologists have used quantitative methods to analyze the social ecology of Cairo (Abu-Lughod, 1969), Alexandria (Latif, 1974a and 1974b), and Izmir (Keleş, 1972).

Abu-Lughod used Cairo "census tract" data from the 1947 and 1960 population censuses of Egypt to identify different types of social areas in this city. She shows that "the population of Cairo, diversified as it is, can be divided roughly into three main types. . . (1) the rural; (2) the traditional urban; (3) the modern or industrial urban . . . each following the tune of a different piper and each with a somewhat different prospect for the future" (1971, p. 218). The following conclusion by Khalaf and Kongstad supports Abu-Lughod's arguments and findings and questions the assumptions of Western urban sociology (1973, p. 134):

> Tentative as the nature of the evidence is, it may still be suggested that urbanization in Beirut thus far has not been associated with a large measure of decline in kinship or weakening of traditional ties and communal attachments. Nor has it created a depersonalized and atomized society. One may perhaps infer that the intensity and increasing scale of urbanization has not been accompanied by a proportional degree of urbanism as a way of life.

Adam (1968) has described in great detail the demographic and economic changes experienced by Casablanca and has analyzed the accompanying processes of social and personal disorganization and social reorganization. He considers the emergence of class and class consciousness rather than the kinship group as being the most important phase of social reorganization. Finally, a few Maghrebi sociologists have focused on the analysis of the current processes of social disorganization and reorganization (Stambouli, 1971; Boukraa, 1971) as well as various aspects of the precolonial social structure (Stambouli and Zghal, 1972) of North African cities.

The social and ecological aspects of Middle Eastern cities, villages, and tribal groups have been extensively studied by Orientalists, historians, anthropologists, and human geographers (cf. Lapidus, 1970; Brown, 1973; Hourani and Stern, 1970). Though the contributions of historians have been assessed by Albert Hourani and those of anthropologists by Richard T. Antoun elsewhere in this volume, some attention should be given here to the work of human geographers. The two themes of a conference on the geography of the Maghreb, modernization of agriculture and interaction between cities and rural areas, could be considered to be among the dominant concerns of the human geography of the Middle East. Another major interest has been the study of the urban morphology and spatial structure of Middle Eastern cities.

In the light of many national programs of land reform and redistribution, farm mechanization, and rural cooperatives or corporations, the concern with agricultural modernization is not surprising. According to Naderi (1973), the interdisciplinary study of the impact of rural development is one of the major programs of research of Tehran University's Institute of Social Studies and Research. As suggested in the following observation by Makhlouf, a Tunisian geographer, it is important to distinguish between national goals and actual accomplishments (1968, p. 51):

> The development plan had as its objective the modernization of *all* agriculture. Modernization effectively occurs in production cooperatives and in the state

> domain destined to be transformed into cooperatives. For different reasons, private agriculture, whether large or small, modern or traditional, remains attached to its techniques and its traditions.

According to Paul Ward English "geographers have played a major role in contributing to recognition" of the importance of studying the "interacting nature of city, village and tribe in systems of spatial and social organization" (1973, p. 38). His own monograph on *City and Village in Iran* is a model of the type of study that is needed. He expressed as follows the theme of his monograph (1966, p. xviii):

> The existence of (the) regional organization of human activity is a major theme of this study. It identifies the Persian landscape as a product of a feudal rather than folk society. Villages are not isolated from the city or from one another. There are strong patterns of interrelatedness between every village and the city, and weaker social and economic ties among villages.

The changing interrelations between cities and rural areas in Algeria, Tunisia, and Morocco have been explored by Maghrebi and French geographers. For example, two Tunisian geographers, Fakhfakh (1968) and Fahem (1968), have explored the effects of population growth, the decline in traditional industry, the attraction of the primate city of Tunis, and national agricultural policies on the relationships between Sfax and Sousse and their rural regions.

There are a number of studies of individual Middle Eastern cities by geographers including the studies of Kirman and Herat by English (1966), Sale by Naciri (1963), Shiraz by Clarke (1963), Kermanshah by Clarke and Clark (1963), Khartoum by Hamdan (1960), and Amman by Hacker (1960). The following summary statement by English indicates that geographers are not only interested in delineating the urban morphology of traditional Middle Eastern cities but also in identifying the elements and nature of changes in this morphology (1973, pp. 11, 14, and 17):

> The spatial patterning of . . . Middle Eastern cities until recently differs markedly from that of industrial centers of the modern world. Several characteristics which consistently reappear in these cities, from Morocco to Afghanistan are: 1) an emphasis on enclosure and security both in urban plans and domestic architecture, 2) the allocation of central space to a mosque bazaar complex, and 3) organization of residential space into semi-autonomous quarters (*haráh*) and streets (*darb*) usually with some degree of ethnic, occupational, or religious unity. . . . This traditional Middle Eastern urban setting has been reshaped by the introduction of Western transportation and communication systems, by the development of new attitudes, values, and ideologies, and by the spreading availability of Western technology. . . . Internally, these new cities are being restructured on new premises, not simply physically but socially as well.

The Family. Since the family has been the object of much legislation in the Middle East and since it constitutes the key social group not only in villages but also in cities, we could expect it to attract the attention of many social scientists (e.g., Allman, Achour, and Stone, 1974; Nedjati, 1974). Partly because of their orientation as well as their focus on the small community, anthropologists have contributed much more than sociologists to an understanding of kinship and family structure and of its social functions. On the other hand, sociologists have been much more quantitative and global in their study of the family and have tended to rely on national census data and the results of special surveys (Prothro, 1961; Prothro and Diab, 1974; Timur, 1972; Kongar, 1972; Touba, 1972; Belghiti, 1971). Sociologists have generally focused on quantitative analyses of the following aspects of the family: (1) the structural processes of family formation, growth, and dissolution; (2) types of family; (3) the sociopsychological patterns of social interaction and role differentiation within the family; and (4) the place of the family in the given social structure of a society. There have been a number of descriptive studies of variations in age at marriage, polygyny, and divorce, but there is a need to develop a more systematic perspective on the process of family formation and dissolution. Timur (1972) has organized her analysis of the Turkish data around types of family and has provided unusual evidence of urban–rural and regional variations in family types. Hinderink and Kıray have explored the interrelations between economic development and family types, intrafamilial authority, and the role of lineage in four Turkish villages. Their conclusion is worth quoting since it provides further support for the aguments advanced by Khalaf, Farsoun, and others (1970, p. 242):

> We also studied the interdependency between agroeconomic development and family kinship and organization. Our observations showed that the composition of households is changing under the impact of newly emerging subsistence patterns, without losing the family's main function of providing security and mutual help, since no other institutions have appeared to take care of these functions. As far as authoritarian intrafamily relations are concerned, no evidence has been found to prove that these stand in the way of development.

Prothro and Diab (1974) have documented the generational and socioeconomic variations in the main features of the Arab family including family formation and dissolution, family size, and extended family ties on the basis of surveys carried out under their direction in Amman, Damascus, Tripoli, Beirut and the two villages of Artas and Buarij studied earlier by Granqvist and Fuller. Prothro and Diab also used census information and data tabulated from the records of the religious Sunni courts of Tripoli and Sidon.

A lengthy annotated bibliography on "Women in the Middle East" prepared by Ayad al-Qazzaz suggests that one popular topic of study has been women's social roles within and outside the family. Though most of these studies have been descriptive in nature, with particular emphasis on villages, there have been a few attempts to examine systematically the determinants of women's role definition and performance. Prothro and Diab have explored the relationship between modesty and the role of women and have documented the extent of changes in the wearing of the veil, patterns of education, employment outside the home, and recreation. Youssef has compared the nature and extent of women's labor force participation in the Middle East and Latin America (1974). Finally, Sertel (1972) has studied quantitatively the interrelations between women's roles and patterns of urbanization and modernization. A theoretically important observation is that "the process of economic development has, so far, motivated the sexes differentially," and that "the impact of such development has not been sufficiently great to break the community norms and social values that limit the ability of females to make full use of what is available to their villages and households" (1972, p. 67).

Social Stratification. Middle Eastern sociologists have placed a high priority on the analysis of various aspects of social stratification and on the impact of independence, urbanization, industrialization, and modernization on the distribution of status, power, and wealth. For example, the theme of the Mediterranean conference held in Hammamet, Tunisia in 1965 was "social stratification and development" (Kıray, 1973). Tunisian, Turkish, Moroccan, Lebanese, and Egyptian sociologists participated in this conference. Topics discussed included the formation, evolution, and political role of the proletariat in Egypt (Wassef, 1973), the role, characteristics, or patterns of recruitment of administrative, political, and industrial elites in Tunisia (Zghal, 1973; Stambouli, 1973; Charrad, 1973; and Hermassi, 1973), and the characteristics of the new middle class in Jordan (Qutub, 1973). In his research on Beirut, Khalaf has also described the salient features of the "new middle class," which because of the "survival of traditional and communal attachments . . . remains relatively diffuse and amorphous as a social group" (Khalaf and Kongstad, p. 73). Political scientists such as Halpern (1969) have also been interested in the nature and political role of the "new middle class."

At the first conference of Maghrebi sociologists in Rabat in 1967, Tunisian sociologists showed their continued interest in the study of elites. Moroccan sociologists such as Pascon and Khatibi focused on the analysis of contemporary stratification and social mobility. Both Maghrebi and Turkish sociologists have emphasized the power and economic aspects of class and have recognized the possibility of class conflict. On the other hand, with few exceptions, the prestige dimension of stratification is more important in studies of Lebanese rural and urban communities. For example, Khuri (1969) used

Warner's reputational technique in a study of social classes in a Lebanese village. Khuri notes the absence of class consciousness and class conflict in this village. The same reputational technique was used by Abu-Laban (1970) to identify leaders in Sidon, Lebanon. The use of this procedure has been challenged by Hinderink and Kıray, who argue that the "status" aspect of stratification is less important than the "power aspect" in an investigation of the influence of "social stratification on development." They summarize as follows their findings of this influence in four Turkish villages (1970, p. 243):

> It was found that the real obstacle to true social and economic development in the villages lies in the existing power relationships. In the least-developed village, the old power relations, although changing, have not yet been replaced by new ones. In the transitional village, a very definite change has taken place that has led to the appearance of a landless group controlled by the newly emerging richer landowners. In the technologically most-developed villages, although theoretically the social system has changed from a feudal landlord-sharecropper relationship into a large-scale commercial farming-contractual wage labor relationship, the essential power relations have remained the same.

Partly because of their importance in the process of political and economic change, national elites throughout the Middle East have been extensively studied, particularly by American political scientists (cf. Zonis, 1971; Waterbury, 1970; Binder, 1962). A number of sociologists such as Berger (1960), Ben Salem (1970), Hermassi (1973), Heper (in press), Khatibi (1970), al-Qazzaz (1971), and Zghal (1973) have also focused on this aspect of stratification. The techniques used to identify and study elites and the problems explored have varied widely and there are no particular disciplinary orientations. Both sociologists and political scientists have carried out intensive interviews of leaders and elite members, whereas others have relied mainly on available information on certain elites (administrative, military, etc.).

There is a real need, however, to go beyond the study of elites and to study patterns of social stratification at the level of a nation or at least a region. This is a task that sociologists should assume. Although population censuses do provide a rich source of information on occupational, educational, and income differentiation at the national level as well as in urban and rural areas, there are few detailed and systematic analyses of these data from a social stratification perspective. New national surveys are needed to identify the nature, determinants, and consequences of social differentiation and mobility. Of particular importance would be studies of occupational prestige, achievement, and mobility.

Other Sociological Fields and Topics. There are a number of other fields such as complex and large-scale organizations, religious structure and behavior, and deviant behavior which have been relatively neglected by sociologists of the Middle East. A sociology of the sociology of the Middle East would be needed to reveal the reason for this neglect.

The increasing importance of complex and large-scale organization in government, business, industry, and labor should have inspired many more systematic and theoretically oriented studies of the recruitment and attitudes of members of these organizations, of formal and informal structure, and of the articulation of complex organizations with other social groups, particularly kinship groups. Of particular importance would be the development of a set of hypotheses pertaining to the relationship between the growth of large-scale organizations and the process of modernization. The pioneer study in this field is Berger's *Bureaucracy and Society in Modern Egypt* (1957). Berger's findings were compared with similar data obtained for Turkish bureaucrats by Roos, Jr. and Roos (1971). A joint venture by Irani and Tunisian sociologists sponsored by UNESCO provides extensive data on the recruitment, characteristics, and attitudes of industrial workers, but unfortunately, few tests of hypotheses (Tehran University, 1965; Sebag, Bouhdiba, and Camilleri, 1968). Other studies of relevance here include the research on dock workers in Tunis by Hermassi (1966), on industrial workers in Alexandria by el-Saaty and Hirabayashi (1959) and in Tunisia by Stambouli (1968), and on industrial unions and family firms and family associations by Khalaf (1971).

There is a vast literature on the nature of Islam and the place of Islam in Middle Eastern societies. Thus of the nearly 5000 titles in English, French, Italian, or German in the bibliography on *Arab Culture and Society in Change* covering the period from the 1910s to 1971, more than a third are on Islam (Center for the Study of the Modern Arab World, 1973). It is surprising, therefore, to find so few studies of Islamic religious behavior, norms, and organization by sociologists. In a review of the evidence on Muslim religious behavior in North Africa, it was asserted that "the type of sociological research which is common in Christian countries has barely begun to be applied to Islam" (anonymous, 1971, p. 38). There are, however, a few excellent examples of the kind of theoretically oriented research that is needed. These include Berger's (1970) quantitative and structural study of religious organization in Egypt, Gilsenan's (1973) description and analysis of a Sufi order in Egypt, Stone's (1974) study in the Weberian tradition of religious ethic and spirit of capitalism in Tunisia, and the analyses of the role of Mullas in Iran by Ferdows (1969) and of the Maqased benevolent association by Khalaf (1969). The sociological study of Islam poses a number of theoretical problems that need to be resolved. For example, Gilsenan states that in the study of Sufi orders "formal typologies developed in a sociological tradition centered in the study of Christianity are just as likely to hinder as to help" (1973, p. 5). The insights and observations of anthropologists such as Gilsenan (1973),

Antoun (1966), Barclay (1963), Gellner (1970), Fakhouri (1972), Geertz (1968), and Fahim (1973), as well as the insights and contributions of other scholars such as Van Nieuwenhuizje (1971), von Grunebaum (1962), Gibb (1970), Mardin (1969), Rahman (1966), Nasr (1966), Berque (1966) and Charnay (1966 and 1972) should help to resolve in part these theoretical problems as well as provide a basis for the development of sociological theories about Islam in the contemporary Middle East.

The work of the Egyptian National Center of Social and Criminological Research and of some Turkish sociologists (Tezcan, 1975) suggests that there is a lively and practical interest in the study of deviant behavior in some Middle Eastern countries. Unfortunately, there are few attempts to deal analytically either with the practical or theoretical issues involved. The type of studies that are needed are illustrated by Khalaf's study of prostitution in Beirut (1965b), Katchadourian's extensive work on mental illness in Lebanon (1969), Bouhdiba's study of juvenile delinquency in Tunisia (1969), and Ammar and Ledjri's (1973) analysis of the familial determinants of schizophrenia in Tunisia. Racy (1970) has published an extensive and annotated bibliography of mental illness in a number of Arab countries.

This brief survey of the sociological literature on the Middle East cannot be concluded without some reference to the many sociological studies of youth and students. Some studies document the ways in which social change is affecting the roles and values or the problems of youth in Egypt (Shafshak, 1968; Hamza et al., 1969), in Morocco (Pascon and Bentahar, 1971), in Tunisia (Camilleri, 1973), and in a number of Middle Eastern countries (Gardner, 1972). Others have focused on certain topics such as the socioeconomic ranking of occupations by Iraqi college students (Alzobaie and El-Ghannam, 1968), the educational aspirations of Lebanese (Abu-Laban, 1968) or Iraqi (Baali, 1967) youth, the occupational aspirations of college students in various Middle Eastern countries (Stone, 1971), the attitudes of Lebanese college students toward the Palestinian Resistance Movement (Barakat, 1971), the perceived reference-group support of students in a Lebanese college (Tomeh, 1970), or the attitudes of secondary-school students in Cairo toward women's emancipation (Dodd, 1968). Obviously, many of these studies could have also been included in the discussion of contributions to such subfields as the family and social stratification.

FUTURE NEEDS

We can identify at least three different ways of establishing priorities for sociological work on the Middle East. The first and most obvious one is to approach the problem from a strictly *disciplinary* perspective and to emphasize topics or questions that have been relatively neglected. Thus the preceding discussion of the state of research in various sociological subfields has indicated some of the existing gaps in sociological studies of population, the family, urban and rural communitees, social stratification, formal organization, religion, and deviance. Though priorities should be specified in terms of sociological subfields or theoretical and methodological problems of greatest relevance to the sociological study of Middle Eastern societies, it is not clear how these priorities are to be established (Gardner, 1973).

The second strategy is to focus on specific *social problems* that are of concern to Middle Easterners and to emphasize the topics or questions which relate in some ways to these problems. Priorities would be established in terms of those social problems which are of greatest concern. Though disciplinary boundaries are obviously irrelevant in such an approach, it may be possible to specify the nature of the contributions of sociology. At the present stage of the development of the sociology of the Middle East, this would seem to be the most realistic and fruitful strategy. But, as suggested by Khalaf, there remains the "critical question" of deciding whether or not Middle East "social scientists are exploring the truly most troublesome problems and issues their societies are facing" (1973a).

Finally, it may be possible to specify *broad areas* of general concern to all disciplines, including sociology, which reflect in part the Middle Eastern experience. Though the emphasis is on the interdisciplinary study of such broad areas as Islam and social change, some of the questions that are raised would undoubtedly be of relevance to specific social problems.

The following discussion presents a brief review of some of the disciplinary or social problem-oriented topics and broad areas that would seem to be of highest priority in terms of the Middle Eastern experience.

Disciplinary Topics

Hermassi has argued that "the bulk of sociological research in the Maghreb remains theoretically weak, purposeless and usually eclectic" and has attributed this tendency to two constraints. One constraint that we have already discussed is the cultural dependency on France. He describes the second constraint as follows (1973, p. 9):

> The kind of scientific community which can enforce the norms of scientific achievement is simply lacking. A proclivity for each man "doing his thing" tends to pervade the research institutions. Techniques are employed regardless of their adequacy . . . and theoretical shortcomings persist unnoticed.

Hermassi's comments suggest the need for both theoretically relevant research as well as for research aimed at testing the adequacy of various research techniques that are mostly Western in origin. One serious problem has been the uncritical use of paper-and-pencil tests and questionnaires. Similarly, many surveys and censuses carried out by governmental agencies have included questions that are identical to those used in Western countries. This is not to say that sociologists and government agencies are not aware of problems involved in using particular research techniques or particular questions, but the process of testing their applicability may be almost as complex as the original research itself. Furthermore, there is strong pressure to "produce" substantive results. A simple example will indicate the complexity of this issue. "Date of birth" or "age at last birthday" is one of the questions used in all Middle Eastern censuses and in most surveys. Field observations or questioning would quickly reveal that many adult villagers in a country such as Morocco do not know or have only an approximate idea of their ages. In a survey carried out in Morocco in 1961–1963 it was decided to rely on a calendar of historical events and thus use on a large scale a technique often employed on a small scale by anthropologists. This is, of course, a procedure that is more costly than the use of a simple question on age or birth date. A methodological analysis by Scot and Sabagh (1970) suggests, however, that it does not necessarily yield better data.

The objective of methodological studies would not only be to explore the problems involved in the applicability of Western techniques of social research but also to develop procedures that are more adapted to conditions in various Middle Eastern population groups. The tape recording of approximately 800 census interviews during the 1971 census of Morocco is one example of the type of studies that is needed (Rachidi, Abzahd, and Housni, 1973). Though these tapes provide a rich source of information on how census data are *produced*, their analysis is fairly complex and requires much ingenuity. An analysis of some data from these tapes by Anna Quandt (1973), reveals, for example, the difficulties involved in defining a household and establishing a roster of household members. Khalaf and his associates "met the same difficulty in identifying and interviewing household units" in their study of *Hamra* (1973a). The methodological problems in carrying out survey research in the Middle East have been explored by Timur (1971) and Kâğitçibaşi (1971) in Turkey, by Zaki and Mahmoud (1965) in Egypt, and by Tessler (1973) in Tunisia. It is significant that the first annual volume to be published by the Egyptian Sociological Association will be focused on discussions of field and other methods of social research.

There is no doubt that if outside funding were available, Middle Eastern governmental agencies such as Divisions of Statistics or Health Ministries would be responsive to proposals for methodological research. A good example is provided by the Centre d'Etudes et de Recherches Démographiques which was recently established in the Moroccan Division of Statistics with partial funding from AID and in collaboration with the International Program of Laboratories for Population Studies of the University of North Carolina (Rachidi, Abzahd, and Housni, 1973). The main objective of this center is to test various methods of collecting vital data. It should be noted that the tape recording of census interviews was done with the help of this center.

The discussion of the preceding sections has provided some indication of substantive sociological areas or topics where the need for additional or new research is greatest. As Morroe Berger as well as others have suggested, it is important that this research be sensitive to the social experience of the Middle East. Whereas an obsession with Western "methodological tools and research designs and techniques" may be counterproductive, an "obsession with Western conceptual models and perspectives" is far more serious. It is essential that the concepts and categories of analysis emerge and be pertinent to the Middle Eastern experience (Khalaf, 1973a). For example, a study of prostitution should start from a Middle Eastern interpretation of sexual misconduct of women in terms of honor and shame rather than from a Western perspective. One "indiscretion" may be sufficient for a woman to "fall" all the way to the bottom.

The study of "sex roles" is of high priority from the standpoints of both anthropology and sociology. The Chapter by Richard T. Antoun in this volume has spelled out in detail some of the reasons for the need to emphasize sex roles and some of the directions of research. The approach to this problem should be both structural and sociopsychological. One important question raised by the work of Youssef (1974) and others is the low rate of labor-force participation of women in the Middle East. However, the definition of the labor force is essentially Western, and a proper answer to this question would require a redefinition of the work situation in terms of nature and extent of contacts between men and women.

Social stratification is another area where much more work needs to be done, particularly in terms of identifying those aspects of ranking that emerge out of the Middle Eastern experience. One important question is the extent to which programs of agrarian reform and development modify the system of ranking and the distribution of privileges and wealth in villages. Another important problem pertains to the possibility of distinguishing different patterns of occupational hierarchies ("traditional," "modern," etc.) and occupational mobility in urban areas. As suggested by Antoun, there is also a need to explore the effects of industrialization and bureaucratization of the relation between occupational and ethnic differentiation.

Social Problems

In a paper on "Middle Eastern and North African Studies: Development and Needs" published in 1967 (*M.E.S.A. Bulletin*), Morroe Berger has stressed the need for interdisciplinary research on "specific problems emerging from recent social change." He lists the following problems as worthy of study: (a) extent of and obstacles to *economic development*, (b) the nature and characteristics of *leaders* and the relationships between leaders and *masses*, (c) the problems posed by rapid increase in *population*, (d) the nature and implications of the new secular and modern *education*, (e) consequences of *nationalism*, and (f) the effects of the oil industry. More recently, Stone (1973) has also suggested the need for research dealing "with the recent phenomena of social change in the area." For example, such research might focus on "the impact of oil income on the social structure, social welfare programs and other aspects of middle eastern societies" as well as on the social impact of the ongoing and rapidly changing Arab–Israeli conflict, including social changes among Palestinians in Israel and outside of Israel" (Stone, 1973).

Ahmed Abou Zeid (1973) has also stated that the first priorities in anthropological and sociological research are now given to "the persistent problems which impinge on the society" and which include the problem of population growth and family planning, the social effects of urbanization and industrialization, the settlement of newly reclaimed land, and the sedentarization of nomads. Social scientists in Iran are faced with a similar set of priorities. Nader Naderi (1973), Director of Teheran University's Institute of Social Studies and Research indicates that research on the following problems are of greatest need: (a) rapid urbanization without industrialization, (b) the impact of various rural development programs on village social and economic structure, and (c) the settlement of nomads. Although many of these priorities are established by the government which supports and finances all social science research, some attention should be given to the problems as they are perceived by the general population. He also stresses the fact that this research as well as the methodology that is adopted or devised "should help the local social scientists to build up their own theoretical framework."

On the basis of the discussions by Berger, Abou Zeid, Naderi, and others it is possible to outline some of the needed problem-oriented research. Clearly, this research has to be designed and conducted from a Middle Eastern perspective.

In a speech delivered in 1971, President Sadat of Egypt expressed himself as follows on the "phenomenon" of rapid population growth (AUFS, 1972):

> This phenomenon if it continues would not only condemn all our hopes for evolution and progress, but threaten the simple maintenance of our present level. . . . And when I say family planning is one of the most important political

> concerns, that is because it is a political and social cause. . . . Perhaps, one of the reasons we have not succeeded in treating this problem has been our overreliance on the purely medical side.

These comments clearly suggest the need for interdisciplinary research whose objective would be to identify the structural conditions and the socio-psychological variables that help sustain a high fertility and may account for the lack of success of family planning programs. One significant topic would be the study of "sex roles," particularly as these pertain to the process of decision making in the family. Another topic would be the role of mass media and the formal educational system in increasing an awareness of this problem.

An important problem pertains to the massive rural–urban migration and all its consequences for urban and rural areas. The concerted efforts of geographers, anthropologists, and sociologists will be needed to assess the volume, direction, and characteristics of this migration. Another related problem is the nature and effectiveness of the social and economic assimilation of villagers in cities. If it is true that a city like Cairo is made of many different villages, then we need to consider the social networks and patterns of interrelations between these different "social worlds" of the metropolis. The possible effects of this migration on village social and economic structure and the potentials for rural economic development need to be considered.

There are a number of problems that relate to the process of education, and particularly higher education in the Middle East. In the Maghreb the most crucial problem has been the process of decolonialization of the educational system. In other Middle Eastern countries such as Egypt the problem has been defined in terms of the "overproduction" and "underemployment" of university graduates.

Finally, urban planners, architects, engineers, and various government offices have been concerned with the many problems created by rapid urban growth, including urban congestion, haphazard developments and squatter settlements, and increasing demand for urban services. More than 10 years ago a conference on "The New Metropolis in the Arab World" brought together social scientists and urban planners to discuss these many problems and formulate priorities for research. In a more recent conference on Middle Eastern Urbanism held in Chicago, January 13–14, 1973, one of the recommendations indicated as follows the need for research that is relevant to the solution of urban problems:

> Topics like the politics of planning, the role of bidonvilles in shaping the structure and functions of Middle Eastern cities in the future, the common goals shared by transformers and the transformed, and specific urban problems like overcrowding and urban health merit immediate attention. Urban planning is being practiced even if it is not discussed. It is essential, therefore, that means of translating

knowledge into forms that can be implemented be given high ranking on any list of research priorities.

Broad Areas of Study

In the same article published in 1967, Morroe Berger also emphasized the need for "broad inquiries into basic institutions" and particularly the study of political, economic, and religious institutions. Similar views have been expressed by Khalaf and Hermassi. Khalaf states his views as follows (1973):

> One central interdisciplinary topic of general nature which should be given priority . . . is the explanation of continuity and change; fixity and structural transformation. This could be explored at all levels: demographic, urban and rural systems, social stratification, economic and political systems, kinship patterns, education and communication, values and cultural expressions, etc. . . . The effort would be to identify, document, and account for the survival of so-called "traditional" forms and networks in all such subfields and analyze their transformation through time and interplay with seemingly "modern" and secular institutions. Only by doing so can we begin to disavow ourselves from the tyranny of Western models and perspectives and study the relevant dimensions of Arab society without distorting its socio-historical reality.

Hermassi (1973) stresses the need to focus on the study of "regime organization, national integration, and structural change." By "regime organization" he means the involvement of the state in "nation building" and the extent to which the state "is capable of mobilizing (or inhibiting) societal resources for developmental goals." Reacting to the colonial policies of "divide and rule," many sociologists have emphasized the analysis of the process of national integration, and have shown, for example, that movements of "rural unrest and regional discontent" involved "the use of traditional means in pursuit of modern ends." Now that national integration has been achieved, "more attention should be given to internal diversities." Finally, according to Hermassi, "there is a significant commitment, by individual sociologists and by most research institutes, to the study of structural changes in the rural society." The concern is "with genuinely developmental issues" and with finding answers to the folowing types of questions: "to what extent is agricultural development affected by social structure, value system, land tenure system, technological transformation? How is the revenue distributed?"

There is no doubt that historians, political scientists, social anthropologists, geographers, and sociologists could agree that the study of Islam is a broad subject of common concern. Even though each discipline would want to study Islam from its own perspective and using its own methods, it should be possible to specify a number of questions which they can all agree to explore.

For example, as suggested by the work of Hermassi, Lapidus, and others, one question would be the changing relationship between Islam and government, the nature of this relation in the more explicitly "Islamic" states, and the role of politico-religious movements such as Wahhabism and Mahdism. In his chapter Albert Hourani suggests that the "institutions and politics of even the most explicitly 'Islamic' states cannot be explained without taking into account also such factors as geographical position, economic needs, and the interest of dynasties and rulers." A number of questions could be asked both in a historical context and in the contemporary Middle East about the social and political role of the ᶜulamâ. Finally, the changing interrelation between social and religious norms could be another subject of interdisciplinary interest.

BIBLIOGRAPHY

Aardes (Association Algérienne pour la Recherche Démographique, Economique et Sociale). 1972. *Natalisme et Natalité. Enquête Socio-Démographique Rapport de Synthèse.* Algiers: 1972.

Abou-Zeid, Ahmed. Personal Communication, 1973.

Abu-Laban, Baha. "Sources of College Aspirations of College Youth," *The Journal of Developing Areas*, **2** (1968), 225–240.

———. "Social Change and Local Politics in Sidon, Lebanon," *The Journal of Developing Areas*, **5** (1970), 27–42.

Abu-Lughod, Ibrahim and Baha Abu-Laban, eds. *Settler Regimes in Africa and the Arab World: The Illusion of Endurance.* Wilmette, Ill.: Medina University Press International, 1974.

Abu-Lughod, Janet. "Migrant Adjustment to City Life: The Egyptian Case," *The American Journal of Sociology*, **67** (1961), 22–32.

———. "Urban-Rural Differences as a Function of the Demographic Transition: Egyptian Data and An Analytical Model," *The American Journal of Sociology*, **69** (1964), 476–490.

———. "Testing the Theory of Social Area Analysis: The Ecology of Cairo, Egypt," *American Sociological Review*, **34** (1969), 198–211.

———. *Cairo. 1001 Years of the City Victorious.* Princeton: Princeton University Press, 1971.

———. "Rural Migration and Politics in Egypt." In *Rural Politics and Social Change in the Middle East.* Richard T. Antoun and Iliya Harik, eds. Bloomington, Ind.: Indiana Univ. Press, 1972.

Adam, André. *Casablanca: Essai sur la transformation de la société marocaine au contact avec l'Occident.* Paris: Editions du Centre National de la Recherche Scientifique, 1968.

———. "Un aperçu de la recherche sociologique sur l'Afriqué du Nord," *Maghreb*, **52** (1972), 34–41.

Adlakha, Arjun. "Model Life Tables: An Empirical Test of Their Applicability to Less Developed Countries," *Demography*, **9** (1972), 589–601.

Albaum, Melvin and Christopher S. Davies. "The Spatial Structure of Socio-economic Attributes of Turkish Provinces," *International Journal of Middle East Studies*, **4** (1973), 288–310.

Allman, James, Cherifa Ben Achour, and Toby Stone. *A Bibliography of Recent Social Science Research on the Family in the Arab States.* Paris: Department of Social Sciences UNESCO, 1974.

Alzobaie, Abadul Jalil and M. A. El-Ghannam. "Iraqi Student Perceptions of Occupations," *Sociology and Social Research,* **52** (1968), 231–236.

American Sociological Association. *Graduate Guide to Sociology Departments 1974.*

Ammar, Hamed. *Growing up in an Egyptian Village.* New York: Grove Press, 1954.

Ammar, Sleim and Habib Ledjri. *Les conditions familiales de développement de la schizophrénie.* Paris: Masson et Cie, 1972.

Anonymous. *Social Change in Izmir, 1925—1965.* Undated.

Anonymous. "Situation actuelle de l'Islam Maghrébin," *Maghreb,* **47** (1971), 30–46.

Anonymous. "Cross National Study of the Social-Psychological Impact of Modernization," *Sociology and Eastern Europe,* **5** (1973), 9–11.

Anonymous. "Middle East Seminar on Population Policy." In *Search of Population Policy.* Washington: National Academy of Sciences, 1974.

Antoun, R. T. "The Social Significance of Ramadan in an Arab Village," *The Muslim World,* **58** (1968), 36–42, 95–104.

———, and Iliya Harik, eds. *Rural Politics and Social Change in the Middle East.* Bloomington, Ind.: Indiana University Press, 1972.

Ari, Oğuz. "Some Indications of Labour Commitment and Adjustment to the Social Milieu. A Turkish Case Study." In *Social Stratification and Development.* M. B. Kıray, ed. The Hague: Mouton, 1973.

Armstrong, Lincoln. "Middle East," *Contemporary Sociology,* Joseph S. Roucek, ed. New York: Philosophical Library, 1958. (a)

———. "The Influence of American Sociology in the Middle East," *Sociology and Social Research,* **42** (1958), 176–184. (b)

Ashford, Douglas E. "Succession and Social Change in Tunisia," *International Journal of Middle East Studies,* **4** (1973) 23–39.

Atiyeh, George N. *The Contemporary Middle East 1948–1973. A Selective and Annotated Bibliography.* Boston, Mass.: G. K. Hall and Co., 1975.

Attia, Habib. "Croissance et migrations des populations sahéliennes," *Revue Tunisienne de Sciences Sociales,* **7**, 23 (1970), 91–118.

AUFS (American Universities Field Staff). *Field Staff Reports.* Northeast Africa Series 17 No. 2, 1972.

Awad, Mohammed Hashim. "The Evolution of Landownership in the Sudan," *The Middle East Journal,* **25** (1971), 212–228.

Ayrout, Henri. *Moeurs et coutumes des fellahs.* Paris: Payot, 1938.

Baali, Fuad. "Social Factors in Iraqi Rural-Urban Migration," *American Journal of Economics and Sociology,* **25** (1966), 359–364.

———. "Educational Aspirations Among College Girls in Iraq," *Sociology and Social Research,* **51** (1967), 485–493.

El-Badry, M. A. "Trends in the Components of Population Growth in the Arab Countries of the Middle East: A Survey of Present Information," *Demography,* **2** (1965), 140–186.

Baer, Gabriel. *Studies in the Social History of Modern Egypt.* Chicago: The University of Chicago Press, 1969.

Balkan, Behire. *Türkiye Nüfus Bibliyografyası Kitaplar: 1928–1967.* Ankara: Hacettepe Üniversitesi Yayınları, 1967.

Barakat, Halim. "Social Factors Influencing Attitudes of University Students in Lebanon Toward the Palestinian Resistance Movement," *Journal of Palestine Studies*, **1** (1971), 87–112.

Barclay, H. B. "Muslim Religious Practice in a Village Suburb of Khartoum," *The Muslim World*, **53** (1963), 205–211.

Baum, Samuel, K. Dopkowski, W. G. Duncan, and P. Gardner. "The World Fertility Survey Inventory: Major Fertility and Related Surveys Conducted in Asia 1960–1973," *WFS Occasional Papers*, No. 4, 1974.

B'Chir, Mongi. "Les Migrations dans une métropole régionale: Sousse," *Revue Tunisienne de Sciences Sociales*, **9**, 28/29 (1972), 107–130.

Bean, Lee L. "The Population of Pakistan: An Evaluation of Recent Statistical Data," *The Middle East Journal*, **28** (1974), 177–184.

Beeley, Brian W. *Köysel Türkiye Bibliyografyası.* Ankara: Hacittepe Üniversitesi Nüfus Etütleri, 1969.

Belghiti, Malika. "Les relations féminines et le statut de la femme dans la famille rurale." In *Etudes sociologiques sur le Maroc.* Abdelkebir Khatibi, ed. Rabat: Societé d'Etudes Economiques, Sociales et Statistiques, 1971.

Ben Salem, Lilia. "Quelques reflexions sur le devenir de la sociologie (en Marge du colloque de Neuchâtel)," *Revue Tunisienne de Sciences Sociales*, **5**, 14 (1968), 235–237.

———. "Les cadres de l'économie locale en Tunisie." In *Social Stratification and Development*, M. B. Kıray, ed. The Hague: Mouton, 1973.

Berger, Morroe. *Bureaucracy and Society in Modern Egypt.* Princeton: Princeton University Press, 1957.

———. *Military Elite and Social Change: Egypt Since Napoleon.* Princeton: Princeton University Press, 1960.

———. *The Arab World Today.* Garden City, N.Y.: Doubleday, 1962.

———. *Islam in Egypt Today: Social and Political Aspects of Popular Religion.* New York: Cambridge University Press, 1970.

Berque, Jacques. "Cent vingt-cinq ans de sociologie maghrébine," *Annales, Economies, Sociétés, Civilisations*, **11** (1950), 296–324.

Bill, James A. "Class Analysis and the Dialectics of Modernization in the Middle East," *International Journal of Middle East Studies*, **3** (1972), 417–434.

———. "The Plasticity of Informal Politics: The Case of Iran," *The Middle East Journal*, **27** (1973), 131–151.

Binder, Leonard. *Iran: Political Development in a Changing Society.* Berkeley: University of California Press, 1962.

Blackman, W. S. *The Fellahin of Upper Egypt: Their Religious, Social, and Industrial Life, with Special Reference to Survivals from Ancient Times.* London: Harrap, 1927.

Bouhdiba, Abdelwahab. "Quelques aspects de la délinquance juvénile en Tunisie," *Revue Tunisienne de Sciences Sociales*, **6**, 19 (1969), 40–67.

———. *La Sociologie du développement africain.* The Hague: Mouton, 1971.

Boukraa, R. "Urbanisation, communication de masse et système social," *Revue Tunisienne de Sciences Sociales*, **8**, 26 (1971), 21–78.

Brown, George F. "Moroccan Family Planning Program—Progress and Problems," *Demography*, **5** (1968), 627–631.

Brown, L. Carl. *From Madina to Metropolis: Heritage and Change in the Near Eastern City*. Princeton: The Darwin Press, 1973.

Brown, T. "Social Distance: Jordanian and Israeli Students, 1968," 2. *Sociology and Social Research*, **53** (1969), 344–362.

Burke, Jean T. *An Annotated Bibliography of Books and Periodicals in English Dealing with Human Relations in the Arab States of the Middle East with Special Emphasis on Modern Times (1945–1954)*. Beirut: American University of Beirut, 1956.

Cairo Demographic Center. *Fertility Trends and Differentials in Arab Countries*. Cairo: 1971.

Camilleri, Carmel. *Jeunesse, famille et développement. Essai sur le changement socio-culturel dans un pays du Tiers Monde (Tunisie)*. Paris: Centre National de la Recherche Scientifique, 1973.

Center for the Study of the Modern Arab World. *Arab Culture and Society in Change*. Beirut: Dar El-Mashreq, 1973.

Charnay, Jean-Paul. "Jeux de miroirs et crises de civilisations. Réorientations du rapport Islam/Islamologie," *Archives de Sociologie des Religions*, **33** (1972), 135–174.

Charrad, M. "Les cadres politiques au niveau local en Tunisie." In *Social Stratification and Development*, M. B. Kıray, ed. The Hague: Mouton, 1973.

Chatilia, Kh. *Le mariage chez les musulmans en Syrie: étude de sociologie*. Paris: Geuthner, 1934.

Clerget, M. *Le Caire: étude de géographie urbaine et d'histoire économique*. Cairo: E. and R. Schindler, 1934.

Clarke, John Innes. *The Iranian City of Shiraz*. Durham: University of Durham Department of Geography, 1963.

Clarke, J. I. and B. D. Clark. *Kermanshah: an Iranian Provincial City*. Durham: University of Durham Dept. of Geography, 1963.

Clarke, J. I. and W. B. Fisher. *Populations of the Middle East and North Africa: A Geographical Approach*. New York: Africana Publishing Corp., 1972.

De Jong, F. "Sociology in a Developing Country. The United Arab Republic: Orientation and Characteristics," *The Sociological Review*, **19** (1971), 241–252.

Divine, Donna Robinson. "The Modernization of Israeli Administration," *International Journal of Middle East Studies*, **5** (1973), 295–313.

Dodd, Peter C. "Youth and Women's Emancipation in the United Arab Republic," *The Middle East Journal*, **22** (1968), 159–172.

Dodd, Peter and Halim Barakat. *River Without Bridges: a Study of the Exodus of the 1967 Palestine Arab Refugees*. Beirut: Institute for Palestine Study, 1961.

Dodd, Peter C. "Family Honor and the Forces of Change in Arab Society," *International Journal of Middle East Studies*, **4** (1973), 40–54.

Dunham, H. Warren and Abdulla Lutfiyya. "Sociology in Egypt," *Journal of Asian and African Studies*, **6** (1971), 118–126.

Duvignaud, Jean. "La Pratique de la sociologie dans les pays décolonisés," *Cahiers Internationaux de Sociologie*, **10** (1963), 165–174.

Davis, James F. "The Two Way Mirror and the U Curve: Americans as Seen by Turkish Students Returned Home," *Sociology and Social Research*, **56** (1971), 29–43.

Eickelman, Dale F. "Is There an Islamic City? The Making of a Quarter in a Moroccan Town," *International Journal of Middle East Studies*, **5** (1974), 274–294.

Eisenstadt, S. N. *Modernization: Protest and Change.* Englewood Cliffs, N.J.: Prentice-Hall, 1966.

Enayat, Hamid. "The State of Social Sciences in Iran," *Middle East Studies Association Bulletin,* **8**, 3 (1974), 1–12.

English, Paul Ward. *City and Village in Iran.* Madison: University of Wisconsin Press, 1966.

———. "Geographical Perspectives on the Middle East: The Passing of the Ecological Trilogy." Paper presented at the Chicago Symposium of Geography and Foreign Area Study, 1973.

Entelis, John P. "Structural Change and Organizational Development in the Lebanese Kata'ib Party," *The Middle East Journal,* **27** (1973), 21–35.

Fahem, Abdelkader. "Un exemple de relations villes-campagnes: Sousse et le Sahel tunisien," *Revue Tunisienne de Sciences Sociales,* **5**, 15 (1968), 275–294.

Fahim, Hussein M. "Change in Religion in a Resettled Nubian Community," *International Journal of Middle East Studies,* **4** (1973), 163–177.

Fahmy, Noha. "L'Adaptation sociale des vieillards," *The National Review of Social Sciences,* **4**, 2 (1967), 181–197.

Fakhfakh, Mohammed. "Evolution des relations entre Sfax et sa région," *Revue Tunisienne de Sciences Sociales,* **5**, 15 (1968), 263–273.

Fakhouri, Hani. *Kafr El-Elow. An Egyptian Village in Transition.* New York: Holt, Rinehart & Winston, 1972.

Farsoun, Samih K. "Family Structure and Society in Modern Lebanon," In *Peoples and Cultures of the Middle East,* Vol. 2. Louise E. Sweet, ed. Garden City, N.Y.: The Natural History Press, 1970.

Ferdows, Amir H. "The Mullas: Their Role in the Process of Political Socialization of the Iranian Populace." Abstracts of the Papers delivered at the Third Annual Meeting of the Middle East Studies Association, 1969.

Firoozi, Ferydoon. "Iranian Censuses 1956 and 1966," *The Middle East Journal,* 24 (1970), 220–228.

Fişek, Nusret H. and Frederic C. Shorter. "Fertility Control in Turkey," *Demography,* **5** (1968), 578–589.

Frey, Frederic W. "Surveying Peasant Attitudes in Turkey," *Public Opinion Quarterly,* **27** (1963), 335–355.

Gadalla, Saad M. *Land Reform in Relation to Social Development in Egypt.* Columbia: University of Missouri Press, 1962.

Gardner, George H. "Modernization and Role Redefinition Pressures." In *Medieval and Middle Eastern Studies.* S. A. Hanna, ed. Leiden: E. J. Brill, 1972.

———. Personal communication. 1973.

Geertz, Clifford. *Islam Observed: Religious Development in Morocco and Indonesia.* New Haven: Yale University Press, 1968.

Geiser, Peter. "Some Differential Factors Affecting Population Movement: The Nubian Case," *Human Organization,* **26** (1967), 164–177.

Gellner, Ernest. "Pouvoir politique et fonction religieuse dans l'Islam marocain," *Annales Economies-Sociétés-Civilisations* **25** (1970), 699–713.

Gilsenan, Michael. *Saints and Sufis in Modern Egypt: An Essay in the Sociology of Religion.* Oxford University Press, 1973.

Gokalp, Catherine. "L'émigration turque en Europe at particulièrement en France," *Population*, **28** (1973), 335–360.

Goldberg, Harvey. "Ecologic and Demographic Aspects of Rural Tripolitania Jewry: 1835–1949," *International Journal of Middle East Studies*, **2** (1971), 245–360.

Goode, William J. *World Revolution and Family Patterns*. Glencoe, Ill.: The Free Press, 1963.

Granqvist, H. *Birth and Childhood among the Arabs: Studies in a Muhammedan Village in Palestine*. Helsinki: 1947.

Gubser, Peter, "The Zu'ama' of Zahlah: the Current Situation in a Lebanese Town," *The Middle East Journal*, **27** (1973), 173–189.

Hacker, June M. *Modern 'Amman: a Social Study*. Durham: University of Durham, 1960.

Halpern, M. "Egypt and the New Middle Class: Reaffirmation and New Explorations," *Comparative Studies in Society and History*, **11** (1969), 97–108.

——— *The Politics of Social Change in the Middle East and North Africa*. Princeton: Princeton University Press, 1963.

Hamza, M. "Analysis of the Employment Situation Among the Educated Classes in the U.A.R.," *The National Review of Social Sciences*, **6**, 3 (1967), 138–171.

Harik, Iliya F. *Political Mobilization of Peasants*. Bloomington: Indiana University Press, 1974.

Heper, Metin. "Political Modernization as Reflected in Bureaucratic Change: The Turkish Bureaucracy and a 'Historical Bureaucratic Empire' Tradition," *International Journal of Middle East Studies*, in press.

Hermassi, Abid Elbaki. "Sociologie du milieu docker," *Revue Tunisienne de Sciences Sociales*, **3**, 7 (1966), 153–179.

———. "Notes on the State of Sociology in the Maghrib." Paper prepared for the State of the Arts project and presented in part at a public lecture at U.C.L.A., 1973. (a)

———. "Elite et Sociétié en Tunisie. Intégration et mobilisation." In *Social Stratification and Development*. M. B. Kıray, ed. The Hague: Mouton, 1973. (b)

Hinderink, Jan, and Mubeccel B. Kiray. *Social Stratification as an Obstacle to Development: A Study of Four Turkish Villages*. New York: Praeger, 1970.

Hourani, A. H. and S. M. Stern, eds. *The Islamic City*. Oxford: Bruno Cassirer, 1970.

Hudson, Bradford, Mohammed K. Barakat, and Rolfe Laforge. "Problems and Methods of Cross-Cultural Research," *Journal of Social Issues*, **15** (1959), 5–19.

Ibn Khaldun. *The Muqaddimah. An Introduction to History*. Translated from the Arabic by Franz Rosenthal. 3 Vols. New York: Pantheon Books, 1958.

Ibrahim, Saad-Eddin. "Urbanization in the Arab World," *Population Bulletin of the United Nations Economic Commission for Western Asia*, **7** (1974), 74–102.

Inkeles, Alex. "Making Men Modern: On the Causes and Consequences of Individual Change in Six Developed Countries," *American Journal of Sociology*, **75** (1969), 208–225.

El-Islam, Fakhr and M. M. Shaalan. "The Marriage and Fertility of Neurotics," *The National Review of Social Sciences*, **6**, 2 (1969), 90–99.

Janowitz, M. "The Comparative Analysis of Middle Eastern Military Institutions." In *Military Intervention*. M. Janowitz and J. van Doorn, eds. Rotterdam: Rotterdam University Press, 1971.

Kâğitiçibaşi, Çiğdem. "Sosyal Ilim Metodolojisi: Köy ve Nüfus Araştımaları, Izmir Araştırması." In *Türkiye' de Sosyal Araştırmaların Gelişmesi.* Ankara: Doğuş Matbaacılık, 1971.

Karpat, Kemal. "Social Effects of Farm Mechanization in Turkish Villages," *Social Research,* **27** (1960), 83–103.

———, ed. *Political and Social Thought in the Contemporary Middle East.* New York: Frederich A. Prager, 1968.

———. and Contributors. *Social Change and Politics in Turkey. A Structural-Historical Analysis.* Leiden: Brill, 1973.

———. "Structural Change, Historical Stages of Modernization, and the Role of Social Groups in Turkish Politics." In *Social Change and Politics in Turkey.* K. H. Karpat, ed. Leiden: Brill, 1973.

Kassem, M. Sami. "Business Executives in Egypt, India and the U.S.: Social Backgrounds and Careers," *International Journal of Comparative Sociology,* **12** (1971), 101–113.

Katchadourian, H. A. and C. W. Churchill. "Social Class and Mental Illness in Urban Lebanon," *Social Psychiatry,* **4** (1969), 49–55.

Katz, Elihu and Brenda Danet. "Petitions and Persuasive Appeals: A Study of Official-Client Relations," *American Sociological Review,* **6** (1966), 811–821.

Katz, Elihu, Michael Gurevitch, and Hadassah Haas. "On the Use of the Mass Media for Important Things," *American Sociological Review,* **38** (1973), 164–165.

Kazamias, Andreas M. *Education and the Quest for Modernity in Turkey.* Chicago: The University of Chicago Press, 1966.

Keddie, Nikki R. "The Iranian Power Structure and Social Change 1800–1969: An Overview." *International Journal of Middle East Studies,* **2** (1971), 3–20.

Keleş, Ruşen. *Izmir Mahalleleri.* Ankara: Ayylidiz Matbaasi A.S., 1972.

Kennedy, John. "Nubian Zar Ceremonies as Psychotherapy," *Human Organization,* **26** (1967), 185–194.

Khalâf, Samir. "Lebanon." In *Nashât al-ᶜArab fî al-ᶜulûm al-ijtimâᶜiyya fî mi'at Sana.* Beirut: American University, 1965. (a)

———. *Prostitution in a Changing Society: a Sociological Survey of Legal Prostitution in Beirut.* Beirut: Khayats, 1965. (b)

———. "Islamic Reform in Lebanon: The Emergence of the Maqased Benevolent Society." Abstracts of papers delivered at the Third Annual Meeting of the Middle East Studies Association, 1969.

———. "Family Associations in Lebanon," *Journal of Comparative Family Studies,* **2**, 2 (1971), 235–250.

———. "Adaptive Modernization: The Case For Lebanon." In *Economic Development and Population Growth in the Middle East,* Charles A. Cooper and Sidney S. Alexander, eds. New York: American Elsevier, 1972.

———. and Per Kongstad. *Hamra of Beirut: A case of Rapid Urbanization.* Leiden: E. J. Brill, 1973. (a)

———. Personal communication, 1973. (b)

Khatibi, Abdelkabir. *Bilan de la sociologie au Maroc.* Rabat: Association pour la Recherche en Sciences Humaines, 1967.

Khatibi, Abdelkabir. "Etat et classes sociales." In *Etudes Sociologiques du Maroc.* M. Belghiti et al., eds. Rabat: Publication du Bulletin Economique et Social du Maroc, 1971.

———. "Stratification sociale au Maroc. Esquisse d'un modèle." In *Social Stratification and Development*. M. B. Kıray, ed. The Hague: Mouton, 1973.

Khuri, Fuad. "A Comparative Study of Migration Patterns in Two Lebanese Villages," *Human Organization*, **26** (1967), 206–213.

———. "The Changing Class Structure of Lebanon," *The Middle East Journal*, **23** (1969), 29–44.

———. *From Village to Suburb: Order and Change in Greater Beirut*. Chicago: Chicago University Press, 1974.

Kıray, Mübeccel Belik. *Örgutleşemyen Kent: İzmir'de İs Hayatinin Yapısı ve Yerlesme Duzeni*. Ankara: Ayyildiz Matbaasi A.Ş., 1972.

———., ed. *Social Stratification and Development in the Mediterranean Basin*. The Hague: Mouton, 1973.

Klaff, Vivian Z. "Ethnic Segregation in Israel," *Demography*, **10** (1973), 161–184.

Kolars, John. "The Integration of the Villagers into the National Life of Turkey." In *Social Change and Politics in Turkey*. K. H. Karpat, ed. Leiden: E. J. Brill, 1973.

Kongar, Emre. *Izmir'de Kentsel Aile*. Ankara: Ayyildiz Matbaasi A.Ş., 1972.

Krane, Ronald E. *Manpower Mobility Across Cultural Boundaries: Social Economic and Legal Aspects. The Case of Turkey and West Germany*. Leiden: E. J. Brill, 1975.

Kremer, A. Von. *Aegypten*. Leipzig: 1863.

Kuroda, Yasamusa. "Young Palestinian Commandos in Political Socialization Perspective," *The Middle East Journal*, **26** (1972), 253–270.

Lambert, Richard D. "Language and Area Studies Review," Social Science Research Council *Items*, **27** (1973), 17–20.

Lapham, Robert J. "Family Planning and Fertility in Tunisia," *Demography*, **7** (1970), 241–253.

———. "Modernisation et contraception au Maroc central. Illustration de l'analyse des données d'une enquête C.A.P.," *Population*, **26** (1971), 79–104.

———. "Population Policies in the Maghrib," *The Middle East Journal*, **26** (1972), 1–10.

Lapidus, Ira, ed. *Middle Eastern Cities*. Berkeley: University of California Press, 1970.

Latif, A. H. "Residential Segregation and Location of Status and Religious Groups in Alexandria, Egypt." In *Comparative Urban Structure Studies in the Ecology of Cities*. Kent P. Schwirian. Lexington, Mass.: D. C. Heath, 1974.

———. "Factor Structure and Change Analysis of Alexandria, Egypt, 1947 and 1960." In *Comparative Urban Structure Studies in the Ecology of Cities*. Kent P. Schwirian. Lexington, Mass.: D. C. Heath, 1974.

Lerner, Daniel. *The Passing of Traditional Society: Modernizing the Middle East*. New York: Macmillan, 1964.

Lutfiyya, Abdulla M. *Baytīn. A Jordanian Village*. The Hague: Mouton, 1966.

Magnarella, Paul J. "From Village to Townsmen in Turkey," *The Middle East Journal*, **24** (1970), 229–240.

Makhlouf, Ezzedine. "La Modernisation de l'agriculture en Tunisie," *Revue Tunisienne de Sciences Sociales*, **5**, 15 (1961), 17–53.

———. "Les changements récents dans le contenu socio-économique de l'exode rural," *Revue Tunisienne de Sciences Sociales*, **9**, 28/29 (1972), 33–72.

Mardin, Şerif A. *Din Ve Ideoloji*. Ankara: Sevinc Matbaasi, 1969.

———. "Ideology and Religion in the Turkish Revolution," *International Journal of Middle East Studies*, **2**, (1971), 197–211.

Marx, E. "The Social Structure of the Negev Bedouin," *The New East*, **7** (1957), I–IV.

Matras, Judah. "Religious Observance and Family Formation in Israel: Some Intergenerational Changes," *The American Journal of Sociology*, **69** (1964), 464–475.

McClelland, David C. "National Character and Economic Growth in Turkey and Iran." In *Communications and Political Development*, Lucian W. Pye, ed. Princeton: Princeton University Press, 1963.

MESA (Middle East Studies Association). *Abstracts of Papers Delivered at the Sixth Annual Meeting of the Middle East Studies Association*, 1972.

Michaux-Bellaire, M. E. "Sociologie marocaine," *Archives Marocaines*, **27** (1927), 293–311.

Michel, André. *The Modernization of North African Families in the Paris Area*. The Hague: Mouton, 1974.

Mitchell, William A. "Turkish Villages in Interior Anatolia and von Thünen's 'Isolated State'; A Comparative Analysis," *The Middle East Journal*, **25** (1971), 355–369.

Moore, Richard, Khalif Asayesh, and Joel Montague. "Population and Family Planning in Iran," *The Middle East Journal*, **28** (1974), 396–408.

Nachmias, David. "Status Inconsistency and Political Opposition: A Case Study of an Israeli Minority Group," *The Middle East Journal*, **27** (1973), 456–470.

Naciri, Mohammed. "Salé: Etude de géographie urbaine," *Revue de Géographie du Maroc*, 3–4 (1963), 13–82.

Naderi, Nader Afshar. Personal communication, 1973.

Nagi, Mostafa H. "Internal Migration and Structural Changes in Egypt," *The Middle East Journal*, **28** (1974), 261–282.

Nakhleh, Emile A. "The Anatomy of Violence: Theoretical Reflections on Palestinian Resistance," *The Middle East Journal*, **25** (1971), 180–200.

Naraghi, Ehsan. "La Sociologie et la société en Iran," *Revue Française de Sociologie*, **8** (1967), 184–188.

Nasr, Seyyed H. *Ideals and Realities of Islam*. London: Allen and Unwin, 1966.

Nedjati, Suzanne. *Etude bibliographique: la famille et la dynamique de population en Turquie et en Iran*. Paris: Department of Social Sciences UNESCO, 1974.

Neyzi, Nezih. "The Middle Classes in Turkey." In *Social Change and Politics in Turkey*. K. H. Karpat, ed. Leiden: E. J. Brill, 1973.

Nicolas, Georges. "La Sociologie rurale au Maroc pendant les cinquantes dernières années," *Tiers-Monde*, **2** (1968), 527–543.

Noin, Daniel. *La Population rurale du Maroc*, 2 volumes. Paris: Presses Universitaires de France, 1970.

Oren, Stephen. "Continuity and Change in Israel's Religious' Parties," *The Middle East Journal*, **27** (1973), 36–54.

Pascon, Paul. *Cours de Sociologie Rurale*. Rabat: Centre de formation d'ingénieurs de travaux statistiques, 1962–1963.

Paydarfar, Ali A. "Differential Life-Styles Between Migrants and Nonmigrants: A Case Study of the City of Shiraz, Iran," *Demography*, **11** (1974), 509–520.

Peres, Yochanon. "Ethnic Relations in Israel," *American Journal of Sociology*, **76** (1971), 1021–1047.

Petersen, Karen Kay. "Villagers in Cairo: Hypotheses versus Data," *American Journal of Sociology*, **77** (1971), 560–573.

Picouet, Michel. "Aperçu des migrations intérieures en Tunisie," *Population*, **26** (1971), 125–148.

Planck, Ulrich. "Die Ländliche Soziologie In Der Türkei," *Sociologia Ruralis*, **12** (1972), 181–196.

Povey, Warren G. and George E. Brown. "Tunisia's Experience in Family Planning," *Demography*, **5** (1968), 620–626.

Prothro, Edwin Terry. *Child Rearing in the Lebanon*. Cambridge, Mass.: Harvard University Press, 1961.

Prothro, Edwin Terry and Lutfy Najib Diab. *Changing Family Patterns in the Arab East*. Beirut: American University of Beirut, 1974.

Quandt, Anna. *The Social Production of Census Data: Interviews from the 1971 Moroccan Census*. Ph.D. Thesis. University of California at Los Angeles: 1973.

al-Qazzaz, Ayad. "Army Officers and Land Reforms in Egypt, Iraq, and Syria," *Sociological Bulletin*, **20** (1971), 159–177.

———. "Sociology in Underdeveloped Countries," *The Sociological Review*, **20** (1972), 93–103.

———. "Some Impressions About the Status of Sociology in Iraq." Paper prepared for the State of the Arts Project, 1973. (a)

———. Personal communication, 1973. (b)

Qutub, Ishaq. "The Rise of the Middle Class in a Transitional Society. The Case of Jordan." In *Social Stratification and Development*. M. B. Kıray, ed. The Hague: Mouton, 1973.

Rachidi, M., M. Abzahd, and E. Housni. "Les Objectifs, le programme et les premières experiences du C.E.R.E.D.," *As Soukan*, 1 (1973), 4–25.

Racy, John. *Psychiatry in the Arab East*. Acta Psychiatrica Scandinavica. Supp. 211, 1970.

Rahman, Fazlur. 1966. "The impact of modernity on Islam," *Islamic Studies*, **5** (1966), 113–128.

———. "Islamic Modernism: Its Scope, Method and Alternative," *International Journal of Middle East Studies*, **1** (1970), 317–333.

Ramazani, Rouhollah K. "Iran's 'White Revolution': A Study in Political Development," *International Journal of Middle East Studies*, **5** (1974), 124–130.

Rizk, Hanna. "National Fertility Sample Survey for Jordan, 1972. The Study and Some Findings," *Population Bulletin of the United Nations Economic and Social Office in Beirut*, 5 (1973), 14–31.

———. "Social and Psychological Factors Affecting Fertility in the United Arab Republic," *Marriage and Family Living* **25** (1963), 69–73.

Rodinson, Maxime. "Sociologie de l'Islam," *L'Annee Sociologique* **16**, (1965), 365–370.

Roos, Leslie L., Jr., and Noralou P. Roos. *Managers of Modernization: Organizations and Elites in Turkey*. Cambridge: Harvard University Press, 1971.

Rosen, Laurence. "Muslim-Jewish Relations in a Moroccan City," *International Journal of Middle East Studies*, 3 (1972), 435–449.

Rosenfeld, Henry. "Processes of Change and Factors of Conservation, in the Rural Arab Family in Israel," *The New East*, **19** (1969), 208–218.

Rugh, William. "Emergence of a New Middle Class in Saudi Arabia," *Thr Middle East Journal*, **27** (1973), 7–20.

El-Saaty, Hassan and Gordon K. Hirabayashi. *Industrialization in Alexandria*. Cairo Social Research Center, American University at Cairo, 1959.

———. "Development of the School of Sociological Thought Since 1952," *The National Review of Social Sciences*, **1**, 1 (1964), 142–146.

Sabagh, Georges and C. Scott. "A Comparison of Different Survey Techniques for Obtaining Vital Data in a Developing Country," *Demography*, **4** (1967), 759–772.

Sabagh, Georges. "The Demography of the Middle East." *Middle East Studies Association Bulletin*, **4** 2 (1970), 1–19.

Saltzman, Philip C. "National Integration of the Tribes in Modern Iran," *The Middle East Journal*, 25 (1971), 325–336.

Sardari, A. M. and R. Keyhan. "The Prospect of Family Planning in Iran." *Demography*, **5** (1968), 780–784.

Sayigh, Yusif A. "Problems and Prospects of Development in the Arabian Peninsula," *International Journal of Middle East Studies*, **2** (1971), 40–58.

Schmelz, U. "Demographic Development of the Arab Countries," *The New East*, **23** (1973), 22–58.

Schnaiberg, Allan. "Rural-Urban Residence and Modernism: A Study of Ankara Province, Turkey," *Demography* **7** (1970), 71–85.

———. "Measuring Modernism: Theoretical and Empirical Explorations," *The American Journal of Sociology*, **76** (1970), 399–425.

Scott, Christopher and Georges Sabagh. "The Historical Calendar as a Method of Estimating age: The Experience of the Moroccan Multi-Purpose Sample Survey of 1961–63," *Population Studies*, **34** (1970), 93–107.

Sebag, Paul, Abdelwahab, Bouhdiba and Carmel Camilleri. *Les Préconditions sociales de l'industrialisation dans la région de Tunis*. Tunis: Cahier du Centre d'Etudes et de Recherches Economiques et Sociales, 1968.

Seeman, Melvin. "The Signals in '68: Alienation in Pre-Crisis France," *American Sociological Review*, **37** (1972), 385–402.

Seklani, Mahmoud. "La mobilité intérieure dans le Sud Tunisien," *Revue Tunisienne de Sciences Sociales*, **7**, 23 (1970), 91–118.

Sertel, Ayşe Kurdat. "Sex Differences in Status and Attitudes in Rural Turkey," *Hacattepe Bulletin of Social Sciences and Humanities*, **4** (1972), 48–79.

Shafshak, Mahmoud A. R. "The Role of the University in Egyptian Elite Recruitment: A Comparative Study of Al-Azhar and Cairo University," *The National Review of Social Science*, **5** (1968), 329–454.

Shoham, S. and M. Hovar. "B'nei Tovim, Middle Class and Upper Class Delinquency in Israel," *Sociology and Social Research*, **48** (1963), 454–468.

Shoham, Shlomo and Leon Shaskolsky. "An Analysis of Delinquents and Non Delinquents in Israel: A Cross-Cultural Perspective," *Sociology and Social Research*, **53** (1969), 333–343.

Smelser, Neil J. and James A. Davis. *Sociology*. Englewood Cliffs, N.J.: Prentiss-Hall, 1969.

Shuval, Judith Y. "Perceived Components of Nursing in Israel," *American Sociological Review*, **28** (1963), 37–46.

Srikantan, K. S. "Regional and Rural-Urban Socio-Demographic Differences in Turkey," *The Middle East Journal*, **27** (1973), 275–300.

SSRC (Social Science Research Council). *Items*, **26** (1972), 31.

Stambouli, Fredj. "Les grandes orientations de la sociologie au Congrès d'Evian," *Revue Tunisienne de Sciences Sociales*, **4**, 9 (1967), 189–193.

———. "Systeme d'autorité et mode de communication au sein de l'enterprise industrielle tunisienne moderne," *Revue Tunisienne de Sciences Sociales*, **5** 14 (1968), 33–68.

———. "Ibn Khaldoun et le système social traditional maghrébin," *Revue Tunisienne de Sciences Sociales*, **7** 20 (1970), 215–237.

———. "Tradition et modernité à travers les processus d'urbanisation en Tunisie," *Revue Tunisienne de Sciences Sociales*, **8**, 26 (1971), 9–20.

Stambouli, F. and A. Zghal. "La Vie urbaine dans le Maghreb pré-colonial," *Annuaire de l'Afrique du Nord*, **11** (1972), 191–214.

Stone, Russell A. Personal communication, 1973.

———. "Religious Ethic and Spirit of Capitalism in Tunisia," *International Journal of Middle East Studies*, **5** (1974), 260–273.

Stookey, Robert W. "Social Structure and Politics in the Yemen Arab Republic, *The Middle East Journal*, **28** (1974), 248–260.

Stycos, J. Mayone and Robert H. Weller. "Female Working Roles and Fertility," *Demography*, **4** (1967), 210–217.

Sweet, Louise. "A Survey of Recent Middle Eastern Ethnology," *The Middle East Journal*, **23** (1969), 221–232.

Talmon, Yonina. "Mate Selection in Collective Settlements," *American Sociological Review*, **29** (1964), 491–508.

Talha, Larbi. "L'evolution du mouvement migratoire entre le Maghreb et la France," *Maghreb-Machrek*, **61** (1974), 17–34.

Tannous, Afif I. *The Arab Community in the Middle East*. Washington, D. C.: Smithsonian Reports, 1943.

Tehran University, Institute d'Etudes et de Recherches Sociales. *Origine des ouvriers de Teheran*. Tehran: 1965.

Tessler, Mark A. "Problems of measurement in Comparative Research: Perspectives from an African Survey," *Social Science Information*, **12** (1973), 29–43.

Tezcan, Mahmut. *Türk Sosyologi Bibliografyasi 1928–1968*. Ankara: Başnur Matbaasi, 1969.

———. Personal communication, 1975.

Timur, Serim. *Türkiye'de Aile Yapısı*. Ankara: Doğuş Maatbacılık, 1972.

Tomeh, Aida K. "Reference-Group Support Among Middle Eastern College Students," *Journal of Marriage and the Family*, **32** (1970), 156–166.

———. "Patterns of Moral Behavior in Two Social Structures," *Sociology and Social Research*, **55** (1971), 149–160.

Toppozada, H. K. "Progress and Problems of Family Planning in the United Arab Republic," *Demography*, **5** (1968), 590–597.

Touba, Jacqueline R. "The Relationship Between Urbanization and the Changing Status of Women in Iran 1956–1966," *Iranian Studies*, **5** 1 (1972), 25–36.

Treadyway, Roy C. "Gradients of Metropolitan Dominance in Turkey: Alternative Models," *Demography*, **9** (1972), 13–33.

Tuma, Elias. "Population, Food and Agriculture in Arab Countries." *The Middle East Journal*, **28** (1974) 381–395.

Ülken, H. Z. "La sociologie rurale en Turquie." *Sosyoloji Dergisi*, **6** (1950), 104–116. (a).

———. "Sociology in Turkey," *Sosyoloji Dergisi*, **6** (1950), 140–149. (b)

Van Nieuwenhuijze. C. A. O. *Sociology of the Middle East: A Stocktaking Interpretation.* Leiden: E. J. Brill, 1971.

Von Allmen-Joray, Malik and France. "Attitudes concernant la taille de la famille et la régulation des naissances," *Population*, **26** (1971), 47–78.

Von Grunebaum, G. E. *Modern Islam: The Search for Cultural Identity.* Berkeley: University of California Press, 1962.

Wardi, 'Ali. *Dirasat fi Tabi'at al-Mujtamaa al-Iraqi.* Baghdad: Ani Press, 1966.

al-Wardi, 'Ali. *Soziologie des Nomadentums: Studie Über die iraquische Gesellschaft.* G. Weirauch and I. al-Haidari, trans. Neuwied: 1972.

Wassef, Wissa. "Le Prolétariat et le sous-prolétariat industriel et agricole dans la Republique Arabe Unie: formation, évolution, role politique." In *Social Stratification and Development.* M. B. Kıray, ed. The Hague: Mouton, 1973.

Waterbury, John. *The Commander of the Faithful: The Moroccan Political Elite.* New York: Columbia University Press, 1970.

Weiker, Walter F. "Social Sciences in Contemporary Turkey," *Middle East Association Bulletin*, **5** (1971), 72–82.

Weller, Leonard, *Sociology in Israel.* Westport, Conn.: Greenwood Press, 1974.

Weintraub, D. and F. Bernstein. "Social Structure and Modernization: A comparative Study of Two Villages," *The American Journal of Sociology*, **72** (1966), 509, 521.

Weulersse, Jacques. *Paysans de Syrie et du Proche-Orient.* Paris: Gallimard, 1946.

Yasa, Ibrahim. "The Impact of Urbanization on the Occupational and Expenditure Patterns of an Agricultural Village Within the Last 25 Years," *Development and Change*, **1** (1969–1970), 51–63.

———. "The Impact of Rural Exodus on the Occupational Patterns of Cities: The Case of Ankara." In *Social Stratification and Development.* M. B. Kıray, ed. The Hague: Mouton, 1973.

Yaukey, David. *Fertility Differences in a Modernizing Country: A Survey of Lebanese Couples.* Princeton: Princeton University Press, 1961.

Youssef, Nadia Haggag. "Social Structure and the Female Labor Force: The Case of Women Workers in Muslim Middle Eastern Countries," *Demography*, **8** (1971), 427–439.

———. "Women's Status and Fertility in Muslim Countries of the Middle East and Asia." Paper Presented at Annual Meetings of the American Psychological Association, 1974. (a)

———. *Women and Work in Developing Societies.* Berkeley: University of California, 1974. (b)

Yuchtman, Ephraim. "Reward Distribution and Work Role Attractiveness in the Kibbutz Reflections on Equity Theory," *American Sociological Review*, **37** (1972), 581–595.

Zaki, Gamal and Noha Fahmy. "Study of Housing Conditions of Rural Areas Guiza Governorate," *The National Review of Sociale Sciences*, **2**, 3 (1965), 89–151.

Zaki, Gamal and Abdel-Halim Mahmoud. "Assessment of the Interview as a Technique of Collecting Data from Egyptian Rural Areas," *The National Review of Social Sciences*, **2**, 2 (1965), 150–166.

Zghal, Abdelkader. "La Participation de la paysannerie maghrébine à la construction nationale," *Revue Tunisienne de Sciences Sociales*, **7** (1970), 125–161.

———. "L'Élite administrative et la paysannerie en Tunisie." In *Social Stratification and Development*. M. B. Kiray, ed. The Hague: Mouton, 1973 (a)

———. Personal communication, 1973. (b)

———. and Hachmi Karoui. "Decolonization and Social Science Research: The Case of Tunisia," *Middle East Studies Association Bulletin*, **7** (1973), 11–25.

Zonis, Marvin. *The Political Elite of Iran*. Princeton: Princeton University Press, 1971.

CHAPTER ELEVEN

Economics

JOHN SIMMONS

Although a comprehensive view of economic research would include the calculations used by the Achaemenids and Egyptians in their construction projects and the models used to predict the price elasticities of demand for crude oil in the year 2000, the task of this paper is to focus not on such a thorough review of past research but rather on future research criteria and priorities. However, in order to establish the context for future research, the published findings of the past 15 years are first discussed under three headings: historical, macro, and country studies; sectoral, micro, and topical, e.g., finance; and international and interdisciplinary. With this work in mind and guided by the results of a questionnaire, future research is discussed. Finally a word is said about the problems and responsibilities of the producers and consumers of research.

Since this paper is intended for, among others, undergraduate and graduate students, representatives of funding agencies, and economists familiar with the region, it is obvious that not all the relevant aspects of the subject can be treated in equal depth. We will consider, however, that one of the major goals of the project has been achieved if this paper stimulates further research for these special audiences.

This project was initiated while I was a Research Fellow, The Woodrow Wilson School, Princeton University. It was funded by a grant from the Ford Foundation to the Middle East Studies Association (MESA). Carl Dahlman, Jose Abiseid, and Fatima el Taleeb provided able assistance. I would also like to thank the correspondents who guided the initial steps of this project, the respondents to the questionnaire, the participants at the meetings at the Center for the Advanced Study of the Behavioral Sciences, and Charles Issawi, Thomas Stauffer, and a reviewer who also commented on the draft.

SCOPE

The Discipline

Development is a field of economics that traces its history back to Adam Smith's *Wealth of Nations* and his concern for economic growth. Since the end of World War II research published in this area has increasingly focused on the developing countries, but not to the exclusion of the developed countries. Development economics, in its attempt to explain why some countries grow and develop and some do not, draws on all the fields of economic inquiry ranging from economic theory to agriculture. Although growth has been a major preoccupation of development economists, other issues have received increasing attention in the past 10 years. How efficiently is growth being achieved? Who benefits from the growth?[1] The initial answers to these questions suggest that the proportions of capital and labor, often based on imported technology, are and seem destined to remain inefficient. Furthermore, we find that not only is the gap between the lowest- and highest-income groups widening in many countries, but the poor are getting poorer. Finally, there is renewed concern for understanding the economic behavior of individuals for such crucial issues as the determinants of fertlility, labor productivity and satisfaction, and rural savings.

Is development economics based on universal theories and policies that vary only in degree across regions and countries? Is the topic of the economic development of the Middle East seen as a legitimate one by development economists? The models of Middle Eastern economic phenomena do not differ in kind from models for Latin America. Although the results from the application of data to the models may differ among countries, that is due to different resource structures. However, as we learn more about the function and structure of the poor economies we *may* find that regional- or country-specific models are required.

If development theory and policies are not regionally specific, is it valid to have economists who are specialists in the Middle Eastern region? Not only is it legitimate to have these specialists, but it is clearly essential so that our understanding of both the better- and lesser-known economies of the region may be maximized in the shortest time. Only through the work of these specialists, and those concentrating on other regions in the world, will it be possible to broaden and deepen our understanding of both general developmental models and the topic of comparative economic systems.

Some topics in development economics like micro, sectoral, and commodity studies have benefited from the knowledge of the physical and social sciences. Communications theory has been as essential in understanding the farmer innovation processes as engineering has been for understanding the physical efficiency of phosphate mining. Moreover, one of the more promising areas for future economic research will result from further collaboration with the health and social sciences to better understand the contribution of human capital to development. If collaborative work is to progress, it is a useful digression to learn how economists are perceived by their colleagues.

Through informal discussion several perceptions of development economists emerged.[2] Most important was the observation about the inadequate and often harmful results of economic planning, even in countries that had placed a high priority on their human and equity objectives. Some anthropologists felt that their involvement in action-oriented research softened the harmful effects of the economists' planned change and social engineering. Urban populations have benefited from the economists at the expense of villagers and nomads. A related complaint was that economists were concerned with material, not human, values in their efforts. In their desire to maximize the rates of economic growth, for example, economists ignored the effects that building a capital-intensive shoe industry would have on the lives of shoe artisans who would be thrown out of work. The crucial problem seemed to be that economists were action-oriented without having a sufficient understanding of what actions to take and how, as well as not knowing enough about the effects that these actions would have on people. Though some of the opinions reflect neither the diversity within economics about the questions that are raised, nor some present trends, they should give pause for reflection.

The Region

Since this chapter is about the study of economic phenomena in the Middle East and North Africa, it is useful to describe briefly the economically important characteristics of that region to distinguish it from other major geographical regions. Social, political, and geographic factors as well as economic are considered.

Four geographic features dominate an economic characterization of the region: the rivers and seacoasts along which most of the population lives; the deserts and semiarid plateaus which have the lowest man/land ratios in the world; a major mineral resource, oil; and the geostrategic importance of a land mass lying astride the most efficient land and water routes between Europe and Asia (more important for early development than for the present), including the possession of warm-water ports that have been coveted by Central Asian powers. The combination of these economically important geographic factors distinguishes the region from other regions of the world.

Socially, few other areas of the world enjoy the homogeneity of the Middle East. A single language, Arabic, is spoken by a majority of the more than

200 million inhabitants, although there are differences between local dialects. And countries like Turkey, Iran, Israel, and Afghanistan, which do not share Arabic, have a single language which most of the population speaks. Relative language homogeneity is an important economic factor that the Middle East shares with no other poor region in the world. Even Latin America, apparently Spanish and Portuguese speaking, still has many tribal languages spoken by large proportions of the population.

The structure of Middle Eastern society both within and across national frontiers also shows remarkable similarity. Patrilineal family structure, tribal and village organization, landholding practices, and urban class structure, while showing some variance, tend to be more similar than different for those social groups between Gibraltar and the Khyber Pass. Most groups share common cultural and historical experiences based on Islamic and Ottoman influences.

Political factors have interacted with economic processes to contribute to the uniqueness of the Middle Eastern economic structure. First, since most of the countries in the area were part of the Ottoman Empire for periods extending up to 500 years, the political/administrative structure of those countries enjoyed substantial similarity when the Empire dissolved. Second, the post-Ottoman colonial experience of the countries was quite different from the more intensive experience of India or Senegal. Iraq, Syria, and Lebanon had a protectorate government which lasted only between the two world wars. Whereas in the eastern Arab countries some army officers went to St. Cloud and Sandhurst and the sons of the bourgeoisie to the London School of Economics and the Sorbonne, a growing number of the future elite attended ᶜAyn Shams, American University of Beirut, or Aleppo College. Arabs of North Africa until recently have tended to go to France for higher education. The effect of both the rigid educational specifications which success in the colonial administration and society required, and the role models provided by the massive number of expatriates, from civil servants to taxi drivers, which were the rule in many non-Middle Eastern colonies, were much less strong in most of the Middle East. Algeria would be one of the exceptions. One could speculate that this less intense colonial experience might be reflected in how the Middle Easterners are beginning to deal with the issue of economic dependence on the rich countries, and their relative success in organizing the oil producers compared to the attempts of other ex-colonial countries to organize their commodities. It could of course be wholly due to the leverage of a product with a low price elasticity of demand and low elasticity of substitution. The colonial experience should also have affected the extent to which trade relations were quickly expanded beyond the original colonial partners.

Third, the Soviet–Western competition for influence in the areas encouraged sizable unearned transfers and concessionary loans for the area. Much of this foreign assistance contributed to escalating the arms race between Arab states as well as with Israel. Although the Soviet–Western conflict dates from the 1920s, it was not until after the World War II that the United States organized the Central Treaty Organization (CENTO) to link the states from Turkey to Pakistan in common defense against the Soviet Union.

At the ideological level the Soviet–Western confrontation was reflected in domestic debate on economic models for development. For the first 10 years or so after 1945 a major political issue was whether a country should have a capitalistic or socialistic economy. By the time that Nasser, Kassem, and the Bacth party had come to power, the issue became whether or not Arab socialism was different, or could be different, from the socialism of the Communist countries. To oversimplify the debate, the right argued that the concept of private ownership of the means of production and distribution was compatible with Arab socialism, while the left argued that it was not. As the left gained ascendancy over the right in some countries, they imported the Eastern European models of public control of production and centralized authority.

The issue of land management illustrates both the effect of political ideology on economic models in some countries and the diversity between the socialist countries avowing socialist objectives. Syria and Tunisia grouped small farms into state-managed enterprises, thus turning peasant farmers into wage laborers. In both countries, production and peasants suffered. Both Iraq and Egypt divided large farms among peasants and the landless, but in Iraq the farmers were organized into state cooperatives that offered little freedom of action. In Egypt, however, they were given more freedom and the state organized ancillary services. Over the decade of the 1960s Egyptian production and yields showed significant improvement compared to the Iraqi figures. Algeria chose a system of self-management of the ex-colonial farms. It profited by a better historical awareness of both its own conditions and the experience of Tunisia and Syria with Polish and Yugoslav models. In these latter countries rigorous economic analysis of the local agricultural conditions was not carried out prior to the decisions. Urban politicians, often with military backgrounds, had little awareness of production and marketing problems in their own villages, let alone in the socialist countries that were supplying the models for reform. Economists' advice tended to be based on theory and thirdhand experience of the Communist countries, rather than observation of collective models and study of local conditions. Thus these early decisions on land management were the result of political ideology being applied to economic planning with little adjustment to local conditions.

The oil sector provides an example of the acceptance until just recently by these same socialist countries like Algeria, Syria, and Tunisia of the model of the foreign-owned capitalist firm. After the failure of the Iranian experience in the early 1950s to nationalize successfully the production and marketing of their oil, the countries were unwilling to collar the goose that was laying the golden eggs. It took another 20 years of experience with the multinational corporations and the resulting increase in confidence for the countries to begin, in 1973 and 1974, to exercise greater control over their most valuable resource.

The final economic factor of political significance is the oil reserves. Their protection for Western consumers and shareholders was a major reason for the CENTO treaty of the Cold War. The political status quo of these countries became of prime concern to the U.S. Government. When the first Communist joined the Syrian cabinet in the middle 1950s, he got front-page headlines not only in Damascus but also in Dublin and Dubuque. It is not a coincidence that the two countries in the world with the highest per capita aid levels for most of the 1950s and 1960s were Middle Eastern: Jordan and Tunisia. The other strategically important countries in the Middle East were either not far behind in aid transfers or had oil income. Where economic arm twisting failed, intervention succeeded. It was either overt, such as landing the U.S. Marine in Lebanon, or covert, such as the CIA-assisted coup in Iran or military espionage in Syria. And finally, both the Soviet Union and the major Western powers used the threat of withholding arms as one more weapon in their political arsenal for maintaining the status quo.

In the above discussion of social, political, and geographic characteristics of economic significance we have already included some of the economic characteristics that make the region different from others in the world, but they are summarized here.

The export and transit trade, for which the Levant has been known throughout recorded history, has affected the development of the coastal as well as the riverine areas in the eastern countries. Phoenician sailors provisioned Mediterranean cities. Syrians filled Roman granaries. Iraqi farmers along the Euphrates began to export wheat to Europe after the opening of the Suez Canal. Commodities produced outside the area were either transshipped across the area or, like Argentine beef going to France, merely purchased en route by Lebanese insurers. And by the 1930s oil exports began their growth to present dominance. The export trade remains a major factor in the economic growth of the oil countries.

Oil exports have produced a second important economic characteristic of the area. At least five major countries, and a larger number of small states, have an enormous surplus on both their domestic account and balance of payments. Until early 1974 most of the surplus found a home abroad in investments ranging from London gold certificates to Miami real estate. As we have seen since 1973, the organization of the Arab nations around this export has become a source of significant political and economic power.

Finally, we should examine the economic maturity of these oil states which have a high per capita income, but retain the economic structure of countries with much lower per capita incomes. A large proportion of the population is still in agriculture, and manufacturing provides a small contribution to value added.

A VIEW OF PAST RESEARCH

We include in this section four main categories of studies. These include Ph.D. dissertations; consultant and other unpublished studies; studies by the United Nations and other international agencies of limited circulation; and finally, books and articles. If we consider research to be the course of critical and scientific inquiry, we have a definition that would exclude some works from each of the categories since they are either uncritical or unscientific. If we refine the definition to exclude those works which, in my opinion, do not significantly extend the frontiers of knowledge, the field for review becomes notably smaller. If we further exclude inaccessible materials, only the category of books and articles is left for review.[3] This somewhat arbitrary process does an injustice to some good work. The broader nature of this chapter, however, leads us to give an impression of past research rather than a comprehensive review.[4]

Historical, Country, and Macroeconomic Research

Research in this category either examines macro data at one point in time, cross-section analysis, or over a specific period, time-series analysis. Economic studies that concentrate on pre-twentieth century periods have required historical rather than econometric skills in dealing with archival materials and languages. For a review of research on economic history, see Issawi (1968).

A distinction cannot be easily drawn between historical studies of the last 150 years and other macroeconomic work, for the latter also provides historical insight. Macroeconomic work is often focused on quantified processes, but historical studies frequently go beyond the numbers to analyze the major economic interrelationships as well as to examine the interaction with social and political factors rather than assuming their effects constant. There are two basic questions underlying all this research: what is the composition of national income, and why does the rate of growth of national income vary over time?

Obviously, the quality of the country studies is mainly a function of the researchers' ability, but it is also dependent on several other factors. The size of the population seems to influence the quality: the best of the studies for the Middle East concern Algeria, Egypt, and Turkey, whereas studies for the smaller countries are of lesser quality. Israel is the exception. The quality and quantity of data available are also important, and the macro work on Libya is not of the same rigor as that on Egypt for this reason. Furthermore, among the better studies the work on Egypt is often on a par with the best country studies for other areas of the world, partly because of the existence of time series extending into the nineteenth century and partly because of the caliber of economists who have been drawn to the country either by its historical importance or through consulting on the early development plans. The collection of country studies by Cooper and Alexander presents a recent concise overview.

The econometric work occupies only a small part of the available research materials. Some of the more interesting work has been done in the past five years. There is not space to mention all this work but the research by Blitzec et al. (Turkey), Evans (Israel), and Tintner and Farghali (Egypt) is representative of the quality and imagination. More routine modeling as part of plan preparations like input–output matrices is often summarized in plans or detailed in unpublished papers. Some of the historical and macro studies also make econometric estimations. In Egypt the work of Hansen and Marzouk, Issawi (1963), Landes, O'Brien, and Owen is comparable in analytic rigor to the best country and macro research in Latin America or Asia. The publications of Amuzegar and Fekrat, Bharier, and Issawi (1971) are significant; the research of both Amin and Tiano provides useful insight on Algeria. The recent work by Peck challenging the idea that capital transfers are at the heart of Israeli expansion exemplifies the solid and imaginative work for Israel; and the research of Hershlag provides an example of the competent work undertaken on Turkey.

Topical, Sectoral, and Microeconomics

Though it is easy theoretically to separate topical, sectoral, and microeconomic research, the literature for the Middle East, which is virtually all empirical, does not allow the same clear distinctions. Most of the economic research on the Middle Eastern topics falls within this area. The publications of the last 15 years indicate that agriculture has been studied twice as much as industry or labor, which are next in frequency. Other subjects like public finance, income distribution, education, or transport have received less attention. Many of these topics are also covered in the country studies.

It is easy to criticize the work of the 1950s from the vantage point of 1975, with its improved data, analytic techniques, and computing facilities. Still the descriptive and critical works by Langley (1961) and Finnie (1958), remain important. There are, however, more recent and consequently more rigorous industrial studies—Hirsch for Israel, Avramovic for Iran, and de Bernis for Algeria. The UN's study of small-scale industry is the first comprehensive piece on a crucial topic. The political implications and economic distortions caused by the multinational firms, both Arab and non-Arab, have been little studied. The work by Viralov and Tanzer is an important exception.

Though several of the above authors have dealt with oil questions, this topic requires separate discussion. Oil research also has implications ranging from the micro to the international and thus defies easy classification. Examples of the better, broader works include Schurr and Homan, Issawi and Yeganeh, and Sayegh (1968). More rigorous analyses are found in the work of Adelman, Meyer, and Penrose.

As development objectives have begun to shift from economic growth to employment and income distribution for a larger number of countries, the literature on labor as a factor of production increases in importance. Whereas labor research traditionally focused on productivity, wages, and training, it has now broadened to include mobility (internal and external), trade unions, manpower planning, and social security. There is a growing awareness that, in contrast to rich countries, the blue collar and gray collar workers are an economic elite when compared to the large percentage of the population whose earnings are lower and less stable. Critical examinations of a range of labor problems are found in the research by Bartsch, Nagi, and the UAR Institute of National Planning (1966). The work by Beling and Salah-Beye are examples of trade union research. The increasingly important topic of worker management has received little attention outside of Algeria (Clegg) and Israel (Schregle). More analysis of manpower within an industry needs to be done to complement the work by Badre and Siksek on oil and Simmons (1973) on shoes. Rural employment has received little attention, but many of the questions that need further work have been raised in the publications of Warriner (1970) and the UAR Institute of National Planning (1968). The behavior of entrepreneurs, although ignored by recent economists, is central to the growth process. Yusif Sayegh's excellent research on Lebanon raises important questions for future work. Finally we come to the question of labor mobility. Though there is little on the economics of internal migration, Trebous examines emigration and related training questions.

Increasing agricultural yields have long been considered a crucial factor in growth and development of the Middle Eastern countries. With the increased interest in spreading the effects of investment to the low-income groups this objective has become even more important. Unlike the other sectors and topics, agricultural research and problems have been carefully reviewed by Taylor for the Eastern countries (1968) and Foster (1966) for the Western. They concluded that, as with other developing regions of the world, the main research has been of a descriptive rather than an analytic nature.

The Taylor and Foster reviews isolate a number of priority policy issues and unanswered questions. These issues include water resource development, farm mechanization, land reform and consolidation, agricultural credit, planning and administration, and farm management including private and collective control. The major lacunae in the literature are farm management and farm level production function work, and modeling of the optimization of social welfare from the rural investment package. Exceptions to these lacunae are the farm management studies in Israel by Mundlak (1964b) and in Lebanon by Ward et al. Robinson and Karpat have begun exploring the socioeconomic impact of mechanization at the village level. Gabriel and Klat have examined the inefficiency of scattered landholdings. The infrequent use of institutional agricultural credit is identified in the work of Sadaka, Loomis, and Taylor; further work needs to explore to what extent this is due to supply or demand factors. The effectiveness of agricultural planning and administrative mechanisms depends on tools ranging from supply and demand projection series comparable to the research by Asfour for Saudi Arabia, Palmer for Turkey, and Mundlak (1964a) for Israel, to the evaluation research by Gittinger and Simmons (1965, 1971). Nomadic pastoralism and cattle raising received some interesting analysis by Malhouk, Stauffer, and Zghal but these studies only begin to explore important policy questions.

We have mentioned the more important research on country studies, agriculture, industry, and labor to give the reader an impression of the state of the art. These topics include more than 80% of the published materials in the economics of the Middle East. Limited space prevents the discussion of other important topics such as finance, income distribution, transport, construction, education, and health.

International and Interdisciplinary

International research includes regional integration, trade, aid, and multinational firms. Studies of the international trade in Middle Eastern goods and services are usually part of global studies for which the Middle East is only one region. Examples include major exports like money, cotton, oil, and skilled manpower as well as the full range of imports. Both the country and oil studies mentioned above devote major efforts to these subjects. Though some work has been published on regional integration, it has been mainly political in orientation and content. Significant rigorous work remains to be done.

Aid has received more attention, although some of the basic questions have not been carefully examined. These include the capacity of the countries and the sectors within them to absorb the aid, and the distortions that foreign aid may have caused, for example, exacerbating an uneconomic bias toward capital intensity or rural–urban migration. The work by El-Naggar, Amuzegar, and Kazemian are examples of a comprehensive treatment for Egypt and Iran. Lanfer has reviewed the impact of Israeli assistance on the African and Latin American countries.

Multinational corporations have received attention in the micro studies by Finnie and Meyer, but little work has been done on their impact within the wider context of an industry and the economy. To what extent do capital-intensive and foreign controlled firms work against the national objectives of employment creation and economic independence? Should agricultural land be sold or leased to produce cash crops for export while the landed peasantry become agricultural laborers? This is a high-priority research topic.

Some economists might argue that to have ignored some of the above subjects and then used valuable space to discuss interdisciplinary work approaches blasphemy. I contend that it is the purists who are in error. The problems of development do not respect the boundaries between disciplines. The primitiveness of the guidelines for the integration of the theories and tools of disciplines is an important reason why our understanding of development processes is often naïve. The psychology of consumer behavior is still treated as a constant in the estimates of consumption function. Understanding the effect of pressure groups and economic elites on distorting resource allocation requires the careful modeling of social and political determinants. Although interdisciplinary work has some support, it has received much less effort, money, or journal space than is needed. As long ago as 1951, the work of Katona defined some of the crucial psychological issues.

Better economic and interdisciplinary research, for example, might help explain why some countries have had impressive rates of growth in national income, but little development measured by significantly improved incomes of the lowest income groups or social services available to that group. The addition of social class, interest groups, and behavioral variables would help explain why the sons and daughters of upper-income groups tend to get more years of schooling than low-income groups, and why some farmers adopt innovations more rapidly than others. These questions are evidence of the need for joining social and political analysis to the economic and technical processes. Hinderink and Keray-belik (1970) suggest in their recent study of Turkish rural life that the more we learn about the political relationships between the rural elites and the peasants through the production and marketing relationships, the better we will understand why the poor remain poor. At the national level Cohn and Jacobs examine similar forces for Turkey and Iran. At the sectoral and firm level the work by Khalaf on Lebanon explores important questions relative to industrial efficiency, while Bourdieu, using different methods, has undertaken similar research on Algeria.

FUTURE RESEARCH TOPICS

Let us assume there are two types of research, empirical and theoretical, and that they are not mutually exclusive. Then empirical research can be divided into two categories: (1) that which meets the immediate needs of decision makers and (2) that which expands our knowledge. Identifying the needs of the decision maker is a complicated process, and yet that crucial link must be made if economic research is going to improve its social utility.

In January 1972 a letter was sent to several economists eliciting their reactions to some research topics that might be prominent in the next 10 years. Their replies were used as a basis for a draft questionnaire which was prepared in November 1972. This was then sent to a wider group for their comment. Their suggestions were incorporated into the final version of the questionnaire. Copies were mailed to more than 70 economists and development specialists whose names were obtained from the list of MESA fellows, the Society for International Development, and contributors to the literature. Only 24% responded. Even allowing for those questionnaires that may never have reached their destination, this was a disappointing, though not unusual, return. However, the opinions of 17 may be more valuable to the reader than those of one.

The largest proportion of respondents was affiliated with institutions in North America and Europe, and 25% was in the Middle East. Sixty-five percent of the 17 respondents gave a university affiliation, 24% government, and 12% public or private firms. Language competence was extensive. Fifty-eight percent said that they had ability in both Middle Eastern and European languages; only 36% did not have a research knowledge of a Middle Eastern language. The majority of respondents received their B.S.s in Europe or the Middle East—only 12% had American B.A.s—and obtained their higher degrees in the U.S. (53%) and Europe (29%).

The questionnaire asked about areas in which the respondents had published, were presently doing research, or had done consulting work. Although they are quite distinct activities, the responses to the questions were aggregated because their composite experience would be more important than any of the individual activities in suggesting research topics. The largest number of replies related to planning activities, and then to general economics; agriculture, oil, and finance followed. Finally came education and health, business, transport and communications, and construction.

The questionnaire asked for the respondents' opinions about the economic literature. Several took this to include literature that dealt with areas other than the Middle East. It asked them to list, as specifically as possible, "the best literature (books and articles) on the topics in which you have a research interest." There was space for three topics and three references for each topic. Two of the 17 did not list any literature. Eleven listed references for only one topic, and nine listed references for all three possibilities. (It is likely that this question, which was on the first page of the questionnaire, discouraged many of the recipients from completing it.)

The topics that received the most comments were planning and finance. Oil, agriculture, and trade were close behind. Topics least mentioned were transport and communications, construction, industry, econometric methods, and business.

Criteria for the Selection of Research Topics

The respondents were asked to rank in order of importance four criteria that might be used in selecting research projects. The criteria included the following:

1. Researchability, including either of the following or both: (*a*) data exist or can be collected at a reasonable cost; (*b*) the models can be developed at reasonable cost.
2. Extending the frontiers of knowledge.
3. Satisfying policy needs.
4. Low opportunity costs of research project, i.e., under $15,000.

Respondents were also given an opportunity to suggest additional criteria, but none took the opportunity.

Although the small number of respondents does not permit a forceful generalization about preference for different criteria, some tendencies do emerge from Table 1. From the "Total" column we see that "researchability" was considered to be most important by seven of the respondents and least important by only two. "Satisfying policy needs" had six votes for the most important criterion. Four respondents felt that "extending the frontiers of knowledge" was most important, and five felt it was the least important criterion. Most felt that low cost research should not be a factor in selecting research projects.

The figures in columns 1 and 2 suggest that the responses for individuals living in the region and those outside are consistent. Perhaps surprisingly, a larger proportion of outsiders than insiders felt that the criterion of satisfying policy needs was more important.

TABLE I
Research Criteria and the Address of Respondent

Criterion		North America and Europe (1)	Middle East (2)	Total (3)
Researchability				
Least important	(1)	2	0	0
↓	(2)	2	2	4
	(3)	2	0	2
Most important	(4)	3	4	7
Extending frontiers of knowledge				
Least important	(1)	3	2	5
↓	(2)	3	1	4
	(3)	2	1	3
Most important	(4)	2	2	4
Satisfying policy needs				
Least important	(1)	2	2	4
↓	(2)	2	0	2
	(3)	2	2	4
Most important	(4)	4	2	6
Low opportunity costs of research				
Least important	(1)	0	3	3
↓	(2)	4	1	5
	(3)	2	1	3
Most important	(4)	1	1	2

Priority Topics for Economic Research

The nature of the questionnaire makes it possible to bias the results. To reduce this possibility, a letter and then a draft of the questionnaire were distributed, eliciting the widest range of suggestions. We recognize nevertheless that the order in which the priority topics appeared in the questionnaire inevitably affected the results. Finally, we tried to avoid the restrictions of a close-ended questionnaire by encouraging individuals to list additional subjects that they felt should have priority.[5]

The results in Table 2 show that research on industrialization and trade should have highest priority for future research. Next in importance came education and manpower, urban migration, and the politics of economic decisions. Subjects that got the lowest priority included public health, village level studies, nomadic pastoralism, and the economics of small states. The

TABLE 2
Priority Topics for Research

Topic	Ranking None (0)	Low (1)	High (2)	Highest (3)	Rank Order
Industrialization	5	0	3	8	1
Trade	7	2	3	5	2
Politics of economic decisions	9	2	2	3	3
Education and manpower	12	1	1	3	3
Urban migration	9	2	2	3	3
Economic history	8	3	4	2	4
Oil and mining	11	1	3	2	4
Intermediate technology	10	1	4	2	4
Employment and unemployment	11	1	3	2	4
Income distribution	11	0	4	2	4
Public finance	10	3	1	2	4
Economic planning	9	3	1	2	4
Agriculture	9	2	3	1	5
Institutional management factor	11	0	3	1	5
Development objectives	11	1	2	1	5
Public health	13	3	0	0	6
Village level	12	3	1	0	6
Nomadic pastoralism	13	2	0	0	6
Economics of small states	13	3	0	0	6

reader should also see the suggestive subjects within each topic in Table 3. These subjects should not be considered as limiting the important subtopics.

Respondents were asked to assign highest priority to no more than three topics, high priority to no more than two topics, and low priority to no more than two topics. The rank order was determined by the greatest frequency of "highest" rankings. For example, the subject of industrialization got eight votes and trade got five. The "none" category could be rank-ordered between the low and high category. It is interesting to note that no topics received a large number of low-priority rankings. Slightly different priorities emerge if the high and highest are summed, or if the low and none are summed.

Do these results simply reflect the specialities of the respondents? The most frequently mentioned areas of research and consulting were, in descending order of frequency, planning, general economics, oil, and finance. The topics picked for research in descending order were industrialization, trade, the politics of economic decisions, education and manpower, and urban migration. We may surmise that the respondents were not limited by their special interests.

TABLE 3
Subtopics as Listed in the Questionnaire

1. *Economic history*
   a. Role of institutions in economic development
   b. Comparative studies; e.g., Egypt/Iran, Algeria/Syria, Turkey/Iraq
   c. Long-run production functions: capital and labour input to discover past sources of growth
2. *Oil and mining*
   a. Development and growth prospects of oil economies
   b. Welfare impact of oil production
   c. Forward linkages for the hard minerals
3. *Industrialization*
   a. The economic impact of the multinational firms: oil, manufacturing, and finance
   b. The effects of industrialization on growth and development
   c. Backward and forward linkages of intermediate products
   d. The impact of economic integration on particular industries
   e. Specific industries: internal efficiency including management, labor, and organization
   f. Technological change: the factors constraining efficient industrialization
4. *Intermediate technology*
   a. The research and development expenditures of governments and firms on technology
   b. The incentives and obstacles to regional industrial development
   c. Alternative production functions for labor absorption
5. *Trade: international and intraregional*
   a. The effects of protection
   b. Trade relations between Middle Eastern countries
   c. Administrative obstacles to improved trade
   d. An Arab common market
6. *Education and manpower*
   a. Evaluation of the internal and external efficiency of educational expenditures in 1950s and 1960s
   b. The links between schooling and worker productivity
   c. Employment generation through investment in education
   d. The oversupply of secondary, technical, and university graduates
   e. The determination of the demand for critical skills: policy models

Table 3 (contd.)

7. *Employment and unemployment*
   a. Public works programs
   b. Investment alternatives to create jobs
8. *Public health*
   a. Private and social rate of return to investment in family planning
   b. Cost-benefit estimates for alternative delivery systems
9. *Urban migration and emigration*
   a. Rural migrants in the service sector: are there gains in productivity?
   b. The economics of urbanization
   c. Optimum transport systems
   d. Social costs of interregional migration
   e. The costs and benefits of emigration
10. *Agriculture*
    a. The efficiency of small versus large farms
    b. Optimum research and delivery systems for agricultural information
    c. The backward and forward linkage effects of investment in alternative commodities
    d. The political constraints to increasing income and outputs of peasants and nomads
11. *Village level*
    a. Optimal allocations at the village level
    b. Is there a common model?
    c. Political economy of village decisions
    d. Nonmonetary cost benefits to village life
    e. The economics of self-help
12. *Nomadic pastoralism*
    a. Contribution to value added
    b. Interdependencies with farm and town
    c. Is there a common model?
    d. The economics of settlement
    e. Marketing efficiency under state and private control
13. *The institutional/management factor*
    a. The effects of institutional reforms
    b. Management as the missing factor
    c. The economics of "institution building"
14. *Politics of economic decisions*
    a. Planning and implementation at the local level
    b. Top down versus bottom up planning
15. *The economics of small states*
    a. What are the special problems?
    b. Is there a common model?
16. *Income distribution*
    a. The fallacy of the trickle-down effect from high rates of economic growth
    b. The contribution of investment in education

Table 3 (contd.)

c. The role of public finance mechanisms
d. The effect of the redistribution of assets

17. *Public finance*
    a. The impact of the Middle Eastern capital markets on Middle Eastern development
    b. The equity of present systems of taxation
    c. Foreign exchange as a constraint to development
    d. The impact of development banks on growth and income distribution
18. *Development objectives*
    a. Westernization/industrialization reconsidered
    b. How are objectives established, and for whom?
19. *Economic planning*
    a. Realistic tools and implementation
    b. Examples of bottom up planning

The major surprise was the lack of interest in the topic of income distribution, although no one gave it a low rating, and the three rural topics: agriculture, nomadic pastoralism, and village level information. It is the rural poor who have missed the development benefits in most of the countries. Perhaps it is a reflection of the fact that only two respondents were agricultural economists, or conversely, that the urban respondents are not confronted by and therefore are not conscious of the problem.

Analysis of Research Priorities

This section has three objectives:

1. Setting standards for distinguishing new or problem-solving contributions from routine continuations of established traditions.
2. Directing new scholars toward questioning the received scholarly traditions.
3. Recommending to funding agencies, both governmental and private, as well as centers and research institutes, what their priorities and criteria might be. These guidelines were provided by the MESA committee and repeated in the covering letter for the questionnaire.

SETTING THE STANDARDS. It is clear from a review of past work and the available tools that future economic research should be more analytic. This is not to discount past research, because these descriptive studies form a useful foundation for more rigorous work. However, in future the question why, rather than what, should dominate. Theories of causality should be tested. Analytic tools developed by economic theory during the past 100 years, and given quantitative shape in the past 20 years, should be increasingly used in the Middle East as they have been in other regions of the world.

Methods of model building and testing are taught in most university economics departments and should be applied to the problems of the Middle East. Using these techniques would take the literature a quantum jump toward both the research frontiers and meeting policy needs. The danger is that models and hypotheses based on the economic processes in the Western countries will be tested without adaptation to the conditions of Middle East. The responsibility for seeing that the research is well designed to meet either basic or policy research needs rests both with the funding agency and researcher, as well as the research and policy community in the Middle Eastern country. As obvious as this sounds, this process has been honored in the breach in the past. A method for putting this responsibility into effect is suggested below.

In short, the standards exist for guiding future economic research. They range from neo-Marxian theory to Bayesian statistics. The major problem is deciding which methods will most effectively increase our understanding of research questions.

QUESTIONING THE SCHOLARLY TRADITION. This dimension of our view of the state of the art is mainly covered in the comments above on analytic work and the types of research suggested in the next section. It should be noted that imaginative application of present research to the economic realities of different types of poverty and the extremes of resource endowment in the Middle East could substantially refine those Western conceived theories.

The significant policy research in the future including both the theoretical and empirical dimension will result from using the techniques of the physical sciences: direct observation and experimentation. Economists need to experience the result of the subject they are studying in order to explain what has been ignored or held constant in the past. This means work on farms, in factories, and in the presidential councils. There is no shortcut to either improved theory or practice. We have relied far too long on the statistical office rather than on our own powers of observation.

CRITERIA AND PRIORITIES. Based on the sample of respondents, the important criteria are those of policy orientation and researchability. Furthermore, these would appear to be the logical criteria, given the available resources and the nature of area studies. (If social science is going to have a social utility, then it is in the application of its knowledge to the problems of people.)

Priority topics were suggested by the respondents and appear in Table 2. It is important to use these data in concordance with the subheadings for each topic found in Table 3. Of course, a strong case could be made for working on the low-priority topics if the research design met policy needs.

Personal Views

Several of my own biases about future research should be shared with the reader.

1. The research question that most directly affects the growth of the Middle East in the next 5–40 years has little to do with the Middle East. This is the long-term availability of alternative energy forms in the West. A related question is the extent to which technical and economic conservation is feasible. Dramatic technological breakthroughs, for example, as with the substitute for natural rubber, would alter long-term growth prospects.
2. A second research issue that needs emphasis is how the rate of expenditure, at the high levels envisaged in the major oil exporting countries, will affect the rates of inflation, growth, and income distribution. Even the theory related to this question is inadequate.
3. What are the implicit or explicit research objectives, and what should they be? Social scientific research has the twin objectives of the advancement of knowledge and the welfare of people. Though these two objectives are shared by the physical and health sciences, research for the direct welfare of people occupies a less prestigious place in the hierarchy of social scientists. It occupies a smaller proportion of space in the better journals and thus attracts fewer good students. In medicine and law the direct welfare dimensions of the research are a high priority. This may be a function of the relative immaturity of economics. To speed up the maturation process incentives to promote welfare research and complement the criteria of journal editors and tenure committees are required. If development economics wishes to gain in legitimacy, it must increase the importance of the welfare objective in its research.
4. If research focuses on welfare questions, then the priorities have to arise from the problems of the people, both rich and poor, rather than be imposed on them by researchers who often have had little first-hand experience with those problems. (It could be argued that this Chapter further illustrates the crucial question, with researchers "second guessing" one another about the problems that need research.) Some of the researchers may be right because they are close enough to some segments of the population, like villagers or unemployed or small businessmen, to understand the

needs. Health research priorities are set in part by focusing on those diseases that kill the largest proportion of the population. In a similar fashion, economic research could well focus on that segment of the population which is benefiting least from development efforts, and begin by surveying their needs as the poor see them. There has been sufficient rhetoric about bottom up planning. It is now time to push aside the easily accessible statistical tables and ascertain the facts from the villages and bidonvilles themselves.

5. What type of economic research about the region should be encouraged for the next 10 years or so? What research would both heighten our understanding of the uniqueness and universality of Middle Eastern growth and development, and contribute to improving the field of development economics? First, even though the data available for most countries in the region have improved recently, their present and future quality and extent preclude the use of most of the econometric techniques that graduate training teaches. Second, the types of hypotheses that many researchers are interested in testing do not even have data. Third, accurate macro analysis and policy work require a much better understanding of micro phenomena than we now have. As Henry Bruton has suggested, "The heart of the growth process is so easily shrouded by aggregation." Given these three observations, micro research offers several advantages for improving both theoretical and policy knowledge. First, micro analysis facilitates using experimental techniques. Parameters can be changed and the effect more accurately understood than with cross-sectional or historical time-series data. Second, micro analysis permits the collection of data to test more elaborate models of economic behavior. No longer is it necessary to assume constant variables that significantly affect results. Psychological and political research provides measures useful for refining economic models. Agricultural and educational production functions are logical applications for these refinements.

6. Returns to scale exist in research as in other production processes. They need to be encouraged by concentrating economic research on several countries of the area selected for (*a*) the representative nature of either their structure of area economies, e.g., oil vs. non-oil, small vs. large populations, or area economic problems; and (*b*) the nature of the research climate, e.g., the local research capacity and freedom of access to data. The second criterion is the limiting one. From preliminary investigations it would seem that only in Lebanon, Israel, Kuwait, and Tunisia does the research climate approach minimum standards. Research on special subjects would be an exception.

By concentrating efforts in several countries, insights quickly deepen as study builds upon previous study in a synergistic fashion. As this pyramid of new knowledge mounts, additional scholars are attracted to it because of this foundation. The quality research which has resulted from the pyramid of analyses based on the Ottoman archives is analogous. It is difficult to make a case for repeating similar research in each country. The economic structures and function do not vary that much. For example, studies of educational and agricultural production functions do not have to be repeated in every country to suggest patterns.

ISSUES RELATED TO FUTURE RESEARCH

Though it is easy to suggest future research priorities, the problem of completing the research and then communicating the results of policy research to decision makers remains.

Should time and money be spent on a thorough review of the economic literature of the region on a topical or other basis? Researchers are already provided with sufficient bibliographical assistance to locate references they need. And the better books, articles, and dissertations have made initial appraisals of sections of the literature. It would be useful for the several economic journals of the region to begin to publish abstracts with the articles. These abstracts could be later collected into an annotated bibliography and used by other retrieval systems.

Should there be an effort made to produce good country studies on all the countries in the region? Let us assume that there are two types of country studies: those that mainly deal with the present and, for certain questions, the past 20 years; and other country studies that cover longer time periods. The decision on this latter type of study should be left to the economic historians. The contemporary studies face a different problem. Because of the absence of sufficient data mentioned in the preceding section,[6] it is probably too early to expect that many good economists would be attracted to do country studies. Furthermore, if country studies are to be both broad in scope and as analytic as possible, they require considerable skill and judgment with a number of tools. Finally, most economists who are recent graduates of doctoral programs tend to be more interested in narrower topics than country studies, which may reflect a weakness in their training.[7] Thus recent country studies would have a low priority. As much as this may limit our understanding of the functioning of the economy, this is probably the correct priority, given the importance of other topics.

Why are there so few economists working on the Middle East compared to other regions in the world? The quality and quantity of economic research on sub-Saharan Africa, a region with about the same total population as the Middle East and North Africa, is significantly higher than that of the Middle East. Two immediate causes can be indicated. In the first place, there has been more funding available for North American scholars for sub-Saharan Africa than other regions. In the second place, language plays a determining part; Arabic is as important in the Middle East as English is in India or East Africa; and the use of French economic publications in the Middle Eastern countries is as extensive as the use of English. An equally important deterrent is the high-risk fieldwork. The chances of a researcher being expelled from the country or being unable to collect data or interview the necessary officials are higher for Middle Eastern countries than for any other region. Even economists with area experience and contacts sometimes hesitate to recommend that doctoral students undertake fieldwork in the area. Finally, and most important, the quality and quantity of data available for most of the countries in the region are inferior to the quality of the data and analytic studies available for countries like India and Mexico. It is to countries like these that economists turn to test their models.

If the data are so poor for some of the countries, is it worthwhile considering a program which would encourage the collection and organization of data at both the country and regional levels? This topic is sufficiently important that it should be explored more carefully than can be done here. Several points should suffice. The quality and quantity of data is improving every year, but most of it does not get into research libraries either in or outside the concerned country. "Published" data often appear in very limited editions that are soon out of print. The collection of unpublished data requires visiting the firms and government ministries, and if a researcher arrives a month too early or too late the limited edition is no longer available. A study in progress may be little known or copies unavailable. In fact, governments have even had to recommission studies, either because the memories of their ministries are too short or their information systems so unorganized.

Because of the cost of organizing published and unpublished data, one cannot be optimistic that realistic solutions can be found that would significantly reduce the researcher's time and expense spent locating data.[8] Given this disclaimer, there are several suggestions. First, a study should be commissioned to explore the many facets of the collection and use of such data. This would include a survey of the major North American and European collections of data. Second, representatives of these data collections, both multilateral agencies and universities, as well as economists with an interest in the region, should meet to discuss the results of the survey of the data. Duplication of effort should be reduced. Third, ways of collaboration should be explored that might include sharing the responsibility for collecting and cataloging the data from one or two countries with a major university research center. As information retrieval systems become more efficient and less costly, the data can be more efficiently stored and used than is now possible, but first they have to be collected.

A separate issue is posed by the storage of economic data on magnetic tape for computer reading. The type of data ranges from population and industrial census to sample survey data of consumers and firms. The census data, for example, have a significantly improved utility if they are available to social scientists on tape rather than in printed tables since the tape format permits the manipulation of the individual observations according to the needs of hypothesis testing rather than the usual demographic needs. Survey data are usually collected to test a limited number of hypotheses, but can often be reanalyzed to test other hypotheses or serve as background data in the preparation for other studies. That both survey and census data are not easily available to researchers is the greatest single waste of resources spent in the production of information. A major reason that the information is not more fully used or made available is that the individuals who are responsible for collecting it have neither an understanding of its value for reanalysis nor the responsibility for seeing that it is made more accessible. Another reason is the lack of an organization to make it available.[9] Until economic data on the Middle East are better organized and made available to researchers, including noneconomists, particularly survey and census data, graduate students and senior researchers will continue to look elsewhere to test their hypotheses. A major project to organize the economic data for Latin American is already underway.[10]

Are incentives missing which are needed to improve the quality of research on the Middle East? A full answer to this question would require a survey of the state of economic research incentives in the other regions of the world. However, two pertinent observations can be made. First, at a time when research funds for universities are declining, funding agencies have increased leverage with the funds that remain. Second, as agencies have concentrated their funding in a limited number of centers for Middle Eastern studies in North America, it is consistent to consider trying to establish within certain of these centers a strong economics section. The importance of interaction with other development economists predetermines that these centers should be established at universities that already have strong sections on development economics in their economics departments. Another incentive to improve the quality of research would be the establishment of collaborative relations with the economic research sections of universities in the region. A basic element in this program of long-term collaboration would be an exchange of scholars and information. This exchange should include graduate students, who presently tend to gravitate toward faculty with secure sources of graduate research funds. Most of these, unfortunately, are not professors interested in the Middle East. A final dimension to increasing quality of research relates to the nature of present fellowship programs for either Westerners or Middle Easterners. It is practically impossible to find a program now which would permit two years of postdoctoral fieldwork, including one half or one quarter time teaching, plus the opportunity to return to the country for several months to check the results and review the drafts. Without such opportunities, it is difficult to produce imaginative and revealing research. The Social Science Research Council has made important strides in this direction, especially with the collaborative grants program, but more needs to be done. The concentration of funding and data collection efforts, plus the establishment of strong collaborative relations with researchers and their institutions in the region indicate the nature of the incentives which would improve regional research.

Are the intellectual and social responsibilities of economists doing research on a developing country's regional topics any different from the responsibilities of researchers working on the developed countries or economic theory? This question has many ramifications, many of which have been explored elsewhere. Furthermore, it is a question, like religion, that has important personal dimensions. An example may illustrate the dilemmas concerning intellectual and social responsibilities. A recent Ph.D. whose thesis was on price theory is asked by the Planning Commission of an Arab country to study the efficiency of small farms. Does he neglect his interest in price theory and put all his energies into understanding farm efficiency? What are his intellectual responsibilities? One could argue that his social responsibility lies with farm efficiency since his findings there could more immediately affect the welfare of the farmers as well as consumers.

Researchers who live in the region more often feel the responsibility to engage in research with a social welfare impact than those living outside the region. Extremes in poverty, inequality, and misallocation confront them daily. Funds for doing research are usually tied to planning activities. There are, however, forces that tend to encourage researchers to work on topics that are in vogue in the *developed* countries, some of which may be more relevant than others for the developing countries. These forces include past training, criteria for publishing in the more prestigious journals, and the criteria for promotion and tenure. These distortions are the basis for the allegation of autocolonialism leveled at some local researchers.

Researchers who live outside the region do not experience the same sanctions as those who live inside. The absence of some sanctions may lead to abuses of research practices. These include the unauthorized use of data, the excessive amounts of time required of already overworked officials, and the failure to send copies of the finished work for either comment or cataloging. Backed by funding beyond levels afforded by local researchers and by the reputations of prestigious institutions, foreigners often have access to data that are denied local researchers. These abuses form the basis for the valid charge of academic imperialism that is leveled at visiting scholars. Unless foreign researchers become more aware of these abuses, they risk having these privileges denied them as in some African and Asian countries.

What are the supply and demand conditions for researchers? The Middle East has not suffered from the rapidly inflating costs of hiring economists that we see in some Latin American countries. If the cost of their services does increase owing to demands for consulting, evaluation, and planning, then few, if any, will be available for most research at present salaries. Also there is the wastage of economists who are trained in research techniques but who have received neither the additional funding nor apprentice possibilities to develop sufficiently their techniques. When they return from obtaining their M.A. or Ph.D. degrees, they are given a full teaching load or a new five-year plan to write, and there end their research careers. Some prefer it that way, but others, who are motivated and gifted for research work, need an environment in which to work. Important attempts to provide this environment are being made at the Economic Research Institute at the American University of Beirut, the Institute of National Planning in Cairo, and the Center for Enonomic and Social Research at the University of Tunis. Either through government or private contracts, and direct budgetary support, researchers are provided with partial or full funding.

Could better coordination improve the quality and utility of future research? There are at least three basic problems. First, economic research in many of the countries has a modest reputation among policy makers either because its analytic level is low ("Aren't they stating the obvious?") or because the policy implications do not exist or are not drawn. Second, researchers from foreign universities, mainly Ph.D. students, often do not have a clear idea of their topics when they arrive in the region, let alone the even more necessary knowledge of what research is being conducted locally. They work quietly for six months to two years, either disturbing as few people as possible or returning to their universities. Furthermore, their topics may be determined more by their professors' interests or the Ph.D. job market in the United States than the needs of the country. This is a major reason why some Ph.D. research seems either irrelevant or repetitive. Third, many organizations are also sponsoring research. In agriculture alone there are more than 50 for the Middle East. For these several reasons, there is a significant need for joint effort by the producers and consumers of economic research first to identify problems where research can make a contribution and then coordinate the required efforts. Because this coordination function is now lacking in most of the countries, a tremendous amount of research is done which does not reach the potential consumers, who, in consequence, may repeat the work.

One mechanism to facilitate the coordination might be a committee of research advisors attached to the office of the planning minister or prime minister. Members could be the representatives from the various ministries, universities, and the private sector. The committee would have two major objectives: to assist researchers in their search for relevant topics and other information, and to assess and publish the national research needs. These two functions should no longer be the sole responsibility, often by default, of foreign agencies and researchers. The committee could establish research priorities and guidelines to promote more efficient research, to avoid incidents which might jeopardize the research, to maintain a file of ongoing research projects, and to ensure that copies of the final product are distributed to the interested parties.

In the developed countries whose agencies fund much of the research on the Middle East, steps should be taken to fund the priorities as perceived by researchers from the area. The Social Science Research Council, for example, has taken the important step of adding Middle Easterners to its review committees.

In conclusion it might be useful to suggest for discussion a strategy for improving the quality and quantity of research on the Middle East and North Africa. The major effort has to come from a joint initiative of the researchers and policy makers in the region. They are close to the problems, and some of the countries have not only the funding potential but also the research manpower. A first step in a research strategy would be to assess problem areas where research could assist decision making. Second, the talent available to do the work should be reviewed, including researchers across national boundaries and students in M.A. and doctoral programs. Third, opportunities for coordination and cooperation should be explored with interested agencies and universities both in and out of the region. And fourth, a mechanism should be established by members of the university and of the private and public sectors to assist in coordinating research efforts and to assure that the producers and consumers of research maintain a dialogue. If proper incentives for implementing that strategy could be developed, it could offer a low-cost approach to improving the quality and quantity of economic research on the Middle East and North Africa.

NOTES

1. For a review of the equity issue, see Chenery, Duloy, and Jolly (1974).

2. This subject is sufficiently important that a more formal study would be useful. It could be broadened to include the consumer of economic research.

3. Dissertations from United States universities are an exception since most of them can be obtained readily through University Microfilms, Ann Arbor, Michigan.

4. The more comprehensive bibliographies which concentrate on economic sources include Issawi (1968), Bartsch and Bharier, and Landau. See also Economic Research Institute of the American University of Beirut, *Middle East Journal*, *La Revue Bibliographique du Moyen Orient*, School of Oriental and African Studies, and the U.S. Department of State. The Development Center of the Organization for Economic Cooperation and Development has reviewed the research institutes and programs of the area, and Berger has revealed the context of area studies. Dissertations on the Middle East have been collected by Selim. Development policy literature which is not region-specific has been reviewed by Healey. See recent issues of the *Journal of Economic Literature* for review articles on relevant theoretical and empirical topics.

5. The additional subjects were mainly in the area of employment, economic history, and agriculture.

6. The International Monetary Fund, the World Bank, and the specialized agencies of the United Nations have regularly published macro data. However, these agencies, particularly the first two, have a tremendous amount of data which are not available to the private research community but are available to more than 140 multinational agencies and governments. Although the World Bank is beginning to publish country studies again, often only after strenuous negotiations to obtain the country's agreement, much more could be done to reduce waste, duplication, and inefficient exploitation of data by sharing this information.

7. An exception to this statement is the Yale Growth Center, whose publications reflect a successful effort to direct Ph.D. candidates to country studies.

8. Important efforts at systematizing published data are being made in a collaborative effort at the University of Durham and the School of Oriental and African Studies, University of London.

9. The Roper Center, Williamstown, Mass., and the Survey Research Center, Ann Arbor, Mich, are examples of organizations that collect and distribute data tapes of American information.

10. The Brookings Institution in collaboration with Latin American research centers started a major project for data collection and analysis several years ago.

BIBLIOGRAPHY

Adelman, Morris, A. *The World Petroleum Market*. Baltimore: Johns Hopkins University Press, 1972.

Amin, S. *L'Economie du Maghreb*, 2 vols. Paris: Editions de Minuit, 1966.

Amuzegar, Jahangir. *Technical Assistance in Theory and Practice: the Case of Iran*. New York: Praeger, 1966.

——— and M. Ali Fekrat. *Iran: Economic Development Under Dualistic Conditions*. Chicago: University of Chicago Press, 1971.

Arlis, J. P. "Manpower Mobilization and Economic Growth: An Assessment of Moroccan and Tunisian Experience," *International Labor Review*, **94**, 1 (July 1966), 121.

Asfour, Edmund. *Long Term Projections of Supply and of Demand for Agricultural Products*. Beirut: American University of Beirut, 1965.

———. *Syria: Development and Monetary Policy*. Cambridge, Mass.: Harvard University Press, 1959.

Avramovic, D. "Industrialization of Iran: The Records, the Problems, and the Prospects," *Tahqiqate Eqtesadi*, **7**, 18 (1970), 14–17.

Badre, Albert Y. and Simon G. Siksek. *Manpower and Oil in Arab Countries*. Beirut: Economic Research Institute, American University of Beirut, 1960.

Bartsch, William. "The Industrial Labor Force of Iran; Problems of Recruitment, Training, and Productivity," *Middle East Journal*, **25**, 1.

Bartsch, William and Julian Bharier. *The Economy of Iran, 1940–1970: A Bibliography*. Durham: University of Durham, 1971.

Beling, Willard A. *Modernization and African Labor: A Tunisian Case Study*. New York: Praeger, 1965.

Berger, M. "Middle Eastern and North African Studies: Development and Needs," *Middle East Studies Association Bulletin*, **1**, 2 (1967), 18.

Bharier, Julian. *Economic Development in Iran, 1900–1970*. (New York: Oxford University Press, 1971.

Blitzec, C., et al. "A Dynamic Five-Sector Model for Turkey, 1967–1982," *American Economic Review*, **60**, 2 (May 1970).

Bourdieu, Pierre. *Travail et Travailleurs en Algerie*. Paris: Mouton, 1963.

Bruno, Michael. *Economic Development Problems of Israel, 1970–1980, RM-5975-FF*. Santa Monica, Calif.: Rand Corporation, 1970.

Bruton, Henz, J. *Principles of Development Economics*. Englewood Cliffs, N.J.: Prentice-Hall, 1965.

Chenery, Hollis, John Duloy, and Richard Jolly. *Redistribution with Growth: An Approach to Policy*. New York: Oxford University Press, 1974.

Clawson, Marion, Hans H. Landsberg, and Lyle T. Alexander. *The Agricultural Potential of the Middle East*. New York: American Elsevier, 1971.

Clegg, Ian. *Worker Self-Management in Algeria*. New York: Monthly Review Press, 1972.

Cohn, Edwin, J. *Turkish Economic, Social and Political Change*. New York: Praeger, 1970.

Cook, M. A., ed. *Studies in the Economic History of the Middle East: From the Rise of Islam to the Present Day*. New York: Oxford University Press, 1970.

Cooper, Charles A., and Sidney S. Alexander, eds. *Economic Development and Population Growth in the Middle East*. New York: American Elsevier, 1971.

de Bernis, Destanne G. "Les Industries Industrialisantes et Les Options Algeriennes," *Revue Tiers Monde*, **12**, 47 (June 1971).

Department of State. *Point Four: Near East and Africa. A Selcted Bibliography of Studies on Economically Underdeveloped Countries*. Ed. by U.S. Library Division. New York: Greenwood Press, 1969.

Evans, N. "An Econometric Model of the Israeli Economy, 1957–1965," *Econometrics*, **38**, 5 (September 1970), 624–660.

Fatemi, Ali Mohammed. *Political Economy of the Middle East*. Akron, Ohio: University of Ohio Press, 1970.

Finnie, David H. *Desert Enterprise*. Cambridge, Mass.: Harvard University Press, 1958.

Foster, Philips W. *Research on Agricultural Development in North Africa*. New York: Agricultural Development Council, 1967.

Gabriel, Abbas. "Consolidation of Agricultural Holdings in Lebanon." FAO Conference, Salahuddin, Iraq, 1955, CP-11-B.

Gittinger, J. P. "Planning and Agricultural Policy in Iran: Program Effects and Indirect Effects," *Economic Development and Cultural Change*, **16**, 1 (1967), 107–118.

Hansen, Bent, and Giris A. Marzouk. *Development and Economic Policy in the U.A.R. (Egypt)*. Amsterdam: North Holland, 1966.

Healey, Derek T. "Development Policy: New Thinking About an Interpretation," *Journal of Economic Literature*, **10**, 3 (September 1972).

Hershlag, Z. Y. *Turkey: The Challenge of Growth*. Leiden: Brill, 1968.

Hinderink, Jan, and Keray-belik, Mubeccel. *Social Stratification as an Obstacle to Developement: A Study of Four Turkish Villages*. New York: Praeger, 1970.

Hirsch, Seev. *The Export Performance of Six Manufacturing Industries: A Comparative Study of Denmark, Holland and Israel*. New York: Praeger, 1970.

Issawi, Charles. *The Economic History of Iran 1800–1914*. Chicago: University of Chicago Press, 1971.

———. "Economic History of the Middle East to 1914," *Middle East Studies Association Bulletin*. **2**, 2 (May 1968).

———. *Egypt in Revolution: An Economic Analysis*. London: Oxford University Press, 1963.

——— and Mohammed Yeganeh. *Economics of Middle Eastern Oil*. New York: Praeger, 1962.

Jacobs, Norman. *Sociology of Development: Iran as an Asian Case Study*. New York: Praeger, 1966.

Karpat, Kemal H. "Social Effects of Farm Mechanization in the Rest of Villages," *Social Research*, **27**, 1 (1960), 83–124.

Katona, George. *The Psychological Analysis of Economic Behavior*. New York: McGraw-Hill, 1951.

Kazemian, Gholam H. *Impact of U.S. Technical Aid on the Rural Development of Iran*. New York: Gaus, 1968.

Khalaf, Nadim G. *Economic Implications of the Size of Nations*. Leiden: Brill, 1971.

Khalaf, Samir G. "Industrial Conflict in Lebanon," *Human Organization*, **24**, 1 (Spring 1965), 25–33.

Klat, Paul J. "Musha Holdings and Land Fragmentation in Syria," *Middle East Economic Papers* (1957), 12–41.

Lambton, A. K. S. *The Persian Land Reform 1926–66*. New York: Oxford University Press, 1964.

Landes, David S. *Bankers and Pashas: International Finance and Economic Imperialism in Egypt*. New York: Harper & Row, 1969.

Landau, Jacob M. "Israeli Studies on the Middle East," *Middle East Journal*, **4**, 3 (1965), 354–362.

Langley, Kathleen M. *The Industrialization of Iraq*. Cambridge, Mass.: Harvard University Press, 1961.

Laufer, Leopold. *Israel and the Developing Countries: New Approaches to Cooperation*. New York: Twentieth Century Fund, 1967.

Malhouk, Adnan. "Recent Agricultural Development and Behavior Settlement in Syria," *Middle East Journal*, **10**, 2 (1956). 167–176.

Meyer, A. J. *Middle Eastern Capitalism*. Cambridge, Mass.: Harvard University Press, 1959.

Mundlak, Yair. *Long Term Projects of Supply and Demand for Agricultural Products in Israel*. Jerusalem: Falk Project, 1964. (a)

———. *An Economic Analysis of Established Family Farms in Israel 1953–58*. Jerusalem: Falk Project, 1964. (b)

Nagi, Mostafa H. *Labor Force and Employment in Egypt: A Demographic and Socioeconomic Analysis*. New York: Praeger, 1971.

El-Naggar, Sa'id. *Foreign Aid and the Economic Development of the United Arab Republic*. Princeton, N.J.: Princeton University Press, 1965.

O'Brien, Patrick. *The Revolution in Egypt's Economic System: From Private Enterprise to Socialism.* London: Oxford University Press, 1966.

Owen, E. R. J. *Cotton and the Egyptian Economy 1820–1914: A Study in Trade and Development.* London: Oxford University Press, 1969.

Peck, Howard. *Structural Change and Economic Policy in Israel.* New Haven, Conn.: Yale University Press, 1971.

Palmer, Edgar Z. *Agriculture in Turkey: Long Term Projections of Supply and Demand.* Belck, Istanbul: Roberts College, 1966.

Penrose, Edith. *The Growth of Firms, Middle East Oil and Other Essays.* London: Frank Cass, 1971.

La Revue Bibliographique du Moyen Orient. (November 1961).

Robinson, Richard. "Tractors in the Village: A Case Study in Turkey." *Journal of Farm Economics,* **34**, 4 (1952), 451–462.

Sadaka, R., C. Loomis, and D. Taylor. *A Study of the Problems of Obtaining Credit and Using it Productively on Some Farms in Northern Beqa'a.* Beirut: Faculty of Agricultural Sciences, American University of Beirut, 1966.

Salah-Beye, Anisse. "Trade Unions and Social Development in the Maghreb,"*International Labor Review.* **94**, 4 (October 1966).

Sayegh, Kamal S. *Oil and Arab Regional Development.* New York: Praeger, 1968.

Sayegh, Yusif. *Entrepreneurs of the Lebanon.* Cambridge, Mass.: Harvard University Press, 1952.

School of Oriental and Africa Studies, University of London: *A Cumulation of a Selected and Annotated Bibliography of Economic Literature on the Arab-Speaking Countries of the Middle East, 1938–1960.* Boston: Hall, 1967.

Schregle, J. "Worker's Participation in Management," *Industrial Relations,* **9**, 2 (February 1970), 117–123.

Schurr, Sam H., and Paul T. Homan. *Middle Eastern Oil and the Western World.* New York: American Elsevier, 1971.

Selim, G. D. *American Doctoral Dissertations on the Arab World, 1883–1968.* Washington, D.C.: Library of Congress, 1970.

Simmons, John. *The Determinants of Earnings: A Socioeconomic Model.* Washington, D.C.: The World Bank, 1973.

———. "Agricultural Development in Iraq: Planning and Management Failures," *Middle East Journal,* **19**, 2 (1965), 141.

———. "Agricultural Cooperatives and Tunisian Development," *Middle East Journal,* **24**, 4 (1970), 455 and **25**, 1 (1971), 45.

Stauffer, Thomas. "The Economics of Nomadism," *Middle East Journal,* **19**, 3 (1965), 284.

Tanzer, Michael. *The Political Economy of International Oil and the Underdeveloped Countries.* Boston: Beacon Press, 1969.

Taylor, Donald C. *Research on Agricultural Development in Selected Middle Eastern Countries.* New York: Agricultural Development Council, 1968.

Tiano, A. "Le Maghreb entre les Mythes." In *L'Economie Nord-Africaine Depuis l'Independence.* Paris: Presses Universitaires de France, 1967.

Tintner, G. and S. Farghali. "The Application of Stochastic Programming to the U.A.R. First Five Year Plan," *Kyklos,* **20**, 3 (1967).

Trebous, Madeleine. *Migration and Development: The Case of Algeria: Manpower Requirements in Algeria and Vocational Training in Europe.* Paris: OECD, Development Centre Studies, 1970.

Tuma, Elias H. "Agrarian Reform and Urbanization in the Middle East," *Middle East Journal*, **24**, 2 (1970), 163.

———. "Agriculture and Economic Development in the Middle East," *MESA Bulletin*, **5**, 3 (October 1971), 1–20.

UAR Institute of National Planning. *Research Report on Employment Problems in Rural Areas UAR: Report on Methodology, Field Work and Documentation*. Cairo: INP, 1966, p. 258.

UAR Institute of National Planning. *Final Report on Employment in Rural Areas UAR.* Cairo: INP, 1968.

UN. *Small Scale Industry in Arab Countries of the Middle East.* New York: United Nations, 1970.

Ustunel, B. "Problems of Development Financing: The Turkish Case," *Journal of Development Studies*, **3**, 2 (January 1967), 130–154.

Viralov, A. G. "Foreign and National Capital in the Industry of Morocco," *KSINA*, **81** (1964), 106–122. (in Russian)

Ward, Gordon H., et al. *Economic Analyses of the Production of Oranges and Bananas in Damour and South Lebanon.* Beirut: Faculty of Agricultural Sciences, American University of Beirut, 1965.

Warriner, Doreen. "Employment and Income Aspects of Recent Agrarian Reforms in the Middle East," *International Labor Review*, **101**, 6 (June 1970), 705–726

———. *Land Reform and Development in the Middle East.* Oxford: Oxford University Press, 1962.

Wirty, Raanan and Avshalom Rokash. *Agricultural Development: Planning and Implementation. An Israeli Case Study.* Dordrecht: Reidel, 1968.

Yenal, Oktay. *Development of the Financial System.* London: Frank Cass, 1967.

Zghal, Abdelkader. *Modernization de l'Agriculture et Populations Semi-nomades*. The Hague: Mouton, 1967.

The subject and name indexes were prepared at the University of Chicago by Jerrold D. Green and Khalil Jahshan, candidates in Political Science, and Bruce Masters, candidate in History. They were assisted by David Creagan, Benjamin A. Frankel, Bereket Haregot, and Mohammad Amien Rais. Claudia Rex typed the index and helped in many ways to coordinate the collective effort.

Author Index

Subject Index